Mar '10

MICHA

Buyer's Guide
to New Zealand
Wines

2010

To Dad

HAPPY 60th BIRTHDAY

Lots of love

Eleanor ☺

H
M
Hodder Moa

A catalogue record for this book is available from the National Library of New Zealand

ISBN 978-1-86971-173-3

A Hodder Moa Book
Published in 2009 by Hachette New Zealand Ltd
4 Whetu Place, Mairangi Bay
Auckland, New Zealand

Designed and produced by Hachette New Zealand Ltd
Printed by Griffin Press, Australia

The 2009 edition

'The *Buyer's Guide* is an essential book for anyone wishing to cut through the fluff and get a fast, honest appraisal of practically any wine made in New Zealand. If a wine doesn't rate well, Cooper tells you why, and if it gains five stars his praise is lavish. . . . This is a book for the novice and the connoisseur, the wine student and wine professional, the collector and the drinker.'
– *New Zealand House & Garden*

'He is really respected and seen as being very, very fair. A lot of people buy that book. It's a little bible by which they buy wine. To get recognised with one of your wines says it is really good and at a good price point.'
– Paul Mooney, Mission Estate winemaker, *Hawke's Bay Today*

'It just gets bigger and better.'
– *Daily News*

'This is New Zealand's most widely read wine book; a guide not only to the wines that are available but to their quality, cost, value for money, taste and all those other things you need or want to know before you buy. It is, quite simply, an indispensable tool for anyone interested in wine, even for those who think they know it all.'
– *Southland Times*

'Essential for anyone interested in wine, whether looking for a cheap and cheerful, good-value wine or something top-flight for a special occasion.'
– *Otago Daily Times*

'Michael Cooper's *Buyer's Guide to New Zealand Wines* is firmly established as the most comprehensive and authoritative annual guide to local wines.'
– *Wanganui Chronicle*

'Whenever I stand in front of the Chardonnay section at my local Glengarry's wine store and feel overwhelmed by the hundred or so New Zealand Chardonnays on display there, I wonder how I could ever make a choice if I didn't have with me the current edition of Cooper's invaluable guide. I never buy wine without having it with me. It is totally indispensable and the best guide on the market by a country mile.'
– *Beattie's Book Blog*

Michael Cooper is New Zealand's most acclaimed wine writer, with 33 books, hundreds of magazine and newspaper articles, and several major literary awards to his credit, including the Montana Medal for the supreme work of non-fiction at the 2003 Montana New Zealand Book Awards for his magnum opus, *Wine Atlas of New Zealand*. In the 2004 New Year Honours, Michael was appointed an Officer of the New Zealand Order of Merit for services to wine writing.

Author of the country's biggest-selling wine book, the annual *Michael Cooper's Buyer's Guide to New Zealand Wines*, now in its 18th edition, he was awarded the Sir George Fistonich Medal in recognition of services to New Zealand wine in 2009. The award is made each year at the country's largest wine competition, the New Zealand International Wine Show, to a 'living legend' of New Zealand wine. He is the New Zealand editor of Australia's *Winestate* magazine and chairman of its New Zealand tasting panel, and is the wine columnist for the *New Zealand Listener*.

In 1977 he obtained a Master of Arts degree from the University of Auckland with a thesis entitled 'The Wine Lobby: Pressure Group Politics and the New Zealand Wine Industry'. He was marketing manager for Babich Wines from 1980 to 1990, and since 1991 has been a full-time wine writer.

Cooper's other works include the fully updated and much-extended second edition of *Wine Atlas of New Zealand* (2008); *Classic Wines of New Zealand* (second edition 2005); *The Wines and Vineyards of New Zealand* (published in five editions from 1984 to 1996); *Michael Cooper's Buyer's Guide to Imported Wines*; and *Pocket Guide to Wines of New Zealand*. He is the New Zealand consultant for Hugh Johnson's annual, best-selling *Pocket Wine Book* and the acclaimed *World Atlas of Wine*.

Contents

White Wines 32

Sweet White Wines 323

Sparkling Wines 343

Rosé Wines 355

Red Wines 371

Index of Wine Brands 583

6

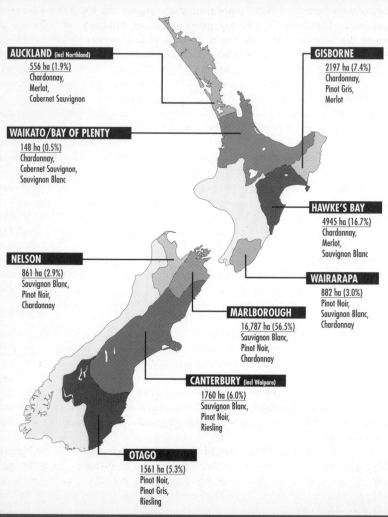

The Winemaking Regions of New Zealand

Area in producing vines 2009 (percentage of national producing vineyard area)

AUCKLAND (incl Northland)
556 ha (1.9%)
Chardonnay,
Merlot,
Cabernet Sauvignon

GISBORNE
2197 ha (7.4%)
Chardonnay,
Pinot Gris,
Merlot

WAIKATO/BAY OF PLENTY
148 ha (0.5%)
Chardonnay,
Cabernet Sauvignon,
Sauvignon Blanc

HAWKE'S BAY
4945 ha (16.7%)
Chardonnay,
Merlot,
Sauvignon Blanc

NELSON
861 ha (2.9%)
Sauvignon Blanc,
Pinot Noir,
Chardonnay

WAIRARAPA
882 ha (3.0%)
Pinot Noir,
Sauvignon Blanc,
Chardonnay

MARLBOROUGH
16,787 ha (56.5%)
Sauvignon Blanc,
Pinot Noir,
Chardonnay

CANTERBURY (incl Waipara)
1760 ha (6.0%)
Sauvignon Blanc,
Pinot Noir,
Riesling

OTAGO
1561 ha (5.3%)
Pinot Noir,
Pinot Gris,
Riesling

These figures are extracted from the *New Zealand Winegrowers Statistical Annual 2008*, published by New Zealand Winegrowers. During the five-year period 2006 to 2011 the total area of producing vines is projected to expand from 22,617 to 34,739 hectares – a rise of nearly 54 per cent.

Preface

What's happening on the New Zealand wine scene? During 2009, Nobilo Marlborough Sauvignon Blanc topped the charts in the US; the bottom dropped from under Gisborne's Chardonnay growers; George Fistonich, of Villa Maria, became the country's first wine knight; William Hill, a pioneering Central Otago winery, slid into receivership; a Nelson vineyard released the country's first wine to be certified biodynamic – Richmond Plains Aries 2008; and the industry harvested another bumper crop, ensuring the supply of New Zealand wine would continue to outstrip demand and that retail prices would keep plummeting.

New Zealand wine of good quality has never been more widely available or cheaper. I recently bought a bottle of Woodman's Bend Marlborough Sauvignon Blanc 2008 for $5.99, and was surprised by its quality. Pinot Noir from Central Otago is suddenly everywhere. Not only are the wineries based in the region launching increasingly affordable, second- and third-tier labels but around New Zealand countless other producers are adding one or two Central Otago Pinot Noirs to their portfolio.

Spare a thought for the winegrowers, enduring tough times. 'For wineries, it is incredibly competitive,' says Philip Gregan, chief executive officer of New Zealand Winegrowers. 'Nobody is making money domestically. There is a lot of downward price pressure for a variety of reasons. Our supply situation is just part of it. The recession is another.' Yet just three years ago, anyone eager to establish a Sauvignon Blanc vineyard in Marlborough couldn't, unless they had ordered the vines well in advance. Nurseries were cleaned out by the soaring demand for plants, reflecting feedback from the major exporting wineries that they couldn't get enough Marlborough Sauvignon Blanc.

But the industry expanded too fast. Between 2000 and 2009, the country's area of bearing vineyards tripled, its production soared from less than 7 million cases to over 22 million cases, and 300 new wineries opened for business. Exports expanded at an exhilarating rate, from $125 million to $1 billion, but still not fast enough to keep pace with the surging output.

The media is full of 'doom and gloom' wine stories. Not only are wine prices falling, so are the prices for grapes, established vineyards and land suitable for viticulture. In 2009, in several regions, grapes were left unpicked. Some vineyards are expected to be uprooted.

It's not all bad news. Oyster Bay Marlborough Sauvignon Blanc is the biggest-selling white wine of all – based on volume and value – in Australia. The quality and value of Hawke's Bay's claret-style reds, based on Merlot and Cabernet Sauvignon, are finally being appreciated. The 2009 Marlborough Sauvignon Blancs, in their infancy, look aromatic, intense and zingy.

Enjoy the bargains while you can. Senior industry executives predict the supply of New Zealand wine will exceed demand for at least another couple of years.

– Michael Cooper

Vintage Charts 2000–2009

WHITES	Auckland	Gisborne	Hawke's Bay	Wairarapa	Nelson	Marlborough	Canterbury	Otago
2009	4	6–7	4	5	6	5	6	3–5
2008	5–6	3–4	3–5	5–7	4	2–5	3–6	5–6
2007	6	7	6	4–5	5	5–6	5–6	4–6
2006	6–7	4–5	6	5	5	4–5	5	5–6
2005	7	5	4	3	4	4–5	5	3–4
2004	6	5–6	5–6	5	5	6	3–6	3
2003	5–6	4	3–4	6	5–6	5	4–6	5
2002	6	7	6	6	6–7	4–6	4–7	5–7
2001	3–5	4	4–5	5	6	6–7	6	4–6
2000	7	5	6	7	5–6	5–7	3–6	4–5

REDS	Auckland	Gisborne	Hawke's Bay	Wairarapa	Nelson	Marlborough	Canterbury	Otago
2009	5	6–7	6	5	6	6	6	3–5
2008	5–7	3–4	3–5	5–7	4	2–5	3–6	5–6
2007	3–5	7	6	4–5	5	4–6	5–6	4–6
2006	4–5	4–5	4–5	5	5	4–5	5	5–6
2005	7	5	4–6	3	4	4–5	5	4–5
2004	5–7	6	5–6	5	4	4–5	4–6	3–4
2003	4–6	4	3–4	7	5–7	5	4–7	5–6
2002	6	7	5–6	4	5–7	4–7	3–6	5–6
2001	4–5	4	4	6	6	5–7	7	6
2000	6–7	5	5–7	6	5–6	5–7	4–6	4

7 = Outstanding   6 = Excellent   5 = Above average   4 = Average   3 = Below average   2 = Poor   1 = Bad

2009 Vintage Report

New Zealand's 2009 grape crop totalled 285,000 tonnes – identical to the massive 2008 harvest, which was a 39 per cent leap on the previous record.

New Zealand Winegrowers reported a 'very good growing season this year. Some early humidity and weather pressure in February was replaced by a superb March and April.' Pinot Noir production fell by 16 per cent, but despite much-publicised work on reducing Sauvignon Blanc yields, the crucial Sauvignon Blanc harvest was actually 5 per cent larger than in 2008.

After generally favourable weather during bud-burst and flowering, most regions reported satisfactory grape yields. The average crop around the country dropped from 9.8 to 9.2 tonnes of grapes per hectare, but this was offset by an increased producing area, up from 29,000 hectares in 2008 to 31,000 hectares in 2009. However, due to the current wine surplus, not all of the grapes were harvested – from Gisborne to Central Otago, thousands of tonnes were left on the vines.

Spring weather was dominated by more anticyclones than usual, bringing mild, sunny and dry conditions to the north and east of the country. After a warm, dry and sunny early–mid-summer in most regions, the East Coast was on a 'red alert' for fire. During mid to late February, the weather turned cool and wet, but March, although still cool, was extremely dry and sunny. April was a mixed bag around the country, but in the principal grapegrowing regions on the East Coast, the weather stayed dry and cool.

Of the national grape harvest, over half (57 per cent) was of one variety from one region: Marlborough Sauvignon Blanc. If you add Sauvignon Blanc from other regions, giving a total of 177,647 tonnes (compared to 169,613 tonnes in 2008), Sauvignon Blanc accounted for almost 63 per cent of the country's total harvest.

The Chardonnay vintage of 34,393 tonnes (up 3 per cent on 2008, reflecting a return to 'normal' yields in Hawke's Bay) was well ahead of Pinot Noir's 27,547 tonnes (a 16 per cent drop on 2008, reflecting markedly smaller crops in Marlborough and Central Otago).

Merlot, in fourth place, had a production level (11,723 tonnes in 2009) 15 per cent higher than in 2008, due to the improved Hawke's Bay harvest. Pinot Gris (11,410 tonnes) followed in fifth place, down by 8 per cent on 2008, but well ahead of Riesling (6316 tonnes), Cabernet Sauvignon (2304 tonnes) and Gewürztraminer (2123 tonnes).

In 2009, over 80 per cent of New Zealand wine flowed from two regions – Marlborough (68 per cent) and Hawke's Bay (14.5 per cent). Gisborne (8.2 per cent) was the third-largest producing region, followed by Nelson (2.7 per cent), Otago (2.2 per cent), Canterbury (1.9 per cent) and Wairarapa (1.6 per cent).

Have you noticed that, from one year to the next, around the country, vintage reports from regional bodies and wineries are consistently upbeat? It pays to be sceptical. As Darryl Soljan, of Ascension Vineyard at Matakana, stated last year: 'A winemaker talking honestly about the weather – that's daring to be different.'

Northland

So rare is Northland wine, less than 0.1 per cent of the country's 2009 grape harvest was grown in the region. The total crop of 148 tonnes (down steeply from 204 tonnes in 2008) equates to little more than 10,000 cases.

A dry, cool December and dry January were followed by a wet February, with more than double the average rainfall. Autumn got off to a great start, with record sunshine in March, but in April the rains returned, with below-average sunshine hours.

Auckland

Auckland wine-growers harvested 1615 tonnes of grapes in 2009 – just ahead of the previous year's record of 1604 tonnes, but only 0.6 per cent of the national total. The prospect is for some excellent reds.

Warm, settled weather at flowering led to a good fruit set, according to Shayne Cox, of Corazon. 'Bud-burst was very even and the early-season weather gave the vines a great start,' reported Man O' War, on Waiheke Island. 'Flowering and fruit set took place under calm blue skies, leading to a heavier than normal crop,' necessitating shoot and bunch removal.

Early–mid-summer was 'intensely hot and dry,' says Man O' War. On 12 February, Auckland sweltered in its highest temperature for over a century, 32.4°C. However, the weather cooled markedly in the second half of February, when 'an unseasonal cold Antarctic blast confused the vines,' reported Te Whau, on Waiheke Island. Rainfall for the month was above average.

In March, 'summer returned with a vengeance,' says Te Whau, bringing record sunshine hours. April was less sunny than usual, but the weather stayed relatively dry.

Some varieties were hit by the poor weather in late February. A top producer at Matakana abandoned two-thirds of his Pinot Gris crop to rot, while Merlot was 'a tad affected by the cold snap,' Te Whau admits. However, Man O' War reports wines of 'unparalleled purity and concentration'.

At Matakana, where Heron's Flight picked its biggest-ever crop, David Hoskins singled out his Dolcetto: 'A monster of a wine, deeply coloured, which will take some taming over the next year while in barrels.' Te Whau was excited about Cabernet Sauvignon and Cabernet Franc, which achieved 'lovely, ripe, concentrated flavours'.

Waikato

With 202 tonnes of grapes (under 0.1 per cent of the national total), Waikato recorded its second-smallest crop of the past decade, just ahead of last season's 192 tonnes. Five to 10 years ago, the region's wine-growers usually harvested about 500 tonnes.

In late summer, Dr Rainer Eschenbruch, of Birchwood Lane Vineyard, Tamahere, reported a good crop 'and was considering bringing harvest forward as a result of the fine, warm weather'. Although February rainfall in the Waikato was more than double the average, in March the weather was much drier (less than half the average).

In Taranaki, Kairau Lodge and Vineyard, owners of the Mountain Road brand, reported a 'great' season: 'Good, ripe fruit this year, as the grapes could stay on the vines longer with the great autumn weather.'

Gisborne

Just prior to the turmoil surrounding the announcement of Pernod Ricard NZ's severe cutbacks to its grapegrowing contracts – mostly for Chardonnay – in Gisborne, the region's wine-growers reported a 'stunning' vintage. With an average-sized crop of 23,093 tonnes (down slightly on 23,911 tonnes in 2008), Gisborne accounted for 8.2 per cent of the national harvest.

'A dry spring and early summer saw a strong, even bud-burst and set the vines up for an excellent flowering,' reported Pernod Ricard. 'Pinot Gris, in particular, had a good set.'

A dry December was followed by high rainfall in early January, which increased berry size. In February, Pernod Ricard reported 'very even ripening, especially in red varieties such as Merlot', and noted that Gisborne had missed the widespread rain in southern regions.

In mid-April, parts of the East Coast were declared a drought area. Gisborne Winegrowers noted that 2009 was similar to the outstanding 2007 vintage, in terms of heat during the ripening season, but also drier.

The 2009 vintage was 'awesome', enthused Andy Nimmo, of Hihi, 'with excellent flavours throughout the varietal range'. At Vinoptima, which called the vintage 'outstanding', Gewürztraminer specialist Nick Nobilo opted to leave 25 per cent of his fruit on the vines to produce a Noble Late Harvest style.

Hawke's Bay

'2009 was the hottest season for the last 10 years and the driest since 1973, giving us another superb quality vintage,' reported Te Mata. Some Chardonnay and Sauvignon Blanc on heavy sites were adversely affected by a wet spell in late February and early March, but, according to Esk Valley, the 2009 Hawke's Bay reds 'show off the heat of the summer, not the vagaries of the autumn'.

At 40,985 tonnes, the 2009 harvest was the second-largest yet, 20 per cent bigger than in 2008, and close to the record 2007 crop of 41,963 tonnes. Hawke's Bay accounted for 14.5 per cent of the national harvest.

'Mild spring weather led to bud-burst occurring about 10 days earlier than usual, in early September,' says Te Mata. 'The rest of September continued mild and dry, with some days reaching 25°C.'

Some vineyards reported damaging frosts in late September. 'As usual, the earlier varieties, Chardonnay and Gewürztraminer, suffered most,' observed Stonecroft. However, a dry, warm October was followed by a 'fairly warm, dry and settled' November, says Paul Mooney, of Mission Estate. 'This gave us pretty good conditions for flowering and set.'

After a warm, dry December and January and warm but much wetter February, the harvest at Te Mata began on 26 February, one of the earliest starts yet. 'We often get years when one of the three summer months is cooler than average,' noted Mooney. 'This can impact on the vintage, especially for the reds, but that was not the case in 2009.' During January, the temperatures in the Mission's Gimblett Gravels vineyards often exceeded 30°C, climbing to 39°C on 1 February.

In February, however, Hawke's Bay received over double its average rainfall. At the end of the month, 'cool, wet conditions took the gloss off some blocks of ripening Chardonnay on heavier soils,' Pernod Ricard noted. One producer reported that persistent rainfall between 20 February and 6 March created 'significant botrytis pressure on the white varieties. We had to start harvesting Chardonnay on 8 March. There was botrytis pressure on Sauvignon Blanc as well.'

A cool March, which dried out as the month progressed, led into a sunny, settled April. Some winemakers enthused about their white wines ('the whites show verve and a fresh, lively nature,' says Gordon Russell, of Esk Valley), but most producers were especially excited about their reds.

'The Bordeaux varieties pumped,' says Mission. 'We pulled most of our red fruit off at 24–25 brix. The tannins are really ripe. The palates of these wines have amazing, plush fruit. This will be a very good Cabernet Sauvignon vintage . . . [and] our Syrahs are as good as 2007, in some cases better.'

Pernod Ricard agreed: 'The pick of the bunch . . . would have to be the Bordeaux varieties of Merlot, Malbec, Cabernet Franc and Cabernet Sauvignon.' Chris Scott, of Church Road, predicts 2009 will yield elegant, rather than blockbuster, reds. 'The hot summer meant we achieved early physiological ripeness on most varieties before sugars got out of control, so we should make wines that are slightly more moderate in alcohol.'

Wairarapa

Wairarapa wine-growers picked 4421 tonnes of grapes in 2009, which surpassed the previous record of 4105 tonnes, set in 2008, but still accounted for only 1.6 per cent of the national harvest. Excellent wine is likely: 'Not since 1996 have we seen the elements that form a growing season line up so favourably for quality and quantity,' declared Roger Parkinson, of Nga Waka.

Dry River reported that September brought 'a cold start to spring, followed by a heavy frost with limited damage to our Chardonnay'. Further north, Gladstone Vineyard experienced a frost-free spring, setting the vines 'up strongly for bud-burst and flowering'.

Early December proved 'calm, dry and warm,' says Dry River, 'providing for an excellent flowering and the potential for good crop levels.' January was also dry, with well below average rainfall, and unusually hot. Nga Waka recorded 21 days with temperatures reaching or exceeding 30°C.

February, however, was wetter than usual – Urlar Wines, at East Taratahi, near Masterton, received an 'unheard-of' 130 mm of rain. 'Drought-breaking rain in late February did produce some botrytis,' says Nga Waka, but the dry autumn meant the big crop was able to be harvested 'without any weather or botrytis issues'.

In mid-March, Allan Johnson, of Palliser Estate, declared the crop was looking good. Earlier, many of the vineyards in the region had 'thinned grapes from the vines to achieve better tonnage levels, because there was more fruit than was ideal'.

Late summer and early autumn were dry and cooler than average, according to Nga Waka. Gladstone Vineyard reported frosts in late April, but after most of the crop had been picked.

The winemakers are upbeat about quality. Nga Waka, at Martinborough, picked Chardonnay at an average of 24 brix and Pinot Noir at 25 brix. 'The crop was fantastic,' says Paddy Borthwick, at East Taratahi, 'with nicely balanced yields and disease-free.' Gladstone Vineyard reported 'a magical vintage, with yields up, exceptional fruit quality and some stunning wines. . . . Our Pinot Noir fruit came in with the highest consistent quality we have yet seen.'

Nelson

After a 'challenging' season, says Woollaston Estate, Nelson growers harvested a record 7740 tonnes of grapes, accounting for 2.7 per cent of the national grape crop.

According to *New Zealand Winegrower*, 'rain in November resulted in lighter fruit set in some varieties, Gewürztraminer in particular and Pinot Noir to a lesser extent'. December was wetter than usual, but January was drier.

'While the long, hot, dry spell after New Year was welcomed by holiday-makers, it caused some temporary water stress to the vines in our Upper Moutere vineyards,' says Woollaston Estate. *New Zealand Winegrower* noted a 'heatwave in January, when temperatures reached 35°C-plus, providing perfect mid-season conditions'. However, February delivered 'a few challenges', with above-average rain.

After an autumn described by *New Zealand Winegrower* as 'extended, warm and sunny', Andrew Sutherland, of Woollaston Estate, declared the 2009 vintage was 'the most stable he could recall, with no rain during the six-week harvest period. Allowing fruit to have the ultimate hang-time has resulted in fantastic flavour profiles.'

Neudorf Vineyards, at Upper Moutere, reported 'brilliant stuff' with a 'small crop but in great condition'.

Marlborough

The 2009 vintage was 'somewhat challenging,' reports Sam Weaver, of Churton. After a slightly wet growing season (with 15 per cent more rainfall than usual, coupled with average heat and sunshine hours), the region's wine-growers harvested 192,128 tonnes of grapes – just 1 per cent less than the record 194,639 tonnes picked in 2008, and over two-thirds (68.1 per cent) of the total national grape crop.

'A very wet winter set the vines up for a great bud-burst,' according to Pernod Ricard NZ. Spring was 'generally cloudy and mild,' reported Winegrowers of Ara. A cloudy, rainy September was followed by a cool, wet October and a warm but wet November.

Flowering (in early–mid-December) coincided with favourably warm conditions, says Winegrowers of Ara. 'As a result [we] embarked on an extensive crop-thinning programme in December and January, spending thousands of man hours manually removing green bunches to readjust yields.'

January was sunny (the sixth sunniest January since 1930), with just 20 per cent of normal rainfall, bringing a rapid drop in soil moisture. In February, however, the weather turned cool and very cloudy, with more than double the average monthly rainfall, delaying the harvest and encouraging canopy growth, berry-swelling and botrytis outbreaks.

Despite February's wetness, the total rainfall over the January–March period was below average. March was cool, sunny and extremely dry (the driest since 1969). 'The low rainfall was exactly what the grape industry in Marlborough needed following the high rainfall in February that got botrytis established in many grape crops,' says Rob Agnew, of Plant and Food Research.

A warm, sunny April followed. Rainfall was slightly above average, but 90 per cent fell in the last four days of the month. 'It was the vintage from heaven, hot and dry, perfect for ripening,' reported Al Soper, of Highfield. 'It also allowed us to pick where and when we wanted without having to race against any rain. We are stoked with the fruit we have.'

Despite the industry concern about the need to slash crops in response to market pressures, the average yield in Marlborough dropped only from 12 tonnes per hectare in 2008 to 11 tonnes per hectare in 2009, according to *Winepress*. Pernod Ricard reported Sauvignon Blanc possessing 'intense flavours with cool-climate pungency', and Wither Hills rated its Chardonnay as 'the best yet'. Wine Marlborough also reported 'a great deal of excitement about the range of botrytised and late-harvest wines'.

The prospects are for excellent Pinot Noir. 'Yields of Pinot Noir are down across the board,' reported Wine Marlborough, 'with the berry size being described as much smaller than in previous years. The upside of that, though, is an increase in colour and riper flavours.' Winemaker Josh Scott, of Allan Scott, described the quality of his Pinot Noir as 'at an all-time high'.

Canterbury

Canterbury wine-growers harvested 5476 tonnes of grapes, 20 per cent less than the record 2008 vintage of 6881 tonnes, but still the region's second-largest crop on record. Overall, the vineyards at Waipara and on the Canterbury Plains accounted for 1.9 per cent of the country's total harvest.

Weka River, at Waipara, reported that spring and early summer brought 'endless days of clear blue skies, with hot and dry weather day after day and no rain, which allowed one of the best flowerings in 25 years over all varieties'. *New Zealand Winegrower*, however, noted that a November frost on the Canterbury Plains 'wiped out the complete crop of some vineyards'.

In early summer, the threat of drought was intensified by high temperatures and strong north to north-west winds. December, sunnier and drier than usual in North Canterbury, was followed by a similarly warm, dry January, although *New Zealand*

Winegrower reported that a hailstorm at Waipara in early January caused 'considerable localised damage to vineyards in the south-east of the region'.

Ripening slowed during February, when temperatures fell and Canterbury had more than double its average rainfall. However, March was extremely dry in North Canterbury, with average temperatures, and in April the weather stayed dry.

After an early harvest, Pegasus Bay praised 2009 as 'an exceptional vintage for both red and white wines'. Pernod Ricard, which produces Waipara wine under its Camshorn brand, reported its Pinot Gris was 'rich and textural', and its Pinot Noir was 'looking stunning: rich, dark and flavoursome'.

Otago

After 'a challenging vintage from start to finish', according to Rippon Vineyard, Otago wine-growers picked 6218 tonnes of grapes, 35 per cent less than in 2008, but still their second-largest crop ever. The vineyards, mostly clustered in Central Otago, but also extending to the Waitaki Valley, in North Otago, yielded just 2.2 per cent of the national grape harvest.

In spring, October was 'peppered with frosts,' says Bald Hills, at Bannockburn, and October and November frosts also reduced the potential crop in the Waitaki Valley. In November a Cromwell Basin grower reported being 'hit with three frosts in a row last week, culminating in the damaging frost [of 8 November] which seemed to affect almost everyone down here to some extent'. After a crippling –5°C frost, Black Ridge at Alexandra lost a third of its crop.

'With some good weather during flowering, a positive fruit set was found across the region,' according to *New Zealand Winegrower*. Wanaka reported record low December temperatures, but January in Otago was warmer and drier than average.

Late summer brought below-average temperatures and over double the normal rainfall. Black Ridge reported a 'grumpy, cool, wet February, which is usually our hottest month . . . The consequence of this lack of heat is that we're later for harvest by nearly a fortnight.' At the end of summer, Grant Taylor, of Valli, was 'worried about the grapes ripening'.

March, however, proved extremely dry, with a return to normal temperatures. 'These last three weeks of warm weather have made a huge difference,' Taylor enthused on 23 March. 'They've ripened that fruit.' However, frost struck the Gibbston district in late March, followed by more frosts in the region in early April.

The 2009 wines are expected to be of highly variable quality. 'There will be some mixed results out of Central,' says a top Pinot Noir producer, 'and it may be a year when site selection and vineyard management are shown up.'

Grant Taylor was enthusiastic about fruit quality: 'It's looking as good as we've seen . . . great colour, the sugars are where we want them and we have smaller berries.' In North Otago, Waitaki Braids reported low yields, 'but what we ended up picking was exceptional'.

Nick Mills, of Rippon Vineyard, sums up: 'Variability in quality is expected to express itself from site to site.'

Best Buys of the Year

Best White Wine Buy of the Year

Eradus Awatere Valley Marlborough Sauvignon Blanc 2009
★★★★★, $18.95

The 2008 scooped several gold medals and five-star ratings on both sides of the Tasman, and the past three vintages each waltzed away from the Air New Zealand Wine Awards with a gold medal. So why is the 2009 so cheap?

'If you over-deliver on quality, it's so much easier to sell the wine,' says Michiel Eradus.

When I first tasted this wine, I jotted down: 'Weighty, rich, rounded, with sweet-fruit characters, notably concentrated gooseberry/lime flavours, hints of tomato stalk, and a slightly minerally streak.' After its identity was revealed, I added: 'Priced sharply.'

Eradus attributes his wine's quality, above all else, to the Awatere Valley, 'just a wonderful place. Anyone who visits in the height of summer will instantly understand why many grapes from here are so delicious.' I've done exactly that. After a long, hot, sun-baked day, around midnight I stepped out from a friend's house into the darkness – and a key lesson on the Awatere's grape-growing climate. It was freezing.

Eradus sees the valley as a source of Sauvignon Blancs with 'complexity, intrigue and certain unique characters. The characters I mention are a mineral and flinty backbone, in addition to clean and racy acidity, followed by a crisp and lingering finish.' He also fairly describes his wine as possessing 'concentration, but with delicacy, elegance and femininity'.

Michiel and his wife Hanna took over the reins of Michiel's parents' vineyard in the lower Awatere Valley in 2004. Har and Sophie Eradus spent 20 years in the flower industry before they launched the Eradus label in 2002.

The company-owned Breloft Vineyard, in the lower Dashwood, runs for 2 kilometres alongside the Awatere River, in a series of undulating terraces. Of the total 12 hectares of vines, 7 hectares are devoted to Sauvignon Blanc. Eradus also draws grapes from a friend's Te One vineyard, 3 kilometres down the road.

Key members of the Eradus production team include viticulturist Jeremy Hyland and winemaker Jules Taylor. With a production level of 12,500 cases, the wine is distributed nationwide, mostly through independent retailers, but it can also be found in some supermarkets.

Peter Thornley, executive chef at Kermadec Restaurant, in Auckland, especially recommends it with whitebait.

Best Red Wine Buy of the Year

Thornbury Hawke's Bay Merlot 2007

★★★★★, $19.95

Offering unrivalled value, this Gimblett Gravels red is deliciously dark and fragrant, with layers of blackcurrant, plum, liquorice, spice and nut flavours. In major tastings featuring many Hawke's Bay reds twice its price, this wine stands out for its richness and sheer class, yet you can buy it for under $20.

When I tasted it blind in mid-2009, I jotted down: 'Dense, bold colour. Complex, nutty bouquet. Almost supercharged, with cassis, plum, spice and nut flavours, warm and dense. Lovely texture. Tight, youthful and very classy. Should be a 10-year wine.'

Other judges have poured top accolades on this moderately priced wine. Rated five stars in *Winestate* magazine, it won a gold medal at the 2009 Royal Easter Show Wine Awards, and another gold medal in October at the 2009 Liquorland Top 100 International Wine Competition.

Thornbury is a brand owned by Villa Maria. Winemaker Simon Fell earlier worked at the company's two Hawke's Bay wineries, Esk Valley and Vidal. Appointed winemaker for Thornbury in 2006, he was given the task of producing outstanding varietal wines from regions around the country.

After the driest season for a decade, hopes were high from the start that 2007 would yield Hawke's Bay's best-ever reds. 'The flavours in the Merlot are superb,' Fell blogged on 2 May 2007. 'There are those ripe plum and underlying redcurrant and violet notes which are very typical of Merlot from the Gimblett Gravels. The colours and tannin profiles have been awesome.'

The hand-harvested grapes were de-stemmed, crushed to open-top fermenters and hand-plunged four times daily for a month, to ensure good extraction of colour, tannin and flavour from the skins. The wine, a blend of Merlot (89 per cent), Cabernet Sauvignon (9 per cent) and Malbec (2 per cent), was then matured for 16 months in French and American oak barriques.

Simon Fell suggests serving this arrestingly rich, stylish red with roast lamb, pasta, pizza, BBQ fare or venison, and expects it to mature well over the next five years. But if you want some, act now – it won't be around for long.

Other shortlisted wines
Whites:
Selaks Winemaker's Favourite Hawke's Bay Chardonnay 2008 (★★★★☆, $20.99)
Tohu Marlborough Sauvignon Blanc 2009 (★★★★☆, $18.95)
Reds:
Church Road Hawke's Bay Merlot/Cabernet Sauvignon 2007 (★★★★☆, $26 – but the average retail price in supermarkets is $16)
Grasshopper Rock Central Otago Pinot Noir 2008 (★★★★★, $29.95)
Vidal Hawke's Bay Merlot/Cabernet Sauvignon 2007 (★★★★★, $19.95)

The Wine Glut

How much cheaper can it get? Marlborough Sauvignon Blanc was rarely seen under $15 until a few years ago – if you wanted a bottle of white wine for less than $10, you bought an Aussie Chardonnay. Then popular brands such as Montana Marlborough Sauvignon Blanc and Villa Maria Private Bin Marlborough Sauvignon Blanc started dipping under $10 on 'special'. Now, supermarkets are promoting brands of Marlborough Sauvignon Blanc none of us have ever heard of before, at prices we have never heard of before – $6.99 or even $5.99.

After more than two decades of swift, relentless expansion, there's a new air of caution in the New Zealand wine industry. Key, sobering trends include falling wine consumption in the industry's key markets, at home and abroad, and a surge in the proportion of exports shipped as bulk wine.

A couple of years ago, if you visited one of the country's throng of wineries, you'd find a positive feeling in the air. 'Over the past decade, we have made many projections about sales growth,' enthused Stuart Smith, chair of New Zealand Winegrowers, at the start of his 2008 annual report. 'Each year we have seen them fulfilled and even surpassed. This year is no exception; the industry is right on track for $1 billion of exports by 2010.'

Why did the industry flourish for so long? Smith, part-owner of Fairhall Downs winery in Marlborough, believes it stuck to its guns on three key issues: 'quality, a strong and unified national brand, and fulfilling the expectations of ever more discerning retailers and consumers'.

The figures tell the story. Between 2000 and 2008, the area of bearing vines spread from 10,197 to 27,416 hectares; the number of wineries leapt from 358 to over 600; and the country's total production soared from 6.69 million cases to 22.8 million cases of wine.

The signs of expansion are everywhere. Peter Yealands, who launched his Yealands Estate range from the 2008 vintage, recently established New Zealand's largest privately owned vineyard, draped across 1000 hectares of the lower Awatere Valley, from the foothills of the Kaikoura Ranges to bluffs overlooking Cook Strait.

Following a bumper harvest in 2008, winemakers were smiling in many regions. In the Wairarapa, the 2008 crop was more than twice as big as the frost-devastated 2007; in Central Otago, it was nearly three times larger; in Canterbury, four times larger.

Overall, New Zealand's wine-growers harvested 285,000 tonnes in 2008, a 39 per cent leap on the previous record, set in 2007. After the heaviest-yielding vintage of the decade, Sauvignon Blanc, Pinot Gris, Riesling, Gewürztraminer, Viognier and Pinot Noir were all in record supply.

But after doubling their output in four years, in 2008 many winemakers began to question the rate of growth. 'In the short term, it lays down a challenge to the industry to sell through a larger than expected quantity without undermining New Zealand's position in the market,' admitted New Zealand Winegrowers.

By late 2008, a growing number of vineyards were for sale, especially in Marlborough and Central Otago. Yealands calculated that vineyard planting in 2008 slowed to just 10 per cent of the previous year's pace, and predicted that wine companies would start exercising clauses in their supply contracts with growers, to limit maximum grape yields per hectare.

In early 2009, fears surfaced in Marlborough that the region's image would be tarnished if export markets were flooded with cheap wine. John Forrest, of Forrest Estate, told the *Marlborough Express* that most wineries crushed more fruit than they needed in 2008. About 20 per cent, he estimated, was of poor quality.

'How do we save the Marlborough and New Zealand wine industry from slipping down to a bulk white-wine producer you can buy for around three pounds to five pounds in the UK, like Chile is?' pondered Forrest. However, his solution for dealing with the surplus ('Tip it') was unlikely to appeal to his colleagues.

Then came the 2009 harvest of 285,000 tonnes – just as big as the massive 2008 vintage, which has caused major oversupply problems and downward pressure on prices. After many years of not being able to supply demand, in 2008 wineries were eager to take the extra fruit, but a large amount of that 2008 wine remains unsold.

According to *Winepress*, the 2009 crop could easily have been even bigger – 300,000 to 400,000 tonnes. At a December 2008 meeting in Marlborough, attended by more than 500, Philip Gregan, CEO of New Zealand Winegrowers, called for grape-growers and wine company representatives to work together to avoid another oversupply by reducing their crops.

Vineyard workers swung into action on millions of vines, removing canes and thinning shoots and bunches. According to vineyard contractor Ken Prouting, 'It's quite devastating for us to be dropping all that fruit.'

It's a sobering fact, however, that several New Zealand wine companies made no wine in 2009. With tanks, barrels and warehouses brimming with wine from 2008 and previous seasons, they sold their grapes or simply left them unpicked.

Wine sales are immune to economic trends, according to a popular school of thought. Even if we can't find a reason to celebrate, we'll drink to drown our sorrows.

So much for that theory. After many years of steadily rising consumption, Kiwis are drinking *less* wine. Gregan says consumers are faced with a choice: 'Is it petrol for the car or wine for the table? The car needs to be driven.' He first noticed in 2007 that the industry's domestic demand was levelling out, 'and then from January 2008 it really dipped'.

The good news is that New Zealand winemakers are now grabbing a rising share of their domestic market. Bulk wine imports are dropping, reflecting the huge volume of New Zealand wine produced in the past couple of vintages and its availability at lower and lower prices.

But wine drinkers are trading down. Simon Mackenzie, of Point Wines on Auckland's North Shore, reports a marked drop in sales of $30-plus white wines and $40-plus reds. 'We're offering a lot more specials.'

As consumers trade down, many wineries are reducing prices to retain demand.

'There are so many specials around that drinkers are able to maintain the quality of wine they buy, even though they are paying less,' says Jeff Poole, of Fine Wine Delivery Company. To protect their principal brands from discounting, many wine companies are launching second- and even third-tier brands at lower prices.

Exports are still expanding swiftly, but according to New Zealand Winegrowers, 'the sales growth hides some big issues'. The biggest concern is the trend to bulk wine exports. In mid-2009, nearly 20 per cent of New Zealand's wine exports were in bulk, up from 5 per cent the previous year. In the UK, where New Zealand first carved out its international reputation, 99 per cent of the recent growth was due to bulk exports.

'It is all centred around Sauvignon Blanc and it is cannibalising bottled wine and other varietal sales,' says New Zealand Winegrowers. 'These bulk sales threaten to undermine New Zealand's super-premium reputation and price point.' Supermarkets in the UK are currently selling 'house brand' Marlborough Sauvignon Blancs at less than £4 per bottle.

Sauvignon Blanc producers aren't the only ones hurting. 'Bottom falls from local grape industry, growers sacked,' screamed the headline in the *Gisborne Herald* on 19 June. It was a 'black day' for Gisborne, following a 'shock announcement that Pernod Ricard NZ [formerly Montana] no longer wants a substantial amount of the grapes it takes from this district'. Growers were to be offered three options: business as usual for a lucky few; two years' notice; or immediate termination with compensation.

The key problem for Gisborne, the self-proclaimed 'Chardonnay capital of New Zealand', is that too many of us have switched from drinking Chardonnay to Sauvignon Blanc, a classic cool-climate variety for which Gisborne is too warm.

The biggest issue facing the industry, according to Gregan, is the runaway expansion of vineyards in Marlborough. 'We currently have too many vines for the markets we are predicting.'

With Marlborough Sauvignon Blanc traditionally in short supply, prices for the region's wines, grapes and land stayed high, but now that the wine supply exceeds demand, prices for all three are softening. The average price of Sauvignon Blanc grapes plunged from $2322 a tonne in 2008 to $1635 in 2009.

The value of land in Marlborough suitable for viticulture soared from $70,000 per hectare in 2000 to more than $250,000 in 2007, but is now falling. Many vineyards are for sale around the country, but there are few buyers. 'This year, for lifestyle viticulture, has been the slowest ever,' says Dick Nardella of Century 21, after 13 years in real estate.

Some blocks will be uprooted. 'We have too many grapes planted in Marlborough,' believes Smith, 'and some vineyards may have to be pulled out, just as apple and kiwifruit orchards have been in the recent past.'

The wine lake will not be drained quickly. In 2010, Gregan has calculated the industry will still be sitting on 30 million litres of surplus 2008 wine. 'Vintage 09 will produce another surplus, maybe just over 15 million litres. The good news is we have cut last year's surplus in half, but the problem is we have added to the 08 surplus, meaning we have an overall surplus of around 45 million litres [60 million bottles].'

Central Otago Vintners, a company set up to be one of New Zealand's largest Pinot Noir producers and owner of the McArthur Ridge brand, slipped into receivership in late 2008. The pioneering William Hill Winery at Alexandra, which has also marketed wine under the brand Shaky Bridge, was placed in receivership in May 2009, followed two months later by Daniel Schuster Wines, in Waipara.

Steve Green, part-owner of Carrick winery, in Central Otago, says established wineries in the region are facing greater competition than ever before. 'A lot of new wineries are putting cheaper wine on the market, without any long-term approach.'

More failures are inevitable. 'For wineries it is incredibly competitive,' says Gregan. 'Nobody is making money domestically. . . . Our supply situation is just part of it; the recession is another. So, yes, I think we are going to see change. There is no doubt about it.'

Classic Wines of New Zealand

A crop of four new Super Classics (Seresin Marlborough Sauvignon Blanc, Lawson's Dry Hills Marlborough Gewürztraminer, Clos de Ste Anne Chardonnay Naboth's Vineyard and Villa Maria Reserve Marlborough Pinot Noir), 13 new Classics and 14 Potential Classics are the features of this year's extensively revised list of New Zealand wine classics.

What is a New Zealand wine classic? It is a wine that in quality terms consistently ranks in the very forefront of its class. To qualify for selection, each label must have achieved an outstanding level of quality for at least three vintages; there are no flashes in the pan here.

By identifying New Zealand wine classics, my aim is to transcend the inconsistencies of individual vintages and wine competition results, and highlight consistency of excellence. When introducing the elite category of Super Classics, I restricted entry to wines which have achieved brilliance in at least five vintages (compared to three for Classic status). The Super Classics are all highly prestigious wines, with a proven ability to mature well (even the Sauvignon Blancs, compared to other examples of the variety).

The Potential Classics are the pool from which future Classics will emerge. These are wines of outstanding quality which look likely, if their current standards are maintained or improved, to qualify after another vintage or two for elevation to Classic status. All the additions and elevations on this year's list are identified by an asterisk.

An in-depth discussion of New Zealand's greatest wines (what they taste like, how well they mature, the secrets of their success) can be found in the second edition of my book *Classic Wines of New Zealand* (Hodder Moa, 2005), which grew out of the *Buyer's Guide*'s annually updated list of New Zealand wine classics.

Super Classics

Branded and Other White Wines
Cloudy Bay Te Koko

Chardonnay
Ata Rangi Craighall; Clearview Reserve; ***Clos de Ste Anne Naboth's Vineyard; Kumeu River Estate; Kumeu River Mate's Vineyard; Neudorf Moutere; Sacred Hill Riflemans; Te Mata Elston

Gewürztraminer
Dry River; ***Lawson's Dry Hills Marlborough

*** New Super Classic*

Pinot Gris
Dry River

Riesling
Dry River Craighall Vineyard; Felton Road; Pegasus Bay

Sauvignon Blanc
Cloudy Bay; Palliser Estate; Saint Clair Wairau Reserve; ***Seresin Marlborough

Sweet Whites
Dry River Late Harvest Craighall Riesling; Villa Maria Reserve Noble Riesling

Branded and Other Red Wines
Esk Valley The Terraces; Goldwater Goldie; Te Mata Coleraine

Cabernet Sauvignon-predominant Reds
Stonyridge Larose Cabernets

Merlot
Esk Valley Winemaker's Merlot-predominant blend

Pinot Noir
Ata Rangi; Dry River; Fromm Fromm Vineyard; Martinborough Vineyard; Pegasus Bay; ***Villa Maria Reserve Marlborough

Syrah
Te Mata Estate Bullnose

Classics

Chardonnay
Babich Irongate; Church Road Reserve; Cloudy Bay; Coopers Creek Swamp Reserve; **Dog Point Vineyard; Dry River; Esk Valley Winemakers Hawke's Bay; Fromm Clayvin Vineyard; Martinborough Vineyard; Montana 'O' Ormond; Pegasus Bay; **Seresin Reserve; **Stonecroft Hawke's Bay; **Te Whau Vineyard Waiheke Island; **Vidal Reserve; **Villa Maria Reserve Barrique Fermented Gisborne; Villa Maria Reserve Marlborough; Wither Hills Wairau Valley Marlborough

Chenin Blanc
Millton Te Arai Vineyard

Gewürztraminer
**Johanneshof Marlborough; Stonecroft Old Vine

Pinot Gris
**Martinborough Vineyard; **Villa Maria Single Vineyard Seddon

Riesling
Palliser Estate

Sauvignon Blanc
Lawson's Dry Hills Marlborough; Nga Waka; Te Mata Cape Crest; Villa Maria Reserve Clifford Bay; Villa Maria Reserve Wairau Valley

Sweet Whites
**Forrest Estate Botrytised Riesling; Glazebrook Regional Reserve Noble Harvest Riesling

Bottle-fermented Sparklings
Deutz Marlborough Cuvée; **Deutz Marlborough Cuvée Blanc de Blancs; Nautilus Cuvée Marlborough; Pelorus

Branded and Other Red Wines
Babich The Patriarch; **Craggy Range Le Sol; Newton Forrest Estate Cornerstone; Unison Selection

Cabernet Sauvignon-predominant Reds
Brookfields Reserve Vintage ['Gold Label'] Cabernet/Merlot; Te Mata Awatea Cabernets/Merlot; Villa Maria Reserve Hawke's Bay Cabernet Sauvignon/Merlot

Merlot
Vidal Reserve Merlot/Cabernet Sauvignon; Villa Maria Reserve Hawke's Bay Merlot

Pinot Noir
Felton Road Block 3; Fromm Fromm Vineyard; Gibbston Valley Reserve; Greenhough Hope Vineyard; Neudorf Moutere; Neudorf Moutere Home Vineyard; Palliser Estate; Wither Hills Marlborough

Syrah
Mills Reef Elspeth; **Passage Rock Reserve; Stonecroft

Potential Classics

Branded and Other White Wines
Craggy Range Les Beaux Cailloux

Chardonnay
*Corbans Cottage Block Hawke's Bay; *Mission Jewelstone Hawke's Bay; Ngatarawa Alwyn; Odyssey Reserve Iliad; Te Awa; Trinity Hill Gimblett Gravels; Villa Maria Single Vineyard Keltern

Gewürztraminer
Cloudy Bay; *Villa Maria Single Vineyard Ihumatao; *Vinoptima Ormond Reserve

Pinot Gris
*Escarpment Martinborough

Riesling
*Carrick Josephine Central Otago; Framingham Classic; Muddy Water Growers' Series James Hardwick Waipara; Neudorf Moutere

Sauvignon Blanc
Astrolabe Marlborough; *Clifford Bay Awatere Valley Marlborough; Clos Henri Marlborough; Greenhough Nelson; Highfield Marlborough; Montana 'B' Brancott Marlborough; Staete Landt Marlborough; Whitehaven Marlborough

Viognier
*Clos de Ste Anne Les Arbres; Trinity Hill Gimblett Gravels; Villa Maria Single Vineyard Omahu Gravels Vineyard

Sweet White Wines
Cloudy Bay Late Harvest Riesling; *Ngatarawa Alwyn Winemaker's Reserve Noble Harvest Riesling

Bottle-fermented Sparklings
Quartz Reef Méthode Traditionnelle Vintage

Rosé
Esk Valley Merlot/Malbec Rosé

Branded and Other Red Wines
Benfield & Delamare; Clearview

Enigma; Craggy Range Sophia; Craggy Range The Quarry; Puriri Hills Reserve; Te Awa Boundary; Tom

Cabernet Sauvignon-predominant Reds
Mills Reef Elspeth Cabernet/Merlot; Mills Reef Elspeth Cabernet Sauvignon; *Sacred Hill Helmsman Cabernet/Merlot

Merlot
Hans Herzog Spirit of Marlborough Merlot/Cabernet Sauvignon; Sacred Hill Brokenstone; Villa Maria Cellar Selection Merlot/Cabernet Sauvignon

Montepulciano
Hans Herzog Marlborough

Pinot Noir
Bannock Brae Barrel Selection; Carrick Central Otago; Dog Point Vineyard Marlborough; Felton Road Block 5; Felton Road Central Otago; Fromm Clayvin Vineyard; *Hans Herzog Marlborough; Kaituna Valley Canterbury The Kaituna Vineyard; Mt Difficulty Single Vineyard Pipeclay Terrace; Muddy Water Slowhand; Olssen's Slapjack Creek; Pegasus Bay Prima Donna; Peregrine Central Otago; *Pisa Range Block Poplar; *Quartz Reef Bendigo Estate Vineyard; Quartz Reef Central Otago; Terravin Hillside Reserve; Villa Maria Cellar Selection Marlborough; Villa Maria Single Vineyard Seddon

Syrah
Bilancia La Collina; *Craggy Range Gimblett Gravels Vineyard Block 14; Passage Rock; Trinity Hill Homage; Vidal Reserve

---

The following wines are not at the very forefront in quality terms, yet have been produced for many vintages, are extremely widely available and typically deliver good to excellent quality and value. They are all benchmark wines of their type – a sort of Everyman's classic.

Chardonnay
Church Road Hawke's Bay; Montana Gisborne; Morton Estate White Label Hawke's Bay; Stoneleigh Marlborough; Stoneleigh Marlborough; Villa Maria Private Bin Marlborough

Gewürztraminer
Seifried Nelson

Riesling
Montana South Island (previously Marlborough); Seifried Nelson

Sauvignon Blanc
Shingle Peak Marlborough; Montana Marlborough; Oyster Bay Marlborough;

Sparklings
Lindauer Brut; Lindauer Special Reserve

Merlot
Church Road Hawke's Bay Merlot/Cabernet

Pinot Noir
Villa Maria Private Bin Marlborough

Cellar Sense

Someone gives you a good bottle of Chardonnay, Riesling, Pinot Noir or Merlot, but it's only a year or two old. Should you drink it or cellar it?

Surveys show that most wine in New Zealand is drunk on the day it is bought and only 1 per cent is cellared for more than a year. Everyone relishes the idea of a personal wine cellar, packed with vintage wines maturing slowly to their peak – but few of us actually do it. Instead, it's three or four bottles in a little rack perched on top of the fridge.

To enjoy many wines at the peak of their powers, you do need to lay them down. Some people keep wine far too long. They *worship* their famous bottles, picking them up from time to time, fondling them, talking about them, but never get around to opening them – until they are well past their best.

A friend called me over a couple of years ago to sort out his cellar, acquired in a burst of enthusiasm 20 years earlier. His interest in wine later faded and the bottles had been lying under his house ever since. 'Bring a corkscrew. I can't find mine any more.'

It was hard going. After several bottles, it was clear that most New Zealand wines don't repay keeping for 20 or 30 years. Nor do most of the world's wines. But another tasting revealed that good New Zealand wines can certainly mature well for a decade.

Opened four years ago, 22 highly rated whites from the 1990 to 1994 vintages, although stored in an uncomfortably hot office, yielded some delicious surprises. Most were still alive, nine were enjoyable and four were magical: Matua Valley Reserve Sauvignon Blanc 1994, grown in West Auckland; Neudorf Moutere Riesling 1994; Dry River Craighall Estate Riesling 1994, from Martinborough; and Dry River Gewürztraminer 1994.

The oldest New Zealand wine I've ever tasted was McWilliam's Hawke's Bay Cabernet Sauvignon 1965. I snapped up a bottle for $20 at an auction several years ago, knowing that the wine once acclaimed as New Zealand's greatest-ever red would be well past its best. A mellow, faded conversation-piece, it was still alive – just.

Others have had more exciting experiences. In 1892, William Beetham planted a 1.2-hectare vineyard at Masterton, mostly in Pinot Noir, Pinot Meunier and Syrah. In 1985, Beetham's descendants broached a rare bottle of his Lansdowne Claret 1903. Geoff Kelly, then the wine columnist for *National Business Review*, enthused that the 82-year-old wine was 'alive and well . . . with the oak standing firm, yet amazing fruit, body and freshness for the age. The finish is superb, long and lingering.'

For my book, *Classic Wines of New Zealand* (second edition 2005), I conducted vertical tastings of over 100 of New Zealand's top wines. In a vertical tasting, several – perhaps all – vintages of a wine are tasted side by side, allowing you to assess the overall quality of a wine, the evolution of its style, the impact of vintage variation, and its maturation potential.

One insight from the tastings was that the best South Island Chardonnays age just as well as those from the most prestigious Chardonnay region, Hawke's Bay. Fromm Clayvin Vineyard Chardonnay, from Marlborough, and Neudorf Moutere Chardonnay, from Nelson, blossom in the bottle for a minimum of five years – every bit as long as such Hawke's Bay classics as Te Mata Elston Chardonnay and Sacred Hill Riflemans Chardonnay.

Another trend in the Chardonnay section was for the wines from cooler vintages to mature better than those from warmer seasons. Crisp, firmly structured Chardonnays may be less seductive in their youth than fleshy, soft models, but they often perform better over the long haul.

Red wines grown in cool-climate regions can be distinctly herbaceous, with green-edged, leafy characters becoming more evident over time, as the toasty, smoky influence of new oak recedes. At a tasting in 2007 in Central Otago, I expressed the view that herbaceous notes are especially evident in the region's mature Pinot Noirs and that they reach their peak earlier than those from Martinborough.

The winemakers responded by sending me a case of 2002 vintage Pinot Noirs to assess. With more than five years under their belt, how well had they matured?

Overall, pretty well. From a light-cropping, early-maturing season in Central Otago, all of the wines were alive and the majority were ripe-tasting, although several were distinctly leafy. Whether the wines were more enjoyable than when they were released four years earlier was a matter of debate. When the region's young vineyards reach maturity, we'll get a clearer idea of the wines' cellaring potential.

So which wines most repay cellaring? First, forget the idea that all wines improve with age. Most New Zealand wine is best drunk young.

I suggest drinking fine-quality New Zealand Sauvignon Blancs at a year to 18 months old; the good news is that screwcaps are preserving the wines' freshness markedly better than corks did. Most Pinot Gris, Gewürztraminers and Viogniers are at their best between 18 months and three years old; fine-quality Chardonnays at two to five years old; and top Rieslings at three to seven years old. Some outstanding examples will flourish for longer, but if you buy a case, it pays to check regularly.

Pinot Noirs and Merlots typically drink well at two to five years old. No one knows yet how well Syrah, the hot new red-wine variety, will mature, but the top Cabernet/Merlot blends from Hawke's Bay and Waiheke Island are still the safest bet for long-term cellaring.

Cellaring Guidelines

Grape variety	Best age to open

White

Grape variety	Best age to open
Sauvignon Blanc	
(non-wooded)	9–18 months
(wooded)	1–3 years
Gewürztraminer	1–3 years
Viognier	1–3 years
Pinot Gris	1–4 years
Sémillon	1–4 years
Chenin Blanc	1–5 years
Chardonnay	2–5 years
Riesling	2–5+ years

Red

Grape variety	Best age to open
Pinotage	1–3 years
Malbec	1–3 years
Cabernet Franc	1–4 years
Merlot	2–5 years
Pinot Noir	2–5 years
Syrah	2–5 years
Cabernet Sauvignon	3–7+ years
Cabernet/Merlot	3–7+ years

Other

Grape variety	Best age to open
Sweet whites	2–4 years
Bottle-fermented sparklings	3–5+ years

How to Use this Book

It is essential to read this brief section to understand how the book works. Feel free to skip any of the other preliminary pages, but not these.

The majority of wines have been listed in the book according to their principal grape variety, as shown on the front label. Lawson's Dry Hills Marlborough Sauvignon Blanc, for instance, can be located simply by turning to the Sauvignon Blanc section. Wines with front labels that do not refer clearly to a grape variety or blend of grapes, such as Cloudy Bay Te Koko or Mills Reef Elspeth One, can be found in the Branded and Other Wines sections for white and red wines.

Most entries are firstly identified by their producer's names. Wines not usually called by their producer's name, such as Drylands Marlborough Sauvignon Blanc (from Constellation New Zealand), or Triplebank Awatere Valley Marlborough Pinot Noir (from Pernod Ricard NZ), are listed under their most common name.

The star ratings for quality reflect my own opinions, formed where possible by tasting a wine over several vintages, and often a particular vintage several times. *The star ratings are therefore a guide to each wine's overall standard in recent vintages*, rather than simply the quality of the latest release. However, to enhance the usefulness of the book, in the body of the text I have also given a *quality rating for the latest vintage of each wine*; sometimes for more than one vintage.

I hope the star ratings give interesting food for thought and succeed in introducing you to a galaxy of little-known but worthwhile wines. It pays to remember, however, that wine-tasting is a business fraught with subjectivity. You should always treat the views expressed in these pages for what they are – one person's opinion.

The quality ratings are:

★★★★★	Outstanding quality (gold medal standard)
★★★★☆	Excellent quality, verging on outstanding
★★★★	Excellent quality (silver medal standard)
★★★☆	Very good quality
★★★	Good quality (bronze medal standard)
★★☆	Average quality
★★	Plain
★	Poor
No star	To be avoided

These quality ratings are based on comparative assessments of New Zealand wines against one another. A five-star Merlot/Cabernet Sauvignon, for instance, is an outstanding-quality red judged by the standards of other Merlot/Cabernet Sauvignon blends made in New Zealand. It is not judged by the standards of overseas reds of a similar style (for instance Bordeaux), because the book is focused solely on New Zealand wines and their relative merits. (Some familiar New Zealand wine brands in recent years have included varying proportions of overseas wine. To be featured in this book, they must still include at least some New Zealand wine in the blend.)

Where brackets enclose the star rating on the right-hand side of the page, for example (★★★), this indicates the assessment is only tentative, because I have tasted very few vintages of the wine. A dash is used in the relatively few cases where a wine's quality has oscillated over and above normal vintage variations (for example ★—★★★).

Super Classic wines, Classic wines and Potential Classic wines (see page 22) are highlighted in the text by the following symbols:

Super Classic	Classic	Potential Classic

Each wine has also been given a dryness-sweetness, price and value-for-money rating. The precise levels of sweetness indicated by the four ratings are:

DRY	Less than 5 grams/litre of sugar
MED/DRY	5–14 grams/litre of sugar
MED	15–49 grams/litre of sugar
SW	50 and over grams/litre of sugar

Less than 5 grams of sugar per litre is virtually imperceptible to most palates – the wine tastes fully dry. With between 5 and 14 grams, a wine has a hint of sweetness, although a high level of acidity (as in Rieslings or even Marlborough Sauvignon Blancs, which often have 4 to 6 grams per litre of sugar) reduces the perception of sweetness. Where a wine harbours over 15 grams, the sweetness is clearly in evidence. At above 50 grams per litre, a wine is unabashedly sweet.

Prices shown are based on the average price in a supermarket or wine shop (as indicated by the producer), except where most of the wine is sold directly to consumers from the winery, either over the vineyard counter or via mail order or the Internet.

The art of wine buying involves more than discovering top-quality wines. The real challenge – and the greatest satisfaction – lies in identifying wines at varying quality levels that deliver outstanding value for money. The symbols I have used are self-explanatory:

–V	=	Below average value
AV	=	Average value
V+	=	Above average value

The ratings discussed thus far are all my own. Many of the wine producers themselves, however, have also contributed individual vintage ratings of their own top wines over the past decade and the 'When to drink' recommendations. (The symbol **WR** indicates Winemaker's Rating, and the symbol **NM** alongside a vintage means the

wine was not made that year.) Only the producers have such detailed knowledge
of the relative quality of all their recent vintages (although in some cases, when the
information was not forthcoming, I have rated a vintage myself). The key point you
must note is that *each producer has rated each vintage of each wine against his or her
highest quality aspirations for that particular label, not against any absolute standard.*
Thus, a 7 out of 7 score merely indicates that the producer considers that particular
vintage to be an outstanding example of that particular wine; not that it is the best-
quality wine he or she makes.

The 'When to drink' (**Drink**) recommendations (which I find myself referring
to constantly) are largely self-explanatory. The **P** symbol for PEAKED means that a
particular vintage is already at, or has passed, its peak; no further benefits are expected
from aging.

Here is an example of how the ratings work:

Mt Difficulty Single Vineyard Pipeclay Terrace Pinot Noir ★★★★★

A powerful, lush Central Otago red with densely packed, cherryish, plummy flavours,
spicy and long. It is grown on a steep, relatively hot slope at Bannockburn, with bony,
gravelly soils. Tasted in late 2008, the 2000 was maturing well, building a savoury,
nutty complexity, while the star 2002 vintage was still fairly youthful in colour, with
beautifully rich plum/cherry flavours, vibrant and harmonious; it's lovely now. There
was no 2006 vintage. The full-coloured 2007 (★★★★☆), matured for 14 months
in French oak barriques, was bottled unfined and unfiltered. Described by the winery
as 'distinctively masculine', it is sturdy, very ripe and sweet-fruited, with a strong
surge of plum, spice and liquorice flavours, braced by firm tannins. One for the
cellar; open 2011+.

Vintage	07	06	05	DRY $90 AV
WR	7	NM	7	
Drink	09-20	NM	11-17	

The winemaker's own ratings indicate that the 2007 vintage is of outstanding quality for the label, and is recommended for drinking between 2009 and 2020.

Describes 'Classic' status, ranging from 🍇🍇🍇 for Super Classic, 🍇🍇 for Classic to 🍇 for Potential Classic. This is a wine that in quality terms ranks in the forefront of its class.

Dryness-sweetness rating, price and value for money. This wine is dry in style (below 5 grams/litre of sugar). At $90 it is average value for money.

Quality rating, ranging from ★★★★★ for outstanding to no star (−), to be avoided. This is generally a wine of outstanding quality.

White Wines

Arneis

Still rare here – so rare it is not listed separately in the New Zealand Vineyard Survey 2008 – Arneis (pronounce the 'neis' as in 'place') is a traditional grape of Piedmont, in north-west Italy, where it yields soft, early-maturing wines with slightly herbaceous aromas and almond flavours. First planted in New Zealand in the late 1990s at the Clevedon Hills Vineyard in South Auckland, its potential is now being explored by Pernod Ricard NZ, Trinity Hill and several other producers. Coopers Creek released the country's first varietal Arneis from the 2006 vintage.

Coopers Creek SV Gisborne Arneis The Little Rascal ★★★★

Who would have thought Arneis would perform so well in Gisborne? The 2008 vintage (★★★★) is a mouthfilling (14.5 per cent alcohol), dryish wine with a subtle, floral bouquet and fresh, lively, citrus and tropical-fruit flavours. It shows very good depth and harmony, with a slightly spicy finish.

MED/DRY $23 AV

The Doctors' Marlborough Arneis (★★★★)

Already drinking well, the debut 2009 vintage (★★★★) from Forrest is floral, fresh and full-bodied, with a basket of ripe-fruit flavours, suggestive of peaches, pears and spices. Off-dry (5 grams/litre of residual sugar), it shows excellent depth.

Vintage	09
WR	6
Drink	09-12

MED/DRY $25 AV

Trinity Hill Hawke's Bay Arneis ★★★★

The 2008 vintage (★★★★) has a fragrant, citrusy, slightly nutty bouquet. A concentrated blend of Arneis (95 per cent) and Viognier (5 per cent), grown in the Gimblett Gravels and mostly fermented in tanks, but also in seasoned French oak barrels, it is weighty (14.5 per cent alcohol), with strong tropical-fruit and spice flavours, showing considerable complexity, and a bone-dry finish.

DRY $19 V+

Branded and Other White Wines

Cloudy Bay Te Koko, Craggy Range Les Beaux Cailloux, Dog Point Vineyard Section 94 – in this section you'll find all the white wines that don't feature varietal names. Lower-priced branded white wines can give winemakers an outlet for grapes like Chenin Blanc, Sémillon and Riesling that otherwise can be hard to sell. They can also be an outlet for coarser, less delicate juice ('pressings'). Some of the branded whites are quaffers, but others are highly distinguished.

Alluviale Blanc (★★★☆)

Weighty and restrained, the 2008 vintage (★★★☆) was grown at Mangatahi, in Hawke's Bay. A blend of Sauvignon Blanc (94 per cent) and Sémillon (6 per cent), partly French oak-fermented, it is full-bodied and dry, with ripe, non-herbaceous fruit flavours, a subtle seasoning of oak and a slightly creamy texture. Still very youthful, it should reward cellaring; open 2010+.

DRY $23 –V

Amor-Bendall The Cru ★★★☆

There's no mention of Chardonnay on the label of the 2006 vintage (★★★☆), but there's no question of this Gisborne wine's varietal origin. Barrel-fermented and lees-stirred weekly, it is fat and soft, with stone-fruit, toffee, caramel and toast flavours in a very upfront style.

DRY $45 –V

Artisan Betty Davis (★★★☆)

Grown in the Tara Vineyard at Oratia, in West Auckland, the debut 2007 vintage (★★★☆) is a barrel-fermented blend of Pinot Gris (85 per cent) and Viognier (15 per cent). The wood subdues Pinot Gris' scentedness, but the wine is weighty, with ripe pear and spice flavours showing very good depth, a hint of nutty oak adding complexity and a dry, rounded finish.

DRY $25 –V

Bell Bird Spring Home Block White (★★★★)

Showing greater complexity than most young aromatic whites, the 2008 vintage (★★★★) is a single-vineyard, Waipara blend of Pinot Gris, Riesling, Muscat and Gewürztraminer, fermented in old oak barriques. Instantly attractive, it's a weighty, medium style (20 grams/litre of residual sugar), rich, spicy and oily, with gentle acidity and excellent flavour depth and harmony.

MED $30 –V

Black Ridge Otago Gold ★★☆

'Great to chill right down', the Alexandra winery's white for summer quaffing is typically floral and light, its citrusy flavours harbouring a distinct splash of sweetness. It's an enjoyable drop, but the big wineries churn out this sort of wine cheaper.

MED $13 AV

Cheeky Little White ★★☆

From Babich, the 2007 vintage (★★☆) was made from Chardonnay, grown in Hawke's Bay. Mouthfilling and smooth, slightly peachy and creamy, with gentle acidity, it's a very easy-drinking style, bargain-priced.

DRY $10 V+

Clearview Endeavour   (★★★★★)

New Zealand's most expensive white wine is grown at Te Awanga, in Hawke's Bay, and bottled exclusively in magnums. Barrel-matured for two and a half years, the 2007 vintage (tasted prior to bottling, and so not rated) is a richly fragrant, powerful wine, sweet-fruited, with highly concentrated flavours of grapefruit, peach and nectarine and a biscuity, mealy complexity. It should be long-lived.

Vintage	07
WR	7
Drink	09-20

DRY $240 (1.5L) –V

Cloudy Bay Te Koko   ★★★★★

Te Koko o Kupe (the oyster dredge of Kupe) is the original name for Cloudy Bay; it is also the name of the Marlborough winery's intriguing oak-aged Sauvignon Blanc. The gorgeous 2006 vintage (★★★★★) was grown at six sites around the Wairau Valley and harvested at an average of 24 brix. Fermented with indigenous yeasts in French oak barrels (only 10 per cent new, to ensure a subtle oak influence), it was matured for 16 months in wood on its yeast lees, and part of the blend went through a softening malolactic fermentation. Beautifully scented, it is powerful, sweet-fruited and silky textured, with highly concentrated, gently oaked flavours and a long, dry, seamless finish. Always fleshy, lush, complex and well-rounded, Te Koko lies well outside the mainstream regional style of Sauvignon Blanc, but is well worth discovering.

Vintage	06	05	04	03
WR	7	7	6	6
Drink	10-13	09-12	09-10	09-11

DRY $53 AV

Craggy Range Les Beaux Cailloux   ★★★★★

Since the debut 2001, Craggy Range's flagship Chardonnay has emerged as an unusually complex Hawke's Bay wine with loads of personality and great texture, mouthfeel and depth. Based on low-yielding Gimblett Gravels vines, it is fermented with indigenous yeasts and lees-aged for up to 17 months in French oak barriques (54 per cent new in 2007), with a full, softening malolactic fermentation. The 2007 vintage (★★★★★) is a majestic, notably refined wine with a beautifully fragrant, complex, mealy bouquet. Weighty (14.5 per cent alcohol), with deep grapefruit and stone-fruit flavours, mealy, nutty notes adding complexity and a hint of butterscotch, it is finely poised, with great texture and harmony. Already drinking well, it's still unfolding.

Vintage	07
WR	7
Drink	10-14

DRY $60 AV

Dada   (★★★★☆)

Labelled simply as 'a blended, dry white wine from New Zealand' but expensive, Dada 1 2007 (★★★★☆) is from a Hawke's Bay producer. Pale lemon/green, with a slightly funky bouquet, it is not labelled as Sauvignon Blanc because that would 'automatically pigeon-hole the wine and the benchmark default to Marlborough Sauvignon Blanc'. Full of personality, it is dry, peachy, spicy and slightly toasty, in a youthful, complex style with a long finish. Alluviale Blanc 2008 (above) is from the same winemakers, Kate Galloway and David Ramonteau.

DRY $50 –V

Dog Point Vineyard Section 94   ★★★★☆

Looking for 'texture, rather than rich aromatics', winemaker James Healy and his partner, Ivan Sutherland, fermented and lees-aged their 2007 (★★★★★) Sauvignon Blanc for 18 months in seasoned French oak casks. Hand-picked in Sutherland's Dog Point Vineyard (for which 'Section 94' was the original survey title) and fermented with indigenous yeasts, it's a mouthfilling, finely structured wine, still unfolding, with a ripely scented, slightly funky bouquet. Mouthfilling, fresh and vibrant, it is very sweet-fruited, with highly concentrated peach and passionfruit flavours, a hint of sweetness (5.6 grams/litre of residual sugar), balanced acidity and a tight finish.

Vintage	07	06	05	04	03
WR	5	6	6	5	6
Drink	09-12	09-11	09-11	09-10	09-10

MED/DRY $33 AV

Hopsbarn White   (★★★)

From Moutere Hills vineyard, the 2007 vintage (★★★) is a Nelson blend of Chardonnay (principally) with Sauvignon Blanc and Pinot Gris. A weighty, flavoursome, dry wine, it is slightly nutty and minerally, with some complexity.

DRY $22 –V

John Forrest Collection The White   ★★★★

With his uniquely diverse blend, winemaker John Forrest is after a 'full-bodied, dry style with fruit intensity and acid definition, but no excess of wood, malolactic fermentation or sugar'. It is billed as an 'uninhibited' marriage of up to seven grape varieties (Viognier, Sauvignon Blanc, Pinot Gris, Chenin Blanc, Riesling, Chardonnay and Gewürztraminer) drawn from Marlborough, Hawke's Bay, Central Otago and the Waitaki Valley. The 2006 vintage (★★★★☆), a full-bodied wine with excellent weight and depth of grapefruit, peach, pear and spice flavours, now developing toasty, bottle-aged notes, is a dryish, fruit-driven style with unusual flavour complexity. The 2007 (★★★☆) is simpler, with good body and depth of slightly herbaceous, lychee and pear flavours, balanced acidity and a fresh, smooth finish (7 grams/litre of residual sugar).

Vintage	07	06
WR	6	6
Drink	10-15	09-11

MED/DRY $50 –V

Millton Les Trois Enfants Clos Monique   (★★★★☆)

The debut 2007 vintage (★★★★☆) is a single-vineyard Gisborne blend of Gewürztraminer, Pinot Gris and Riesling, grown together at Clos Monique, picked together and fermented together. Pale straw, with a complex bouquet, peachy and distinctly spicy, it is impressively full and concentrated, with unobtrusive sweetness (12 grams/litre of residual sugar) and fresh acidity. The Gewürztraminer makes its presence well felt, but the blend possesses more weight, richness and complexity than most 'straight' Gewürztraminers, with a lingering, spicy finish.

Vintage	07
WR	6
Drink	09-10

MED/DRY $27 AV

Moutere Hills Sarau (★★★)

The distinctive 2007 vintage (★★★) is a slightly funky Nelson blend of Chardonnay, Pinot Gris, Sauvignon Blanc and Chenin Blanc, fermented and aged for 10 months in all-new oak barrels. Mouthfilling and vibrant, it looked excellent in its youth, with concentrated, peachy, slightly spicy and minerally flavours and a tight, dry finish. However, when retasted in early 2009, it was past its best.

DRY $42 –V

Paritua Grace ★★★☆

The 2008 vintage (★★★☆) is a medium-bodied Hawke's Bay blend of Sauvignon Blanc and Sémillon, barrel-fermented and oak-aged for 10 months. Fresh, crisp and minerally, it is slightly creamy and nutty, with very good depth and complexity, firm acid spine and a tight, dry finish. Best drinking mid-2010+.

Vintage	08
WR	7
Drink	09-13

DRY $30 –V

Rippon Vineyard Ralph Hotere White Wine ★★☆

Grown on the shores of Lake Wanaka, in Central Otago, this wine is made 'for summer drinking, not sipping'. Since 2006 it has been made from Osteiner (a crossing of Riesling and Sylvaner). It typically tastes like a restrained Riesling – tangy, with light body and slightly sweet lemon, apple and lime flavours cut with fresh acidity.

MED/DRY $17 –V

Seresin Chiaroscuro (★★★★☆)

The debut 2007 vintage (★★★★☆) is a full-bodied, finely textured dry blend of 42 per cent Chardonnay (for 'structure'), 32 per cent Pinot Gris (for 'texture'), 19.5 per cent Riesling (for 'fruity acidity') and 6.5 per cent Pinot Meunier ('spicy interest'). Grown organically in the Home Vineyard at Renwick, in Marlborough, the grapes were hand-picked and co-fermented with indigenous yeasts in French oak barriques. Oak-aged for 17 months, and given a full, softening malolactic fermentation, it's a light yellow, peachy, lemony and spicy wine, with complexity, sweet-fruit delights and a faintly buttery, lingering, well-rounded finish.

DRY $60 –V

Terravin Te Ahu ★★★★☆

Already delicious, the 2008 vintage (★★★★★) is a Sauvignon Blanc from Marlborough vines cropped at 'almost half the regional average'. Fermented and matured in French oak barrels, it is mouthfilling and sweet-fruited, with a ripely scented, gently oaked bouquet, concentrated, ripe tropical-fruit flavours, showing excellent complexity, and a tight, powerful finish. Drink now or cellar.

DRY $36 –V

Te Whare Ra Toru ★★★★

This is a Marlborough blend of three ('toru') varieties – Gewürztraminer, Riesling and Pinot Gris – hand-picked and tank-fermented. The 2007 vintage (★★★★) is full-bodied (13.5 per cent alcohol) and smooth, with ripe pear, spice and slight ginger flavours, gentle sweetness (13 grams/litre of residual sugar) and good delicacy, harmony and depth.

MED/DRY $22 AV

White Cloud Medium White Wine ★★

From Constellation NZ (formerly Nobilo), this was once a huge seller, here and abroad – a sort of New Zealand version of Blue Nun. However, despite the name 'White Cloud' and a picture of what looks like the Southern Alps on the label, the non-vintage bottling (★★) on sale in 2009 is a blend of New Zealand and Australian wines. It's a soft, medium-bodied wine with a distinct splash of sweetness amid its simple lemony, slightly peachy flavours.

MED $9 AV

White Wire ★★☆

From Mount George, a subsidiary of Paritua, the 2008 vintage (★★★) was made mostly from Gisborne and Hawke's Bay Chardonnay, blended with Gewürztraminer (5 per cent), Riesling (5 per cent) and Sauvignon Blanc (4 per cent). It's a good, easy quaffer, fresh, fruity, tasty and smooth (6.5 grams/litre of residual sugar), with citrusy, peachy, slightly spicy flavours.

MED/DRY $15 AV

Wooing Tree Blondie ★★★

This is a *blanc de noir* – a white (or rather faintly pink) Central Otago wine, estate-grown at Cromwell. The 2009 vintage (★★★) was made from Pinot Noir grapes; the juice was held briefly in contact with the skins and then tank-fermented. Enjoyable from the start, it's a fresh, crisp, strawberryish and slightly spicy wine with appetising acidity and a slightly off-dry finish.

DRY $25 –V

Breidecker

A nondescript crossing of Müller-Thurgau and the white hybrid Seibel 7053, Breidecker is rarely seen in New Zealand. There were 32 hectares of bearing vines recorded in 2003, but only 7 hectares in 2009. Its early-ripening ability is an advantage in cooler regions, but Breidecker typically yields light, fresh quaffing wines, best drunk young.

Hunter's Breidecker ★★★

This Marlborough wine is made 'for those who are new to wine'. Grown in the Wairau Valley, it is typically floral, fresh, light and lively, with a distinct splash of sweetness (14 grams/litre of residual sugar in 2008), gentle acidity and ripe flavours of lemons and apples in a very charming style, easy to gulp.

Vintage	09
WR	5
Drink	09-10

MED/DRY $16 AV

Chardonnay

New Zealand Chardonnay has yet to make the huge international impact of our Sauvignon Blanc. Our top Chardonnays are world class, but so are those from numerous other countries in the Old and New Worlds. In the year to mid-2009, Chardonnay accounted for 4.4 per cent by volume of New Zealand's wine exports (far behind Sauvignon Blanc, with 81.1 per cent, and also Pinot Noir with 5.5 per cent).

There's an enormous range to choose from. Most wineries – especially in the North Island and upper South Island – make at least one Chardonnay; many produce several and the big wineries produce dozens. The hallmark of New Zealand Chardonnays is their delicious varietal intensity; the leading labels show notably concentrated aromas and flavours, threaded with fresh, appetising acidity.

Yet Chardonnay is less popular than a few years ago, when it was the country's most prestigious white-wine variety. Sauvignon Blanc now decisively outsells Chardonnay in supermarkets and in restaurants, while Pinot Gris is flying high.

The price of New Zealand Chardonnay ranges from under $10 to $240 (for a magnum of Clearview Endeavour). The quality differences are equally wide, although not always in relation to their prices. Lower-priced wines are typically fermented in stainless steel tanks and bottled young with little or no oak influence; these wines rely on fresh, lemony, uncluttered fruit flavours for their appeal.

Recent vintages have brought a surge of unoaked Chardonnays, as winemakers with an eye on overseas markets strive to showcase New Zealand's fresh, vibrant fruit characters. Without oak flavours to add richness and complexity, Chardonnay handled entirely in stainless steel tanks can be plain – even boring. The key to the style is to use well-ripened, intensely flavoured grapes.

Mid-price wines may be fermented in tanks and matured in oak casks, which adds to their complexity and richness, or fermented and/or matured in a mix of tanks and barrels. The top labels are fully fermented and matured in oak barriques (normally French, with varying proportions of new casks); there may also be extended aging on (and regular stirring of) yeast lees and varying proportions of a secondary, softening malolactic fermentation (sometimes referred to in the tasting notes as 'malo'). The best of these display the arresting subtlety and depth of flavour for which Chardonnay is so highly prized.

Chardonnay plantings have been far outstripped in recent years by Sauvignon Blanc, as wine producers respond to overseas demand, and in 2010 will constitute 12.2 per cent of the bearing vineyard. The variety is spread throughout the wine regions, particularly Hawke's Bay (where 31 per cent of the vines are concentrated), Gisborne (30 per cent) and Marlborough (28 per cent). Gisborne is renowned for its softly mouthfilling, ripe, peachy Chardonnays, which offer very seductive drinking in their youth; Hawke's Bay yields sturdy wines with rich grapefruit-like flavours, power and longevity; and Marlborough's Chardonnays are slightly leaner in a cool-climate, more appley, appetisingly crisp style.

Chardonnay has often been dubbed 'the red-wine drinker's white wine'. Chardonnays are usually (although not always, especially cheap models) fully dry, as are all reds with any aspirations to quality. Chardonnay's typically mouthfilling body and multi-faceted flavours are another obvious red-wine parallel.

Broaching a top New Zealand Chardonnay at less than two years old can be infanticide – the finest of the 2007s will offer excellent drinking during 2010. If you must drink Chardonnay when it is only a year old, it makes sense to buy one of the cheaper, less complex wines specifically designed to be enjoyable in their youth.

3 Stones Hawke's Bay Unoaked Chardonnay   (★★☆)

From Ager Sectus (which also owns Crossroads, The Crossings and Southbank Estate), the 2007 vintage (★★☆) is a Hawke's Bay wine, sturdy and smooth, with lemony, appley flavours woven with fresh acidity. A solid quaffer.

Vintage	07
WR	7
Drink	09-10

DRY $20 –V

Akarua Central Otago Chardonnay   ★★★☆

This is consistently one of the region's best Chardonnays. Estate-grown at Bannockburn and fermented and matured in French oak barriques (30 per cent new), the 2008 vintage (★★★☆) is a finely balanced wine, fresh and crisp, with ripe, citrusy, slightly nutty flavours that linger well.

Vintage	08	07	06	05
WR	6	6	6	6
Drink	09-14	10-11	09-10	P

DRY $27 –V

Akarua Unoaked Chardonnay   ★★☆

Handled in stainless steel tanks, this Central Otago wine is typically lemony, appley and lively, offering simple, easy drinking. Estate-grown at Bannockburn, the 2007 vintage (★★☆) is a medium-bodied wine, pleasantly fresh and crisp.

Vintage	08	07	06
WR	4	5	5
Drink	09-11	09-10	P

DRY $20 –V

Ake Ake Chardonnay Reserve   (★★★☆)

The 2008 vintage (★★★☆) was hand-picked at Kerikeri, in the Bay of Islands, and fermented and matured in a mix of tanks and new American oak barriques, with weekly lees-stirring. It's a mouthfilling wine with very good depth of fresh, ripe, slightly buttery flavours in a moderately complex style, worth cellaring.

Vintage	08
WR	5
Drink	09-11

DRY $29 –V

Alana Estate Martinborough Chardonnay   ★★★★☆

This winery produces consistently stylish Chardonnays that mature well. Hand-harvested and fermented and matured in French oak casks, the 2007 vintage (★★★★☆) has a complex, slightly peachy bouquet. Weighty, with impressively rich stone-fruit flavours, gently seasoned with biscuity oak, it shows good richness, texture and harmony, with a long finish.

Vintage	08	07
WR	5	7
Drink	10-16	09-13

DRY $42 –V

Alexandra Wine Company Feraud's Chardonnay   ★★★☆

The 2007 vintage (★★★☆) was grown at Alexandra, in Central Otago. Fermented in French oak casks (20 per cent new), it is weighty and finely textured, with a fragrant, creamy bouquet and lemony, slightly appley and nutty flavours, showing good drive and immediacy.

Vintage	08	07	06		DRY $21 AV
WR	5	6	5		
Drink	09-11	09-10	09		

Alexia Hawke's Bay Unoaked Chardonnay   (★★★)

The 2007 vintage (★★★) from Jane Cooper, winemaker at Matahiwi Estate, under her own label, is an easy-drinking wine, mouthfilling, with ripe stone-fruit flavours and a smooth, slightly off-dry finish (4.8 grams/litre of residual sugar).

DRY $20 –V

Allan Scott Marlborough Chardonnay   ★★★☆

This label began as a fruit-driven style, but in recent years has shown greater complexity and is now consistently satisfying. The 2008 (★★★☆), matured in French oak barriques (20 per cent new), is a forward vintage, fresh, smooth, citrusy and slightly buttery, with good depth and strong, drink-young appeal.

Vintage	08	07	06	05	04	DRY $22 AV
WR	5	6	6	6	6	
Drink	09-13	09-13	09-12	09-11	09-10	

Allan Scott Unwooded Marlborough Chardonnay   ★★☆

Handled entirely in stainless steel tanks, this is typically a citrusy, appley, creamy-smooth wine, with plenty of flavour in a refreshing, uncomplicated style.

DRY $19 –V

Allan Scott Wallops Marlborough Chardonnay   ★★★★

This single-vineyard wine is typically rich, creamy and complex. Barrel-fermented with indigenous yeasts and given a full, softening malolactic fermentation, the 2008 vintage (★★★★) is a refined wine, still very youthful, with vibrant grapefruit-like flavours, finely integrated oak and fresh, lively acidity. It's a complex style, well worth cellaring.

Vintage	08	07	DRY $29 AV
WR	7	7	
Drink	09-14	09-13	

Alpha Domus AD Chardonnay   ★★★★☆

This is a single-vineyard Hawke's Bay wine, hand-picked, fermented with indigenous and cultured yeasts, and lees-aged, with stirring, for 10 months in French oak barriques (55 per cent new in 2007). The 2007 vintage (★★★★☆) – the first since 2004 – is very fragrant, with mouthfilling body and ripe grapefruit and nut flavours, showing excellent delicacy and concentration. A youthful, very tightly structured and elegant wine, with good acid spine, it should be long-lived.

Vintage	07	06	05	04
WR	7	NM	NM	7
Drink	09-11	NM	NM	P

DRY $35 –V

Alpha Domus Barrique Fermented Chardonnay ★★★☆

This is the Hawke's Bay winery's middle-tier Chardonnay. Estate-grown and fermented and lees-aged for six months in French oak barrels (20 per cent new), the 2006 vintage (★★★☆) is ripe, citrusy and slightly toasty, in a moderately concentrated style with a tight, dry, creamy-smooth finish.

Vintage	08	07	06	05
WR	7	6	6	6
Drink	09-13	09-11	09-10	P

DRY $23 AV

Alpha Domus The Pilot Chardonnay ★★★

This is typically a freshly scented Hawke's Bay wine with crisp, lively lemon and apple flavours, a gentle seasoning of oak and strong drink-young appeal. The 2008 vintage was mostly handled in tanks, but 15 per cent of the blend was oak-aged.

Vintage	08	07	06	05
WR	6	6	6	6
Drink	09-12	09-10	09	P

DRY $19 AV

Amor-Bendall The Cru – see Branded and Other White Wines

Anchorage Nelson Chardonnay ★★★

Estate-grown at Motueka and oak-aged for 10 months, the 2007 vintage (★★★) is slightly creamy, with good body and peachy, buttery, toasty flavours, showing good depth.

DRY $19 AV

Anchorage Reserve Chardonnay (★★★)

The 2008 vintage (★★★) is a Nelson wine, based on young, first-crop vines and fermented initially in tanks, then in French oak barrels (100 per cent new). It's a medium-bodied style with fresh, ripe, lemony, toasty flavours, showing moderate complexity, and a slightly buttery, rounded finish.

DRY $21 –V

Anchorage Unoaked Chardonnay ★★★

From the Motueka-based Drummond family, the 2007 vintage (★★★) is a fresh, lively Nelson wine, made without oak or malolactic fermentation. Mouthfilling, it has crisp, citrusy, slightly peachy flavours, showing good ripeness, balance and depth.

DRY $17 AV

Artisan Geordie's Block Gisborne Chardonnay (★★★☆)

Grown in Geordie Witters' vineyard at Waiohika and mostly handled in tanks (10 per cent was matured in seasoned barrels), the 2006 vintage (★★★☆) is mouthfilling, ripe, fruity and smooth, in a moderately complex style with very good balance and depth. Ready.

DRY $19 V+

Artisan Kauri Ridge Oratia Chardonnay ★★★☆

Grown in the Kauri Ridge Vineyard in West Auckland, the 2006 vintage (★★★☆) was fermented in French oak casks (40 per cent new). A powerful, very full-bodied wine (14.5 per cent alcohol) with dried fig and apricot flavours and a mealy, biscuity complexity, it is ripe, rounded and ready for drinking from now onwards.

Vintage	06
WR	6
Drink	09-11

DRY $23 AV

Ascension The Ascent Reserve Matakana Chardonnay ★★★★

Estate-grown, the 2007 vintage (★★★★) was hand-picked and fermented and lees-aged for 11 months in French oak barriques (25 per cent new). Delicious now, it has a slightly honeyed and toasty bouquet leading into a full-bodied wine with strong, ripe, peachy, slightly buttery and nutty flavours, smooth and rich. Full of personality, it's a high-flavoured style, for drinking now or cellaring.

DRY $35 –V

Ashwell Chardonnay ★★★★

The 2008 vintage (★★★★) is a barrel-fermented Martinborough wine, elegant and youthful, with ripe, sweet-fruit characters, citrusy, mealy flavours and a deliciously creamy texture. Drink now or cellar.

Vintage	08	07	06
WR	6	6	7
Drink	09-13	09-12	09-10

DRY $26 AV

Askerne Hawke's Bay Chardonnay ★★★☆

Estate-grown north of Te Mata Peak, in top vintages such as 2007 (★★★★☆) this is a great buy. The 2008 (★★★) was matured for nine months in French (92 per cent) and American oak casks, with 55 per cent malolactic fermentation. It's a peachy and creamy, slightly honeyed, flavoursome wine, but less rich and complex than usual.

Vintage	08	07	06	05	04
WR	6	7	6	5	6
Drink	09-13	09-12	09-11	P	P

DRY $20 AV

Askerne Reserve Chardonnay ★★★★

Only made in top vintages, this is a refined Hawke's Bay wine, fermented and matured in French oak casks (60 per cent new in 2007). The 2007 (★★★★) has a fragrant bouquet, citrusy, slightly buttery and oaky. Mouthfilling and slightly creamy, it offers concentrated grapefruit and toast flavours, rounded and rich.

Vintage	07
WR	7
Drink	10-14

DRY $30 –V

Aspire Chardonnay   ★★★

From Matariki, this Hawke's Bay wine is estate-grown in the Gimblett Gravels and at Havelock North. It's typically fresh and crisp, with citrusy flavours and a subtle twist of oak. The 2007 vintage (★★★), matured in tanks and seasoned oak barrels, is a mid-weight style with fresh, ripe, citrusy flavours to the fore, a hint of toasty oak and good depth.

Vintage	07	06
WR	6	6
Drink	09-12	09-11

DRY $20 –V

Astrolabe Voyage Marlborough Chardonnay   (★★★★)

The generous 2007 vintage (★★★★) was hand-picked, fermented – partly with indigenous yeasts – in French and American oak casks, wood-aged for 10 months, and given a full, softening malolactic fermentation. Still youthful, it's a stylish wine, mouthfilling and creamy, with vibrant, ripe tropical-fruit flavours, fresh acidity and well-integrated, biscuity notes adding complexity.

Vintage	07
WR	6
Drink	09-14

DRY $27 AV

Ata Rangi Craighall Chardonnay   ★★★★★

This consistently memorable Martinborough wine has notable body, richness, complexity and downright drinkability. Made from a company-owned block of low-yielding, mostly over 20-year-old, Mendoza clone vines in the Craighall Vineyard, it is hand-picked, whole-bunch pressed and fully fermented in French oak barriques (25 per cent new). The 2007 vintage (★★★★★) is one for the cellar. The bouquet is fragrant, mealy and slightly buttery; the palate refined, fresh and vibrant, with sweet-fruit delights and highly concentrated, peachy, slightly toasty flavours, crisp and long. It should be in peak shape from 2010 onwards.

Vintage	07	06	05	04	03	02
WR	7	7	6	6	7	7
Drink	09-15	09-12	09-11	09-10	P	P

DRY $38 AV

Ata Rangi Petrie Chardonnay   ★★★★

This single-vineyard wine is grown south of Masterton, in the Wairarapa. It's not in the same class as its Craighall stablemate (above), but the price is lower. It is typically fragrant and creamy, with rich peach and grapefruit characters, a distinct touch of butterscotch and a well-rounded finish. There was no 2007, due to frost. From a top vintage, the 2008 (★★★★☆) was hand-picked and fermented and lees-aged for seven months in French oak barriques (25 per cent new), with 30 per cent malolactic fermentation. It's an elegant, rich wine, slightly creamy, with finely balanced acidity and concentrated, peachy, sweet-fruit flavours, delicious from the start.

Vintage	06	05	04	03	02
WR	7	6	7	NM	7
Drink	09-10	P	09-10	NM	P

DRY $28 AV

Auntsfield Cob Cottage Marlborough Chardonnay   ★★★★

A consistently rewarding wine. Estate-grown on the south side of the Wairau Valley, hand-picked and fermented (partly with indigenous yeasts) in French oak barriques (40 per cent new), the 2008 vintage (★★★★) is full-bodied and youthful, with rich, ripe, peachy, slightly creamy flavours, good texture and obvious cellaring potential. The classy 2007 (★★★★☆) has a biscuity, mealy bouquet. Weighty and youthful, it is sweet-fruited, with concentrated, vibrant, grapefruit-like flavours, showing good complexity, a hint of butterscotch, and a slightly creamy finish.

Vintage	08	07	06	05	04
WR	6	7	7	6	6
Drink	09-16	09-15	09-14	09-13	09-11

DRY $32 –V

Aurum 45th Parallel Vineyard Chardonnay   (★★★★)

The 2007 vintage (★★★★) was estate-grown in the 45th Parallel Vineyard at Lowburn, in Central Otago, hand-picked, and fermented and lees-aged for 10 months in French oak barrels (25 per cent new) with a full, softening malolactic fermentation. A mouthfilling wine with fresh, strong grapefruit and peach flavours, it has mealy, biscuity characters adding complexity and a crisp, dry finish.

Vintage	07
WR	6
Drink	09-10

DRY $23 V+

Awa Valley Chardonnay   ★★★☆

A consistently enjoyable wine, priced right. Grown at Huapai, in West Auckland, the 2007 vintage (★★★☆) was hand-harvested and barrel-fermented. Full-bodied, with sweet oak aromas and ripe grapefruit and peach flavours, it has mealy, oaky notes adding richness and a dry, smooth finish.

Vintage	07	06	05
WR	6	7	7
Drink	09+	P	P

DRY $20 AV

Awaroa Hawke's Bay Stell Chardonnay   (★★★★)

From a Waiheke Island-based winery, the 2007 vintage (★★★★) was hand-harvested in the Stell Vineyard at Te Awanga, in Hawke's Bay, and matured in French oak casks (40 per cent new). Full-bodied and slightly creamy, with grapefruit and stone-fruit flavours and a subtle seasoning of wood, it's not a showy wine, but quietly satisfying, with excellent harmony, texture and length.

DRY $22 V+

Babich Gimblett Gravels Hawke's Bay Chardonnay   ★★★

The 2007 vintage (★★★☆) was fermented in tanks (80 per cent) and new French oak casks (20 per cent). A fruit-driven style, it is mouthfilling and sweet-fruited, with vibrant, citrusy, appley flavours, and good weight and texture. It's reminiscent of Chablis, except with gentler acidity. The 2008 (★★★) is fresh, fruity and crisp, with vibrant, citrusy, peachy, slightly biscuity flavours, balanced for easy drinking.

Vintage	08	07	06	05	04
WR	4	7	NM	NM	7
Drink	09-12	09-12	NM	NM	P

DRY $20 –V

Babich Irongate Chardonnay   ★★★★★

Babich's flagship Chardonnay. A stylish wine, Irongate has traditionally been leaner and tighter than other top Hawke's Bay Chardonnays, while performing well in the cellar, but the latest releases have more drink-young appeal. It is based on hand-picked fruit from the shingly Irongate Vineyard in Gimblett Road, west of Hastings, whole-bunch pressed, fully barrel-fermented (about 20 per cent new), and lees-matured for up to nine months. Malolactic fermentation was rare up to and including the 2002, but is now a growing influence. The 2006 (★★★★☆) is a rich, creamy wine with citrusy, deftly oaked, slightly minerally flavours, drinking well now. The 2007 (★★★★★) is a top vintage. Very sweet-fruited and rounded, it has deep peach and grapefruit flavours, hints of nuts and biscuits, and excellent complexity and fragrance. Drink now or cellar.

> DRY $35 AV

Babich Lone Tree Unoaked Chardonnay   ★★★

Made with no 'intrusion' of oak flavour, this wine is handled entirely in tanks, with 'a bit of malolactic fermentation and lees-stirring' to add complexity. It is typically finely balanced, with fresh, citrusy flavours showing good delicacy and depth. The 2008 vintage (★★☆), grown in Hawke's Bay, is lemony and crisp, fruity and slightly honeyed, in a pleasant, drink-young style.

> DRY $16 AV

Beach House Hawke's Bay Chardonnay   ★★★★

This rare wine has a strong record in blind tastings. Grown near the coast, at Te Awanga, and French and American oak-fermented, it is typically fleshy and sweet-fruited, with grapefruit-like flavours seasoned with toasty oak in a smooth style, showing excellent harmony and richness.

Vintage	08
WR	7
Drink	09-19

> DRY $23 V+

Bell Bird Bay New Zealand Chardonnay   ★★★☆

Made at Alpha Domus, the 2007 (★★★☆) is a good example of the fruit-driven style. A full-bodied Hawke's Bay wine with ripe, peachy flavours, fresh and finely balanced for easy drinking, it's not complex, but delicious. (The 2008 vintage, also from Hawke's Bay, was mostly handled in tanks, but 10 per cent of the blend was oak-aged.)

Vintage	08
WR	6
Drink	09-12

> DRY $14 V+

Bell Hill Chardonnay   ★★★★★

At its best, as in 2004 (★★★★★), this is a magical wine, extremely rich and minerally. Only one barrel was made of the 2005 vintage (★★★★☆). Grown at Waikari, in North Canterbury, and fermented and aged in 'old oak', with a full, softening malolactic fermentation, it is light yellow, with deep, well-spined flavours, showing some development. Concentrated, with a powerful presence in the mouth, it's drinking well now. Tasted from the barrel (and so not rated), the 2006 is very fragrant, with crisp, rich stone-fruit flavours.

Vintage	05
WR	7
Drink	09-14

> DRY $65 AV

Bensen Block Chardonnay   ★★★

The 2008 vintage (★★★) from Pernod Ricard NZ, grown in Gisborne, was made in a fruit-driven style. It's a flavoursome wine, ripe, slightly buttery and creamy, balanced for easy drinking.

Vintage	08	07	06	05
WR	5	6	6	5
Drink	09-10	P	P	P

DRY $17 AV

Black Barn Barrel Fermented Chardonnay   ★★★★

Grown on the Havelock North hills, hand-picked, fermented with some use of indigenous yeasts in French oak barriques and given a full, softening malolactic fermentation, this is typically a classy wine. The 2007 vintage (★★★★) is an elegant wine, vibrantly fruity, with a strong seasoning of toasty oak (60 per cent new) but fresh, concentrated fruit flavours to match. It should mature gracefully.

Vintage	07	06	05	04
WR	7	6	6	5
Drink	09-14	P	P	P

DRY $35 –V

Black Barn 5 Barrel Chardonnay   (★★★★)

The refined 2007 vintage (★★★★) is a Hawke's Bay wine with strong, grapefruit-like flavours and a nutty, mealy complexity from fermentation and aging in one-year-old barrels. It shows excellent freshness, delicacy and depth, with obvious cellaring potential.

DRY $28 AV

Black Barn Hawke's Bay Chardonnay   ★★★☆

The 2008 vintage (★★★☆) is a barrel-fermented wine with ripe, citrusy flavours seasoned with toasty oak, a slightly creamy texture, and very good complexity and depth. It's an upfront style, already enjoyable.

Vintage	07
WR	6
Drink	09-12

DRY $28 –V

Black Barn Unoaked Chardonnay   (★★☆)

The 2008 vintage (★★☆) is a mouthfilling, dry Hawke's Bay wine with ripe, grapefruit-like flavours. It's a solid wine, but lacks a bit of freshness and vibrancy.

DRY $20 –V

Black Estate Omihi Waipara Chardonnay   ★★★★

The 2007 (★★★★☆) has a rich, toasty, buttery bouquet. A powerful wine (14.5 per cent alcohol), it's highly expressive, with concentrated, peachy, buttery, toasty flavours, woven with fresh acidity, in a bold style, drinking well now. The 2008 vintage (★★★☆) was hand-picked and barrel-fermented, mostly in seasoned oak (8 per cent new). Bright, light yellow-green, it is youthful, tight and crisp, with strong, citrusy, slightly buttery flavours and firm acid spine.

Vintage	08	07
WR	6	6
Drink	10-15	10-13

DRY $30 –V

Blackenbrook Nelson Chardonnay   ★★★☆

This single-vineyard Moutere wine is hand-picked and matured in American and French oak barrels. It is typically robust (the 2006 and 2007 vintages are both 15 per cent alcohol), with strong, ripe stone-fruit flavours seasoned with nutty oak.

Vintage	07	06	05	04
WR	7	7	6	6
Drink	09-11	09-10	09-10	P

DRY $24 AV

Blackenbrook Nelson Reserve Chardonnay   (★★★)

The 2006 vintage (★★★) was harvested at a very ripe 24.8 brix and fermented and matured for a year in barrels, mostly new American. It's a strapping wine (15 per cent alcohol), with concentrated, peachy flavours, but the fruit flavours are slightly overwhelmed by oak. (The previous release, from 2004, was labelled as Barrel Fermented Chardonnay.)

Vintage	07
WR	7
Drink	08-11

DRY $31 –V

Blue Ridge Marlborough Chardonnay   ★★★★

From West Brook. Delicious in its youth, the fully barrel-fermented 2007 (★★★★) is an upfront style with fresh, strong flavours of grapefruit and pears. It's a sweetly oaked wine with a fully dry, slightly creamy finish.

Vintage	07
WR	7
Drink	09-12

DRY $25 AV

Boatshed Bay by Goldwater Marlborough Chardonnay   ★★★☆

Fresh, fruity and slightly creamy, with ripe, citrusy flavours, the 2008 vintage (★★★) was mostly handled in tanks; 10 per cent of the blend was French oak-aged. It's an enjoyable, easy-drinking style, with a touch of complexity.

Vintage	08	07
WR	6	6
Drink	09-11	09-10

DRY $17 V+

Borthwick Vineyard Wairarapa Chardonnay   ★★★☆

The 2007 vintage (★★★☆) was grown in Dakins Road, near Masterton, and fermented with indigenous yeasts in French and American oak casks. It's a full-flavoured wine, ripe and peachy, with hints of butterscotch and toast, fresh acidity and a smooth finish.

DRY $24 AV

Bouldevines Marlborough Chardonnay   ★★★☆

Grown on the south side of the Wairau Valley, the 2006 vintage (★★★★) is a single-vineyard wine, fully oak-aged. Showing good freshness and balance, with ripe grapefruit flavours, subtle oak and a rounded finish, it is maturing well – rich and mealy, with excellent complexity, texture and length.

Vintage	06
WR	5
Drink	09-11

DRY $28 –V

Boundary Vineyards Tuki Tuki Road Hawke's Bay Chardonnay ★★★☆

Pernod Ricard NZ's wine is grown at a 'semi-coastal' site at Te Awanga. Fermented in Hungarian oak barriques (25 per cent new), with over 60 per cent of the blend given a softening malolactic fermentation, the 2008 vintage (★★★☆) is a generous, full-bodied wine with ripe stone-fruit flavours, nutty oak adding complexity, and a well-rounded finish. It's already drinking well.

Vintage	08	07	06	05
WR	5	6	7	5
Drink	09-10	P	P	P

DRY $20 AV

Brightside Nelson Chardonnay ★★☆

From Kaimira Ventures, the 2007 vintage (★★☆) of this lightly oaked wine was grown at Brightwater. It's a medium-bodied wine with fresh acidity, lemony, appley flavours and a slightly buttery, dry finish. The 2008 vintage (★★☆) is mouthfilling (14 per cent alcohol), with citrusy, slightly spicy flavours, showing a hint of toasty oak.

Vintage	08	07
WR	5	6
Drink	09-11	09-11

DRY $16 –V

Brightside Nelson Unoaked Chardonnay ★★☆

From Kaimira Ventures, the 2007 (★★☆) is mouthfilling (14.4 per cent alcohol), with lemony, slightly peachy flavours and creamy, buttery notes adding drink-young appeal. The 2008 vintage (★★☆) is citrusy and appley, with a fresh, crisp finish.

DRY $16 –V

Brightwater Vineyards Lord Rutherford Barrique Chardonnay ★★★★

The 2007 vintage (★★★★) is a single-vineyard Nelson wine, hand-picked and fermented in French oak barriques (25 per cent new). Oak-aged for 10 months, it is weighty and rich, with grapefruit, stone-fruit and butterscotch flavours showing good concentration, finely balanced oak and fresh acidity.

Vintage	07	06
WR	6	6
Drink	09-11	09-11

DRY $30 –V

Brightwater Vineyards Nelson Chardonnay ★★★☆

The stylish 2007 vintage (★★★★) was mostly handled in tanks, but a third of the blend was fermented and lees-aged in French oak barriques. Mouthfilling, vibrantly fruity and creamy, it has subtle, biscuity, leesy notes adding complexity and good weight, depth and roundness.

Vintage	07	06	05
WR	6	5	6
Drink	09-10	P	P

DRY $23 AV

Brookfields Bergman Chardonnay ★★★

Named after the Ingrid Bergman roses in the estate garden, this wine is grown alongside the winery at Meeanee, in Hawke's Bay, hand-picked, and fermented and matured on its yeast lees in seasoned French and American oak casks. The 2008 vintage (★★★☆), oak-aged for eight months, is mouthfilling, with ripe, peachy, slightly buttery flavours, showing good depth, and a dry, rounded finish.

Vintage	08	07	06
WR	7	7	7
Drink	09-13	09-12	09-11

DRY $19 AV

Brookfields Marshall Bank Chardonnay   ★★★★☆

Brookfields' top Chardonnay is named after proprietor Peter Robertson's grandfather's property in Otago. Grown in a vineyard adjacent to the winery at Meeanee and fermented and matured in mostly new French oak barriques, it is a rich, concentrated, strongly oak-influenced Hawke's Bay wine with peachy, toasty, buttery flavours, lush and complex. The 2007 vintage (★★★★) is light yellow/green, very citrusy, mealy and biscuity, with mouthfilling body, distinct grapefruit characters, good complexity and a crisp, dry, lingering finish.

Vintage	07
WR	7
Drink	09-12

DRY $30 AV

Brookfields Unoaked Hawke's Bay Chardonnay   (★★★☆)

Delicious from the start, the estate-grown 2009 vintage (★★★☆) is fresh-scented, with vibrant, ripe stone-fruit flavours, a hint of spice, and a very smooth (5 grams/litre of residual sugar) finish. A good example of the unwooded style, it offers very easy drinking.

Vintage	09
WR	7
Drink	10-12

MED/DRY $19 V+

Brunton Road Gisborne Chardonnay   ★★★☆

The 2008 vintage (★★★☆) of this single-vineyard wine was grown at Patutahi. A barrel-fermented style with fresh, ripe, peachy flavours seasoned with perfumed, toasty oak (French and American) and a creamy-smooth finish, it is moderately complex, with good depth and drink-young appeal.

DRY $25 –V

Bushmere Estate Classic Chardonnay   ★★★★

This is the winery's barrel-fermented, oak-aged style. The stylish 2007 vintage (★★★★) is a classic regional expression – Gisborne in a glass. Hand-picked at 24.5 brix, lees-stirred for six months and matured in French oak casks (46 per cent new) for nine months, it has substantial body, with ripe sweet-fruit characters and rich, citrusy, peachy flavours. A generous, satisfying wine, it's delicious now.

DRY $22 V+

Bushmere Estate Unoaked Gisborne Chardonnay   ★★★

A good example of the style, the 2007 vintage (★★★) was hand-picked at 24 brix and lees-aged briefly. Fresh and full-bodied, it has citrusy, peachy flavours in a simple but lively style, showing good ripeness and depth.

DRY $19 AV

Cable Bay Waiheke Chardonnay   ★★★★☆

Blended from six sites on the island – at Church Bay, Oneroa and Onetangi – this tightly structured wine opens out well with bottle-age. Hand-picked, it is fermented (partly with indigenous yeasts) and matured for 10 months in French oak barriques (around 15 per cent new), with no use of malolactic fermentation. Instantly appealing, the 2007 vintage (★★★★★) has lovely sweet-fruit flavours to the fore, with a delicate seasoning of toasty oak. Very fresh and vibrant, with excellent depth and harmony, it's the best vintage yet.

Vintage	07	06	05	04
WR	7	6	7	7
Drink	09-14	09-11	09-11	P

DRY $34 AV

Cable Station Marlborough Chardonnay   ★★★

From Cape Campbell, the 2007 vintage (★★★) is a lightly wooded style: '50 per cent of the wine had oak contact for seven months'. Vibrantly fruity, with grapefruit characters to the fore, a touch of creaminess and a soft finish, it's enjoyable young.

DRY $19 AV

Cadwalladers Riverside Hawke's Bay Chardonnay   ★★★

The 2007 vintage (★★★) is full-bodied, peachy and faintly honeyed, in a fruity, soft style with drink-young appeal.

DRY $15 V+

Cape Campbell Limited Edition Reserve Marlborough Chardonnay   ★★★★

A rich, upfront style. The 2007 vintage (★★★☆) was grown in the Kernick Vineyard at Rapaura and the Turner Vineyard at Blind River, and fermented in new and once-used American oak casks. The bouquet is mealy and sweetly oaked; the palate toasty, with good weight and depth of peachy, slightly buttery flavour.

Vintage	07
WR	6
Drink	09-11

DRY $25 AV

Cape Campbell Marlborough Chardonnay   ★★★☆

Grown at Rapaura, on the north side of the Wairau Valley, and partly American oak-aged, the 2008 vintage (★★★) is fresh and vibrant, with good depth of citrusy, slightly toasty flavours, finely balanced for early drinking.

DRY $18 V+

Carrick Cairnmuir Terraces EBM Chardonnay   ★★★★☆

From a region that has struggled to produce top Chardonnay, this wine is one of the best. The outstanding 2007 vintage (★★★★★), grown on the Cairnmuir Terraces at Bannockburn, was fermented and matured for 18 months (EBM means 'extended barrel maturation') in French oak barriques (20 per cent new for the first year, then entirely in older barrels). Richly fragrant, it is full-bodied, with citrusy, mealy, biscuity flavours, cool-climate freshness, and impressive complexity and richness.

Vintage	07	06	05	04	03	02
WR	7	5	6	6	7	6
Drink	10-14	09-12	09-11	09-10	09-10	P

DRY $32 AV

Carrick Central Otago Chardonnay ★★★★

A tight, elegant, cool-climate style, this wine is grown at Bannockburn and matured for a year in French oak barriques (15 per cent new). The 2007 vintage (★★★★☆) is impressive. Complex and minerally, it is full-bodied (14 per cent alcohol), with finely integrated oak and excellent depth of vibrant, citrusy, mealy flavours, dry and finely textured.

DRY $25 AV

Catalina Sounds Marlborough Chardonnay ★★★☆

The 2008 vintage (★★★) is a single-vineyard wine, hand-picked in the upper Wairau Valley and barrel-fermented. Still youthful, it's a medium-bodied style (12.5 per cent alcohol) with fresh acidity and citrusy, creamy, moderately complex flavours.

DRY $22 AV

Chard Farm Closeburn Chardonnay ★★★

The winery's second-tier Chardonnay is typically a fresh, vibrant Central Otago wine with appetising acidity. The 2007 vintage (★★★) was, as usual, handled entirely in tanks, with no exposure to oak. Full-bodied, it offers fresh, crisp, citrusy flavours, with minerally and buttery notes adding interest.

DRY $23 –V

Chard Farm Judge and Jury Chardonnay ★★★★

Named after a rocky outcrop overlooking the Gibbston (Central Otago) winery, the 2005 vintage (★★★★) was grown at two sites, at Cromwell and Wanaka, and barrel-fermented. Rich and vibrant, with fresh, citrusy, peachy flavours, showing a good balance of oak and acidity, it's an elegant, cool-climate style, maturing gracefully. (There is no 2006 or 2007.)

Vintage	05	04	03	02
WR	6	5	6	6
Drink	P	P	P	P

DRY $38 –V

Charles Wiffen Marlborough Chardonnay ★★★

Charles and Sandy Wiffen own a vineyard in the Wairau Valley, but their wine is made at West Brook in West Auckland. The 2007 vintage (★★★☆) was French oak-aged for 10 months. It's a vibrantly fruity style with ripe grapefruit, pear and spice flavours, finely integrated oak and a fresh, smooth finish.

DRY $23 –V

Church Road Cuve Chardonnay   (★★★★)

This label was originally reserved for rare wines, made in 'a more Burgundian, less fruit-driven, less oaky' style of Hawke's Bay Chardonnay than its lush and (at that stage) relatively fast-maturing Church Road Reserve stablemate. Since 2006, its production has been expanded and the price reduced significantly. The 2006 vintage (★★★★) was hand-picked, mostly at the company's Korokipo Vineyard, fermented with indigenous yeasts in French oak barriques (28 per cent new), and barrel-aged for over a year. Maturing gracefully, it has generous stone-fruit and toast flavours, with a more overt, toasty oak influence than the earlier releases, but excellent complexity, texture and length. Tasted prior to bottling (and so not rated), the 2008 looked promising – tightly structured, with deep, peachy, mealy flavours.

DRY $26 AV

Church Road Hawke's Bay Chardonnay   ★★★★

This typically mouthfilling, rich wine is made by Pernod Ricard NZ at the Church Road winery in Hawke's Bay. The 2008 vintage (★★★★) was fermented, partly with indigenous yeasts, in French (70 per cent) and Hungarian (30 per cent) oak barriques (a third new), and barrel-aged for 10 months on its full yeast lees, with fortnightly stirring. Fleshy and rounded, it has substantial body and ripe stone-fruit flavours showing good texture, complexity and depth. A forward vintage, it's already drinking well (and great value at its average supermarket price of $16).

Vintage	08	07	06
WR	5	6	7
Drink	09-10	09-10	09-10

DRY $26 AV

Church Road Reserve Chardonnay   ★★★★★

This classy wine is based on the 'pick' of Pernod Ricard NZ's Hawke's Bay Chardonnay crop. It is hand-harvested, fermented with indigenous yeasts in French oak barriques (53 per cent new in 2007), and stays on its yeast lees for the total time in barrel (up to 14 months), with frequent lees-stirring. In recent years, the wine has become more elegant, less 'upfront' in style, and should mature longer. The 2007 vintage (★★★★★) is outstanding. Richly fragrant and full-bodied, with concentrated, well-ripened grapefruit flavours, finely integrated oak and impressive complexity, it is still youthful and unfolding gracefully. (Tasted before bottling, and so not rated, the 2008 is sturdy, with strong, citrusy, peachy flavours, showing a slightly buttery richness.)

Vintage	07	06	05	04	03	02
WR	7	7	6	6	NM	7
Drink	09-10	P	P	P	NM	P

DRY $36 AV

C.J. Pask Declaration Chardonnay   ★★★★☆

The Hawke's Bay winery's top Chardonnay is grown in Gimblett Road and fermented and matured in all-new French oak barriques, with weekly lees-stirring. The 2007 vintage (★★★★) is a classic regional style, with rich, ripe stone-fruit flavours seasoned with French oak and fresh acidity keeping things lively.

Vintage	07	06	05	04
WR	7	7	6	7
Drink	09-11	09-10	P	P

DRY $45 –V

C.J. Pask Gimblett Road Hawke's Bay Chardonnay   ★★★☆

This second-tier Chardonnay is designed to highlight vibrant fruit characters, fleshed out with restrained wood. Maturing very gracefully, the 2007 vintage (★★★★) is mouthfilling and peachy, slightly creamy and nutty, with a hint of oak (30 per cent of the blend was barrel-aged), and fresh, lively fruit flavours shining through.

DRY $20 AV

C.J. Pask Roy's Hill Hawke's Bay Unoaked Chardonnay   ★★☆

Grown in Gimblett Road and handled in stainless steel tanks, the 2008 vintage (★★☆) is a medium-bodied style, fresh and crisp, with straightforward, appley flavours of moderate length.

DRY $15 AV

Clearview Beachhead Chardonnay   ★★★☆

This Hawke's Bay winery has a reputation for powerful Chardonnays, and top vintages of its second-tier label are no exception – big and rich. The lighter 2008 (★★★) was hand-picked at Te Awanga and fermented in seasoned French oak casks. It's a fruit-driven style, fresh-scented, with vibrant, grapefruit-like flavours to the fore, a subtle oak influence and moderate complexity.

Vintage	08
WR	6
Drink	09-14

DRY $25 –V

Clearview Reserve Chardonnay   ★★★★★

For his premium Hawke's Bay Chardonnay label, winemaker Tim Turvey aims for a 'big, grunty, upfront' style – and hits the target with ease. It's typically a hedonist's delight – an arrestingly bold, intense, savoury, mealy, complex wine with layers of flavour. Based on ultra-ripe fruit (hand-harvested at 24–25 brix from Te Awanga vines), the 2008 vintage (★★★★☆) was fermented in all-new barrels (75 per cent French) and lees-aged in oak, with weekly lees-stirring, for 11 months. Highly fragrant, rich and vibrantly fruity, it is weighty, with concentrated, well-ripened stone-fruit flavours, well seasoned with toasty oak, and a fresh, dry finish. It's still very youthful; best drinking mid-2010+.

Vintage	08	07	06	05	04
WR	7	7	7	7	7
Drink	09-18	09-14	09-12	09-11	P

DRY $35 AV

Clearview Unwooded Chardonnay   ★★★☆

This Hawke's Bay wine is a tank-fermented style, simple but full-flavoured. The 2008 vintage (★★★☆) was hand-picked at Te Awanga, on the coast, cool-fermented and lees-stirred, with 30 per cent malolactic fermentation. Instantly appealing, it's a full-bodied wine, not complex, but offering loads of fresh, vibrant, peachy flavour, dry, ripe and smooth.

Vintage	08	07
WR	7	6
Drink	09-15	P

DRY $19 V+

Clearwater Vineyards Waipara Chardonnay   (★★★☆)

Still on sale, the 2004 vintage (★★★☆) was fermented and lees-aged for a year in French oak barriques (40 per cent new). Maturing well, it's a creamy wine with grapefruit, toasty oak and slight butterscotch flavours, woven with fresh acidity, in a distinctly cool-climate style.

DRY $32 –V

Clos de Ste Anne Chardonnay Naboth's Vineyard   ★★★★★

Millton's flagship Chardonnay is based on mature vines in the steep, north-east-facing Naboth's Vineyard in the Poverty Bay foothills, planted in loams overlying sedimentary calcareous rock. Grown biodynamically and hand-harvested, it is fermented in mostly second-fill French oak barrels, and in most vintages it is not put through malolactic fermentation, 'to leave a pure, crisp mineral flavour'. The 2007 (★★★★★) is a powerful, complex Gisborne wine from a top vintage. Still youthful, it is very sturdy, ripe and concentrated, with a lovely array of peachy, slightly nutty, creamy and honeyed flavours, good acid balance and excellent potential. Certified organic.

Vintage	07	06	05	04	03	02
WR	7	7	7	7	6	7
Drink	09-17	09-16	09-15	09-14	P	09-12

DRY $54 AV

Cloudy Bay Chardonnay   ★★★★★

A powerful Marlborough wine with impressively concentrated, savoury, lemony, mealy flavours and a proven ability to mature well over the long haul (at least four years and up to a decade). The grapes, mostly hand-picked, are sourced from numerous company-owned and growers' vineyards in the Wairau and Brancott valleys. All of the wine is fermented (with a high proportion of indigenous yeasts) in French oak barriques (20 per cent new in 2007) and lees-aged in barrels for up to 15 months, and most goes through a softening malolactic fermentation. Still developing, the 2007 vintage (★★★★☆) is citrusy, nutty and minerally, with excellent complexity in a fresh, tight, firmly structured style with cool-climate vibrancy and vigour.

Vintage	07	06	05	04
WR	7	7	5	6
Drink	10-14	09-11	09-10	09-11

DRY $41 AV

Coniglio Hawke's Bay Chardonnay   ★★★★★

Launched by Morton Estate from 1998, Coniglio is one of New Zealand's most expensive Chardonnays. A Rolls-Royce version of the company's famous Black Label Chardonnay, it is typically an arresting wine, powerful and concentrated. Grown in the cool, elevated (150 metres above sea level) Riverview Vineyard at Mangatahi, Hawke's Bay, it is hand-picked from mature vines and fermented and lees-aged in all-new French oak barriques, with malolactic fermentation according to the season. Harvested at a very ripe 25 brix, the bright yellow 2004 vintage (★★★★★) is a refined wine with a highly fragrant, citrusy, nutty bouquet. Mouthfilling and sweet-fruited, with a fine thread of acidity, it's a rich, elegant wine, maturing gracefully and now probably at its peak. (There is no 2005.)

Vintage	05	04	03	02	01	00
WR	NM	7	NM	7	NM	6
Drink	NM	09-12	NM	P	NM	P

DRY $80 –V

Coopers Creek Gisborne Chardonnay/Viognier   (★★★)

The 2007 vintage (★★★) is a very easy-drinking style, full-bodied and fruity, with ripe, peachy flavours and a smooth finish.

DRY $18 AV

Coopers Creek Reserve Gisborne Chardonnay   ★★★★

Designed as a 'full-bodied, oak-influenced style', this single-vineyard wine is fermented and matured in partly new French oak barriques. It is typically weighty, ripe and rounded, with strong, tropical-fruit flavours seasoned with toasty oak in a lush, yet refined, style.

Vintage	07	06	05	04
WR	6	6	6	6
Drink	09-11	P	P	P

DRY $28 AV

Coopers Creek SV The Limeworks Hawke's Bay Chardonnay   ★★★★

The 2008 vintage (★★★★) is a single-vineyard, Havelock North wine, barrel-fermented. It's a full-on style with rich, grapefruit-like flavours, well seasoned with toasty American oak, and a creamy-soft texture (100 per cent malolactic fermentation). Savoury, with good weight, concentration and complexity, it has strong drink-young appeal.

Vintage	08	07	06
WR	6	5	7
Drink	09-12	09-11	P

DRY $20 V+

Coopers Creek Swamp Reserve Chardonnay   ★★★★★

Based on the winery's best Hawke's Bay Chardonnay fruit, this is typically a lush, highly seductive wine with a finely judged balance of rich, citrusy, peachy fruit flavours and toasty oak. Hand-picked in the company's Middle Road Vineyard at Havelock North, it is fully fermented and matured for nine months in French oak barriques (33 to 50 per cent new). The 2006 vintage (★★★★☆) was hand-picked (in two separate 'passes' through the vineyard) and given a full, softening malolactic fermentation. Weighty and ripe, with concentrated grapefruit and butterscotch flavours and a soft, long finish, it's a deliciously rich, well-rounded wine.

Vintage	07	06	05	04
WR	7	6	6	6
Drink	09-11	09-10	P	P

DRY $30 V+

Coopers Creek Unoaked Gisborne Chardonnay   ★★★☆

Coopers Creek no longer matures its popular, moderately priced Gisborne wine in wood, but the recipe still includes maturation on its yeast lees. Still fresh and youthful, the top-vintage, instantly likeable 2007 (★★★★) is vibrantly fruity and mouthfilling, with strong, ripe, peachy flavours, balanced acidity and a smooth (fractionally off-dry) finish.

Vintage	07	06	05	04
WR	6	5	NM	6
Drink	09-10	P	NM	P

DRY $17 V+

Corbans Cottage Block Hawke's Bay Chardonnay   ★★★★★

A consistently classy wine from Pernod Ricard NZ. The superb 2007 vintage (★★★★★) was hand-picked in three company-owned vineyards, fully barrel-fermented with indigenous yeasts, and matured for a year in French oak barriques (new and one year old). A classic regional style, it has a fragrant, complex, nutty, creamy bouquet, leading into a generous, finely textured palate with ripe grapefruit and smoky oak flavours, showing lovely delicacy, complexity and length. Don't miss it – it's a star.

Vintage	07	06	05
WR	7	7	6
Drink	09-12	09-11	09-10

DRY $36 AV

Corbans Homestead Hawke's Bay Chardonnay   (★★☆)

From Pernod Ricard NZ, this dry wine is made without oak in a simple, fruit-driven style. The 2008 vintage (★★☆) is enjoyable now, in a faintly honeyed style with decent depth of ripe, peachy, slightly buttery flavour. (Fine value at its average supermarket price of $10.55.)

Vintage	08	07
WR	5	6
Drink	09-10	P

DRY $17 –V

Corbans Private Bin Hawke's Bay Chardonnay   ★★★★

Hand-picked and barrel-fermented, with indigenous yeasts adding absorbing 'funky' notes, this is typically a great buy. The 2007 vintage (★★★★☆) is weighty and rich, with concentrated, peachy, toasty, nutty flavours, moderate acidity and a slightly creamy texture. Drink now or cellar.

Vintage	07	06	05	04
WR	7	6	6	7
Drink	09-12	09-10	09-10	P

DRY $24 V+

Corbans White Label Chardonnay   (★★☆)

From Pernod Ricard NZ, the 2008 vintage (★★☆) is a regional blend with fresh, citrusy and peachy flavours in a simple style with a smooth, slightly buttery finish. (Good value at its average supermarket price of $7.33.)

MED/DRY $10 V+

Cottle Hill Chardonnay   ★★☆

The Chardonnays from this Northland winery have been of varying quality. At their best, they are fleshy and rich, but some vintages have shown a slight lack of freshness and vibrancy.

DRY $19 –V

Crab Farm Chardonnay   ★★★☆

Grown in Hawke's Bay, the 2007 vintage (★★★☆) is a fruit-driven style, handled without oak. It's a full-bodied wine (14.5 per cent alcohol) with ripe grapefruit-like flavours, a slightly creamy texture and good immediacy.

Vintage	07	06
WR	6	6
Drink	09-10	P

DRY $17 V+

Crab Farm Reserve Chardonnay ★★★★

The 2008 vintage (★★★★) from this small Hawke's Bay winery was hand-picked and aged for eight months in new oak barrels. Pale and youthful in colour, it is mouthfilling and sweet-fruited, with rich, vibrant, peachy, citrusy flavours, oak complexity and good acid spine. Well worth cellaring.

Vintage	08				DRY $25 AV
WR	7				
Drink	09-11				

Craggy Range C3 Kidnappers Vineyard Hawke's Bay Chardonnay ★★★★

Made using 'the traditional techniques of Chablis', the 2008 vintage (★★★★☆) is a gently oaked style, full of interest. Grown near the coast at Te Awanga, and fermented in a mix of tanks, oak cuves and new puncheons, it is weighty and smooth, with fresh, ripe, citrusy, appley flavours, slightly leesy and nutty. A subtle style of Chardonnay, it is refined and persistent.

Vintage	08	07			DRY $25 AV
WR	6	6			
Drink	09-13	09-12			

Craggy Range Gimblett Gravels Vineyard Chardonnay ★★★★

This stylish Hawke's Bay wine is mouthfilling, complex and savoury, with biscuity, nutty characters from fermentation and maturation in French oak barriques (42 per cent new in 2008). The 2008 vintage (★★★★☆) is generous, ripe and rounded, with a fragrant, slightly toasty and mealy bouquet. Mouthfilling, with peachy, biscuity flavours, a hint of butterscotch, good complexity and a rich finish, it's already delicious; drink now or cellar.

Vintage	08	07	06	05	04	DRY $29 AV
WR	6	6	6	6	7	
Drink	09-13	09-13	09-10	09-10	P	

Craggy Range Les Beaux Cailloux – see Branded and Other White Wines

Craggy Range Seven Poplars Vineyard Chardonnay ★★★★☆

Grown on the banks of the Tutaekuri River in the lower Dartmoor Valley, this is typically a refined wine with lovely depth of flavour. The 2006 vintage (★★★★☆) was hand-picked from Dijon clones of Chardonnay at 23.7 brix, and fermented with indigenous yeasts in French oak barriques (45 per cent new). Barrel-aged for 10 months, it's a powerful yet approachable Hawke's Bay wine, robust (14.4 per cent alcohol), with lush, ripe grapefruit flavours, mealy and biscuity, impressive harmony and a lasting finish.

Vintage	08	07	06	05	04	DRY $30 AV
WR	6	6	7	NM	6	
Drink	09-13	09-14	09-12	NM	P	

Crawford Farm Unoaked Chardonnay ★★☆

From Constellation NZ, the 2007 vintage (★★) is citrusy and smooth, but my sample also showed a slight lack of freshness and fragrance.

DRY $22 –V

Croft Chardonnay   (★★★★☆)

The 2006 vintage (★★★★☆) is a refined Martinborough wine, maturing gracefully. Fully barrel-fermented (in 30 per cent new oak), it is bright, light yellow/green, with a fleshy palate showing concentrated, ripe grapefruit-like flavours, integrated nutty oak and a long finish.

Vintage 06   DRY $24 V+
WR   6
Drink   09-11

Croney Three Ton Marlborough Chardonnay   (★★★)

This is an unoaked style, recommended for enjoying with food and friends, 'or just drink it alone in your room'. Hand-picked, tank-fermented and lees-aged, it has a slightly creamy bouquet leading into a full-bodied wine with good depth of ripe, citrusy, peachy flavour and a smooth, dry finish.

                                                            DRY $15 V+

Crossroads Hawke's Bay Chardonnay   ★★★☆

The 2007 vintage (★★★★), the best yet, is delicious now. Eighty per cent of the blend spent 10 months in French oak casks (25 per cent new); the rest was handled in tanks. It's a full-bodied, slightly creamy Hawke's Bay wine, citrusy and peachy, with ripe-fruit flavours, some toasty, mealy touches and a rounded finish.

Vintage 07   DRY $20 AV
WR   7
Drink   09-12

Culley Marlborough Chardonnay   ★★☆

Produced by Neill Culley, a partner in the Cable Bay winery on Waiheke Island, the 2007 vintage (★★☆) is a fruit-driven style with citrusy, appley flavours, fresh and uncomplicated.

                                                            DRY $20 –V

Cypress Hawke's Bay Chardonnay   (★★☆)

Estate-grown at Roy's Hill and tank-fermented, the debut 2007 vintage (★★☆) is a mouthfilling dry wine with decent depth of ripe, citrusy flavours in a pleasant, easy-drinking style.

Vintage 07   DRY $20 –V
WR   5
Drink   09-10

Cypress Terraces Hawke's Bay Chardonnay   (★★★★)

From a sloping, 2-hectare vineyard, the 2008 vintage (★★★★) is a barrel-fermented wine, sturdy (14.5 per cent alcohol) and very ripe-tasting, with sweet-fruit delights of peaches and melons, buttery, toasty notes (French oak, 60 per cent new), gentle acidity, and good complexity and texture. Drink now or cellar.

Vintage 08   DRY $30 –V
WR   6
Drink   09-12

Dashwood Marlborough Chardonnay   ★★★

Vavasour's lower-tier Chardonnay is a drink-young style with fresh, lively fruit flavours and appetising acidity. The 2008 vintage (★★★) is an easy-drinking style with ripe, peachy flavours and slightly toasty, creamy notes adding a touch of complexity.

Vintage	08
WR	6
Drink	09-11

DRY $17 AV

Delegat's Hawke's Bay Chardonnay   ★★★

For Delegat's lower-tier Chardonnay, the idea is: 'let the fruit do the talking'. The 2008 vintage (★★★☆), fermented in tanks and barrels, is flavoursome, peachy and citrusy, in a ripe, vibrantly fruity style, creamy-textured, with strong drink-young appeal.

Vintage	08	07	06
WR	6	7	5
Drink	09-14	09-14	P

DRY $16 AV

Delegat's Reserve Hawke's Bay Chardonnay   ★★★★

The fine-value 2007 vintage (★★★★), grown in the inland Crownthorpe district, was fully barrel-fermented. It's a very elegant, fragrant wine with citrusy, nutty flavours, showing good delicacy and richness, fresh acidity and a lingering finish.

Vintage	08	07	06	05
WR	6	7	6	5
Drink	09-14	09-14	09-12	09-11

DRY $20 V+

Distant Land Hawke's Bay Chardonnay   (★★☆)

From Lincoln, the debut 2007 vintage (★★☆) was grown in the Dartmoor Valley, lees-aged and handled without oak. It's a full-bodied, slightly sweet wine (6 grams/litre of residual sugar) with ripe, citrusy flavours, offering fresh, easy drinking.

MED/DRY $20 −V

Distant Land [Reserve] Hawke's Bay Chardonnay   ★★★★

Note: the word 'reserve' appears only on the back label. The 2007 vintage (★★★★) is an elegant wine, with rich grapefruit and peach flavours, slightly toasty, finely balanced and smooth.

DRY $28 AV

Dog Point Vineyard Marlborough Chardonnay   ★★★★★

This consistently classy, single-vineyard wine is grown on the south side of the Wairau Valley, fermented with indigenous yeasts, matured for 18 to 20 months in French oak barriques (15 to 25 per cent new), and given a full, softening malolactic fermentation. The 2007 vintage (★★★★★) is refined, full-bodied, fresh and rich, with a complex bouquet, lively acidity and concentrated grapefruit, peach and subtle oak flavours, slightly minerally, tight and lingering. Drink now or cellar.

Vintage	07	06	05	04	03
WR	6	6	5	6	5
Drink	09-12	09-12	09-11	09-11	P

DRY $33 V+

Dolbel Estate Hawke's Bay Chardonnay   (★★★★)

The 2007 vintage (★★★★☆) was fermented in French oak barrels (57 per cent new). The bouquet is toasty and creamy; the palate is mouthfilling and rounded, with stone-fruit and nut flavours, concentrated and complex. It's a generous wine, for drinking now onwards.

Vintage	08	07
WR	6	6
Drink	09-12	09-11

DRY $27 AV

Domaine Georges Michel Golden Mile Marlborough Chardonnay   ★★★

Named after 'the central route of the Rapaura area', this wine is tank-fermented and then matured in seasoned French oak casks. It is typically full-bodied and crisp, offering easy, no-fuss drinking. The 2007 vintage (★★★☆) is mouthfilling and vibrantly fruity, with good depth of ripe, peachy flavours, subtle toasty oak and a rounded, creamy-smooth finish. It's drinking well now.

DRY $20 –V

Domaine Georges Michel La Reserve Chardonnay   ★★★

Grown at Rapaura, in Marlborough, this wine is tank-fermented and then matured for a year in new and one-year-old French oak barriques. The 2006 vintage (★★★☆) is a mouthfilling, distinctly creamy wine with fresh acidity and strong grapefruit and nut flavours, showing considerable complexity.

Vintage	06	05
WR	6	6
Drink	09-12	09-11

DRY $25 –V

Drylands Marlborough Chardonnay   ★★★★

From Constellation NZ, this enjoyable wine is an upfront style – fragrant, creamy and full of flavour. The 2007 vintage (★★★★), 'fermented predominantly in French oak barriques', has a toasty bouquet leading into a fleshy, smooth wine with stone-fruit and citrus-fruit flavours, creamy and toasty. Showing good concentration, it's drinking well now.

DRY $22 V+

Dry River Chardonnay   ★★★★★

Elegance, restraint and subtle power are the key qualities of this Martinborough wine. It's not a bold, upfront style, but tight, savoury and seamless, with rich grapefruit and nut flavours that build in the bottle for several years. Based on very low-cropping (typically below 5 tonnes/ hectare) Mendoza clone vines, it is hand-harvested, whole-bunch pressed and fermented in French oak hogsheads (averaging 25 per cent new). The proportion of the blend that has gone through a softening malolactic fermentation has never exceeded 15 per cent. The 2008 vintage (★★★★☆) is rich and subtle, with stone-fruit, apple and spice flavours, finely integrated oak, mealy, complex notes and a tight, lingering finish. Open 2011+.

Vintage	08	07	06	05	04	03	02
WR	7	7	7	6	6	7	7
Drink	11-17	12-18	09-14	09-13	09-11	09-11	P

DRY $52 AV

Elephant Hill Chardonnay   (★★★★☆)

Grown near the coast at Te Awanga, in Hawke's Bay, the 2008 vintage (★★★★☆) is rich, complex and full of personality. Hand-harvested, fermented with indigenous yeasts in French oak barriques (50 per cent new) and lees-aged in oak for 10 months, with no use of malolactic fermentation, it's a sophisticated wine with sweet-fruit delights, highly concentrated grapefruit and stone-fruit flavours seasoned with toasty oak, and a fresh, finely balanced finish. Drink now or cellar.

DRY $26 V+

Emeny Road Tauranga Reserve Chardonnay   ★★★☆

This rare Bay of Plenty wine is grown at Plummers Point, 17 kilometres west of Tauranga. The powerful 2007 vintage (★★★☆) is mouthfilling, with concentrated stone-fruit flavours, toasty oak, a hint of honey and firm acid spine. Drink now.

DRY $23 AV

Escarpment Chardonnay   ★★★★

Due to the light crop in Martinborough, the 2007 vintage (★★★★) is a blend of Martinborough and Hawke's Bay grapes. Fermented and matured in French oak barriques (30 per cent new), it has very satisfying body and depth of grapefruit and peach flavours, seasoned with toasty oak. Finely balanced, with fresh acidity, it's a complex style, likely to age well.

Vintage	07	06
WR	5	7
Drink	09-11	09-10

DRY $35 –V

Esk Valley Hawke's Bay Chardonnay   ★★★★

Top vintages offer fine value. A weighty, rich style with strong drink-young appeal, the 2008 vintage (★★★★) was fermented in a 3:1 split of French oak barrels (20 per cent new) and tanks. It has ripe stone-fruit flavours to the fore, with mealy, biscuity notes and a hint of butterscotch adding complexity, and excellent texture and depth.

Vintage	09	08	07	06
WR	6	7	7	6
Drink	09-12	09-11	09-12	09-10

DRY $23 V+

Esk Valley Winemakers Hawke's Bay Chardonnay   ★★★★★

Often one of the region's most distinguished Chardonnays, this wine was called 'Reserve' rather than 'Winemakers', prior to the 2008 vintage. The 2008 (★★★★☆) is a blend of grapes from two sites – 85 per cent from Bay View, on the coast (which gives 'lush' fruit characters), and 15 per cent from the Gimblett Gravels (which yields a more 'flinty' style). Hand-picked, fermented with indigenous yeasts and matured for a year in French oak barriques (35 per cent new), it is sturdy (14.5 per cent alcohol), with rich peach and grapefruit flavours, complex, deliciously nutty and creamy, but still very youthful; open 2011+.

Vintage	08	07	06	05	04	03	02
WR	7	7	7	7	7	7	7
Drink	09-13	09-14	09-12	09-11	09-12	09-12	09-11

DRY $30 V+

Fairhall Downs Single Vineyard Marlborough Chardonnay   ★★★★

Grown and hand-picked in the Brancott Valley, this wine shows rising form and the 2008 vintage (★★★★) is one of the best yet. Fermented with indigenous yeasts and matured for 10 months in French oak barriques, it's a very open, expressive and well-rounded wine with mouthfilling body and citrusy, peachy, slightly toasty and nutty flavours, showing good complexity. It's already delicious.

Vintage	08	07	06	05	04
WR	6	7	7	NM	7
Drink	09-15	09-13	09-12	NM	P

DRY $30 –V

Fall Harvest Chardonnay   (★★★)

From Constellation NZ, the 2007 vintage (★★★) is drinking well now. Not identified by region, but made from New Zealand grapes, it is pale straw, with good body and plenty of fresh, peachy, slightly spicy flavour, ripe and smooth. There's even a touch of complexity.

DRY $13 V+

Farmgate Hawke's Bay Chardonnay   ★★★☆

From the Ngatarawa winery, this brand is sold directly to consumers via the Farmgate website. The 2008 vintage (★★★) was barrel-aged for 10 months. Full-bodied, with a biscuity bouquet and moderately concentrated flavours, it is peachy and smooth, with a fractionally off-dry finish.

Vintage	08	07	06
WR	7	NM	7
Drink	09-13	NM	09-10

MED/DRY $25 –V

Fat Cat Gisborne Chardonnay   ★★★

Fat Cat is made by Purr Productions of Huapai, a division of Coopers Creek. The goal is 'a fat, alcoholic wine with lots of oak – a wine that's just what the name suggests'. Toasty American oak and buttery 'malo' characters are key parts of the recipe. Those vintages I have tasted have been mouthfilling, peachy and toasty, in a very upfront style.

DRY $15 V+

Felton Road Block 2 Chardonnay   ★★★★

The 2008 vintage (★★★★☆), estate-grown at Bannockburn, in Central Otago, was matured for 18 months in French oak casks (12 per cent new). Light lemon/green, it is highly refined, mouthfilling and youthful, with grapefruit-like flavours, slightly nutty and buttery, in a finely poised, very elegant style, likely to be long-lived. Best drinking mid-2010+.

Vintage	08
WR	7
Drink	09-18

DRY $42 –V

Felton Road Central Otago Chardonnay   ★★★☆

Estate-grown at Bannockburn, this wine is matured in French oak barriques (with limited use of new oak – 12 per cent in 2008). The 2008 vintage (★★★★) is toasty and creamy, with mouthfilling body, cool-climate vigour and strong, citrusy, slightly buttery flavours, woven with fresh acidity. It should mature well.

Vintage	08	07	06	05	04
WR	6	7	6	6	6
Drink	09-18	09-13	09-12	09-11	09-10

 DRY $32 –V

Felton Road Elms Central Otago Chardonnay ★★★★

The finely poised 2009 vintage (★★★★) is full of interest for Chardonnay lovers. Handled without oak, it is weighty and full-flavoured, citrusy and faintly buttery, with balanced acidity and excellent harmony, not at all brash but quietly satisfying, and enjoyable from the start.

Vintage	09
WR	6
Drink	09-17

DRY $24 V+

Fiddler's Green Waipara Chardonnay ★★★★

Still on sale, the 2006 vintage (★★★★) was hand-picked and fermented and matured for nine months in French oak barriques (20 per cent new). It is creamy and mouthfilling, with ripe stone-fruit and citrus flavours, slightly toasty and buttery, and a fully dry, minerally finish.

Vintage	06	05	04	03	02
WR	6	6	6	6	6
Drink	09-10	P	P	P	P

DRY $29 AV

Field of Grace Mahurangi River Matakana Chardonnay (★★★★☆)

The powerful 2007 vintage (★★★★☆) was estate-grown at Mahurangi River Estate, hand-picked, and fermented with indigenous yeasts in French oak barriques (30 per cent new). It has lovely weight, with concentrated, very ripe grapefruit-like flavours, slightly dominated by oak in its youth, and a fine thread of acidity. Rich, mealy and generous, with a long finish, it should flourish with cellaring.

 DRY $39 –V

Firstland Reserve Marlborough Chardonnay ★★★★

The fleshy, richly flavoured 2006 vintage (★★★★) was grown at three sites in the Wairau Valley, partly barrel-fermented and fully oak-aged. Creamy, citrusy and biscuity, with spicy, appley notes and excellent texture and complexity, it's a drink-now proposition.

DRY $29 AV

Five Flax Chardonnay ★★★

A drink-young style, priced right. Made by Pernod Ricard NZ and handled without oak, but lees-aged and lees-stirred, it is typically fresh and smooth, in a vibrantly fruity style, balanced for easy drinking. The 2008 vintage (★★☆) is ripe and peachy, slightly buttery and creamy.

 DRY $15 V+

Forrest Marlborough Chardonnay   ★★★★

John Forrest favours a gently oaked style, looking to very ripe grapes and extended lees-aging to give his wine character. The 2006 vintage (★★★★) was half tank-fermented; the rest was fermented and lees-aged for 10 months in French and American oak casks, with a softening malolactic fermentation. An elegant, cool-climate style with mouthfilling body, strong, ripe grapefruit-like flavours and a gentle seasoning of oak, it is finely balanced and building up good complexity with bottle-age.

Vintage	06	05	04
WR	6	6	5
Drink	09-15	09-11	09-10

MED/DRY $23 V+

Fossil Ridge Nelson Chardonnay   ★★★☆

Still on sale, the 2006 vintage (★★★☆) of this single-vineyard, hand-picked wine was fermented and aged in American and French oak casks. It's a powerful wine (14.5 per cent alcohol) with strong stone-fruit flavours seasoned with sweet, toasty oak in a moderately complex, upfront style.

DRY $23 AV

Fossil Ridge Nelson Unoaked Chardonnay   ★★★

The 2007 vintage (★★★) is fruity and smooth, with plenty of citrusy, slightly limey flavour and a crisp finish. It's drinking well now.

DRY $17 AV

Foxes Island Marlborough Chardonnay   ★★★★☆

This deeply flavoured, finely balanced Chardonnay is consistently impressive. The 2006 vintage (★★★★☆), fully fermented in French oak barriques, has concentrated, grapefruit-like flavours and a subtle seasoning of oak. Tight and complex, with a minerally thread, it shows good cellaring potential.

Vintage	06	05	04	03	02
WR	6	6	6	NM	7
Drink	09-10	P	P	NM	P

DRY $40 –V

Framingham Marlborough Chardonnay   ★★★★

Framingham is best known for Riesling, but the Chardonnay is consistently attractive in a subtle, satisfying style. Grown at several sites in the Wairau Valley, it is fermented in a 50/50 split of tanks and French oak barriques, with lees-aging and some malolactic fermentation. The 2008 vintage (★★★★) has a mealy, slightly creamy bouquet and good weight. Fleshy and finely balanced, it has fresh, ripe grapefruit and slight nut flavours, with a well-rounded finish.

Vintage	08	07	06	05	04
WR	6	6	6	6	7
Drink	09-13	09-12	09-11	09-10	09-10

DRY $23 V+

Freefall Marlborough Chardonnay   ★★★

From High Plains Wine Company, based in Central Otago, the 2007 vintage (★★★) was fermented in a 50/50 split of tanks and old barrels. A crisp, medium-bodied style, it is lemony, appley and dry, with firm acid spine and good freshness and vigour.

DRY $20 –V

Frizzell Hawke's Bay Chardonnay   (★★★☆)

Winemaker Rod McDonald set out to make a 'gutsy' style 'but without too much oak'. The debut 2008 vintage (★★★☆) was lees-aged in barrels and given a full, softening malolactic fermentation. A mouthfilling wine, it has generous, peachy, slightly spicy flavours, a hint of butterscotch, and a well-rounded finish. Enjoyable in its youth, it offers good value.

DRY $19 V+

Fromm Brancott Valley Chardonnay   (★★★★☆)

(Past releases were labelled 'Fromm La Strada Marlborough Chardonnay'.) This stylish wine is grown in the Brancott Valley, on the south side of the Wairau Valley, fermented with indigenous yeasts in French oak casks (a low percentage new), and barrel-aged for well over a year. The 2006 vintage (★★★★☆) has buttery, biscuity aromas leading into a mouthfilling, creamy-textured wine with concentrated grapefruit-like flavours, mealy notes adding complexity, fresh underlying acidity and a tight, dry finish.

Vintage	08	07	06	05
WR	6	6	6	6
Drink	10-14	09-13	09-12	09-11

DRY $42 –V

Fromm Clayvin Vineyard Chardonnay   ★★★★★

Fromm's top Chardonnay is grown on the southern flanks of the Wairau Valley, where the clay soils, says winemaker Hätsch Kalberer, give 'a less fruity, more minerally and tighter character'. Top vintages mature well for up to a decade. Fermented with indigenous yeasts in French oak barriques, with little or no use of new wood, it is barrel-aged for well over a year. The superb 2006 vintage (★★★★★) is rich and elegant, with a fragrant, complex bouquet and beautifully concentrated, grapefruit and slight spice flavours, showing a subtle oak/lees influence, and a long, finely balanced finish.

Vintage	08	07	06	05	04	03	02	01	00
WR	6	7	7	7	6	5	5	7	6
Drink	11-16	10-15	09-14	09-13	09-12	09-10	P	09-10	P

DRY $56 AV

Fromm La Strada Marlborough Chardonnay – see La Strada Marlborough Chardonnay

Gibbston Highgate Estate Heartbreaker Chardonnay   ★★★

The 2008 vintage (★★★) was harvested at 24.8 brix in Central Otago and mostly tank-fermented; 20 per cent of the blend was fermented and lees-aged in new and older French oak casks. It's a distinctly cool-climate style, reminiscent of Chablis, with citrusy, appley flavours, crisp and lively.

Vintage	08	07	06
WR	6	5	6
Drink	10-15	09-12	09-12

DRY $25 –V

Gibbston Valley Greenstone Chardonnay   ★★★

Typically a vibrantly fruity, crisp wine in a distinctly cool-climate style. The 2007 vintage (★★★) was grown at Bendigo, in Central Otago, hand-picked, and fermented in a 50/50 split of tanks and seasoned oak barrels. It shows good depth of fresh, lemony, appley flavours, balanced for easy drinking. (The 2008 is listed simply as 'Greenstone Chardonnay' – see below.)

DRY $24 –V

Gibbston Valley Reserve Chardonnay   ★★★★

This is a more complex style than its stablemate (above). Estate-grown in the Chinaman's Terrace vineyard at Bendigo, in Central Otago, the 2008 vintage (★★★★) was fermented and lees-aged in French oak barriques (20 per cent new). It's a rich, mouthfilling, slightly creamy wine with citrusy, peachy, spice flavours, showing good texture, complexity and harmony.

Vintage	08	07
WR	7	6
Drink	10-14	09-12

DRY $32 –V

Giesen Marlborough Chardonnay   ★★★

Typically a citrusy, slightly buttery and creamy wine, with a touch of complexity and a crisp finish. The 2008 vintage, grown in the Wairau Valley, was mostly handled in tanks, but 35 per cent was barrel-fermented and all of the final blend was lees-aged, with 60 per cent malolactic fermentation.

DRY $16 AV

Glazebrook Regional Reserve Chardonnay   ★★★☆

Ngatarawa's second-tier Chardonnay is named after the Glazebrook family, formerly partners in the Hawke's Bay venture. Grown in The Triangle district and fermented and matured for 11 months in French oak barrels (15 per cent), the 2007 vintage (★★★★) is a drink-now or cellaring proposition. Full-bodied, it has citrusy, peachy flavours showing good richness, finely integrated oak and slightly mealy, buttery notes adding complexity.

Vintage	07	06	05
WR	7	6	6
Drink	09-12	09-11	09-10

DRY $27 –V

Golden Bay Chardonnay   ★★★

Still on sale, the 2005 vintage (★★★) is a single-vineyard Nelson wine, grown at Takaka, hand-picked and fermented in seasoned oak casks. Light yellow, with crisp, citrusy, slightly buttery flavours, it shows some toasty development. Priced sharply.

Vintage	06	05
WR	7	7
Drink	09-10	09-11

DRY $15 V+

Goldridge Estate Gisborne Chardonnay   ★★☆

The pale straw 2007 vintage (★★☆) was partly barrel-fermented. It's a peachy, slightly honeyed wine offering smooth, easy drinking. Ready.

DRY $16 –V

Goldridge Estate Premium Reserve Chardonnay   (★★★)

The easy-drinking 2008 vintage (★★★) is a blend of Matakana (70 per cent) and Hawke's Bay (30 per cent) grapes, fermented and lees-aged for 10 months in predominantly French oak barriques (30 per cent new). Fleshy and smooth, it has plenty of ripe, peachy, slightly toasty and buttery flavour, with a well-rounded finish. Ready.

DRY $19 AV

Goldridge Estate Premium Reserve Hawke's Bay Chardonnay   ★★★

The 2007 vintage (★★★☆) is a single-vineyard wine, barrel-fermented. It's a fragrant wine with moderately rich stone-fruit flavours, some mealy complexity and a well-rounded finish.

DRY $19 AV

Goldwater Marlborough Chardonnay   ★★★★

Typically a finely scented, weighty, vibrantly fruity wine with tropical-fruit characters and subtle use of oak in a highly attractive style. Partly French oak-fermented, the 2008 vintage (★★★★) is a full-bodied style with strong, ripe-fruit flavours, a touch of butteriness and a dry, well-rounded finish. Already drinking well, it shows excellent delicacy, texture, complexity and harmony.

Vintage	08	07	06	05	04
WR	6	7	7	6	6
Drink	09-13	09-10	P	P	P

DRY $21 V+

Goldwater Zell Waiheke Island Chardonnay   ★★★★☆

Grown in the hillside, clay-based Zell Vineyard on Waiheke Island, this is a rich, complex wine with the ripeness and roundness typical of northern Chardonnays. It is hand-picked, whole-bunch pressed and fermented with indigenous yeasts in French oak casks (30 to 40 per cent new), with full malolactic fermentation in 2008. The 2008 vintage (★★★★★), barrel-aged for a year, is one of the finest yet. A lovely, tightly structured wine, it is highly fragrant, with rich stone-fruit flavours, a hint of butterscotch, and excellent vigour, delicacy and length. It should mature well.

DRY $34 AV

Gravitas Reserve Marlborough Chardonnay   ★★★★☆

The 2007 vintage (★★★★☆) was hand-picked and fermented with indigenous yeasts in French oak barriques. Fragrant, with a complex, slightly biscuity bouquet, it is sweet-fruited and rich, with concentrated peach and slight butterscotch flavours woven with fresh acidity. Drink now or cellar.

Vintage	07	06	05	04
WR	7	6	6	6
Drink	09-11	09-10	09-10	P

DRY $29 V+

Greenhough Hope Vineyard Chardonnay ★★★★☆

This impressive wine is estate-grown at Hope, in Nelson, hand-picked and fermented and matured for a year in French oak casks (25 to 30 per cent new). The 2007 vintage (★★★★★) is superb. Peachy, citrusy and nutty, with lovely flavour depth and harmony, it is slightly minerally, very complex, subtle and long.

Vintage	07	06	05	04	03	02
WR	7	6	6	6	6	7
Drink	09-13	09-12	09-12	P	09-11	09-10

DRY $29 V+

Greenhough Nelson Chardonnay ★★★★

This consistently enjoyable wine is fermented and matured in seasoned French oak casks. The 2008 vintage (★★★☆) is fresh and vibrantly fruity, with good body and depth of lemony, appley flavours and a subtle seasoning of oak.

Vintage	08	07	06	05	04
WR	7	6	NM	6	6
Drink	09-13	09-12	NM	09-10	P

DRY $22 V+

Greenstone Central Otago Chardonnay ★★★

Past vintages were called 'Gibbston Valley Greenstone Chardonnay', but the 2008 (★★☆) is just branded as 'Greenstone'. It's a pleasant, lemony wine with strong, creamy, milky notes, balanced for easy drinking.

DRY $24 –V

Grove Mill Marlborough Chardonnay ★★★☆

Typically an attractive, skilfully balanced, flavoursome wine with a subtle oak influence and fresh, crisp acidity. The 2007 (★★★★), fermented in a mix of tanks and barrels (new to five years old), is an elegant, weighty, vibrantly fruity wine with strong grapefruit and slight lime flavours, balanced acidity and a twist of oak. Subtle but not simple, it's a top vintage, enjoyable from the start.

Vintage	08	07
WR	6	6
Drink	10-13	09-12

DRY $18 V+

Gumfields Marlborough Chardonnay (★★☆)

From West Brook, the 2007 vintage (★★☆) was mostly handled in tanks, but 10 per cent was barrel-fermented. It's a vibrantly fruity, simple wine with citrus and passionfruit flavours and fresh acidity, offering easy drinking.

DRY $20 –V

Gunn Estate Chardonnay ★★★

The 2007 vintage (★★★) is a Hawke's Bay wine, fresh and vibrant, with citrusy, slightly spicy and smooth flavours. It's not a complex style, but immediately appealing.

DRY $18 AV

Gunn Estate Skeetfield Chardonnay   ★★★★☆

From Sacred Hill, the 2007 vintage (★★★★) was hand-picked in Hawke's Bay and fermented and lees-aged for 10 months in new and one-year-old French oak barriques. A tight, elegant style, it has rich, citrusy, slightly limey flavours, showing good complexity, and a very fresh, crisp and lively finish. Well worth cellaring.

Vintage	07	06	05	04
WR	7	6	6	7
Drink	12-14	09-11	P	P

DRY $33 AV

Gunn Estate Unoaked Chardonnay   ★★★

Produced by Sacred Hill, the 2007 vintage (★★★☆) is a very good example of the fruit-driven style. A regional blend, it has good depth of citrusy, appley flavours, deliciously fresh and vibrant.

DRY $17 AV

Hans Herzog Marlborough Chardonnay   ★★★★☆

At its best, this is a notably powerful wine with layers of peach, butterscotch, grapefruit and nut flavours and a long, rounded finish. The 2008 vintage (★★★★☆) was hand-picked at 24 brix, fermented with indigenous yeasts in 500-litre French oak puncheons and given a full, softening malolactic fermentation. Oak-aged for a year, it is weighty, rich and sweet-fruited, with concentrated, citrusy flavours, a subtle oak influence, good texture and a rounded finish. It should be at its best mid-2010 onwards.

Vintage	08
WR	7
Drink	09-19

DRY $45 –V

Hay Maker Hawke's Bay Chardonnay   (★★☆)

From Mud House, the 2007 vintage (★★☆) is a fruit-driven style with decent depth of vibrant, citrusy flavours and a fresh, dry finish.

DRY $17 –V

Highfield Marlborough Chardonnay   ★★★★☆

A consistently classy wine. The 2008 vintage (★★★★☆), fully French oak-fermented, has a fragrant, youthful bouquet, citrusy and biscuity. Mouthfilling, it's a rich, elegant wine, tightly structured, with grapefruit-like flavours, slightly nutty, mealy and buttery, and a dry, minerally finish. It should be long-lived.

Vintage	08	07	06	05	04
WR	5	6	6	7	6
Drink	10-14	09-11	09-10	P	P

DRY $32 AV

Himmelsfeld Vineyard Moutere Chardonnay   ★★★★

Nelson wine-grower Beth Eggers gives her single-vineyard, Upper Moutere wines lengthy bottle-age before release: 'They do well with time.' The 2005 vintage (★★★★☆) is still youthful in colour. The bouquet is fragrant and creamy; the palate is mouthfilling (14.5 per cent alcohol), rich and smooth, with concentrated, peachy, slightly toasty flavours and a tight, dry finish. Probably at its peak, it's a powerful, generous wine with loads of personality.

DRY $32 –V

Hinchco Barrel Fermented Matakana Chardonnay   (★★★)

Hand-picked and fermented and lees-aged in new American oak, the 2008 vintage (★★★) is pale straw, with a woody bouquet. It's a peachy, nutty wine with good body and freshness, but less oak would have been better. Open mid-2010+.

DRY $30 –V

Hitchen Road Pokeno Unwooded Chardonnay   (★★★☆)

Priced sharply, the 2009 vintage (★★★☆) was estate-grown at a 'summer-dry' site at Pokeno, in northern Waikato. Fleshy (14.4 per cent alcohol), ripe and rounded, it's a very good example of the unoaked style, with sweet-fruit characters and good depth of stone-fruit flavours, soft and forward.

DRY $17 V+

Huia Marlborough Chardonnay   ★★★★

This full-bodied, creamy-textured wine is hand-picked, fermented with indigenous yeasts and matured in French oak casks, emerging with citrusy, slightly nutty flavours. Understated in its youth, it typically matures well for several years, offering smooth, very satisfying drinking. The 2007 vintage (★★★★) is mouthfilling and rounded, with ripe grapefruit-like flavours, a gentle oak influence, slightly buttery notes, and good harmony and texture. It's a subtle, satisfying wine with a lingering finish.

Vintage	07	06
WR	7	6
Drink	09-15	09-11

DRY $34 –V

Huntaway Reserve Gisborne Chardonnay   ★★★★

From Pernod Ricard NZ, this wine is made in a high-impact, creamy-rich style, delicious in its youth, but top vintages mature well. The 2007 (★★★★☆) was fermented in French oak casks (20 per cent new) and lees-stirred weekly, with a high percentage of malolactic fermentation. Delicious now, it has a fragrant, rich bouquet, with ripe, citrusy, toasty flavours that linger well. Still youthful, it's an elegant, finely textured wine, tightly structured and likely to be long-lived.

DRY $24 V+

Hunter's Marlborough Chardonnay   ★★★☆

From one vintage to the next, this is a good buy, placing its accent on fresh, vibrant fruit flavours, overlaid with subtle, mealy barrel-ferment characters. About 40 per cent of the blend is fermented and lees-aged in new French oak barriques (medium toast); the rest is tank-fermented and then matured in one and two-year-old casks. It is a proven performer in the cellar. The 2008 (★★★☆) is creamy and smooth, with satisfying fullness and depth of grapefruit-like flavours, a slightly nutty complexity and good texture. It's a characterful wine, for drinking now onwards.

Vintage	08	07	06	05	04
WR	6	6	6	5	6
Drink	09-12	09-11	09-10	P	P

DRY $19 V+

Hyperion Helios Matakana Chardonnay   ★★★☆

The 2008 vintage (★★★☆) was estate-grown, hand-picked and fermented and lees-aged for six months in French oak barriques (one year old). Pale yellow, it's a weighty wine with ripe stone-fruit and toasty oak flavours, balanced acidity, fractional sweetness (6 grams/litre of residual sugar) and very good depth.

Vintage	08
WR	6
Drink	09-13

MED/DRY $27 –V

Instinct Hawke's Bay Chardonnay   (★★★)

From C.J. Pask, the easy-drinking 2007 vintage (★★★) was grown in Gimblett Road and mostly tank-fermented, with 'some' barrel fermentation. Mouthfilling, with a citrusy bouquet, it has fresh, lemony flavours to the fore, with hints of toast and butterscotch, lively acidity and a smooth finish.

DRY $17 AV

Isabel Marlborough Chardonnay   ★★★★

This producer is after 'a tight, restrained style'. Clearly the best of recent vintages, the 2006 (★★★★☆) was tank-fermented and then matured for 10 months in seasoned barrels. It is fresh and fragrant, minerally and slightly creamy, with mouthfilling body, generous, ripe-fruit flavours and a finely textured, lingering finish. Delicious drinking now onwards.

Vintage	06	05
WR	7	7
Drink	09-17	08-15

DRY $28 AV

Ivicevich Signature Reserve Waimauku Chardonnay   ★★★★☆

Launched from 2004 (★★★★☆), this is West Brook's estate-grown Chardonnay. The 2006 vintage (★★★★) is youthful and elegant, with grapefruit, pear, spice and nut flavours, showing good complexity, and a smooth finish. The 2007 (★★★★☆) is a baby. Fleshy, with fresh, very delicate pear, grapefruit and spice flavours, it has gentle acidity and lovely texture. Open 2010+.

DRY $39 –V

Jackson Estate Shelter Belt Marlborough Chardonnay   ★★★☆

The 2008 vintage (★★★☆) was estate-grown in the Homestead Vineyard and fully barrel-aged (20 per cent new). Creamy and slightly biscuity on the nose, it is mouthfilling and rounded, with citrusy, peachy flavours, a hint of butterscotch, and very good complexity and depth.

Vintage	08	07	06
WR	6	6	6
Drink	09-14	09-15	09-12

DRY $23 AV

John Forrest Collection Marlborough Chardonnay   (★★★★☆)

Still on sale, the weighty, finely textured 2004 vintage (★★★★☆) was made from clone 95 Chardonnay, grown in the Wairau Valley, and barrel-aged for 14 months, with very little new oak or malolactic fermentation. The bouquet is fragrant, showing toasty, bottle-aged complexity; the palate is sweet-fruited, with developed, grapefruit-like flavours, some creamy notes and a slightly minerally streak.

Vintage	04
WR	7
Drink	09-14

DRY $50 –V

John Forrest Collection Waitaki Valley North Otago Chardonnay   (★★★★)

Handled in seasoned oak barriques, the debut 2008 vintage (★★★★) has a fragrant, creamy bouquet leading into a weighty, citrusy, toasty and buttery wine, with good richness and a rounded finish. It's hard to pin down any distinctive regional characters, but it's a complex wine, already delicious.

Vintage 08
WR   6
Drink   09-12

 DRY $50 –V

Kahurangi Estate Moutere Chardonnay   ★★★

The 2007 vintage (★★★) is a fresh, crisp Nelson wine, mouthfilling (14 per cent alcohol), with peachy, slightly honeyed and toasty flavours, and a hint of butterscotch. It's an upfront style, ready to roll.

 DRY $22 –V

Kaimira Estate Brightwater Chardonnay   ★★★☆

Estate-grown in Nelson and fermented and lees-aged in French oak barriques, the 2008 vintage (★★★☆) is light yellow, with strong, peachy, citrusy, toasty flavours and fresh acidity. Worth cellaring.

Vintage	08	07	06	05
WR	5	5	5	6
Drink	09-12	09-12	09-11	P

DRY $22 AV

Kaituna Valley Canterbury The Kaituna Vineyard Chardonnay   ★★★☆

Grown on Banks Peninsula, this is a consistently characterful and enjoyable wine, priced right. The 2006 vintage (★★★☆) was hand-picked and fermented and matured in French oak barriques (35 per cent new). Slightly creamy on the nose, it is crisp and very citrusy, slightly buttery and mealy, with good harmony and flavour depth.

DRY $22 AV

Karikari Estate Gisborne Chardonnay   (★★★☆)

The 2006 vintage (★★★☆) was fermented in French and American oak barrels. It's a mouthfilling wine with ripe stone-fruit and toasty oak flavours, showing some complexity, and a dry, slightly creamy finish.

DRY $25 –V

Karikari Estate Karikari Peninsula Chardonnay   ★★★★

From New Zealand's northernmost vineyard and winery, this sturdy wine reminds me of a white from the Rhône Valley. The 2007 vintage (★★★★) was fermented and matured for nine months in predominantly French oak barriques. The toasty, creamy bouquet leads into a mouthfilling wine with fresh acidity and ripe sweet-fruit flavours, showing excellent depth.

Vintage 07
WR   7
Drink   09-12

DRY $34 –V

Kawarau Estate Reserve Chardonnay   ★★★★

Certified organic, this consistently excellent, single-vineyard wine is grown at Pisa Flats, north of Cromwell in Central Otago. The 2007 (★★★★) was fermented with indigenous yeasts in French barriques, oak-aged for 10 months and given a full, softening malolactic fermentation. Invitingly fragrant, it is a weighty wine with ripe, concentrated flavours, slightly creamy, harmonious and persistent. The refined 2008 vintage (★★★★) is fresh, lemony and dry, with mouthfilling body, crisp, minerally acidity and nutty oak adding complexity.

Vintage	08	07	06
WR	5	6	5
Drink	10-11	09-11	09-10

DRY $32 –V

Kemblefield The Distinction Chardonnay   ★★★★

This has been the key wine in the Kemblefield range, although it now has a low profile in New Zealand. Estate-grown in the slightly elevated, relatively cool Mangatahi district of Hawke's Bay, French oak-fermented and matured on its yeast lees for up to 14 months, it is typically made in an upfront style with rich toast and butterscotch aromas, substantial body and strong, peachy, toasty flavours.

DRY $22 V+

Kemblefield Vista Chardonnay   (★★★)

Made in a drink-young style, this wine is estate-grown at Mangatahi, in Hawke's Bay, and fermented in a mix of tanks and barrels. It's typically an enjoyable wine with citrusy, peachy flavours, a subtle oak influence and crisp, dry finish.

DRY $17 AV

Kennedy Point Chardonnay Cuvée Eve   (★★★★)

The debut 2008 vintage (★★★★) was grown in the Oakura Bay Vineyard on Waiheke Island, and fermented (with indigenous yeasts) and matured for 15 months in French oak barriques. It's a full-bodied, rich wine with concentrated, ripe stone-fruit flavours, showing good freshness and complexity.

DRY $38 –V

Kerr Farm Limited Release Kumeu Chardonnay   ★★★

Estate-grown in West Auckland and fermented and matured in French and American oak casks, this is typically a full-bodied wine with plenty of ripe, peachy, slightly toasty flavour.

DRY $25 –V

Kew Barrel Fermented Gisborne Chardonnay   ★★★☆

Still on sale, the 2005 vintage (★★★) was hand-picked at Patutahi and fermented and matured for nine months in seasoned French and American oak casks. Yellow-hued, with a slightly oaky bouquet, it is full-bodied, citrusy and smooth, in a moderately complex style.

DRY $22 AV

Kew Virgin Chardonnay   (★★☆)

'Virgin', in this case, means untouched by wood. Grown in Gisborne, it typically has fresh, lemony, appley aromas and flavours in a simple, vibrantly fruity style with a slightly sweet (6 or 7 grams/litre of residual sugar) finish.

MED/DRY $20 –V

Kim Crawford New Zealand Unoaked Chardonnay   ★★★

Blended from Gisborne, Hawke's Bay and Marlborough grapes, the 2008 vintage (★★☆) is an easy-drinking style, pale straw, with simple, vibrantly fruity, faintly honeyed flavours and a rounded finish. Ready.

DRY $23 –V

Kim Crawford SP Tietjen Gisborne Chardonnay   (★★★★)

Made in an upfront style, this is one of the region's boldest Chardonnays, with rich ripe-fruit flavours, strongly seasoned with perfumed, toasty oak. Fermented in American oak casks, it is given a full, softening malolactic fermentation. Less lush than some vintages, the 2007 (★★★☆) is mouthfilling (14.5 per cent alcohol), with ripe, peachy, citrusy, toasty flavours, showing some complexity and very good depth. Drink 2009–10.

DRY $33 –V

Kina Beach Vineyard Reserve Chardonnay   ★★★★☆

This single-vineyard, coastal Nelson wine possesses strong personality. The 2007 vintage (★★★★☆) was grown at Kina Beach and fermented and matured in French oak barriques (one-third new). Bright, light yellow, it's weighty and rich, but also slightly tighter, more elegant and complex than some past vintages, with finely integrated oak and impressive concentration, delicacy and length.

Vintage	07	06	05	04
WR	7	7	7	7
Drink	09-15	09-15	09-10	P

DRY $30 AV

Kono Gisborne Unoaked Chardonnay   (★★★)

From Tohu Wines, the 2007 vintage (★★★) is a smooth, fruit-driven style with lively, citrusy, appley flavours and slightly creamy notes. It offers fresh, easy, enjoyable drinking.

DRY $18 AV

Kumeu River Coddington Chardonnay   ★★★★★

Launched from the 2006 vintage, this wine is grown in the Coddington Vineyard, between Huapai and Waimauku. The grapes, cultivated on a clay hillside, achieve an advanced level of ripeness (described by marketing manager Paul Brajkovich as 'flamboyant, unctuous, peachy'). Powerful, complex and slightly nutty, it's a lusher, softer wine than its Hunting Hill stablemate (below), but the finish is tight-knit, promising plenty of scope for development. Well worth cellaring, the 2007 (★★★★★) is very rich and sweet-fruited, with bold, citrusy, peachy flavours, vibrant and youthful, balanced toasty oak, and a fine thread of acidity.

Vintage	08	07	06
WR	6	7	7
Drink	10-14	09-14	09-13

`DRY $45 AV`

Kumeu River Estate Chardonnay   ★★★★★

Previously called Kumeu River Chardonnay, this wine now ranks fourth in the company's hierarchy of five Chardonnays, after three single-vineyard labels, but is still outstanding. Grown at Kumeu, in West Auckland, it is powerful, with rich, beautifully interwoven flavours and a seductively creamy texture. The key to its quality lies in the vineyards, says winemaker Michael Brajkovich: 'We manage to get the grapes very ripe.' Grown in several blocks around Kumeu, hand-picked, fermented with indigenous yeasts and lees-aged (with weekly or twice-weekly lees-stirring) in Burgundy oak barriques (typically 25 per cent new), the wine also normally undergoes a full malolactic fermentation. The 2007 vintage (★★★★★) is elegant and sweet-fruited, with lovely delicacy and harmony. Its beautifully ripe and pure Chardonnay flavours are fleshed out with subtle oak and slight butterscotch characters, leading to a soft, dry, rounded finish.

Vintage	08	07	06	05	04	03	02
WR	6	7	7	7	7	6	7
Drink	10-14	09-14	09-13	09-10	P	P	P

`DRY $38 AV`

Kumeu River Hunting Hill Chardonnay   ★★★★★

Launched from the 2006 vintage, this single-vineyard wine is grown on the slopes above Mate's Vineyard, directly over the road from the winery at Kumeu. Marketing manager Paul Brajkovich describes the site's Chardonnay fruit characters as 'floral'. A stylish, elegant wine, in its youth it is less lush than its Coddington stablemate (above), but with good acidity and citrusy, complex flavours that build well across the palate. The 2006 (★★★★★) is drinking extremely well now, but still developing. The 2007 (★★★★★) is tight and finely structured, with very intense, crisp, citrusy, slightly nutty flavours. It's very youthful; open 2010+.

Vintage	08	07	06
WR	6	7	7
Drink	10-14	09-14	09-13

`DRY $45 AV`

Kumeu River Mate's Vineyard Kumeu Chardonnay   ★★★★★

This extremely classy single-vineyard wine is Kumeu River's flagship. It is made entirely from the best of the fruit harvested from Mate's Vineyard, planted in 1990 on the site of the original Kumeu River Vineyard purchased by Mate Brajkovich in 1944. Strikingly similar to Kumeu River Estate Chardonnay, but slightly more opulent and concentrated, it offers the same rich and harmonious flavours of grapefruit, peach and butterscotch, typically with a stronger seasoning of new French oak. For winemaker Michael Brajkovich, the hallmark of Mate's Vineyard is 'a pear-like character on the nose, with richness and length on the palate after two to three years'. The powerful yet elegant 2007 vintage (★★★★★) has concentrated stone-fruit flavours, butterscotch, toast, butter and nut characters, and compelling richness and complexity. A tight-knit wine, it's best opened 2010+.

Vintage	08	07	06	05	04	03	02
WR	6	7	7	6	7	6	7
Drink	10-14	09-14	09-13	09-11	09-10	P	P

`DRY $52 AV`

Kumeu River Village Chardonnay ★★★☆

Kumeu River's lower-tier, drink-young wine is made from heavier-bearing Chardonnay clones than the Mendoza commonly used for the top wines, and is fermented with indigenous yeasts in a mix of tanks (principally) and seasoned French oak casks. The 2008 vintage (★★★☆) is mouthfilling, with good depth of ripe, peachy, slightly spicy flavours, fresh, crisp and dry.

DRY $18 V+

Kupe by Escarpment Martinborough Chardonnay (★★★★★)

Likely to be long-lived, the debut 2006 vintage (★★★★★) is Escarpment's top Chardonnay. Fermented and matured in French oak barriques (50 per cent new), it is very refined and elegant, with ripe sweet-fruit characters and intense, vibrant, citrusy, mealy flavours threaded with fresh acidity. There is no 2007, but the 2008 vintage will be released in early 2010.

DRY $55 AV

Lake Chalice Flight 42 Unoaked Chardonnay ★★★

Grown in Marlborough, this is typically a fresh, vibrant wine with good depth of citrusy, appley flavours, crisp and dry. It's not a complex style, but finely balanced for easy drinking. The 2008 vintage (★★☆) is full-bodied, with straightforward, lemony flavours, fresh and smooth.

DRY $20 –V

Lake Chalice Marlborough Chardonnay ★★★☆

This 'black label' wine is typically fresh, vibrant and creamy, with drink-young appeal. The 2007 vintage (★★★☆) was fermented in a mix of tanks and barrels, and given a full, softening malolactic fermentation. Buoyantly fruity, it is citrusy and appley, with a gentle twist of oak, mouthfilling body and a well-rounded finish.

DRY $20 AV

Lake Chalice Platinum Marlborough Chardonnay ★★★★

This lush, rich, complex wine is estate-grown in the Falcon Vineyard at Rapaura. Hand-picked, it is fermented in French and American oak barriques, lees-aged and given a full malolactic fermentation. It typically offers strong, nutty, mealy flavours and a very creamy texture in a fragrant, full-blown Chardonnay style. The powerful 2007 vintage (★★★★) is still youthful, with deep grapefruit and nut flavours, a hint of butterscotch and obvious potential.

Vintage	07
WR	6
Drink	09-10

DRY $29 AV

Landmark Estate Gisborne Chardonnay ★★★

From a long-established West Auckland producer, this wine is typically fleshy and ripe, in an upfront, flavoursome style, slightly honeyed and soft.

DRY $19 AV

La Strada Marlborough Chardonnay (★★★★☆)

Fromm's unoaked Chardonnay, described by winemaker Hätsch Kalberer as 'very Chablis-like', is given extensive aging on lees and a full, softening malolactic fermentation, but no barrel maturation. The 2007 vintage (★★★★☆) is a candidate for the title of New Zealand's finest unoaked Chardonnay. Dry, weighty and concentrated, it offers smooth, citrusy, slightly spicy flavours, finely balanced acidity and a long finish.

Vintage	08	07	06
WR	6	6	6
Drink	10-14	09-13	09-12

DRY $31 AV

Lawson's Dry Hills Marlborough Chardonnay   ★★★★

This is typically a characterful wine with concentrated, peachy, toasty, buttery flavours. Released at about four years old, it gives a rare opportunity to buy a mature Chardonnay at its peak. Still on sale in 2009, the 2004 vintage (★★★★) is aging well. Grown at three sites in the Wairau Valley, it was fermented – partly with indigenous yeasts – and matured for nine months in French oak barriques (25 per cent new). Bright yellow/green, with strong peach and grapefruit flavours, it has toasty, bottle-aged notes adding complexity and a crisp, lively finish.

Vintage	07	06	05	04	03	02
WR	6	7	NM	5	6	7
Drink	09-11	09-10	NM	P	P	P

DRY $27 AV

Lawson's Dry Hills Unoaked Marlborough Chardonnay   ★★★☆

Grown in the company-owned Chaytors Road Vineyard in the Wairau Valley, this wine is cool-fermented in tanks, with daily stirring of its yeast lees 'to add a creamy texture', but malolactic fermentation is avoided. The 2008 vintage (★★★) is mouthfilling and dry, with citrusy, appley aromas and flavours in an uncomplicated but very fresh and vibrant, highly enjoyable style.

Vintage	09	08
WR	6	7
Drink	09-10	P

DRY $20 AV

Lincoln Reserve Chardonnay   ★★★★☆

Lincoln's flagship Chardonnay label. Still on sale, the 2004 vintage (★★★★☆) is a Hawke's Bay wine, hand-picked in the Smith Vineyard in the Dartmoor Valley and fermented and lees-aged for a year in French oak barriques (50 per cent new). Complex and richly flavoured, with vibrant grapefruit and peach characters, well-integrated oak, good acid spine and a dry, lingering finish, it's a very harmonious and elegant wine.

Vintage	04	03	02
WR	6	NM	6
Drink	P	NM	P

DRY $27 V+

Lochiel Estate Mangawhai Chardonnay   (★★★★)

The skilfully crafted, powerful, creamy-textured 2008 vintage (★★★★) was estate-grown in Northland, in the foothills of the Brynderwyn Range, and 80 per cent barrel-fermented (French, 30 per cent new). Light yellow, with a fragrant bouquet mingling ripe-fruit aromas and toasty oak, it is sturdy (14.5 per cent alcohol), with concentrated stone-fruit flavours, good complexity and a rounded finish. A bold, upfront style, it's already drinking well.

Vintage	08
WR	6
Drink	09-12

DRY $25 AV

Lonely Bay Chardonnay   (★★★★)

Grown at Cooks Beach, on the east coast of the Coromandel Peninsula, this label is worth discovering. The 2007 vintage (★★★★) was hand-picked and fermented and matured for six months in French oak barriques. Light straw, with toasty oak aromas, it is full-bodied, ripe and smooth, with good concentration of stone-fruit flavours and a dry, slightly buttery and creamy finish.

 DRY $23 V+

Lonestone Hawke's Bay Chardonnay   ★★★☆

Produced by Auckland-based wine distributor Bennett & Deller, the 2007 vintage (★★★★) was French oak-aged for six months. Delicious now, it's a very harmonious wine, only moderately complex but concentrated, with strong grapefruit and peach flavours and a creamy-smooth texture.

Vintage	07	06
WR	7	7
Drink	09-12	09-11

 DRY $20 AV

Longbush Chardonnay   ★★★

This 'bird series' label is enjoyable young. Grown in Gisborne and French oak-aged for 10 months, the 2008 vintage (★★★) is full-bodied, with a slightly buttery and toasty bouquet, and satisfying depth of peachy, toasty, well-rounded flavour.

Vintage	08	07
WR	6	5
Drink	09-14	09-10

 DRY $18 AV

Longbush Gisborne Oak Free Chardonnay   ★★☆

Priced right, the 2007 vintage (★★★) is a fruity, uncomplicated wine with ripe, peachy, slightly honeyed flavours. Made in an easy-drinking style with a smooth finish, it's maturing soundly.

Vintage	07
WR	7
Drink	09-11

DRY $13 AV

Longridge Hawke's Bay Chardonnay   ★★★

Part of the Pernod Ricard NZ portfolio, this wine showcases fresh, ripe-fruit characters. The 2007 vintage (★★★), partly French and American oak-aged, is an easy-drinking wine with citrusy, slightly buttery flavours, fresh and smooth.

Vintage	07	06	05
WR	6	6	5
Drink	P	P	P

 DRY $18 AV

Longview Estate Northland Chardonnay   (★★)

Estate-grown just south of Whangarei, this wine is matured for five months in French and Hungarian oak barriques. Most vintages I have tasted have been full-bodied and dry, but lacked a bit of freshness and vibrancy.

 DRY $18 –V

Loopline Wairarapa Chardonnay   ★★☆

Grown at Opaki, just north of Masterton, the 2006 vintage (★★★) is a tight, crisp wine, lemony and slightly austere, in a lean style with some flavour intensity.

DRY $21 –V

Mahi Marlborough Chardonnay   (★★★★)

The debut 2007 vintage (★★★★) was hand-harvested at three sites (including 'our 18 rows of the Home Vineyard' at Renwick), fermented with indigenous yeasts and lees-aged for 11 months in French oak barriques. It's a tightly structured, elegant wine with vibrant, citrusy, peachy, slightly nutty flavours, showing good delicacy and harmony.

Vintage	08	07
WR	6	6
Drink	09-14	09-12

DRY $24 V+

Mahi Twin Valleys Vineyard Marlborough Chardonnay   ★★★★☆

The 2008 vintage (★★★★☆) was grown and hand-picked in the Twin Valleys Vineyard, at the junction of the Wairau and Waihopai valleys. Fermented with indigenous yeasts and matured for 10 months in French oak barriques, it's a fleshy, creamy wine with rich grapefruit and nut flavours, showing good complexity. Delicious from the start, it's a very harmonious wine, for drinking now or cellaring.

Vintage	08	07	06
WR	6	6	6
Drink	09-13	09-16	09-12

DRY $34 AV

Maimai Creek Hawke's Bay Chardonnay   ★★☆

The 2007 vintage (★★☆) is a fruit-driven style, partly oak-aged for six months, with peachy flavours, hints of toast and butterscotch, and moderate depth.

DRY $18 –V

Main Divide Chardonnay   ★★★☆

The Main Divide range is from Pegasus Bay. Grown in Marlborough, the 2007 vintage (★★★☆) was fermented with indigenous yeasts and lees-aged for a year in French oak barrels (10 per cent new). It is mouthfilling, with very satisfying depth of fresh, lively, peachy flavours, a hint of butterscotch and good complexity. (The 2008 vintage was grown at Waipara.)

Vintage	08	07	06	05
WR	6	5	6	5
Drink	09-11	09-11	09-10	P

DRY $20 AV

Man O' War Valhalla Waiheke Island Chardonnay   ★★★☆

Grown at the far, eastern end of the island in Auckland's Hauraki Gulf and matured for a year in French oak casks (30 per cent new), the 2007 vintage (★★★☆) is a robust wine (14.5 per cent alcohol), with fresh acidity and concentrated, peachy, toasty, faintly honeyed flavours.

Vintage	08	07
WR	6	6
Drink	10-15	09-10

DRY $40 –V

Man O' War Waiheke Island Chardonnay   ★★★★

Fermented in a mix of tanks and barrels, the immediately appealing 2007 vintage (★★★★) has rich, grapefruit-like flavours, threaded with fresh acidity, a hint of honey and finely integrated oak.

Vintage	08	07
WR	5	6
Drink	09-12	09-10

DRY $28 AV

Margrain Martinborough Chardonnay   ★★★☆

The 2007 vintage (★★★☆), fermented and matured for 10 months in French oak casks (20 per cent new), is crisp, dry and minerally, with strong grapefruit and peach flavours and firm acid spine. It's a slightly austere style, with good intensity. The 2008 (★★★☆) is citrusy, slightly appley and buttery, with a subtle oak influence and a crisp, dry finish.

Vintage	08
WR	6
Drink	09-13

DRY $28 –V

Marsden Bay of Islands Estate Chardonnay   ★★★

This Northland wine is estate-grown at Kerikeri, in the Bay of Islands, and made without any oak or malolactic fermentation. The 2007 vintage (★★★☆) is a weighty, rounded northern style, full-bodied and fleshy, with moderate acidity and very satisfying depth of ripe stone-fruit flavours.

Vintage	07	06
WR	5	7
Drink	P	P

DRY $25 –V

Marsden Black Rocks Chardonnay   ★★★★☆

This Kerikeri, Bay of Islands, wine has lately been in great form. Fermented and matured for a year in French and American oak casks, the instantly appealing 2007 vintage (★★★★★) is sturdy, with concentrated, ripe sweet-fruit flavours well seasoned with toasty oak. A lush, creamy-smooth and fragrant wine, it's delicious now.

Vintage	07	06	05
WR	5	7	7
Drink	09-10	P	P

DRY $35 –V

Martinborough Vineyard Chardonnay   ★★★★★

Mouthfilling, peachy, citrusy and mealy, this is a powerful, harmonious wine, rich and complex. Made entirely from grapes grown on the gravelly Martinborough Terrace, including the original Mendoza clone vines planted in 1980, it is hand-picked, fully fermented (with indigenous yeasts) and lees-aged for a year in French oak barriques (25 per cent new in 2007). Notably weighty and rich, the 2007 (★★★★★) has delicious depth of ripe stone-fruit flavours seasoned with toasty oak. A top vintage, creamy-textured and seamless, it's a drink-now or cellaring proposition.

Vintage	07	06	05	04	03	02
WR	7	7	6	6	7	6
Drink	09-13	09-12	09-11	09-10	P	P

DRY $42 AV

Matahiwi Estate Hawke's Bay Chardonnay   (★★★☆)

The 2008 vintage (★★★☆) is full-bodied, with strong, citrusy flavours, a gentle seasoning of nutty oak, and a slightly creamy finish. Drink now onwards.

DRY $25 –V

Matahiwi Estate Holly Wairarapa Chardonnay   (★★★☆)

The 2008 vintage (★★★☆) is a single-vineyard wine, barrel-fermented and lees-aged for 10 months. The bouquet is toasty and slightly creamy; the palate is mouthfilling, with ripe, peachy, citrusy, slightly buttery flavours, a strong seasoning of toasty oak, and considerable complexity. Best drinking mid-2010+.

DRY $26 –V

Matakana Estate Matakana Chardonnay   ★★★☆

Estate-grown north of Auckland, this wine has shown varying form, but the 2007 vintage (★★★★☆) is one of the finest. Hand-picked and fermented and lees-aged in French oak barriques (40 per cent new), it's a generous, immaculate wine with rich, peachy, slightly toasty and creamy flavours, good complexity and real power through the palate.

DRY $27 –V

Matariki Aspire Chardonnay – see Aspire Chardonnay

Matariki Hawke's Bay Chardonnay   ★★★★

This is a consistently rewarding wine. It is grown in Gimblett Road (principally), with a smaller portion of fruit cultivated in limestone soils on the east side of Te Mata Peak giving 'a flinty, lime character'. Partly French oak-fermented and fully barrel-aged, the 2006 vintage (★★★★) is a tightly structured, complex wine with fresh acidity and strong grapefruit and peach flavours, slightly nutty and toasty.

Vintage	07	06	05	04
WR	6	6	6	6
Drink	09-12	09-11	09-10	P

DRY $27 AV

Matariki Reserve Chardonnay   ★★★★☆

This often outstanding Hawke's Bay wine is grown at the company's sites in the Gimblett Gravels and at Te Mata Peak (see above) and fermented (partly with indigenous yeasts) in French oak barriques (92 per cent new in 2006). The 2006 vintage (★★★★☆) has a fragrant, citrusy, biscuity bouquet. Mouthfilling and slightly creamy, it is very refined, with a core of ripe grapefruit-like flavours, hints of butterscotch and toasty oak, and excellent richness and elegance.

Vintage	07	06	05	04
WR	7	6	7	7
Drink	09-12	09-11	09-10	P

DRY $36 –V

Matua Valley Ararimu Chardonnay   ★★★★☆

Ararimu ('path to the forest') is Matua Valley's premier Chardonnay. It is usually based on low-cropped, hand-picked grapes at Judd Estate in Gisborne, and fermented and matured, with regular lees-stirring, in French oak barriques (55 per cent new in 2007). Already delicious, the 2007 vintage (★★★★☆) is fragrant, complex, rich and rounded. It's a very harmonious wine, concentrated, nutty and creamy, with a long finish.

Vintage	07
WR	7
Drink	09-12

DRY $40 –V

Matua Valley Eastern Bays Chardonnay   ★★★

This moderately priced wine is typically a fruit-driven style, fresh and crisp, with lees-aging and a touch of French and American oak adding depth. (The 2009 vintage was grown in Gisborne.)

DRY $15 V+

Matua Valley Judd Estate Chardonnay   ★★★★

Hand-picked in the company-owned Judd Estate vineyard, this is a softly mouthfilling Gisborne wine with good complexity and the ability to age well. The 2007 vintage (★★★★), fermented and matured for 10 months in French oak barriques (35 per cent new), has a fragrant, ripe, slightly nutty bouquet, leading into a finely textured wine, mouthfilling and smooth, with vibrant peach and grapefruit flavours, slightly toasty, creamy and concentrated. It's already delicious.

Vintage	07
WR	6
Drink	09-12

DRY $25 AV

Matua Valley Matheson Chardonnay   ★★★☆

This Hawke's Bay wine is usually sourced from the company's Matheson Vineyard in The Triangle and barrel-fermented (French, 25 per cent new in 2007). It is typically an upfront style, peachy, toasty and creamy, with some richness and complexity and a rounded finish.

Vintage	07
WR	6
Drink	09-12

DRY $20 AV

Matua Valley Reserve Chardonnay   (★★★☆)

The 2007 vintage (★★★☆) was mostly grown and hand-picked at Judd Estate vineyard, in Gisborne, and fully barrel-fermented. A tightly structured, full-bodied wine with smooth, citrusy, appley flavours, it shows good delicacy, with toasty, creamy notes adding a degree of complexity.

DRY $20 AV

Matua Valley Shingle Peak Marlborough Chardonnay   ★★★

The 2007 vintage (★★★) is a fruit-driven style with melon and citrus characters to the fore. It's a fresh, vibrant wine with slightly leesy, mealy notes and a crisp finish. (For the 2008 vintage, see the entry for Shingle Peak Chardonnay.)

DRY $18 AV

Maven Marlborough Chardonnay ★★★

The 2007 vintage (★★★) was grown in the Wairau Valley and a small component of the blend was barrel-fermented. Fruity, full-bodied and flavoursome, with ripe, citrusy, peachy characters and a smooth finish, it's not complex, but delivers satisfying, easy drinking.

Vintage	07	06
WR	6	5
Drink	09-10	P

 DRY $18 AV

Mill Road Hawke's Bay Chardonnay ★★☆

Priced right, Morton Estate's bottom-tier, non-vintage Chardonnay typically offers lively, citrusy-fruit characters in an uncomplicated style, clean, fresh and crisp. The wine on the market in 2009 (★★) is light yellow, with lemony, slightly honeyed flavours, smooth and ready.

 DRY $13 AV

Mills Reef Elspeth Chardonnay ★★★★☆

Mills Reef's flagship Hawke's Bay Chardonnay is consistently rewarding and a classic regional style. The 2008 vintage (★★★★☆) is a single-vineyard wine, hand-picked and fermented and matured for 11 months in French oak barriques (80 per cent new). Mouthfilling and rounded, it has concentrated, ripe grapefruit and peach flavours, with a hint of butterscotch (50 per cent malolactic fermentation), and excellent texture, complexity and length. Best drinking mid-2010+.

 DRY $32 AV

Mills Reef Hawke's Bay Chardonnay ★★★

Mills Reef's bottom-tier Chardonnay is an easy-drinking Hawke's Bay wine. Grown at Meeanee, the 2007 vintage (★★★☆) is one of the best. It was mostly handled in tanks, but a third of the blend was fermented with indigenous yeasts in seasoned oak barrels and wood-aged for three months. Mouthfilling and slightly buttery, it has very good depth of peachy, slightly toasty flavours, ripe and rounded.

DRY $17 AV

Mills Reef Reserve Hawke's Bay Chardonnay ★★★★

Mills Reef's middle-tier Chardonnay. The 2007 vintage (★★★★) was grown in coastal vineyards at Meeanee and in the Gimblett Gravels, and fermented and matured for 10 months in a 70/30 split of American and French oak barrels (one-third new). It's a fleshy, full-flavoured style, citrusy, peachy and concentrated, with good complexity and harmony and a creamy-smooth finish.

Vintage	07	06	05	04
WR	7	7	7	7
Drink	09-11	09-10	P	P

 DRY $25 AV

Millton Clos de Ste Anne Chardonnay – see Clos de Ste Anne Chardonnay

Millton Gisborne Chardonnay Opou Vineyard   ★★★★

This is Millton's middle-tier Chardonnay, barrel-fermented and certified organic. A top vintage, the 2007 (★★★★☆) is rich, dry and complex, with peachy, nutty, slightly buttery flavours and a hint of butterscotch. Refined and slightly minerally, it's drinking well now.

Vintage	07	06	05	04
WR	7	6	6	7
Drink	09-14	09-12	09-10	09-10

DRY $27 AV

Millton Gisborne Chardonnay Riverpoint Vineyard   (★★★)

A good example of the unoaked style, the 2007 vintage (★★★) was grown organically near the sea, hand-picked and fermented in tanks. Fresh and fruity, it's an uncomplicated wine with citrusy, slightly spicy flavours and an off-dry (5.3 grams/litre of residual sugar), crisp and lively finish.

Vintage	07	06
WR	6	5
Drink	09-10	09-10

MED/DRY $21 –V

Mission Hawke's Bay Chardonnay   ★★★

Hawke's Bay winemaker Paul Mooney knows how to make Chardonnay taste delicious at just a few months old. The 2008 vintage (★★★) is a full-bodied, lightly oaked style with good depth of ripe, peachy, citrusy, slightly toasty flavours and a smooth, dry finish. Ready.

DRY $17 AV

Mission Jewelstone Hawke's Bay Chardonnay   ★★★★★

This wine has shone since the super-stylish 2002 vintage (★★★★★), grown in Central Hawke's Bay. The 2007 (★★★★★), grown at Te Awanga, near the coast, was hand-picked and matured on its yeast lees for 17 months in French oak barriques (40 per cent new). The bouquet is highly attractive – rich, mealy, nutty and complex. Powerful, weighty and tightly structured, it has highly concentrated stone-fruit flavours woven with appetising acidity, and lovely length.

Vintage	07	06	05	04
WR	6	5	6	5
Drink	09-13	09-11	09-11	P

DRY $34 AV

Mission Reserve Chardonnay   ★★★★

For Mission's middle-tier Chardonnay, the style goal is a Hawke's Bay wine that 'emphasises fruit characters rather than oak, but offers some of the benefits of fermentation and maturation in wood'. Grown in the Gimblett Gravels, the 2008 vintage (★★★★) was fermented and lees-aged in French oak casks (25 per cent new). It's a skilfully made wine with strong, citrusy flavours to the fore, a subtle seasoning of nutty oak, and a slightly buttery finish. Rich and concentrated, it's worth cellaring. (Note: the word 'Reserve' appears only on the back label.)

Vintage	08	07	06	05	04
WR	7	7	5	5	5
Drink	09-15	09-11	09-10	P	P

DRY $23 V+

Mission Vineyard Selection Chardonnay ★★★☆

Grown in the Gimblett Gravels and fermented and lees-aged for seven months in French oak casks (10 per cent new), the 2008 vintage (★★★☆) is mouthfilling, with strong grapefruit-like flavours, hints of limes and honey, and good complexity. Drink now or cellar.

DRY $18 V+

Moana Park Vineyard Selection Grange Block Chardonnay (★★☆)

The 2008 vintage (★★☆) was grown in Hawke's Bay and mostly handled in tanks, but 30 per cent of the blend was barrel-fermented. Mouthfilling, fruity and smooth, it's an uncomplicated wine with fresh, citrusy, appley flavours. A drink-young style, priced right.

Vintage	08
WR	5
Drink	09-12

DRY $15 AV

Moana Park Vineyard Tribute Chardonnay ★★★☆

The 2007 vintage (★★★☆) was grown in Hawke's Bay and fermented with indigenous yeasts in French oak barriques (30 per cent new). It's a fat, big-bodied wine, peachy, nutty and creamy, made in a soft, upfront style.

Vintage	07
WR	6
Drink	09-10

DRY $25 –V

Momo Marlborough Chardonnay (★★★☆)

From Seresin, the 2008 vintage (★★★☆) was grown organically and fermented with indigenous yeasts in seasoned oak barrels. Already drinking well, it is fresh, fruity and softly textured, with the slightly earthy aromas of 'wild' yeasts and plenty of citrusy, slightly nutty flavour.

DRY $20 AV

Monkey Bay Gisborne Chardonnay ★★☆

From Constellation NZ, the 2007 vintage (★★★) is a fresh and lively, no-fuss wine that rests its case on its buoyantly fruity, peachy flavours. A good example of the unoaked style, it's ready to roll. The 2008 (★★☆) is vibrantly fruity, with slightly buttery and creamy notes and a very smooth finish.

MED/DRY $15 AV

Montana Gisborne Chardonnay ★★☆

From Pernod Ricard NZ, this long-popular Chardonnay is an undemanding style, fresh, fruity and smooth. The 2008 vintage (★★☆) was tank-fermented, with no oak, but 4 per cent Viognier was added for its 'lovely apricot flavours' and 'enticing texture'. It's a lemony, appley, faintly honeyed wine in a straightforward style, crisp, fresh and dry. (Note: at its average price in supermarkets of $10.70, it delivers value.)

DRY $18 –V

Montana 'O' Ormond Chardonnay   ★★★★★

This is the flagship Gisborne Chardonnay from Pernod Ricard NZ, made for cellaring. Grown at three sites, two at Ormond and the third at Patutahi, it is hand-harvested, whole-bunch pressed, fermented in French oak barriques (40 to 50 per cent new) and matured on its yeast lees for 10 to 11 months. It has a proven ability to age well for a decade. The 2006 (★★★★★) is very elegant, with a complex bouquet and fresh acidity enlivening its grapefruit and subtle oak flavours, which are finely balanced and lingering. The 2007 vintage (★★★★★) is rich and poised, with grapefruit and peach flavours, slightly creamy and toasty, and good drive and complexity. Best drinking mid-2010+.

Vintage	07	06	05	04	03	02	01	00
WR	7	6	6	6	NM	7	NM	7
Drink	09-12	09-11	09-10	09	NM	08-10	NM	P

DRY $33 V+

Montana Reserve Chardonnay   ★★★☆

Past releases were sourced from Marlborough, but the 2007 vintage (★★★★) is from Hawke's Bay and the 2008 (★★★☆) is from Gisborne. Grown in company-owned vineyards, it was partly tank-fermented, but 60 per cent of the blend was fermented in French and Hungarian oak barriques (25 per cent new). It's a mouthfilling wine, crisp and elegant, with good depth of ripe-fruit flavours and a subtle seasoning of oak.

DRY $23 AV

Montana Terroir Stuart Block Gisborne Chardonnay   ★★★★

Grown in the relatively cool Patutahi district, the 2006 vintage (★★★★) was fermented and matured in French oak barriques (30 per cent new). A fragrant wine with well-ripened, tropical-fruit and toasty oak flavours, fresh acidity and considerable elegance, it's maturing well.

Vintage	06
WR	6
Drink	P

DRY $29 AV

Montana Terroir Waihirere Gisborne Chardonnay   ★★★★

Grown in the relatively warm, inland Ormond district, this wine is hand-picked and fermented in French oak barriques. The 2006 vintage (★★★★) has a fragrant, slightly creamy bouquet leading into a generous, mouthfilling wine with concentrated, ripe grapefruit and nut flavours, harmonious and rich. Delicious now.

Vintage	06
WR	7
Drink	P

DRY $29 AV

Morton Estate Black Label Hawke's Bay Chardonnay   ★★★★☆

Grown principally in the company's cool, elevated Riverview Vineyard at Mangatahi, this can be a very classy Chardonnay, although the latest releases have not quite achieved the standard of a decade ago. At its best, it's a powerful wine, robust and awash with flavour, yet also highly refined, with beautifully intense citrusy fruit, firm acid spine and the structure to flourish with age. It is fully barrel-fermented, and given the wine's concentrated fruit characters, the French oak barriques are 100 per cent new. The 2002 was the first to include fruit from Matapiro – over the river from Riverview. The 2006 vintage (★★★★) is pale straw and mouthfilling, with strong peach and grapefruit flavours, hints of honey and toast, and a slightly oily richness. It's a relatively forward vintage; drink now onwards.

Vintage	06	05	04	03	02
WR	5	NM	6	NM	7
Drink	09-12	NM	09-10	NM	P

DRY $35 –V

Morton Estate Coniglio Chardonnay – see Coniglio Hawke's Bay Chardonnay

Morton Estate Private Reserve Hawke's Bay Chardonnay ★★☆

The golden 2005 (★★) is distinctly honeyed, with a clear botrytis influence, and past its best. The 2006 (★★☆), oak-aged, is mouthfilling, with simple, peachy, slightly honeyed flavours.

Vintage	06	05
WR	5	6
Drink	09-12	09-11

DRY $21 –V

Morton Estate Riverview Hawke's Bay Chardonnay ★★★★

Grown at the same site at Mangatahi as the famous Black Label Chardonnay and fermented in French oak barriques, the 2005 vintage (★★★★) is an elegant wine, mouthfilling and generous, with rich, smooth, grapefruit-like flavours and biscuity, mealy notes adding complexity.

Vintage	05	04	03	02
WR	5	7	NM	7
Drink	09-10	P	NM	P

DRY $20 V+

Morton Estate Three Vineyards Hawke's Bay Chardonnay ★★★☆

The 'three vineyards' include Tantallon, Morton's warmest vineyard, down on the Heretaunga Plains (which gives 'a more tropical, fruit-forward style'), and the cooler Kinross and Riverview vineyards. Fermented in a mix of tanks and barrels, the 2007 vintage (★★★☆) is fresh, with lively acidity and citrusy, gently oaked flavours, showing very good delicacy and depth.

Vintage	07
WR	6
Drink	09-12

DRY $20 AV

Morton Estate White Label Hawke's Bay Chardonnay ★★★☆

Morton Estate's best-known Hawke's Bay Chardonnay is typically a good buy. Fermented and lees-aged in French oak barriques, the 2008 (★★★) is pale yellow, mouthfilling and smooth, with peachy, citrusy, slightly honeyed flavours, showing good depth, and a touch of biscuity oak adding complexity. It's a forward vintage, ready to roll.

Vintage	08
WR	6
Drink	09-12

DRY $18 V+

Mountford Estate Chardonnay ★★★★

In top vintages, this Waipara wine offers strikingly rich flavour, with a commanding mouthfeel. The 2006 vintage (★★★★☆) is an opulent, lush wine, very powerful (14.5 per cent alcohol), with highly concentrated, peachy, faintly honeyed flavours. Drink now to 2010.

DRY $49 –V

Mount Maude Central Otago Chardonnay   ★★★

The 2007 vintage (★★☆) is a single-vineyard Wanaka wine, fermented with indigenous yeasts and matured for 10 months in oak puncheons. It's a very lightly wooded wine with fresh, straightforward, citrusy, appley flavours and appetising acidity.

DRY $25 –V

Mount Michael Bessie's Block Central Otago Chardonnay   ★★★☆

Estate-grown on a site overlooking Cromwell, the 2007 vintage (★★★) is mouthfilling and crisp, with vibrant, citrusy, appley flavours, showing good depth, but only moderate complexity.

DRY $27 –V

Mount Riley Marlborough Chardonnay   ★★★

Mount Riley is named after the dominant peak in the Richmond Range, on the northern flanks of the Wairau Valley. The 2007 vintage (★★★) is a fruit-driven style, 40 per cent fermented in French (mostly) and American oak casks (one and two-year-old). Lively and smooth, it offers satisfying depth of citrusy, limey flavours and a slightly buttery finish.

Vintage	08	07	06	05
WR	4	5	7	5
Drink	P	09-11	P	P

DRY $19 AV

Mount Riley Seventeen Valley Marlborough Chardonnay   ★★★☆

Still on sale, the 2005 vintage (★★★) was hand-picked at Renwick and in the company's Seventeen Valley Vineyard, south of Blenheim, and fermented with indigenous yeasts in mostly new French oak casks. It shows some botrytis-derived, honeyed notes, but also good body, richness and complexity.

Vintage	05	04	03	02
WR	7	7	6	7
Drink	09-10	P	P	P

DRY $30 –V

Moutere Hills New Zealand Chardonnay   (★★★★)

The 2007 vintage (★★★★) is a tight, Chablis-style Nelson wine with a minerally bouquet. Barrel-fermented, it is weighty and dry, with firm acidity threaded through its citrusy, appley, mealy, biscuity flavours. Flinty and tautly structured, it's an obvious candidate for cellaring.

DRY $38 –V

Mt Difficulty Central Otago Chardonnay   ★★★☆

Grown in three vineyards at Bannockburn, the 2007 vintage (★★★) was fully barrel-fermented and 70 per cent went through a softening malolactic fermentation. It's not fragrant but mouthfilling, with satisfying depth of citrusy, slightly nutty and minerally flavours and some complexity.

Vintage	07	06
WR	7	7
Drink	10-12	09-12

DRY $35 –V

Mt Hector Hawke's Bay Chardonnay (★★☆)

From Matahiwi, the 2007 vintage (★★☆) is full-bodied and fruity, with decent depth of citrusy, slightly limey flavours in a solid, no-fuss style, priced right.

DRY $13 AV

Mudbrick Vineyard Reserve Waiheke Island Chardonnay ★★★★

The youthful 2008 vintage (★★★★☆) was fermented – with some use of indigenous yeasts – and matured for 10 months in French oak barriques (30 per cent new). The best wine yet under this label, it is mouthfilling (14.5 per cent alcohol), lush and sweet-fruited, with rich, yet delicate, grapefruit and nut flavours, showing very good complexity. Best drinking mid-2010+.

Vintage	08
WR	7
Drink	09-12

DRY $36 –V

Muddy Water Chardonnay ★★★☆

The 2007 vintage (★★★★) was hand-picked at Waipara at over 24 brix, fermented with indigenous yeasts and matured for 11 months in French oak barriques and puncheons (10 per cent new). Light yellow/green, with a lemony bouquet, it's a fresh, tightly structured wine with finely integrated oak and good intensity of citrusy, slightly buttery flavour.

Vintage	07	06	05	04
WR	7	7	7	6
Drink	09-15	09-12	09-12	09-10

DRY $30 –V

Mud House Swan Marlborough Chardonnay ★★★★

The 2007 vintage (★★★★) was fermented and lees-aged for 10 months in French oak barriques. A high-impact style, offering concentrated, stone-fruit flavours strongly seasoned with toasty oak, it is mouthfilling, rich, peachy and slightly creamy, with loads of personality.

DRY $25 AV

Murdoch James Blue Rock Unoaked Chardonnay ★★☆

Grown in Martinborough, the 2008 vintage (★★★) is an unwooded style, full-bodied, fresh and vibrantly fruity, with good depth of smooth, lemony, appley flavours and a dry finish.

Vintage	08	07	06
WR	6	7	6
Drink	09-11	09-10	09-10

DRY $20 –V

Nautilus Marlborough Chardonnay ★★★★

This stylish wine has fresh, strong, citrusy flavours and finely integrated oak. The 2007 vintage (★★★★☆) was mostly estate-grown at Renwick, hand-picked and fermented (partly with indigenous yeasts) and lees-aged in French oak barriques (25 per cent new). It's a mouthfilling, creamy-textured wine with rich yet delicate grapefruit, nut and toast flavours, slightly minerally and finely poised. Well worth cellaring; open mid-2010+.

Vintage	08	07	06	05	04
WR	7	7	6	6	6
Drink	10-13	09-12	09-11	P	P

DRY $29 AV

Nest, The, Marlborough Chardonnay   (★★★)

From Lake Chalice, the debut 2008 vintage (★★★) is an easy-drinking style, grown in the Wairau Valley and fermented in a mix of tanks and barrels (French and American). Given a full, softening malolactic fermentation, it is creamy and faintly nutty, with citrusy, slightly peachy flavours and a well-rounded finish.

DRY $20 –V

Neudorf Moutere Chardonnay   ★★★★★

Superbly rich but not overblown, with arrestingly intense flavours enlivened with fine acidity, this rare, multi-faceted Nelson wine enjoys a reputation second to none among New Zealand Chardonnays. Grown in clay soils threaded with gravel at Upper Moutere, it is hand-harvested from vines up to 29 years old, fermented with indigenous yeasts, and lees-aged for up to a year in French oak barriques (27 per cent new in 2007). The 2007 vintage (★★★★★), grown in the Home Vineyard (mostly) and 'across the road' in the Beuke Vineyard, was picked at 23.8 to 24.2 brix. A forward, already very open and expressive vintage, it has a highly fragrant, complex bouquet, with rich, ripe grapefruit-like flavours, slightly nutty and minerally, and a creamy-smooth finish.

Vintage	08	07	06	05	04	03	02	01	00
WR	6	7	7	6	6	7	6	6	6
Drink	09-16	09-15	09-16	09-15	09-14	09-13	09-13	09-11	09-10

DRY $55 AV

Neudorf Nelson Chardonnay   ★★★★☆

Overshadowed by its famous stablemate (above), this regional blend is a fine Chardonnay in its own right. Grown at Upper Moutere (mostly), but also at Kina, on the coast, and at Brightwater, on the Waimea Plains, it is fermented with indigenous yeasts in French oak casks (20 per cent new in 2007), and given a full, softening malolactic fermentation. The 2007 vintage (★★★★☆) is highly fragrant, impressively weighty and harmonious, with a distinct hint of butterscotch. It has ripe grapefruit and toast flavours, woven with fresh acidity, and excellent structure and complexity. As a classy wine for drinking young, it's hard to beat.

Vintage	08	07	06	05	04	03	02
WR	6	6	7	7	6	6	
Drink	09-16	09-15	09-14	09-13	09-12	09-12	09-11

DRY $30 AV

Ngatarawa Alwyn Chardonnay   ★★★★★

Ngatarawa's flagship Hawke's Bay Chardonnay is based on estate-grown, hand-picked grapes, supplemented since 2000 with fruit from a neighbouring grower's vineyard. Fermented and lees-aged for a year in French oak barriques, with no use of malolactic fermentation, it is typically an arrestingly bold, highly concentrated wine that takes years to reveal its full class and complexity. The 2007 vintage (★★★★★) is youthful in colour, with very rich, stone-fruit flavours, balanced toasty oak and a bone-dry, finely structured finish. It's a finely poised wine, for drinking now or cellaring.

Vintage	08	07	06
WR	NM	7	7
Drink	NM	09-12	09-11

DRY $35 AV

Ngatarawa Glazebrook Chardonnay – see Glazebrook Regional Reserve Chardonnay

Ngatarawa Silks Chardonnay   ★★★

The 2008 vintage (★★★) is basically a Hawke's Bay wine (with 8 per cent Gisborne fruit). Ready to roll, it is full-bodied, with fresh, citrusy, peachy flavours, a touch of biscuity oak and a slightly off-dry finish.

Vintage	08	07	06
WR	7	6	6
Drink	09-12	09-11	09-10

MED/DRY $20 –V

Ngatarawa Stables Chardonnay   ★★☆

Ngatarawa's lower-tier Chardonnay is made for easy drinking. The 2009 vintage (★★☆) is an East Coast blend of Hawke's Bay and Gisborne grapes, fresh and fruity, with pleasant, peachy flavours and a smooth finish.

Vintage	08	07	06
WR	6	6	6
Drink	09-11	09-10	P

DRY $16 –V

Nga Waka Home Block Chardonnay   ★★★★☆

This single-vineyard Martinborough wine is based on mature vines and fermented and lees-aged in French oak barriques. At its best, it is an authoritative wine, weighty and concentrated, with grapefruit and toast flavours, a fresh, minerally character and great personality. The 2006 vintage (★★★★★) is a powerful wine, showing lovely fruity sweetness, with very rich peachy, citrusy, toasty, slightly minerally flavours. Classy, complex and finely poised, it's a drink-now or cellaring proposition.

Vintage	06	05	04	03	02
WR	7	7	6	7	6
Drink	10+	09+	P	P	P

DRY $35 –V

Nga Waka Martinborough Chardonnay   ★★★★☆

Following the launch of the flagship label (above), the price of this consistently rewarding wine was trimmed and it now offers great value. Hand-harvested and French oak-fermented, the 2008 vintage (★★★★☆) has a fragrant, biscuity, rich bouquet, concentrated grapefruit and peach flavours, and excellent complexity. Drink now or cellar.

Vintage	08	07	06	05	04
WR	7	7	7	7	6
Drink	10+	P	P	P	P

DRY $25 V+

Nikau Point Reserve Hawke's Bay Chardonnay   ★★★☆

The 'One Tree Hill Vineyards' in small print is a division of Morton Estate. The 2008 vintage (★★★☆) is fresh and vibrant, with strong grapefruit and peach flavours and a slightly creamy texture. It should mature well.

Vintage	08
WR	7
Drink	09-10

DRY $17 V+

Nikau Point Unoaked Hawke's Bay Chardonnay   ★★☆

The 2007 vintage from Morton Estate (★★☆) is fresh and fruity, with pleasant, simple, citrusy flavours.

Vintage	07
WR	6
Drink	P

DRY $16 –V

Nobilo Regional Collection East Coast Chardonnay   ★★★

Top vintages – until 2006 called Poverty Bay, rather than East Coast – were delicious and offered good value, but the label now has a low profile in New Zealand. Still on sale in 2009, the 2005 (★★☆) was mostly tank-fermented, but a portion was barrel-fermented and the wine is strongly 'malo'-influenced (which has a softening effect). Yellow-hued, with buttery aromas and flavours, it's a smooth, flavoursome wine, peachy, creamy and toasty, in an upfront style, but now slightly past its best.

DRY $17 AV

Northfield Frog Rock Waipara Chardonnay   (★★★☆)

The 2007 vintage (★★★☆) is an upfront style, peachy, spicy and creamy, with a seasoning of sweet oak (French and American), some mealy complexity and a well-rounded finish.

DRY $25 –V

Obsidian Waiheke Island Chardonnay   ★★★★

The powerful 2008 vintage (★★★★) was fermented and lees-aged for seven months in French oak barriques (33 per cent new). Still very youthful, it's a sturdy (14.5 per cent alcohol), fresh and lively wine with rich, ripe, peachy, slightly toasty flavours, good complexity and a slightly creamy, rounded finish. Open mid-2010+.

Vintage	08	07
WR	6	6
Drink	10-14	09-12

DRY $33 –V

Odyssey Gisborne Chardonnay   ★★★

A drink-young style, this is typically a crisp, fruity, often slightly honeyed wine, flavoursome and smooth. The 2007 vintage (★★★), grown in the Kawatiri Vineyard, is weighty and rounded, with plenty of smooth, ripe, peachy flavour in a forward style, ready now.

Vintage	08	07
WR	6	6
Drink	09-11	09-10

DRY $19 AV

Odyssey Reserve Iliad Gisborne Chardonnay   ★★★★★

Top vintages represent Gisborne Chardonnay at its finest. Grown in the Kawatiri Vineyard at Hexton and fermented and lees-aged in French oak barriques, the 2006 vintage (★★★★☆) is fleshy, with rich citrus, tropical-fruit and toasty oak flavours, showing excellent texture and concentration. A powerful wine, it's also elegant and tightly structured.

Vintage	07	06	05	04	03	02
WR	6	6	6	7	6	6
Drink	09-11	09-10	P	P	P	P

DRY $32 V+

Ohinemuri Estate Reserve Patutahi Chardonnay ★★★

Fermented in barrels (60 per cent) and tanks (40 per cent), the 2007 vintage (★★★☆) is full-bodied, with sweet-fruit characters and ripe, citrusy, slightly creamy flavours showing good depth.

Vintage	07
WR	6
Drink	09-12

DRY $24 –V

Okahu Chardonnay ★★☆

The 2007 vintage (★★★☆) was estate-grown in Northland and 60 per cent barrel-fermented (in French and American oak, partly new). Mouthfilling, with a rich, slightly toasty bouquet, it has ripe, citrusy, slightly nutty flavours, showing very good depth, fresh acidity and considerable complexity.

DRY $27 –V

Okahu Chardonnay/Viognier Unoaked (★★☆)

Grown in Northland, the 2007 vintage (★★☆) is 'unhindered by oak'. It's a solid but fairly plain wine, appley, slightly peachy, mouthfilling and dry, with fresh acidity.

DRY $26 –V

Old Coach Road Nelson Chardonnay ★★★

Tank-fermented and mostly American oak-matured, with lots of lees-stirring, this affordable wine from Seifried Estate has won many awards, in New Zealand and the UK. It's an upfront style, typically citrusy and sweetly wooded, slightly creamy, buttery and smooth.

DRY $17 AV

Old Coach Road Unoaked Nelson Chardonnay ★★☆

Seifried Estate's low-priced Chardonnay typically appeals for its freshness and vigour. The 2008 vintage (★★☆) is vibrantly fruity, with citrusy, slightly appley flavours, crisp, simple and lively. The 2009 (★★☆) is similar – fresh and crisp, appley and limey, in a style akin to Sauvignon Blanc.

DRY $15 AV

Olssen's Charcoal Joe Chardonnay ★★★☆

Named after a nineteenth-century goldminer, this wine is hand-picked at Bannockburn, in Central Otago, and fermented and matured in French oak barriques. The 2008 vintage (★★★), harvested at 23.7 brix and oak-aged for 11 months, is fresh, lemony, buttery and crisp, with good depth of vibrant, citrusy, slightly toasty flavours.

DRY $25 –V

Omaka Springs Falveys Marlborough Chardonnay   ★★★

The 2007 (★★★), lees-aged for a year in French oak barriques, is a moderately complex wine, fleshy, flavoursome and distinctly buttery. The 2008 vintage (★★☆) is lemony and toasty, with a soft, slightly buttery finish.

Vintage	08
WR	7
Drink	09-12

DRY $22 –V

Omihi Road Waipara Chardonnay   ★★★☆

Ready now, the 2006 vintage (★★★) of this North Canterbury wine from Torlesse is a cool-climate style with mouthfilling body, citrusy, slightly peachy flavours, threaded with fresh acidity, and some minerally complexity.

DRY $21 AV

One Tree Hawke's Bay Chardonnay   ★★★

Made by Capricorn Wine Estates (a division of Craggy Range), the 2007 vintage (★★★☆) is a fruit-driven style with mouthfilling body and a slightly creamy texture. Peachy and full-flavoured, it's delicious now. Good value.

Vintage	07
WR	6
Drink	09-10

DRY $15 V+

Onyx Reserve Hawke's Bay Chardonnay   (★★★★☆)

From wine distributor Bennett & Deller, the 2007 vintage (★★★★☆) is full of personality. French oak-aged for a year, it is mouthfilling and concentrated, with vibrant, sweet-fruit flavours, a hint of butterscotch, a fine thread of acidity, and excellent delicacy and richness. Drink now or cellar.

Vintage	07
WR	7
Drink	09-11

DRY $29 V+

Orinoco Vineyards Nelson Chardonnay   (★★★☆)

The 2007 vintage (★★★☆) is a creamy, upfront style, fermented in a 50/50 split of tanks and barrels. Peachy, with toast and butterscotch characters, it has underlying acidity and very good depth.

DRY $20 AV

Oyster Bay Marlborough Chardonnay   ★★★☆

From Delegat's, this wine sets out to showcase Marlborough's pure, incisive fruit flavours. Only 50 per cent of the blend is barrel-fermented, but all of the wine spends six months in casks (mostly French), with weekly lees-stirring. It typically offers ripe grapefruit flavours, slightly buttery and crisp, with creamy, toasty elements adding complexity. The 2008 vintage (★★★★) is weighty, with ripe, peachy, citrusy flavours, finely integrated oak, balanced acidity, and impressive elegance and length.

Vintage	08	07	06	05
WR	6	6	7	5
Drink	09-14	09-13	09-13	09-11

DRY $20 AV

Palliser Estate Martinborough Chardonnay   ★★★★

Rather than sheer power, the key attributes of this wine are delicacy and finesse. A celebration of rich, ripe, citrusy fruit flavours, it is gently seasoned with French oak, producing a delicious wine with subtle winemaking input and concentrated varietal flavours. It is fermented in French oak barriques (34 per cent new in 2007). The 2007 vintage (★★★★) is fleshy, slightly toasty and buttery, with concentrated, ripe citrus and tropical-fruit flavours enriched but not dominated by spicy, nutty oak. It's a deliciously flavoursome, finely balanced wine, drinking well now.

Vintage	08	07	06	05
WR	7	6	6	5
Drink	09-12	09-12	09-11	09-10

DRY $28 AV

Palliser Pencarrow Chardonnay – see Pencarrow Martinborough Chardonnay

Paritua Hawke's Bay Chardonnay   ★★★★☆

The 2007 vintage (★★★★★) is maturing superbly. The 2008 (★★★★) was hand-picked and fermented (60 per cent with indigenous yeasts) in French oak barriques (60 per cent new). Fragrant, with a toasty, nutty bouquet, it is weighty and concentrated, with ripe stone-fruit flavours, strongly seasoned with oak, and a well-rounded finish. It needs more time to achieve balance, but shows good complexity, texture and richness.

Vintage	08
WR	6
Drink	09-13

DRY $30 AV

Parr & Simpson Limestone Bay Barrique Fermented Chardonnay   ★★★☆

From a site overlooking Golden Bay, in Nelson, the 2007 vintage (★★★) was hand-picked and fermented and lees-aged in French oak barriques (30 per cent new). A tightly structured, lemony wine with considerable complexity and good flavour depth, it is slightly austere, with high acidity. The much more approachable, rounder 2008 (★★★★) is a refined wine, citrusy, nutty and slightly buttery, with excellent complexity, texture and length. A label worth discovering.

DRY $20 AV

Passage Rock Barrel Fermented Gisborne Chardonnay   (★★★☆)

The 2007 vintage (★★★☆) was fermented and matured for six months in French oak casks. Full-bodied and smooth, with generous lemon/apple flavours and hints of pears and spice, it's a gently wooded wine, with good body, texture and depth.

DRY $20 AV

Passage Rock Waiheke Island Chardonnay   (★★★★)

The 2008 vintage (★★★★) is a powerful wine with an oaky bouquet, substantial body and ripe grapefruit and peach flavours, slightly nutty and youthful.

DRY $30 –V

Pegasus Bay Chardonnay   ★★★★★

Strapping yet delicate, richly flavoured yet subtle, this sophisticated wine is one of the country's best Chardonnays grown south of Marlborough. Muscular and taut, it typically offers a seamless array of fresh, crisp, citrusy, biscuity, complex flavours and great concentration and length. Estate-grown at Waipara, it is based almost entirely on mature Mendoza clone vines, fermented with indigenous yeasts, given a full, softening malolactic fermentation and matured for a year on its yeast lees in barrels (French oak puncheons, 30 per cent new in 2007). The 2007 vintage (★★★★★) is straw-hued, with a complex bouquet, slightly funky and nutty. Mouthfilling and rich, with stone-fruit flavours, dry, complex and long, it's a firm, powerful yet elegant wine, with loads of personality.

Vintage	07	06	05	04
WR	6	6	6	6
Drink	09-16	09-14	09-12	09-11

DRY $36 AV

Pegasus Bay Virtuoso Chardonnay   ★★★★★

The 2006 vintage (★★★★☆) represents the 'four best barrels' made from the company's 22-year-old Mendoza clone vines at Waipara. Fermented with indigenous yeasts, lees-aged for a year in French oak puncheons (30 per cent new), then matured in tanks on light lees for a further six months before bottling, it was then bottle-aged prior to its release in 2009. Still youthful in colour, with a fresh, complex bouquet and taut palate, it is very crisp and vibrant, with firm acid spine and unusual complexity. A slightly austere, thought-provoking wine, it should be very long-lived; open 2011 onwards.

Vintage	06	05
WR	6	7
Drink	09-18	09-13

DRY $49 AV

Pencarrow Chardonnay   ★★★☆

Pencarrow is Palliser Estate's second-tier label. The 2007 vintage (★★★☆) is a great buy. Grown in Martinborough, it's a fleshy, softly structured wine with generous, grapefruit-like flavours, some oak complexity and a slightly creamy texture.

DRY $15 V+

Penny Lane Hawke's Bay Unoaked Chardonnay   (★★★)

From Morton Estate, the very easy-drinking 2007 vintage (★★★) is fresh and smooth, with a sliver of sweetness amid its ripe, passionfruit-like flavours.

Vintage	07
WR	7
Drink	09-10

MED/DRY $16 AV

Peregrine Central Otago Chardonnay   ★★★★

Fermented in stainless steel tanks and French oak barriques, this is typically a full-bodied, cool-climate style with strong grapefruit, butterscotch and biscuit flavours and a crisp, lively finish. The 2008 vintage (★★★★) is mouthfilling, peachy, slightly creamy and toasty, with a hint of butterscotch, and excellent body, texture and depth. Drink now onwards.

DRY $25 AV

Ransom Barrique Chardonnay   ★★★☆

Grown at Mahurangi, north of Auckland city, at its best this is a stylish wine with rich fig/melon
flavours, fleshed out with mealy, nutty characters. The 2006 vintage (★★★☆) was fermented
and matured for nine months in new and seasoned French oak barrels, with partial malolactic
fermentation. It's a generous wine with fresh acidity and strong, peachy, nutty, faintly honeyed
flavours.

DRY $25 –V

Ransom Gumfield Chardonnay   ★★★☆

Grown at Mahurangi, near Matakana, the 2006 vintage (★★★☆) was hand-harvested and tank-
fermented. It has good intensity of citrusy, slightly appley and minerally flavours in a Chablis-
like style, crisp and dry.

DRY $20 AV

Ra Nui Marlborough Chardonnay   ★★★☆

The 2007 vintage (★★★☆) was mostly handled in tanks, but 10 per cent of the blend was
fermented in new barrels. It's a mouthfilling, easy-drinking wine, with fresh, peachy, citrusy
flavours, slightly mealy and nutty, and good harmony and depth.

DRY $20 AV

Rapaura Springs Marlborough Chardonnay   (★★★★)

The 2008 vintage (★★★★) is already delicious. Barrel-fermented and lees-aged for six months,
it is mouthfilling and vibrantly fruity, with generous, sweet-fruit flavours, a subtle oak influence
and a rounded, slightly buttery finish. Drink now or cellar.

Vintage	08
WR	5
Drink	09-12

DRY $22 V+

Redmetal Vineyards Hawke's Bay Chardonnay   (★★★☆)

Made in an easy-drinking but satisfying style, the 2007 vintage (★★★☆) is full-bodied and
vibrantly fruity, with a 'minimal' oak influence. It offers plenty of ripe, peachy, citrusy flavour,
fresh acidity to keep things lively, and a smooth finish.

Vintage	07
WR	6
Drink	P

DRY $20 AV

Renato Nelson Chardonnay   ★★★☆

Estate-grown on the Kina Peninsula and fully barrel-fermented (French, 15 per cent new), the
2008 vintage (★★★☆) is a citrusy, slightly nutty and creamy wine, moderately concentrated,
with ripe fruit and well-integrated oak.

Vintage	08	07
WR	6	NM
Drink	10-12	NM

DRY $25 –V

Revington Vineyard Estate Chardonnay   ★★★

Fresh and lively, the 2007 vintage (★★★☆) is a Gisborne wine with plenty of ripe, peachy, toasty, faintly honeyed flavour and a smooth finish.

Vintage	07
WR	7
Drink	09-14

DRY $23 –V

Richmond Plains Nelson Chardonnay   ★★★

The 2008 vintage (★★★) is crisp and youthful, in a fruit-driven style with satisfying depth of fresh, dry, citrusy, appley flavours. Certified organic.

Vintage	08	07	06
WR	5	6	5
Drink	09-12	09-11	P

DRY $20 –V

Rimu Grove Nelson Chardonnay   ★★★★☆

Estate-grown near the coast in the Moutere hills, the light-yellow 2007 vintage (★★★★☆) is a full-bodied, high-flavoured wine, fermented and matured on its yeast lees for 11 months in French oak barrels (50 per cent new). Full of personality, it is peachy, toasty, slightly buttery and minerally, with excellent complexity and richness.

Vintage	07	06	05	04
WR	7	7	7	7
Drink	09-21	09-20	09-12	09-10

DRY $28 V+

Riverby Estate Marlborough Chardonnay   ★★★★☆

This single-vineyard wine is grown in the heart of the Wairau Valley. Harvested from 20-year-old vines, the 2008 vintage (★★★★) was fully fermented and lees-aged in French oak barrels (20 per cent new), and 50 per cent went through a softening malolactic fermentation. It's a powerful wine (14.5 per cent alcohol), with ripe, peachy, toasty flavours, good complexity and a creamy, rounded finish.

Vintage	07	06
WR	7	7
Drink	09-11	09-10

DRY $25 V+

Riverstone Chardonnay   (★★☆)

From Villa Maria, the non-vintage wine (★★☆) on sale in 2009 is fresh and fruity, with plenty of smooth, slightly honeyed flavour, balanced for easy drinking.

MED/DRY $12 V+

Rockburn Central Otago Chardonnay   ★★★

The 2007 (★★★), grown at Parkburn and Gibbston, is a distinctly cool-climate style with decent depth of peachy, citrusy flavours and a crisp, minerally streak. The 2008 vintage (★★☆), hand-picked and mostly handled in tanks (14 per cent of the blend was barrel-fermented), is a pale, fruit-driven style with uncomplicated, citrusy, appley flavours, fresh and lively.

Vintage	08	07
WR	5	7
Drink	10-14	09-14

DRY $24 –V

Rock Ferry Marlborough Chardonnay   (★★★)

The 2006 vintage (★★★) is weighty, with grapefruit-like flavours woven with flinty acidity and seasoned oak adding a touch of complexity. (The 2007 vintage was handled in French oak, 20 per cent new.)

Vintage	07	06	05
WR	5	6	5
Drink	09-14	09-12	09-12

 DRY $32 –V

Rongopai East Coast Chardonnay   ★★☆

From Babich (which now owns the Rongopai brand), the 2007 vintage (★★★) is a fruit-driven style with crisp, citrusy, appley flavours, simple but enjoyably fresh and lively. The 2008 (★★☆) is fruity and straightforward, with crisp, peachy, slightly honeyed flavours.

 DRY $14 V+

Rose Tree Cottage Gisborne Chardonnay   ★★★☆

From Constellation NZ, the 2006 vintage (★★★★) is a skilfully balanced wine, grown in the Dixon Vineyard, French oak-fermented and given a full, softening malolactic fermentation. Full of charm, it is fragrant, with strong, ripe citrus and stone-fruit flavours seasoned with toasty oak and a well-rounded finish. A classic regional style, it's now at its peak.

DRY $23 AV

Ruben Hall Chardonnay   (★★★)

From Villa Maria, the non-vintage bottling (★★★) on sale in 2009 is a blend of New Zealand and Australian wines. Light lemon/green, it's a very satisfying quaffer, mouthfilling and slightly creamy, with ripe tropical-fruit aromas and flavours, and even a hint of toasty oak. Worth buying.

DRY $11 V+

Ruby Bay Vineyard SV Chardonnay   ★★★☆

The 2007 vintage (★★★☆) was grown at a coastal site in Nelson, hand-picked and handled in a mix of tanks (75 per cent) and new French oak (25 per cent). It's an elegant, fruit-driven style with lively acidity, fresh, vibrant, grapefruit-like flavours and a subtle seasoning of oak.

DRY $24 AV

Running Hare Chardonnay   (★★)

From RH Wines, based in Mt Albert, Auckland, the 2005 vintage (★★) was still on sale in 2009, when I tasted it. Bright, light lemon/green, it's a solid but plain wine, maturing solidly, with pleasant, citrusy, peachy flavours and a smooth finish.

MED/DRY $10 AV

Sacred Hill Barrel Fermented Chardonnay   ★★★☆

A typically attractive wine, sturdy, with strong, ripe tropical/citrus-fruit flavours fleshed out with mealy, lees-stirred characters and toasty oak. The 2008 vintage (★★★☆) is vibrantly fruity, with substantial body, plenty of fresh, peachy, slightly toasty flavour, some oak-derived complexity and a dry finish.

Vintage	08	07
WR	6	7
Drink	09-11	09-12

Sacred Hill Riflemans Chardonnay   ★★★★★

Sacred Hill's flagship Chardonnay is one of New Zealand's greatest Chardonnays – powerful yet elegant, with striking intensity and outstanding cellaring potential. Grown in the cool, inland, elevated (100 metres above sea level) Riflemans Vineyard in the Dartmoor Valley of Hawke's Bay, it is hand-picked from mature, own-rooted, Mendoza clone vines, whole-bunch pressed, and fermented with indigenous yeasts in French oak barriques (90 per cent new in 2007), with some malolactic fermentation. The 2007 vintage (★★★★★) is mouthfilling, with gentle acidity and beautifully ripe, delicate flavours of stone-fruit and finely integrated toasty oak that build across the palate to a rich, well-rounded finish. Silky-textured and harmonious, it's best cellared to mid 2010+.

Vintage	07
WR	7
Drink	09-12

Sacred Hill The Wine Thief Series Hawke's Bay Chardonnay   ★★★★

A classic regional style, the 2008 vintage (★★★★) was hand-harvested in the Ohiti Valley, barrel-fermented and lees-aged for a year. Full-bodied, with fresh, ripe citrus and stone-fruit flavours, seasoned with toasty French oak (50 per cent new), and a well-rounded finish, it's still youthful; open mid-2010+.

Vintage	08	07
WR	7	7
Drink	09-12	09-12

Saint Clair Marlborough Chardonnay   ★★★☆

This smooth, full-flavoured, early-drinking wine is fermented and lees-aged in a mix of tanks and new and older French and American oak casks. The 2008 (★★★★) is a top vintage. Delicious already, it is mouthfilling, with fresh, ripe peach and grapefruit flavours, finely integrated, biscuity oak and a well-balanced, dry finish.

Vintage	08	07
WR	6	6
Drink	09-12	09-10

Saint Clair Omaka Reserve Marlborough Chardonnay   ★★★★☆

A proven show-stopper, this is a fat, creamy wine, weighty and rich, in a strikingly bold, upfront style. It is hand-picked, mostly in the company's vineyard in the Omaka Valley, and fermented and lees-aged in American oak casks, with a full, softening malolactic fermentation. The 2008 vintage (★★★★★) has a creamy, toasty bouquet. Weighty and concentrated, with ripe, peachy fruit characters and a clear but not dominating oak influence, it's a better-balanced wine than some past vintages, with good texture and harmony, and a long finish.

Vintage	08
WR	7
Drink	09-12

DRY $33 AV

Saint Clair Pioneer Block 4 Sawcut Marlborough Chardonnay ★★★★

Grown in the Ure Valley, half-way between Blenheim and Kaikoura, the 2008 vintage (★★★★) was matured for 10 months in French oak casks (50 per cent new). Weighty, it's an elegant, very harmonious wine with fresh acidity, good concentration of citrusy, peachy flavours and a creamy-smooth finish.

Vintage	08	07
WR	7	7
Drink	09-13	09-11

DRY $30 –V

Saint Clair Pioneer Block 10 Twin Hills Marlborough Chardonnay ★★★★☆

The outstanding 2008 vintage (★★★★★) is a single-vineyard, Omaka Valley wine, hand-picked and fermented and matured for nine months in French oak casks (50 per cent new). Mouthfilling, with excellent concentration of ripe, peachy, toasty flavours, it is finely textured, biscuity and creamy, with notable depth and complexity.

Vintage	08	07
WR	6	6
Drink	09-13	09-11

DRY $30 AV

Saint Clair Pioneer Block 11 Cell Block Marlborough Chardonnay ★★★★

Grown in the 'slightly cooler' Dillons Point district, east of Blenheim, the 2008 vintage (★★★★) shows exuberant use of oak – it was matured for 10 months in French oak casks, 100 per cent new. Fresh, ripe, citrusy, peachy, nutty and buttery, with impressively concentrated fruit flavours, it's a rich, upfront style, likely to be at its best from mid-2010.

Vintage	08	07
WR	7	7
Drink	09-11	09-10

DRY $30 –V

Saint Clair Pioneer Block 13 B & B Block Marlborough Chardonnay (★★★★)

Made in an 'old world style', the debut 2007 vintage (★★★★) was grown on the seaward side of Rapaura, fermented with indigenous yeasts and handled entirely without oak. Fresh, vibrant and youthful, it's a very age-worthy wine with delicate, citrusy, appley flavours that build well across the palate to a slightly minerally and nutty finish. There is no 2008.

Vintage	08	07
WR	NM	7
Drink	NM	09-10

DRY $30 –V

Saint Clair Unoaked Marlborough Chardonnay ★★★

This refreshing wine is cool-fermented in tanks, using malolactic fermentation to add complexity and soften the acidity. The 2007 vintage (★★★) is fresh and flavourful, with a core of ripe citrus and peach characters, crisp and lively, a hint of butterscotch, and an easy-drinking appeal.

Vintage	07
WR	6
Drink	09-10

DRY $21 –V

Saint Clair Vicar's Choice Marlborough Chardonnay   ★★★

The very user-friendly 2009 vintage (★★★) is a lightly oaked style, full-bodied, with peachy, slightly biscuity and buttery flavours and a fresh, smooth finish.

Vintage	08	07
WR	6	6
Drink	09-11	P

DRY $19 AV

Saints Gisborne Chardonnay   ★★★☆

From Pernod Ricard NZ, this ripe, creamy-smooth wine is always enjoyable. The 2008 vintage (★★★☆), grown at Patutahi and Ormond, was fermented and matured for six months in French (70 per cent) and American oak casks (16 per cent new). Light lemon/green, with sweet oak aromas, it's an upfront style, peachy, citrusy, toasty and crisp, with moderate complexity and plenty of flavour.

Vintage	08	07
WR	5	6
Drink	09-10	P

DRY $20 AV

San Hill Chardonnay   ★★☆

Made at Pukeora Estate, in Central Hawke's Bay, the estate-grown 2008 vintage (★★☆) was hand-picked, blended with Sémillon (8 per cent), and fermented and matured for nine months in French oak barriques. It's a mouthfilling wine with lemony, appley, slightly buttery flavours and fresh acidity.

Vintage	08
WR	4
Drink	09-12

DRY $15 AV

Secret Stone Marlborough Chardonnay   ★★★☆

From Foster's, which also owns Matua Valley, the 2008 vintage (★★★☆) is mouthfilling, creamy and buttery, with citrusy, slightly limey and nutty flavours, showing very good texture and depth. Drink now onwards.

DRY $20 AV

Seifried Nelson Chardonnay   ★★★☆

The quality of this wine has risen in recent years. Partly fermented and matured in American oak barriques (new to two-year-old), the 2008 vintage (★★★) is a slightly honeyed wine, mouthfilling and crisp, peachy, toasty and flavoursome. It's a forward vintage, for drinking now to 2010.

Vintage	08	07	06	05	04
WR	6	6	6	6	7
Drink	09-14	09-13	09-10	09-10	P

DRY $21 AV

Seifried Winemaker's Collection Barrique Fermented Chardonnay   ★★★★

This is always a bold style, concentrated and creamy, with lashings of flavour. The 2007 vintage (★★★★☆) is a tightly structured wine, grown in Nelson and fermented and lees-aged for a year in American oak barriques (new and one year old). It's a typically upfront style, with a toasty bouquet and strong, ripe peach and grapefruit flavours, well seasoned with oak. Fresh and concentrated, it should mature well.

Vintage	07	06	05	04
WR	6	6	6	7
Drink	09-15	09-15	09-12	09-11

DRY $28 AV

Selaks Founders Reserve Hawke's Bay Chardonnay   ★★★★☆

The 2007 vintage (★★★★★), estate-grown in Constellation NZ's Corner 50 Vineyard, was fermented in French oak barriques, partly with indigenous yeasts, and lees-aged in oak for nine months. A notably refined and rich wine, for enjoying now or cellaring, it has a fragrant, complex, savoury bouquet, with rich, grapefruit-like flavours, tight, mealy and finely balanced with toasty oak. Still vibrant and youthful, it has excellent delicacy, complexity and length.

DRY $28 V+

Selaks Premium Selection Marlborough Chardonnay   ★★★

The 'standard' Chardonnay from Selaks usually shows a touch of class. It is tank-fermented and matured 'on' (read: not barrel-aged) a combination of French and American oak, with lees-aging and full malolactic fermentation. It is typically citrusy and slightly nutty, with plenty of flavour, a slightly creamy texture and crisp, dryish finish.

MED/DRY $16 AV

Selaks Winemaker's Favourite Hawke's Bay Chardonnay   ★★★★

This soft, creamy-rich wine from Constellation NZ is always a bargain. Grown 'predominantly' in the company's Corner 50 Vineyard, next to the winery, and fermented and lees-aged for eight months in French oak barriques (partly new), the 2008 vintage (★★★★☆) is a rich, upfront style with a fragrant, toasty bouquet. Generous, with concentrated, ripe stone-fruit flavours, showing good complexity, and a deliciously smooth finish, it's already drinking well.

DRY $21 V+

Seresin Chardonnay   ★★★★☆

This stylish Marlborough wine is designed to 'focus on the textural element of the palate rather than emphasising primary fruit characters'. It is typically a finely balanced, full-bodied and complex wine with good mouthfeel, ripe melon/citrus characters shining through, subtle toasty oak and fresh acidity. The outstanding 2007 vintage (★★★★★) was hand-picked in the Home and Raupo Creek vineyards, fermented with indigenous yeasts in French oak barriques (15 per cent new), and lees-aged for 11 months, with full malolactic fermentation. A fragrant, fresh, complex bouquet leads into a very elegant wine, citrusy, slightly toasty and buttery, with a minerally streak and finely poised, long finish. A good buy.

Vintage	07	06	05	04
WR	6	7	6	6
Drink	09-12	09-10	P	P

DRY $28 V+

Seresin Chardonnay Reserve   ★★★★★

Finesse is the keynote quality of this classy Marlborough wine. Estate-grown at Renwick and in the Raupo Creek Vineyard, hand-picked, French oak-fermented with indigenous yeasts and lees-aged in oak (15 per cent new in 2007) for a year, it is typically a powerful wine, toasty and nutty, with citrusy, mealy, complex flavours of great depth. The 2007 vintage (★★★★★) is pale yellow, with a complex bouquet. It has a powerful presence in the mouth, with impressive weight, finely balanced acidity and highly concentrated, peachy, slightly toasty flavours, deliciously nutty and complex.

Vintage	07	06	05	04
WR	7	7	6	7
Drink	09-13	09-12	09-10	P

DRY $39 AV

Shaky Bridge Central Otago Chardonnay   ★★☆

The 2008 vintage (★★☆) was estate-grown at Alexandra. Hand-picked, it was mostly handled in tanks then blended with 'a small amount of lightly oaked wine'. It's a fruity, simple wine, smooth, lemony and appley, with crisp acidity and a fractionally off-dry finish.

DRY $20 –V

Shepherds Ridge Marlborough Chardonnay   ★★★☆

From Wither Hills, the 2008 vintage (★★★☆), 60 per cent French oak-aged, is mouthfilling, fresh and fruity, with vibrant, citrusy, slightly toasty and buttery flavours, showing a touch of complexity and very good depth.

DRY $20 AV

Shingle Peak Chardonnay   ★★★

The 2008 vintage (★★☆) no longer features the Matua Valley logo and is no longer identified as a Marlborough wine. 'New Zealand' in origin, it is fruity, citrusy, fresh and simple, in an easy-drinking style with reasonable depth.

DRY $18 AV

Shingle Peak Marlborough Chardonnay – see Matua Valley Shingle Peak Marlborough Chardonnay

Shipwreck Bay New Zealand Chardonnay   ★★☆

The 2008 vintage (★★☆) from Okahu Estate is a blend of Gisborne (80 per cent) and Northland grapes. 'Uncluttered by oak', it's a medium-bodied wine, fresh and fruity, with straightforward, lemony, appley flavours and a crisp finish.

DRY $18 –V

Sileni Cellar Selection Hawke's Bay Chardonnay   ★★★

Partly barrel-fermented, the 2008 (★★☆) is a slightly honeyed wine with solid depth of citrusy, peachy flavours. It's a forward vintage, now ready.

Vintage	08	07
WR	4	5
Drink	09-11	09-10

DRY $19 AV

Sileni The Lodge Hawke's Bay Chardonnay ★★★★

Estate-grown at the Plateau Vineyard at Maraekakaho and hand-picked, this wine gets the works in the winery, including fermentation and lees-aging in French oak barriques. The 2007 vintage (★★★★☆) is soft and rich, with concentrated, peachy, toasty flavours in a powerful style with upfront appeal. The 2008 (★★★☆), a slightly honeyed wine with mouthfilling body and stone-fruit and oak flavours, shows very good depth, but is a relatively forward vintage, probably at its best during 2010.

Vintage	08	07	06	05	04
WR	4	5	6	6	6
Drink	09-12	09-12	09-11	P	P

DRY $35 –V

Sleeping Giant Vineyards Hill Block Chardonnay ★★★★

Grown at the foot of Te Mata Peak ('the sleeping giant'), in Hawke's Bay, the 2006 vintage (★★★★☆) is a powerful, sturdy wine with highly concentrated, grapefruit-like flavours, creamy, minerally notes adding complexity, and a tight finish.

DRY $38 –V

Soho Carter Waiheke Island Chardonnay (★★★★)

An excellent debut, the 2008 vintage (★★★★) was fermented and matured in French oak barriques (15 per cent new). It's a mouthfilling, refined and harmonious wine with peach, grapefruit and biscuity oak flavour, showing good complexity, and the structure to age. Open mid-2010+.

DRY $38 –V

Soljans Barrique Reserve Chardonnay ★★★☆

The 2006 vintage (★★★★) is a single-vineyard, Hawke's Bay wine, matured for 20 months in oak casks (26 per cent new). Pale yellow, it is maturing gracefully, with mouthfilling body, strong grapefruit and nut flavours, showing good complexity, and a slightly buttery, dry finish.

Vintage	06
WR	6
Drink	09-11

DRY $25 –V

Southbank Estate Hawke's Bay Chardonnay ★★★☆

Maturing well, the 2007 vintage (★★★★) was mostly (80 per cent) matured for eight months in French oak casks (25 per cent new). It's a mouthfilling wine with a fragrant, citrusy bouquet and ripe grapefruit and nut flavours. Slightly creamy, it shows excellent delicacy, complexity and length.

Vintage	07	06	05
WR	7	6	6
Drink	09-12	09-12	P

DRY $20 AV

Southern Cross Hawke's Bay Chardonnay   (★★★)

From One Tree Hill Vineyards, a division of Morton Estate, the 2007 vintage (★★★) is an easy-drinking style with mouthfilling body and ripe grapefruit and stone-fruit flavours, still fresh and creamy-smooth. Enjoyable now, it offers fine value.

Vintage	07
WR	6
Drink	09-10

DRY $13 V+

Spinyback Nelson Chardonnay   ★★★☆

From Waimea Estates, the 2008 vintage (★★★☆) is a partly barrel-fermented style with high alcohol (14.5 per cent) and sweet-fruit flavours, peachy, citrusy, fresh and smooth. A dry, full-flavoured wine, it offers top value.

Vintage	08	07	06
WR	7	6	6
Drink	09-12	09-11	P

DRY $15 V+

Spy Valley Envoy Marlborough Chardonnay   ★★★★★

Launched from the 2005 vintage (★★★★★), this distinguished wine is estate-grown in the Waihopai Valley, hand-picked, fermented with indigenous yeasts and lees-aged in French oak barriques (mostly seasoned) for up to 18 months. The 2006 (★★★★★) is poised and immaculate. Pale straw, with a fresh, slightly nutty bouquet, it is mouthfilling and youthful, with rich, ripe peach and grapefruit flavours, subtle oak and a long, harmonious finish. A very classy wine, it's still unfolding and likely to be at its peak around 2010.

Vintage	06	05
WR	7	7
Drink	09-12+	09-11+

DRY $36 AV

Spy Valley Marlborough Chardonnay   ★★★★

A consistently attractive, bargain-priced wine. The 2007 vintage (★★★★) was fermented (mostly with indigenous yeasts) and lees-aged for 10 months in French oak barrels. A mouthfilling wine with strong grapefruit and stone-fruit flavours, it shows good weight and concentration, with a dry, lingering finish.

Vintage	08	07	06	05	04
WR	6	6	6	7	6
Drink	10-12	09-12	09-11	09-10	P

DRY $20 V+

Spy Valley Marlborough Unoaked Chardonnay   ★★★

The 2008 vintage (★★★), estate-grown and lees-aged for four months, is a fruity, easy-drinking, off-dry style (6.9 grams/litre of residual sugar) with mouthfilling body and fresh, ripe, peachy flavours.

Vintage	09	08	07
WR	7	5	6
Drink	10-12	09-10	P

MED/DRY $18 AV

Squawking Magpie Gimblett Gravels Chardonnay   ★★★★

Squawking Magpie is the label of Gavin Yortt, co-founder of the Irongate Vineyard in Gimblett

Road, Hawke's Bay. Also grown in Gimblett Road, the 2007 vintage (★★★★) is a savoury style, full and rich, with melon and grapefruit flavours and finely integrated oak adding complexity. It's still youthful.

DRY $33 –V

Staete Landt Marlborough Chardonnay ★★★★☆

This consistently impressive, single-vineyard wine is grown in the Rapaura district, hand-picked and fermented with partial use of indigenous yeasts in French oak barriques (20 per cent new). The 2007 vintage (★★★★) spent an unusually long period of 18 months in barrels. Pale straw, it's an elegant, cool-climate style, mouthfilling, with fresh citrus and stone-fruit flavours, balanced toasty oak, good concentration and complexity, and a tight, dry finish. Best drinking mid-2010+.

Vintage	07	06
WR	6	6
Drink	09-13	09-12

DRY $29 V+

Stafford Lane Estate Nelson Chardonnay ★★★

Handled in tanks, with some exposure to oak, the estate-grown 2007 vintage (★★★) has matured well. Still fresh and lively, it's a fleshy, weighty wine (14.5 per cent alcohol) with crisp, lemony, slightly buttery flavours, not highly complex, but showing some elegance and richness.

DRY $20 –V

Stone Bridge Gisborne Chardonnay (★★★★☆)

Estate-grown, the 2007 vintage (★★★★) was fermented in a 50/50 split of seasoned French and new French and American oak barrels. Mouthfilling, with excellent concentration and complexity, it is peachy and toasty, with sweet-fruit delights, in a generous, upfront but also refined style, drinking well now.

DRY $24 V+

Stone Bridge Unoaked Chardonnay ★★☆

The 2007 vintage (★★☆) of this Gisborne wine was matured on its yeast lees for three months in tanks. It's a solid but simple, lemony, appley, crisp wine.

DRY $20 –V

Stonecroft Hawke's Bay Chardonnay ★★★★★

Alan Limmer aimed for a 'restrained style of Chardonnay with elegance and complexity which ages well'. His wine also has impressive weight and flavour richness. The 2007 (★★★★★) is concentrated and seamless, with a power and complexity reminiscent of a good Meursault. Sweet-fruited, with a slightly oily texture, it offers concentrated peach and grapefruit flavours, with hints of butterscotch and nuts. However, the 2007 vintage is likely to be the last. (The rich, elegant 2002 is now at its peak. Limmer's last bottle of his debut, 1987 vintage, opened in early 2009, was still alive, with mellow flavours of peaches, tea and honey.)

Vintage	08	07	06
WR	NM	7	6
Drink	NM	09-16	09-15

DRY $38 AV

Stonecroft Old Vine Chardonnay   ★★★★★

Still unfolding, the 2007 vintage (★★★★★) is fleshy and rich, with deep, delicate flavours of peaches and grapefruit, subtle, integrated oak and finely balanced acidity. Concentrated and finely structured, with richness through the palate, it's a classic cellaring style; open 2010 onwards.

DRY $40 AV

Stoneleigh Marlborough Chardonnay   ★★★★

Made by Pernod Ricard NZ, this wine is typically highly enjoyable. Fermented in a mix of tanks (40 per cent) and French oak casks (60 per cent), the 2007 (★★★★) is fleshy, rich and lingering, in an instantly appealing style with fresh, grapefruit-like flavours seasoned with toasty oak. The 2008 vintage (★★★☆) is fresh, mouthfilling and smooth, with grapefruit and peach flavours, a subtle oak influence, moderate complexity, and good body and depth.

Vintage	08	07
WR	5	6
Drink	09-10	P

DRY $22 V+

Stoneleigh Rapaura Series Marlborough Chardonnay   ★★★★☆

The 2007 vintage (★★★★☆) brought a change to a more 'fruit forward' style, involving briefer oak maturation. Fermented and lees-aged for four months in new and one-year-old French oak casks, the 2008 (★★★★) is rich, mealy and finely textured, with generous, ripe-fruit flavours, creamy, cashew notes and a long finish.

DRY $27 V+

Stone Paddock Hawke's Bay Chardonnay   ★★★

From Paritua, the 2007 (★★★) is a partly (60 per cent) barrel-fermented style with ripe, peachy flavours and a slightly creamy texture. It's drinking well now. The 2008 vintage (★★☆), 40 per cent French oak-fermented, is fresh and fruity, with straightforward, slightly honeyed flavours and an off-dry (5.1 grams/litre of residual sugar) finish.

Vintage	08
WR	7
Drink	09-12

MED/DRY $20 −V

Stop Banks Hawke's Bay Chardonnay   (★★★)

From a Marlborough-based producer, the 2008 vintage (★★★) is a fruit-driven style with ripe, peachy flavours, not complex, but vibrant and well-rounded. Drink young.

DRY $18 AV

Summerhouse Marlborough Chardonnay   ★★★★

This single-vineyard label is worth discovering. The 2008 vintage (★★★★) was fully fermented and lees-aged for 10 months in French oak barriques. It's a full-bodied (14.5 per cent alcohol), well-rounded wine with ripe grapefruit and slight butterscotch flavours, showing excellent depth and complexity. Drink now or cellar.

DRY $27 AV

Tasman Bay New Zealand Chardonnay ★★★☆

This seductively soft, creamy-smooth wine can be irresistible at only 18 months old. Fermented entirely in stainless steel tanks, with full malolactic fermentation, it is not barrel-aged, but oak staves are immersed in the wine. Still on sale, the 2006 vintage (★★★★), grown in Nelson, has a fragrant, sweetly oaked bouquet. High-flavoured and smooth, it has strong, ripe, peachy, slightly buttery and toasty flavours, in a delicious drink-young style.

DRY $18 V+

Te Awa Chardonnay ★★★★★

Top vintages of this Hawke's Bay wine are very classy. Hand-harvested in the Gimblett Gravels district, it is fermented and lees-aged for 11 to 15 months in French oak barriques (30 to 35 per cent new); malolactic fermentation is avoided. It typically displays intense grapefruit and nut characters, with excellent weight, texture and harmony. The 2006 vintage (★★★★☆) has a slightly oaky, creamy bouquet. Mouthfilling and concentrated, with sweet-fruit delights, it's a powerful wine with ripe, grapefruit-like flavours and balanced acidity in a classic regional style.

DRY $30 V+

Te Awa Windmill Chardonnay ★★★☆

The 2007 vintage (★★★☆) was estate-grown in Hawke's Bay, fermented in seasoned French oak barrels and lees-aged for eight months, but shows little sign of wood. Fresh and vibrantly fruity, with citrusy, peachy flavours, it is delicious young.

DRY $20 AV

Te Henga The Westie Chardonnay (★★★)

From Babich, the 2007 vintage (★★★) is an unoaked style, mouthfilling and smooth, with good depth of ripe, peachy flavours and a dry finish. Drinking well now, it offers fine value.

DRY $13 V+

Te Kairanga Casarina Reserve Chardonnay ★★★★

Estate-grown in the Casarina Block at Martinborough, the 2006 vintage (★★★★) was harvested at 23 brix and fermented and lees-aged for 10 months in French oak barriques (35 per cent new), with no malolactic fermentation. Light yellow, it is elegant and rich, with strong, grapefruit-like flavours, slightly buttery, toasty and minerally. The 2007 (★★★★) is a refined, citrusy wine with a slightly nutty bouquet. Savoury and slightly minerally, it is woven with fresh acidity, with good fruit/oak balance and a lingering finish.

Vintage	07	06	05
WR	6	6	5
Drink	09-13	09-12	09-11

DRY $29 AV

Te Kairanga Gisborne Chardonnay ★★☆

This is typically a drink-young style with vibrant fruit characters and restrained oak. The 2008 vintage (★★★) is ripely scented, with fresh, peachy flavours and a crisp finish.

Vintage	08
WR	6
Drink	09-12

DRY $18 –V

Te Kairanga Martinborough Chardonnay   ★★★☆

Te Kairanga's second-tier Chardonnay. The 2007 vintage (★★★★) was fermented and matured for 10 months in French oak barriques (20 per cent new). A crisp, slightly minerally style, drinking well now, it has a toasty, citrusy bouquet, showing some development, and a rich, flavoursome palate, with grapefruit and peachy characters and deftly judged, nutty oak.

Vintage	07	06	05
WR	6	4	6
Drink	09-13	09-12	P

DRY $22 AV

Te Mania Nelson Chardonnay   ★★★

The 2008 vintage (★★☆) is an easy-drinking style, lightly oaked, with fresh, lemony scents and flavours and a crisp, smooth finish.

Vintage	08	07	06
WR	5	7	6
Drink	09-12	09-10	P

DRY $20 –V

Te Mania Reserve Chardonnay   ★★★☆

Typically a powerful Nelson wine with heaps of oak seasoning concentrated ripe-fruit flavours and a creamy-smooth texture. The 2008 vintage (★★★☆) was fermented and matured for 10 months in French and American oak barriques (30 per cent new). A mouthfilling wine with strong, citrusy flavours wrapped in toasty oak, it's still youthful; open mid-2010+.

Vintage	08	07
WR	5	7
Drink	09-13	09-12

DRY $28 –V

Te Mata Elston Chardonnay   ★★★★★

One of New Zealand's most illustrious Chardonnays, Elston is a stylish, intense, slowly evolving Hawke's Bay wine. At around four years old, it is notably complete, showing concentration and finesse. The grapes are grown principally at two sites in the Te Mata hills at Havelock North, and the wine is fully fermented in French oak barriques (35 per cent new), with full malolactic fermentation. The 2008 vintage (★★★★★) is weighty, generous and complex, with rich, ripe peach and slight fig flavours showing excellent delicacy, a fine thread of acidity, well-integrated oak and a tight, long finish. It's a highly concentrated wine, likely to be long-lived.

Vintage	08	07	06	05	04	03	02
WR	7	7	7	7	7	7	7
Drink	09-13	09-12	09-11	09-10	09-10	P	P

DRY $34 V+

Te Mata Estate Woodthorpe Chardonnay   ★★★★

This bargain-priced Hawke's Bay wine is grown in the company's inland Woodthorpe Vineyard in the Dartmoor Valley. Fermented and lees-aged in a mix of tanks (50 per cent) and French oak barrels, it is typically a harmonious wine with sweet, ripe grapefruit characters enriched with biscuity oak and very good richness and complexity. The 2007 vintage (★★★★) is fragrant, full-bodied, fresh and vibrant, with peachy, citrusy, slightly toasty flavours, a hint of butterscotch, and good complexity and harmony. It's an elegant wine, drinking well now.

Vintage	08
WR	7
Drink	09-11

`DRY $19 V+`

Terravin Chardonnay   ★★★★☆

The debut 2007 vintage (★★★★☆) was grown in the Omaka Valley, in Marlborough, hand-picked and fermented with indigenous yeasts in seasoned French oak puncheons. It is powerful, with mouthfilling body, very ripe, peachy, citrusy flavours, good fruit/oak balance and a rich, harmonious finish.

`DRY $35 –V`

Te Whare Ra Marlborough Chardonnay   ★★★☆

Barrel-fermented and given a full, softening malolactic fermentation, this is typically a weighty wine with a creamy bouquet, strong grapefruit and peach flavours and a dry finish.

`DRY $26 –V`

Te Whau Vineyard Waiheke Island Chardonnay   ★★★★★

For its sheer vintage-to-vintage consistency, this is Te Whau's finest wine. Full of personality, it has beautifully ripe fruit characters showing excellent concentration, nutty oak and a long, finely poised finish. Hand-picked, fermented with indigenous yeasts and lees-aged for a year in French oak barriques (partly new), the 2008 vintage (★★★★★) is softly mouthfilling, with great texture and rich, ripe stone-fruit flavours, highly concentrated, complex and rounded.

Vintage	08	07
WR	7	7
Drink	09-13	09-12

`DRY $85 –V`

Thornbury Gisborne Chardonnay   ★★★★

From Villa Maria, the 2008 vintage (★★★☆) was fermented in a mix of tanks and barrels, and barrel-aged for eight months. A fruit-driven style with very good depth of ripe, citrusy, slightly honeyed flavours, biscuity notes adding complexity and a well-rounded finish, it's a very harmonious wine, for drinking now onwards. Tasted prior to bottling, and so not rated, the 2009 looked excellent – fresh and crisp, with ripe grapefruit-like flavours, a slightly creamy texture and a subtle twist of oak.

Vintage	09
WR	6
Drink	09-15

`DRY $21 V+`

Three Paddles Martinborough Chardonnay   (★★★)

From Nga Waka, the 2009 vintage (★★★) has vibrant fruit aromas, good body and plenty of peachy, slightly limey and spicy flavour. Crisp and lively, it has a Sauvignon Blanc-like freshness and immediacy.

Vintage	09
WR	7
Drink	10+

`DRY $18 AV`

Three Stones Hawke's Bay Chardonnay –

see 3 Stones Hawke's Bay Chardonnay (at the start of the Chardonnay section)

Timara Chardonnay   (★★☆)

The 2008 vintage (★★☆) from Pernod Ricard NZ is a fresh, fruit-driven style with ripe, peachy flavours, balanced for smooth, easy drinking. Good value.

DRY $11 V+

Ti Point Hawke's Bay Chardonnay   (★★★)

French oak-aged, this is typically an attractive, uncomplicated wine with vibrant, citrusy, appley flavours showing good depth.

DRY $21 –V

Tiritiri Estate Chardonnay   ★★★☆

From 'New Zealand's smallest vineyard', the 2007 vintage (★★★☆) was grown in Gisborne, hand-picked and fermented and lees-aged in French oak barriques. Light gold, it is weighty, peachy, toasty and rounded, in a forward style with a hint of honey. It's fairly developed for such a young wine, but shows good body, flavour depth and personality. Ready.

Vintage	07	06	05	04	03
WR	6	NM	NM	6	NM
Drink	09-11	NM	NM	P	NM

DRY $40 –V

Tiritiri Reserve Chardonnay   ★★★★☆

Duncan and Judy Smith's tiny (0.27-hectare), organically-managed vineyard is in the Waimata Valley, 25 kilometres from the city of Gisborne. French oak-fermented, the 2007 vintage (★★★★☆) is pale gold, rich and soft, with highly concentrated, peachy, slightly buttery flavours, nutty and complex. Fat and powerful, with sweet-fruit delights, it's already delicious.

Vintage	07
WR	6
Drink	09-11

DRY $75 –V

Tohu Gisborne Unoaked Chardonnay   ★★★

Made in a drink-young style, the 2007 vintage (★★★) was handled entirely in stainless steel tanks. It's a fresh, lively wine with mouthfilling body and satisfying depth of ripe, citrusy, peachy flavours.

DRY $19 AV

Tohu Marlborough Unoaked Chardonnay   ★★★

The 2009 vintage (★★★) is a drink-young style, mouthfilling and dryish (5 grams/litre of residual sugar). Given a full, softening malolactic fermentation, it is fleshy and fruity, with a slightly creamy texture and a well-rounded finish.

MED/DRY $19 AV

Tom Chardonnay   (★★★★★)

Maturing very gracefully, the debut 2006 vintage (★★★★★) from Pernod Ricard NZ was made at the Church Road winery, in Hawke's Bay. Light lemon/green, it is very rich and fleshy, with sweet-fruit delights, tight peach and grapefruit flavours, nutty, mealy and complex, and a well-rounded finish. Drink now or cellar.

DRY $70 AV

Torlesse Waipara Chardonnay   ★★★

The 2007 vintage (★★☆) was fermented in tanks (60 per cent) and barrels (40 per cent). It's a citrusy, appley, faintly honeyed wine with pleasant, simple flavours and fresh, crisp acidity.

Vintage	07
WR	5
Drink	09-12

DRY $17 AV

Trinity Hill Gimblett Gravels Chardonnay   ★★★★★

The flagship Chardonnay from John Hancock is typically a very stylish, intense, finely structured wine. Grown in the Gimblett Gravels district of Hawke's Bay, it is hand-picked, barrel-fermented and matured on its yeast lees in French oak barriques (30 per cent new). The 2008 (★★★☆) has a peachy, faintly honeyed bouquet. Full-flavoured and finely textured, it has balanced acidity and some creamy richness, but lacks the weight and concentration of a top vintage.

Vintage	08	07	06	05
WR	5	6	6	5
Drink	10-12	09-13	09-11	09-11

DRY $30 V+

Trinity Hill Hawke's Bay Chardonnay   ★★★

The 2007 vintage (★★★) was mostly handled in tanks, but a small percentage of the blend was oak-aged. Matured on its yeast lees for eight months, it's a fresh, citrusy, appley wine, medium-bodied and skilfully balanced, with a crisp, dry finish.

DRY $19 AV

Trinity Hill Hawke's Bay Chardonnay/Viognier   (★★★)

The debut 2008 vintage (★★★) is a fruit-driven blend of Chardonnay (86 per cent) and Viognier (14 per cent). Slightly honeyed, it has fresh fruit aromas, subtle citrus and melon flavours, enlivened by fresh acidity, and a dry finish.

DRY $19 AV

Trout Valley Nelson Chardonnay   (★★★)

From Kahurangi Estate, the 2007 vintage (★★★) is an unoaked style, crisp and lively, with citrusy, appley, slightly limey flavours showing good vigour and freshness.

DRY $17 AV

Tukipo River Estate Fat Trout Chardonnay   (★★★☆)

Grown at Takapau, in Central Hawke's Bay, the 2007 vintage (★★★☆) is full-bodied and creamy, with subtle, citrusy, slightly limey flavours and fresh acidity. Showing considerable complexity, it's well worth cellaring.

DRY $26 –V

TW CV Chardonnay/Viognier   ★★★

The 2008 vintage (★★★☆) is a Gisborne blend of Chardonnay (70 per cent) and Viognier (30 per cent), partly handled in old oak casks. Full-bodied, fruity and smooth, with peach, pear and slight spice flavours, it is a soft, very easy-drinking style, showing good freshness, depth and charm.

DRY $20 –V

TW Estate Chardonnay   ★★★

Not oak-aged, this Gisborne wine is typically full-bodied and citrusy, with ripe, uncomplicated flavours and a creamy-smooth finish.

DRY $17 AV

TW Gisborne Chardonnay   ★★★★

'TW' stands for Paul Tietjen and Geordie Witters, vastly experienced Gisborne grape-growers. Typically excellent, this wine is fermented and matured in French and American oak barriques, with partial malolactic fermentation. The 2007 vintage (★★★★☆) is a lovely wine, with ripe peach and pear flavours, showing excellent delicacy and depth, finely integrated oak and impressive complexity. Drink now or cellar.

Vintage	07
WR	7
Drink	09-17

DRY $27 AV

Twin Islands Marlborough Chardonnay   ★★★

From Nautilus Estate, this is a lightly wooded, drink-young style, priced right. 'Lightly oaked', the 2007 vintage (★★★☆) is a full-bodied, slightly buttery wine with crisp, grapefruit-like flavours, a touch of complexity and good harmony.

DRY $17 AV

Two Thieves Hawke's Bay Chardonnay   (★★★☆)

From Two Thieves Wines (linked to Squawking Magpie), the 2007 vintage (★★★☆) is a fruit-driven style, enjoyable in its youth. It is fresh and vibrant, with ripe, citrusy characters to the fore, a hint of butterscotch and some elegance.

DRY $17 V+

Two Tracks Marlborough Chardonnay   ★★★☆

From Wither Hills, the 2008 vintage (★★★☆) was mostly handled in tanks, but 20 per cent of the blend was wood-aged. It's a fruit-driven style, fresh, crisp and lively, with peachy, slightly toasty flavours, showing very good vigour and depth.

Vintage	08
WR	5
Drink	09-11

DRY $20 AV

Vavasour Awatere Valley Chardonnay ★★★★☆

A powerful Marlborough wine, rich and creamy. The 2008 vintage (★★★★☆) was hand-picked, fermented with indigenous yeasts in French oak barriques (35 per cent new), and oak-aged for nine months, with weekly lees-stirring. Fleshy and rich, it's mouthfilling (14.5 per cent alcohol), with deep stone-fruit and toasty oak flavours, finely balanced acidity, and excellent complexity and harmony. Already highly enjoyable, it's a drink-now or cellaring proposition.

Vintage	08	07	06	05	04
WR	6	7	7	7	7
Drink	09-13	09-12	09-12	09-10	P

DRY $26 V+

Vidal Hawke's Bay Chardonnay ★★★

This is typically a fruit-driven style with plenty of flavour. The 2008 vintage (★★☆) was 45 per cent fermented and matured in French oak barriques (7 per cent new); the rest was handled in tanks. It's a mouthfilling, peachy, slightly buttery wine in a fresh, simple, vibrantly fruity style.

Vintage	08	07	06
WR	6	7	6
Drink	09-11	09-10	P

DRY $19 AV

Vidal Reserve Chardonnay ★★★★★

At its best, this is one of Hawke's Bay's finest Chardonnays, with a string of top wines stretching back to the mid-1980s. The 2008 vintage (★★★★☆) was hand-picked, in the Gimblett Gravels and at Ohiti, and fermented, mostly with indigenous yeasts, in French oak barriques (40 per cent new). It's a weighty, powerful wine, sweet-fruited, with peachy, slightly biscuity flavours, showing excellent complexity and depth.

Vintage	08	07	06	05	04
WR	6	7	7	7	7
Drink	09-13	09-12	09-12	09-10	P

DRY $30 V+

Villa Maria Cellar Selection Hawke's Bay Chardonnay ★★★★

Typically rich and good value. The 2007 vintage (★★★★) was hand-picked and fermented in a mix of tanks and French oak barriques (new and seasoned); all components were lees-aged and stirred. It's a refined wine, fragrant and finely balanced, with ripe, concentrated, stone-fruit flavours, slightly buttery and toasty, and a long finish.

Vintage	07	06	05	04
WR	6	7	7	7
Drink	09-12	09-12	09-11	P

DRY $23 V+

Villa Maria Cellar Selection Marlborough Chardonnay   ★★★★

A consistently stylish, good-value wine. The 2008 vintage (★★★★) was fermented and matured in French oak barriques (20 per cent new). Instantly likeable, with mouthfilling body and strong, ripe, citrusy flavours, it is fresh and vibrant, with toasty, creamy notes adding considerable complexity, and excellent balance for early drinking.

Vintage	08	07	06	05	04
WR	6	6	6	6	6
Drink	09-14	09-12	09-12	09-11	P

DRY $23 V+

Villa Maria Private Bin East Coast Chardonnay   ★★★☆

A drink-young, fruit-driven style with a touch of class. The 2008 vintage (★★★☆) was mostly grown in the North Island regions of Gisborne and Hawke's Bay, but a small portion of the blend came from Marlborough. It was mostly lees-aged in tanks, but partly barrel-aged. Drinking well now, it has ripe stone-fruit flavours, slightly honeyed and toasty, with good depth and a well-rounded, dry finish.

Vintage	08	07	06	05	04
WR	5	6	6	6	6
Drink	09-12	09-11	09-10	P	P

DRY $18 V+

Villa Maria Reserve Barrique Fermented Gisborne Chardonnay   ★★★★★

The term 'Barrique Fermented' was reinstated from the 2004 vintage (the lush, multiple award-winning Barrique Fermented Chardonnay, launched in the 1980s but not produced from 2001 to 2003, was usually – but not always – made from Gisborne grapes). Fermented in French oak barriques (with a high percentage new), it is grown in the company's Katoa and McDiarmid Hill vineyards. The 2008 vintage (★★★★☆) is already drinking well. Soft, ripe, concentrated and creamy, it has delicious depth of peachy, slightly buttery flavours, dry, rounded and rich.

Vintage	08	07	06
WR	6	7	7
Drink	09-13	09-16	09-15

DRY $36 AV

Villa Maria Reserve Hawke's Bay Chardonnay   ★★★★☆

Hand-picked in the Waikahu Vineyard at Maraekakaho, the 2008 vintage (★★★★★) was fermented and matured in French oak barriques (55 per cent new). It's an authoritative wine, fleshy and forward, with substantial body (14.5 per cent alcohol) and highly concentrated stone-fruit flavours, rounded and creamy. It's already delicious.

Vintage	08
WR	7
Drink	09-14

DRY $31 AV

Villa Maria Reserve Marlborough Chardonnay   ★★★★★

With its rich, slightly mealy, citrusy flavours, this is a distinguished wine, very concentrated and finely structured. A marriage of intense, ripe Marlborough fruit with premium French oak, it is one of the region's greatest Chardonnays. It is typically grown in the warmest sites supplying Chardonnay grapes to Villa Maria, in the Awatere and Wairau valleys. The grapes are hand-picked and the wine is fermented with cultured and indigenous yeasts in French oak barriques (20 per cent new in 2007). Built to last, the 2007 vintage (★★★★★) is a quietly classy wine, still youthful, with subtle grapefruit and nutty oak flavours, showing lovely delicacy, poise and length.

Vintage	07	06	05	04	03	02
WR	7	7	7	7	6	7
Drink	09-14	09-13	09-12	09-12	09-10	09-10

DRY $31 V+

Villa Maria Single Vineyard Ihumatao Chardonnay   ★★★★★

This outstanding Chardonnay is estate-grown at the winery, near Auckland International Airport, low-cropped and fermented with indigenous yeasts in French oak barriques (typically a high percentage new). The 2008 vintage (★★★★☆) is a tightly structured, elegant, youthful wine, with strong, ripe grapefruit, peach and nutty oak flavours, very harmonious and long. One for the cellar.

Vintage	08	07	06	05
WR	6	7	7	7
Drink	09-13	09-14	09-13	09-12

DRY $36 AV

Villa Maria Single Vineyard Keltern Chardonnay   ★★★★★

Grown at the Keltern Vineyard, a warm, inland site east of Maraekakaho in Hawke's Bay, this wine is hand-picked, fermented with indigenous yeasts and lees-aged in French oak barriques (partly new). The 2008 vintage (★★★☆) is powerful and tightly structured, with mouthfilling body and concentrated, peachy, toasty flavours showing excellent ripeness and complexity. Open 2011+.

Vintage	08	07
WR	6	7
Drink	09-16	09-17

DRY $36 AV

Villa Maria Single Vineyard Taylors Pass Chardonnay   ★★★★

Grown in the company's Taylors Pass Vineyard in Marlborough's Awatere Valley, this wine is hand-picked and fermented and matured for a year in French oak barriques (28 per cent new in 2007). The refined 2007 vintage (★★★★) is a mouthfilling wine with subtle, delicate flavours of peaches, grapefruit and slight butterscotch, woven with fresh acidity. It's still very youthful; open mid-2010+.

Vintage	07	06	05
WR	7	7	7
Drink	09-13	09-12	09-11

DRY $36 –V

Villa Maria Single Vineyard Waikahu Chardonnay   ★★★★★

Grown at Maraekakaho, in Hawke's Bay, this fleshy and highly complex wine is hand-harvested, fermented with indigenous yeasts and matured in French oak barriques (typically half new) with lots of *batonnage* (lees-stirring). The 2006 vintage (★★★★★) has a fragrant, creamy, nutty bouquet, mouthfilling body and concentrated, grapefruit-like flavours, delicately seasoned with oak. A fine, elegant style, it shows great richness and length.

Vintage	06	05
WR	7	7
Drink	09-12	09-11

DRY $36 AV

Villa Maria Single Vineyard Waldron Chardonnay ★★★★☆

Grown at a warm site at Rapaura, in Marlborough, this wine is hand-harvested and French oak-fermented. Crisp and lively, with ripe grapefruit flavours seasoned with toasty oak, the 2006 vintage (★★★★) is moderately intense, with mealy, creamy notes adding complexity and good harmony.

Vintage	06	05
WR	6	6
Drink	09-13	09-12

DRY $36 –V

Voss Estate Reserve Chardonnay ★★★★☆

This powerful, richly flavoured Martinborough wine is typically fragrant and mouthfilling, with ripe grapefruit flavours, hints of nuts and butterscotch and a creamy, rounded finish. The 2007 vintage (★★★★☆) was hand-picked from mature vines (15 to 19 years old) and fermented in French oak barriques (10 per cent new). Richly fragrant, it is concentrated and sweet-fruited, with grapefruit and peach flavours, gently seasoned with biscuity oak, and finely balanced acidity. It's already drinking well.

DRY $28 V+

W5 Marlborough Chardonnay ★★★

Sold by blackmarket.co.nz, this is a drink-young style from Mt Olympus, creamy-smooth, with grapefruit and slight butterscotch flavours, lively and finely balanced. It typically offers good value.

DRY $14 V+

Waimarie Gisborne Chardonnay [Green Label] (★★★☆)

From Stephen Nobilo (a third-generation member of the famous wine family), the 2008 vintage (★★★☆) is a good buy. Hand-picked in the Judd Vineyard and cool-fermented in tanks, it is fresh-scented and weighty, with ripe melon, peach, pear and slight spice flavours, deliciously vibrant and lively.

Vintage	08
WR	5
Drink	09-10

DRY $18 V+

Waimarie Gisborne Chardonnay [Yellow Label] (★★★☆)

Grown in the Judd Estate vineyard, hand-picked and two-thirds barrel-fermented (French, 20 per cent new), the 2008 vintage (★★★☆) is mouthfilling, with very good depth of ripe citrus and stone-fruit flavours, well-integrated nutty oak and fresh acidity. Drink now or cellar.

Vintage	08
WR	6
Drink	10-12

DRY $20 AV

Waimarie Muriwai Valley Chardonnay   (★★★★☆)

Grown at Waimauku, in West Auckland, the rare 2008 vintage (★★★★☆) was hand-picked and fermented with indigenous yeasts in a single, one-year-old French oak barrel. It is weighty and rich, with ripe, peachy, sweet-fruit flavours and excellent complexity. A powerful wine, already drinking well, it should also reward cellaring.

Vintage	08
WR	6
Drink	10-13

DRY $48 –V

Waimea Bolitho SV Nelson Chardonnay   ★★★★

Still on sale, the 2005 vintage (★★★☆) is a single-vineyard wine, grown on the coast at Kina and barrel-fermented with indigenous yeasts. Mouthfilling (15 per cent alcohol) and peachy, with crisp acidity and some complexity, it is developed and ready.

Vintage	05	04	03
WR	5	5	7
Drink	09-10	P	P

DRY $25 AV

Waimea Nelson Chardonnay   ★★★★

The 2008 vintage (★★★★) was grown on the Kina Peninsula, hand-picked, barrel-fermented with indigenous yeasts, and given a full, softening malolactic fermentation. It's a full-bodied wine (14.5 per cent alcohol) with strong, peachy, citrusy, toasty flavours, good complexity and a slightly buttery finish. Drink now or cellar.

Vintage	08
WR	6
Drink	09-13

DRY $22 V+

Waipara Downs Chardonnay   ★★★★

This has been the most successful wine grown at Keith and Ruth Berry's farm at Waipara. Still on sale, the 2006 vintage (★★★★), harvested at 23 brix, was fermented and matured for 11 months in French oak barriques. Biscuit and butterscotch aromas lead into a full-bodied wine with strong, citrusy flavours, slightly oily and rich.

DRY $26 AV

Waipara Hills Soul of the South Waipara Chardonnay   (★★★☆)

The 2008 vintage (★★★☆) was grown in the Glasnevin Vineyard, behind the winery, and matured in seasoned oak barrels, with no use of malolactic fermentation. It's an elegant, gently wooded wine with ripe grapefruit and slight spice flavours, showing good concentration, and fresh acidity.

DRY $21 AV

Waipara Hills Southern Cross Selection Waipara Chardonnay   (★★★☆)

Fully fermented and matured for five months in French oak barrels (partly new), the 2008 vintage (★★★☆) was grown behind the winery, in the Glasnevin Vineyard. It's a fresh, vibrantly fruity wine with grapefruit, peach and toasty oak flavours, showing very good depth.

DRY $29 –V

Waipara Springs Premo Chardonnay   ★★★☆

The light yellow 2006 vintage (★★★★) was grown at Waipara and fermented with indigenous yeasts in French oak barriques (30 per cent new). Based on 28-year-old vines, it is tight and intense, with rich, citrusy flavours and firm acid spine in a dry, distinctly cool-climate style, likely to be long-lived.

Vintage	06
WR	6
Drink	09-10

DRY $24 AV

Waipara Springs Premo Old Vine Chardonnay   (★★★★☆)

Recommended for cellaring for over a decade, the 2005 vintage (★★★★☆) was made from 'a quarter of a century old Mendoza clone Chardonnay vines' at Waipara. Matured in all-new French oak barriques, it is yellow-hued, tight and complex, with very citrusy, minerally characters, fresh and toasty, and an extra layer of flavour.

Vintage	05
WR	7
Drink	09-17

DRY $28 V+

Waipara Springs Waipara Chardonnay   (★★★)

French oak-fermented, the 2006 vintage (★★★) is full-bodied and peachy, with slightly buttery notes and fresh acidity.

Vintage	06
WR	4
Drink	09-10

DRY $19 AV

Waipara West Chardonnay   ★★★★

Still on sale, the 2005 vintage (★★★☆) is a mature wine with good weight and depth of peachy, buttery flavour, showing considerable complexity. Ready.

DRY $25 AV

Waipara West Unoaked Chardonnay   (★★★☆)

A good example of the unoaked style, the 2008 vintage (★★★☆) has plenty of peachy, slightly spicy and limey flavour, very fresh and vibrant.

DRY $19 V+

Waipipi Wairarapa Chardonnay   ★★☆

Grown at Opaki, north of Masterton, and matured in new French oak barriques, the 2007 vintage (★★★) is a bright yellow, mouthfilling, peachy wine, slightly honeyed and toasty, in an upfront style, now ready.

Vintage	07	06
WR	5	5
Drink	09-12	09-10

DRY $22 –V

Wairau River Home Block Chardonnay   (★★★★)

Grown on the northern side of the Wairau Valley, in Marlborough, and barrel-matured for nine months, the 2007 vintage (★★★★) is an elegant, mouthfilling wine, sweet-fruited, with ripe, citrusy, slightly nutty flavours, showing excellent harmony, roundness and depth. It's delicious now.

Vintage	07
WR	6
Drink	09-11

DRY $28 AV

Wairau River Marlborough Chardonnay   ★★★☆

The 2008 vintage (★★★) was mostly handled in tanks, but 30 per cent was oak-aged. It's a fruit-driven style with vibrant, lemony, slightly biscuity flavours, showing good freshness and depth.

Vintage	08
WR	5
Drink	09-11

DRY $20 AV

Waitiri Creek Central Otago Chardonnay   ★★★☆

Still on sale, the 2006 vintage (★★★★) is a single-vineyard wine, fermented and matured for six months in French oak barriques (25 per cent new). It's fleshy and elegant, with strong, vibrant, citrusy flavours and buttery, creamy notes adding richness.

DRY $30 –V

West Brook Barrique Fermented Chardonnay   ★★★☆

The 2007 vintage (★★★☆) is a blend of Marlborough and estate-grown, Waimauku (West Auckland) grapes, fully barrel-fermented. With its vibrant, grapefruit-like flavours, fresh and strong, and tight finish, it should mature well.

DRY $20 AV

White Cliff Chardonnay   (★★★)

From Sacred Hill, the 2007 vintage (★★★) is an above-average quaffer. Light lemon/green, it is very fresh, vibrantly fruity and smooth, with good depth of peachy, citrusy flavour in an easy-drinking style. Top value.

DRY $10 V+

Whitehaven Marlborough Chardonnay   ★★☆

The 2007 vintage (★★☆) was 80 per cent barrel-fermented. Fruity and smooth, it's a pleasant wine, citrusy, lively, crisp and dry, offering simple, easy drinking.

Vintage	07	06	05	04
WR	6	6	5	5
Drink	09-11	09-10	P	P

DRY $20 –V

Wicked Vicar, The, Chardonnay   ★★★

The 2007 vintage (★★★) was grown at Waipara and matured in French oak casks (10 per cent new). Bright, light lemon/green, it's a lemony, buttery, slightly toasty wine, full-flavoured, in a slightly austere style with flinty acidity.

Vintage	07	06
WR	6	6
Drink	09-13	09-12

DRY $26 –V

Wild Rock Hawke's Bay Chardonnay   (★★★☆)

Sold only in supermarkets, the 2008 vintage (★★★☆) is mouthfilling and vibrantly fruity, with ripe, peachy, citrusy flavours gently seasoned with toasty oak, a slightly creamy texture, and a rounded finish.

DRY $19 V+

Wild Rock Pania Hawke's Bay Chardonnay   ★★★★

Wild Rock is a division of Craggy Range. Partly barrel-fermented, the 2008 vintage (★★★★) is an instantly appealing, drink-young style with a fragrant bouquet of peaches and butterscotch. Creamy and mouthfilling, it has fresh, ripe stone-fruit and slight toasty flavours, showing excellent depth.

Vintage	08	07
WR	7	6
Drink	09-12	09-11

DRY $20 V+

Wild South Marlborough Chardonnay   ★★☆

The 2008 vintage (★★★) from Sacred Hill was mostly estate-grown in the Waihopai Valley and handled entirely in tanks. It's a mouthfilling, fully dry wine with vibrant, citrusy, appley flavours, fresh acidity and good drink-young appeal.

DRY $19 –V

Wishart Reserve Chardonnay   ★★★☆

Still on sale, the 2005 vintage (★★★☆) is a powerful Hawke's Bay wine, hand-picked and barrel-fermented. Deep yellow/green, with a developed bouquet, it has rich grapefruit and toast flavours, leading to a rounded, slightly honeyed finish. It's an upfront style, ready now.

DRY $25 –V

Wishart Te Puriri Chardonnay   ★★☆

Grown in Hawke's Bay and partly barrel-fermented, the 2006 vintage (★★☆) is a smooth wine with ripe, citrusy, peachy, slightly buttery flavours and a touch of bottle-aged complexity. Verging on three stars. Ready.

DRY $20 –V

Wishart Te Puriri Unoaked Chardonnay   ★★★

Estate-grown at Bay View, in Hawke's Bay, and lees-aged for six months, the 2007 vintage (★★★) is fresh and lively, with grapefruit and slight spice flavours.

DRY $19 AV

Wither Hills Wairau Valley Marlborough Chardonnay ★★★★★

This is a classy wine with a formidable track record in shows. A powerful, upfront style in the past, it showed a toasty, biscuity complexity from fermentation and lees-aging in French oak casks (typically 50 per cent new), coupled with the intense flavours of Marlborough fruit. Under Ben Glover, appointed as chief winemaker in 2007, the company is keen to produce a less wood-influenced style. The 2007 vintage (★★★★★) was fermented, partly with indigenous yeasts, in French oak barriques (20 per cent new). An elegant, tightly structured wine with a complex bouquet, it has concentrated, ripe, citrusy, slightly toasty flavours and a long, finely textured, creamy finish. The slightly less intense 2008 (★★★★) is an elegant, vibrantly fruity wine with mouthfilling body, very good depth of peachy, citrusy flavours, a subtle oak influence (all French, 20 per cent new), and a faintly buttery, finely balanced finish. It's ready to roll.

		DRY $20 V+
Vintage	08	
WR	7	
Drink	09-13	

Wooing Tree Central Otago Chardonnay ★★★☆

The 2008 vintage (★★★☆) was hand-picked at Lowburn and fermented in French oak barriques. It's a fleshy, rounded wine with a creamy, slightly toasty bouquet and lots of peachy, toasty flavour, showing good complexity.

DRY $28 –V

Wrights GW Chardonnay (★★★)

Approved by the Vegetarian Society, the 2007 vintage (★★★) is a single-vineyard wine, grown at Patutahi and not oak-aged. It's a medium-bodied style with lively, citrusy, appley flavours, fresh, crisp and dry.

DRY $20 –V

Chenin Blanc

Today's Chenin Blancs are far riper, rounder and more enjoyable to drink than the typically thin, sharply acidic and austere wines of a decade ago. Yet this great grape variety is still struggling for an identity in New Zealand. In recent years, several labels have been discontinued – not for lack of quality or value, but lack of buyer interest.

A good New Zealand Chenin Blanc is fresh and buoyantly fruity, with melon and pineapple-evoking flavours and a crisp finish. In the cooler parts of the country, the variety's naturally high acidity (an asset in the warmer viticultural regions of South Africa, the United States and Australia) can be a distinct handicap. But when the grapes achieve full ripeness here, this classic grape of Vouvray, in the Loire Valley, yields sturdy wines that are satisfying in their youth yet can mature for many years, gradually unfolding a delicious, honeyed richness.

Only three wineries have consistently made impressive Chenin Blancs over the past decade: Millton, Margrain and Esk Valley. Many growers, put off by the variety's late-ripening nature and the susceptibility of its tight bunches to botrytis rot, have uprooted their vines. Plantings have plummeted from 372 hectares in 1983 to 48 hectares of bearing vines in 2010.

Chenin Blanc is the country's eleventh most widely planted white-wine variety (behind even Reichensteiner, a bulk-wine variety), with plantings concentrated in Gisborne and Hawke's Bay. In the future, winemakers who plant Chenin Blanc in warm, sunny vineyard sites with devigorating soils, where the variety's vigorous growth can be controlled and yields reduced, can be expected to produce the ripest, most concentrated wines. New Zealand winemakers have yet to get to grips with Chenin Blanc.

Esk Valley Hawke's Bay Chenin Blanc   ★★★★

This is one of New Zealand's best (and few truly convincing) Chenin Blancs, with the ability to mature well for several years. Grown mostly at Moteo Pa (80 per cent), but also in the Gimblett Gravels (20 per cent), the 2008 vintage (★★★★) was mostly fermented and lees-aged in tanks, but 20 per cent of the blend was fermented with indigenous yeasts in seasoned French oak casks. Showing lots of personality, it's an immaculate, finely balanced wine, fleshy, very fresh and vibrant, with ripe tropical-fruit flavours, a touch of complexity and a tight, dryish (5.5 grams/litre of residual sugar), crisp finish. Well worth cellaring.

Vintage	09	08	07	06
WR	6	7	7	6
Drink	09-14	09-14	09-14	09-12

MED/DRY $23 AV

Farmgate Hawke's Bay Chenin Blanc   (★★★☆)

Grown in the Gimblett Gravels and partly barrel-fermented, the 2008 vintage (★★★☆) is a mouthfilling, minerally wine with good depth of pear, citrus fruit and apple flavours and a crisp, dry finish. Finely balanced, it should mature well. (Sold directly to consumers by Ngatarawa from the Farmgate website.)

Vintage	08
WR	6
Drink	09-14

DRY $22 AV

Forrest Gibsons Creek Marlborough Chenin Blanc   ★★★

This is an extremely rare beast – a Chenin Blanc grown in the South Island. The 2007 vintage (★★★) is light (11 per cent alcohol) and fresh, with smooth, delicate lemon/apple flavours and a distinct splash of sweetness (14 grams/litre of residual sugar).

MED/DRY $20 –V

Margrain Martinborough Chenin Blanc   ★★★★

When Margrain bought the neighbouring Chifney property in 2001, they acquired Chenin Blanc vines now around 30 years old. The 2008 vintage (★★★★) is medium-bodied, very fresh and vibrant, with good harmony of ripe citrus, melon and pineapple flavours, a splash of sweetness (18 grams/litre of residual sugar) and appetising acidity. It's enjoyable now, but should blossom with cellaring.

Vintage	08
WR	7
Drink	09-19

MED $30 –V

Millton Chenin Blanc Te Arai Vineyard   ★★★★★

This Gisborne wine is New Zealand's greatest Chenin Blanc. It's a richly varietal wine with concentrated, fresh, vibrant fruit flavours to the fore in some vintages (2006, 2007); nectareous scents and flavours in others (2005). The grapes are grown organically and hand-picked at different stages of ripening, culminating in some years ('It's in the lap of the gods,' says James Millton) in a final harvest of botrytis-affected fruit. Fermentation is in tanks and large, 620-litre French oak casks, used in the Loire for Chenin Blanc. The 2007 vintage (★★★★★) has fresh, pineapple and honey aromas and flavours, with a sliver of sweetness (10 grams/litre of residual sugar) and excellent balance, intensity and varietal expression. A luscious wine, it's already enjoyable, but tightly structured and likely to be long-lived.

Vintage	07	06	05	04	03	02
WR	7	7	6	7	5	7
Drink	09-15	09-20	09-10	09-14	P	09-12

MED/DRY $30 AV

Flora

A California crossing of Gewürztraminer and Sémillon, in cool-climate regions Flora produces aromatic, spicy wine. Some of New Zealand's 'Pinot Gris' vines were a few years ago positively identified as Flora, but the country's total area of bearing Flora vines in 2009 was just 2 hectares.

Artisan Kauri Ridge Oratia Flora ★★★

Estate-grown in the Kauri Ridge Vineyard at Oratia, in West Auckland, the 2007 vintage (★★★) is an easy-drinking, distinctly medium style (40 grams/litre of residual sugar), medium-bodied, lemony, appley and crisp.

MED $20 –V

Ascension The Rogue Flora ★★★

Grown at Matakana, this is typically a floral, weighty wine with grapey, slightly sweet and spicy flavours in a smooth, easy-drinking style.

MED/DRY $27 –V

Omaha Bay Vineyard The Impostor Matakana Flora ★★★☆

The 2008 vintage (★★★★) is the best yet. A full-bodied wine (over 13 per cent alcohol), it is gently sweet, with generous, citrusy, spicy flavours, a hint of apricots and a tight finish. Showing good weight and depth, it should mature well.

Vintage	08	07	06
WR	6	6	6
Drink	09-12	09-12	P

MED $27 –V

Gewürztraminer

Only a trickle of Gewürztraminer is exported (16,222 cases in the year to mid-2009, 0.1 per cent of total wine shipments), and the majority of New Zealand bottlings lack the power and richness of the great Alsace model. Yet this classic grape is starting to get the respect it deserves from grape-growers and winemakers here.

For most of the 1990s, Gewürztraminer's popularity was on the wane. Between 1983 and 1996, New Zealand's plantings of Gewürztraminer dropped by almost two-thirds. A key problem is that Gewürztraminer is a temperamental performer in the vineyard, being particularly vulnerable to adverse weather at flowering, which can decimate grape yields. Now there is proof of a strong renewal of interest: the area of bearing vines has surged from 85 hectares in 1998 to 316 hectares in 2009. Most of the plantings are in Gisborne (33 per cent of the national total), Marlborough (27 per cent) and Hawke's Bay (18 per cent).

Slight sweetness and skin contact have been commonly used in the past to boost the flavour of Gewürztraminer, at the cost of flavour delicacy and longevity. Such outstanding wines as Dry River have revealed the far richer, softer flavours and greater aging potential that can be gained by reducing crops, leaf-plucking to promote fruit ripeness and avoiding skin contact.

Gewürztraminer is a high-impact wine, brimming with scents and flavours. 'Spicy' is the most common adjective used to pinpoint its distinctive, heady aromas and flavours; tasters also find nuances of gingerbread, freshly ground black pepper, cinnamon, cloves, mint, lychees and mangoes. Once you've tasted one or two Gewürztraminers, you won't have any trouble recognising it in a 'blind' tasting – it's the most forthright, distinctive white-wine variety of all.

Allan Scott Marlborough Gewürztraminer   ★★★★

The 2008 vintage (★★★★) is a perfumed, softly mouthfilling wine, fermented in tanks and old barrels. It offers impressively ripe lychee and spice flavours, with a hint of ginger, some complexity, and very good delicacy and depth. Drink now or cellar.

Vintage	08
WR	5
Drink	09-15

MED/DRY $22 AV

Anchorage Nelson Gewürztraminer   (★★★)

Grown at Motueka, the 2008 vintage (★★★) is a soft, forward wine with lychee and spice flavours, a distinct splash of sweetness (13.9 grams/litre of residual sugar) and gentle acidity. It's enjoyable young.

MED/DRY $18 AV

Askerne Hawke's Bay Gewürztraminer   ★★★★

This small winery has an excellent track record with Gewürztraminer. The 2008 vintage (★★★) is a dry wine (4 grams/litre of residual sugar), estate-grown near Havelock North and principally handled in tanks; 15 per cent was matured in old French oak casks. Moderately perfumed, fleshy and soft, with light yellow colour and citrusy, slightly spicy and gingery flavours, it's ready to roll.

Vintage	08	07	06	05	04
WR	6	7	7	6	7
Drink	09-12	09-11	P	P	P

DRY $20 V+

Askerne Reserve Hawke's Bay Gewürztraminer   (★★★★)

The exotically perfumed, light yellow 2008 vintage (★★★★) was harvested at 27 brix and 15 per cent barrel-fermented. It has concentrated, slightly gingery and honeyed flavours in a forward, gently sweet style (22 grams/litre of residual sugar), rich, rounded and ready.

Vintage	08
WR	6
Drink	09-12

MED $25 –V

Astrolabe Voyage Marlborough Gewürztraminer   (★★★★)

The richly scented 2008 vintage (★★★★), grown at Grovetown and in the Waihopai Valley, has a slightly oily texture and a distinct splash of sweetness (22 grams/litre of residual sugar) amid its lush, extroverted flavours. It's a softly mouthfilling, rich wine, delicious now.

Vintage	08
WR	6
Drink	09-13

MED $22 AV

Ataahua Gewürztraminer   (★★★)

Hand-picked at 23.2 brix in Waipara from first-crop vines, the 2008 vintage (★★★) is a dry style (4 grams/litre of residual sugar) with mouthfilling body and plenty of spicy, slightly gingery flavour.

DRY $20 –V

Babich Gimblett Gravels Gewürztraminer   ★★★

Grown in the company's vineyard in Gimblett Road, Hawke's Bay, and fully fermented in old oak casks, the 2007 vintage (★★★) is a softly mouthfilling, slightly sweet style (8 grams/litre of residual sugar) with citrusy, spicy flavours and a well-rounded finish. Ready.

Vintage	07	06	05
WR	7	6	6
Drink	09-15	09-14	09-13

MED/DRY $20 –V

Beach House Hawke's Bay Gewürztraminer   (★★★)

Grown at Te Awanga, the 2008 vintage (★★★) was hand-picked and fermented to dryness (3 grams/litre of residual sugar). It's a mouthfilling (14 per cent alcohol), rounded wine with a gently spicy bouquet, good palate weight and satisfying depth of ripe lychee and spice flavours.

Vintage	08
WR	6
Drink	09-15

DRY $22 –V

Bird Marlborough Gewürztraminer   ★★★☆

Mouthfilling and smooth, the 2008 vintage (★★★☆) is a single-vineyard wine, grown in the Omaka Valley. Vibrantly fruity, slightly sweet (5.9 grams/litre of residual sugar), fresh and crisp, it has a ripe, spicy bouquet and very good depth of lychee, pear and spice flavours.

Vintage	08	07	06
WR	6	4	5
Drink	09-12	P	09-10

MED/DRY $23 –V

Blackenbrook Vineyard Nelson Gewürztraminer   ★★★★☆

A consistently delicious wine. The estate-grown, exotically perfumed 2008 vintage (★★★★☆)
is an Alsace style, hand-picked very ripe (over 24 brix), with substantial body (14.5 per cent
alcohol) and a sliver of sweetness (8 grams/litre of residual sugar). It has fresh pear and spice
aromas, and the flavours show lovely delicacy, harmony and richness.

Vintage	08	07	06	05
WR	7	NM	7	6
Drink	09-11	NM	09-10	P

MED/DRY $27 AV

Blackenbrook Vineyard Nelson Reserve Gewürztraminer   ★★★★☆

The beautifully perfumed, softly mouthfilling (14.8 per cent alcohol) 2008 vintage (★★★★☆)
was harvested at 25.6 brix. Intensely varietal, it has very ripe peach, lychee and spice flavours,
showing lovely depth and delicacy, and a slightly sweet (12 grams/litre of residual sugar), well-
rounded finish.

Vintage	08	07
WR	7	7
Drink	09-13	09-13

MED/DRY $31 –V

Bladen Marlborough Gewürztraminer   ★★★☆

Hand-picked in the Tilly Vineyard, the 2008 vintage (★★★☆) is a mouthfilling, slightly sweet
style with a floral bouquet, a slightly oily texture and good depth of citrus fruit, lychee and spice
flavours.

MED/DRY $24 –V

Bouldevines Marlborough Gewürztraminer   (★★★☆)

Ripely scented and mouthfilling, the 2009 vintage (★★★☆) is a single-vineyard, finely textured
wine with good depth of lychee and spice flavours, gentle acidity and a dryish finish.

MED/DRY $27 –V

Brookfields Gewürztraminer   ★★★☆

Grown in stony soils in Ohiti Road, inland from Fernhill, this is typically a weighty Hawke's
Bay wine with plenty of character. The 2008 vintage (★★★☆), harvested at 24 brix, is very full-
bodied (14.5 per cent alcohol), with soft, ripe lychee and spice flavours in a creamy-textured,
relatively dry style (5 grams/litre of residual sugar) with a well-rounded finish.

Vintage	08	07	06	05	04
WR	7	7	7	7	7
Drink	09-12	09-11	09-10	09-10	P

MED/DRY $20 AV

Brunton Road Gisborne Gewürztraminer   ★★★☆

Grown in the Searle Vineyard at Patutahi, the 2008 vintage (★★★) was hand-harvested and
stop-fermented in an off-dry style (5 grams/litre of residual sugar). It's a mouthfilling wine (14
per cent alcohol) with ripe lychee, pear and spice flavours, gentle acidity and a slightly gingery,
rounded finish.

MED/DRY $23 –V

Bushmere Estate Gisborne Gewürztraminer   ★★★☆

The generous 2007 vintage (★★★★) is a medium-dry style (12 grams/litre of residual sugar), hand-harvested at 24 brix. Mouthfilling and fleshy, it has Turkish delight aromas and rich, ripe, spicy flavours, well-rounded and harmonious.

MED/DRY $22 –V

Cable Bay Marlborough Gewürztraminer   ★★★☆

The 2008 vintage (★★★☆) was grown at the Brentwood Vineyard, in the warm Rapaura district. It's a mouthfilling wine with smooth, ripe flavours of citrus fruits, lychees and spices, showing good delicacy, depth and harmony.

Vintage	08	07
WR	6	7
Drink	09-10	09-10

MED/DRY $25 –V

Cape Campbell Limited Edition Reserve Gewürztraminer   ★★★☆

The 2007 vintage (★★★☆) is floral and fleshy, with strong lychee, pear and spice flavours, slightly sweet (9 grams/litre of residual sugar) and rounded.

Vintage	07	06
WR	5	7
Drink	09-11	P

MED/DRY $25 –V

Chard Farm Central Otago Gewürztraminer   ★★★★

The ripely scented 2007 vintage (★★★★☆) is a delicious wine, blended from estate-grown, Gibbston grapes, supplemented by fruit from a grower at Cromwell. Softly mouthfilling, with gentle acidity, it has ripe flavours of citrus fruits, lychees and spices, showing excellent varietal definition, delicacy and depth.

MED/DRY $26 –V

Clayridge Marlborough Gewürztraminer   (★★★★)

The richly perfumed 2008 vintage (★★★★) is a single-vineyard wine, hand-picked and fermented in tanks (55 per cent) and seasoned French oak barriques. It's a mouthfilling, slightly sweet wine (9 grams/litre of residual sugar), with rich citrus fruit, lychee, apricot and spice flavours, showing considerable complexity.

Vintage	08
WR	5
Drink	09-11

MED/DRY $24 AV

Clearview Estate Gewürztraminer   ★★★

The 2008 vintage (★★★) is a mouthfilling, smooth blend of Gisborne and young-vine Te Awanga (Hawke's Bay) grapes. Gently sweet (6 grams/litre of residual sugar), it has ripe lychee and spice flavours showing good delicacy and depth. The 2009 (★★★), grown at Te Awanga, is a fully dry style, perfumed, with pear, citrus fruit and spice flavours. It's not concentrated, but has good varietal character and freshness.

Vintage	09	08	07
WR	7	6	7
Drink	09-15	09-12	09-10

DRY $19 –V

Cloudy Bay Marlborough Gewürztraminer ★★★★★

To experience the Cloudy Bay magic at its most spellbinding, try the rare, less fashionable wines, made in small volumes. Top vintages of this wine are distinctly Alsace-like – highly perfumed, weighty, complex and rounded. The 2007 (★★★★☆), fermented and matured for six months in old French oak barrels, is light lemon/green, with a voluminous bouquet. Mouthfilling, with greater complexity than most New Zealand Gewürztraminers, it's a medium-dry style (8.6 grams/litre of residual sugar), with a rich array of lychee, ginger and spice flavours, gentle acidity and a well-rounded finish.

Vintage	05	04	03	02
WR	6	6	6	5
Drink	09-10	09	P	P

MED/DRY $35 AV

Coopers Creek Gisborne Gewürztraminer ★★★☆

A single-vineyard wine, grown at Patutahi, the 2007 vintage (★★★★) is richly perfumed, with deep lychee, spice and ginger flavours, a slightly oily texture and a slightly sweet finish (6 grams/litre of residual sugar). It's a weighty (14.5 per cent alcohol) and concentrated wine, already delicious. There is no 2008.

Vintage	08	07
WR	NM	6
Drink	NM	P

MED/DRY $18 V+

Corbans Private Bin Hawke's Bay Gewürztraminer ★★★★☆

The 2007 vintage (★★★★) from Pernod Ricard NZ has a perfumed, musky bouquet, good weight and concentrated flavours, soft and rich. The 2008 (★★★★), grown at Haumoana, is mouthfilling and rounded, with ripe, spicy, gingery flavours, a sliver of sweetness and good length.

Vintage	08	07	06	05	04
WR	6	7	6	NM	7
Drink	09-11	09-11	09-10	NM	P

MED/DRY $24 V+

Crab Farm Hawke's Bay Gewürztraminer ★★★☆

The 2008 vintage (★★★☆) has a spicy bouquet, leading into a medium to full-bodied wine (12 per cent alcohol) with very good depth of citrus fruit, lychee, pear and spice flavours, slightly sweet and crisp.

Vintage	08
WR	7
Drink	09-12

MED/DRY $17 V+

Crawford Farm New Zealand Gewürztraminer/Riesling (★★★☆)

The 2007 vintage (★★★☆) from Constellation NZ is a blend of Waipara Riesling and Gisborne Gewürztraminer. It's a medium-dry style (6 grams/litre of residual sugar) with strong, spicy notes in an easy-drinking style, delicious young.

MED/DRY $23 –V

Crossroads Hawke's Bay Gewürztraminer   ★★☆

The 2006 vintage (★★☆) is a medium-bodied style with moderate depth of fresh lychee, apple and spice flavours and a distinct splash of sweetness (20 grams/litre of residual sugar).

Vintage   06
WR   6   `MED $20 –V`
Drink   P

Distant Land Gisborne Gewürztraminer   (★★★☆)

From Lincoln, the 2007 vintage (★★★☆) is a single-vineyard wine, lees-aged and made in a slightly sweet (10.5 grams/litre of residual sugar) style. The bouquet is perfumed and gingery; the palate is full-bodied (14 per cent alcohol), ripe, citrusy and spicy, with very good balance and flavour depth.

`MED/DRY $20 AV`

Dry River Estate Gewürztraminer   ★★★★★

This intensely perfumed and flavoured Martinborough Gewürztraminer is one of the country's finest. Medium-dry or medium in most years, in top vintages it shows a power and richness comparable to Alsace's *vendange tardive* (late-harvest) wines. Always rich in alcohol and exceptionally full-flavoured, it is also very delicate, with a tight, concentrated, highly refined palate that is typically at its most seductive at two to four years old, although it can mature well for more than a decade. The 2008 vintage (★★★★☆) is labelled 'Amaranth', meaning it is highly recommended for cellaring. A powerful, mouthfilling wine (14 per cent alcohol) with a very ripe, slightly musky bouquet, it has intensely varietal lychee, pear and spice flavours, slightly sweet (12 grams/litre of residual sugar) and concentrated. Open mid-2010+.

Vintage	08	07	06	05	04
WR	7	NM	6	NM	6
Drink	10-15	NM	09-12	NM	09-10

`MED $48 AV`

Dry River Lovat Vineyard Gewürztraminer   ★★★★★

Grown in the Lovat Vineyard in Martinborough, a few hundred metres down the road from the winery, the 2008 (★★★★★) is weighty and richly perfumed. It's a very Alsace-like wine, with concentrated flavours of citrus fruits, lychees and spice, a hint of ginger, gentle acidity and considerable sweetness (20 grams/litre of residual sugar). The 2009 vintage (★★★★☆) is highly perfumed, mouthfilling and soft, with fresh lychee and spice flavours, a distinct splash of sweetness (24 grams/litre of residual sugar) and a soft, rich finish. It's already delicious.

Vintage	09	08
WR	7	7
Drink	10-14	09-15

`MED $39 AV`

Farmgate Hawke's Bay Gewürztraminer   ★★★☆

From Ngatarawa, the 2008 vintage (★★★☆) is a mouthfilling, ripely perfumed wine with lychee, spice and ginger flavours in a medium-dry style with very good varietal character and depth.

Vintage	08	07
WR	7	7
Drink	09-13	09-11

`MED $22 –V`

Forrest The Valleys Wairau Gewürztraminer   (★★★★)

Delicious from the start, the 2008 vintage (★★★★) was grown in the middle of the Wairau Valley and in the Brancott Valley. Full-bodied and smooth, it has concentrated, delicate flavours of lychees, pears and spices, gentle sweetness (14 grams/litre of residual sugar) and lovely harmony.

Vintage	08	07	06
WR	6	7	7
Drink	09-12	09-10	09-10

MED/DRY $25 –V

Fossil Ridge Nelson Gewürztraminer   ★★★☆

From an elevated site at Richmond, the 2008 vintage (★★★★) is perfumed and full-bodied, with a distinct splash of sweetness (14 grams/litre of residual sugar) and very good depth of ripe lychee, pear, spice and slight ginger flavours. Full of personality, it's delicious now.

MED/DRY $20 AV

Framingham Marlborough Gewürztraminer   ★★★★☆

This label has shown excellent form of late. Already very expressive, the 2008 vintage (★★★★☆) is a single-vineyard wine, mostly handled in tanks, but 20 per cent of the blend was aged in old barrels. A medium-dry style (11 grams/litre of residual sugar), exotically perfumed, mouthfilling and rounded, it offers lychee, spice and ginger flavours, with a slightly oily texture, and impressive delicacy and richness.

Vintage	08	07	06	05	04	03
WR	7	6	6	6	6	5
Drink	10-13	09-11	P	P	P	P

MED/DRY $28 AV

Gibbston Valley La Dulcinée The Expressionist Series Gewürztraminer   (★★★★☆)

Just 35 cases were made of the 2008 vintage (★★★★☆), from 'old', company-owned vines at Gibbston. Richly perfumed and weighty (14 per cent alcohol), it has concentrated, peachy, spicy, faintly buttery flavours, with a slightly sweet finish (12 grams/litre of residual sugar), offering delicious drinking from now onwards.

Vintage	08
WR	7
Drink	10-15

MED/DRY $45 –V

Gibson Bridge Reserve Marlborough Gewürztraminer   ★★★☆

A single-vineyard wine, grown at Renwick, the 2007 vintage (★★★) is an easy-drinking, gently perfumed, medium to full-bodied wine with good depth of slightly sweet lychee and spice flavours.

MED/DRY $22 –V

Greenhough Nelson Gewürztraminer   ★★★☆

Grown at two sites, at Mapua and Hope, and partly barrel-fermented (25 per cent), the 2008 vintage (★★★★) has a ripely scented, spicy, gingery bouquet, substantial body (14.5 per cent alcohol) and slightly sweet (8.5 grams/litre of residual sugar) pear, lychee, peach and spice flavours. It's a powerful, concentrated wine, already highly enjoyable.

Vintage	08	07	06
WR	7	6	5
Drink	09-12	09-11	09-10

MED/DRY $22 –V

Greystone Waipara Gewürztraminer   ★★★★☆

The 2009 vintage (★★★★☆) is a medium style (21 grams/litre of residual sugar), perfumed and mouthfilling, very fresh and vibrant, with rich lychee, pear and spice flavours, a hint of ginger, a slightly oily texture and a lasting finish. A richly varietal wine, it should unfold well during 2010.

MED $24 V+

Huia Marlborough Gewürztraminer   ★★★☆

This is a consistently characterful wine. The 2008 vintage (★★★☆) is a fully dry style, mostly handled in tanks; 10 per cent of the blend was fermented in old French oak casks. Full-bodied (14 per cent alcohol), it is softly textured, with some complexity and good depth of pear and spice flavours.

Vintage	08	07	06	05	04
WR	7	6	6	5	6
Drink	09-19	09-13	09-11	09-10	P

DRY $28 –V

Huntaway Reserve Gisborne Gewürztraminer   ★★★★

The 2007 vintage (★★★★) from Pernod Ricard NZ was grown at Riverpoint. Most of the blend was fermented initially in tanks, then in a large oak cuve, but 24 per cent was fermented in seasoned French oak barrels. Perfumed, with excellent weight and harmony, it's a mouthfilling wine with ripe lychees and spice flavours, showing some complexity, a slightly oily texture and a smooth, dryish finish (5.9 grams/litre of residual sugar).

MED/DRY $24 AV

Hunter's Marlborough Gewürztraminer   ★★★★☆

Hunter's produces a consistently stylish Gewürztraminer, with impressive weight, flavour depth and fragrance. Delicious from the start, the 2008 vintage (★★★★☆) was harvested at a ripe 24 brix. Exotically perfumed, it is weighty, with fresh, concentrated lychee and spice flavours, balanced acidity and a dryish, rich finish.

Vintage	09	08	07	06	05	04
WR	6	6	6	5	6	5
Drink	10-13	09-12	09-10	09-10	P	P

MED/DRY $23 V+

Johanneshof Marlborough Gewürztraminer   ★★★★★

This beauty ranks among New Zealand's greatest Gewürztraminers. The 2009 vintage (★★★★★) is a medium style with a heady, exotically perfumed bouquet and lovely richness, delicacy and harmony. Finely poised, with beautifully ripe lychee and spice flavours and gentle acidity, it should unfold superbly during 2010.

Vintage	09	MED $27 V+
WR	6	
Drink	09-14	

Johanneshof Marlborough Gewürztraminer Trocken/Dry   (★★★★☆)

The 2008 vintage (★★★★☆) is a mouthfilling, unusually dry Gewürztraminer with a perfumed, gingery bouquet and strongly spicy, gingery flavours. Weighty, slightly oily and rich, it's a good food wine.

Vintage	08	DRY $27 AV
WR	4	
Drink	09-11	

Kaimira Estate Brightwater Gewürztraminer   ★★★

The 2008 vintage (★★★) is a dryish (5.3 grams/litre of residual sugar) Nelson wine, attractively perfumed, with substantial body (14 per cent alcohol) and plenty of spicy, slightly gingery flavour.

MED/DRY $20 –V

Landmark Estate Gisborne Gewürztraminer   (★★★☆)

From the Vitasovich family, based at Henderson, the 2006 vintage (★★★☆) is bright yellow, with mouthfilling body and strong, citrusy, spicy flavours. A dryish style with good varietal character, it's drinking well now.

MED/DRY $19 AV

Lawson's Dry Hills Marlborough Gewürztraminer   ★★★★★

This is consistently one of the country's most impressive Gewürztraminers. Grown near the winery in the Lawson's Dry Hills and nearby Woodward vineyards, at the foot of the Wither Hills, it is typically harvested at over 24 brix and mostly cool-fermented in stainless steel tanks, but a small component (7.5 per cent in 2008) is given 'the full treatment', with a high-solids, indigenous yeast ferment in seasoned French oak barriques, malolactic fermentation and lees-stirring. The 2008 (★★★★☆) is fleshy and soft, with ripe lychee, ginger and spice flavours, pure, intensely varietal and very harmonious, but fractionally less intense than in a top vintage.

Vintage	08	07	06	05	04	DRY $27 V+
WR	7	7	7	6	7	
Drink	09-13	09-12	09-11	P	09-10	

Longbush Gewürztraminer [Bird Series]   (★★★)

The 2008 vintage (★★★) is a full-bodied Gisborne wine (14.4 per cent alcohol) with gently sweet (10 grams/litre of residual sugar) lychee and spice flavours, fresh and lively. It's drinking well now.

Vintage	08	MED/DRY $18 AV
WR	6	
Drink	09-12	

Longbush Gisborne Gewürztraminer   (★★★)

The 2008 vintage (★★★) is mouthfilling, with plenty of spicy, gingery flavour, off-dry (8 grams/litre of residual sugar), and drink-young appeal.

Vintage   08
WR   5
Drink   09-11

MED/DRY $13 V+

Maimai Creek Hawke's Bay Gewürztraminer   ★★★☆

The 2008 vintage (★★★☆) is full-bodied, with lots of spicy, slightly sweet and gingery flavour. Good value.

MED/DRY $18 V+

Matua Valley Judd Estate Gisborne Gewürztraminer   ★★★☆

Estate-grown, the 2007 vintage (★★★) is a medium-dry style (8 grams/litre of residual sugar) with good but not great depth of lemony, appley, gently spicy flavour. It lacks real richness, but is still very fresh and lively.

MED/DRY $20 AV

Misha's Vineyard The Gallery Central Otago Gewürztraminer   (★★★★☆)

The debut 2008 vintage (★★★★☆) was hand-picked at Bendigo at over 26 brix and mostly handled in tanks, but 14 per cent was fermented with indigenous yeasts in seasoned oak casks. It's a mouthfilling (14.4 per cent alcohol), medium-dry style (14 grams/litre of residual sugar) with strong, spicy flavours, showing good delicacy, a touch of complexity and a deliciously soft texture.

MED/DRY $26 AV

Mission Hawke's Bay Gewürztraminer   ★★★☆

Typically good value. The 2009 vintage (★★★☆) is a fruity, medium-dry style (14 grams/litre of residual sugar), with ripe lychee and spice aromas and flavours, gentle acidity and a slightly oily texture. It's enjoyable from the start.

MED/DRY $16 V+

Moana Park Vineyard Tribute Taché Gewürztraminer   (★★★☆)

The faintly pink 2008 vintage (★★★☆) is a powerful wine with strong, peachy, slightly gingery and spicy flavours, fresh and vibrant. Fully dry, it shows good body (14 per cent alcohol) and depth.

Vintage   08
WR   6
Drink   09-12

DRY $20 AV

Montana 'P' Patutahi Gisborne Gewürztraminer   ★★★★

Full of character, at its best this is a mouthfilling wine with a musky perfume and intense pepper and lychees-like flavours, delicate and lush. Grown mostly hard against the hills inland from the city of Gisborne, at Patutahi, supplemented by fruit from Riverpoint Estate, the 2007 vintage

(★★★★) was hand-picked at 24.8 brix and stop-fermented in a medium style (17 grams/litre of residual sugar). It's a soft, rich wine with abundant sweetness and strong pear, lychee and spice flavours, showing good delicacy and texture.

MED $36 –V

Montana Reserve Gisborne Gewürztraminer   ★★★☆

The 2008 (★★★) was lees-aged for several months. Fresh, with citrus fruit and lychee flavours, slightly spicy and gingery, it's an easy-drinking, dryish wine with good depth, but lacks the richness of a top vintage.

MED/DRY $24 –V

Montana Terroir Series McLoughlin Block Gewürztraminer   ★★★☆

Grown at Patutahi, further from the sea and cooler at night than Riverpoint (see below), the 2007 vintage (★★★☆) has a perfumed, spicy bouquet leading into a finely balanced Gisborne wine with very good depth of citrusy, spicy flavours, ripe and gently sweet.

Vintage	07	06	05
WR	7	6	6
Drink	P	P	P

MED/DRY $24 –V

Montana Terroir Series Riverpoint Gewürztraminer   ★★★★☆

Grown on the same site (now owned by Pernod Ricard NZ) as Denis Irwin's original Matawhero Gewürztraminers of the 1970s, the finely textured 2007 vintage (★★★★☆) is a richer Gisborne wine than its McLoughlin Block stablemate (above). Perfumed and ripe, it has lush, concentrated lychee, apricot and spice flavours, a splash of sweetness and a soft finish. Delicious now.

Vintage	07
WR	7
Drink	P

MED/DRY $25 AV

Morton Estate White Label Hawke's Bay Gewürztraminer   ★★★☆

The 2009 vintage (★★★☆) is a powerful wine (14.5 per cent alcohol), ripely perfumed, with strong pear, lychee, ginger and spice flavours, already quite open and expressive.

Vintage	09
WR	7
Drink	09-11

MED/DRY $19 AV

Mystery Creek Gewürztraminer   (★★★☆)

The 2007 vintage (★★★☆), labelled as a 'galloping good Gisborne Gewürztraminer', was hand-picked, fermented with indigenous yeasts and made in a medium-dry style (13 grams/litre of residual sugar). It's a full-bodied wine with fresh, crisp acidity and citrusy, spicy, gingery flavours showing very good depth.

Vintage	07
WR	5
Drink	09-11

MED/DRY $20 AV

Ohinemuri Estate Matawhero Gewürztraminer   ★★★☆

The 2008 vintage (★★★☆) was grown in Gisborne and mostly fermented in tanks, but 20 per cent of the blend was barrel-fermented. It's a medium style (18 grams/litre of residual sugar), with mouthfilling body and strong, peachy, spicy, slightly gingery flavours. Ready.

Vintage	08	07	06		MED $23 –V
WR	6	7	6
Drink	09-11	09-11	P

Olssen's Central Otago Gewürztraminer   ★★★

Estate-grown at Bannockburn, the 2008 vintage (★★☆) is an easy-drinking, medium-dry wine (6 grams/litre of residual sugar), partly barrel-fermented (15 per cent), with good body, restrained, citrusy, appley, gently spicy flavours and a rounded finish.

MED/DRY $24 –V

Omihi Road Waipara Gewürztraminer   ★★★★

The generous 2008 vintage (★★★★) from Torlesse is exotically perfumed, with mouthfilling body, an oily texture and strong, slightly sweet flavours of citrus fruits, lychees and spices, ripe and smooth. With bottle-age, it's opening out well.

Vintage	08		MED/DRY $24 AV
WR	6
Drink	09-12

Passage Rock Gisborne Gewürztraminer   (★★★)

The 2008 vintage (★★★) from this small, Waiheke Island-based producer has an attractively perfumed bouquet. It's a medium-bodied, gently sweet wine with lychee, spice and ginger flavours, balanced for easy drinking.

MED $20 –V

Pyramid Valley Growers Collection Orton Vineyard Hawke's Bay Gewürztraminer   (★★★★★)

From 30-year-old vines, since uprooted, the 2007 vintage (★★★★★) was hand-picked, fermented with indigenous yeasts in French oak puncheons (20 per cent new), and bottled unfined and unfiltered. Light gold, it's a striking wine, full-bodied (14.5 per cent alcohol), with an intensely spicy perfume and flavours. Very powerful and concentrated, with a rounded, dry finish (1.7 grams/litre of residual sugar), it's drinking superbly now.

DRY $39 AV

Ra Nui Wairau Valley Marlborough Gewürztraminer   ★★★★

The 2009 vintage (★★★★) is a distinctive, dry style. Hand-picked in the Cob Cottage Vineyard, it is attractively perfumed and fleshy, with ripe lychee and spice flavours, showing good harmony and concentration.

DRY $21 V+

Revington Vineyard Gisborne Gewürztraminer   ★★★★

The Revington Vineyard in Gisborne's Ormond Valley yields a rare wine that has ranked among the country's finest Gewürztraminers. Full of personality, the 2007 vintage (★★★★☆) has a scented, gingery bouquet, showing good complexity. Delicious now, it is mouthfilling (14 per cent alcohol), with concentrated, spicy, gingery flavours, a hint of honey, and a slightly sweet (16 grams/litre of residual sugar) finish.

Vintage	07
WR	7
Drink	09-14

MED $30 –V

River Farm Godfrey Road Marlborough Gewürztraminer   (★★★★☆)

Full of interest, the 2009 vintage (★★★★☆) was hand-picked at 24.5 brix, partly fermented with indigenous yeasts in seasoned French oak casks, and made in a fully dry style. Mouthfilling (14.5 per cent alcohol), it is fleshy and ripe, with strong citrus fruit, lychee and spice flavours, showing a touch of complexity, and excellent harmony.

DRY $25 AV

Rockburn Central Otago Gewürztraminer   ★★★

The bone-dry 2008 vintage (★★★) was grown at Parkburn, in the Cromwell Basin, and fermented and lees-aged in tanks. It's a sturdy wine (14.4 per cent alcohol) with a perfumed, musky bouquet, ripe lychee and spice flavours and a fully dry finish.

Vintage	08
WR	5
Drink	09-11

DRY $24 –V

Saint Clair Pioneer Block 12 Lone Gum Gewürztraminer   ★★★★

Grown in a warm site in Marlborough's lower Omaka Valley, the 2008 vintage (★★★★) was late-harvested and made in a medium-dry (13.8 grams/litre of residual sugar) style. Softly seductive, it is perfumed and full-bodied, with rich, ripe lychee and spice flavours and a well-rounded finish.

Vintage	08	07
WR	6	6
Drink	09-12	09-12

MED/DRY $23 AV

Saint Clair Reserve Godfrey's Creek Gewürztraminer   ★★★☆

Grown in the Godfrey's Creek Vineyard, in the Brancott Valley, the 2008 vintage (★★★☆) is a distinctly medium style (28 grams/litre of residual sugar), harvested from first-crop vines. Rich and soft, it's a gently perfumed wine with ripe peach, lychee and spice flavours, gentle acidity and drink-young appeal.

Vintage	08
WR	6
Drink	09-11

MED $27 –V

Saints Gisborne Gewürztraminer   ★★★☆

Grown at Patutahi, at its best Pernod Ricard NZ's wine is rich and flavour-packed. Already drinking well, the 2008 vintage (★★★☆) is mouthfilling, with plenty of spicy, gingery flavour and a smooth finish.

MED/DRY $20 AV

Sanctuary Marlborough Gewürztraminer   (★★☆)

From Grove Mill, the debut 2008 vintage (★★☆) is a medium-bodied style with solid depth of lemon, lychee and slight apple flavours. Fresh and smooth, it lacks intensity, but is a well-balanced, easy-drinking style (10 grams/litre of residual sugar).

Vintage	08
WR	7
Drink	09-10

MED/DRY $17 –V

Seifried Nelson Gewürztraminer   ★★★★

Typically a floral, well-spiced wine, of excellent quality. The 2009 vintage (★★★☆) is aromatic and gently sweet (16 grams/litre of residual sugar), in a medium-bodied style (12.5 per cent alcohol) with fresh, crisp lychee and spice flavours, balanced for easy drinking.

Vintage	09
WR	6
Drink	09-13

MED $21 V+

Seifried Winemaker's Collection Nelson Gewürztraminer   ★★★★☆

This is typically a rich wine with loads of character. Based on the oldest vines in the company's Redwood Valley Vineyard, the 2009 vintage (★★★★) is exotically perfumed, with a splash of sweetness (11 grams/litre of residual sugar) amid its soft lychee and apricot flavours, which show excellent delicacy and depth.

Vintage	09	08	07	06
WR	6	6	6	7
Drink	09-14	09-12	09-10	P

MED/DRY $23 V+

Selaks The Favourite Marlborough Gewürztraminer   (★★★★)

The 2007 vintage from Constellation NZ is a single-vineyard wine, made in a basically dry style (4 grams/litre of residual sugar). Perfumed and mouthfilling, with ripe, citrusy, spicy, slightly gingery flavours, showing a touch of complexity, it's intensely varietal, with impressive richness and a smooth finish. Delicious now.

DRY $21 V+

Seresin Marlborough Gewürztraminer   ★★★☆

This wine is hand-picked in the Raupo Creek Vineyard, in the Omaka Valley. The 2008 vintage (★★★☆) is a medium-dry style (7 grams/litre of residual sugar), partly fermented in old French oak barriques. A mouthfilling wine with a touch of complexity, it is fleshy and ripe, with peachy, spicy flavours, showing very good depth.

MED/DRY $27 –V

Shaky Bridge Central Otago Gewürztraminer   ★★★

Grown at Alexandra, the 2008 vintage (★★☆) was hand-picked in the Pioneer Vineyard. It's a pleasant, medium-dry style (6 grams/litre of residual sugar) with solid depth of lychee, pear and spice flavours and a soft finish.

MED/DRY $24 –V

Shaky Bridge Pioneer Series Central Otago Gewürztraminer   (★★★)

The 2008 vintage (★★★) was estate-grown in the Alexandra Basin and hand-picked. Made in a slightly sweeter style (11 grams/litre of residual sugar) than its stablemate (above), it's a perfumed, moderately concentrated wine with lychee, spice and slight ginger flavours, drinking well now.

MED/DRY $19 –V

Soljans Gisborne Gewürztraminer   ★★★

Drinking well now, the 2006 vintage (★★★☆) is a medium style (26 grams/litre of residual sugar), with good depth of lychee and spice flavours, ripe and rounded.

MED $20 –V

Spy Valley Envoy Marlborough Gewürztraminer   ★★★★☆

The 2007 vintage (★★★★), estate-grown in the lower Waihopai Valley, was hand-picked at over 25 brix, and fermented and lees-aged for seven months in large German oak ovals. Restrained in its youth but opening out now, it has soft citrus fruit, lychee, spice and orange flavours, a splash of sweetness (19 grams/litre of residual sugar), gentle acidity and good weight, complexity and texture.

Vintage	08	07	06
WR	6	6	6
Drink	10-13	09-12	09-11

MED $29 AV

Spy Valley Marlborough Gewürztraminer   ★★★★☆

Estate-grown in the Waihopai Valley, this wine consistently offers great value. The 2008 vintage (★★★★☆) was harvested at 22.6 to 24.9 brix and partly fermented in seasoned oak barrels. It's a full-bodied wine with soft, slightly sweet (10 grams/litre of residual sugar) pear, citrus fruit and spice flavours, a hint of ginger, and excellent depth, varietal character and harmony.

Vintage	09	08	07	06
WR	7	6	6	6
Drink	10-12	09-11	09-10	P

MED/DRY $20 V+

Stafford Lane Nelson Gewürztraminer   (★★☆)

The 2009 vintage (★★☆) is a medium-bodied wine, fresh, crisp and lively, with decent depth of lemon, apple and spice flavours and an off-dry (6.7 grams/litre of residual sugar) finish.

MED/DRY $19 –V

Stone Bridge Gisborne Gewürztraminer   ★★★

The 2007 vintage (★★★) was harvested at 24 brix and stop-fermented with 11 grams/litre of residual sugar, creating a slightly sweet style. It's a medium-bodied wine with clear-cut varietal character and plenty of fresh, gently spicy flavour.

DRY $23 –V

Stonecroft Hawke's Bay Gewürztraminer   ★★★★★

The outstanding 2008 vintage (★★★★★) was hand-picked from 15 and 25-year-old vines, which due to frost only yielded a tiny crop of grapes (1 tonne/hectare). It's a beautifully perfumed, rich wine with very ripe lychee, pear and spice flavours, showing lovely delicacy, depth and roundness. An intensely varietal wine, still youthful, it should flourish with cellaring. (Tasted in early 2009, the deep gold 1988 Late Harvest was still giving pleasure, with concentrated, apricot-like flavours, and the 1996 and 2000 are both in superb condition.)

Vintage	08	07	06
WR	7	7	6
Drink	09-20	09-15	09-15

MED/DRY $45 AV

Stonecroft Old Vine Gewürztraminer   ★★★★★

The Gewürztraminers from this tiny Hawke's Bay winery are striking and among the finest in the country. This 'Old Vine' wine, introduced from the 2004 vintage, is made entirely from grapes hand-picked from the original Mere Road plantings in 1983. The 2007 vintage (★★★★☆), handled entirely in tanks, is concentrated and soft, with good complexity of lychee, pear and spice flavours, gentle acidity and a slightly sweet (7 grams/litre of residual sugar) finish. Weighty, finely textured and rich, it's well worth cellaring.

Vintage	07	06	05
WR	6	6	6
Drink	10-20	09-20	09-15

MED/DRY $40 AV

Summerhouse Marlborough Gewürztraminer   (★★★☆)

The debut 2009 vintage (★★★☆) looked promising in its infancy. A single-vineyard wine, it is weighty (14.5 per cent alcohol), with ripe pear, lychee and spice flavours showing good delicacy and depth, and an off-dry finish.

DRY $27 –V

Te Kairanga Six Sons Gisborne Gewürztraminer   (★★★★)

The debut 2008 vintage (★★★★) is ripely scented, with mouthfilling body and fresh, finely balanced lychee and spice flavours. It's a medium-dry style (12 grams/litre of residual sugar), with excellent depth.

Vintage	08
WR	6
Drink	09-12

MED/DRY $22 AV

Te Whare Ra Marlborough Gewürztraminer   ★★★☆

This was once an arrestingly powerful, hedonistic wine that crammed more flavour into the glass than most other Gewürztraminers from the region, but the latest releases are less magical. The 2007 vintage (★★★) was harvested at 25.5 brix from '14 rows in the old block which were planted in 1979 and are some of the oldest vines in Marlborough'. Restrained in its youth, it has delicate, appley aromas and flavours, and plentiful sweetness (22 grams/litre of residual sugar). Give it time.

MED $32 –V

Three Miners Earnscleugh Gewürztraminer   ★★★

Grown in Central Otago, the 2007 vintage (★★★☆) was handled entirely in tanks. It's an easy-drinking wine with a splash of sweetness (22 grams/litre of residual sugar) and soft, spicy, slightly appley flavours, building up well with age. (The 2008 is a markedly drier style, with 5 grams/litre of residual sugar.)

Vintage	08
WR	5
Drink	09-12

MED $21 –V

Torlesse Waipara Gewürztraminer   ★★★★

The 2008 vintage (★★★★) is a perfumed, gently sweet (18 grams/litre of residual sugar) wine with excellent body, texture and richness of lychee, pear and spice flavours. The 2009 (★★★★) is also fresh and lively, in an intensely varietal style with spicy, concentrated flavours.

MED $20 V+

Villa Maria Cellar Selection East Coast Gewürztraminer   ★★★★☆

The 2007 vintage (★★★★★) is an exotically perfumed beauty, blended from Auckland, Gisborne, Hawke's Bay and Marlborough grapes, and lees-aged for five months. Softly mouthfilling (14.5 per cent alcohol), with lush, rich flavours of lychees, spices and ginger, it is musky, weighty, oily and concentrated, with an off-dry (13 grams/litre of residual sugar), long finish.

Vintage	07	06
WR	7	7
Drink	09-11	P

MED/DRY $24 V+

Villa Maria Private Bin East Coast Gewürztraminer   ★★★★

This deservedly popular wine is a vibrantly fruity, well-spiced, medium-dry style, bargain-priced. The 2009 vintage (★★★★) has a perfumed, intensely varietal bouquet of lychees and spices. Weighty and rounded, it has excellent body and depth of fresh lychee, pear and spice flavours, dryish (7.5 grams/litre of residual sugar) and lingering.

Vintage	09	08	07
WR	6	6	6
Drink	09-12	09-11	09-10

MED/DRY $19 V+

Villa Maria Reserve Gewürztraminer   ★★★★☆

The 2007 vintage (★★★★★) is a strikingly rich blend of Gisborne (Katoa Vineyard) and Marlborough (Waihopai Valley) grapes. It has soaring, musky scents, with lovely delicacy and intensity of fresh, soft lychee, Turkish delight and spice flavours.

MED/DRY $29 AV

Villa Maria Single Vineyard Ihumatao Gewürztraminer   ★★★★★

The 2008 vintage (★★★★☆) is an exotically perfumed, estate-grown wine from Mangere, in South Auckland, mostly handled in tanks, but 15 per cent of the blend was fermented with indigenous yeasts in seasoned French oak barriques. The bouquet is musky, with fresh, ripe, slightly sweet (8.5 grams/litre of residual sugar) flavours, showing excellent ripeness, delicacy and cellaring potential.

Vintage	08
WR	6
Drink	09-13

MED/DRY $31 AV

Vinoptima Ormond Reserve Gewürztraminer   ★★★★★

Launched from 2003, this memorable wine flows from Nick Nobilo's vineyard at Ormond, in
Gisborne, devoted exclusively to Gewürztraminer, and is partly fermented in large, 1200-litre
German oak ovals. The lovely 2006 vintage (★★★★★) is mouthfilling and rich, with notable
delicacy, spiciness, concentration and harmony. The 2004 (★★★★★) is the other outstanding
vintage to date.

Vintage	06	05	04	03
WR	6	5	7	5
Drink	09-17	09-12	09-12	09-10

MED $55 –V

Waimea Nelson Gewürztraminer   ★★★★

Estate-grown on the Waimea Plains, the 2008 vintage (★★★★) was hand-picked at 23–26
brix. It's a full-bodied (14.5 per cent alcohol) wine, exotically perfumed, with fresh acidity, rich,
well-spiced, slightly gingery flavours, showing some complexity, and an off-dry (6.3 grams/litre
of residual sugar), smooth finish.

Vintage	08
WR	6
Drink	09-11

MED/DRY $22 AV

Waipara Springs Premo Gewürztraminer   (★★★★)

The 2008 vintage (★★★★) is a medium style, full-bodied and finely textured, with peachy,
spicy flavours, showing a touch of complexity, lively acidity and impressive intensity.

MED $24 AV

Wairau River Marlborough Gewürztraminer   ★★★☆

The 2009 vintage (★★★★) is a medium style (15 grams/litre of residual sugar), 10 per cent oak-
aged. Ripely scented, it has good weight and texture, with rich lychee, pear, apricot and spice
flavours, showing excellent delicacy, roundness and depth. Delicious from the start.

Vintage	09	08
WR	6	5
Drink	09-12	P

MED $23 –V

Whitehaven Marlborough Gewürztraminer   ★★★★

The 2009 vintage (★★★★) is mouthfilling and soft, with indigenous yeast fermentation in old
barriques for part of the blend adding a touch of complexity. Already delicious, it has strong
lychee, spice and slight ginger flavours, fresh and ripe, in an off-dry style (9 grams/litre of
residual sugar) with lovely texture.

Vintage	08
WR	5
Drink	09-12

MED/DRY $23 AV

Yealands Estate Marlborough Gewürztraminer   ★★★★

Estate-grown in the Awatere Valley, the 2008 vintage (★★★★) is a richly varietal wine with a
perfumed, spicy, slightly gingery bouquet. It's a slightly off-dry style with fresh, strong stone-fruit
and spice flavours. The 2009 (★★★★) is similar – intensely varietal, very fresh and vibrant, with
slightly sweet (8 grams/litre of residual sugar) flavours of lychees and spices, showing good intensity.

MED/DRY $24 AV

Grüner Veltliner

Dubbed 'Gru Vee' by its fast-expanding fan clubs in the UK and US, Grüner Veltliner is Austria's flagship white-wine variety. Its vibrantly fruity, spicy dry wines are enjoyable in their youth, but top examples mature well for several years. Interest is starting to stir here, but according to the New Zealand Vineyard Survey 2008, only 1 hectare of Grüner Veltliner will be bearing in 2010.

Coopers Creek SV The Groover Gisborne Grüner Veltliner   (★★★☆)

The 2008 vintage (★★★☆), New Zealand's first Grüner Veltliner, is a rare beast – only 840 bottles were produced. A medium-bodied style with a gently floral bouquet, hinting at nuts and spices, it has very good depth of ripe, citrusy, peachy, slightly spicy flavours and a dryish finish.

MED/DRY $21 AV

Müller-Thurgau

Not long ago New Zealand's most commonly planted variety by far, Müller-Thurgau is now an endangered species.

Most likely a crossing of Riesling and Sylvaner, Müller-Thurgau became extremely popular in Germany after the Second World War, when it was prized for its ability to ripen early with bumper crops. In New Zealand, plantings started to snowball in the early 1970s, and by 1975 it was our most widely planted variety. Today, however, there are only 78 hectares of bearing vines – down from 1873 hectares in 1983. Two-thirds of the vines are clustered in Gisborne.

Müller-Thurgau should be drunk young, at six to 18 months old, when its garden-fresh aromas are in full flower. To attract those who are new to wine, it is typically made slightly sweet. Its fruity, citrusy flavours are typically mild and soft, lacking the crisp acidity and flavour intensity of Riesling.

Corbans White Label Müller-Thurgau   ★★★

This cheap, easy-drinking wine from Pernod Ricard NZ is typically smooth and lemon-scented, with gentle sweetness balanced by moderate acidity in a light-bodied style with greater character and depth than most Müller-Thurgaus of the past. The 2008 vintage (★★★) is light (10.5 per cent alcohol) and lively, with citrusy, limey flavours, showing good depth and harmony.

MED $9 V+

Jackman Ridge Müller-Thurgau   ★★

The non-vintage wine (★★) from Pernod Ricard NZ on sale in 2009 harbours 12 per cent alcohol, making it a slightly fuller-bodied style than its stablemate (above). The bouquet is restrained; the palate is plain, lemony and slightly appley, with a gently sweet, smooth finish.

MED $7 AV

Muscat

Muscat vines grow all over the Mediterranean, but Muscat is rarely seen in New Zealand as a varietal wine, because it ripens late in the season, without the lushness and intensity achieved in warmer regions. Of New Zealand's 125 hectares of bearing Muscat vines in 2009, 99 hectares were clustered in Gisborne. Most of the grapes are used to add a musky, aromatic richness to low-priced sparkling wines, modelled on the Muscat-based Asti Spumantes of northern Italy.

Millton Te Arai Vineyard Muskats @ Dawn ★★★

Modelled on Moscato d'Asti, the 2008 vintage (★★★) of this Gisborne wine was handled entirely in stainless steel tanks and stop-fermented with low alcohol (9.3 per cent) and plentiful sweetness (40 grams/litre of residual sugar). Perfumed, Muscat aromas lead into a fresh, light wine with lemony, appley, lively flavours, showing good delicacy and liveliness. Easy, summer sipping.

Vintage	08
WR	7
Drink	P

MED $28 –V

Pinot Blanc

If you love Chardonnay, try Pinot Blanc. A white mutation of Pinot Noir, Pinot Blanc is highly regarded in Italy and California for its generous extract and moderate acidity, although in Alsace and Germany, the more aromatic Pinot Gris finds greater favour.

With its fullness of weight and restrained, appley aroma, Pinot Blanc can easily be mistaken for Chardonnay in a blind tasting. The variety is still rare in New Zealand, but between 2004 and 2009 the area of bearing vines expanded from 12 to 17 hectares, mostly in Canterbury and Central Otago.

Bentwood Pinot Blanc ★★★

Grown at Tai Tapu, south of Christchurch, in Canterbury, the 2007 vintage (★★★) was harvested at 23.5 brix and partly barrel-fermented. Slightly honeyed on the nose, it is mouthfilling, with strong, peachy flavours, showing a hint of oak and a distinct touch of botrytis.

MED/DRY $24 –V

Bracken's Order Central Otago Pinot Blanc (★★★★)

The 2008 vintage (★★★★) was grown at Gibbston and mostly handled in tanks, but 30 per cent of the blend was fermented in new French oak casks. Fleshy, with some complexity, it is scented and lively, with citrusy, slightly spicy flavours, a sliver of sweetness and good acid spine. Drink 2009–10.

MED/DRY $20 V+

Clayridge Marlborough Pinot Blanc ★★★★

The 2008 vintage (★★★★), 30 per cent fermented with indigenous yeasts in seasoned French oak barriques, is a basically dry style (4.5 grams/litre of residual sugar), with mouthfilling body and fresh peach, pear and slightly spicy flavours, showing a touch of complexity and good concentration.

Vintage	08
WR	6
Drink	09-10

DRY $24 AV

Gibbston Valley Central Otago Pinot Blanc ★★★☆

The 2008 vintage (★★★☆) was estate-grown at Bendigo, fermented – 50 per cent with indigenous yeasts – in old French oak casks, and lees-aged for nine months. It's a mouthfilling, rather Chardonnay-like wine, youthful, peachy and dry, with good acid spine and aging potential.

Vintage	08
WR	7
Drink	10-12

DRY $27 –V

Greenhough Hope Vineyard Pinot Blanc ★★★★☆

From vines planted at Hope, in Nelson, in the late 1970s, the impressive 2008 vintage (★★★★☆) was harvested at 25 brix, fermented in seasoned French oak barriques and produced in a dry style (2.9 grams/litre of residual sugar). It's a highly concentrated, slightly Chardonnay-like wine, sturdy (14 per cent alcohol), with rich stone-fruit and spice flavours, finely integrated oak, good complexity and a long finish. Drink now or cellar.

Vintage	08	07	06	05	04
WR	7	7	6	NM	6
Drink	09-13	09-12	09-12	NM	09-10

DRY $29 AV

Pyramid Valley Vineyards Growers Collection Kerner Estate Vineyard Marlborough Pinot Blanc ★★★★

Grown in the Waihopai Valley, the 2007 vintage (★★★☆) was hand-picked, fermented with indigenous yeasts in old French barrels, and bottled unfined and unfiltered. Pale gold, it is fleshy and smooth, with ripe, peachy, slightly spicy flavours, showing very good depth and complexity, and a dry finish. Ready.

DRY $30 –V

Pinot Gris

Pinot Gris has soared in popularity in recent years, making this one of the fastest-growing sections of the *Buyer's Guide*. The wines are also starting to carve out an international reputation. Over 226,000 cases were exported in the year to mid-2009 – nearly 17 times the volume shipped five years ago.

At *Winestate* magazine's 2008 Wine of the Year Awards in Adelaide, the trophy for champion Pinot Gris was awarded to Greystone Waipara Pinot Gris 2007. Also among the top five Pinot Gris of the year were wines from Hawke's Bay (Sileni Cellar Selection 2008), Central Otago (Rockburn 2007) and Marlborough (Villa Maria Single Vineyard Seddon 2007).

Spinyback Nelson Pinot Gris 2008, from Waimea Estates, won the trophy for White Single Varietal in the under £10 category at the Decanter World Wine Awards 2009, judged in London.

The variety is spreading like wildfire – from 130 hectares of bearing vines in 2000 to 1460 hectares in 2009 – and will account for 5 per cent of the national producing vineyard area in 2010. Having recently overhauled Riesling, Pinot Gris now ranks as the country's third most extensively planted white-wine variety, trailing only Sauvignon Blanc and Chardonnay.

A mutation of Pinot Noir, Pinot Gris has skin colours ranging from blue-grey to reddish-pink, sturdy extract and a fairly subtle, spicy aroma. It is not a difficult variety to cultivate, adapting well to most soils, and ripens with fairly low acidity to high sugar levels. In Alsace, the best Pinot Gris are matured in large casks, but the wood is old, so as not to interfere with the grape's subtle flavour.

What does Pinot Gris taste like? Imagine a wine that couples the satisfying weight and roundness of Chardonnay with some of the aromatic spiciness of Gewürztraminer. As a refined, full-bodied, dryish white wine – most New Zealand versions are fractionally sweet – that accompanies a wide variety of dishes well, Pinot Gris is worth getting to know.

In terms of style and quality, however, New Zealand Pinot Gris vary widely. Many of the wines lack the enticing perfume, mouthfilling body, flavour richness and softness of the benchmark wines from Alsace. These lesser wines, typically made from heavily cropped vines, are much leaner and crisper – more in the tradition of cheap Italian Pinot Grigio.

Popular in Germany, Alsace and Italy, Pinot Gris is now playing an important role here too. Over half of the country's plantings are concentrated in Marlborough (31 per cent) and Hawke's Bay (24 per cent), but there are also significant pockets of Pinot Gris in Gisborne, Otago, Canterbury, Nelson, Auckland and Wairarapa.

3 Stones New Zealand Pinot Gris (★★★)

From Ager Sectus (which also owns Crossroads, The Crossings and Southbank), the 2008 vintage (★★★) is a regional blend. Freshly scented, it's a medium-bodied wine with good depth of citrusy, slightly spicy flavour, slightly sweet and lively.

MED/DRY $20 –V

36 Bottles Central Otago Pinot Gris (★★★)

From Mt Aspiring Wines, the 2008 vintage (★★★) was grown in the Cromwell Basin and made in a medium-dry style. Fresh pear and spice aromas lead into a mouthfilling, vibrantly fruity, easy-drinking wine with good depth and a smooth finish.

MED/DRY $25 –V

12,000 Miles Wairarapa Pinot Gris (★★★)

From Gladstone Vineyard, the 2008 vintage (★★★) was grown in Dakins Road, tank-fermented and lees-aged. It's a robust wine with good depth of lychee, pear and spice flavours and a soft, dry (2.5 grams/litre of residual sugar) finish.

DRY $21 –V

Akarua Central Otago Pinot Gris   ★★★☆

Grown at Bannockburn, the 2008 vintage (★★★★) is a finely balanced wine, mostly handled in tanks, but 30 per cent was fermented in old barrels. Mouthfilling, with moderate acidity, it is vibrantly fruity, with ripe, peachy, slightly spicy flavours, showing good varietal character, and a hint of apricots.

Vintage 08
WR 6
Drink 09-11

`DRY $27 –V`

Allan Scott Marlborough Pinot Gris   ★★★

The 2008 vintage (★★★) is a medium-bodied style, with a sliver of sweetness (7 grams/litre of residual sugar). It was mostly handled in tanks, but 10 per cent was matured in old oak. Peachy and smooth, it's a softly textured wine, moderately concentrated, offering very easy drinking.

Vintage 08
WR 5
Drink 09-13

`MED/DRY $27 –V`

Amisfield Central Otago Pinot Gris   ★★★★

The 2008 vintage (★★★★) was estate-grown in the Cromwell Basin, harvested at 23.8 to 27 brix, and mostly fermented in tanks; 20 per cent was fermented with indigenous yeasts in large (600-litre) French oak casks. Richly scented, with mouthfilling body and ripe flavours of citrus fruits, lychees and spices, showing good complexity, it is fresh, crisp and vibrantly fruity, with an off-dry (6.5 grams/litre residual sugar), long finish.

Vintage	09	08	07	06
WR	5	7	5	4
Drink	11-14	10-20	09-12	09-11

`MED/DRY $35 –V`

Anchorage Nelson Pinot Gris   ★★★☆

The 2008 vintage (★★★) is medium-bodied, with lemon, lychee and spice flavours, fresh, crisp and fully dry. It's a Pinot Grigio style, maturing very soundly.

`DRY $19 AV`

Anthem Central Otago Pinot Gris   (★★★★)

Estate-grown at Gibbston, the 2007 vintage (★★★★) is still youthful in colour, with a fresh-scented bouquet. A vibrantly fruity wine with gentle sweetness and strong peach, pear and spice flavours, threaded with crisp acidity, it's balanced for easy drinking and delicious now.

`MED/DRY $20 V+`

Artisan The Far Paddock Marlborough Pinot Gris   ★★★☆

Grown at Spring Creek, the 2007 vintage (★★★☆) is basically dry (4 grams/litre of residual sugar), with a gently spicy bouquet. Mouthfilling and smooth, it has pear, spice and slight apricot flavours, in an easy-drinking style with good depth.

 `DRY $21 AV`

Ashwood Estate Gisborne Pinot Gris   (★★★★)

One of Gisborne's finest Pinot Gris to date, the 2008 vintage (★★★★) is from a partnership between grower Murray McPhail and winemaker Nick Nobilo, of Vinoptima. Pale straw, it's a weighty wine with concentrated peach and slight apricot flavours, an oily texture and a slightly sweet (8 grams/litre of residual sugar), distinctly spicy, lingering finish.

MED/DRY $25 AV

Askerne Hawke's Bay Pinot Gris   (★★★)

The 2009 vintage (★★★) was hand-picked and fermented in tanks (90 per cent) and old French oak barrels (10 per cent). Medium-bodied, it has ripe pear, spice and slight apricot flavours, showing good varietal character and freshness, and a smooth, slightly sweet (12 grams/litre of residual sugar) finish.

Vintage	09
WR	6
Drink	09-11

MED/DRY $20 –V

Astrolabe Discovery Awatere Pinot Gris   (★★★☆)

Hand-picked in the lower Awatere Valley, the 2008 vintage (★★★☆) is a full-bodied (14.5 per cent alcohol), moderately concentrated wine with fresh citrus-fruit, pear and spice flavours, showing good delicacy and purity, a slightly oily texture and a crisp, dryish (5.6 grams/litre of residual sugar) finish.

Vintage	08
WR	6
Drink	08-13

MED/DRY $24 –V

Astrolabe Voyage Marlborough Pinot Gris   (★★★)

Grown in the Waihopai and Awatere valleys, the 2008 voyage (★★★) is a mouthfilling, off-dry style (6.2 grams/litre of residual sugar) with fresh acidity and good depth of pear, lychee and spice flavours.

Vintage	08
WR	6
Drink	08-13

MED/DRY $21 –V

Ata Rangi Lismore Pinot Gris   ★★★★☆

Grown in the Lismore Vineyard in Martinborough, 400 metres from the Ata Rangi winery, the 2008 vintage (★★★★☆) is attractively scented, rich, ripe and rounded (9 grams/litre of residual sugar). Delicious from the start, it's a mouthfilling, harmonious, Alsace-style wine with concentrated stone-fruit and spice flavours and a smooth, long finish.

Vintage	08	07	06	05	04
WR	6	6	7	7	7
Drink	08-12	09-10	P	P	P

MED/DRY $28 AV

Aurora Vineyard Bendigo Pinot Gris   (★★★☆)

The fleshy, distinctive 2008 vintage (★★★☆) was estate-grown at Bendigo and 75 per cent barrel-fermented. Mouthfilling (14.5 per cent alcohol), it's a slightly Chardonnay-like wine with strong, ripe, stone-fruit flavours and creamy, leesy notes adding complexity.

DRY $28 –V

Aurum Central Otago Pinot Gris   ★★★☆

Estate-grown at Lowburn, the 2008 vintage (★★★☆) is a medium-bodied, off-dry style (7 grams/litre of residual sugar) with fresh, clearly varietal aromas and good depth of pear, lychee and spice flavours, balanced by lively acidity.

Vintage	08	07
WR	5	6
Drink	09-12	09-10

MED/DRY $23 –V

Awatere River Marlborough Pinot Gris   (★★★★)

The 2008 vintage (★★★★) is an attractively scented blend of Awatere Valley and Wairau Valley grapes, with excellent delicacy and depth. Hand-picked and partly handled in seasoned French oak barriques, it is mouthfilling, fresh, ripe and rounded, with an oily texture and pear/lychee flavours, slightly sweet and rounded. Aromatic and youthful, it shows good potential.

MED/DRY $22 V+

Babich Marlborough Pinot Gris   ★★★☆

Grown at Rapaura, on the north side of the Wairau Valley, and in the Waihopai Valley, the 2008 vintage (★★★☆) was 15 per cent fermented and lees-aged in old French oak casks; the rest was handled in tanks. It's an attractively scented wine, full-bodied, with very good depth of ripe stone-fruit and spice flavours, finely balanced acidity and a dry finish.

Vintage	08	07	06	05	04
WR	7	7	7	7	6
Drink	09-11	09-10	P	P	P

DRY $20 AV

Bald Hills Pinot Gris   ★★★

From a small block of vines at Bannockburn, in Central Otago, the 2008 vintage (★★★☆) has gently spicy aromas. Enlivened by fresh acidity, it's a dry style (3.4 grams/litre of residual sugar) with a slightly creamy texture and fresh, vibrant, citrusy, slightly appley and spicy flavours, showing good depth.

Vintage	09	07	06	05	04
WR	7	6	5	6	6
Drink	09-14	11-13	10-12	09-11	09-10

DRY $25 –V

Bensen Block Pinot Gris   (★★★)

The 2008 vintage (★★★) from Pernod Ricard NZ is not identified by region, but the grapes were grown in Gisborne. Full-bodied, it offers plenty of citrusy, slightly appley and spicy flavour, with a dryish (6.5 grams/litre of residual sugar), crisp finish.

MED/DRY $17 AV

Bilancia Hawke's Bay Pinot Gris   ★★★★

From Lorraine Leheny and Warren Gibson (winemaker at Trinity Hill), the 2008 vintage (★★★★) is a dry style (3 grams/litre of residual sugar) with a peachy, spicy bouquet, good weight (14 per cent alcohol) and strong, ripe peach, pear and spice flavours. A generous, finely textured wine, showing excellent depth and harmony, it's drinking well now.

Vintage	08
WR	6
Drink	09-14

DRY $25 AV

Bilancia Reserve Pinot Gris   ★★★★★

Grown at Haumoana, near the Hawke's Bay coast, this is a vineyard selection of grapes from the most heavily crop-thinned, later-harvested vines. The classy 2008 vintage (★★★★★) is mouthfilling (14.5 per cent alcohol), with deep stone-fruit and spice flavours, gentle acidity, a sliver of sweetness (7 grams/litre of residual sugar), a slightly oily texture and lovely harmony. It's a distinctly Alsace-style wine, for drinking now or cellaring.

Vintage	08
WR	7
Drink	10-16

MED/DRY $35 AV

Bird Marlborough Pinot Gris   ★★★☆

Very pale pink, the 2008 vintage (★★★) is a mouthfilling wine with strawberry and spice aromas, a hint of apricots, plenty of flavour and a dry (3 grams/litre of residual sugar) finish.

Vintage	08	07	06
WR	6	4	4
Drink	09-11	P	P

DRY $23 –V

Bishops Head Waipara Valley Pinot Gris   (★★★☆)

The 2008 vintage (★★★☆) is a youthful, citrusy, slightly peachy wine, medium-bodied, with very good depth of flavour, slightly sweet and crisp.

MED/DRY $20 AV

Black Barn Vineyards Single Vineyard Pinot Gris   (★★★★)

The 2008 vintage (★★★★) is a Hawke's Bay wine, hand-harvested and made with a 'subtle' oak influence. It's a mouthfilling wine (14 per cent alcohol) with good concentration of pear and spice flavours, finely integrated oak, a sliver of sweetness (5 grams/litre of residual sugar) and a touch of complexity. Drink now onwards.

Vintage	08
WR	6
Drink	09-12

MED/DRY $25 AV

Blackenbrook Vineyard Nelson Pinot Gris   ★★★★☆

The powerful 2008 vintage (★★★★☆) was estate-grown, hand-picked at over 25 brix and lees-aged in tanks. It's a weighty wine (harbouring 15 per cent alcohol), floral and very ripely scented, with concentrated peach, pear and spice flavours in a distinctly late-harvest style with apple strudel and honey notes.

Vintage	09	08	07	06	05	04
WR	6	7	7	6	6	6
Drink	09-12	09-12	09-10	09-10	P	P

MED/DRY $27 AV

Bladen Marlborough Pinot Gris   ★★★

The 2008 vintage (★★★) was hand-picked in the Bladen and Gifford vineyards. It's a fresh, aromatic wine, medium-bodied, with crisp, lively lemon, apple and spice flavours, showing good length.

MED/DRY $24 –V

Boreham Wood Single Vineyard Awatere Valley Pinot Gris   (★★★★)

Showing good personality and immediacy, the 2008 vintage (★★★★) is a mouthfilling, vibrantly fruity wine with fresh pear, lychee and spice flavours, a minerally streak and a dry (3.9 grams/litre of residual sugar), finely balanced finish.

Vintage	09	08
WR	7	6
Drink	10-14	09-12

DRY $24 AV

Bouldevines Marlborough Pinot Gris   (★★★)

Full-bodied and smooth, the 2008 vintage (★★★) is a clearly varietal wine with decent depth of pear and spice flavours, a slightly oily texture and an off-dry finish.

MED/DRY $27 –V

Boundary Vineyards Paper Lane Waipara Pinot Gris   (★★★☆)

From Pernod Ricard NZ, the 2008 vintage (★★★☆) is a mouthfilling Waipara wine with fresh, vibrant pear and spice flavours, showing clear-cut varietal characters, and a splash of sweetness (7.9 grams/litre of residual sugar) giving easy-drinking appeal.

MED/DRY $20 AV

Brick Bay Matakana Pinot Gris   ★★★☆

At its best, this wine is impressively weighty, rich and rounded. Hand-picked, lees-aged and made in an off-dry style, the 2008 vintage (★★★☆) is full-bodied and fresh, with vibrant, ripe pear, lychees and spice flavours and a smooth finish.

Vintage	08	07	06	05	04
WR	7	7	7	6	7
Drink	09-11	09-10	P	P	P

MED/DRY $29 –V

Brightside Nelson Pinot Gris   ★★★☆

From Kaimira Estate, the good-value 2008 vintage (★★★☆) is a powerful wine, sturdy (14 per cent alcohol), with strong, dryish (7.9 grams/litre of residual sugar) flavours of lychees, pears and spices.

MED/DRY $18 V+

Bronte by Rimu Grove Nelson Pinot Gris   ★★★★

In the past labelled 'Rimu Grove Bronte', this is the winery's second-tier Pinot Gris – but it's still impressive. The 2008 vintage (★★★★) was hand-picked in the Moutere Hills and mostly handled in tanks, but 18 per cent of the blend was fermented in seasoned French oak barrels. Fresh, vibrant and slightly sweet (10 grams/litre of residual sugar), it shows excellent depth and delicacy, with strong pear and spice flavours, a slightly oily texture and a well-rounded finish.

Vintage	08
WR	6
Drink	09-13

MED/DRY $24 AV

Brookfields Robertson Hawke's Bay Pinot Gris   ★★★☆

The 2009 vintage (★★★) is a slightly sweet wine (11 grams/litre of residual sugar), full-bodied, with peachy, appley, spicy flavours, in an easy-drinking style with a smooth finish.

Vintage	09	08	MED/DRY $19 AV
WR	7	7	
Drink	10-13	09-11	

Brunton Road Gisborne Pinot Gris   ★★★

A single-vineyard wine, grown at Patutahi, the 2008 vintage (★★★) is a mouthfilling, pleasantly fruity wine, citrusy, slightly appley and spicy, with a fresh, crisp, dryish (4 grams/litre of residual sugar) finish.

DRY $21 –V

Burnt Spur Martinborough Pinot Gris   ★★★★

Fleshy and rich, in the classic Alsace style, the 2008 vintage (★★★★) was estate-grown in the Burnt Spur Vineyard, hand-picked, and lees-aged in tanks. Strong pear and spice aromas lead into a mouthfilling wine with concentrated pear and spiced apple flavours and a lingering finish. It's a youthful, tightly structured wine, with cellaring potential.

Vintage	08	07	MED/DRY $27 –V
WR	7	7	
Drink	09-13	09-12	

Butterfish Bay Northland Pinot Gris   (★★★☆)

The debut 2009 vintage (★★★☆) from winemaker Mark Rattray was hand-harvested on Paewhenua Island, a peninsula reaching into Mangonui Harbour. Enjoyable from the start, it's a medium to full-bodied wine, freshly aromatic, with good depth of ripe peach, pear and lychee flavours, a sliver of sweetness (9 grams/litre of residual sugar) and a well-rounded finish.

Vintage	09	MED/DRY $28 –V
WR	6	
Drink	09-11	

Camshorn Waipara Pinot Gris   ★★★★

Grown in Pernod Ricard NZ's hillside vineyard in North Canterbury, the easy-drinking 2008 vintage (★★★★) is an enticingly scented wine, oily and rich, with strongly varietal pear, lychee and spice flavours, pure, gently sweet and smooth. Tasted prior to bottling (and so not rated), the 2009 was fresh-scented, with strong, vibrant pear/spice flavours and a crisp, lingering finish.

Vintage	08	07	MED/DRY $27 –V
WR	5	5	
Drink	P	P	

Cape Campbell Marlborough Pinot Gris   ★★★☆

The 2008 vintage (★★★☆) is fresh and lively, with a floral bouquet, medium body and slightly sweet, pear and spice flavours that linger well.

Vintage	08	07	06
WR	6	7	6
Drink	09-11	09-10	P

MED/DRY $19 AV

Carrick Central Otago Pinot Gris ★★★★

The 2008 vintage (★★★★) was grown at Bannockburn and 20 per cent fermented in very old casks; the rest was handled in tanks. It's a mouthfilling wine (13.5 per cent alcohol), with a hint of sweetness (7 grams/litre of residual sugar) amid its concentrated stone-fruit and spice flavours, which show excellent ripeness and depth. Drink now or cellar.

MED/DRY $25 AV

Castaway Bay Marlborough Pinot Gris (★★☆)

From Maven, the 2008 vintage (★★☆) was hand-harvested in the Wairau and Omaka valleys, and part of the blend was fermented with indigenous yeasts in seasoned French oak barriques. It's a medium-bodied wine, slightly sweet, with moderate depth of flavour, a slightly creamy texture and a soft finish.

MED/DRY $15 AV

Catalina Sounds Marlborough Pinot Gris (★★★)

The debut 2007 vintage (★★★) is pale pink, with good depth of lychee, pear and spice flavours, a distinct hint of apricot, and a dryish (6.7 grams/litre of residual sugar), crisp finish.

MED/DRY $25 –V

Chard Farm Central Otago Pinot Gris ★★★★

Hand-picked in Cromwell vineyards, the 2008 vintage (★★★★) is a seductive, easy-drinking wine with slightly sweet flavours of peaches, pears and lychees, showing excellent ripeness and depth. Smooth, with a slightly oily texture, it's a great drink-young style, with some cellaring potential.

MED/DRY $28 –V

Charles Wiffen Marlborough Pinot Gris (★★★★)

The 2008 vintage (★★★★) is an auspicious debut. Estate-grown and made in an off-dry style (7 grams/litre of residual sugar), it's an intensely varietal wine, floral and full-bodied, with fresh pear, spice and lychee flavours showing excellent delicacy and depth.

MED/DRY $23 AV

Church Road Cuve Hawke's Bay Pinot Gris ★★★☆

Grown 300 metres above sea level in Pernod Ricard NZ's cool, inland site at Matapiro, the debut 2007 vintage (★★★★) was harvested at 23.8 to 24.5 brix and lees-aged for 10 months. Fleshy and soft, it is concentrated, peachy and slightly spicy, with gentle sweetness (7 grams/litre of residual sugar) and good texture. The very forward 2008 (★★★) is richly scented but slightly flabby, with strong, peachy, spicy flavours and a slightly sweet, soft finish.

MED/DRY $27 –V

Church Road Hawke's Bay Pinot Gris   ★★★☆

Grown mostly at Pernod Ricard NZ's cool, elevated, inland site at Matapiro, this wine is mostly lees-aged in tanks; a small portion is fermented in seasoned French oak barrels. The 2008 vintage (★★★★) is elegant, with good weight, concentrated stone-fruit flavours, a slightly oily texture and a rich, dryish finish.

DRY $26 –V

Clayridge Marlborough Pinot Gris   ★★★★☆

The 2008 vintage (★★★★☆) was grown at two sites and part of the blend was fermented with indigenous yeasts and lees-aged in seasoned French oak barriques. Scented and mouthfilling, it's a dryish wine (5.8 grams/litre of residual sugar) with stone-fruit and spice flavours, faintly honeyed and rich.

Vintage	08	07
WR	7	7
Drink	09-12	09-12

MED/DRY $24 V+

Clearwater Vineyards Waipara Pinot Gris   (★★★)

From Sherwood, the non-vintage bottling (★★★) on sale in 2009 is a blend of 2006 and 2007 wines. Gently sweet and full-bodied (14 per cent alcohol), it has citrusy, slightly honeyed aromas and flavours.

MED/DRY $20 –V

Cloudy Bay Marlborough Pinot Gris   (★★★★)

The 2008 vintage (★★★★) was handled in a mix of tanks (30 per cent) and seasoned French oak barrels (70 per cent). Mouthfilling and smooth, with pear, spice and lychee aromas and flavours, it's a moderately concentrated wine, off-dry (5.3 grams/litre of residual sugar) with a touch of complexity, good texture and length.

MED/DRY $35 –V

Coney Piccolo Martinborough Pinot Gris   (★★★★☆)

An excellent debut, the 2008 vintage (★★★★☆) is fleshy, mouthfilling and rich. A dryish, well-rounded and strongly varietal wine, it has concentrated, ripe lychee, pear and spice flavours, hints of apricots, and a slightly oily texture. Drink now onwards.

MED/DRY $22 V+

Coopers Creek New Zealand Pinot Gris   ★★★

The early releases were estate-grown at Huapai, in West Auckland, then Gisborne grapes were added, and the 2008 vintage (★★★) also includes Marlborough fruit. It's an easy-drinking, medium to full-bodied wine with decent depth of citrus-fruit, pear and spice flavours, slightly sweet, fresh and crisp.

Vintage	08	07	06
WR	6	7	6
Drink	09-10	P	P

MED/DRY $18 AV

Corbans Homestead Gisborne Pinot Gris   ★★★

The 2008 vintage (★★★) from Pernod Ricard NZ was lees-aged for four months in tanks and stop-fermented in a medium-dry style. Offering very easy drinking, it's medium to full-bodied, with soft, peachy flavours, showing good depth.

MED/DRY $17 AV

Corbans Private Bin Hawke's Bay Pinot Gris   ★★★☆

The 2007 vintage (★★★☆) was picked in Pernod Ricard NZ's inland, elevated Matapiro Vineyard, and 50 per cent of the blend was fermented in seasoned French oak barriques. A mouthfilling wine with an oily texture, good depth of peach, pear and spice flavours and a dryish (8 grams/litre of residual sugar) finish, it is scented, with good vigour and a touch of complexity.

Vintage	07	06
WR	6	5
Drink	P	P

MED/DRY $24 –V

Cracroft Chase Single Vineyard Grey Pearl Canterbury Pinot Gris   ★★★

Grown in the Port Hills at Christchurch, the 2008 vintage (★★★) is a dry style, mostly handled in tanks, but 20 per cent of the blend was lees-aged in mature barrels. It's a lemony, crisp wine, with slightly funky notes, but lacks fragrance and richness.

DRY $18 AV

Craggy Range Otago Station Vineyard Waitaki Valley Pinot Gris   (★★★☆)

Likely to mature well, the 2008 vintage (★★★☆) is fresh, vibrant and mouthfilling, with lemony, slightly appley and spicy flavours, and an off-dry (7.4 grams/litre of residual sugar) finish.

Vintage	08
WR	6
Drink	09-14

MED/DRY $35 –V

Crater Rim, The, Waipara Pinot Gris   ★★★☆

The 2008 vintage (★★★☆) was fermented with indigenous yeasts and partly barrel-fermented. Light yellow, with a honeyed bouquet, it's a fleshy, peachy wine with a clear botrytis influence and good richness.

MED/DRY $28 –V

Crawford Farm New Zealand Pinot Gris   (★★★)

The 2008 vintage (★★★) from Constellation NZ is a regional blend. A medium to full-bodied style with a splash of sweetness amid its fresh, crisp lemon, apple and spice flavours, it's a smooth, easy-drinking wine with decent depth.

DRY $22 –V

Crossroads Hawke's Bay Pinot Gris   (★★☆)

The estate-grown 2008 vintage (★★☆) has solid depth of peach, pear and spice flavours. It's a fully dry style (2 grams/litre of residual sugar).

Vintage	08	
WR	6	DRY $20 –V
Drink	09-12	

Culley Marlborough Pinot Gris   (★★★)

The debut 2008 vintage (★★★) has fresh pear, spice and apricot flavours, slightly sweet and crisp. It's a clearly varietal, moderately concentrated wine, enjoyable from the start.

MED/DRY $19 AV

Cypress Hawke's Bay Pinot Gris   (★★★★)

The debut 2008 vintage (★★★★) was hand-picked and tank-fermented. Sturdy and ripe, with concentrated, stone-fruit and spice flavours, substantial body and a creamy texture, it's a good food wine, mouthfilling, dry (3 grams/litre of residual sugar) and well-rounded.

Vintage	08	
WR	6	DRY $25 AV
Drink	09-11	

Dashwood Marlborough Pinot Gris   (★★★☆)

Grown in the Awatere Valley, the fine-value 2008 vintage (★★★☆) is scented and softly mouthfilling, with vibrant pear, citrus-fruit, lychee and spice flavours, gentle sweetness (8 grams/litre of residual sugar), and very good depth.

Vintage	08	
WR	6	MED/DRY $17 V+
Drink	09-12	

Desert Heart Central Otago Pinot Gris   (★★)

Grown at Bannockburn, the 2008 vintage (★★) was matured for five months in old oak barrels. Very pale, it has light lemon, apple and pear flavours, but lacks real fragrance, ripeness and richness.

MED/DRY $25 –V

Devil's Staircase Central Otago Pinot Gris   (★★★☆)

From Rockburn, the debut 2008 vintage (★★★☆) was grown in the Cromwell Basin and at Gibbston. Full-bodied, with fresh, spicy aromas, it has fresh, slightly sweet (13 grams/litre of residual sugar) pear, lychee and spice flavours, showing good length.

Vintage	08	
WR	6	MED/DRY $20 AV
Drink	09-11	

Distant Land Marlborough Pinot Gris   ★★★☆

The 2008 vintage (★★★☆) from Lincoln was grown in the Wairau Valley and 10 per cent of the blend was fermented in old French barrels. It's a mouthfilling, ripely scented wine with soft, peachy, slightly spicy flavours, showing very good depth. The 2009 (★★★★), not oak-aged, is delicious from the start, with an attractively scented bouquet and fresh, rich nectarine and pear flavours, showing good harmony.

MED/DRY $20 AV

Drumsara Central Otago Ventifacts Block Pinot Gris   ★★★★

The 2008 vintage (★★★★), estate-grown at Alexandra, has strong personality. Hand-picked at 23.5 brix, it's a dry wine (3.9 grams/litre of residual sugar), with a scented bouquet, moderate acidity and ripe stone-fruit flavours, showing good concentration.

Vintage	09	08
WR	6	5
Drink	09-13	09-12

DRY $28 –V

Dry Gully Walkers Block Central Otago Pinot Gris   (★★★☆)

Grown at Alexandra, the 2008 vintage (★★★☆) is a fleshy, sturdy (14.5 per cent alcohol) wine, attractively scented, with fresh peach, pear, lychee and spice flavours, showing very good depth, and a dry finish.

Vintage	08
WR	5
Drink	09-12

DRY $20 AV

Dry River Pinot Gris   ★★★★★

From the first vintage in 1986, for many years Dry River towered over other New Zealand Pinot Gris, by virtue of its exceptional body, flavour richness and longevity. A sturdy Martinborough wine, it has peachy, spicy characters that can develop great subtlety and richness with maturity (at around five years old for top vintages, which also hold well for a decade). It is grown in the estate vineyard and nearby Craighall Vineyard; the majority of the vines are over 25 years old. To avoid any loss of varietal flavour, it is not oak-aged. The seamless 2008 vintage (★★★★☆) is fleshy, very harmonious and well-rounded, with ripe, peachy, citrusy flavours. Gently floral, it builds well across the palate, with a slightly oily texture, good concentration and a medium-dry (12 grams/litre of residual sugar) finish.

Vintage	08	07	06	05	04	03	02	01
WR	7	7	7	7	7	7	NM	6
Drink	10-18	10-17	09-18	09-13	09-15	09-10	NM	P

MED/DRY $50 AV

Drylands Marlborough Pinot Gris   ★★★

The 2007 vintage (★★★) was mostly grown in the Awatere Valley and made in a dryish style (5 grams/litre of residual sugar). Faintly pink, it is peachy and spicy, with fresh, lively acidity.

MED/DRY $22 –V

Edge, The, Martinborough Pinot Gris   ★★★

From Escarpment, the 2008 vintage (★★★) is crisp and lively, with vibrant citrus-fruit and pear flavours, and a sliver of sweetness balanced by appetising acidity.

MED/DRY $19 AV

Eradus Awatere Valley Marlborough Pinot Gris ★★★

Enjoyable young, the 2009 vintage (★★★☆) is a mouthfilling, rounded wine, freshly aromatic, with very good depth of peachy, slightly spicy flavours, slightly sweet (10 grams/litre of residual sugar) and balanced for easy drinking.

Vintage	09
WR	5
Drink	09-11

MED/DRY $19 AV

Escarpment Martinborough Pinot Gris ★★★★★

This distinctive, 'Burgundian inspired' Pinot Gris is fermented and matured in oak casks. The 2007 vintage (★★★★★), grown in Te Muna Road, is full-bodied (14 per cent alcohol) and richly scented, with strong, ripe flavours of stone-fruit, lychees and spice, a subtle twist of oak, and a dryish (5 grams/litre of residual sugar), long finish. Very refined and concentrated, it offers delicious drinking.

Vintage	07	06	05	04	03	02
WR	5	7	6	6	7	6
Drink	09-10	09-10	P	P	P	P

MED/DRY $29 V+

Esk Valley Hawke's Bay Pinot Gris ★★★★

The 2008 vintage (★★★★) was hand-picked at several sites, with some 'noble rot' infection, and fermented, partly with indigenous yeasts, in tanks and old, neutral oak barriques. Fleshy, with rich pear/spice flavours, showing a hint of honey, it has excellent mouthfeel, texture and depth. The 2009, tasted prior to bottling (and so not rated), is a medium-dry style, 40 per cent barrel-fermented, with mouthfilling body and rich, rounded pear/spice flavours.

Vintage	09	08	07	06	05
WR	7	6	7	6	6
Drink	09-14	09-13	09-12	09-10	09-10

MED/DRY $24 AV

Fairhall Downs Single Vineyard Marlborough Pinot Gris ★★★☆

Grown in the Brancott Valley, the 2009 vintage (★★★☆) was mostly tank-fermented; 23 per cent was handled in seasoned French oak casks. Already enjoyable, it is mouthfilling and well-rounded, with vibrant, ripe pear, lychee and spice flavours, fresh acidity and a dry, finely textured finish.

DRY $25 –V

Fiddler's Green Waipara Pinot Gris (★★★☆)

The 2008 vintage (★★★☆) was fermented with indigenous yeasts and lees-aged in tanks. It's a medium-dry style (10 grams/litre of residual sugar), softly textured, with peachy, slightly buttery flavours, offering very easy drinking.

Vintage	08
WR	6
Drink	09-12

MED/DRY $23 –V

Five Flax Pinot Gris (★★☆)

A blend of New Zealand and Australian wines, the 2008 vintage (★★☆) from Pernod Ricard NZ is a very easy-drinking style with pear, spice and slight honey flavours, smooth and ready.

MED/DRY $15 AV

Forrest Marlborough Pinot Gris   ★★★☆

The 2007 vintage (★★★☆) has lifted, strongly spicy aromas leading into a softly mouthfilling wine with a distinct splash of sweetness (17 grams/litre of residual sugar). It's a slightly Gewürztraminer-like wine with a creamy texture and peachy, well-spiced flavours. (The 2009 is significantly drier, with 7 grams/litre of residual sugar.)

Vintage	09
WR	4
Drink	09-11

MED/DRY $25 –V

Framingham Marlborough Pinot Gris   ★★★★

The 2008 vintage (★★★★) was mostly handled in tanks, but 20 per cent was fermented in a mix of old oak casks and small, stainless steel 'barrels'. Ripely scented, it's a mouthfilling wine, slightly sweet (7 grams/litre of residual sugar), with moderate acidity, an oily texture and rich stone-fruit, lychee and spice flavours.

Vintage	08	07	06	05	04
WR	6	7	6	6	6
Drink	10-12	09-11	09-10	09-10	P

MED/DRY $28 –V

Gibbston Highgate Estate Dreammaker Pinot Gris   ★★★

From a vineyard at Gibbston, in Central Otago (not associated with the Gibbston Valley winery), the 2008 vintage (★★★) was harvested at 22.7 brix and mostly handled in tanks; 20 per cent was barrel-fermented. Scented, it's a dry wine (2.3 grams/litre of residual sugar) with satisfying depth of citrusy, appley flavour.

Vintage	08	07	06
WR	5	5	7
Drink	09-12	09-10	09-12

DRY $25 –V

Gibbston Valley Central Otago Pinot Gris   ★★★☆

At its best, this wine is full of personality. The 2008 vintage (★★★★) was grown at Bendigo (95 per cent) and Gibbston, and mostly handled in tanks; 15 per cent of the blend was fermented in old oak barrels. Floral and full-bodied (14 per cent alcohol), it's an almost dry wine (4.9 grams/litre of residual sugar) with fresh pear and spice flavours, showing good texture and depth.

Vintage	08	07	06
WR	7	7	6
Drink	09-12	09-11	09-10

DRY $27 –V

Gibbston Valley La Dulcinée The Expressionist Series Pinot Gris   ★★★★★

The 2008 vintage (★★★★★) was grown in the School House Vineyard at Bendigo, in Central Otago, and handled in stainless steel 'barriques'. A medium-dry style (7 grams/litre of residual sugar), it is powerful, weighty and rounded, with highly concentrated peach, pear and spice flavours, showing excellent complexity, balanced acidity and a long finish. Drink now or cellar.

Vintage	08	07
WR	7	7
Drink	12-16	09-15

MED/DRY $45 AV

Gibson Bridge Cellar Selection Marlborough Pinot Gris   (★★☆)

The 2008 vintage (★★☆) was hand-picked and mostly handled in tanks, but a small portion of the final blend was barrel-fermented. It's an off-dry style, fresh, citrusy and slightly spicy, with mouthfilling body, but when tasted twice in late 2008, lacked harmony.

MED/DRY $29 –V

Gibson Bridge Reserve Marlborough Pinot Gris   ★★★★

Fresh and softly textured, with an easy-drinking charm, the 2008 vintage (★★★☆) is an unwooded style, attractively scented, with mouthfilling body and very good depth of pear and spice flavours.

MED/DRY $29 –V

Gladstone Vineyard Wairarapa Pinot Gris   ★★★☆

Developing well, the 2008 vintage (★★★★) was mostly fermented and lees-aged for five months in tanks, but 30 per cent of the blend was barrel-fermented. It's a fleshy wine with ripe stone-fruit and spice aromas and flavours, a slightly creamy texture, good richness and a smooth, dryish finish (4.9 grams/litre of residual sugar).

DRY $24 –V

Glasnevin Pinot Gris   ★★★★☆

From a company owned by Fiddler's Green, the 2008 vintage (★★★★☆) is a rich Waipara wine, fermented with indigenous yeasts and matured for nine months in French oak barriques (20 per cent new). It's a concentrated wine with peachy, spicy flavours showing excellent complexity, an oily texture, and a finely balanced, dry (4 grams/litre of residual sugar), well-rounded finish.

Vintage	08
WR	7
Drink	09-14

DRY $28 AV

Glazebrook Regional Reserve Hawke's Bay Pinot Gris   ★★★☆

From the Ngatarawa winery, the 2008 vintage (★★★☆) was grown at Bridge Pa, in The Triangle district, and tank-fermented to dryness. Fresh, crisp and mouthfilling, with very good depth of citrus and stone-fruit flavours and a hint of spice, in style it sits half-way between the classic Pinot Gris of Alsace and the Pinot Grigio of northern Italy.

Vintage	08	07	06
WR	5	6	6
Drink	09-11	09-10	P

DRY $22 AV

Goldridge Estate Pinot Gris   (★★☆)

Grown 'predominantly' at Matakana and partly barrel-aged, the 2008 vintage (★★☆) is a smooth, easy-drinking wine, citrusy, slightly peachy and honeyed, with moderate flavour depth.

MED/DRY $16 AV

Goldridge Estate Premium Reserve Matakana Pinot Gris   ★★★

The 2008 vintage (★★★) is a dry Matakana wine with refreshing acidity and good depth of citrusy, slightly honeyed flavour.

DRY $19 AV

Greenstone Central Otago Pinot Gris   (★★★)

From Gibbston Valley, the 2008 vintage (★★★) is a fresh, full-bodied wine, dryish, citrusy and slightly spicy, with clear-cut varietal character and decent depth.

MED/DRY $18 AV

Greystone Waipara Pinot Gris   ★★★★☆

Benchmark stuff, the 2009 vintage (★★★★★) is beautifully scented, rich and rounded. Mouthfilling, fresh and finely poised, it's a gently sweet style (15 grams/litre of residual sugar), vibrantly fruity, with excellent concentration of peach, pear and spice flavours, showing lovely richness and harmony.

Vintage	09
WR	7
Drink	09-13

MED $28 AV

Greystone Winemaker's Series Waipara Pinot Gris   (★★★★)

Powerful, with rich stone-fruit flavours, the 2008 vintage (★★★★) was fermented in a 50/50 mix of tanks and barrels and fully barrel-aged. Weighty and soft, with a slightly oily texture, it's already drinking well.

DRY $31 –V

Grove Mill Marlborough Pinot Gris   ★★★★

Grove Mill is a key pioneer of Pinot Gris in Marlborough, since 1994 producing a richly flavoured style with abundant sweetness. The 2008 vintage (★★★☆), partly French oak-fermented, is a distinctly medium style (29 grams/litre of residual sugar) with a lower level of alcohol than usual (12.5 per cent, compared to the customary 13.5 per cent). It's a scented, medium-bodied wine with very good depth of vibrant peach, pear and spice flavours, already enjoyable.

Vintage	08	07	06	05
WR	7	7	6	7
Drink	09-12	P	P	09-10

MED $24 AV

Gunn Estate Pinot Gris   ★★★

From Sacred Hill, the 2007 vintage (★★★) is a blend of Italian and New Zealand wines. Tasted in mid-2009, it's a medium-bodied style (12.5 per cent alcohol), still fresh, with distinctly citrusy, slightly appley flavours, slightly sweet and well balanced for easy drinking.

MED/DRY $17 AV

Hans Herzog Marlborough Pinot Gris   ★★★★☆

Grown on the north side the Wairau Valley, the 2008 vintage (★★★★☆) was hand-picked at 23.5 brix and mostly tank-fermented; 20 per cent of the blend was fermented and matured for 10 months in French oak puncheons. Pale yellow, with a gently spicy fragrance, it is mouthfilling, with vibrant, sweet-fruit characters, rich stone-fruit and spice flavours, a touch of oak-derived complexity and a long, dry finish. Drink now or cellar.

Vintage	08
WR	7
Drink	09-14

DRY $43 –V

Harwood Hall Marlborough Pinot Gris   (★★★★)

From winemakers Bill ('Digger') Hennessy and Corey Hall, the debut 2008 vintage (★★★★) was grown at Renwick and mostly handled in tanks; 15 per cent of the blend was barrel-fermented with indigenous yeasts. It's a scented, weighty wine with excellent texture and depth of peachy, spicy flavours and a dry finish (3 grams/litre of residual sugar). Good value.

DRY $20 V+

Hawkshead Central Otago Pinot Gris   (★★★☆)

Grown at Bendigo, the 2008 vintage (★★★☆) has an attractively scented bouquet. A vibrantly fruity, dryish wine (5 grams/litre of residual sugar), it has fresh, finely balanced pear/spice flavours, showing very satisfying purity and depth.

MED/DRY $28 –V

Hay Maker Gisborne Pinot Gris   (★★☆)

From Mud House, the 2008 vintage (★★☆) was grown at Patutahi, tank-fermented and briefly lees-aged. It's a medium-dry style (6 grams/litre of residual sugar), with a light bouquet, peachy, faintly honeyed flavours, showing solid depth, and crisper acidity than most Pinot Gris.

MED/DRY $17 –V

Huia Marlborough Pinot Gris   ★★★★

The 2008 vintage (★★★★) was grown at Wairau Valley sites and fermented in tanks (70 per cent) and old French oak casks (30 per cent). It's a dryish style (5 grams/litre of residual sugar), mouthfilling and fresh, with very good depth of ripe stone-fruit flavours, showing some complexity, and a slightly oily richness.

Vintage	08	07
WR	6	6
Drink	09-19	09-11

MED/DRY $28 –V

Huntaway Reserve Gisborne Pinot Gris   ★★★

The 2008 vintage (★★★) from Pernod Ricard NZ was blended with Gewürztraminer (6 per cent) and aged on its light yeast lees in tanks and large oak cuves. It's a medium to full-bodied style with good vigour, a sliver of sweetness (6 grams/litre of residual sugar) and pleasing depth of pear, lemon and spice flavours.

Vintage	08	07	06
WR	5	6	6
Drink	09-10	P	P

MED/DRY $23 –V

Hyperion Phoebe Matakana Pinot Gris   ★★☆

Estate-grown north of Auckland, the 2007 vintage (★★★) is mouthfilling and fleshy, with ripe lychee, citrus-fruit and pear flavours and a rounded, dryish (5 grams/litre of residual sugar) finish. It has some idiosyncratic notes, but it's a clearly varietal, characterful wine.

Vintage	07	06	05	04
WR	6	6	6	6
Drink	09-12	09-10	P	P

MED/DRY $25 –V

Isabel Marlborough Pinot Gris   ★★★☆

The 2007 vintage (★★★☆) is a very pale pink, medium-bodied style, grown in the Isabel Estate
and McGinley vineyards. It offers lots of peachy, spicy flavour, with a sliver of sweetness (7
grams/litre of residual sugar) and fresh acidity.

Vintage	09	MED/DRY $20 AV
WR	7	
Drink	09-14	

Johanneshof Marlborough Pinot Gris Medium   ★★★☆

The 2008 vintage (★★★☆) is a gently sweet style, faintly pink, mouthfilling and smooth, with
good depth of stone-fruit and spice flavours, fresh, ripe and soft.

Vintage	08	07	MED $27 –V
WR	5	7	
Drink	09-13	09-11	

Johanneshof Marlborough Pinot Gris Trocken/Dry   ★★★☆

The pale pink 2008 vintage (★★★☆) has a peachy, spicy bouquet, leading into a dryish wine
with good depth of ripe stone-fruit and spice flavours and a rounded finish.

Vintage	08	07	06	MED/DRY $27 –V
WR	4	6	5	
Drink	09-13	09-11	P	

Johner Wairarapa Pinot Gris   ★★★

Grown at Gladstone, the 2009 vintage (★★★★) is clearly the best yet. It's an elegant, rich wine,
mouthfilling, with fresh acid spine and slightly sweet, peachy, spicy flavours, showing good
concentration and harmony.

MED/DRY $22 –V

Junction Central Hawke's Bay Pinot Gris   (★★★★)

Grown on the Takapau Plains, the 2007 vintage (★★★★) is 'thoroughly drinkable any old
time', claims the back label. One of Central Hawke's Bay's finest wines yet, it's robust and fleshy
(14.5 per cent alcohol), impressively weighty and rich. Its strong peach, pear and spice flavours
show a hint of honey, leading to a slightly sweet, finely balanced finish.

MED/DRY $23 AV

Jurassic Ridge Pinot Grigio   ★★★

Grown at Church Bay, on Waiheke Island, and tank-fermented, the 2009 vintage (★★★) is a
distinctive style. Pale pink/orange, it is a medium-bodied wine (11.8 per cent alcohol), with
spicy, slightly earthy aromas and strawberryish, spicy flavours, refreshingly crisp and dry.

Vintage	09	08	DRY $29 –V
WR	7	6	
Drink	09-11	09-10	

Kaimira Estate Brightwater Pinot Gris ★★★☆

Grown in Nelson, the 2008 vintage (★★★☆) is a powerful wine, robust (14.5 per cent alcohol), with a spicy bouquet and loads of peachy, spicy flavour, dryish (5.2 grams/litre of residual sugar) and rounded. Ready.

MED/DRY $20 AV

Kaituna Valley Canterbury Summerhill Vineyard Pinot Gris ★★★☆

Grown at Tai Tapu, on Banks Peninsula, the 2008 vintage (★★★) has a slightly honeyed bouquet, with crisp, slightly sweet (10 grams/litre of residual sugar) pear, lime and spice flavours, showing good depth.

Vintage	08
WR	6
Drink	09-12

MED/DRY $24 –V

Kaituna Valley Marlborough The Awatere Vineyard Pinot Gris ★★★★

Grown in the Awatere Valley, the 2008 vintage (★★★★) is scented and mouthfilling, with good concentration of citrus-fruit, pear and spice flavours, a splash of sweetness (12 grams/litre of residual sugar) and lively acidity.

Vintage	08
WR	5
Drink	09-10

MED/DRY $24 AV

Kawarau Estate Central Otago Pinot Gris ★★★☆

Certified organic, the 2008 vintage (★★★) was hand-picked at Pisa Flats, in the Cromwell Basin, fermented with indigenous yeasts and lees-aged in tanks. It's a creamy-smooth wine with mouthfilling body, solid depth of peachy, slightly spicy flavours and a slightly off-dry (4.9 grams/litre of residual sugar) finish.

Vintage	08	07
WR	6	5
Drink	09-11	09-10

DRY $25 –V

Kim Crawford New Zealand Pinot Gris ★★★

From 'selected vineyards across New Zealand', the 2008 vintage (★★☆) from Constellation NZ is a medium to full-bodied wine with solid depth of peachy, slightly honeyed flavour, fresh acidity and a slightly sweet finish. Ready.

MED/DRY $23 –V

Kim Crawford SP Boyszone Marlborough Pinot Gris ★★★★

The 2007 vintage (★★★★) from Constellation NZ is a partly barrel-fermented wine with lychee, pear and spice flavours, showing good texture and richness, and an off-dry finish (5 grams/litre of residual sugar).

MED/DRY $33 –V

Koura Bay Sharkstooth Marlborough Pinot Gris   ★★★☆

Typically a fragrant Awatere Valley wine with good body and depth of flavour. The 2009 vintage (★★★☆) is fresh-scented, mouthfilling and vibrantly fruity, with peach, pear and spice flavours, a sliver of sweetness and lively acidity.

Vintage	09	08	07	06
WR	6	5	7	6
Drink	10-12	10-11	09-10	P

MED/DRY $22 AV

Kumeu River Pinot Gris   ★★★★☆

This consistently attractive wine is grown at Kumeu, in West Auckland, matured on its yeast lees, but not oak-matured. Made in a medium-dry style, it is typically floral and weighty, with a slightly oily texture, finely balanced acidity and peach, pear and spice aromas and flavours, vibrant and rich. The 2008 vintage (★★★★☆) is mouthfilling and concentrated, with ripe stone-fruit and spice flavours, unobtrusive sweetness and fresh, balanced acidity. It's already delicious, but well worth cellaring.

Vintage	08	07	06	05	04
WR	7	7	7	7	7
Drink	09-12	09-11	P	P	P

MED/DRY $27 AV

Lake Chalice Eyrie Vineyard Marlborough Pinot Gris   ★★★☆

Grown principally in the Eyrie Vineyard in the Waihopai Valley, the 2008 vintage (★★★☆) is fresh and crisp, with vibrant flavours of citrus fruits, lychees and limes, showing good depth, and a dry (3.5 grams/litre of residual sugar) slightly spicy finish.

DRY $20 AV

Lake Hayes Central Otago Pinot Gris   ★★★☆

From Amisfield, the 2009 vintage (★★★☆) was grown alongside the cellar door at Lake Hayes and at another site in Gibbston, and lees-aged in tanks. Fresh, crisp and vibrantly fruity, it has very good depth of peachy, limey, slightly spicy flavours, slightly sweet (7.5 grams/litre of residual sugar), tight and youthful.

Vintage	09	08	07
WR	5	6	5
Drink	09-11	09-10	09-10

MED/DRY $25 –V

Lamont Pinot Gris   ★★★☆

A single-vineyard wine, hand-picked at Bendigo, in Central Otago, the 2007 vintage (★★★☆) is fresh, vibrantly fruity and mouthfilling, with very good depth of pear and spice flavour and a dryish (5.8 grams/litre of residual sugar) finish.

Vintage	07
WR	7
Drink	09-12

MED/DRY $26 –V

Latitude 41 Pinot Gris   ★★★

From Spencer Hill, the 2008 vintage (★★★) is a South Island regional blend, given some exposure to new French oak. It offers plenty of vibrant, appley, slightly minerally and toasty flavour, with an off-dry (7 grams/litre of residual sugar) finish.

MED/DRY $20 –V

Lawson's Dry Hills Marlborough Pinot Gris   ★★★★☆

The 2008 vintage (★★★★) was grown mostly in the Chaytors Road Vineyard and harvested at 23.5 to 24 brix, with a small percentage of noble rot. Twenty-five per cent of the blend was fermented with indigenous yeasts in seasoned French oak casks; the rest was handled in tanks. It's a mouthfilling, medium-dry wine (6.5 grams/litre of residual sugar), fleshy and concentrated, with soft, ripe, peachy flavours showing good complexity, roundness and richness.

Vintage	09	08	07	06
WR	7	5	7	6
Drink	09-11	P	P	P

MED/DRY $27 AV

Lime Rock Central Hawke's Bay Pinot Gris   ★★★☆

The 2008 vintage (★★★☆) was grown at Waipawa, hand-picked and fermented and lees-aged in three-year-old French oak barriques. It's a youthful, mouthfilling wine with ripe, peachy, citrusy, slightly spicy flavours, a subtle oak influence, fresh acidity, good depth and a smooth, dry finish. Worth cellaring.

DRY $25 –V

Locharburn Central Otago Pinot Gris   (★★★☆)

Grown at Lowburn and harvested at 24 to 25 brix, the 2008 vintage (★★★☆) was mostly handled in tanks, but 20 per cent was fermented in French oak puncheons. It's a fresh-scented, full-bodied wine with very satisfying depth of lemony, appley, slightly spicy flavour, a dryish finish (5 grams/litre of residual sugar) and good harmony.

Vintage	08
WR	6
Drink	09-11

MED/DRY $25 –V

Lonestone Marlborough Pinot Gris   (★★★☆)

From wine distributors Bennett & Deller, the bargain-priced 2008 vintage (★★★☆) was grown in the Waihopai Valley. A basically dry style (4 grams/litre of residual sugar), it is mouthfilling, peachy, slightly spicy and honeyed, with very good balance and flavour depth.

DRY $16 V+

Longbush Pinot Gris   (★★★)

The 'bird series' 2008 vintage (★★★) was grown in Gisborne and made in a slightly sweet (12 grams/litre of residual sugar) style. Light yellow, it's a slightly honeyed wine, fruity and forward, with plenty of peachy, slightly spicy flavour. It's drinking well now.

Vintage	08
WR	6
Drink	09-12

MED/DRY $18 AV

Longridge Hawke's Bay Pinot Gris   (★★★☆)

The 2009 vintage (★★★☆) from Pernod Ricard NZ is a mouthfilling wine with refreshing pear and spice flavours, good varietal character and a finely balanced, smooth, dry finish.

DRY $18 V+

Maimai Creek Hawke's Bay Pinot Gris   (★★★☆)

Priced sharply and enjoyable from the start, the 2008 vintage (★★★☆) is a floral, weighty wine (14.5 per cent alcohol) with very good depth of peachy, spicy, slightly sweet flavours, balanced for easy drinking.

MED/DRY $18 V+

Man O' War Ponui Island Pinot Gris   (★★★)

From a smaller island near the eastern coast of Waiheke, in Auckland, the straw-coloured 2007 vintage (★★★) is a Chardonnay-like wine, fleshy, with good depth of stone-fruit flavours, slightly spicy and minerally, and a dry finish.

Vintage	07
WR	6
Drink	09-10

DRY $28 –V

Man O' War Waiheke Island Pinot Gris   ★★★

Grown on relatively cool, south-facing slopes at the eastern end of the island, the 2007 vintage (★★★☆) is pale straw, with a slightly earthy, rather than floral, bouquet. Full-bodied and dry, it has a Chardonnay-like weight and roundness, with strong, peachy, spicy flavours.

Vintage	07
WR	5
Drink	09-10

DRY $28 –V

Maori Point Central Otago Pinot Gris   ★★★

Grown at Tarras, north of Lake Dunstan, the 2008 vintage (★★★☆) is a mouthfilling, single-vineyard wine, partly (one-third) barrel-fermented, with citrusy, appley flavours in a slightly sweet style (5.3 grams/litre of residual sugar) with a clearly varietal fragrance. Well worth cellaring.

Vintage	09	08	07
WR	6	6	6
Drink	09-14	09-12	09-10

MED/DRY $23 –V

Margrain Martinborough Pinot Gris   ★★★☆

The 2008 vintage (★★★) is a bone-dry wine with crisp pear and green-apple flavours and a minerally streak. It's an austere style of Pinot Gris, but may reward cellaring.

Vintage	08	07	06	05	04
WR	7	7	7	6	6
Drink	09-16	09-13	09-12	09-11	09-10

DRY $30 –V

Marsden Bay of Islands Pinot Gris   ★★★

In favourable seasons, this Kerikeri, Bay of Islands winery produces an impressive Pinot Gris. The 2008 (★★★) was made principally from Pinot Gris (90 per cent), but includes 7 per cent Flora and 3 per cent Chardonnay. It's a fresh, mid-weight style with slightly sweet, citrusy, appley flavours, crisp acidity and a floral bouquet.

Vintage	08
WR	5
Drink	09-10

MED/DRY $27 –V

Martinborough Vineyard Pinot Gris   ★★★★★

This powerful, concentrated wine is one of the finest Pinot Gris in the country. It is hand-picked and fermented with a high percentage of indigenous yeasts, and lees-aged, partly in seasoned French oak casks (50 per cent in 2008), in a bid to produce a 'Burgundian style with complexity, texture and weight'. The outstanding 2008 vintage (★★★★★) was harvested at 23.4 to 24.7 brix. Pale lemon/green, it's a mouthfilling wine (14.5 per cent alcohol), with lovely, vibrant peach, pear and spice fruit characters shining through, a subtle oak influence, and notable complexity and harmony. Already delicious, it's a drink-now or cellaring proposition.

Vintage	08	07	06	05	04
WR	7	6	6	7	6
Drink	09-13	09-12	09-11	P	P

DRY $45 AV

Matakana Estate Matakana Pinot Gris   ★★★☆

Estate-grown north of Auckland, the ripe, smooth 2008 vintage (★★★☆) was 20 per cent barrel-fermented and made in a dry style. It's a finely balanced, slightly Chardonnay-like wine with very good depth of peachy, citrusy, slightly toasty flavour, showing good complexity and roundness.

DRY $27 –V

Matua Valley New Zealand Pinot Gris   (★★☆)

The 2008 vintage (★★☆) is part of the company's 'Regional Series', but is not labelled by region (apparently the grapes were grown in Marlborough). It's a medium-bodied wine with pleasant, lemony, slightly spicy and honeyed flavours and a crisp, dry (3 grams/litre of residual sugar) finish.

DRY $15 AV

Maude Central Otago Pinot Gris   (★★★)

Fresh and lively, the 2008 vintage (★★★) has moderately ripe, appley, lemony flavours and a crisp, medium-dry finish.

MED/DRY $22 –V

Maven Marlborough Pinot Gris   ★★★☆

The attractive 2007 vintage (★★★☆) was mostly handled in tanks, but 10 per cent of the blend was fermented with indigenous yeasts in seasoned French oak barriques. It's a scented, fleshy, slightly sweet wine with ripe peach and pear flavours showing a hint of oak and some richness.

Vintage	07	06	05
WR	6	6	5
Drink	P	P	P

MED/DRY $24 –V

Michael Ramon Matakana Pinot Gris   (★★☆)

Grown on the Tawharanui Peninsula, harvested at 24.5 brix and given 'some' oak aging, the 2008 vintage (★★☆) is a pale straw wine, medium to full-bodied, with peachy, citrusy, slightly spicy flavours, showing moderate depth.

MED/DRY $30 –V

Mills Reef Reserve Hawke's Bay Pinot Gris   (★★★)

The 2009 vintage (★★★) is an easy-drinking style, fermented and lees-aged for three months in seasoned oak casks. It's a dry style (3 grams/litre of residual sugar) with mouthfilling body, peachy, slightly spicy flavours and a very smooth finish.

DRY $25 –V

Misha's Vineyard Dress Circle Central Otago Pinot Gris   (★★★★☆)

The debut 2008 vintage (★★★★☆) was hand-picked at Bendigo at 22.8 brix and mostly handled in tanks; 28 per cent of the blend was fermented with indigenous yeasts in seasoned oak barrels. It's a rich, youthful wine with concentrated, pure stone-fruit and spice flavours, a touch of complexity and excellent freshness, vigour and harmony. Worth cellaring.

MED/DRY $26 AV

Mission Hawke's Bay Pinot Gris   ★★★

The Mission has long been a standard-bearer for Pinot Gris. The 2009 vintage (★★★) is full-bodied and fresh, with satisfying depth of peachy, slightly spicy flavour and a finely balanced, dry finish.

DRY $16 V+

Mission Vineyard Selection Ohiti Road Pinot Gris   ★★★

The 2008 vintage (★★★) is a Hawke's Bay wine, full-bodied (14 per cent alcohol), with soft, ripe, peachy, gently spicy flavours. Moderately concentrated, it's a dry style, but offers very easy drinking. The 2009 (★★★☆), grown organically, is mouthfilling and smooth, with a slightly oily texture and good depth of peach and lychee flavours.

DRY $18 AV

Moana Park Vineyard Selection Pinot Gris   (★★★)

Grown in the Dartmoor Valley, in Hawke's Bay, the 2008 vintage (★★★) is pale straw, with ripe, peachy, slightly gingery flavours and a slightly sweet, crisp finish. Medium-bodied, it's already drinking well and bargain-priced.

Vintage	08
WR	6
Drink	09-11

MED/DRY $15 V+

Momo Marlborough Pinot Gris   (★★★☆)

From Seresin, the 2008 vintage (★★★☆) was hand-harvested at three sites and mostly handled in tanks, but 30 per cent was aged for three months in old French barriques. The bouquet is slightly earthy; the palate is vibrant, with a slightly oily texture, gentle sweetness (6 grams/litre of residual sugar), and citrusy, appley, spicy flavours, showing a touch of complexity.

MED/DRY $20 AV

Moncellier Marlborough Pinot Gris   (★★★★)

From winemaker Greg Rowdon and Bill Spence (co-founder of Matua Valley), the debut 2008 vintage (★★★★) is a single-vineyard wine, grown on the banks of the Wairau River and lees-aged for three months. A dry style (3.9 grams/litre of residual sugar), it is mouthfilling and creamy, with stone-fruit and spice flavours, a hint of apricot, and good texture and richness.

Vintage	09
WR	6
Drink	10-14

MED/DRY $25 AV

Monkey Bay Gisborne Pinot Gris   ★★☆

From Constellation NZ, the 2008 vintage (★★☆) is a light style of Pinot Gris with fresh pear and spice aromas and flavours. It's a pleasant, all-purpose wine with a slightly sweet finish.

MED/DRY $16 AV

Monowai Pinot Gris   (★★★☆)

The 2007 vintage (★★★☆) of this Hawke's Bay wine was estate-grown inland, at Crownthorpe, tank-fermented and lees-aged. Light lemon/green, with citrusy, spicy aromas and flavours, showing a minerally streak, it's a tightly structured wine, developing well.

MED/DRY $22 AV

Montana North Island Pinot Gris   ★★★

Balanced for easy drinking, the 2008 vintage (★★★) of this regional blend was mostly grown in Gisborne and a small amount of Gewürztraminer was added, 'enhancing the aromatics and flavour'. Mouthfilling and smooth, it has ripe, peachy, spicy flavours, with a sliver of sweetness (6.5 grams/litre of residual sugar), moderate acidity and good depth.

Vintage	08
WR	6
Drink	P

MED/DRY $18 AV

Montana Reserve Hawke's Bay Pinot Gris   ★★★☆

The 2008 vintage (★★★☆) was grown mostly at Matapiro, a cool, elevated, inland district, and matured on its yeast lees in tanks for three months. It's a full-bodied, fresh and lively wine, finely textured, with very good depth of citrusy, slightly appley flavours, a touch of sweetness (6.5 grams/litre of residual sugar) and balanced acidity.

Vintage	08	07
WR	7	7
Drink	P	P

MED/DRY $24 –V

Morton Estate White Label Hawke's Bay Pinot Gris   ★★★

Grown at the company's inland Kinross Vineyard, the 2008 vintage (★★★☆) is scented, with mouthfilling body and good depth of fresh, citrusy, slightly spicy flavours. It's drinking well now.

Vintage	08	07	06
WR	6	6	7
Drink	09-12	09-10	P

DRY $19 AV

Mount Dottrel Central Otago Pinot Gris   ★★★★

The 2009 vintage (★★★★) from Mitre Rocks is an attractively scented, dry wine with fresh, pure lychee, pear and spice flavours. It shows excellent vibrancy, delicacy and depth.

Vintage	09	08	DRY $23 AV
WR	6	6	
Drink	09-12	09-11	

Mount Riley Marlborough Pinot Gris   ★★★

The 2008 vintage (★★★) is fresh, with satisfying depth of pear, apple and spice flavours and a slightly sweet (11 grams/litre of residual sugar), smooth finish.

Vintage	08	07	06	MED/DRY $18 AV
WR	6	6	6	
Drink	09-11	09-10	09	

Mount Vernon Marlborough Pinot Gris   (★★★★)

From Lawson's Dry Hills, the bargain-priced 2008 vintage (★★★★) is a mouthfilling, finely textured wine with good depth and purity of peach, pear and spice flavours, sweet-fruit characters, crisp acidity and a floral bouquet.

MED/DRY $20 V+

Moutere Hills Nelson Dry Pinot Gris   (★★★★)

From vines cropped deliberately at 'ridiculously low' levels, the 2007 vintage (★★★★) was partly barrel-fermented with indigenous yeasts. Sturdy (14.4 per cent alcohol), with well-ripened stone-fruit flavours, slightly nutty and minerally, it's a distinctive, bone-dry style, still fresh and maturing well.

DRY $35 –V

Mt Difficulty Pinot Gris   ★★★★

Grown at Bannockburn, in Central Otago, the 2008 vintage (★★★★) was hand-picked at 23.6 to 23.9 brix, tank-fermented and lees-aged for three months. It's a mouthfilling wine (14 per cent alcohol) with strong peach, pear and spice flavours, vibrant and finely balanced, and a crisp, dry finish (4 grams/litre of residual sugar).

DRY $25 AV

Mt Difficulty Roaring Meg Central Otago Pinot Gris   ★★★☆

Tasted in its infancy, the 2009 vintage (★★★☆) is a gently sweet style (9 grams/litre of residual sugar), very fresh and vibrant, with crisp acidity, pure varietal flavours of pears and spices, and good delicacy and depth.

MED/DRY $20 AV

Mt Difficulty Single Vineyard Mansons Farm Pinot Gris   ★★★★

The 2007 vintage (★★★★) was late-picked at Bannockburn, in Central Otago, and produced in a medium style (25 grams/litre of residual sugar). Ripely scented, it is sturdy and ripe, with lush, citrusy, peachy, faintly honeyed flavours, still very vibrant and youthful. Well worth cellaring.

MED $35 –V

Mt Rosa Central Otago Pinot Gris ★★★☆

The 2008 vintage (★★★☆) is a scented wine, grown at Gibbston, with mouthfilling body, good depth of peachy, spicy flavours, a touch of complexity and a dry finish.

DRY $26 –V

Murdoch James Wairarapa Pinot Gris ★★★☆

From grapes hand-picked at Martinborough and Masterton, the 2008 vintage (★★★☆) is mouthfilling (13.5 per cent alcohol), with crisp, citrusy, appley, slightly spicy flavours, showing cool-climate freshness and vigour, and a dryish (5.4 grams/litre of residual sugar) finish. It's maturing well.

Vintage	08	MED/DRY $20 AV
WR	6	
Drink	09-11	

Nautilus Marlborough Pinot Gris ★★★☆

Typically a citrusy, spicy, clearly varietal wine with a subtle oak influence (15 per cent barrel-fermented), very good depth of dryish flavour (5 grams/litre of residual sugar in 2008), and substantial body.

Vintage	08	07	06	05	04
WR	6	7	6	7	6
Drink	10-12	09-12	09-10	P	P

MED/DRY $29 –V

Ned, The, Waihopai River Marlborough Pinot Gris ★★★☆

From Waihopai River Vineyard, the 2008 vintage (★★★☆) is faintly pink, with pleasing fullness of body and strong peach, apricot and spice flavours, ripe and smooth.

MED/DRY $17 V+

Neudorf Maggie's Block Nelson Pinot Gris ★★★★

The 2008 vintage (★★★★) replaced the former Brightwater Pinot Gris. A single-vineyard wine, grown on the Waimea Plains, it was hand-picked and mostly lees-aged in tanks; 15 per cent of the blend was French oak-fermented. It's a dry style (4 grams/litre of residual sugar) with ripe pear, lychee and spice flavours, showing good delicacy and depth, a hint of apricot and fresh, crisp acidity. Weighty (14.5 per cent alcohol) and still very youthful, it's worth cellaring.

Vintage	08	07	DRY $22 V+
WR	5	5	
Drink	09-13	09-12	

Neudorf Moutere Pinot Gris ★★★★☆

The 2008 vintage (★★★★★) is full of personality. A single-vineyard wine, hand-picked at 23.8 to 24.7 brix, it was 60 per cent fermented in old French barrels (the rest was handled in tanks), and made in a medium-dry style (12 grams/litre of residual sugar). Attractively scented, it is fleshy, very fresh, vibrant and harmonious, with ripe stone-fruit and spice flavours, showing impressive complexity and richness, good acid spine and a finely poised, long, tight finish, suggesting it will reward cellaring.

Vintage	08	07	06	05	04	03	02
WR	6	7	6	7	5	NM	5
Drink	09-17	09-17	09-16	09-15	09-10	NM	09-10

DRY $26 AV

Nevis Bluff Central Otago Pinot Gris   ★★★★

A consistently impressive wine. The 2007 vintage (★★★★) was hand-picked at over 24 brix in the Cromwell Basin and at Gibbston, tank-fermented and lees-aged for nine months. Pale straw, it's a full-bodied wine (14 per cent alcohol), fresh and vibrant, with ripe peach and slight apricot flavours, balanced acidity and a long, dry (2 grams/litre of residual sugar) finish.

Vintage	07
WR	6
Drink	09-13

DRY $27 –V

Nevis Bluff Pinot Gris Second Edition   (★★★★)

(Note: the words 'Second Edition' appear only in small letters on the back label.) Still on sale, the 2006 vintage (★★★★) was grown at Gibbston and Cromwell, tank-fermented with indigenous yeasts, and lees-aged for nine months (three months longer than the First Edition, now sold out). Weighty and slightly oily, with peachy, slightly spicy flavours, it's a dry style (3 grams/litre of residual sugar), with good texture and depth.

Vintage	06
WR	5
Drink	09-11

DRY $28 –V

Oak Hill Matakana Pinot Gris   (★★★☆)

The 2008 vintage (★★★☆) is a fully dry style with impressive weight, strong, ripe fruit flavours and a slightly oily texture. An obvious oak influence gives it a slightly Chardonnay-like feel, but the wine is fleshy and rich.

DRY $39 –V

Odyssey Marlborough Pinot Gris   ★★★

Grown in the Odyssey Vineyard, in the Brancott Valley, the 2008 vintage (★★★) was hand-picked and mostly handled in tanks; a third of the blend was fermented in seasoned French oak casks. It's a mouthfilling, well-rounded wine with fresh, ripe peach and lychee flavours, a touch of complexity and a dry finish.

Vintage	08	07
WR	6	6
Drink	09-11	09-10

DRY $25 –V

Old Coach Road Nelson Pinot Gris   (★★★)

From Seifried, the 2009 vintage (★★★) is a freshly scented, full-bodied wine, harvested at 23.6 brix, mostly in the Redwood Valley. An easy-drinking style, it has satisfying depth of pear and spice flavours, with a sliver of sweetness (4.5 grams/litre of residual sugar) balanced by lively acidity. Priced right.

DRY $16 V+

Omaha Bay Vineyard Matakana Pinot Gris   ★★★☆

The 2007 vintage (★★★☆) was fermented in seasoned oak barrels. A dry wine with an earthy, rather than floral, bouquet, it is mouthfilling (14 per cent alcohol) and slightly Chardonnay-like, with stone-fruit flavours showing some complexity. The 2008 (★★★☆) is similar, with very good depth and complexity in a dry, mouthfilling style, peachy and faintly oaked.

Vintage	08	07	06
WR	6	6	5
Drink	09-13	09-12	09-11

DRY $30 –V

Omaka Springs Marlborough Pinot Gris   ★★★

Grown in the Omaka Valley, the 2008 vintage (★★☆) is a crisp, slightly sweet style (16 grams/litre of residual sugar), medium-bodied (12 per cent alcohol), with citrusy, appley flavours, balanced for easy drinking.

Vintage	08
WR	6
Drink	09-13

MED $19 AV

Omihi Road Waipara Pinot Gris   ★★★☆

From Torlesse, the 2008 vintage (★★★★) was harvested at 24 to 26 brix. Fermentation was initially in tanks, then barriques. Attractively scented, it has strong, ripe citrus-fruit and apple strudel flavours and a fresh, crisp, off-dry finish.

Vintage	08
WR	6
Drink	09-12

MED $20 AV

Omori Estate Lake Taupo Pinot Gris   (★★★☆)

Grown on the south-west shores of the lake, hand-picked and lees-aged in tanks, the 2008 vintage (★★★☆) is ripely scented, with peachy, faintly spicy and honeyed flavours, showing good depth. It's an easy-drinking wine, finely textured and lingering.

DRY $25 –V

One Tree Otago Pinot Gris   (★★★★)

A great buy, the 2008 vintage (★★★★) is from Capricorn Wine Estates, a division of Craggy Range. Partly oak-aged, it's a mouthfilling wine, fresh-scented and vibrantly fruity, with strong, peachy, citrusy, slightly spicy flavours, a sliver of sweetness (8.5 grams/litre of residual sugar), fresh underlying acidity – and loads of drink-young charm.

MED/DRY $16 V+

Opawa Marlborough Pinot Gris   (★★★☆)

The 2008 vintage (★★★☆) was made in a 'lighter, crisper' style than its Nautilus Estate stablemate. Hand-picked in the Wairau Valley and tank-fermented, it is full-bodied and dryish (5 grams/litre of residual sugar), with lemony, slightly spicy flavours, showing good delicacy and depth.

MED/DRY $23 –V

Opihi Pinot Gris   ★★★☆

Grown on a north-facing slope inland from Timaru, in South Canterbury, this is typically a highly attractive wine, hand-picked and made with some use of indigenous yeasts and lees-stirring. The 2006 vintage (★★★) has good weight and fresh pear/spice flavours, with a touch of sweetness (11 grams/litre of residual sugar) balanced by crisp, lively acidity. There is no 2007, but the label returns from 2008.

MED/DRY $22 AV

Ostler Audrey's Waitaki Valley Pinot Gris   ★★★★

The 2008 vintage (★★★★) was estate-grown, 20 per cent barrel-fermented and made in a dry style (2.7 grams/litre of residual sugar). Bright, light lemon/green, it is richly scented and mouthfilling, with ripe stone-fruit and spice flavours, finely balanced and generous. Drink now onwards.

Vintage	06
WR	6
Drink	P

DRY $35 –V

Ostler Grower Selection Blue House Vines Waitaki Valley Pinot Gris   (★★★☆)

The 2008 vintage (★★★☆) was grown in Grants Road and made in a medium-dry style (14 grams/litre of residual sugar). Attractively scented, it is very fresh and vibrant, with peachy, slightly limey flavours and good acid spine.

MED/DRY $29 –V

Palliser Estate Martinborough Pinot Gris   ★★★★

The 2007 vintage (★★★★☆), 5 per cent oak-aged, is a delicious wine, fleshy, with excellent depth of ripe pear, lychee and spice flavours, dryish (7 grams/litre of residual sugar) and well-rounded.

MED/DRY $26 –V

Parr & Simpson Limestone Bay Pinot Gris   (★★★★)

A single-vineyard Nelson wine from Pohara, in eastern Golden Bay, the 2008 vintage (★★★★) is full of interest. Blended with 8 per cent Gewürztraminer and handled in tanks, it is not highly scented but weighty and dry (3.7 grams/litre of residual sugar), with finely balanced acidity, concentrated stone-fruit flavours and an almost Chardonnay-like richness. Priced sharply.

DRY $20 V+

Pasquale Alma Mater Hakataramea Valley Pinot Gris/Riesling/Gewürztraminer   (★★★☆)

Grown in South Canterbury, the 2008 vintage (★★★☆) is a highly aromatic wine with very good depth of citrusy, spicy flavour, a touch of complexity from aging in old oak casks, and a splash of sweetness (10.9 grams/litre of residual sugar) balanced by crisp acidity.

MED/DRY $27 –V

Passage Rock Waiheke Island Pinot Gris   ★★★

The 2009 vintage (★★★) is a mouthfilling wine (14 per cent alcohol), easy-drinking, with soft peach, pear and slight spice flavours, fresh, vibrant and smooth.

MED/DRY $23 –V

Peregrine Central Otago Pinot Gris   ★★★☆

The 2008 vintage (★★★☆) was hand-picked and tank-fermented. It's a weighty, finely textured wine with very good depth of peach, pear and spice flavours and a dryish (6 grams/litre of residual sugar), lingering finish.

MED/DRY $25 –V

Peter Yealands Marlborough Pinot Gris   (★★★)

The 2009 vintage (★★★) is scented, with fresh, vibrant flavours of peaches, lemons and spices, and a crisp, basically dry (4 grams/litre of residual sugar) finish.

DRY $19 AV

Pisa Moorings Central Otago Pinot Gris   (★★★☆)

The debut 2008 vintage (★★★☆) is invitingly scented, with mouthfilling body (14 per cent alcohol) and ripe, peachy, gently spicy flavours. Fresh and vibrant, with a sliver of sweetness (5 grams/litre of residual sugar), moderate acidity and a well-rounded finish, it's a full-flavoured wine, drinking well now.

MED/DRY $22 AV

Pisa Range Estate Central Otago Pinot Gris   (★★★☆)

The debut 2007 vintage (★★★☆) is a single-vineyard wine, grown in the Cromwell Basin, and was lees-aged in tanks for five months. It's a sturdy wine (14.5 per cent alcohol) with good depth of fresh, citrusy, peachy, slightly spicy flavours and a moderately crisp, dry finish.

DRY $27 –V

Poderi Crisci Pinot Grigio   ★★★

Grown on Waiheke Island, the 2008 (★★★) is light and lively, with lemony, spicy flavours, fresh, crisp and dry. The 2009 vintage (★★★) was handled in a 50/50 split of tanks and seasoned French oak casks. It's a gently spicy wine, full-bodied (13.5 per cent alcohol), with ripe, peachy flavours and a crisp, bone-dry finish.

Vintage	09
WR	7
Drink	09-12

DRY $29 –V

Pohangina Valley Estate Pinot Gris   ★★★★

This ground-breaking Manawatu wine flows from a stony river terrace in the Pohangina Valley, north-east of Palmerston North. The refined 2007 vintage (★★★★) is fleshy and rounded, with ripe stone-fruit and spice flavours showing clear-cut varietal characters and excellent depth.

Vintage	07	06
WR	5	7
Drink	09-11	09-10

DRY $30 –V

Prophet's Rock Central Otago Pinot Gris ★★★★

Grown at Pisa, in the Cromwell Basin, the 2008 vintage (★★★★) was fermented with indigenous yeasts and lees-aged. Made in a medium-dry style, it is weighty and concentrated, with youthful pear, lychee and spice flavours, balanced acidity, a touch of complexity, and obvious cellaring potential.

MED/DRY $35 –V

Quartz Reef Bendigo Central Otago Pinot Gris ★★★★

The 2008 vintage (★★★★) was estate-grown and hand-picked at Bendigo, fermented dry and lees-stirred in tanks. It's a pale, mouthfilling wine (14.5 per cent alcohol), crisp and dry, with citrusy, spicy flavours showing good intensity, vigour and length.

Vintage	08	07	06
WR	6	6	6
Drink	09-11	09-10	P

DRY $26 –V

Rabbit Ranch Central Otago Pinot Gris ★★★

Awarded five stars by 'Roger Rabbit', this wine is made by Chard Farm in a smooth, off-dry style with lychee, pear and spice flavours. It is typically fleshy and forward, in a very user-friendly style.

MED/DRY $24 –V

Ransom Clos De Valerie Pinot Gris ★★★☆

Estate-grown at Mahurangi, near Warkworth, north of Auckland, this wine is named after the road on which the vineyard lies – Valerie Close. The 2007 vintage (★★★☆) is full-bodied and dry, in a restrained but attractive style with a slightly oily texture and fresh, lemony flavours that linger well.

DRY $23 –V

Ra Nui Marlborough Wairau Valley Pinot Gris ★★★☆

The 2009 vintage (★★★☆) was hand-picked in the Cob Cottage Vineyard, near Blenheim. It is mouthfilling, with very good depth of peach, pear and slight spice flavours, and a finely textured, dry finish.

DRY $21 AV

Red Tussock Central Otago Pinot Gris (★★★)

From Mark Mason, originally involved with Sacred Hill, the 2008 vintage (★★★) is a fresh, dryish wine, still youthful, with good body and depth of peachy, slightly spicy flavours. The 2007 (★★★☆) is drinking well now – scented, with peachy, citrusy, slightly honeyed flavours.

MED/DRY $20 –V

Redoubt Hill Vineyard Nelson Pinot Gris ★★★

Grown at Motueka, the 2008 vintage (★★★) has a gently floral bouquet and good depth of citrusy, appley, spicy flavours. The pale, youthful 2009 (★★★) has pear, lychee and spice aromas leading into a medium-bodied wine, vibrant and slightly sweet (6.8 grams/litre of residual sugar). It's not intense, but shows good varietal character and should open out over the summer of 2009–10.

MED/DRY $25 –V

Renato Nelson Pinot Gris   ★★★☆

Grown on the Waimea Plains, hand-picked and lees-aged, the refined 2009 vintage (★★★★) is a slightly sweet style, scented and mouthfilling, with very good depth of peach, pear and spice flavours, showing excellent delicacy and harmony. It's a finely poised wine that should age well.

Vintage	09	08	07	06	05
WR	6	6	6	6	6
Drink	10-13	09-12	09-11	09-10	P

MED/DRY $23 –V

Ribbonwood Marlborough Pinot Gris   (★★★☆)

From Framingham and sold exclusively by blackmarket.co.nz, the 2008 vintage (★★★☆) is attractively scented and fleshy, with peachy, spicy flavours showing clear-cut varietal character and moderate concentration. It's a mouthfilling, ripe and well-rounded wine with drink-young appeal.

MED/DRY $18 V+

Richardson Central Otago Pinot Gris   (★★★☆)

Fresh, lively and youthful, the 2007 vintage (★★★☆) is a single-vineyard wine. Most of the blend was tank-fermented and then barrel-aged, but 30 per cent was fermented with indigenous yeasts in seasoned oak barriques. It's a medium to full-bodied style with good depth of lychee and apple flavours and a crisp, off-dry (6.4 grams/litre of residual sugar) finish. (The 2008 was 15 per cent barrel-fermented.)

MED/DRY $27 –V

Rimu Grove Bronte Pinot Gris – see Bronte by Rimu Grove Pinot Gris

Rimu Grove Nelson Pinot Gris   ★★★★☆

A consistent winner. The 2008 vintage (★★★★☆) is weighty and very harmonious, with concentrated peach, pear and spice flavours, slightly sweet (7 grams/litre of residual sugar), and deliciously rich and rounded.

Vintage	09	08	07	06	05
WR	7	7	7	6	6
Drink	10-17	09-15	09-12	09-10	P

MED/DRY $29 AV

Riverby Estate Marlborough Pinot Gris   (★★★)

A single-vineyard wine, grown in Jacksons Road, in the heart of the Wairau Valley, the 2008 vintage (★★★) is a crisp, medium-dry style (9 grams/litre of residual sugar), with lemon, apple and spice flavours, fresh and vibrant, good texture and an aromatic bouquet.

Vintage	08
WR	6
Drink	09-12

MED/DRY $22 –V

Riverstone Pinot Gris   (★★)

From Villa Maria, the easy-drinking, non-vintage wine (★★) on sale in 2009 is a blend of Italian and New Zealand wines. Pale, it's a restrained, slightly sweet, medium-bodied style with moderate depth of lemony, slightly spicy flavours and a smooth finish.

MED/DRY $12 AV

Road Works Waiheke Island Pinot Gris   (★★★)

From Man O' War, the 2008 vintage (★★★) is not highly aromatic, but the palate is sturdy (14 per cent alcohol), with plenty of ripe, citrusy, peachy, slightly spicy flavour and a dry finish.

DRY $18 AV

Rockburn Central Otago Pinot Gris   ★★★☆

Grown at Parkburn, in the Cromwell Basin, and at Gibbston, the 2008 vintage (★★★) was handled in tanks. A gently sweet style (15 grams/litre of residual sugar), it is medium-bodied (12.9 per cent alcohol), fresh, crisp and vibrant, with lemon, apple and pear flavours, balanced for easy drinking.

Vintage	08
WR	6
Drink	09-11

MED $20 AV

Ruby Bay Vineyard Pinot Gris   ★★★☆

The 2009 vintage (★★★) is a single-vineyard Nelson wine, hand-picked. Pale and gently aromatic, it's a fresh, medium-bodied wine (12.3 per cent alcohol) with pure, delicate, pear-like flavours and an off-dry (5 grams/litre of residual sugar) finish.

Vintage	09
WR	5
Drink	09-12

DRY $24 –V

Sacred Hill Marlborough Vineyards Pinot Gris   ★★★★

Grown in the company's Hell's Gate Vineyard, in the Waihopai Valley, the 2008 vintage (★★★★) is an immaculate wine, with fresh, pure varietal flavours of peaches, pears and spices, a slightly oily texture and a long, dryish finish. Fine value.

Vintage	07
WR	7
Drink	P

MED/DRY $21 V+

Saddleback Central Otago Pinot Gris   (★★★☆)

From Peregrine, the 2008 vintage (★★★☆) is a fleshy, gently sweet style (9.6 grams/litre of residual sugar), with mouthfilling body and very good depth of lemon and pear flavours, balanced for easy drinking.

MED/DRY $20 AV

Saint Clair Godfrey's Creek Reserve Pinot Gris   ★★★☆

The 2008 vintage (★★★☆) was grown at two sites, principally the Godfrey's Creek Vineyard, at the mouth of the Brancott Valley, and mostly tank-fermented, with some handling in old French oak barrels. An off-dry style (5.5 grams/litre of residual sugar), it is a generous, mouthfilling wine, ripely flavoured, with a touch of complexity and a rounded finish.

Vintage	08	07	06
WR	6	6	6
Drink	09-11	09-10	P

MED/DRY $25 –V

Saint Clair Marlborough Pinot Gris   ★★★☆

The 2008 vintage (★★★☆) was partly fermented with indigenous yeasts in old oak barrels and made in a medium-dry style (7.3 grams/litre of residual sugar). It has finely balanced peach, pear and spice flavours, fresh, vibrant and smooth.

Vintage	08
WR	6
Drink	09-10

MED/DRY $21 AV

Saint Clair Pioneer Block 5 Bull Block Pinot Gris   (★★★★)

Grown in the southern Omaka Valley, the 2007 vintage (★★★★) is a fleshy, distinctly medium style (24 grams/litre of residual sugar), with ripe, smooth flavours of lychees and pears and good harmony. Weighty, with an oily texture and a long finish, it's delicious now. (There is no 2008.)

Vintage	08	07
WR	NM	7
Drink	NM	09-12

MED $25 AV

Saint Clair Vicar's Choice Marlborough Pinot Gris   ★★☆

The easy-drinking 2008 vintage (★★☆) is medium-bodied, with slightly sweet (7.7 grams/litre of residual sugar) lychee and spice flavours, showing solid depth.

Vintage	08
WR	6
Drink	09-10

MED/DRY $19 –V

Saints Gisborne Pinot Gris   ★★☆

From Pernod Ricard NZ, the 2008 vintage (★★☆) is a medium-dry style (7 grams/litre of residual sugar), fresh, citrusy and appley, but it lacks real richness, with moderate flavour depth.

Vintage	08
WR	6
Drink	P

DRY $18 –V

Sanctuary Marlborough Pinot Gris   ★★☆

From Grove Mill, the 2008 vintage (★★☆) is fresh and vibrantly fruity, with moderate flavour depth and a sliver of sweetness (6 grams/litre of residual sugar) giving it a smooth, easy-drinking appeal.

Vintage	09	08	07
WR	7	5	6
Drink	09-11	P	P

MED/DRY $15 AV

San Hill Pinot Gris   ★★☆

From Pukeora Estate, this wine is grown at Waipukurau, in Central Hawke's Bay. Maturing well, the 2008 vintage (★★★) is a bone-dry wine, 50 per cent fermented in seasoned oak barrels. From low-cropping vines (2 tonnes/hectare), it is citrusy and peachy, in a tight, Pinot Grigio style with a hint of toasty oak adding complexity and a fresh, crisp finish. (The 2009 vintage was handled entirely in tanks.)

Vintage	09	08
WR	5	5
Drink	09-11	09-10

DRY $20 –V

Seifried Nelson Pinot Gris   ★★★☆

Grown mostly in the Redwood Valley, where the vines are up to 26 years old, the 2009 vintage (★★★☆) is a full-bodied wine with lively acidity and a sliver of sweetness (8 grams/litre of residual sugar) amid its peachy, spicy, slightly gingery flavours, which show very good depth.

Vintage	09	08	07	06
WR	6	6	6	6
Drink	09-11	09-10	P	P

DRY $21 AV

Selaks Premium Selection New Zealand Pinot Gris   (★★☆)

From Constellation NZ, the debut 2007 vintage (★★☆) is a regional blend, full-bodied, fresh and citrusy, with satisfying flavour depth and an off-dry, slightly peachy and spicy finish.

MED/DRY $17 –V

Selaks Winemaker's Favourite Moteo and Te Tua Vineyards Pinot Gris   (★★★★)

The Alsace-style 2008 vintage (★★★★) from Constellation NZ was grown in the Te Tua Vineyard, on the Heretaunga Plains, and mostly handled in tanks; 5 per cent was barrel-aged. Mouthfilling, with ripe stone-fruit and spice flavours, a sliver of sweetness (6 grams/litre of residual sugar) and fresh, lively acidity, it shows excellent varietal character, richness and harmony.

 MED/DRY $21 V+

Seresin Marlborough Pinot Gris   ★★★★

One of the region's most distinctive Pinot Gris. The 2008 vintage (★★★★) was hand-picked at 25 brix in the Home Vineyard and the hillside Raupo Creek Vineyard, fermented with indigenous yeasts, and lees-aged for six months in seasoned French oak barriques. It's a powerful, peachy, spicy, basically dry wine (4 grams/litre of residual sugar) with substantial body (14.5 per cent alcohol) and excellent flavour depth.

Vintage	08	07	06	05	04
WR	7	7	7	6	6
Drink	09-14	09-13	09-10	09-10	P

DRY $28 –V

Shaky Bridge Pioneer Series Central Otago Pinot Gris   (★★★)

The 2008 vintage (★★★) was grown at Alexandra. It's a fresh, full-bodied wine, slightly sweet, with peach, lychee and spice flavours, vibrant and crisp. Enjoyable now.

MED/DRY $19 AV

Sherwood Estate Waipara Pinot Gris   (★★★★)

The 2008 vintage (★★★★) is scented, with vibrant peach, pear and spice flavours, showing good richness, fresh acidity and a lingering finish.

MED/DRY $20 V+

Shingle Peak Reserve Marlborough Pinot Gris   ★★★☆

The 2008 vintage (★★★☆) is mouthfilling and fleshy, with strong, ripe pear and spice flavours and a slightly sweet finish.

MED/DRY $20 AV

Sileni Cellar Selection Hawke's Bay Pinot Gris   ★★★

The 2009 vintage (★★★) is a refreshing Pinot Grigio style, medium-bodied (12.5 per cent alcohol), with peach, pear and spice flavours, crisp and dry.

DRY $19 AV

Vintage	08	07	06
WR	6	6	5
Drink	09-11	09-10	P

Soho Marlborough Pinot Gris   ★★★☆

Enjoyable from the start, the 2008 vintage (★★★☆) is freshly scented, with mouthfilling body and vibrant flavours of peaches, pears and spices, showing very good depth, delicacy and roundness. The 2009 (★★★☆) is moderately concentrated, with ripe, peachy, slightly spicy flavours, a hint of apricot, and good freshness and balance (7 grams/litre of residual sugar).

MED/DRY $26 –V

Soljans Kumeu Pinot Gris   ★★★

Estate-grown in West Auckland, the 2009 vintage (★★★) is a medium-bodied wine with fresh, vibrant flavours of pears, lychees and spices and a smooth finish.

MED/DRY $20 –V

Southbank Estate East Coast Pinot Gris   ★★★

The 2008 vintage (★★★) offers fresh peach, pear and spice flavours, with a crisp, dry finish (2 grams/litre of residual sugar).

DRY $20 –V

Vintage	08	07
WR	6	7
Drink	P	09-10

Southern Cross Hawke's Bay Pinot Gris   (★★☆)

From One Tree Hill Vineyards, a division of Morton Estate, the 2008 vintage (★★☆) is mouthfilling, with a scented, slightly honeyed bouquet and peachy, slightly spicy and honeyed flavours. A decent quaffer, priced right.

DRY $13 V+

Vintage	08
WR	6
Drink	09-11

Spinyback Nelson Pinot Gris   ★★★☆

From Waimea Estate, the 2009 vintage (★★★☆) was harvested on the Waimea Plains at 22 to 24 brix, tank-fermented and lees-stirred. Full-bodied (14 per cent alcohol), it has crisp, slightly sweet (5.8 grams/litre of residual sugar) flavours of peaches and spices, showing good depth. It should unfold well during 2010.

Vintage	09	08	07	06
WR	7	7	6	6
Drink	09-12	09-11	09-10	P

MED/DRY $18 V+

Spy Valley Envoy Marlborough Pinot Gris   ★★★★☆

The 2007 vintage (★★★★☆) was estate-grown in the Waihopai Valley, hand-picked at 26 brix, and fermented and lees-aged for seven months in large German oak ovals. Lush, with a soft texture and rich, peachy, gently sweet flavours (17 grams/litre of residual sugar), it is fleshy and very harmonious, with greater complexity than most New Zealand Pinot Gris and obvious cellaring potential. (The 2008 vintage is a medium-sweet style, with 39 grams/litre of residual sugar.)

Vintage	08	07	06
WR	6	6	6
Drink	10-12	09-12	09-11

MED $29 AV

Spy Valley Marlborough Pinot Gris   ★★★★

A consistently good and sometimes great buy. The 2008 vintage (★★★★) was harvested at 23.2 to 24.7 brix and partly fermented in old oak. It's ripely scented and mouthfilling, with slightly sweet (10 grams/litre of residual sugar), peachy, spicy flavours, strongly varietal and very harmonious. Delicious from the start.

Vintage	09	08	07	06	05	04
WR	7	6	6	7	6	5
Drink	10-12	09-11	09-10	P	P	P

MED/DRY $20 V+

Squawking Magpie The Chatterer Pinot Gris   ★★★☆

Grown in a single Hawke's Bay vineyard, the 2007 vintage (★★★★) is building up well with bottle-age. Scented and mouthfilling, it has good richness of pear and spice flavours, a slightly oily texture and a finely balanced, rounded finish.

MED/DRY $20 AV

Staete Landt Marlborough Pinot Gris   ★★★★

This single-vineyard wine is hand-harvested at Rapaura and fermented and matured on its yeast lees in old French oak puncheons. It is typically weighty and concentrated, with a slightly nutty complexity. The 2008 vintage (★★★★☆) is full-bodied and bone-dry, with deep stone-fruit and spice flavours, sweet-fruit delights, complexity from the restrained oak influence and a deliciously soft, rich finish.

Vintage	08	07
WR	7	6
Drink	09-13	09-12

DRY $29 –V

Stafford Lane Nelson Pinot Gris   ★★☆

The 2008 vintage (★★☆) is fresh and vibrant, with solid depth of citrusy, spicy, slightly sweet, crisp flavour. The 2009 (★★) is light-bodied, with restrained, lemony, spicy flavours and a slightly sweet (8.3 grams/litre of residual sugar) finish.

MED/DRY $19 –V

Starborough Marlborough Pinot Gris   ★★★☆

Full of promise, the 2009 vintage (★★★★) is a blend of Wairau Valley (70 per cent) and Awatere Valley (30 per cent) fruit, mostly handled in tanks, but 10 per cent barrel-fermented. Skilfully crafted, it is mouthfilling, ripe and rounded, with peach, pear and spice flavours showing good concentration, a slightly oily texture and good harmony.

DRY $23 –V

Stone Bridge Gisborne Pinot Gris   (★★★)

Estate-grown and picked from first-crop vines, the 2008 vintage (★★★) is freshly scented and medium-bodied, with vibrant pear and spice flavours and a slightly sweet (7.8 grams/litre of residual sugar), crisp finish.

MED/DRY $22 –V

Stonecutter Martinborough Pinot Gris   ★★★

Lemony and crisp, the 2007 vintage (★★★) was handled in tanks and made in a virtually dry style (4.5 grams/litre of residual sugar). It shows good flavour depth, with hints of spices and honey, and fresh acidity keeping things lively.

Vintage	07
WR	5
Drink	09-11

DRY $25 –V

Stoneleigh Marlborough Pinot Gris   ★★★

The 2008 vintage (★★★☆) from Pernod Ricard NZ is fresh and finely balanced, with a scented bouquet and good depth of citrus, pear and spice flavours, slightly sweet and smooth. Tasted prior to bottling (and so not rated), the 2009 is fragrant, with lively acidity and fresh, strong pear/spice flavours.

Vintage	08	07
WR	6	6
Drink	P	P

DRY $23 –V

Stoneleigh Rapaura Series Marlborough Pinot Gris   ★★★★☆

Made in a richer, sweeter style than its Stoneleigh stablemate (above), the 2008 vintage (★★★★★) was grown at Rapaura, harvested at 21.5 to 22.5 brix, and aged on its yeast lees in tanks for three months. A fleshy, concentrated wine with a slightly honeyed fragrance, ripe pear and spice flavours, good texture and real power through the palate, it's a deliciously aromatic wine, slightly sweet (11.5 grams/litre of residual sugar), oily and rich.

Vintage	08	07
WR	7	5
Drink	09-10	P

MED/DRY $27 AV

Takatu Matakana Pinot Gris   ★★★★☆

Grown on a north-facing hillside above Matakana, this is a sophisticated wine, fermented and lees-aged in old French oak puncheons. The 2008 vintage (★★★★☆) is ripely scented, mouthfilling and bone-dry, with sweet-fruit characters, citrusy and peachy, fine acidity, and unusual complexity for Pinot Gris. Tight and youthful, with a subtle seasoning of oak, it is finely textured and long. Drink now or cellar.

Vintage	08	07	06	05
WR	7	7	7	6
Drink	09-12	09-10	P	P

DRY $33 –V

Tasman Bay New Zealand Pinot Gris ★★★

The 2007 vintage (★★★) from Spencer Hill is an easy-drinking blend of Nelson and Marlborough grapes, briefly oak-aged. It's a medium to full-bodied style with fresh citrus-fruit and pear aromas, and citrusy, faintly honeyed, smooth flavours. The 2008 (★★★) is scented, slightly sweet and crisp, offering very easy drinking.

MED/DRY $19 AV

Tattybogler Otago Pinot Gris ★★★★

From Forrest, the 2009 vintage (★★★★) was grown at Bannockburn, in the Cromwell Basin, and the Waitaki Valley (hence the 'Otago' statement of origin on the label, rather than 'Central Otago'). Tasted soon after bottling, it's a powerful, rounded wine, 10 per cent barrel-fermented, with mouthfilling body and strong lychee, pear and spice flavours, finely textured and rounded (7 grams/litre of residual sugar).

Vintage	09	08
WR	5	6
Drink	09-12	09-10

MED/DRY $ 29 –V

Te Henga The Westie Premium Marlborough Pinot Gris (★★★☆)

Produced by Babich for the West Auckland licensing trusts, the 2008 vintage (★★★☆) is fresh-scented, with very good body and depth of ripe, peachy, faintly honeyed flavours. A generous wine, already drinking well, it offers fine value.

MED/DRY $16 V+

Te Kairanga Swing Bridge Gisborne Pinot Gris (★★★☆)

Enjoyable from the start, the 2008 vintage (★★★☆) is a crisp, vibrantly fruity wine with pear and spice flavours showing good delicacy, a slightly oily texture and a dry (3 grams/litre of residual sugar) finish.

Vintage	08
WR	6
Drink	09-12

DRY $19 AV

Te Mania Nelson Pinot Gris ★★★

The 2008 vintage (★★★), hand-picked and tank-fermented, is a fleshy wine (14 per cent alcohol), with fresh, peachy, slightly spicy flavours, showing decent depth.

Vintage	09	08	07
WR	6	5	6
Drink	09-12	09-10	P

MED/DRY $22 –V

Te Mara Central Otago Pinot Gris   (★★★★★)

The superb 2008 vintage (★★★★★) was grown on the Wanaka Road (between Cromwell and Wanaka), tank-fermented and stop-fermented just short of dryness. Highly scented, it is mouthfilling and rich, with concentrated peach, pear and spice flavours, very vibrant and harmonious, a sliver of sweetness, a slightly oily texture, and excellent delicacy and length.

MED/DRY $26 V+

Terrace Edge Waipara Valley Pinot Gris   (★★★★☆)

Richer and more complex than most New Zealand Pinot Gris, the 2008 vintage (★★★★☆) was fermented with indigenous yeasts in aged barrels. Fragrant, with a citrusy, slightly spicy bouquet, it is mouthfilling, with strong stone-fruit and spice flavours, a hint of honey, gentle sweetness (13 grams/litre of residual sugar), and excellent texture and length. Great value.

MED/DRY $19 V+

Terrain East Coast Pinot Gris   (★★★)

Sold at New World and PAK'nSAVE (it's a Foodstuffs brand), the 2008 vintage (★★★) is a fresh, medium to full-bodied wine with good varietal character and a hint of sweetness amid its peach, pear and spice flavours, which linger to a smooth finish.

MED/DRY $13 V+

Terravin Marlborough Pinot Gris   ★★★★☆

The 2008 vintage (★★★★) was estate-grown in the Omaka Valley, hand-picked, fermented with indigenous yeasts and lees-aged in old French oak barrels. Fleshy and complex, it is not highly aromatic but weighty, with rich, ripe peach, pear and spice flavours, good mouthfeel, texture and harmony, and a rounded, dryish finish (6 grams/litre of residual sugar).

MED/DRY $35 –V

Te Whare Ra Marlborough Pinot Gris   (★★★☆)

The 2007 vintage (★★★☆) was estate-grown at Renwick, harvested at 24 brix and mostly handled in tanks; 25 per cent was fermented and lees-stirred in old French barrels. It shows good weight and delicacy, with fresh pear and spice aromas and flavours, ripe, slightly sweet (7 grams/litre of residual sugar) and rounded.

MED/DRY $26 –V

Thornbury Waipara Pinot Gris   ★★★☆

The 2009 vintage (★★★★) from Villa Maria is a full-bodied, dryish style (5 grams/litre of residual sugar), with fresh, strongly varietal flavours of peaches, pears and spices, showing good richness and harmony. It's already drinking well.

Vintage	09
WR	7
Drink	09-12

MED/DRY $21 AV

Tinpot Hut Marlborough Pinot Gris   (★★★☆)

The floral 2008 vintage (★★★☆) is mouthfilling and smooth, with dryish pear, lychee and spice flavours, showing good depth, vibrancy and youthful impact.

MED/DRY $21 AV

Ti Point Hawke's Bay Pinot Gris   (★★★)

Grown at Mangatahi, the 2008 vintage (★★★) is a dry (3 grams/litre of residual sugar) style with fresh citrus-fruit, pear and spice flavours and a crisp, tight finish.

DRY $21 –V

Tohu Nelson Pinot Gris   ★★★☆

The 2009 vintage (★★★★) is the best yet. Grown in the Whenua Matua Vineyard and partly barrel-fermented, it is ripely scented, weighty and rounded, with strong stone-fruit, spice and pear flavours, a touch of complexity and a dryish (5 grams/litre of residual sugar), finely balanced finish. Fine value.

MED/DRY $19 AV

Torlesse Waipara Pinot Gris   ★★★★

The 2009 vintage (★★★★☆) is scented, mouthfilling and finely poised, with vibrant lychee and spice flavours showing lovely purity, richness and roundness. A good buy.

MED/DRY $20 V+

Torrent Bay Nelson Pinot Gris   (★★☆)

From Anchorage, the 2008 vintage (★★☆) is a light, dry wine (4 grams/litre of residual sugar), with fresh, vibrant, lemony, appley flavours that lack a bit of ripeness and richness.

DRY $21 –V

Tranquil Valley Matakana Pinot Gris   (★★☆)

From Huasheng Wines, linked to Matakana Estate, the 2008 vintage (★★☆) is an easy-drinking wine, citrusy, peachy and slightly honeyed, with moderate depth and a smooth finish.

MED/DRY $25 –V

Tresillian Pinot Gris   (★★★☆)

Estate-grown at West Melton, the 2008 vintage (★★★☆) is a medium-bodied Canterbury wine (12.5 per cent alcohol) with good depth of citrusy, peachy flavour, fresh acidity to balance its slight sweetness (5 grams/litre of residual sugar) and a lingering finish. Well worth cellaring.

MED/DRY $25 –V

Trinity Hill 'Black Label' Hawke's Bay Pinot Gris   ★★★★

The 2008 vintage (★★★★) was grown in the Gimblett Gravels (46 per cent), at Haumoana (37 per cent) and at Mangaorapa Station, in Central Hawke's Bay (17 per cent). Hand-picked, tank-fermented and lees-aged, it's a dry wine (3 grams/litre of residual sugar), rich and full-bodied. It shows excellent balance and depth, with a lifted fragrance of pears and spices.

Vintage	08	07	06
WR	6	5	5
Drink	09-10	09-10	P

DRY $29 –V

Trinity Hill Hawke's Bay Pinot Gris   (★★★)

The 'white label' 2008 vintage (★★★) was grown at four sites, tank-fermented and lees-aged for four months. It's a full-bodied, flavoursome wine, ripe, peachy and slightly spicy, with a rounded, dry finish (3 grams/litre of residual sugar).

DRY $19 AV

Triplebank Awatere Valley Marlborough Pinot Gris   ★★★★

Pernod Ricard NZ's wine is typically aromatic and flavour-packed. The 2008 vintage (★★★★) was harvested at 21.6 brix and lees-aged for two months in tanks. A mouthfilling, slightly sweet wine (8.5 grams/litre of residual sugar) with vibrant pear and spice flavours and fresh, balanced acidity, it's a delicious mouthful – creamy-textured and floral.

Vintage	08	07	06
WR	6	6	6
Drink	09-10	P	P

MED/DRY $24 AV

Trout Valley Nelson Pinot Gris   (★★★)

From Kahurangi Estate, the 2008 vintage (★★★) is a scented, slightly Riesling-like wine with good depth of vibrant lemon, apple and spice flavours, slightly sweet and fresh.

MED/DRY $17 AV

Turanga Creek New Zealand Pinot Gris   (★★★☆)

Grown at Whitford, in South Auckland, the debut 2008 vintage (★★★☆) is an attractively scented, medium-bodied wine, fresh and vibrant, with ripe peach, citrus-fruit and spice flavours, showing very good depth, and a finely balanced, dry finish (3 grams/litre of residual sugar).

DRY $24 –V

Tussock Nelson Pinot Gris   ★★★☆

From Woollaston Estates, the 2009 vintage (★★★) is a dry style (3 grams/litre of residual sugar), fleshy and slightly buttery, with ripe, peachy, rounded flavours.

DRY $18 V+

TW Gisborne Pinot Gris   (★★★)

Fleshy, peachy and slightly buttery, the 2007 vintage (★★★) was matured in old oak casks. Light straw, with stone-fruit flavours, ripe and rounded, it's a Chardonnay-like style with some complexity.

DRY $22 –V

Two Rivers Marlborough Wairau Selection Pinot Gris   ★★★☆

Floral and finely balanced, the 2008 vintage (★★★☆) was mostly handled in tanks, but 7 per cent of the blend was barrel-fermented. It's a fresh, easy-drinking style with ripe stone-fruit and spice flavours, showing very good depth.

MED/DRY $26 –V

Two Sisters Central Otago Pinot Gris   (★★★★)

Hand-picked at Lowburn, the 2008 vintage (★★★★) was barrel-fermented with indigenous yeasts. Pale straw, it's a mouthfilling, gently sweet style, softly textured, with good concentration of peachy, spicy flavour and excellent complexity and harmony, in an Alsace style, drinking well now.

MED $30 –V

Two Tracks Marlborough Pinot Gris   (★★★)

From Wither Hills, the debut 2008 vintage (★★★) is fresh, vibrantly fruity and smooth, with balanced acidity and clearly varietal, pear and spice flavours showing good depth. Enjoyable from the start.

Vintage	08
WR	6
Drink	P

MED/DRY $19 AV

Urlar Gladstone Pinot Gris   (★★★☆)

The creamy, toasty 2008 vintage (★★★☆) was grown near Masterton, in the Wairarapa, and barrel-fermented. Slightly Chardonnay-like, with mouthfilling body and good complexity, it's a well-rounded wine, still youthful and worth cellaring.

DRY $28 –V

Vavasour Marlborough Pinot Gris   ★★★★

The 2007 vintage (★★★★) was estate-grown in the Awatere Valley, hand-picked and mostly handled in tanks, but 15 per cent was fermented with indigenous yeasts and lees-stirred in seasoned French oak barriques. Floral and slightly minerally, it's a mouthfilling, finely textured wine, slightly sweet (6.6 grams/litre of residual sugar), with lychee, apple and spice flavours showing impressive purity, vibrancy and length.

Vintage	08	07	06
WR	7	6	6
Drink	09-13	09-10	P

MED/DRY $25 AV

Vidal East Coast Pinot Gris   ★★★☆

The 2009 vintage (★★★☆) is a blend of Hawke's Bay, Marlborough and Gisborne grapes. It's an off-dry style (5 grams/litre of residual sugar), vibrantly fruity and finely balanced, with fresh, delicate pear and spice flavours that linger well.

Vintage	09	08
WR	6	6
Drink	09-11	09-10

MED/DRY $19 AV

Villa Maria Cellar Selection Marlborough Pinot Gris   ★★★★

From warmer sites in the Awatere Valley, the 2009 vintage (★★★★) is a full-bodied, basically dry style (4.5 grams/litre of residual sugar) with strong pear, lychee and spice flavours. Fresh, with excellent depth, texture and harmony, it should unfold well.

Vintage	09
WR	7
Drink	09-13

DRY $23 AV

Villa Maria Private Bin East Coast Pinot Gris   ★★★★

Often one of the country's top-value Pinot Gris. The 2009 vintage (★★★☆) was grown in Gisborne (58 per cent), Hawke's Bay (22 per cent) and Marlborough (20 per cent), lees-aged for two months in tanks, and made in a dryish (4.8 grams/litre of residual sugar) style. It's a mouthfilling, clearly varietal wine, distinctly spicy, with good flavour depth and a creamy-smooth finish.

Vintage	09	08	07
WR	6	6	6
Drink	09-11	09-10	P

DRY $19 V+

Villa Maria Single Vineyard Seddon Pinot Gris   ★★★★★

One of the country's top Pinot Gris, this Awatere Valley, Marlborough wine is typically sturdy, beautifully scented and intense. The 2008 vintage (★★★★☆) was tank-fermented and lees-aged for eight months. It's a medium-dry style (7.5 grams/litre of residual sugar), powerful (14.5 per cent alcohol), with fresh, impressively concentrated pear, lychee and spice flavours, a hint of honey and a well-rounded finish.

Vintage	08	07	06
WR	7	7	6
Drink	09-14	09-13	09-11

MED/DRY $31 AV

Villa Maria Single Vineyard Taylors Pass Pinot Gris   ★★★★☆

Grown in the Awatere Valley, this is typically a floral Marlborough wine with pear/spice flavours in a medium-dry style with lovely texture and richness. The 2007 vintage (★★★★★) was hand-picked and fermented and lees-aged for five months, with weekly stirring, in tanks. Enticingly scented, it is weighty (14 per cent alcohol), with highly concentrated, vibrant flavours of pears, lychees, spices and apricots, a sliver of sweetness (10.3 grams/litre of residual sugar) and a very harmonious, rich and rounded finish. Benchmark stuff.

Vintage	07	06
WR	7	6
Drink	09-13	09-11

MED/DRY $31 –V

Vin Alto Pinot Grigio Riserva   ★★★☆

Estate-grown at a cool, elevated site at Clevedon, in South Auckland, the 2007 (★★★★) is from an ultra-low-yielding season. Made in a slightly sweet (9 grams/litre of residual sugar) style, it has rich, well-ripened flavours, while retaining the fresh acidity typical of the vineyard's Pinot Gris.

MED/DRY $27 –V

Waimea Bolitho SV Pinot Gris   ★★★★

The 2007 vintage (★★★☆) was estate-grown on the Waimea Plains, in Nelson, hand-harvested at an average of 25.2 brix, and cool-fermented and lees-stirred for six weeks in tanks. A gently sweet style (25 grams/litre of residual sugar), it offers plenty of peachy, spicy flavour, in an attractive, moderately concentrated, easy-drinking style.

Vintage	07	06	05
WR	7	7	6
Drink	09-12	09-11	09-10

MED $25 AV

Waimea Nelson Pinot Gris   ★★★★

From one vintage to the next, this is one of the best-value Pinot Gris in the country. The 2008 vintage (★★★★) is fleshy, with concentrated, ripe, peachy, slightly spicy flavours and a hint of sweetness (6.8 grams/litre of residual sugar). Rich and faintly honeyed, it's a finely balanced wine, delicious now.

Vintage	08	07	06	05
WR	7	7	6	7
Drink	09-12	09-11	09-10	P

MED/DRY $22 V+

Waipara Hills Equinox Waipara Pinot Gris   (★★★★)

The 2007 vintage (★★★★) is a weighty, slightly sweet style with excellent intensity of ripe pear, spice and slight ginger flavours.

MED/DRY $43 –V

Waipara Hills Soul of the South Waipara Pinot Gris   (★★★☆)

Grown in the Pilgrim and Glasnevin vineyards, the 2008 vintage (★★★☆) is a slightly sweet wine with fresh, pure citrus-fruit, pear and spice flavours, crisp and lingering.

MED/DRY $25 –V

Waipara Hills Southern Cross Selection Waipara Pinot Gris   (★★★★)

From the Glasnevin Vineyard, adjacent to the winery, the 2008 vintage (★★★★) is a fresh, full-bodied wine, finely textured, with impressively concentrated citrus-fruit, pear and spice flavours.

MED/DRY $29 –V

Wairau River Marlborough Pinot Gris   ★★★★

The 2008 vintage (★★★★) is a medium-dry style (6 grams/litre of residual sugar), with mouthfilling body (13 per cent alcohol) and good texture and concentration of pear, apple and spice flavours, showing some complexity.

Vintage	09	08
WR	6	4
Drink	09-12	P

MED/DRY $23 AV

Waitaki Braids Waitaki Valley Pinot Gris   (★★★★)

The youthful 2008 vintage (★★★★) was hand-harvested in the Otago Station Vineyard and tank-fermented. Mouthfilling (14 per cent alcohol), it's a rich wine with tight, citrusy, slightly minerally flavours that build well across the palate to a tight, dry finish (2.5 grams/litre of residual sugar). Best drinking mid-2010+.

DRY $45 –V

Weka River Waipara Valley Pinot Gris   (★★★☆)

The 2008 vintage (★★★☆) is scented, with fresh, vibrant, slightly sweet pear and spice flavours, showing very good depth.

MED/DRY $22 AV

Whitehaven Marlborough Pinot Gris   ★★★☆

Mouthfilling, with fresh pear, lychee and spice flavours, gentle sweetness (7 grams/litre of residual sugar) and a slightly oily texture, the 2009 vintage (★★★☆) is a very easy-drinking style with good depth.

Vintage	09	08	07	06
WR	7	6	6	7
Drink	09-11	09-10	P	P

MED/DRY $23 –V

Wild Earth Central Otago Pinot Gris   ★★★★

Estate-grown at Bannockburn, the 2008 vintage (★★★★☆) was hand-harvested and mostly handled in tanks, but 20 per cent of the blend was fermented in French oak barrels. Very fresh and pure, it's a full-bodied style with incisive, slightly sweet (11 grams/litre of residual sugar) pear and spice flavours, showing lovely balance and immediacy.

MED/DRY $27 –V

Wild Rock Otago Pinot Gris   (★★★☆)

Sold only in supermarkets, the easy-drinking 2008 vintage (★★★☆) is from a subsidiary of Craggy Range. Full-bodied, it is slightly sweet, with peachy, spicy flavours showing good freshness and vibrancy, a slightly creamy texture and a well-rounded finish.

MED/DRY $19 AV

Wild Rock Sur Lie Pinot Gris   (★★★★)

From a Craggy Range subsidiary, the 2008 vintage (★★★★) is a refined Hawke's Bay wine. Mostly handled in tanks, but 7 per cent French oak-matured, it has mouthfilling body and pure, peachy, slightly spicy and leesy flavours. It shows good mouthfeel and texture, with a dryish (5.4 grams/litre of residual sugar), lingering finish.

Vintage	08
WR	6
Drink	09-11

MED/DRY $20 V+

Wild South Marlborough Pinot Gris   ★★★

From Sacred Hill and grown in the Waihopai Valley, the 2008 vintage (★★★) is a finely balanced, easy-drinking style with good depth of pear/spice flavours and a fully dry finish.

DRY $19 AV

Wither Hills Wairau Valley Marlborough Pinot Gris   ★★★☆

The 2008 vintage (★★★☆) was mostly handled in tanks, but a small portion was fermented with indigenous yeasts in old French oak casks. Ripely scented, it is mouthfilling (14.5 per cent alcohol), with a slightly oily texture, fresh, vibrant stone-fruit and spice flavours, showing lively acidity, and good depth.

Vintage	08	07
WR	6	7
Drink	09-10	P

MED/DRY $20 AV

Wooing Tree Central Otago Pinot Gris   (★★★☆)

The 2008 vintage (★★★☆) was grown in the Cromwell Basin, hand-picked and barrel-fermented. Fleshy and rounded, it's a creamy-textured wine with good depth of fresh, dryish, peachy, slightly toasty flavours, maturing well.

MED/DRY $28 –V

Woollaston Burke's Bank Nelson Pinot Gris   ★★★★

Grown at Burke's Bank, Hope, the 2007 vintage (★★★★) was hand-picked and made in a dry style (3.9 grams/litre of residual sugar). A strapping wine (over 15 per cent alcohol), it has low acidity and ripe flavours of stone-fruit and spices, slightly honeyed, concentrated and soft.

DRY $22 V+

Woollaston Nelson Pinot Gris   ★★★★

The 2009 vintage (★★★★) is a slightly sweet wine (6 grams/litre of residual sugar), with good weight and strong, fresh, vibrant flavours of stone-fruit and spices.

MED/DRY $20 V+

Yealands Estate Marlborough Pinot Gris   ★★★

Estate-grown in the Awatere Valley, the 2009 vintage (★★★) is mouthfilling, with strong, lemony flavours, hints of pears and spices, and a basically dry (4 grams/litre of residual sugar), crisp finish.

DRY $23 –V

Yealands Marlborough Pinot Gris   (★★★)

Estate-grown at Seaview, in the Awatere Valley, the debut 2008 vintage (★★★) is a fresh, finely balanced wine, crisp and vibrant, with plenty of citrusy, peachy, slightly spicy flavour and an off-dry (5 grams/litre of residual sugar) finish.

MED/DRY $19 AV

Riesling

Riesling isn't yet one of New Zealand's great successes in overseas markets – the 86,222 cases shipped in the year to June 2009 accounted for just 0.7 per cent of our total wine exports. Many New Zealand wine lovers also ignore this country's Rieslings.

Scentedness and intense lemon/lime flavours enlivened by fresh, appetising acidity are the hallmarks of the top New Zealand Rieslings. Around the world, Riesling has traditionally been regarded as Chardonnay's great rival in the white-wine quality stakes, well ahead of Sauvignon Blanc. So why are wine lovers here slow to appreciate Riesling's lofty stature?

Riesling is usually made in a slightly sweet style, to balance the grape's natural high acidity, but this obvious touch of sweetness runs counter to the fashion for 'dry' wines. And fine Riesling demands time (at the very least, a couple of years) to unfold its full potential; drunk in its infancy, as it so often is, it lacks the toasty, minerally, honeyed richness that is the real glory of Riesling.

After recently being overhauled by Pinot Gris, Riesling ranks as New Zealand's fourth most extensively planted white-wine variety. Between 2007 and 2010, its total area of bearing vines is expanding slowly, from 868 to 934 hectares.

The great grape of Germany, Riesling is a classic cool-climate variety, particularly well suited to the cooler growing temperatures and lower humidity of the South Island. Its stronghold is Marlborough, where well over 40 per cent of the vines are clustered, but the grape is also extensively planted in Nelson, Canterbury and Central Otago.

Riesling styles vary markedly around the world. Most Marlborough wines are medium to full-bodied (12 to 13.5 per cent alcohol), with just a touch of sweetness. However, a new breed of Riesling has recently emerged – lighter (only 7.5 to 10 per cent alcohol) and markedly sweeter. These refreshingly light, sweet Rieslings offer a more vivid contrast in style to New Zealand's other major white wines, and are much closer in style to the classic German model.

Alana Estate Martinborough Riesling   ★★★★

The 2008 vintage (★★★★) is ripely scented, with crisp grapefruit, lime and passionfruit flavours in a medium-dry style (7 grams/litre of residual sugar), showing good intensity and cellar potential.

Vintage	09	08	07
WR	6	6	7
Drink	15-20	14-20	09-15

MED/DRY $30 –V

Alexia Martinborough Riesling   (★★★☆)

From Jane Cooper, winemaker at Matahiwi, the 2008 vintage (★★★☆) is tangy and slightly minerally, with good depth of lemon/lime flavours and a gently sweet, crisp finish.

MED/DRY $20 AV

Allan Scott Marlborough Riesling   ★★★★

A typically impressive wine, sourced partly from vines in the heart of the Wairau Valley approaching 30 years old. The 2008 vintage (★★★☆) is scented and mouthfilling (13.5 per cent alcohol), with very good depth of citrusy, slightly appley flavours, in a medium-dry style (7 grams/litre of residual sugar) woven with fresh, appetising acidity.

Vintage	08
WR	6
Drink	09-18

MED/DRY $20 V+

Allan Scott Moorlands Marlborough Riesling   ★★★★☆

A basically dry style (6 grams/litre of residual sugar), the distinctive 2008 vintage (★★★★) was mostly handled in tanks, but 5 per cent was aged in old casks. It's a concentrated, complex wine with an array of grapefruit, pear, lime and spice flavours, a faint hint of honey and a rounded finish.

Vintage	08
WR	6
Drink	09-18

MED/DRY $27 V+

Amisfield Dry Riesling   ★★★★

Estate-grown in the Cromwell Basin of Central Otago, the 2009 vintage (★★★★☆) was hand-picked and fermented to a medium-dry style (7 grams/litre of residual sugar). It's an intense wine, lemony and limey, with lovely vibrancy, delicacy and harmony, and a zingy, long finish. It's already approachable, but should be at its best 2011+.

Vintage	09	08	07	06
WR	6	6	5	5
Drink	09-17	09-12	09-12	09-11

MED/DRY $30 –V

Amisfield Rocky Knoll Riesling – see Sweet White Wines

Anchorage Classic Riesling   (★★★★)

Maturing gracefully, the 2007 vintage (★★★★), grown in Nelson, is a tightly structured, medium style (18 grams/litre of residual sugar) with lemony, slightly spicy flavours showing excellent vigour and intensity. Still youthful, with good harmony, it is fresh, floral and lingering.

MED $16 V+

Anchorage Nelson Riesling   ★★☆

The 2008 vintage (★★☆) is a light wine (8.5 per cent alcohol), with abundant sweetness (20 grams/litre of residual sugar) and moderate depth of crisp, lemony, appley flavours.

Vintage	08	07	06
WR	6	6	4
Drink	09-13	09-12	09-12

MED $16 AV

Astrolabe Voyage Marlborough Dry Riesling   (★★★★)

The 2008 vintage (★★★★) is a single-vineyard, Waihopai Valley wine with a citrusy, slightly minerally bouquet and good flavour intensity. Floral and elegant, it has a rich, dryish finish (6.5 grams/litre of residual sugar).

Vintage	08
WR	6
Drink	09-13

MED/DRY $23 AV

Aurora Vineyard, The, Bendigo Riesling   ★★★★

From Bendigo, in Central Otago, the 2008 vintage (★★★) was estate-grown and hand-picked at 23 brix. The bouquet is restrained, but the palate is better – lemony, tight and crisp, with good depth and a slightly sweet (10 grams/litre of residual sugar) finish.

Vintage	08	07
WR	6	6
Drink	09-13	09-12

MED/DRY $24 AV

Aurum Central Otago Riesling   ★★★★

Estate-grown at Lowburn, in the Cromwell Basin, the 2008 vintage (★★★★) is a mouth-wateringly crisp, cool-climate style with a lemony, slightly toasty bouquet. Lively with a distinctly minerally streak, it has good intensity of vibrant, slightly sweet (7.9 grams/litre of residual sugar) lemon/lime flavours and a tangy, lingering finish.

Vintage	08	07
WR	6	6
Drink	10-15	09-15

MED/DRY $23 AV

Babich Marlborough Riesling Dry   ★★★☆

Typically a well-crafted wine with good drinkability. Grown in the Wairau and Waihopai valleys, the 2008 vintage (★★★) is lemony and slightly minerally, with some early development showing. Crisp and dryish, it's for drinking now onwards.

MED/DRY $20 AV

Bald Hills Last Light Riesling   ★★★★

Hand-picked from a 1-hectare plot at Bannockburn, in Central Otago, the 2008 vintage (★★★☆) is a full-bodied style (14 per cent alcohol) with strong, fresh, lemony scents and good depth of citrusy, peachy, slightly spicy flavour. Slightly sweet and crisp, it's likely to mature well.

Vintage	09	08	07	06
WR	6	6	6	6
Drink	09-12	11-14	10-13	09-12

MED/DRY $23 AV

Bannock Brae Goldfields Dry Riesling   ★★☆

This Central Otago wine 'exhibits the characteristics of a bygone age'. The 2008 vintage (★★☆) was grown at Bannockburn and fully barrel-fermented, with lees-stirring and partial malolactic fermentation. It's a more 'oxidative', less vibrantly fruity wine than most, lemony, dryish (6 grams/litre of residual sugar) and mellow.

MED/DRY $24 –V

Beach House Hawke's Bay Riesling   ★★★★

A single-vineyard Hawke's Bay wine, grown near the sea at Te Awanga, the 2008 vintage (★★★★) is light and lively, with a fresh, appley, minerally bouquet, good acid spine and strong, lemony, slightly sweet flavours (8 grams/litre of residual sugar).

Vintage	08
WR	6
Drink	09-25

MED/DRY $17 V+

Bird Marlborough Riesling   ★★★★

A single-vineyard wine, estate-grown at Omaka, the 2007 vintage (★★★★) is almost fully dry (4.5 grams/litre of residual sugar). Finely scented, it is full-bodied (13.5 per cent alcohol), with fresh, strong lemon and lime flavours, delicate and lingering. Finely balanced, it carries the dry style well.

Vintage	07	06
WR	5	6
Drink	09-12	P

DRY $23 AV

Bishops Head Reserve Riesling   (★★★☆)

The 2007 vintage (★★★) was grown at Waipara and 25 per cent barrel-fermented. It's an off-dry style (8.6 grams/litre of residual sugar) with strong, crisp, lemony, slightly spicy flavours, seasoned with nutty oak.

MED/DRY $23 –V

Bishops Head Waipara Riesling   ★★★☆

The 2008 vintage (★★★☆) is a zingy, medium style (20 grams/litre of residual sugar), 10 per cent barrel-aged, with good depth of lemon/apple flavours, crisp and youthful.

MED $19 AV

Black Barn Vineyards Single Vineyard Riesling   (★★★)

Pale yellow, with a slightly honeyed and toasty bouquet, the 2007 vintage (★★★) is a fleshy, rounded Hawke's Bay wine, slightly sweet (10 grams/litre of residual sugar), citrusy and appley, in a forward style, ready now onwards.

MED/DRY $25 –V

Black Estate Omihi Waipara Riesling   (★★★☆)

Hand-picked at Waipara but not estate-grown, the easy-drinking 2008 vintage (★★★☆) is a slightly honeyed wine with a clear botrytis influence. A medium-bodied style (11 per cent alcohol) with citrus-fruit and passionfruit flavours, gently sweet and crisp, it's drinking well now.

Vintage	08
WR	7
Drink	10-15

MED $22 AV

Blackenbrook Vineyard Nelson Riesling   ★★★★☆

Full of potential, yet already drinking well, the estate-grown 2008 vintage (★★★★★) is tight and rich, with substantial body, a sliver of sweetness (10 grams/litre of residual sugar), and lovely depth of citrusy, slightly spicy flavours. From the earliest harvest to date, it's still youthful, with notable ripeness, delicacy and length. (The 2009 is sweeter, with 23 grams/litre of residual sugar.)

Vintage	09	08	07	06	05
WR	7	7	7	NM	6
Drink	09-12	09-11	09-10	NM	P

MED/DRY $23 V+

Boreham Wood Single Vineyard Marlborough Riesling   (★★★★)

The vivacious, light 2008 vintage (10 per cent alcohol) was hand-harvested in the Awatere Valley from first-crop vines. Lemony, minerally scents lead into a gently sweet style (30 grams/litre of residual sugar) with rich, citrusy, faintly honeyed flavours, threaded with appetising acidity. Finely balanced and lingering.

Vintage	09	08
WR	7	7
Drink	10-14	09-13

MED $24 AV

Borthwick Vineyard Wairarapa Riesling   ★★★☆

Estate-grown at Gladstone, the 2008 vintage (★★★★) is a single-vineyard wine with strong, citrusy, limey flavours, appetising acidity and a long, dryish finish. It shows good freshness, richness and harmony.

MED/DRY $24 –V

Bouldevines Marlborough Riesling   ★★★☆

Grown on the south side of the Wairau Valley, the 2009 vintage (★★★☆) is a single-vineyard wine, fresh, crisp and medium-bodied, with ripe, lemony, appley, slightly spicy flavours and a dryish finish.

MED/DRY $20 AV

Brightside Brightwater Riesling   ★★★

From Kaimira Estate, the 2009 vintage is a medium style (15 grams/litre of residual sugar) with ripe, citrusy, appley flavours, balanced for easy drinking. (Tasted shortly after bottling, it was clearly bottle-shocked, so is not rated.) Enjoyable now, the 2008 (★★★), labelled 'Nelson Riesling', is slightly honeyed, with good depth of citrusy, medium-dry flavour (12.7 grams/litre of residual sugar).

Vintage	09	08
WR	6	5
Drink	09-14	09-12

MED $16 V+

Brightwater Vineyards Lord Rutherford Dry Riesling   (★★★★☆)

Dry (4 grams/litre of residual sugar) but not austere, the debut 2007 vintage (★★★★☆) is punchy, with mouthfilling body and concentrated, very ripe grapefruit, lime and peach flavours. It shows excellent potential.

Vintage	07
WR	6
Drink	09-10

DRY $25 AV

Brightwater Vineyards Nelson Riesling   ★★★★

Estate-grown on the Waimea Plains, this wine is always full of personality. The 2009 vintage (★★★★) is a distinctly medium style (18 grams/litre of residual sugar), handled entirely in tanks. A mouthfilling, vibrantly fruity wine with strong citrusy, limey flavours, a hint of passionfruit and appetising acidity, it's well balanced for easy drinking.

Vintage	09	08	07	06	05	04
WR	5	5	6	6	6	4
Drink	09-12	09-11	09-10	P	P	P

MED $20 V+

Brookfields Ohiti Estate Riesling   ★★★☆

Grown at Ohiti, inland from Fernhill, the 2008 vintage (★★★☆) is a slightly sweet (11 grams/litre of residual sugar) Hawke's Bay wine, medium-bodied, lemony and slightly minerally, with good harmony and drink-young appeal.

Vintage	08
WR	7
Drink	09-13

MED/DRY $20 AV

Camshorn Waipara Classic Riesling   ★★★★

The 2008 vintage (★★★★) from Pernod Ricard NZ is immaculate, finely textured and very harmonious, with gently sweet, lemon/apple flavours showing impressive delicacy, purity and persistence. Tasted prior to bottling (and so not rated), the 2009 was similar – punchy, with vibrant lemon/lime flavours, finely balanced for easy drinking.

Vintage	08	07
WR	5	6
Drink	09-10	P

MED $27 –V

Camshorn Waipara Dry Riesling   ★★★★

The 2007 vintage (★★★★) from Pernod Ricard NZ is a classic dry style (4.5 grams/litre of residual sugar), with rich, ripe grapefruit and peach flavours and a rounded finish. Still fresh, it's maturing very gracefully, with toasty, bottle-aged notes adding complexity.

Vintage	07	06	05
WR	6	6	6
Drink	09-12	09-10	P

DRY $27 –V

Canadoro Martinborough Riesling   ★★☆

The hand-picked 2007 vintage (★★☆) is a medium-bodied style with solid depth of lemony, limey flavours and a slightly sweet (7 grams/litre of residual sugar), crisp finish.

MED/DRY $18 –V

Carrick Central Otago Dry Riesling   (★★★★)

Dry (4 grams/litre of residual sugar) but not austere, the 2008 vintage (★★★★) was grown at Bannockburn. A tight, medium to full-bodied wine, it's very youthful, with searching, lemony, appley flavours, a minerally thread and appetising acidity. A classic cellaring style; open mid-2010+.

Vintage	08
WR	6
Drink	10-14

DRY $21 V+

Carrick Central Otago Riesling   ★★★★

Consistently classy and good value. Grown at Bannockburn, the 2008 vintage (★★★★) is a medium style (18 grams/litre of residual sugar) with intense, vibrant lemon, apple and lime flavours, slightly minerally, crisp and long. It should mature well.

Vintage	08	07	06	05	04
WR	6	6	6	7	6
Drink	10-14	09-13	09-12	09-12	09-10

MED/DRY $21 V+

Carrick Josephine Central Otago Riesling   ★★★★★

The 2008 vintage (★★★★★) was grown in the Lot 8 Vineyard, on the Cairnmuir Terraces at Bannockburn, hand-picked and stop-fermented in a low-alcohol (9.5 per cent), medium-sweet style (49 grams/litre of residual sugar). Showing lovely lightness, richness and harmony, it is tight and concentrated, with fresh grapefruit, passionfruit and lime flavours, good acid spine and instant appeal. Drink now or cellar.

MED $26 V+

Catalina Sounds Marlborough Riesling   (★★★★)

Grown mostly in the Ant's Nest Vineyard, high on a ridge of the Waihopai Valley, the 2007 vintage (★★★★) is a dry style (3.8 grams/litre of residual sugar) with a highly scented, lemony bouquet. Light (11.5 per cent alcohol) and lively, citrusy and slightly minerally, it carries the dry style well and shows strong personality.

DRY $21 V+

Charles Wiffen Marlborough Riesling   ★★★★

The 2007 vintage (★★★★) is finely balanced, with lemon/lime flavours, slightly sweet (9 grams/litre of residual sugar) and youthful. It shows good intensity, with a long finish. The 2008 (★★★★) is very similar – a refined young wine, scented and full-flavoured, in a medium-dry style with obvious potential.

MED/DRY $19 V+

Clayridge Marlborough Wild Riesling   ★★★☆

Grown in the Escaroth Vineyard, high in Taylors Pass, and in the Omaka Valley, the 2008 vintage (★★★★) was fermented with indigenous yeasts in tanks. Scented, light-bodied (11.5 per cent) and lively, it's a distinctly medium style (22 grams/litre of residual sugar) with vibrant peach, lemon and apple flavours, showing very good intensity. It's already delicious.

Vintage	08	07
WR	6	5
Drink	09-18	09-17

MED $24 –V

Clearwater Vineyards Waipara Riesling   (★★★★)

Still on sale in 2009, the 2005 vintage (★★★★) from Sherwood Estate is maturing well, with bright, light lemon/green colour and strong, ripe, citrusy flavours, slightly minerally and long.

MED/DRY $24 AV

Clifford Bay Estate Marlborough Riesling   ★★★★

Grown in the Awatere Valley, the 2007 vintage (★★★★) is lemon-scented, with mouthfilling body, a sliver of sweetness (7 grams/litre of residual sugar), and fresh, pure lemon/apple flavours, showing good potential.

MED/DRY $20 V+

Cloudy Bay Riesling   ★★★★☆

Released at over four years old, the 2005 vintage (★★★★☆) was grown in Marlborough and fermented with indigenous yeasts in old French oak barrels. Light yellow/green, it is highly scented, with the minerally, toasty notes of classic bottle-aged Riesling. Poised and tight, with rich grapefruit, lime and spice flavours, an unobtrusive splash of sweetness (5.4 grams/litre of residual sugar) and good acid spine, it shows good complexity and lovely harmony. Drink now or cellar.

MED/DRY $35 –V

Coney Ragtime Riesling   ★★★☆

This characterful Martinborough wine is made in a medium-dry style. The 2008 vintage (★★★☆) has ripe-fruit aromas leading into a mouthfilling wine (13 per cent alcohol) with strong, ripe, citrusy flavours, fresh acidity and a hint of marmalade.

Vintage	08	07	06	05
WR	7	5	6	5
Drink	09-11	09-10	09	P

MED/DRY $20 AV

Coney Rallentando Riesling   ★★★

This Martinborough wine is a drier style than its stablemate (above). Pale lemon/green, the 2007 vintage (★★★☆) has good depth of lemony, spicy flavours, tight and crisp. It's developing well, but best opened 2010+.

Vintage	07	06	05
WR	5	6	5
Drink	10-15	09-12	09-10

DRY $20 –V

Corbans Homestead Waipara Riesling   (★★★)

The 2009 vintage (★★★) flowed from Pernod Ricard NZ's vineyards in North Canterbury. Balanced for easy drinking, it has passionfruit and citrus-fruit flavours, showing good depth, and a slightly sweet, crisp finish.

MED/DRY $17 AV

Corbans White Label Johannisberg Riesling   ★★☆

Some past vintages have been trans-Tasman blends, but the 2008 (★★☆) from Pernod Ricard NZ was made entirely from New Zealand grapes. Enjoyable in its youth, it's a lemon-scented, gently sweet wine with light, fresh, citrusy flavours, a hint of honey and crisp acidity. Good value.

MED $9 V+

Crab Farm Hawke's Bay Riesling   (★★★★)

Already drinking well, the rich 2008 vintage (★★★★) offers top value. Crisp and gently sweet (14 grams/litre of residual sugar), it has good intensity of citrusy, limey, faintly honeyed flavour.

Vintage	08
WR	7
Drink	09-12

MED/DRY $17 V+

Craggy Range Fletcher Family Vineyard Riesling   ★★★☆

Past vintages have matured well. The 2008 (★★★☆) was grown on the Rocenvin Estate, in Marlborough's Wairau Valley. Fresh and tightly structured, with moderate alcohol (11.4 per cent), gentle sweetness and appetising acidity, it's an obvious candidate for cellaring.

Vintage	09	08	07	06	05
WR	7	6	6	7	6
Drink	09-16	09-15	09-12	09-14	09-10

MED/DRY $23 –V

Craggy Range Glasnevin Gravels Vineyard Waipara Riesling   ★★★★

Like its predecessors, the 2008 vintage (★★★★) was modelled on the slender but intensely flavoured Rieslings of the Mosel. It has low alcohol (10 per cent), with penetrating, lemony, appley flavours, sweetish, slightly minerally and long.

Vintage	09	08
WR	6	7
Drink	09-16	09-13

MED $23 AV

Craggy Range Otago Station Vineyard Riesling   (★★★★)

Grown in the Waitaki Valley, North Otago, the 2008 vintage (★★★★) is still very youthful, with pure, vibrant lemon/lime flavours, crisp, gently sweet (23 grams/litre of residual sugar) and slightly minerally. Open mid-2010+.

Vintage	08
WR	6
Drink	09-15

MED/DRY $35 –V

Craggy Range Te Muna Road Vineyard Riesling   ★★★☆

Hand-picked in Martinborough, the 2008 vintage (★★★★) was cool-fermented to a medium-dry style and lees-aged for four months. Invitingly scented, it has good intensity of fresh lemon, apple and lime flavours, tight, finely balanced and appetisingly crisp. Drink now or cellar.

Vintage	08	07	06	05
WR	6	6	7	6
Drink	09-15	09-12	09-13	09-10

MED/DRY $26 –V

Crater Rim, The, Canterbury Riesling   (★★☆)

Grown at Waipara, the 2008 vintage (★★☆) is a hand-picked, single-vineyard wine. Appley and limey, it's a medium style (22 grams/litre of residual sugar), pale, light (10.5 per cent alcohol) and reasonably flavoursome, but it lacks the scentedness of fine Riesling.

MED $20 –V

Crater Rim, The, Waipara Riesling   ★★★☆

The 2008 vintage (★★★☆) is a distinctly medium style (45 grams/litre of residual sugar), with light body (9.5 per cent alcohol) and crisp, lemony flavours, fresh and strong.

MED $21 AV

Crossroads Marlborough Riesling   (★★☆)

The 2008 vintage (★★☆) is pale and light, with lemony, appley flavours, gentle sweetness (10.3 grams/litre of residual sugar) and mouth-watering acidity. It's a lean, slightly austere wine in its youth, but should age solidly.

MED/DRY $20 –V

Culley Marlborough Riesling   ★★★

The 2008 vintage (★★☆) is pale, with appley aromas leading into a light, slightly sweet wine with appetising acidity and moderate depth.

MED/DRY $19 AV

d'Akaroa Dry Riesling   (★★★)

Grown at French Farm Bay, on Banks Peninsula, in Canterbury, the 2008 vintage (★★★) is scented and youthful, with tight, very lemony flavours, woven with fresh acidity, and a dryish (6 grams/litre of residual sugar) finish. Worth cellaring.

MED/DRY $20 –V

Dancing Water Kamaka Riesling   (★★★☆)

Grown at Waipara, the 2008 vintage (★★★☆) is already enjoyable, in a light-bodied style (10 per cent alcohol) with very good depth of lemony, limey, gently sweet (28 grams/litre of residual sugar) flavour, fresh and crisp.

MED $28 –V

Daniel Schuster Waipara Riesling   ★★★☆

The 2007 vintage (★★★★) is a medium style, attractively scented, with light body (10.7 per cent alcohol) and strong, lemony, limey, spicy flavours, slightly sweet (17 grams/litre of residual sugar) and crisp. Fresh and vibrant, it's a vivacious young wine, for drinking now or cellaring.

Vintage	08	07
WR	6	6
Drink	P	P

MED $23 –V

Desert Heart Central Otago Riesling   ★★★☆

The 2008 vintage (★★★★) was hand-harvested at Bannockburn and fermented entirely with indigenous yeasts. Made in a medium-dry style (14 grams/litre of residual sugar), it's a concentrated, vibrantly fruity wine, bright, light lemon/green, with fresh, rich lemon/lime flavours, already delicious. Drink now or cellar.

Vintage	08	07	06
WR	6	5	4
Drink	09-15	09-16	09-11

MED/DRY $25 –V

Discovery Point Marlborough Dry Riesling (★★★★★)

From wine distributor Bennett & Deller, the 2008 vintage (★★★★★) is a great buy. A single-vineyard wine, grown at Omaka, it is a virtually dry style (5 grams/litre of residual sugar), invitingly scented, with medium body (12.5 per cent alcohol), good acid spine and fresh, searching, lemony, limey flavours, very finely textured and lingering. Perfectly poised for current enjoyment, it's a distinctive, satisfyingly dry wine – and exactly the style that could turn Kiwis onto Riesling.

Vintage	08	MED/DRY $22 V+
WR	6	
Drink	11-13	

Divine Daughter, The, Riesling ★★★☆

From The Old Glenmark Vicarage, at Waipara, the 2008 vintage (★★★☆) is light-bodied and tangy, with slightly sweet lemon/apple flavours, showing good depth. It's a finely poised wine, slightly minerally and refreshing, with cellaring potential.

Vintage	08	07	MED $23 –V
WR	7	7	
Drink	09-11	09-10	

Doctors', The, Riesling ★★★★

From Forrest Estate, this very low alcohol, medium-sweet style is like biting into a fresh, crunchy Granny Smith apple. The 2009 vintage (★★★★), harvested at 18 brix, was stop-fermented with 8.5 per cent alcohol and 35 grams/litre of residual sugar. Attractively scented, it is light and lively, with lemony, appley flavours, showing excellent delicacy, poise and harmony. Best drinking 2011+.

Vintage	08	07	06	MED $22 V+
WR	7	6	6	
Drink	09-20	09-10	09-10	

Domain Road Central Otago Riesling ★★★☆

Grown at Bannockburn, the 2009 vintage (★★★☆) is a single-vineyard wine, finely balanced, with very good depth of fresh, vibrant, lemony, appley, spicy flavours, slightly sweet and minerally.

Vintage	09	08	MED/DRY $24 –V
WR	6	6	
Drink	10-15	09-14	

Drylands Marlborough Dry Riesling ★★★★

The 2007 vintage (★★★★) from Constellation NZ is lemon-scented and dry (3.8 grams/litre of residual sugar), with fresh, strong, citrusy flavours and a floral bouquet. Past vintages have matured well, at three to four years old offering rich, toasty, minerally flavours in a classic dry Riesling style.

DRY $22 V+

Dry River Craighall Vineyard Riesling   ★★★★★

Winemaker Neil McCallum believes that, in quality terms, Riesling is at least the equal of Pinot Noir in Martinborough. His Craighall Riesling, one of the finest in the country, is a wine of exceptional purity, delicacy and depth, with a proven ability to flourish in the cellar for many years: 'It's not smart to drink them at less than five years old,' says McCallum. The grapes are sourced from a small block (0.8 hectares) of vines, mostly 15 to 20 years old, in the Craighall Vineyard, with yields limited to an average of 6 tonnes per hectare, and the wine is stop-fermented just short of dryness. The finely balanced 2009 vintage (★★★★) is restrained in its youth. Fresh and crisp, with just a sliver of sweetness (5 grams/litre of residual sugar), it has pure, delicate flavours of lemons and limes, fresh, zingy acidity and obvious potential. Open 2011+.

Vintage	09	08	07	06	05	04	03	02
WR	6	7	7	7	6	6	7	6
Drink	11-16	10-15	09-14	09-12	09-10	09-10	09-10	P

MED/DRY $44 AV

Dusky Sounds South Island Riesling   (★★★)

From Waipara Hills, the 2007 vintage (★★★) is a medium style with fresh, ripe lemon and passionfruit flavours, a distinct splash of sweetness and a hint of honey. It's an enjoyable, drink-young style.

MED $19 AV

Esk Valley Marlborough Riesling   (★★★★)

The 2009 (★★★★) is the winery's first Marlborough Riesling – past vintages were grown in Hawke's Bay. Hand-picked in the Wairau and Awatere valleys, it's a medium-dry style (6.7 grams/litre of residual sugar), lemon-scented, with tight, immaculate flavours of lemons and limes, still very youthful. Finely poised, it's worth cellaring to 2011+.

Vintage	09
WR	6
Drink	09-14

MED/DRY $23 AV

Fallen Angel Marlborough Riesling   ★★★☆

The 2009 vintage (★★★☆) from Stonyridge Vineyard is worth cellaring. A medium-bodied style, it is crisp and slightly sweet (9 grams/litre of residual sugar), with strong, lemony, appley flavours, showing good freshness, delicacy and harmony.

MED/DRY $25 –V

Felton Road Block 1 Riesling – see Sweet White Wines

Felton Road Dry Riesling   ★★★★☆

Based on low-yielding vines in schisty soils at Bannockburn, in Central Otago, this wine is hand-picked and fermented with indigenous yeasts. The 2009 vintage (★★★★★) is full of personality, but still a baby. Bright, light lemon/green, it is mouthfilling (13 per cent alcohol), with concentrated, vibrant lemon/lime flavours, slightly spicy and minerally. Dry but not austere, it's crying out for cellaring to at least 2011.

Vintage	09	08	07	06	05	04
WR	6	6	7	6	6	6
Drink	09-19	09-18	09-17	09-16	09-15	09-14

DRY $26 AV

Felton Road Riesling   ★★★★★

Estate-grown on mature vines at Bannockburn, in Central Otago, this is a gently sweet wine with deep flavours cut with fresh acidity. It offers more drink-young appeal than its Dry Riesling stablemate, but invites long-term cellaring. Tank-fermented mostly with indigenous yeasts, it is bottled with 20 to 50 grams per litre of residual sugar. The 2009 vintage (★★★★★) is finely balanced and racy, with lovely lightness (10 per cent alcohol), vivacity and intensity of lemon/lime flavours, gently sweet, crisp and harmonious. It's already quite expressive.

Vintage	09	08	07	06	05	04
WR	6	6	7	6	6	6
Drink	09-29	09-23	09-22	09-16	09-15	09-14

MED $26 V+

Fiddler's Green Waipara Classic Riesling   (★★★★)

The very fresh, crisp and zingy 2008 vintage (★★★★) is light (11.5 per cent alcohol) and vibrantly fruity, in a distinctly medium style (22 grams/litre of residual sugar) with lemony, appley flavours showing good intensity.

Vintage	08
WR	6
Drink	09-13

MED $20 V+

Fiddler's Green Waipara Dry Riesling   (★★★★)

Crisp, tight and lively, the 2008 vintage (★★★★) has good intensity of lemon, lime and passionfruit flavours and a hint of honey. It's a basically dry style (5 grams/litre of residual sugar), finely balanced.

Vintage	08
WR	6
Drink	09-15

MED/DRY $23 AV

Five Flax East Coast Riesling   ★★★

The 2008 vintage (★★★) from Pernod Ricard NZ is not labelled by region. It's an easy-drinking style with fresh, crisp, citrus-fruit and passionfruit flavours, slightly sweet and crisp. A good buy on special at around $11.

MED/DRY $15 V+

Floating Mountain Waipara Riesling   (★★★☆)

Fresh, tight and lively, the 2007 vintage (★★★☆) has strong, appley flavours, abundant sweetness (21 grams/litre of residual sugar) and appetising acidity. Partly barrel-fermented, it has good flavour depth, vigour and aging potential.

MED $22 AV

Forrest Collection Riesling – see John Forrest Collection Riesling

Forrest Marlborough Riesling   ★★★☆

John Forrest believes Riesling will one day be Marlborough's greatest wine, and his own wine is helping the cause. The 2009 vintage (★★★★) is attractively scented, in a vibrant, gently sweet style (14 grams/litre of residual sugar) with very good depth of crisp, lemony, appley flavours, balanced for easy drinking.

Vintage	09	08	07
WR	7	6	7
Drink	09-20	09-12	09-15

 MED/DRY $20 AV

Forrest The Doctors' Riesling – see Doctors', The, Riesling

Forrest The Valleys Brancott Riesling ★★★★☆

The 2007 vintage (★★★★☆) is a light Marlborough wine with fresh, pure, citrusy, appley flavours, slightly sweet and finely balanced. Showing lovely delicacy and harmony, it should mature superbly. The 2004 vintage (★★★★★), retasted in March 2009, is maturing superbly, with great texture and complexity. The 2008 (★★★★☆) is rich, with gently sweet (12 grams/litre of residual sugar), ripe citrus and peach flavours, showing impressive concentration and harmony.

Vintage	07
WR	7
Drink	09-15

MED/DRY $25 AV

Forrest The Valleys Wairau Dry Riesling ★★★★

The 2008 vintage (★★★★) is a low-alcohol wine (10.5 per cent) with a restrained, youthful bouquet. The palate is tight and almost bone-dry (3 grams/litre of residual sugar), but quite weighty, and crying out for more time. It offers pure, lemony, slightly minerally flavours, finely poised and not austere. Well worth cellaring.

Vintage	08	07
WR	5	6
Drink	09-20	09-20

 DRY $29 –V

Forrest The Valleys Wairau Library Release Dry Riesling (★★★★★)

On sale in 2009, the 2001 vintage (★★★★★) was first released as Forrest Estate Dry Riesling. Light lemon/green, it has a beautifully scented, rich fragrance, leading into a dry, citrusy, slightly toasty palate, not at all austere. A great example of the benefits of cellaring.

 DRY $30 AV

Foxes Island Marlborough Riesling ★★★★☆

The 2008 vintage (★★★★) is a rich, ripe style, estate-grown, hand-picked at 22 brix in the Old Ford Road Vineyard, in the Awatere Valley, and lees-aged for three months. Full-bodied and finely balanced, it's a scented, youthful wine, worth cellaring, with concentrated, peachy, slightly limey flavours, gentle sweetness and fresh, lively acidity.

MED/DRY $34 –V

Framingham Classic Riesling ★★★★★

Top vintages of this Marlborough wine are strikingly aromatic, richly flavoured and zesty. The 2008 (★★★★☆) is ripely scented, with fresh, vibrant lemon/lime flavours, gently sweet (17.5 grams/litre of residual sugar), crisp and minerally. Intense and still very youthful, it's best cellared to at least mid-2010+.

Vintage	08	07	06	05	04
WR	6	7	7	7	7
Drink	10-15	09-13	09-11	09-10	P

 MED $23 V+

Framingham Dry Riesling
★★★★☆

Still on sale, the 2004 (★★★★☆) is a classic, slow-maturing dry style (5 grams/litre of residual sugar) from Marlborough. Bright light lemon/green, with a toasty, very minerally bouquet, it has grapefruit, lime and spice flavours, still tense and slightly austere. The 2005 vintage (★★★★) has lemony, appley, toasty aromas and flavours, developing good fragrance and complexity.

Vintage	04	MED/DRY $28 AV
WR	7	
Drink	10-13+	

Fromm Riesling Dry
★★★★☆

Typically a beautifully poised, delicate Marlborough wine with citrusy, minerally flavours and a zingy, lasting finish. The 2008 vintage (★★★★☆) is a fractionally off-dry style with highly concentrated, ripe, appley and spicy flavours, tangy, minerally and sustained. A refined, finely balanced wine, it's already approachable, but should be long-lived.

Vintage	09	08	07	06	05	04	03	DRY $24 V+
WR	6	6	6	7	6	7	6	
Drink	10-15	10-14	10-13	10-14	10-11	10-12	10-11	

Gibbston Valley Central Otago Riesling
★★★★

At its best, this is a deliciously zingy wine, awash with lemon/lime flavours. The 2008 vintage (★★★★), grown at Bendigo, is medium-dry (7.9 grams/litre of residual sugar). A full-bodied, weighty wine, it has good acid spine and fresh, citrusy, appley aromas and flavours, dryish (7.9 grams/litre of residual sugar), slightly minerally, tense and lively.

Vintage	08	07	06	05	04	MED/DRY $27 –V
WR	7	6	6	7	4	
Drink	10-14	09-14	09-14	09-10	P	

Gibbston Valley Le Fou The Expressionist Series Riesling
★★★★☆

Grown in the Home Block at Gibbston, in Central Otago, this is a lower alcohol, sweeter style than its stablemate (above). The 2008 vintage (★★★★☆) has abundant sweetness (40 grams/litre of residual sugar), balanced by mouth-watering acidity. Light (9 per cent alcohol) and racy, it shows excellent intensity of lemony, appley flavours, vibrant and minerally, with good complexity.

Vintage	08	07	MED $35 –V
WR	7	7	
Drink	10-20	09-18	

Gladstone Wairarapa Riesling
★★★

Typically citrusy and appley in its youth, with a minerally streak and a crisp, dryish finish (7 grams/litre of residual sugar in 2008). It matures well, developing toasty, honeyed notes at around three years old.

MED/DRY $20 –V

Glasnevin Classic Riesling
(★★★★)

From Fiddler's Green, the 2008 vintage (★★★★) was fermented with indigenous yeasts and lees-aged in tanks. Pale lemon/green, it's a medium-sweet style (43 grams/litre of residual sugar), light (9.5 per cent alcohol) and lively, with good intensity of lemony, appley flavours, showing excellent delicacy and poise. Drink now or cellar.

Vintage	08
WR	6
Drink	09-14

MED $24 AV

Glenmark Riesling Medium ★★★☆

Still on sale in 2009, the 2004 vintage (★★★☆) has strong, very citrusy flavours, crisp and tangy. It should be long-lived.

MED $21 AV

Goldridge Estate Marlborough Riesling ★★☆

The 2008 vintage (★★☆) is a full-bodied, medium-dry wine with solid depth of crisp, citrusy, appley flavours.

MED/DRY $16 AV

Greenhough Apple Valley Nelson Riesling ★★★★☆

Grown in a coastal vineyard at Mapua and made in a low-alcohol, medium style, the 2009 vintage (★★★★☆) is light (10 per cent alcohol) and sweetish (32 grams/litre of residual sugar), with intense, lemony, appley flavours, showing lovely delicacy and purity. It's a very finely poised wine, slightly minerally and lingering.

Vintage	09	08	07
WR	6	6	6
Drink	09-15	09-14	09-13

MED $22 V+

Greenhough Hope Vineyard Riesling ★★★★☆

This Nelson wine is hand-picked from vines planted in 1979. The 2008 vintage (★★★★) is pale yellow, with slightly honeyed aromas. Mouthfilling, it has ripe grapefruit and slight spice flavours, showing good richness, in a forward style, drinking well from now onwards.

Vintage	08	07	06	05	04
WR	7	7	6	6	6
Drink	09-13	09-12	09-11	09-11	09-10

MED $23 V+

Greystone Waipara Dry Riesling ★★★☆

The 2009 vintage (★★★★) is an off-dry style (6 grams/litre of residual sugar), invitingly scented, with good weight and intensity of ripe peach, passionfruit and spice flavours, fresh and already drinking well.

Vintage	09
WR	6
Drink	09-16

MED/DRY $26 –V

Greystone Waipara Riesling ★★★★

Estate-grown and hand-harvested, the 2009 vintage (★★★★) is a medium style (33 grams/litre of residual sugar) with excellent depth of lemony, appley flavour, balanced for easy drinking. Floral and focused, with appetising acidity, it should unfold well.

Vintage	09	08	07
WR	6	6	5
Drink	09-16	09-12	09-11

MED $24 AV

Grove Mill Marlborough Riesling   ★★★☆

Typically a finely balanced wine with strong fruit flavours, a distinct splash of sweetness (14 grams/litre of residual sugar in 2008) and appetising acidity. The 2008 vintage (★★★☆) is attractively scented and light (11.5 per cent alcohol), with pure, delicate flavours of lemons, apples and limes.

Vintage	08	07	06	05	04
WR	6	7	7	6	7
Drink	10-14	09-14	09-13	09-10	09-12

MED/DRY $18 V+

Hawkshead Central Otago Riesling   (★★★★)

Grown at Bendigo, the 2008 vintage (★★★★) is opening out well. Mouthfilling and dryish (9.5 grams/litre of residual sugar), with strong, citrusy, slightly spicy flavours that linger well, it is a vibrantly fruity, tightly structured wine that should mature gracefully over the long haul.

MED/DRY $25 AV

Hay Maker Waipara Riesling   ★★★☆

Estate-grown by Mud House, the 2008 vintage (★★★☆) is a light-bodied (11 per cent alcohol), medium style (23 grams/litre of residual sugar), instantly appealing, with lots of citrusy, slightly spicy flavour. A drink-young style.

MED $17 V+

Highfield Marlborough Riesling   ★★★★

The 2008 vintage (★★★★) was hand-picked in the Omaka Valley and stop-fermented with 9.5 per cent alcohol and 30.5 grams per litre of residual sugar. It's a perfumed wine with a lemony, minerally bouquet and pure, ripe lemon, apple and spice flavours, already very harmonious and expressive.

Vintage	08	07	06	05	04
WR	5	6	6	NM	5
Drink	09-11	09-10	09-10	NM	P

MED $19 V+

Hudson RPM Martinborough Riesling   ★★☆

Grown south of Martinborough, the 2007 vintage (★★☆) is a medium-bodied style with creamy notes on the nose and palate that slightly overwhelm the wine's crisp, citrusy fruit flavours. The 2008 (★★★) is fresh and gently sweet, with mouthfilling body and decent depth of lemony, appley flavours.

MED/DRY $22 –V

Hudson Wharekaka Martinborough Dry Riesling   (★★★)

The 2008 vintage (★★★) is a full-bodied style (13 per cent alcohol), with citrusy, slightly minerally flavours, basically dry, showing a touch of complexity and some development.

DRY $22 –V

Huia Marlborough Riesling   ★★★☆

Zingy and lively, the 2008 vintage (★★★☆) is a fresh, medium-bodied wine (12.5 per cent alcohol) with minimal sweetness (5 grams/litre of residual sugar), balanced acidity, and very good harmony and depth.

Vintage	08							MED/DRY $28 –V
WR	6							
Drink	09-19							

Hunter's Marlborough Riesling   ★★★★

This wine is consistently good – and good value. The 2008 vintage (★★★★) was picked at 21.2 brix in the Wairau Valley. Pale lemon/green, it is fresh, crisp, tight and lively, with intense, youthful flavours, lemony, slightly sweet (6.6 grams/litre of residual sugar) and rich. It should mature well.

Vintage	09	08	07	06	05	04	03	02	MED/DRY $20 V+
WR	5	6	6	6	6	5	6	6	
Drink	10-14	10-13	09-11	09-10	09-10	P	P	P	

Isabel Marlborough Dry Riesling   ★★★☆

The 2007 vintage (★★★☆) was estate-grown and fermented almost to full dryness (4 grams/litre of residual sugar). It has good body and carries the dry style well, with strong, fresh flavours, rounded for Riesling.

Vintage	08	07		DRY $20 AV
WR	6	6		
Drink	09-17	09-14		

John Forrest Collection Riesling   ★★★★★

The 2006 vintage (★★★★★) is very intense and refined. Grown at two sites in the Brancott and Wairau valleys, it was picked from low-yielding vines (4 to 6.7 tonnes/hectare) and stop-fermented in a medium-dry style (12 grams/litre of residual sugar). Finely structured, with great delicacy, it has a scented, floral bouquet and fresh, pure lemon/apple flavours, slightly minerally, intense and harmonious.

Vintage	06	MED/DRY $50 –V
WR	6	
Drink	09-20	

Johner Estate Wairarapa Riesling   ★★★☆

The 2009 vintage (★★★★) is a refined wine, fresh and vibrantly fruity, with ripe, citrusy, faintly honeyed flavours, good acid spine, a gentle splash of sweetness, and excellent harmony. It's already delicious.

MED $16 V+

Julicher Martinborough Riesling   ★★★★☆

Still on sale, the beautifully poised, rich 2006 vintage (★★★★★) is a winner. Zingy and tightly structured, it's an intense, dry style (3.5 grams/litre of residual sugar), with deliciously concentrated citrus-fruit and passionfruit flavours, slightly minerally, toasty and honeyed.

Vintage	06	05	DRY $20 V+
WR	6	6	
Drink	09-12	09-12	

Jumper, The, Marlborough Riesling   ★★★☆

A good buy from Spring Creek Estate. The 2007 vintage (★★★) is an easy-drinking style with ripe, citrusy, appley, slightly spicy flavours, a splash of sweetness and satisfying depth.

MED/DRY $15 V+

Junction Central Hawke's Bay Riesling   (★★★☆)

Grown on the Takapau Plains, the 2007 vintage (★★★☆) shows good intensity of peach, lemon and lime flavours, in a slightly sweet style with fresh, bracing acidity. It's well worth cellaring.

MED/DRY $22 AV

Kahurangi Dry Riesling   ★★★☆

The 2006 vintage (★★★★) was grown at Upper Moutere, in Nelson. It's a fleshy, generous wine with a hint of honey enriching its fresh, dryish, crisp flavours of ripe grapefruit and limes.

MED/DRY $19 AV

Kahurangi Estate Moutere Riesling   ★★★

From 'some of the South Island's oldest Riesling vines', the 2006 vintage (★★★) is a fleshy, minerally Nelson wine with citrusy, appley aromas and flavours, slightly sweet and crisp.

MED/DRY $18 AV

Kahurangi Estate Mt Arthur Moutere Reserve Riesling   (★★★☆)

The 2006 vintage (★★★☆) is a full-bodied, flavoursome wine from early-ripening, coastal sites at Tasman and Ruby Bay. Fleshy, with a touch of sweetness amid its lemony, appley flavours, it shows good balance, depth and potential.

MED/DRY $19 AV

Kaimira Estate Brightwater Riesling   ★★★★

This wine typically ages well. The 2008 vintage (★★★★) is full-bodied and finely balanced, with a sliver of sweetness (6.5 grams/litre of residual sugar) and good intensity of citrusy, slightly limey flavours. Generous, with a lingering finish, it should be at its best mid-2010+.

Vintage	08	07	06	05
WR	7	5	6	5
Drink	09-13	09-12	09-11	09-10

MED/DRY $20 V+

Kim Crawford SP The Mistress Waipara Riesling   (★★★★)

Still on sale, the 2005 vintage (★★★★) is a fleshy, finely balanced North Canterbury wine with good intensity of pure, ripe, citrusy flavours. Threaded with crisp, lively acidity, it has a just off-dry finish (5 grams/litre of residual sugar).

MED/DRY $33 –V

Kingsmill Tippet's Race Riesling   ★★★★

The 2008 vintage (★★★★) is a single-vineyard Central Otago wine, hand-picked at Bendigo. It's a tightly structured, dryish style (6 grams/litre of residual sugar), full-bodied and very youthful, with crisp, citrusy, appley, slightly minerally flavours, showing good intensity and vigour.

MED/DRY $25 AV

Konrad Marlborough Riesling   ★★★

Estate-grown in the Waihopai Valley, the 2008 vintage (★★☆) was made in a medium-dry style (8.9 grams/litre of residual sugar). It's a crisp, lemony, appley wine, but lacks richness.

Vintage	08	07	06	05	04
WR	4	4	6	6	5
Drink	09-12	09-11	09-11	09-10	P

MED/DRY $18 AV

Kurow Village Waitaki Valley Riesling   (★★★☆)

The 2008 vintage (★★★☆) is a light to medium-bodied wine, attractively scented, with citrusy, gently sweet flavours (16.7 grams/litre of residual sugar), slightly minerally and crisp. Drink now or cellar.

MED $20 AV

Lake Chalice Marlborough Riesling   ★★★☆

Grown in the company's Falcon Vineyard at Rapaura, the 2008 vintage (★★★☆) is a medium style (15 grams/litre of residual sugar), full-bodied (13 per cent alcohol) and crisp, with strong, lemony, limey flavours.

MED $20 AV

Lamont Riesling Dry   (★★★☆)

Still on sale, the 2006 vintage (★★★☆) is a single-vineyard Central Otago wine, grown at Bendigo. It's citrusy and finely balanced (5.6 grams/litre of residual sugar), in a ripe, moderately intense style with good delicacy and roundness, drinking well now.

MED/DRY $22 AV

Lawson's Dry Hills Marlborough Riesling   ★★★★

The 2007 vintage (★★★☆) is ripely scented, with tight, dryish flavours, slightly toasty and minerally, showing good vigour.

Vintage	08	07	06	05	04
WR	7	6	7	6	6
Drink	09-12	09-10	09-10	P	P

MED/DRY $20 V+

Maimai Creek Hawke's Bay Riesling   ★★★

Priced sharply, the 2008 vintage (★★★) is scented and light-bodied (11.5 per cent alcohol), with fresh, dryish flavours, citrusy, appley and tangy.

MED/DRY $15 V+

Main Divide Waipara Valley Riesling   ★★★★☆

From Pegasus Bay, this is always a bargain. The 2008 vintage (★★★★) is a concentrated wine with fairly sweet (30 grams/litre of residual sugar), rich citrus, passionfruit and lime flavours and botrytis-derived, marmalade notes. Crisp and lively, it's a drink-now or cellaring proposition.

Vintage	08	07
WR	7	7
Drink	09-15	09-15

MED $20 V+

Margrain Proprietors Selection Riesling   ★★★☆

The tightly structured 2008 vintage (★★★☆), grown in Martinborough, is a medium-dry style (12 grams/litre of residual sugar) with crisp, lemony, appley flavours showing good freshness, vigour and depth. It should mature well.

Vintage	08	MED/DRY $24 –V
WR	6	
Drink	09-17	

Martinborough Vineyard Jackson Block Riesling   ★★★★☆

One of the jewels of the range. The 2008 vintage (★★★★★), based on 18-year-old vines in the Jackson Vineyard, near the winery, is a daringly dry style (4 grams/litre of residual sugar), but pulls it off well. Showing real power and potential, it has intense, ripe flavours of citrus fruits and limes, with a hint of passionfruit, and a long, finely balanced finish. It should flourish for a decade.

MED/DRY $26 AV

Martinborough Vineyard Manu Riesling   ★★★★

The 2008 vintage (★★★★) was grown in the Jackson Vineyard. A distinctly medium style (25 grams/litre of residual sugar), with a gentle botrytis influence, it is citrusy and slightly honeyed, with mouthfilling body (13 per cent alcohol), rich ripe-fruit flavours and drink-young appeal.

MED $26 –V

Matua Valley Shingle Peak Marlborough Riesling   ★★★

The easy-drinking 2007 vintage (★★★) is lemon-scented and full-bodied, with decent depth of dryish, lemony, appley flavours, ripe and rounded.

Vintage	06	MED/DRY $18 AV
WR	4	
Drink	P	

Mills Reef Hawke's Bay Riesling   ★★★

The 2009 vintage (★★★) is a full-bodied, dry style (4 grams/litre of residual sugar), with good depth of lemony, slightly spicy flavours and a fresh, crisp finish.

DRY $18 AV

Millton Opou Vineyard Riesling   ★★★★

Typically finely scented, with rich, lemony, often honeyed flavours, this is the country's northernmost fine-quality Riesling. Grown in Gisborne (some of the vines are over 25 years old), it is gently sweet, in a softer, less racy style than the classic Marlborough wines. The grapes, grown organically in the Opou Vineyard at Manutuke, are hand-harvested over a month at three stages of ripening, usually culminating in a final pick of botrytis-affected fruit. The 2008 vintage (★★★★) is gently floral, with citrus-fruit, apple and passionfruit flavours showing very good delicacy and depth. Light (8.5 per cent alcohol) and lively, with abundant sweetness (39 grams/litre of residual sugar), it's still very youthful; open 2010+.

Vintage	08	07	06	05
WR	7	5	6	6
Drink	09-14	09-12	09-10	P

MED $26 –V

Misha's Vineyard Limelight Riesling   (★★★★☆)

The debut 2008 vintage (★★★★☆) is a single-vineyard Central Otago wine, partly barrel-fermented and made in a medium style (29 grams/litre of residual sugar). A beautifully balanced wine with strong personality, it has rich, citrusy flavours, with a touch of complexity, and excellent delicacy and texture. Drink now or cellar.

MED $27 AV

Mission Hawke's Bay Riesling   ★★★

Mission's Rieslings offer good value. The 2008 (★★★) has a slightly developed bouquet, with hints of toast and honey. Crisp and mouthfilling, it has good depth of slightly sweet, citrusy flavours. The lemon-scented 2009 vintage (★★★), grown in Ohiti Road, is balanced for enjoyable summer sipping, with a splash of sweetness (11 grams/litre of residual sugar) amid its fresh, vibrant, lemony, appley flavours.

MED/DRY $16 V+

Momo Marlborough Riesling   ★★★

From Seresin, the 2008 vintage (★★★) has a scented, lemony bouquet and gently sweet (12 grams/litre of residual sugar), citrusy flavours, balanced for easy drinking and showing good depth.

Vintage	08
WR	5
Drink	09-12

MED/DRY $18 AV

Mondillo Central Otago Riesling   ★★★☆

Estate-grown at two Bendigo sites, the 2008 vintage (★★★☆) is an off-dry style (5.5 grams/litre of residual sugar), mouthfilling (13.5 per cent alcohol) and crisp, with citrusy, slightly peachy flavours, firm acid spine, and very good vigour and depth. Drink now or cellar.

Vintage	08	07
WR	7	6
Drink	09-11	09-10

MED/DRY $25 –V

Montana Reserve Waipara Riesling   ★★★☆

The easy-drinking, finely poised 2008 vintage (★★★) is a lemony, medium-bodied wine with a splash of sweetness (11.5 grams/litre of residual sugar), fresh, lively acidity and good but not great depth.

MED/DRY $24 –V

Montana South Island Riesling   ★★★☆

This good-value wine has evolved from the long-popular Montana Marlborough Riesling, no longer produced. A blend of Waipara (mostly) and Marlborough grapes, the 2008 vintage (★★★☆) is intensely varietal, with very good depth of citrusy flavour, slightly sweet (13 grams/litre of residual sugar) and mouth-wateringly crisp.

MED/DRY $18 V+

Morton Estate Stone Creek Marlborough Riesling   ★★★☆

The 2007 vintage (★★★) is a mouthfilling (14 per cent alcohol) wine with ripe, citrusy, peachy flavours and a slightly sweet, rounded finish. It's enjoyable now.

Vintage	07	06
WR	6	6
Drink	09-17	09-12

MED/DRY $21 AV

Morton Estate White Label Marlborough Riesling   ★★☆

The 2007 vintage (★★☆) is slightly honeyed, with mouthfilling body (13.5 per cent alcohol) and peachy, slightly spicy flavours, showing some development. Ready; no rush.

Vintage	07	06
WR	6	6
Drink	09-16	09-12

DRY $18 –V

Mount Edward Central Otago Riesling   ★★★★

The 2007 vintage (★★★★) is a single-vineyard wine from Lowburn, in the Cromwell Basin. Still very youthful, it is finely textured and slightly sweet, with strong, citrusy flavours and a lingering finish. A tightly structured wine, it should mature well; open 2011+.

Vintage	07	06
WR	6	6
Drink	09-14	09-13

MED/DRY $25 AV

Mount Riley Nelson/Marlborough Riesling   ★★★☆

The 2007 vintage (★★★) of this two-regions blend is full-bodied, with good vigour and depth of ripe, citrusy, slightly sweet flavours (8 grams/litre of residual sugar).

Vintage	07	06	05	04
WR	6	6	6	5
Drink	09-11	09-10	P	P

MED/DRY $18 V+

Mount Riley Seventeen Valley Marlborough Riesling   (★★★★)

Still on sale, the 2005 vintage (★★★★) is a single-vineyard wine, hand-picked in the heart of the Wairau Valley and fermented with indigenous yeasts. It's maturing very gracefully, in a tight, dry style with citrusy, slightly toasty flavours, showing very good delicacy and depth.

DRY $22 V+

Mt Beautiful North Canterbury Riesling   ★★★☆

Grown at Cheviot, north of Waipara, the 2007 vintage (★★★★) is an elegant wine, light and lemony, with hints of apples and spices, slight sweetness (11.5 grams/litre of residual sugar), and excellent texture, delicacy and depth. The 2008 (★★★) has lemon, apple and slight passionfruit flavours, crisp and slightly flinty.

MED/DRY $24 –V

Mt Difficulty Dry Riesling   ★★★☆

Grown at Bannockburn, in Central Otago, this is a wine for purists – steely and austere in its youth, but rewarding (almost demanding) time. The 2008 vintage (★★★☆) carries t he dry style well. Pale, light and lively, it is lemony, slightly spicy and minerally, with good depth and immediacy.

DRY $25 –V

Mt Difficulty Single Vineyard Long Gully Central Otago Riesling – see Sweet White Wines

Mt Difficulty Target Gully Riesling ★★★★

Grown mostly in the Target Gully Vineyard at Bannockburn, in Central Otago, the 2008 vintage (★★★★) is a distinctly medium style (38 grams/litre of residual sugar). A vivacious wine, it is light (11 per cent alcohol), tangy and intense, with lemon/lime flavours, lively and long. Drink now or cellar.

MED $25 AV

Mt Rosa Central Otago Riesling ★★★★

Grown at Gibbston, the 2007 vintage (★★★★) is full of personality. A full-bodied, medium-dry style (8 grams/litre of residual sugar) with generous, citrusy, slightly earthy and spicy flavours and distinct overtones of Alsace, it's now starting to soften and offer great drinkability.

Vintage	07
WR	4
Drink	09-10

 MED/DRY $22 V+

Muddy Water Dry Riesling ★★★★☆

The 2008 vintage (★★★★) was hand-harvested at Waipara, hand-sorted to eliminate botrytis and fermented with indigenous yeasts to near dryness (6.6 grams/litre of residual sugar). It's still a baby. Slightly austere in its youth, but with obvious cellaring potential, it has good intensity of grapefruit, lemon and lime flavours, with a firm backbone of acidity adding a minerally streak.

Vintage	08
WR	7
Drink	09-15

MED/DRY $28 AV

Muddy Water Growers' Series James Hardwick Waipara Riesling ★★★★★

The 2008 vintage (★★★★) was hand-picked with no botrytis and fermented with indigenous yeasts. It's a medium-dry style (14 grams/litre of residual sugar), full-bodied and crisp, with good intensity of grapefruit and slight spice flavours, showing good harmony and length. Worth cellaring.

Vintage	08	07	06	05	04
WR	7	7	7	7	7
Drink	09-15	09-12	09-10	P	P

 MED $28 V+

Muddy Water Growers' Series Lough Vineyard Riesling (★★★★☆)

Grown at Waipara, the debut 2008 vintage (★★★★☆) was hand-picked and stop-fermented in a medium style (27 grams/litre of residual sugar). Ripely scented, it is mouthfilling (13 per cent alcohol) and ripe, with good complexity of citrusy, spicy, peachy flavours, well-rounded and generous. It's already delicious.

 MED $24 V+

Muddy Water Riesling Unplugged – see Sweet White Wines

Mud House Waipara Riesling   ★★★★☆

The 2008 vintage (★★★★★) is notably intense and vibrant, with lemon/lime flavours, finely poised and punchy. It's still youthful, but already highly expressive.

MED/DRY $20 V+

Murdoch James Blue Rock Martinborough Riesling   ★★★

The 2008 vintage (★★★) is a slightly sweet style (7.9 grams/litre of residual sugar), citrusy and crisp, with good varietal character and vigour and some toasty, bottle-aged notes starting to emerge.

Vintage	08	07	06
WR	6	4	5
Drink	09-14	09-13	09-12

MED/DRY $20 –V

Mystery Creek Gisborne Riesling   (★★☆)

The 2007 vintage (★★☆) was grown at Patutahi and made in a gently sweet (16 grams/litre of residual sugar) style. It's a medium-bodied wine (11.5 per cent alcohol) with lemony flavours, faintly honeyed and crisp, and some developed, toasty notes.

Vintage	08	07
WR	5	4
Drink	10-12	09-11

MED $14 AV

Neudorf Brightwater Riesling   ★★★★

Grown at Brightwater, on Nelson's Waimea Plains, this is a consistently rewarding wine. The 2007 vintage (★★★★) was hand-picked and made in a medium-dry style (10 grams/litre of residual sugar). Light-bodied (11 per cent alcohol), with crisp lemon and slight passionfruit flavours, showing good delicacy and intensity, it is fresh, finely poised and racy.

Vintage	08	07	06	05	04
WR	5	6	6	6	5
Drink	09-14	09-13	09-12	09-11	P

MED/DRY $23 AV

Neudorf Moutere Riesling   ★★★★★

A copybook cool-climate style with excellent intensity, estate-grown at Upper Moutere and tank-fermented with indigenous yeasts. The 2007 vintage (★★★★☆) was hand-picked in mid-May from young vines in the Beuke Block, on a hill overlooking the Home Vineyard. Light lemon/green, with a minerally bouquet, it is light (10 per cent alcohol) and vivacious, sweetish (40 grams/litre of residual sugar) and poised, with strong, citrusy, appley, slightly spicy flavours, still youthful. (The 2008 is a similar style, with 47 grams/litre of residual sugar.)

Vintage	08	07	06	05	04	03	02
WR	6	6	7	7	NM	6	5
Drink	09-17	09-17	09-16	09-15	NM	09-12	09-10

MED $28 V+

Nga Waka Martinborough Riesling   ★★★★☆

A consistently rich, long-lived wine with bone-dry flavours. The 2004 vintage (★★★★☆) is a classic dry style. Harvested at 21.4 brix from very low-yielding vines (3.75 tonnes/hectare), it is finely balanced, with minerally, toasty and complex flavours, building to a rich, rounded finish.

DRY $25 AV

Northburn Station Riesling ★★★☆

Grown on the eastern side of Lake Dunstan, in Central Otago, the 2008 vintage (★★★☆) is floral, crisp and slightly minerally, with lemony, appley, medium-dry flavours (12 grams/litre of residual sugar) showing good purity, texture and length.

Vintage	08	
WR	5	
Drink	09-12	

MED/DRY $24 –V

Northfield Waipara Valley Riesling (★★★☆)

The tangy 2007 vintage (★★★☆) has some intensity of lemon/lime flavours, woven with tight, minerally acidity.

MED/DRY $22 AV

Ohinemuri Estate Marlborough Riesling (★★☆)

Waikato-based winemaker Horst Hillerich until recently drew his Riesling grapes from Gisborne, but the 2007 vintage (★★☆) is from Marlborough. It's a briefly oak-aged wine made in a medium style (15 grams/litre of residual sugar), with restrained lemon/lime flavours and a crisp, tight finish. (The 2008 was grown in Gisborne and briefly oak-matured.)

Vintage	08	07
WR	6	5
Drink	09-12	09-12

MED $19 –V

Old Coach Road Nelson Riesling ★★★☆

Skilfully crafted for easy drinking, the 2009 vintage (★★★☆) from Seifried is a medium-dry style (14 grams/litre of residual sugar) with plenty of lemony, appley flavour, a hint of passionfruit, and good acidity to balance its appealing splash of sweetness. Very fresh and vibrant, it should open out well. The attractively scented 2008 (★★★☆) offers equally good value.

Vintage	09	08
WR	6	7
Drink	09-14	09-12

MED/DRY $17 V+

Olssen's Central Otago Riesling ★★★★

The 2008 vintage (★★★☆) was estate-grown at Bannockburn. Mouthfilling, it has very good vigour and depth of fresh lemon, apple and lime flavours, with a crisp, almost dry finish (6 grams/litre of residual sugar).

MED/DRY $23 AV

Omaka Springs Marlborough Riesling ★★☆

The 2007 vintage (★★) is a solid but plain wine, lemony and appley, but lacking real fragrance, delicacy and richness.

Vintage	07
WR	5
Drink	09-13

MED/DRY $18 –V

Omihi Road Waipara Riesling   ★★★★

From Torlesse, this is typically a scented, vibrant North Canterbury wine with pure, ripe, lemon/lime flavours, showing excellent delicacy and depth. Both the 2005 (★★★★) and 2006 (★★★★) vintages showed good purity and richness.

MED/DRY $20 V+

Orinoco Vineyards Nelson Riesling   ★★★☆

The skilfully made, very harmonious 2008 vintage (★★★★) is a medium-dry style (12 grams/litre of residual sugar), with low alcohol (10.5 per cent) but plenty of body. Immediately appealing, it is fresh and crisp, with strong lemon, lime and slight passionfruit flavours, intense and tangy.

MED $19 AV

Ostler Grower Selection Blue House Vines Waitaki Valley Riesling   (★★★☆)

From the Blue House Vineyard, in Grants Road, the 2008 vintage (★★★☆) is fresh, light, lemony and crisp, with gentle sweetness (8 grams/litre of residual sugar) and lively, appley flavours, tight and youthful. Best drinking mid-2010+.

MED/DRY $28 –V

Palliser Estate Martinborough Riesling   ★★★★★

In top vintages, this is a beautifully scented wine with intense, slightly sweet flavours and a racy finish. It is made from mature vines on the Martinborough Terrace and matures well for five to eight years; sometimes longer. The 2007 (★★★★) is fresh and finely poised (7 grams/litre of residual sugar), with citrusy, minerally flavours showing good balance, spine and intensity.

MED/DRY $18 V+

🍇🍇

Paritua Central Otago Riesling   ★★★

The 2008 vintage (★★★) from this Hawke's Bay-based producer is light-bodied (11.5 per cent alcohol) and lemony, with crisp, slightly sweet (12 grams/litre of residual sugar) flavours, fresh, lively and balanced for easy drinking.

Vintage	08
WR	6
Drink	09-16

MED/DRY $28 –V

Pegasus Bay Aria Late Harvest Riesling – see Sweet White Wines

Pegasus Bay Bel Canto Riesling Dry   ★★★☆

The 2008 vintage (★★★☆) is the first Riesling Dry to be labelled Bel Canto ('beautiful singing'). Late-harvested at Waipara from mature vines and produced with some influence from noble rot, indigenous yeasts and barrel aging, it's a dryish (8 grams/litre of residual sugar), mouthfilling wine (14 per cent alcohol), crisp, spicy, gingery and honeyed. A very distinctive style, it's best enjoyed young.

Vintage	08	07
WR	7	7
Drink	09-12	09-10

MED/DRY $32 –V

Pegasus Bay Riesling ★★★★★

This is classy stuff. Estate-grown at Waipara, in North Canterbury, it is richly fragrant and thrillingly intense, with flavours of citrus fruits and honey, complex and luscious. Based on mature vines and stop-fermented in a distinctly medium style, it breaks into full stride at two or three years old and most vintages keep well for a decade. The 2008 (★★★★☆) is mouthfilling (13 per cent alcohol), with a slightly honeyed bouquet, reflecting some 'noble rot' influence. Ripe citrus, passionfruit and slight apricot flavours, gently sweet (25 grams/litre of residual sugar) and tangy, create a powerful impression on the palate. It's a concentrated, youthful wine, for drinking 2010+.

Vintage	08	07	06	05	04	03	02	01
WR	7	7	6	6	7	6	6	6
Drink	09-19	09-18	09-16	09-16	09-15	09-14	09-12	09-10

MED $28 V+

Peregrine Central Otago Riesling ★★★★

A dryish style with pure lemon/lime flavours, the 2007 vintage (★★★★) shows good texture and length, with a touch of bottle-aged toastiness. Full-bodied, tight and immaculate, it's maturing well. (In a vertical tasting of the 2002–2006 vintages, held in late 2008, the star was the 2004 – generous, complex and lovely now.) The 2005 (★★★☆), still on sale, is maturing solidly, with bright, light lemon/green colour, strong, lemony, slightly toasty flavours and a dry finish (4 grams/litre of residual sugar).

Vintage	07
WR	6
Drink	09-14

MED/DRY $23 AV

Peregrine Rastasburn Riesling ★★★★

Grown in the Cromwell Basin, this Central Otago wine is made in a medium style. The 2006 vintage (★★★★) is gently sweet (18 grams/litre of residual sugar), with a scented bouquet and excellent depth, delicacy and harmony. Maturing very gracefully, it's drinking well now.

Vintage	07
WR	6
Drink	09-14

MED $22 V+

Pond Paddock Harvest Moon Riesling ★★★

The 2007 vintage (★★★) was grown in Te Muna Road, Martinborough and harvested at 17.5 brix. It's a tightly structured wine, light to medium-bodied (11.5 per cent alcohol), with a splash of sweetness (13 grams/litre of residual sugar) and fresh, crisp, green-apple flavours.

MED/DRY $20 –V

Prophet's Rock Central Otago Dry Riesling ★★★★

The 2008 vintage (★★★★) was hand-harvested at Pisa, fermented with indigenous yeasts and lees-aged. Crisp, with a dryish feel, it is citrusy and slightly spicy, with good purity and length and fresh, racy acidity. Best drinking 2011+.

MED/DRY $35 –V

Pyramid Valley Vineyards Growers Collection Lebecca
Vineyard Marlborough Riesling   (★★★★)

The 2007 vintage (★★★★) was hand-picked at Rapaura, fermented with indigenous yeasts and lees-aged for eight months. It's a light (11 per cent alcohol), medium style (34 grams/litre of residual sugar) with strong, ripe, citrusy flavours, finely balanced for current enjoyment.

MED $27 –V

Pyramid Valley Vineyards Growers Collection
Riverbrook Vineyard Marlborough Riesling   (★★★☆)

Grown in the Brancott Valley, the 2007 vintage (★★★☆) was hand-picked (15 per cent of the fruit was late-harvested, with noble rot) and fermented with indigenous yeasts. Light yellow/green, it's a medium style (20 grams/litre of residual sugar) with concentrated, lemony, slightly honeyed flavours. Drink now onwards.

MED $27 –V

Pyramid Valley Vineyards Growers Collection Rose
Vineyard Marlborough Riesling   (★★★☆)

Hand-picked at Rapaura, the 2007 vintage (★★★☆) was fermented with indigenous yeasts in tanks and old oak casks. Mouthfilling and dryish (9 grams/litre of residual sugar), it's a fleshy, very individual wine, not highly scented, but generous, ripe and well-rounded.

MED/DRY $27 –V

Rabbit Ranch Central Otago Riesling   (★★★)

Enjoyable now, the 2007 vintage (★★★) is a full-bodied style (13.5 per cent alcohol) with plenty of citrusy, gently sweet, slightly spicy flavour, showing some toasty, bottle-aged development. Ready.

MED/DRY $23 –V

Redoubt Hill Vineyard Nelson Riesling   (★★★★)

Fleshy and ripe, the 2008 vintage (★★★★) is a single-vineyard wine, grown at Motueka and fermented to dryness (3 grams/litre of residual sugar). It's a classy wine, ripely scented, with good body and depth of citrusy, minerally flavours, showing excellent delicacy and concentration. Dry but not austere, finely poised, tight and immaculate, it should mature well.

Vintage	08
WR	6
Drink	09-12

DRY $29 –V

Ribbonwood Marlborough Riesling   (★★★)

The easy-drinking 2008 vintage (★★★) was made by Framingham for blackmarket.co.nz. Medium-bodied, it is fresh, slightly sweet and crisp, with a hint of marmalade and drink-young appeal.

MED/DRY $18 AV

Richmond Plains Nelson Riesling   (★★★★)

Impressive in its infancy, the 2009 vintage (★★★★) is fresh and vibrant, with good intensity of lemony, limey flavour, slightly sweet (8 grams/litre of residual sugar) and crisp. It's a very harmonious wine, likely to age well.

Vintage	09
WR	6
Drink	09-14

MED/DRY $20 V+

Rippon Jeunesse Young Vines Riesling   ★★★★

The 2008 vintage (★★★★☆) is full of personality and lovely now. Grown at Lake Wanaka, in Central Otago, it has a richly scented, citrusy bouquet. Mouthfilling, with concentrated, citrusy flavours, it's an off-dry style with slight marmalade notes, firm acidity adding a minerally streak, and impressive complexity and harmony.

MED/DRY $25 AV

Rippon Riesling   ★★★★☆

This single-vineyard, Lake Wanaka, Central Otago wine is a distinctly cool-climate style, steely, long-lived and penetratingly flavoured. Based on mature vines, the 2008 vintage (★★★★★) was fermented with indigenous yeasts and given extended lees-aging. At this stage more restrained on the nose than the Jeunesse, it offers striking depth of citrusy, appley, spicy flavour, dryish, complex, layered and long. An authoritative wine with a firm thread of acidity, it's a top candidate for cellaring.

Vintage	08	07	06	05	04
WR	7	7	6	7	6
Drink	09-17	09-17	09-16	09-15	09-10

MED/DRY $32 –V

Riverby Estate Marlborough Riesling   ★★★☆

The 2008 vintage (★★★) is a hand-picked style (3 grams/litre of residual sugar) with light, appley flavours and a dryish finish (2.5 grams/litre of residual sugar). It's a solid wine, but less rich than the 2007 (★★★★).

DRY $20 AV

Riverby Estate Sali's Block Marlborough Riesling   (★★★★)

Balanced for easy drinking, the 2008 vintage (★★★★) is a medium style (15 grams/litre of residual sugar) with rich, ripe, citrusy flavours and a hint of honeysuckle (from a small percentage of botrytis). It's a lush, well-rounded wine with good length.

Vintage	08
WR	7
Drink	09-11

MED $19 V+

Riverstone Riesling   (★★)

From Villa Maria, the non-vintage bottling (★★) on sale in 2009 is a blend of Australian and New Zealand wines. A medium-bodied wine with crisp, slightly sweet, citrusy flavours, it's a plain quaffer, but priced right.

MED/DRY $12 AV

Rockburn Central Otago Parkburn Riesling   ★★★☆

The youthful 2007 vintage (★★★) was estate-grown in the Cromwell Basin and produced in a medium style. It has fresh, citrusy, appley flavours and a crisp, lingering finish. The 2008 (★★★☆) is very youthful, with crisp, lemony, limey flavours, slightly sweet (15 grams/litre of residual sugar), strong, tight and tangy.

Vintage	08	07	06
WR	5	7	6
Drink	10-15	09-15	09-13

MED $23 –V

Rock Face Waipara Riesling   (★★★)

The 2007 vintage (★★★) is priced sharply. It's a gently sweet wine (15 grams/litre of residual sugar) with fresh acidity and citrusy, rounding flavours.

MED $15 V+

Rock Ferry Marlborough Riesling   ★★★

The 2007 vintage (★★★☆) was hand-picked in the Corners Vineyard, in the heart of the Wairau Plains, and fermented in tanks and barriques. Fresh and lively, it's a crisp, dryish style (6.4 grams/litre of residual sugar), with lemony, appley flavours showing good depth, a touch of complexity and a floral bouquet.

MED/DRY $24 –V

Rocky Point Central Otago Riesling   ★★★☆

From Prophet's Rock, the 2007 vintage (★★★☆) was grown at Bannockburn, fermented with indigenous yeasts in tanks (mostly) and old oak casks (20 per cent), and made in a medium style (18 grams/litre of residual sugar). Drinking well from the start, it's citrusy and flavoursome, with good freshness and harmony.

MED $22 AV

Ruby Bay Vineyard Nelson Riesling   ★★★

The 2009 vintage (★★★) is a Nelson wine, estate-grown, hand-picked and lees-aged. It's a light-bodied style with good varietal character and depth of lemony, appley, slightly spicy flavours, dry (4.5 grams/litre of residual sugar) and youthful. Best drinking mid-2010+.

Vintage	09
WR	4
Drink	09-12

DRY $24 –V

Saddleback Central Otago Riesling   (★★★☆)

From Peregrine, the 2008 vintage (★★★☆) offers fine value. Pale lemon/green, it's a medium-bodied style (12 per cent alcohol) with fresh, vibrant, citrusy, slightly spicy flavours and a hint of apricot, balanced for easy drinking.

MED/DRY $18 V+

Saint Clair Marlborough Riesling   ★★★☆

This is typically an attractive wine, grown in the Dog Point area, on the south side of the Wairau Valley. The 2008 vintage (★★★) is a medium-bodied, slightly sweet style (8 grams/litre of residual sugar), lightly floral, with satisfying depth of citrusy, appley flavours threaded with fresh acidity.

Vintage	08	07	06	05	04
WR	6	6	6	6	6
Drink	09-11	09-11	09-10	P	P

MED/DRY $21 AV

Saint Clair Pioneer Block 9 Big John Riesling   ★★★★☆

Grown in the lower Brancott Valley, Marlborough, the 2008 vintage (★★★★) is a punchy, single-vineyard wine with moderate alcohol (10 per cent) and plentiful sweetness (48 grams/litre of residual sugar). Light-bodied, with strong lemon/apple aromas and flavours and fresh, racy acidity, it's already enjoyable.

Vintage	08	07
WR	7	7
Drink	09-13	09-12

MED $25 AV

Saint Clair Vicar's Choice Marlborough Riesling   ★★★

The 2008 vintage (★★☆) is a slightly honeyed, medium-bodied wine, crisp and slightly sweet (7 grams/litre of residual sugar), with a distinct touch of botrytis. It's best drunk young.

Vintage	08	07	06
WR	6	6	6
Drink	09-11	P	P

MED/DRY $19 AV

Sandihurst Riesling Halbtrocken   (★★★)

Still on sale, the 2006 vintage (★★★) was hand-picked at West Melton and Burnham, south-west of Christchurch, and matured on its yeast lees for six months. It's a light, lemony, appley Canterbury wine, gently sweet (16 grams/litre of residual sugar) and crisp, with good flavour depth and slight earthy notes adding a touch of European-style complexity.

Vintage	06
WR	6
Drink	09-15

MED $25 –V

Seifried Nelson Riesling   ★★★☆

Seifried is a key pioneer of Riesling in New Zealand. The 2008 vintage (★★★☆) is full-bodied (13.5 per cent alcohol) and fruity, in a distinctly medium style with peachy, citrusy, slightly spicy and honeyed flavours. It's already drinking well.

Vintage	09	08
WR	6	6
Drink	09-14	09-12

MED/DRY $19 AV

Seresin Marlborough Riesling   ★★★★☆

Still on sale, the 2005 vintage (★★★★) was grown at the estate vineyard, near Renwick, and the elevated Raupo Creek Vineyard, on the south side of the Wairau Valley. The bouquet is lemony and minerally; the palate is tight, dry (3 grams/litre of residual sugar), lemony and appley, with a hint of honey and good weight and harmony.

Vintage	05	04	03	02	01
WR	6	5	6	5	6
Drink	09-12	09-11	09-10	P	09-10

DRY $23 V+

Seresin Memento Riesling   ★★★★

Harvested by hand from mature vines in the Home Vineyard at Renwick, in Marlborough, this is a medium-sweet style. The 2008 vintage (★★★★) is light (10.5 per cent alcohol), with fresh, vibrant lemon/apple flavours, showing good intensity, and a distinct splash of sweetness (45 grams/litre of residual sugar), finely balanced by racy acidity. It should be long-lived.

Vintage	08
WR	5
Drink	09-18

MED $28 –V

Shaky Bridge Central Otago Riesling   ★★★☆

Grown and hand-picked at Alexandra, the 2007 vintage (★★★☆) is a mouthfilling wine (13.5 per cent alcohol), made in a medium-dry style (12 grams/litre of residual sugar). It offers strong, citrusy, appley flavours, ripe and rounded, with good balance and drink-young appeal.

MED/DRY $20 AV

Shingle Peak Marlborough Riesling – see Matua Valley Shingle Peak Marlborough Riesling

Shipwreck Bay Riesling   (★★★)

From Okahu Estate, the 2008 vintage (★★★) is a Marlborough wine, full-bodied (13.5 per cent alcohol) and citrusy, with hints of passionfruit and spice, and a slightly sweet, crisp finish. It's ready for drinking.

MED/DRY $18 AV

Sileni Cellar Selection Hawke's Bay Riesling   ★★★

The 2008 vintage (★★★) is enjoyable now, with ripe citrus and tropical-fruit flavours, crisp and slightly toasty.

Vintage	08	07	06	05
WR	5	6	5	4
Drink	09-12	09-12	P	P

MED/DRY $19 –V

Sileni The Don Hawke's Bay Riesling   ★★★★☆

One of the region's best Rieslings yet, the 2007 vintage (★★★★☆) is a single-vineyard wine, grown close to the winery in The Triangle. Hand-picked, tank-fermented and lees-aged, it's basically a dry style (5.4 grams/litre of residual sugar), but very finely balanced, with intense lemon/lime aromas and flavours, racy and long. The 2009 (★★★★) is youthful and tightly structured, with concentrated, grapefruit-like flavours, finely poised and lingering. It's already approachable, but offers best drinking 2011+.

MED/DRY $25 AV

Soma Nelson Riesling   ★★★★

The great-value 2007 vintage (★★★★) was 'made in the Alsace style of natural stabilisation over time, approximately one year, until bottling'. Grown at Mapua and on the Waimea Plains, it is lemon-scented, with gently sweet (17 grams/litre of residual sugar) grapefruit and lime flavours that show lovely purity, poise and length.

Vintage	07	06	05
WR	7	6	6
Drink	09-15	09-13	09-12

MED $17 V+

Spinyback Nelson Riesling   ★★★☆

A youthful wine from Waimea Estate, the 2008 vintage (★★★☆) has citrusy, appley, limey flavours, vibrant and strong, and a splash of sweetness (13.7 grams/litre of residual sugar) balanced by appetising, zesty acidity. Bargain-priced.

Vintage	08	07
WR	7	7
Drink	09-13	09-12

MED/DRY $14 V+

Spring Creek Estate Marlborough Riesling   (★★★★)

The great-value 2007 vintage (★★★★) was grown at Rapaura. It has a slightly honeyed bouquet, with crisp, ripe, slightly sweet (8.4 grams/litre of residual sugar) flavours of citrus fruits, spice and passionfruit.

MED/DRY $15 V+

Spy Valley Marlborough Riesling   ★★★★

Always a good buy. The 2008 vintage (★★★☆) is a medium style (15 grams/litre of residual sugar) with good body and depth of ripe, citrusy, slightly spicy flavour, crisp and tangy, and slight botrytis adding a hint of marmalade.

Vintage	09	08	07	06	05	04
WR	6	6	7	6	7	6
Drink	10-14	09-12	09-11	09-10	P	P

MED $20 V+

Staete Landt Marlborough Riesling Dry   ★★★★

The classy 2008 vintage (★★★★☆) was estate-grown at Rapaura, hand-picked, fermented in old French oak puncheons, then oak-aged for a further five months. It's a medium-dry style (11 grams/litre of residual sugar), intensely varietal and very finely balanced, with rich, ripe, lemon/lime flavours, a touch of complexity, and excellent harmony and length.

Vintage	08
WR	7
Drink	09-14

MED/DRY $24 AV

Stafford Lane Estate Riesling   ★★★

The 2009 vintage (★★) is an off-dry Nelson wine, pale and light, crisp, lemony and appley, but it lacks flavour depth.

MED/DRY $18 AV

Stoneleigh Marlborough Riesling   ★★★★

Deliciously fragrant in its youth, this is typically a refined wine from Pernod Ricard NZ with good body, incisive lemon/lime flavours and a crisp, long finish. The 2008 vintage (★★★☆) is tight and crisp, with slightly sweet, lemony flavours, finely balanced and floral. The 2009 (★★★★) is enjoyable from the start, with strong lemon/lime flavours, showing excellent delicacy and harmony.

Vintage	08	07	06
WR	5	6	6
Drink	09-10	P	P

MED/DRY $23 AV

Summerhouse Marlborough Dry Riesling   (★★★☆)

Estate-grown and hand-picked, the 2009 vintage (★★★☆) is full-bodied, fresh and very youthful, with good depth of lemony, appley, slightly spicy flavours. It carries the dry style well. Open mid-2010+.

DRY $27 –V

Te Kairanga East Plain Martinborough Riesling   ★★★★

A consistently good wine, priced right. Scented, toasty, lemony, limey and honeyed, the 2006 vintage (★★★★) is delicious now. The 2008 (★★★★) is floral, vibrant and rich, with lemony, limey, slightly minerally flavours, a touch of sweetness (7.8 grams/litre of residual sugar) and lively acidity. Drink now or cellar.

Vintage	08	07	06
WR	7	7	7
Drink	09-15	09-14	09-12

MED/DRY $22 V+

Te Mania Nelson Riesling   ★★★☆

A bargain. Harvested from mature vines in the Home Block, the 2008 vintage (★★★★) has a slightly honeyed bouquet, leading into a very crisp and lively wine with slightly sweet (8 grams/litre of residual sugar), lemony, limey flavours, showing good intensity.

Vintage	09
WR	6
Drink	09-14

MED/DRY $19 AV

Terrace Edge Waipara Valley Riesling   (★★★★)

A youthful wine with obvious potential, the 2008 vintage (★★★★) is crisp and full-flavoured, with good vigour and strong lemon/lime characters, slightly sweet (18 grams/litre of residual sugar) and minerally.

Vintage	08
WR	6
Drink	09-12

MED $19 V+

Terrain Marlborough Riesling   (★★☆)

Sold in New World supermarkets, the 2007 vintage (★★☆) is a pale yellow, easy-drinking wine with lemony, slightly honeyed flavours and a gently sweet, rounded finish. Ready.

MED $13 V+

Thornbury Waipara Riesling   (★★★☆)

From Villa Maria, the 2008 vintage (★★★☆) is medium-bodied (12 per cent alcohol), with ripe, citrusy, slightly spicy flavours, showing good depth, and a gentle splash of sweetness (7.9 grams/litre of residual sugar). Tasted prior to bottling (and so not rated), the 2009 looked promising, with tight, vibrant, lemony, crisp flavour, showing good intensity.

MED/DRY $21 AV

Three Miners Earnscleugh Valley Riesling   (★★★)

A dryish style (8 grams/litre of residual sugar) from Alexandra, in Central Otago, the 2007 vintage (★★★) is medium-bodied, with lemony, appley flavours showing decent depth. It's not intense, but maturing well.

MED/DRY $22 –V

Three Paddles Martinborough Riesling   ★★★☆

From Nga Waka, the 2009 vintage (★★★★) is very fresh and vibrant, with strong, citrusy, limey flavours, a hint of apricot, and a distinct splash of sweetness. It's a very harmonious wine, delicious young.

Vintage	09	08
WR	7	7
Drink	10+	09+

MED $18 V+

Timara Riesling   ★★☆

The 2007 vintage (★★) from Pernod Ricard NZ is a regional blend with moderate depth of citrusy, slightly peachy flavours, woven with fresh acidity. It's a slightly sweet wine, offering plain, easy drinking.

MED/DRY $12 V+

Tohu Marlborough Riesling   ★★★★

Grown in the Waihopai Valley, the 2009 vintage (★★★★) is a fresh, vibrant, medium-dry style (6 grams/litre of residual sugar), showing good intensity of lemony, limey, slightly minerally flavour. Finely balanced, with excellent delicacy and length, it offers good value.

MED/DRY $19 V+

Torlesse Waipara Riesling   (★★★★)

The stylish 2008 vintage (★★★★) has strong, citrusy flavours, a distinct splash of sweetness (25 grams/litre of residual sugar) and lively acidity. It shows excellent intensity, freshness and harmony, and is priced sharply.

Vintage	08
WR	7
Drink	09-15

MED $18 V+

Tresillian Dry Riesling   (★★★★)

Picked from first-crop Canterbury vines, the 2008 vintage (★★★★) has a Germanic lightness and intensity, with strong, pure, lemony flavours, slightly sweet (10 grams/litre of residual sugar), very lively and harmonious.

MED/DRY $20 V+

Tresillian Riesling   (★★★☆)

From Swannanoa, in Canterbury, the 2008 vintage (★★★☆) is light (9.2 per cent alcohol), lemony and appley, with gently sweet (22 grams/litre of residual sugar), finely balanced flavours, still very youthful.

MED $20 AV

Trout Valley Nelson Riesling   (★★★)

Made from 'the South Island's oldest Riesling vines' at Kahurangi Estate, in Upper Moutere, the 2007 vintage (★★★) is a mouthfilling wine with citrusy, appley flavours showing good varietal character, and a crisp, slightly sweet (7.4 grams/litre of residual sugar) finish.

MED/DRY $17 AV

Two Rivers Marlborough Wairau Selection Riesling   ★★★☆

Hand-picked and lees-aged for 11 months, the 2008 vintage (★★★☆) is a finely balanced wine with very good depth. Medium-bodied, it has a minerally streak through its lemony, appley flavours and a dryish, harmonious finish.

MED/DRY $22 AV

Two Sisters Central Otago Riesling   ★★★★☆

From a steep, north-facing slope at Lowburn, in the Cromwell Basin, the 2007 vintage (★★★★☆) was hand-picked, fermented with indigenous yeasts, and made in a medium style (16 grams/litre of residual sugar). It is scented and full-bodied (13 per cent alcohol), tightly structured and yet highly expressive, with vibrant, concentrated, citrusy, limey flavours, good sugar/acid balance and a lasting finish. Still very youthful, the 2008 (★★★★☆) is fresh, punchy and zingy, with intense, pure, lemony flavours, vibrant and racy. Drink 2011+.

MED $27 AV

Urlar Gladstone Riesling   (★★★★)

Hand-picked at East Taratahi and tank-fermented, the 2008 vintage (★★★★) is a punchy Wairarapa wine with mouthfilling body (13 per cent alcohol) and very fresh, vibrant lemon/lime flavours, with hints of passionfruit and apricot. It's a medium-dry style with finely balanced acidity and good intensity.

MED/DRY $22 V+

Valli Old Vine Otago Riesling   ★★★★☆

The 2008 vintage (★★★★☆) was made from vines planted at Black Ridge, in Alexandra, in 1980. Picked at 23.4 brix, it is a powerful, mouthfilling wine (13 per cent alcohol), slightly austere in its infancy, but tight and intense, with concentrated, citrusy, limey flavours and a bone-dry, minerally, lasting finish. It needs time; open 2010+.

Vintage	08	07
WR	7	5
Drink	09-19	09-13

DRY $28 AV

Vavasour Marlborough Riesling   ★★★★

Still on sale, the 2006 vintage (★★★★) should theoretically be in the sweet wines section of the *Guide*, but it's packaged in a full (750-ml) bottle and only tastes medium-sweet (with 52 grams/litre of residual sugar). Estate-grown and hand-picked in the Awatere Valley, it has a pale, youthful colour, with a finely scented, slightly toasty bouquet. Light-bodied (10.5 per cent alcohol), with rich, lemony, limey flavours, showing excellent delicacy and harmony, it is starting to develop bottle-aged complexity and should be long-lived.

Vintage	06	SW $21 V+
WR	7	
Drink	09-12	

Vidal Marlborough Riesling   ★★★☆

The 2008 (★★★★) is a tight, youthful wine, medium-bodied, with penetrating, citrusy, limey flavours and a hint of passionfruit. Crisp and fresh, it has good sugar/acid balance (8.4 grams/litre of residual sugar) and obvious potential. The 2009 vintage (★★★☆) is lemon-scented, with fresh, vibrant, lemony, slightly spicy flavours, gently sweet (8 grams/litre of residual sugar) and crisp.

Vintage	09	08	07	06	05	04	MED/DRY $20 AV
WR	7	7	7	7	7	6	
Drink	09-15	09-13	09-12	09-10	09-10	P	

Villa Maria Cellar Selection Marlborough Riesling   ★★★★

The 2008 vintage (★★★★) is light, lively and finely balanced, with good intensity of crisp, citrusy, slightly sweet flavours. The 2009, tasted prior to bottling (and so not rated), is light (11.5 per cent alcohol), with fresh, ripe, citrusy, limey flavours, slightly sweet (8 grams/litre of residual sugar), appetisingly crisp and lingering.

Vintage	09	MED/DRY $23 AV
WR	7	
Drink	09-17	

Villa Maria Private Bin Marlborough Riesling   ★★★☆

The 2008 vintage (★★★) is a lemony wine with gentle sweetness giving an easy-drinking balance and good but not great depth. The 2009, tasted prior to bottling (and so not rated), was grown in the Awatere and Wairau valleys and made in a medium-dry style (9 grams/litre of residual sugar). Perfumed, with citrus and tropical-fruit flavours, it shows good balance and depth.

Vintage	09	MED/DRY $20 AV
WR	7	
Drink	09-14	

Villa Maria Reserve Marlborough Riesling   ★★★★☆

The 2007 (★★★★☆) has a distinct splash of sweetness (29 grams/litre of residual sugar). The bouquet is rich and minerally; the palate is light, with lemony, limey, finely poised flavours, crisp, zingy and intense. The 2008 vintage (★★★★☆) was grown in the Waldron Vineyard, in the Wairau Valley. Gently sweet (25 grams/litre of residual sugar), it's a tightly structured, elegant wine, finely poised, citrusy, light (10.5 per cent alcohol) and lovely.

Vintage	08	07	06	MED $26 AV
WR	7	7	7	
Drink	09-17	09-17	09-18	

Villa Maria Single Vineyard Fletcher Vineyard Marlborough Riesling   (★★★★☆)

Hand-picked in the middle of the Wairau Valley, the 2008 vintage (★★★★☆) was stop-fermented in a medium style (28 grams/litre of residual sugar) with low alcohol (9.5 per cent). It shows excellent intensity of lemon and apple flavours, with gentle sweetness balanced by lively acidity and a long, slightly minerally finish.

Vintage	08
WR	7
Drink	09-20

MED $26 AV

Villa Maria Single Vineyard Taylors Pass Riesling   ★★★☆

Grown in the Awatere Valley of Marlborough, the 2007 vintage (★★★☆) is a distinctly medium style (27 grams/litre of residual sugar), light, with citrusy, appley flavours and good acid spine.

MED $30 –V

Voss Estate Riesling   ★★★☆

Worth cellaring, the 2008 vintage (★★★) is a medium-bodied wine (11 per cent alcohol) from Martinborough with slightly sweet (7 grams/litre of residual sugar), lemony flavours, fresh, finely balanced and youthful. There is no 2009.

Vintage	09	08	07	06
WR	NM	6	NM	5
Drink	NM	09-18	NM	09-12

MED/DRY $20 AV

Vynfields Classic Riesling   ★★★★

Certified organic, the 2008 vintage (★★★★) of this Martinborough wine offers forward, easy drinking, in a soft, sweetish style with strong, lemony flavours, showing some lushness.

MED $29 –V

Vynfields Dry Classic Riesling   (★★★★)

Dryish (5.4 grams/litre of residual sugar) but not austere, the 2007 vintage (★★★★) was grown organically in Martinborough. Weighty (13.5 per cent alcohol) and minerally, it has strong lemon/lime flavours, crisp and finely balanced.

MED/DRY $29 –V

Waimea Bolitho SV Nelson Riesling   ★★★★

The 2006 vintage (★★★★) is a lemony, slightly toasty wine with elegant, complex flavours that linger well. Full, rounded and finely balanced, it's a medium-dry style (13.8 grams/litre of residual sugar), offering good drinking from now onwards and likely to be long-lived.

Vintage	07	06	05
WR	7	7	7
Drink	09-17	09-16	09-15

MED/DRY $22 V+

Waimea Classic Riesling   ★★★★

Balanced for easy drinking, this Nelson wine is consistently impressive and delivers great value. The 2008 vintage (★★★★★) is a very generous wine with rich lemon/lime flavours, abundant sweetness (21.8 grams/litre of residual sugar) and lively acidity. Refined and concentrated, it's already a lovely mouthful.

Vintage	08	07
WR	7	7
Drink	09-16	09-17

MED $18 V+

Waimea Dry Riesling ★★★★

Grown on the Waimea Plains of Nelson, the 2006 vintage (★★★☆) is a tight, youthful wine, dry (3.7 grams/litre of residual sugar) with a minerally streak and lemony, appley flavours that linger well. Drink now or cellar.

Vintage	06	05	04
WR	7	5	6
Drink	09-16	09-10	09-10

MED/DRY $18 V+

Waipara Hills Equinox Waipara Riesling (★★★★☆)

Finely scented and light-bodied (11 per cent alcohol), the 2007 vintage (★★★★☆) has intense grapefruit, apple and lime flavours, fresh, crisp and minerally. A beautifully poised wine, it should flourish with cellaring.

MED $43 –V

Waipara Hills Waipara Riesling ★★★★☆

The 2007 vintage (★★★★☆) is very fresh and intense, with citrusy, limey flavours that linger well.

MED/DRY $20 V+

Waipara Springs Premo Dry Riesling ★★★★

The highly distinctive 2007 vintage (★★★★☆) was made with some use of botrytis-affected fruit, indigenous yeasts and barrel fermentation (40 per cent of the blend spent three months in old barrels). The bouquet is slightly honeyed; the palate is very rich, with peachy, lemony, spicy, faintly sweet flavours (6 grams/litre of residual sugar), harmonious and well-rounded. Drink now or cellar.

Vintage	07	06
WR	7	7
Drink	09-12	09-11

MED/DRY $22 V+

Waipara Springs Riesling ★★★☆

The 2007 vintage (★★★☆) is a light Waipara wine (10.5 per cent alcohol). Lemon and apple-scented, it is crisp and lively, with a splash of sweetness (25 grams/litre of residual sugar) and very good delicacy and depth.

Vintage	07	06
WR	6	5
Drink	09-11	09-10

MED $19 AV

Wairau River Marlborough Riesling ★★★☆

The 2008 (★★★☆) is a medium-dry style with good depth of lemon/lime flavours, tight and crisp. The 2009 vintage (★★★☆), 10 per cent barrel-aged, is tight and crisp, with lemony, appley flavours, a splash of sweetness (11.5 grams/litre of residual sugar) and a slightly spicy, lingering finish.

Vintage	09	08
WR	6	4
Drink	09-12	09-10

MED/DRY $20 AV

Wairau River Summer Riesling (★★★☆)

'Sup with frivolous frivolity' urges the back label on the 2009 vintage (★★★☆), grown in Marlborough. Light (9.5 per cent alcohol) and sweetish (35 grams/litre of residual sugar), it is tense and very youthful, with good depth of flavour, appley and tangy. Best drinking mid-2010+.

Vintage	09
WR	5
Drink	09-10

MED $20 AV

Weka River Waipara Valley Riesling ★★★★

The 2008 vintage (★★★★) is an elegant, concentrated, single-vineyard wine with good acid spine. Made in a medium style (28 grams/litre of residual sugar), it has strong lemon and slight nectarine flavours, finely balanced and tightly structured. Drink now or cellar.

MED $22 V+

West Brook Marlborough Riesling ★★★★

The 2008 (★★★☆) is full-bodied, with gentle sweetness (11 grams/litre of residual sugar) and plenty of crisp, lemony, limey flavour, balanced for easy drinking. The 2009 (★★★★) is attractive from the start. Showing good vigour and intensity, it has strong, ripe lemon, lime and passionfruit flavours, gently sweet, crisp, finely balanced and lingering. Drink now or cellar.

MED/DRY $20 V+

Whitehaven Marlborough Riesling ★★★

Full-bodied, the 2009 vintage (★★★) has dryish (5 grams/litre of residual sugar), lemony, slightly spicy flavours, showing decent depth and good delicacy and harmony. It should mature well.

Vintage	09
WR	7
Drink	09-14

MED/DRY $19 AV

Wild Earth Central Otago Riesling ★★★★

The finely poised 2008 vintage (★★★★☆) was fermented in 'a single, small tank'. Rich and tightly structured, with intensely varietal, ripe lemon and peach flavours, it has good acid spine and a slightly sweet (14 grams/litre of residual sugar), minerally, lingering finish.

MED $27 –V

Wild South Marlborough Riesling   ★★★☆

The vivacious 2007 vintage (★★★★) from Sacred Hill is a single-vineyard wine, grown in the Awatere Valley. Fresh and punchy, with ripe-fruit aromas, it's a gently sweet style with vibrant peach, lemon and lime flavours.

Vintage 08
WR   6
Drink   09-11

MED/DRY $19 AV

Wither Hills Marlborough Riesling   (★★★★)

The debut 2007 vintage (★★★★) is a single-vineyard wine, grown at Dillons Point, in the lower Wairau Valley. It has fresh, pure flavours of lemons, limes and passionfruit, slightly sweet (9 grams/litre of residual sugar), finely balanced and lingering.

Vintage 07
WR   6
Drink   09-10

MED/DRY $25 AV

Woollaston Nelson Riesling   ★★★★

The 2009 vintage (★★★★) shows excellent potential. Mouthfilling, it has strong citrusy, limey flavours, showing very good delicacy and purity, a sliver of sweetness (8.5 grams/litre of residual sugar) and a fresh, crisp, long finish.

MED/DRY $19 AV

Yealands Estate Marlborough Riesling   (★★★☆)

The tightly structured 2008 vintage (★★★☆) is a single-vineyard Awatere Valley wine with crisp, ripe, citrusy flavours that linger well. A medium-dry style (11 grams/litre of residual sugar) with good acid spine, it's still unfolding.

MED/DRY $23 –V

Yealands Marlborough Riesling   (★★★)

The debut 2008 vintage (★★★) is an easy-drinking style, grown in the Awatere Valley. It has fresh, citrusy flavours, with a hint of passionfruit, a distinct splash of sweetness (13 grams/litre of residual sugar), and good delicacy and depth.

MED/DRY $18 AV

Sauvignon Blanc

Sauvignon Blanc is New Zealand's key calling card in the wine markets of the world. At the 2009 International Wine Challenge, in London, the trophy for champion Sauvignon Blanc was awarded to Clifford Bay Awatere Valley Sauvignon Blanc 2008. Oyster Bay Marlborough Sauvignon Blanc is the most popular white wine in Australia, regardless of variety, and the biggest-selling Sauvignon Blanc in the US is Nobilo Marlborough Sauvignon Blanc.

The rise to international stardom of New Zealand Sauvignon Blanc was remarkably swift. Government Viticulturist Romeo Bragato imported the first Sauvignon Blanc vines from Italy in 1906, but it was not until 1974 that Matua Valley marketed New Zealand's first varietal Sauvignon Blanc. Montana established its first Sauvignon Blanc vines in Marlborough in 1975, allowing Sauvignon Blanc to get into full commercial swing in the early 1980s. In the year to June 2009, 81.1 per cent by volume of all New Zealand's wine exports were based on Sauvignon Blanc.

Sauvignon Blanc is by far New Zealand's most extensively planted variety, in 2010 comprising 49.9 per cent of the bearing national vineyard. Over 85 per cent of all vines are concentrated in Marlborough, with further significant plantings in Hawke's Bay, Nelson, Wairarapa and Waipara. Between 2005 and 2010, the area of bearing Sauvignon Blanc vines will more than double, from 7277 hectares to 14,844 hectares.

The flavour of New Zealand Sauvignon Blanc varies according to fruit ripeness. At the herbaceous, under-ripe end of the spectrum, vegetal and fresh-cut grass aromas hold sway; riper wines show capsicum, gooseberry and melon-like characters; very ripe fruit displays tropical-fruit flavours.

Intensely herbaceous Sauvignon Blancs are not hard to make in the viticulturally cool climate of the South Island and the lower North Island (Wairarapa). 'The challenge faced by New Zealand winemakers is to keep those herbaceous characters in check,' says Kevin Judd, formerly chief winemaker at Cloudy Bay. 'It would be foolish to suggest that these herbaceous notes detract from the wines; in fact I am sure that this fresh edge and intense varietal aroma are the reason for its recent international popularity. The better of these wines have these herbaceous characters in context and in balance with the more tropical-fruit characters associated with riper fruit.'

There are two key styles of Sauvignon Blanc produced in New Zealand. Wines handled entirely in stainless steel tanks – by far the most common – place their accent squarely on their fresh, direct fruit flavours. Alternatively, many top labels are handled principally in tanks, but 5 to 10 per cent of the blend is barrel-fermented, adding a touch of complexity without subduing the wine's fresh, punchy fruit aromas and flavours.

Another major style difference is regionally based: the crisp, incisively flavoured wines of Marlborough contrast with the softer, less pungently herbaceous Hawke's Bay style. These are wines to drink young (traditionally within 18 months of the vintage) while they are irresistibly fresh, aromatic and tangy, although the oak-matured, more complex wines sometimes found in Hawke's Bay (currently an endangered species, despite their quality) can mature well for several years.

The recent swing from corks to screwcaps has also boosted the longevity of the wines. Rather than running out of steam, many are now highly enjoyable at two years old.

3 Stones Marlborough Sauvignon Blanc ★★★

From Ager Sectus (owner of The Crossings, Crossroads and Southbank brands), the 2008 vintage (★★☆) is a medium-bodied wine with fresh, grassy aromas and flavours and a crisp, dry finish.

Vintage	08	07	06	
WR	6	7	6	DRY $20 AV
Drink	P	P	P	

12,000 Miles Sauvignon Blanc ★★★

From Gladstone Vineyard, the 2008 vintage (★★★) is a fresh Wairarapa wine with melon and green-capsicum flavours, crisp and dry.

DRY $17 AV

Akarua Marlborough Sauvignon Blanc   ★★★☆

The 2008 vintage (★★★☆) from this Central Otago winery was grown in the Awatere and Wairau valleys. It's a dry style (2.4 grams/litre of residual sugar), with fresh 'tomato stalk' aromas leading into a medium to full-bodied, vibrant, ripely herbaceous wine showing very good delicacy and depth. Tight and punchy, it lingers well.

DRY $22 AV

Alana Estate Martinborough Sauvignon Blanc   ★★★☆

The 2008 vintage (★★★☆) is a single-vineyard wine with a fresh, ripely herbaceous bouquet. Fleshy and soft, it has vibrant, tropical-fruit flavours, dry (3 grams/litre of residual sugar) and showing very good depth.

Vintage	09
WR	6
Drink	09-14

DRY $25 –V

Alexia Wairarapa Sauvignon Blanc   ★★★☆

From Jane Cooper, winemaker at Matahiwi, the 2008 vintage (★★★☆) is medium-bodied and balanced for easy drinking, with crisp, freshly herbaceous flavours, showing very good depth and liveliness.

DRY $20 AV

Allan Scott Marlborough Sauvignon Blanc   ★★★☆

The Scotts aim for a 'ripe tropical-fruit' Sauvignon – a style typical of the Rapaura area of the Wairau Valley, where most of the company's vineyards are clustered. The 2008 vintage (★★★☆), the 21st, is medium-bodied, with ripe passionfruit and lime flavours, showing very good delicacy and depth, and a crisp, basically dry (4 grams/litre of residual sugar) finish.

Vintage	09	08	07
WR	6	6	7
Drink	09-11	P	P

DRY $20 AV

Allan Scott Millstone Marlborough Sauvignon Blanc   (★★★☆)

From a company-owned vineyard 'in conversion to organic', the 2008 vintage (★★★☆) is a medium-bodied (12.5 per cent alcohol), fully dry wine (5 per cent oak-aged), with very good depth of ripe melon and lime flavours, and some funky notes adding a touch of complexity.

Vintage	08
WR	6
Drink	09-12

DRY $27 –V

Allan Scott Moorlands Marlborough Sauvignon Blanc   ★★★★

Based on vines planted in 1980, next to the winery at Rapaura, the 2008 vintage (★★★★) was mostly handled in tanks, but 5 per cent of the blend was fermented in old barrels. It's a bone-dry style, tight and youthful, with a slightly creamy texture and ripe tropical-fruit flavours, showing good concentration.

Vintage	08
WR	6
Drink	09-12

DRY $27 –V

Alpha Domus The Pilot Hawke's Bay Sauvignon Blanc   ★★★☆

The 2008 vintage (★★★) is a typical regional style with mouthfilling body and plenty of fresh, ripe passionfruit/lime flavour, crisp, dry and lively.

Vintage	08
WR	6
Drink	09-12

DRY $20 AV

Amisfield Central Otago Sauvignon Blanc   ★★★★

The 2009 vintage (★★★★) was estate-grown at Lowburn and mostly handled in tanks, but 5 per cent of the blend was fermented in old French oak barriques. Mouthfilling, with a distinct touch of complexity, it is crisp, vibrant and limey, with good intensity and a sliver of sweetness (4 grams/litre of residual sugar) to balance its fresh, appetising acidity. It's not cheap, but highly enjoyable.

Vintage	09	08	07
WR	5	5	6
Drink	09-11	09-10	P

DRY $30 –V

Anchorage Nelson Sauvignon Blanc   ★★★

Estate-grown at Motueka, in Nelson, the 2008 vintage (★★★☆) was harvested from first-crop vines. It has grassy aromas, medium body and strong, fresh, dry (3.4 grams/litre of residual sugar) melon/capsicum flavours, woven with lively acidity.

DRY $17 AV

Ara Composite Marlborough Sauvignon Blanc   ★★★★

From Winegrowers of Ara, the 2008 vintage (★★★★) is a concentrated, lively wine with fresh, tropical-fruit flavours, showing excellent ripeness and depth. Pineappley and limey, it has good vigour and a fully dry, lingering finish.

Vintage	08
WR	6
Drink	09-10

DRY $22 V+

Ara Pathway Marlborough Sauvignon Blanc   (★★★☆)

The sharply priced 2008 vintage (★★★☆) shows good weight and flavour depth. Mouthfilling, it has ripe tropical-fruit flavours and a crisp, fully dry finish.

DRY $16 V+

Ara Resolute Marlborough Sauvignon Blanc – see Resolute Marlborough Sauvignon Blanc

Artisan The Sands Block Marlborough Sauvignon Blanc   ★★★☆

A single-vineyard wine, grown at the eastern (cooler) end of the Wairau Valley, this is typically fresh-scented and crisp, with ripe melon and lime flavours, finely balanced, lively and punchy.

DRY $19 V+

Ash Ridge Hawke's Bay Barrel Fermented Sauvignon Blanc   (★★★☆)

Grown in The Triangle, the 2009 vintage (★★★☆) is a single-vineyard wine, fermented (partly with indigenous yeasts) in old oak barrels. Ripely scented, with vibrant, tropical-fruit characters to the fore, it is medium-bodied (12 per cent alcohol), with very good depth of flavour, showing some complexity, and a finely balanced, dry finish. A good food wine.

Vintage	09			DRY $23 AV
WR	5			
Drink	09-14			

Ashwell Sauvignon Blanc   ★★★☆

This Martinborough wine is typically good, with mouthfilling body and ripely herbaceous flavours, fresh and strong. The 2009 vintage (★★★☆) is ripely scented and full-bodied, with good depth of passionfruit and lime flavours and a smooth, dry finish.

Vintage	09	08	07	DRY $20 AV
WR	6	6	7	
Drink	09-10	P	P	

Askerne Hawke's Bay Sauvignon Blanc   ★★★☆

This small Havelock North winery makes a good, often excellent Sauvignon. The 2009 vintage (★★★☆), handled without oak and made in a bone-dry style, is mouthfilling (14 per cent alcohol), with ripe tropical-fruit flavours, showing good texture and depth. Priced sharply.

Vintage	09	08	07	06	DRY $16 V+
WR	6	6	6	6	
Drink	09-11	09-10	P	P	

Aspire Hawke's Bay Sauvignon Blanc   ★★★

From Matariki, the 2008 vintage (★★★) is a typical regional style, grown in the Gimblett Gravels. Mouthfilling, it has good depth of fresh, tropical-fruit and gooseberry flavours, ripe and rounded (4 grams/litre of residual sugar).

Vintage	08			DRY $20 AV
WR	5			
Drink	09-10			

Astrolabe Discovery Awatere Sauvignon Blanc   ★★★★☆

Aromatic, nettley and punchy, the 2008 vintage (★★★★☆) has freshly herbaceous aromas leading into a distinctive Awatere Valley style with lively, intense melon and green-capsicum flavours, pure, incisive and long. It's maturing well.

Vintage	08	07		DRY $24 V+
WR	6	6		
Drink	09-12	P		

Astrolabe Discovery Kekerengu Sauvignon Blanc   (★★★★)

Grown on a limestone site at Kekerengu, half-way between Blenheim and Kaikoura, the 2008 vintage (★★★★) is still unfolding. Tight and minerally, it's a youthful, quietly classy Marlborough wine, ripely herbaceous, with good body and a sustained, bone-dry finish. Best drinking mid-2010+.

Vintage	08			DRY $26 –V
WR	6			
Drink	09-12			

Astrolabe Voyage Marlborough Sauvignon Blanc   ★★★★★

This label has recently acquired cult status, and the 2008 vintage (★★★★★) is another striking wine. Grown at seven sites in the Awatere, Waihopai and Wairau valleys, it is weighty and rich, with a lovely interplay of tropical-fruit and herbaceous flavours, woven with fresh but not high acidity. Impressively intense, it's a dry wine (3.3 grams/litre of residual sugar), with a very long finish.

Vintage	08	07	06
WR	6	6	6
Drink	09-12	P	P

DRY $21 V+

Ata Rangi Martinborough Sauvignon Blanc   ★★★★

A consistently attractive wine, with ripe tropical-fruit rather than grassy, herbaceous flavours. From a 'near perfect season', the 2008 (★★★★☆) was mostly handled in tanks, but 10 per cent of the blend was fermented and lees-aged in seasoned oak barrels. Mouthfilling, it is very intense and zingy, with a strong surge of melon/lime flavour, a touch of complexity from the oak and lees-aging, and fresh, crisp acidity enlivening the finish.

Vintage	08	07	06
WR	7	6	6
Drink	09-11	09-10	09-10

DRY $24 AV

Ataahua Waipara Sauvignon Blanc   ★★★★

The 2008 vintage (★★★★) is a single-vineyard wine with a complex, slightly funky bouquet. The palate is tight, with a sliver of sweetness (4 grams/litre of residual sugar) balanced by crisp acidity, good weight and tight, rich, non-herbaceous flavours. It shows strong personality.

DRY $20 V+

Auntsfield Long Cow Sauvignon Blanc   ★★★★☆

Grown and hand-harvested near the Long Cow paddock on the south side of the Wairau Valley, where Marlborough's first wines were made in the 1870s, the 2008 vintage (★★★★★) was 20 per cent fermented in seasoned French oak barriques. Lovely in its youth, it has ripe, slightly 'sweaty' aromas, leading into a mouthfilling, sweet-fruited wine, with a real touch of complexity. Finely textured, fresh and vibrant, it is deliciously rich, ripe and rounded.

Vintage	08	07	06
WR	7	7	5
Drink	09-10	P	P

DRY $22 V+

Awatere River Marlborough Sauvignon Blanc   (★★★★)

The label on the 2008 vintage (★★★★) doesn't say categorically that this wine was grown in the Awatere Valley, but its fresh, strong, nettley aromas are certainly typical of the sub-region. Mouthfilling, vibrant and zingy, it's a full-bodied wine with gooseberry and green-capsicum flavours, showing excellent delicacy and depth.

DRY $22 V+

Babich Black Label Marlborough Sauvignon Blanc   ★★★★☆

Aimed at the restaurant trade, this is a consistently excellent wine. The 2009 vintage (★★★★★) was mostly handled in tanks, but a small part of the blend was fermented in seasoned oak casks.

It has real presence in the mouth, with mouthfilling body, a touch of complexity, and crisp, concentrated flavours of melons and capsicums, deliciously rich, vibrant and zingy.

DRY $23 V+

Babich Individual Vineyards Cowslip Valley Marlborough Sauvignon Blanc   (★★★★☆)
From the Waihopai Valley, the 2009 vintage (★★★★☆) has slight 'sweaty armpit' aromas, leading into a weighty, rounded wine with ripe tropical-fruit flavours, showing excellent delicacy, texture and depth. It's a very harmonious wine with fine acidity and lovely flow and richness.

DRY $25 AV

Babich Individual Vineyards Headwaters Organic Block Marlborough Sauvignon Blanc   (★★★☆)
Certified organic, the 2009 vintage (★★★☆) is a bone-dry wine, pale, with gentle, limey aromas. Subtle and restrained in its infancy, with good fruit sweetness and delicacy, and a slightly minerally streak, it should mature well; open mid-2010+.

DRY $25 –V

Babich Lone Tree Hawke's Bay Sauvignon Blanc   ★★★
Grown in Hawke's Bay, the 2008 vintage (★★☆) is still fresh and lively, with crisp apple and tropical-fruit flavours.

DRY $16 V+

Babich Marlborough Sauvignon Blanc   ★★★★
Joe Babich favours 'a fuller, riper, softer style of Sauvignon Blanc. It's not a jump out of the glass style, but the wines develop well.' The latest releases reflect a rising input of grapes from the company's Cowslip Valley Vineyard in the Waihopai Valley, which gives less herbaceous fruit characters than its other Marlborough vineyards. The 2009 vintage (★★★★) is weighty and dry, with refreshing acidity and ripe passionfruit and lime flavours, showing good richness and immediacy.

DRY $20 V+

Babich Winemakers Reserve Marlborough Sauvignon Blanc   ★★★☆
A good example of gently wooded Marlborough Sauvignon Blanc, with very ripe flavours and great drinkability. Grown in the Waihopai and Awatere valleys, it is mostly handled in tanks, but 10 per cent is fermented and lees-aged in French oak barriques. The 2008 vintage (★★★☆) is enjoyable now, with good depth of ripe tropical-fruit flavours, a subtle seasoning of toasty oak and a smooth finish.

DRY $25 –V

Bel Echo Terroir Portrait Marlborough Sauvignon Blanc   ★★★☆
From Clos Henri, the 2008 vintage (★★★★) was hand-picked, tank-fermented and matured on its yeast lees for seven months. Mouthfilling, it has slightly 'sweaty' aromas, in a fleshy style with generous tropical-fruit flavours, rounded and rich. The best yet.

Vintage	08	07	06
WR	7	5	6
Drink	09-13	09-10	P

DRY $22 AV

Belmonte Marlborough Sauvignon Blanc ★★★☆

From a company with family links to John Forrest, the 2009 vintage (★★★) is vibrantly fruity, in a fresh, medium-bodied style with good depth of smooth, ripe tropical-fruit flavours, finely balanced for easy drinking.

DRY $17 V+

Bensen Block Sauvignon Blanc ★★★

From Pernod Ricard NZ, the 2008 vintage (★★★) is a Marlborough wine. It's a very easy-drinking style, full-bodied, with ripe tropical-fruit flavours and a soft, well-rounded finish.

Vintage	08	07
WR	7	7
Drink	P	P

DRY $17 AV

Big Sky Te Muna Road Martinborough Sauvignon Blanc (★★★)

Weighty, with ripe melon and lime flavours and gentle acidity, the 2008 vintage (★★★) is a subtle, dry style with a smooth finish.

DRY $22 –V

Bird Marlborough Sauvignon Blanc ★★★★

Estate-grown in the Old Schoolhouse Vineyard, in the Omaka Valley, the 2008 vintage (★★★☆) is crisp and tight, with freshly herbaceous aromas. Full-bodied, it has dry melon, capsicum and lime flavours, showing very good depth.

Vintage	08	07	06
WR	6	5	4
Drink	09-11	09-10	P

DRY $20 V+

Black Barn Vineyards Barrel Ferment Sauvignon Blanc (★★★☆)

Still on sale, the 2007 vintage (★★★☆) was grown in Hawke's Bay and fermented in seasoned French oak barrels. A mouthfilling, dry style, it has ripe tropical-fruit flavours, showing good concentration, and a rich, creamy texture, but the wood influence is assertive.

Vintage	07
WR	6
Drink	09-11

DRY $30 –V

Black Barn Vineyards Hawke's Bay Sauvignon Blanc ★★★☆

Crisp and dry, the 2008 vintage (★★★☆) has ripe tropical-fruit flavours to the fore, with a slight herbal undercurrent. Still very fresh and lively, it has a touch of bottle-aged complexity and is drinking well now.

DRY $20 AV

Blackenbrook Vineyard Nelson Sauvignon Blanc ★★★★

Grown in the Tasman district, harvested by hand and lees-aged in stainless steel tanks, the 2009 vintage (★★★★☆) is a dry style (4 grams/litre of residual sugar). Aromatic, it is fresh, vibrant and punchy, with good intensity of gooseberry and lime flavours, racy and long.

Vintage	09	08	07	06
WR	6	6	7	6
Drink	09-10	P	P	P

Bladen Marlborough Sauvignon Blanc ★★★

The 2008 vintage (★★★) is fleshy and rounded, with good depth of tropical-fruit and herbaceous flavours, balanced for easy drinking.

Blind River Marlborough Sauvignon Blanc ★★★★

The 2008 vintage (★★★★) was estate-grown in the Awatere Valley and mostly handled in tanks; 10 per cent was fermented in seasoned oak barriques. Deliciously fresh and vibrant and punchy, it has the classic 'tomato stalk' aromas of the district's Sauvignon Blancs, in a finely poised, limey, slightly minerally style with excellent intensity and harmony.

Blue Ridge Marlborough Sauvignon Blanc ★★★☆

The 2008 vintage (★★★★) is full of youthful impact. Punchy and vibrant, it has excellent intensity of ripe tropical-fruit flavours, fresh and crisp.

DRY $25 –V

Boreham Wood Jane's Awatere Valley Marlborough Sauvignon Blanc (★★☆)

The 2008 vintage (★★☆) is a single-vineyard wine, tank-fermented and lees-aged for five months. Fresh, fruity and smooth, it's a light, easy-drinking dry wine, not concentrated, but priced right.

Vintage	09	08
WR	7	6
Drink	10-11	09-10

Boreham Wood Marlborough Sauvignon Blanc ★★★☆

This single-vineyard wine is grown in the Awatere Valley. The 2008 vintage (★★★) is crisp and lively, with finely balanced, dry melon, lime and capsicum flavours, showing good depth.

Vintage	09	08	07	06
WR	7	6	7	6
Drink	10-12	09-10	09-10	P

DRY $19 V+

Borthwick Vineyard Wairarapa Sauvignon Blanc ★★★★

Showing excellent richness, the 2008 vintage (★★★★) is a scented and weighty wine with ripe melon, capsicum and lime flavours, showing a touch of complexity and excellent freshness and length.

Boundary Vineyards Rapaura Road Marlborough Sauvignon Blanc   ★★★☆

From Pernod Ricard NZ, this is typically a very ripe and rounded style with distinctly tropical-fruit flavours, smooth and strong. The 2008 vintage (★★★☆) is a medium to full-bodied style, with very good ripeness, dryness and depth. The 2009 (★★★☆) is fleshy and rounded, with ripe passionfruit-like flavours, offering smooth, easy, satisfying drinking.

Vintage	08	07	06	05
WR	6	6	6	6
Drink	09-10	P	P	P

DRY $20 AV

Brightside Brightwater Sauvignon Blanc   ★★☆

The 2009 vintage (★★☆) from Kaimira is the first to be labelled 'Brightwater', rather than 'Nelson'. Priced right, it's a medium-bodied wine with clearly varietal, freshly herbaceous aromas and flavours, showing solid depth, and a smooth (5 grams/litre of residual sugar) finish.

MED/DRY $15 AV

Brightwater Vineyards Lord Rutherford Sauvignon Blanc   ★★★★☆

Grown in Nelson, the 2009 vintage (★★★★☆) has ripe, 'sweaty armpit' aromas, leading into a mouthfilling, smooth wine with concentrated passionfruit and lime flavours, dry (3.4 grams/litre of residual sugar), lively and long.

Vintage	08	07
WR	7	6
Drink	09-10	09-10

DRY $25 AV

Brightwater Vineyards Nelson Sauvignon Blanc   ★★★★

Grown on the Waimea Plains, this is a consistently enjoyable, ripely flavoured wine, fresh and punchy. Grown at two sites, the 2009 vintage (★★★★) is dry (2.9 grams/litre of residual sugar), with mouthfilling body and vibrant passionfruit/lime flavours, crisp and concentrated.

Vintage	08	07	06
WR	6	5	6
Drink	09-10	P	P

DRY $20 V+

Brookfields Ohiti Estate Hawke's Bay Sauvignon Blanc   ★★★

The 2009 vintage (★★★) is mouthfilling and smooth, with good depth of vibrant, tropical-fruit flavours, and a sliver of sweetness (5 grams/litre of residual sugar) balanced by fresh, crisp acidity.

Vintage	09	08
WR	7	7
Drink	10-12	09-10

MED/DRY $19 AV

Burnt Spur Martinborough Sauvignon Blanc   ★★★☆

A delicious, easy-drinking style, the 2008 vintage (★★★★) is a single-vineyard wine from Martinborough Vineyard. Vibrantly fruity, with strong, ripe tropical-fruit flavours and lees-aging characters adding a touch of complexity, it is mouthfilling and finely textured, with a well-rounded finish.

DRY $22 AV

Cable Bay Marlborough Sauvignon Blanc   ★★★☆

Waiheke Island-based winemaker Neill Culley aims for a Sauvignon Blanc with 'restraint and textural interest, to enjoy with food'. The 2008 vintage (★★★★) was grown in the Brancott and Omaka valleys and at Rapaura. Enjoyable from the start, it has a freshly herbaceous bouquet, leading into a mouthfilling wine with strong, ripe gooseberry and capsicum flavours, a touch of complexity, and a crisp, lasting finish.

Vintage	08	07	06
WR	7	7	7
Drink	09-10	P	P

DRY $22 AV

Camshorn Waipara Sauvignon Blanc   (★★★☆)

The 2008 vintage (★★★☆) from Pernod Ricard NZ is medium-bodied, with fresh, crisp tropical-fruit and herbaceous flavours, a slightly minerally streak, and good length. Ready.

DRY $27 –V

Cape Campbell Marlborough Sauvignon Blanc   ★★★☆

The 2008 vintage (★★★☆) was estate-grown at Blind River, south of the Awatere River. Punchy, 'tomato stalk' aromas lead into a medium-bodied wine with fresh, strong melon/capsicum flavours and a basically dry (3.5 grams/litre of residual sugar), crisp finish.

Vintage	08
WR	7
Drink	09-10

DRY $19 V+

Carrick Central Otago Sauvignon Blanc   ★★★

Grown at Bannockburn, this wine is mostly handled in tanks, but 20 to 25 per cent of the blend is fermented in old barrels. The 2008 vintage (★★★) is citrusy and appley, with a touch of complexity and a crisp, dry (4 grams/litre of residual sugar) finish.

DRY $20 AV

Castaway Bay Marlborough Sauvignon Blanc   (★★☆)

From Maven, the 2008 vintage (★★☆) was estate-grown in the Wairau Valley. It's a pleasant but plain wine with a restrained bouquet, ripe passionfruit, pear and lime flavours, and a smooth finish.

DRY $15 AV

Charles Wiffen Marlborough Sauvignon Blanc   ★★★☆

The 2008 vintage (★★★★) is freshly scented, with vibrant, ripely herbaceous flavours. A dry style (3 grams/litre of residual sugar) with excellent depth, it's attractive from the start.

DRY $20 AV

Cheeky Little Sav   (★★☆)

From Babich, the 2008 vintage (★★☆) is an East Coast wine, medium-bodied, with ripe gooseberry/lime flavours, fresh acidity and a smooth finish. It's an easy-drinking style, priced sharply.

DRY $10 V+

Church Road Hawke's Bay Sauvignon Blanc   ★★★★☆

Aiming for a wine that is 'more refined and softer than a typical New Zealand Sauvignon Blanc, with restrained varietal characters', the 2008 vintage (★★★★) was based mostly (78 per cent) on aromatic fruit from Pernod Ricard NZ's elevated Matapiro site (300 metres above sea level), blended with grapes from warmer vineyards on the plains. Partly barrel-fermented, it is a finely balanced, weighty, slightly creamy wine with strong melon and capsicum flavours, a hint of oak, moderate acidity and a fully dry finish. Great drinkability.

Vintage	08	07
WR	7	7
Drink	09-10	P

DRY $26 AV

Churton Marlborough Sauvignon Blanc   ★★★★☆

English wine merchant-turned-winemaker Sam Weaver aims for a style that 'combines the renowned flavour and aromatic intensity of Marlborough fruit with the finesse and complexity of fine European wines'. The 2008 vintage (★★★★) is a subtle, sophisticated wine, mostly handled in tanks (5 to 10 per cent was oak-aged), and late-bottled. Vibrant and fruity, it has ripe melon/lime flavours, showing excellent delicacy and depth, a minerally streak and a bone-dry, lingering finish.

Vintage	08	07	06	05
WR	6	7	6	7
Drink	10-12	09-12	09-10	09-13

DRY $23 V+

C.J. Pask Roy's Hill Sauvignon Blanc   ★★☆

Winemaker Kate Radburnd aims for 'an easy-drinking style with its emphasis on tropical-fruit flavours and a tangy lift'. Grown in Hawke's Bay, it is typically fresh, light, citrusy and limey, with decent depth.

DRY $15 AV

Clark Estate Single Vineyard Awatere Valley Marlborough Sauvignon Blanc   (★★☆)

From the owners of Boreham Wood, the 2008 vintage (★★☆) is medium-bodied, with a slightly funky bouquet, moderate depth of ripe tropical-fruit flavours and a dry finish.

Vintage	09	08
WR	7	6
Drink	10-12	09-10

DRY $18 −V

Clayridge Marlborough Sauvignon Blanc   ★★★★

The 2008 vintage (★★★★), 13 per cent barrel-fermented, is ripely scented and mouthfilling, with generous, distinctly tropical-fruit flavours, showing good texture and richness, and a dry finish (2.1 grams/litre of residual sugar).

Vintage	08
WR	6
Drink	09-10

DRY $21 V+

Clearview Estate Reserve Hawke's Bay Sauvignon Blanc ★★★★

The 2008 vintage (★★★★) was grown principally in the Wilkins Vineyard, near the sea at Te Awanga, hand-picked and fermented and matured for 10 months in seasoned French oak barriques. Slightly creamy and nutty, it has good weight and depth of ripe tropical-fruit flavours, with finely integrated oak and a crisp, fully dry finish.

Vintage	08	07	06	DRY $23 AV
WR	6	7	6	
Drink	10-14	09-11	09-10	

Clearview Estate Te Awanga Sauvignon Blanc ★★★☆

Grown near the coast in Hawke's Bay and handled entirely in tanks, the 2008 vintage (★★★☆) is crisp and dry, with ripe tropical-fruit flavours, showing good freshness, vigour and depth.

Vintage	09	DRY $17 V+
WR	6	
Drink	09-11	

Clearwater Vineyards Waipara Sauvignon Blanc (★★★)

From Sherwood, the 2007 vintage (★★★), still on sale, has nettley aromas and flavours, strongly herbaceous, but showing good freshness and depth.

DRY $20 AV

Clifford Bay Awatere Valley Marlborough Sauvignon Blanc ★★★★★

This is a consistently impressive wine. The 2008 vintage (★★★★★) is mouthfilling, vibrant and punchy, with excellent freshness, vigour and depth of melon and green-capsicum flavours. Pure, crisp and searching, it is basically dry (4 grams/litre of residual sugar), slightly minerally and long.

Vintage	09	08	DRY $21 V+
WR	7	6	
Drink	09-12	09-11	

Clos Henri Marlborough Sauvignon Blanc ★★★★★

The Clos Henri Vineyard near Renwick is owned by Henri Bourgeois, a leading, family-owned producer in the Loire Valley, which feels this wine expresses 'a unique terroir . . . and French winemaking approach'. A sophisticated and distinctive Sauvignon Blanc, in top years it's a joy to drink. The 2008 vintage (★★★★) was hand-picked and most of the blend was fermented and matured for eight months on its fine yeast lees in tanks; 8 per cent was barrel-fermented. Mouthfilling, it is fleshy, ripe and rounded, with tropical-fruit flavours, finely textured, concentrated and fully dry.

Vintage	08	07	06	05	DRY $28 AV
WR	7	5	6	6	
Drink	09-13	10-11	09-12	09-11	

Clos Marguerite Marlborough Sauvignon Blanc ★★★★

Estate-grown in the Awatere Valley, the 2008 vintage (★★★★) is distinctly nettley, with very good depth of fresh gooseberry/lime flavours, crisp, minerally and aromatic.

DRY $25 AV

Cloudy Bay Sauvignon Blanc   ★★★★★

New Zealand's most internationally acclaimed wine is sought after from Sydney to New York and London. Its irresistibly aromatic and zesty style and intense flavours stem from 'the fruit characters that are in the grapes when they arrive at the winery'. It is sourced from company-owned and several long-term contract growers' vineyards in the Rapaura, Fairhall, Renwick and Brancott districts of the Wairau Valley. The juice is cool-fermented in stainless steel tanks; the wine does not have any significant oak maturation, but is aged for up to two months on its yeast lees before bottling. The 2009 vintage (★★★★★) has a punchy, ripely herbaceous bouquet. Deliciously rich and racy, it is vibrant, with an array of fruit flavours – melon, lime, lychee and passionfruit. Weighty and pure, with a long, dry (3 grams/litre of residual sugar), tight finish, it's an authoritative wine, more subtle and sophisticated, less 'in your face' than some of its competitors, with excellent body, complexity and texture. It's the sort of Sauvignon that draws you back for a second glass . . . and a third.

Vintage	09	08	07	06
WR	7	5	6	7
Drink	09-11	09-10	09-11	09-12

DRY $34 AV

Cloudy Bay Te Koko – see Branded and Other White Wines

Coal Pit Central Otago Sauvignon Blanc   ★★★☆

Estate-grown at Gibbston, the 2009 vintage (★★★☆) has a freshly herbaceous bouquet leading into a crisp, medium-bodied wine with strong, vibrant, citrusy, limey flavours, fresh and frisky.

Vintage	09	08
WR	5	7
Drink	10-12	09-11

DRY $25 –V

Cockle Bay Marlborough Sauvignon Blanc   (★★☆)

Sold cheaply in supermarkets, the 2008 vintage (★★☆) was grown in the Wairau and Awatere valleys. Fresh, crisp and lively, with gooseberry and capsicum flavours, showing decent depth, it offers great value.

MED/DRY $7 V+

Composite Marlborough Sauvignon Blanc – see Ara Composite Marlborough Sauvignon Blanc

Cooks Beach Vineyard Sauvignon Blanc   (★★★)

Grown and hand-picked on the Coromandel Peninsula, the 2007 (★★★) is a medium-bodied wine with ripe tropical-fruit flavours, crisp and dry. The 2009 vintage was obviously bottle-shocked when tasted in August 2009, so is not rated, but looked promising, with mouthfilling body and melon/lime flavours, ripe and rounded.

DRY $20 AV

Coopers Creek Marlborough Sauvignon Blanc   ★★★☆

A consistently good wine, priced right. The 2008 vintage (★★★) is fresh, vibrant and smooth, with ripe melon/lime flavours, balanced for easy drinking.

Vintage	08	07
WR	6	6
Drink	09-10	P

DRY $18 V+

Coopers Creek Reserve Marlborough Sauvignon Blanc   ★★★★☆

The 2008 vintage (★★★★☆) was grown at two sites – mostly a mature vineyard in the Brancott Valley, which contributed 'richness and texture', supplemented by a young vineyard in the Awatere Valley, which added 'high notes'. Rich, vibrant and crisp, it's a highly refined wine with melon, capsicum and lime flavours, very pure, fresh and long.

Vintage	08	**DRY $25 AV**
WR	7	
Drink	09-10	

Coopers Creek SV Awatere Marlborough Sauvignon Blanc   (★★★☆)

The debut 2008 vintage (★★★☆) is a single-vineyard wine, grown at Blind River, in the Awatere Valley. The bouquet is nettley; the palate is fresh, with moderately intense, grassy, gooseberryish flavours, vibrant and crisp.

DRY $22 AV

Coopers Creek SV Dillons Point Marlborough Sauvignon Blanc   ★★★★

Harvested from first-crop vines at Dillons Point – between Blenheim and the Cloudy Bay coast – the 2009 vintage (★★★★) is aromatic, with fresh tropical-fruit and herbaceous flavours, youthful, vibrant and punchy.

Vintage	09	08	07	**DRY $20 V+**
WR	7	6	6	
Drink	09-11	09-10	P	

Corazon Single Vineyard Sauvignon Blanc   (★★★☆)

Grown in Marlborough and fermented in tanks (two-thirds) and seasoned oak barrels, the 2008 vintage (★★★☆) has a fresh, limey bouquet. It's a finely balanced wine showing good freshness, ripeness and depth, and a dry (3.5 grams/litre of residual sugar), crisp finish.

Vintage	08	**DRY $20 AV**
WR	6	
Drink	09-11	

Corbans Cottage Block Hawke's Bay Sauvignon Blanc   ★★★★

The 2007 vintage (★★★★) was grown by Pernod Ricard NZ at Matapiro, 40 kilometres inland, and fermented and lees-aged for 10 months in seasoned French oak barrels. The bouquet is slightly oaky; the palate is powerful and creamy-textured, with substantial body and ripe stone-fruit flavours, showing good complexity.

Vintage	07	06	05	**DRY $32 –V**
WR	6	6	5	
Drink	P	P	P	

Corbans Homestead Hawke's Bay Sauvignon Blanc   ★★★

From Pernod Ricard NZ, this is typically a fresh, fruity wine with ripe passionfruit and lime flavours showing good depth and a smooth finish. Drinking well now, the 2008 vintage (★★★) is ripely scented, in a medium to full-bodied style with fresh, vibrant tropical-fruit flavours, balanced for easy drinking.

Vintage	08	07
WR	6	6
Drink	08-09	P

DRY $17 AV

Corbans Private Bin Hawke's Bay Sauvignon Blanc   ★★★☆

The 2008 vintage (★★★★) was grown inland, at the company-owned vineyard at Matapiro. It offers good intensity of ripe tropical-fruit flavours, with a touch of complexity, lively acidity and a fresh, dry finish.

DRY $24 –V

Cottage Block Sauvignon Blanc – see Corbans Cottage Block Hawke's Bay Sauvignon Blanc

Crab Farm Hawke's Bay Sauvignon Blanc   ★★★

The 2008 vintage (★★★) is a very easy-drinking style, full-bodied and fresh, with ripe, passionfruit-like, non-herbaceous flavours, showing good depth.

Vintage	08
WR	7
Drink	P

DRY $17 AV

Craggy Range Avery Vineyard Marlborough Sauvignon Blanc   ★★★☆

Grown at a slightly cooler site in the Wairau Valley than its Old Renwick Vineyard stablemate (below), the 2008 vintage (★★★★) is fresh and lively, with very good depth of melon and green-capsicum flavours, finely balanced, elegant and lingering.

Vintage	09	08	07	06
WR	6	7	6	6
Drink	09-12	09-10	P	P

DRY $20 AV

Craggy Range Old Renwick Vineyard Sauvignon Blanc   ★★★☆

Based on mature, 20-year-old vines in the heart of the Wairau Valley, the 2008 vintage (★★★) offers good but not great depth of slightly appley and limey flavours, and a crisp, dry finish.

Vintage	09	08	07	06
WR	7	7	5	7
Drink	09-12	09-10	P	P

DRY $20 AV

Craggy Range Te Muna Road Vineyard Martinborough Sauvignon Blanc   ★★★★

Grown a few kilometres south of Martinborough township, this wine is mostly fermented and lees-aged in tanks, but typically about 12 per cent of the blend is barrel-fermented with indigenous yeasts. The 2008 vintage (★★★★) is mouthfilling, ripe and rounded, with strong tropical-fruit flavours, good acid balance, a touch of complexity and a fully dry finish.

Vintage	09	08	07
WR	7	7	7
Drink	09-13	09-11	P

DRY $23 AV

Crater Rim, The, Waipara Sauvignon Blanc   ★★★★

The 2008 vintage (★★★★) was mostly handled in tanks, but a small portion of the blend was fermented with indigenous yeasts in barrels. Fleshy and rich, it has concentrated, tropical-fruit flavours, very lively and long.

DRY $23 AV

Crawford Farm Marlborough Sauvignon Blanc   ★★★★

From Constellation NZ, the 2008 vintage (★★★☆) is a freshly herbaceous style with strong gooseberry/lime flavours. Mouthfilling and dry, it has crisp, slightly nettley characters, showing very good depth.

DRY $23 AV

Croft Sauvignon Blanc   (★★★☆)

Grown in Martinborough and mostly handled in tanks (5 per cent was aged in old oak casks), the 2008 vintage (★★★☆) is a fresh, melon and lime-flavoured wine, ripe and smooth, with very good balance and depth.

Vintage	08
WR	5
Drink	09-10

DRY $20 AV

Croney Three Ton Marlborough Sauvignon Blanc   (★★★★)

Offering great value, the 2008 vintage (★★★★) was hand-picked in the Wairau Valley and a 'very small' portion was barrel-fermented; the rest was handled in tanks. Fresh, ripe-fruit aromas lead into a mouthfilling wine with tropical-fruit flavours, showing a touch of complexity, good concentration and plenty of personality.

DRY $15 V+

Crossings, The, Marlborough Sauvignon Blanc   ★★★★

The 2008 vintage (★★★★), grown at three company-owned sites in the Awatere Valley, is tight and punchy, with very fresh, pure and delicate melon/lime flavours, slightly minerally and lingering.

Vintage	08
WR	6
Drink	P

DRY $20 V+

Crossroads Marlborough Sauvignon Blanc   ★★★☆

The 2008 vintage (★★★) is a medium-bodied, dry wine (2.8 grams/litre of residual sugar), with melon, gooseberry and lime flavours, ripely scented and smooth.

Vintage	08
WR	6
Drink	P

DRY $20 AV

Crowded House Marlborough Sauvignon Blanc ★★★☆)

A good buy. The 2008 vintage (★★★☆) is vibrantly fruity, with ripe melon/lime flavours woven with fresh acidity and a dry (3.5 grams/litre of residual sugar) finish.

DRY $18 V+

Culley Marlborough Sauvignon Blanc ★★★☆

A good buy from Waiheke Island-based winery, Cable Bay. Grown at Rapaura and in the Omaka Valley, the 2008 vintage (★★★☆) is instantly appealing – full-bodied and fresh, with melon and green-capsicum flavours, strong and smooth.

DRY $19 V+

Curio Castles Vineyard Awatere Valley Marlborough Sauvignon Blanc (★★★★)

From Mud House and sold mainly in restaurants, the debut 2008 vintage (★★★★) has strong 'tomato stalk' aromas, typical of the Awatere. Mouthfilling and smooth, it's a 'full-on' style with penetrating gooseberry, herb and slight spice flavours, a sliver of sweetness (7 grams/litre of residual sugar) adding smoothness, and good harmony.

MED/DRY $26 –V

Curio Gane's Vineyard Wairau Valley Marlborough Sauvignon Blanc (★★★☆)

The debut 2008 vintage (★★★☆) from Mud House is aimed at the restaurant trade. It's a full-bodied style with lively tropical-fruit flavours showing very good depth and a crisp, dry finish.

DRY $26 –V

Daisy Rock Marlborough Sauvignon Blanc ★★★

From Maven, the 2008 vintage (★★★) is a fresh, crisp, fairly herbaceous style, with gooseberry and green-capsicum flavours to the fore, some tropical-fruit notes and satisfying depth.

DRY $17 AV

Dancing Water Awatere Valley Sauvignon Blanc ★★★☆

The 2008 vintage (★★★) is a single-vineyard wine, crisp and lively, with ripe tropical-fruit and greener, nettley aromas and flavours. Tasted in 2009, the 2007 (★★★☆) is a typical sub-regional style, clearly herbaceous, with hints of asparagus emerging with bottle-age. Ready.

DRY $20 AV

Daniel Schuster Marlborough Sauvignon Blanc ★★★★

Typically a wine with depth and individuality. The 2007 vintage (★★★★) is enjoyable now, with mouthfilling body, tropical-fruit flavours to the fore and a herbal undercurrent. It shows good richness, ripeness, texture and complexity, with a rounded finish.

DRY $24 AV

Darling, The, Marlborough Sauvignon Blanc   (★★★)

The ripely scented 2008 vintage (★★★) from Savvy Wines was mostly handled in tanks; 5 per cent was fermented with indigenous yeasts in oak casks. It's a mouthfilling wine with plenty of citrusy, gently herbaceous flavour, crisp and lively.

DRY $22 –V

Dashwood Marlborough Sauvignon Blanc   ★★★☆

Vavasour's drink-young, unwooded Sauvignon Blanc is typically great value. The 2009 vintage (★★★☆) is a fresh, vibrant, finely balanced blend of Awatere Valley (70 per cent) and Wairau Valley (30 per cent) grapes. Strongly varietal, it has very good delicacy and depth of melon, lime and green-capsicum flavours.

Vintage	08	07	06	05
WR	6	6	6	7
Drink	09	09	P	P

DRY $17 V+

Day Break Gisborne Sauvignon Blanc   (★★★☆)

Unusually punchy for a Gisborne savvy, the 2009 vintage (★★★☆) was made by Nick Nobilo for Day Break Wines and on sale by May 2009. Freshly aromatic, it is crisp, tangy and ripely herbaceous, with strong passionfruit and lime flavours, balanced for early drinking.

DRY $19 V+

Delegat's Marlborough Sauvignon Blanc   ★★★☆

Winemaker Michael Ivicevich aims for 'a tropical fruit-flavoured style, a bit broader and softer than some'. The 2009 vintage (★★★☆) is crisp, with fresh, strong melon/lime flavours, woven with racy acidity. Good value.

Vintage	09	08	07
WR	6	6	7
Drink	09-13	09-12	09-10

DRY $16 V+

Delegat's Reserve Marlborough Sauvignon Blanc   ★★★★

From the Awatere Valley, the 2008 vintage (★★★★) is weighty and dry, with concentrated passionfruit and lime flavours, in a slightly riper, less herbal style than most of the valley's wines.

Vintage	08
WR	6
Drink	09-13

DRY $20 V+

Discovery Point Marlborough Sauvignon Blanc   (★★★★☆)

From wine distributor Bennett & Deller, the 2008 vintage (★★★★☆) was grown at three sites, one in the Awatere Valley and two in the Wairau Valley. It's a fleshy wine with an array of ripe sweet-fruit flavours, intense and slightly minerally, that build well across the palate to a bone-dry, lingering finish.

DRY $22 V+

Distant Land Hawke's Bay Sauvignon Blanc   ★★★

From Lincoln, the 2009 vintage (★★★) is a very easy-drinking wine, medium-bodied, with ripe tropical-fruit flavours, fresh and vibrant, and a splash of sweetness (7.9 grams/litre of residual sugar) to add smoothness.

MED/DRY $18 AV

Distant Land Marlborough Sauvignon Blanc   ★★★☆

The 2009 vintage (★★★☆) from Lincoln was grown in the Wairau Valley. A freshly herbaceous style, it's intensely varietal, with gooseberry and green-capsicum flavours, crisp and strong.

DRY $20 AV

Doctors', The, Marlborough Sauvignon Blanc   (★★★☆)

From Forrest, the debut 2009 vintage (★★★☆) is a low-alcohol style (9.5 per cent), made for 'easy drinking at lunchtime'. Aromatic, it is light and lively, fresh and punchy, with gently herbaceous, limey flavours and a dryish (7 grams/litre of residual sugar), crisp finish. A good apéritif.

Vintage	09
WR	5
Drink	09-11

MED/DRY $22 AV

Dog Point Vineyard Marlborough Sauvignon Blanc   ★★★★

This wine offers a clear style contrast to Section 94, the company's complex, barrel-aged Sauvignon Blanc (see the Branded and Other White Wines section). Hand-picked, it is lees-aged in tanks, with no exposure to oak. The 2008 vintage (★★★★) is mouthfilling, with good weight and depth of vibrant, ripe, limey, slightly leesy flavours, fresh acidity and a smooth (4.8 grams/litre of residual sugar), finely balanced finish.

DRY $25 AV

Dolbel Estate Hawke's Bay Sauvignon Blanc   ★★★★

A label worth discovering. Grown at Springfield Vineyard, on the banks of the Tutaekuri River, and made by Tony Prichard, formerly of Church Road, the 2007 vintage (★★★★) is a barrel-fermented style of Sauvignon Blanc, reminiscent of white Bordeaux. Light lemon/green, it is mouthfilling, complex and smooth, with rich, ripe sweet-fruit flavours, a hint of nutty oak and a dry, deliciously well-rounded finish.

Vintage	08	07	06
WR	6	6	6
Drink	09-12	09-12	09-11

DRY $25 AV

Domain Road Central Otago Sauvignon Blanc   ★★★☆

A single-vineyard wine, grown at Bannockburn, the 2009 vintage (★★★★) is stylish, with good richness. Mouthfilling, it is ripely scented, with vibrant melon and lime flavours, showing a touch of complexity, and excellent delicacy and depth.

DRY $24 –V

Domaine Georges Michel Golden Mile Marlborough Sauvignon Blanc ★★★

Grown in the Rapaura ('golden mile') district of the Wairau Valley, the 2008 vintage (★★☆) is mouthfilling and fleshy, with ripe, restrained tropical-fruit flavours and a smooth, dry finish.

DRY $17 AV

Domaine Georges Michel La Reserve Marlborough Sauvignon Blanc ★★★★

The 2008 vintage (★★★☆) is a ripe style, hand-harvested and fermented and matured for eight months in seasoned French oak barrels. It's not at all herbaceous, with tropical-fruit flavours to the fore, a touch of complexity and a rounded, softly textured finish.

DRY $22 V+

Drylands Marlborough Sauvignon Blanc ★★★☆

This is a consistently enjoyable wine from Constellation NZ, fermented and lees-aged in tanks. It is typically full-bodied and fresh-scented, with an array of melon, gooseberry and capsicum flavours, crisp and strong.

DRY $19 V+

Durvillea Marlborough Sauvignon Blanc (★★★☆)

From Astrolabe, the 2008 vintage (★★★☆) is named after a local seaweed. Pungently herbaceous on the nose, it is mouthfilling, with strong gooseberry, capsicum and lime flavours. Lying at the greener end of the ripeness spectrum, it's a 'full-on' style, now showing slightly toasty, bottle-aged notes.

Vintage 08
WR 6
Drink 09-11

DRY $16 V+

Easthope The Gatecrasher Sauvignon Blanc (★★★★☆)

This Hawke's Bay wine is ambitiously priced, but the 2007 vintage (★★★★☆) is still full of interest. A single-vineyard wine, grown in the Dartmoor Valley, it was hand-picked and fermented with indigenous yeasts in seasoned French oak barriques. It's a fleshy wine, with ripe, slightly nutty, toasty and honeyed flavours, complex and rich.

DRY $56 –V

Elephant Hill Hawke's Bay Sauvignon Blanc ★★★☆

Grown at Te Awanga, the 2009 vintage (★★★☆) has fresh, limey aromas leading into a medium-bodied wine with lively acidity, pure melon and green-capsicum flavours and a crisp, slightly minerally, dry finish. It should provide stimulating drinking over the summer of 2009–10.

DRY $22 AV

Elephant Hill Reserve Hawke's Bay Sauvignon Blanc (★★★☆)

The 2008 vintage (★★★☆) was estate-grown at Te Awanga and oak-aged on its yeast lees for five months. Mouthfilling, it is clearly herbaceous, with a hint of nutty oak and a crisp, dry finish. A tightly structured wine, it should be drinking well during 2010.

DRY $29 –V

Eliot Brothers Marlborough Sauvignon Blanc   (★★★☆)

From an Auckland-based company, the bargain-priced 2008 vintage (★★★☆) is maturing well. Fresh and weighty, it has tropical-fruit flavours, an unobtrusive splash of sweetness (6.6 grams/ litre of residual sugar), and very good liveliness and depth. Drink now.

MED/DRY $15 V+

Eradus Awatere Valley Marlborough Sauvignon Blanc   ★★★★☆

The 2009 vintage (★★★★★) is a weighty, rich and rounded wine with sweet-fruit delights, deep gooseberry and lime flavours, a slightly minerally streak and the 'tomato stalk' characters typical of the Awatere. It's priced very sharply and is the Best White Wine Buy of the Year (see page 16).

Vintage	09
WR	6
Drink	09-11

DRY $19 V+

Esk Valley Marlborough Sauvignon Blanc   (★★★★★)

This Hawke's Bay winery, a key part of the Villa Maria stable, recently switched its Sauvignon Blanc focus from Hawke's Bay to Marlborough – with immediate success. The debut 2009 vintage (★★★★★) is weighty, with punchy gooseberry/lime flavours, showing lovely vigour and intensity, racy acidity and a long, bone-dry finish.

Vintage	09
WR	7
Drink	09-10

DRY $20 V+

Fairbourne Marlborough Sauvignon Blanc   (★★★★)

Outside the mainstream style, the distinctive 2008 vintage (★★★★) was grown at two sites in the Wairau Valley. It's a mouthfilling, subtle wine with ripe tropical and citrus-fruit flavours, very non-herbaceous and finely textured, slightly 'funky' notes, and an uncompromisingly dry, but not austere, finish. Worth discovering.

Vintage	08
WR	5
Drink	09-11

DRY $28 –V

Fairhall Downs Hugo Marlborough Sauvignon Blanc   ★★★★☆

The 2008 vintage (★★★★☆) is a complex style, barrel-fermented with indigenous yeasts and French oak-matured for 10 months. Mouthfilling, it is sweet-fruited, with strong, ripe tropical-fruit flavours, a distinct suggestion of toasty oak, and lively acidity. Best drinking 2010–11.

DRY $30 AV

Fairhall Downs Single Vineyard Marlborough Sauvignon Blanc   ★★★★

Grown at the head of the Brancott Valley, the 2009 vintage (★★★★) is scented, vibrant and punchy, with classic gooseberry, passionfruit and lime flavours, pure, crisp and dry. Fine value.

DRY $20 V+

Fairmont Estate Sauvignon Blanc   ★★☆

The 2008 vintage (★★) from this Wairarapa producer is a simple quaffer, light and plain.

DRY $15 AV

Fall Harvest Sauvignon Blanc   (★★)

The 2007 vintage (★★) from Constellation NZ is a blend of Chilean and New Zealand wines. It's a restrained style, lacking the pungency typical of New Zealand Sauvignon Blanc, with ripe tropical-fruit rather than herbaceous flavours, offering smooth, easy drinking.

DRY $13 AV

Fallen Angel Marlborough Sauvignon Blanc   ★★★★

From Stonyridge Vineyard, on Waiheke Island, the 2009 vintage (★★★★) is mouthfilling, with punchy, ripe passionfruit and lime flavours, showing good intensity and vibrancy, and a dry finish.

DRY $32 –V

Farmgate Hawke's Bay Sauvignon Blanc   ★★★☆

From Ngatarawa, the 2008 vintage (★★★★) was made from first-crop vines and partly fermented in seasoned French oak barriques. A fully dry style, with substantial body and ripe tropical-fruit scents and flavours, it has slight herbal notes adding interest, coupled with fresh acidity and a touch of oak complexity.

Vintage	08	07
WR	7	7
Drink	09-12	09-10

DRY $22 AV

Fiddler's Green Waipara Sauvignon Blanc   ★★★★

A distinctly cool-climate style, typically with excellent vibrancy and depth. Estate-grown and tank-fermented, the 2008 vintage (★★★☆) is crisp and lively, with punchy tropical-fruit/lime flavours.

DRY $22 V+

Five Flax Sauvignon Blanc   ★★☆

From Pernod Ricard NZ, the 2008 vintage (★★☆) is clearly herbaceous, in a medium-bodied style with decent depth of gooseberry and herb flavours, and a smooth finish.

Vintage	08
WR	5
Drink	P

DRY $15 AV

Forrest Marlborough Sauvignon Blanc   ★★★☆

This aromatic, vibrantly fruity wine has recently become noticeably drier, while retaining good drinkability. The 2008 vintage (★★★☆) is fleshy, ripe and smooth, with good depth of non-herbaceous, tropical-fruit flavours and a dry (3 grams/litre of residual sugar) finish.

Vintage	08
WR	5
Drink	09-15

DRY $22 AV

Forrest The Valleys Awatere Marlborough Sauvignon Blanc   (★★★★★)

A top-flight debut, the 2009 vintage (★★★★★) is enticingly scented, with the gooseberry, lime and 'tomato stalk' aromas typical of the Awatere. Full-bodied and smooth, it shows excellent purity, delicacy and depth, with impressive weight and lovely texture and intensity.

DRY $22 V+

Forrest The Valleys Wairau Sauvignon Blanc   (★★★★☆)

The 2007 vintage (★★★★) is mouthfilling, with rich, ripe sweet-fruit flavours of melons and limes, showing excellent delicacy and depth, and a rounded finish.

DRY $35 –V

Foxes Island Marlborough Sauvignon Blanc   ★★★★

The 2008 vintage (★★★★) was hand-picked at 23.5 brix, fermented in tanks (mostly) and new French oak barriques, and lees-aged for three months. Mouthfilling and punchy, with ripe tropical-fruit flavours showing good immediacy and drive, it is fleshy and slightly minerally, with excellent depth.

Vintage	08	07	06
WR	6	6	6
Drink	09-10	P	P

DRY $34 –V

Framingham F Series Marlborough Sauvignon Blanc   (★★★★☆)

The 2008 vintage (★★★★☆) was handled in a 2:1 mix of old oak barrels and stainless steel 'barrels', and 50 per cent of the blend went through a softening malolactic fermentation. Rich, ripe and rounded, with barrel-ferment complexity and some slightly 'funky' notes, it's a very non-herbaceous style, with gentle acidity and a bone-dry, finely textured finish. It shows excellent harmony and is well worth cellaring.

Vintage	08
WR	6
Drink	10-12

DRY $35 –V

Framingham Marlborough Sauvignon Blanc   ★★★★

Winemaker Andrew Hedley favours a dry style with no use of oak: 'Complexity comes from different sites and levels of fruit maturity.' The 2008 vintage (★★★☆) is fresh, full-bodied and smooth (3.5 grams/litre of residual sugar), with lively acidity and good depth and delicacy of melon and green-capsicum flavours.

DRY $22 V+

Frizzell Sauvignon Blanc   (★★★★)

The front label of the debut 2008 vintage (★★★★) warns: 'Please Note: May Contain Traces of Summer.' Grown in the Wairau Valley, Marlborough, and lees-aged over winter, it has a punchy, lifted, herbaceous bouquet. Full-bodied, it has a basket of fruit flavours, with a minerally streak, and very good richness, delicacy and length.

DRY $19 V+

Giesen Marlborough Sauvignon Blanc   ★★★

The largest-volume wine from Giesen has a low profile in New Zealand, but enjoys major export success. It is typically light and lively, with tangy acidity and good depth of fresh melon, capsicum and lime flavours. The 2008 vintage was grown at 28 sites and made in a dry (3.5 grams/litre of residual sugar) style.

DRY $17 AV

Gladstone Vineyard Wairarapa Sauvignon Blanc   ★★★☆

The 2008 vintage (★★★☆) was harvested at four sites near Masterton and mostly handled in tanks; about 2 per cent of the blend was fermented and matured for three months in French oak barrels. It's a fleshy, bone-dry style with tropical-fruit flavours, a touch of leesy complexity, and good depth and vigour.

DRY $23 AV

Glazebrook Marlborough Sauvignon Blanc   ★★★

Grown at three sites in the Wairau Valley, the 2008 vintage (★★★) from Ngatarawa is fleshy and ripe, with passionfruit and lime flavours showing good balance and depth, and a dry (2.8 grams/litre of residual sugar) finish.

Vintage	08	07	06
WR	6	6	5
Drink	09-11	09-10	P

DRY $20 AV

Goldridge Marlborough Sauvignon Blanc   ★★☆

The 2008 vintage (★★☆) is an easy-drinking style with smooth, tropical-fruit flavours, a sliver of sweetness (5.3 grams/litre of residual sugar) and decent depth.

MED/DRY $16 AV

Goldridge Premium Reserve Marlborough Sauvignon Blanc   ★★☆

The 2008 vintage (★★★) is freshly herbaceous and smooth (3.8 grams/litre of residual sugar), with some tropical-fruit notes, lively acidity and good depth.

DRY $19 –V

Goldwater Wairau Valley Sauvignon Blanc   ★★★★

The instantly likeable 2008 vintage (★★★★) is ripely scented, full-bodied and smooth, with ripe tropical-fruit flavours, a herbal undercurrent and creamy-smooth finish.

DRY $22 V+

Grass Cove Marlborough Sauvignon Blanc   (★★★☆)

From an Auckland-based company, the 2008 vintage (★★★☆) is fresh, crisp, citrusy and limey, with good body, flavour depth and vigour, and a tight, dry (3.9 grams/litre of residual sugar) finish.

DRY $17 V+

Greenhough Nelson Sauvignon Blanc   ★★★★★

Andrew Greenhough aims for a 'rich Sauvignon Blanc style with ripe, creamy mouthfeel' — and hits the target with ease. Grown at three sites at Hope, the 2009 vintage (★★★★) was mostly handled in tanks, but 4 per cent of the blend was fermented with indigenous yeasts in new oak casks. Mouthfilling and dry (2.9 grams/litre of residual sugar), it's a finely poised, gently herbaceous wine with strong melon, peach and capsicum flavours, vibrant and crisp. It should open out well during 2010.

Vintage	09	08	07	06
WR	7	7	7	6
Drink	09-13	09-12	09-11	09-10

DRY $20 V+

Greyrock Marlborough Sauvignon Blanc   (★★☆)

From Sileni, the 2008 vintage (★★☆) is a slightly sweet style with crisp melon and lime flavours, showing decent depth.

MED/DRY $14 V+

Greystone Waipara Sauvignon Blanc   ★★★★

The 2009 vintage (★★★★) was 4 per cent fermented in French oak barrels and made in a fully dry style. Ripely scented, it has good weight, fresh, delicate melon and herb flavours, a minerally streak and good intensity.

DRY $22 V+

Greywacke Marlborough Sauvignon Blanc   (★★★★☆)

The debut 2009 vintage (★★★★☆) from Kevin Judd, formerly managing director of Cloudy Bay, was grown at various sites in the Brancott Valley and on the Wairau Plains. Partly barrel-fermented, it is mouthfilling, with punchy, ripe stone-fruit and lime flavours, finely textured, crisp and lingering. It's a tightly structured, elegant wine that should unfold well during 2010.

DRY $26 AV

Grove Mill Marlborough Sauvignon Blanc   ★★★★

At its best, this is a powerful wine, with excellent drinkability. The grapes are drawn from vineyards (both company-owned and growers') scattered across the Wairau Valley, but mostly in the Rapaura and Renwick districts. The wine is fermented and lees-aged for three to four months in tanks, and a portion goes through malolactic fermentation, to improve the blend's complexity and texture. Most vintages mature well for several years. It is typically mouthfilling and punchy, with rich, ripe tropical-fruit flavours to the fore, a herbal undercurrent, and a finely balanced, dry, long finish.

Vintage	08	07	06
WR	7	7	7
Drink	09-10	P	P

DRY $18 V+

Hans Herzog Marlborough Sauvignon Blanc   (★★★★☆)

Far outside the mainstream regional style, the 2008 vintage (★★★★☆) was estate-grown on the north side of the Wairau Valley, hand-picked at 23.8 brix, fermented with indigenous yeasts in French oak puncheons, oak-matured for 11 months, and given a full, softening malolactic fermentation. Mouthfilling, sweet-fruited and complex, it's a fleshy, rich wine with very ripe tropical-fruit and slight nut flavours, a slightly oily texture, and a well-rounded, dry finish.

Vintage	08
WR	7
Drink	09-17

DRY $45 –V

Harwood Hall Marlborough Sauvignon Blanc   (★★★★)

The debut 2008 vintage (★★★★) is a 50/50 blend of Wairau Valley and Awatere Valley fruit. It is fleshy, sweet-fruited and zingy, with 'tomato stalk' notes and a lingering, bone-dry finish.

DRY $19 V+

Harwood Hall Wairau Marlborough Sauvignon Blanc   (★★★☆)

Grown at two sites in the Wairau Valley, the 2008 vintage (★★★☆) is fleshy, with good depth and delicacy of tropical-fruit flavours, showing a hint of 'sweaty armpit', and a bone-dry finish.

DRY $19 V+

Hay Maker Marlborough Sauvignon Blanc   ★★★☆

From Mud House, the 2008 vintage (★★★☆) is freshly aromatic and fleshy, with strong gooseberry and lime flavours, moderate acidity and a dry finish (2.9 grams/litre of residual sugar). Good value.

DRY $17 V+

Heart of Stone Marlborough Sauvignon Blanc   ★★★☆

From Forrest Estate, the 2009 vintage (★★★☆) is already enjoyable. Punchy and ripely herbaceous, it has melon, capsicum and slight 'tomato stalk' characters, showing good vigour, delicacy and depth. Fine value.

DRY $17 V+

Highfield Marlborough Sauvignon Blanc   ★★★★★

Typically a very classy wine – scented and harmonious, with rich, limey fruit flavours and excellent depth. The 2009 vintage (★★★★★) was mostly handled in tanks and given extended lees contact, but 2 per cent of the blend was oak-aged. It shows lovely freshness, balance, delicacy and intensity, with sweet-fruit delights, a complex array of fruit flavours, woven with lively acidity, and a very long finish. Benchmark stuff, it's already delicious.

Vintage	09	08	07
WR	6	4	6
Drink	09-11	09-10	09

DRY $24 V+

Himmelsfeld Vineyard Moutere Sauvignon Blanc   ★★★☆

Still unfolding, the 2008 (★★★☆) is weighty, with fresh gooseberry/lime flavours, good vigour and a crisp, dry finish. The 2007 vintage (★★★★) is now in full stride. Fleshy and generous, it's a powerful wine (14 per cent alcohol) with concentrated, tropical-fruit flavours and a well-rounded finish.

DRY $30 –V

Homer Marlborough Sauvignon Blanc   (★★★)

From Odyssey, the 2008 vintage (★★★) was grown in the Brancott Valley. It's a drink-young style with smooth (4 grams/litre of residual sugar) gooseberry, pear and lime flavours, fresh and moderately concentrated.

Vintage	08
WR	5
Drink	09-10

DRY $16 V+

Hudson Sauvignon Blanc   ★★★

Grown near Martinborough, the 2008 vintage (★★★) is a single-vineyard wine, made in a dryish, easy-drinking style with mouthfilling body and fresh, ripe tropical-fruit flavours woven with lively acidity.

DRY $21 –V

Huia Marlborough Sauvignon Blanc   ★★★☆

Grown at six sites in the Wairau Valley, the 2008 vintage (★★★☆) is full-bodied and smooth, with ripe melon, lime and capsicum flavours. It's a tight, slightly minerally wine with a crisp, dry finish.

Vintage	08
WR	6
Drink	09-11

DRY $22 AV

Huntaway Reserve Marlborough Sauvignon Blanc   (★★★★)

Grown on rich clay soils in the lower Wairau Valley, the debut 2008 vintage (★★★★) is highly scented, with mouthfilling body and vibrant tropical-fruit flavours, ripe and strong. Sweet-fruited and crisp, it's delicious in its youth.

DRY $24 AV

Hunter's Kaho Roa Marlborough Sauvignon Blanc   ★★★★

Based on Hunter's ripest, least-herbaceous grapes, this wine is grown in stony vineyards along Rapaura Road, on the relatively warm, north side of the Wairau Valley. Part of the blend is handled entirely in stainless steel tanks; another is tank-fermented but barrel-aged; and the third is fermented and lees-aged for eight to nine months in new French oak barriques. It typically matures well for up to five years. The 2008 vintage (★★★★) is already delicious. Ripely scented, it has attractive, passionfruit-like flavours, showing excellent depth, delicacy and dryness, gentle acidity and a lingering finish.

Vintage	08	07
WR	5	5
Drink	11-13	10-12

DRY $23 AV

Hunter's Marlborough Sauvignon Blanc   ★★★★☆

Hunter's fame rests on the consistent excellence of this fully dry wine, which exhibits the intense aromas of ripe, cool-climate grapes, uncluttered by any oak handling. The style goal is 'a strong expression of Marlborough fruit – a bell-clear wine with a mix of tropical and searing gooseberry characters'. The grapes are sourced from numerous sites in the Wairau Valley, and to retain their fresh, vibrant characters, they are processed very quickly, with protective anaerobic techniques and minimal handling. The wine is usually at its best between one and two years old. The 2008 vintage (★★★★) is weighty, with dry, tropical-fruit flavours, showing a touch of complexity, good acid balance, and excellent drinkability.

Vintage	09	08
WR	6	5
Drink	10-13	09-12

DRY $20 V+

Instinct Marlborough Sauvignon Blanc   (★★★)

From C.J. Pask, based in Hawke's Bay, the debut 2008 vintage (★★★☆) is ripely scented, with crisp passionfruit/lime flavours, fresh, crisp and lively.

DRY $17 AV

Invivo Marlborough Sauvignon Blanc ★★★☆

From an Auckland-based company, the 2009 vintage (★★★☆) is medium-bodied (12.5 per cent alcohol), with fresh, pure melon and lime flavours, crisp and very finely balanced.

DRY $20 AV

Isabel Marlborough Sauvignon Blanc ★★☆

Grown in the Isabel Estate Vineyard near Renwick, in the heart of the Wairau Valley, and other sites in the Wairau and Omaka valleys, in the past this was a stunning wine, but the latest vintages are less distinguished. About 10 per cent of the blend is barrel-fermented – the majority is cool-fermented in tanks – and some use is made of indigenous yeasts and malolactic fermentation. The 2008 vintage (★★☆) is crisp and full-flavoured, but shows a slight lack of freshness, with a hint of botrytis-derived honey.

Vintage	09
WR	7
Drink	09-14

DRY $20 –V

Jackman Ridge Sauvignon Blanc (★★)

The non-vintage wine (★★) on sale in mid-2009 is slightly honeyed, with moderate depth of ripe tropical-fruit flavours. It's a solid quaffer, priced right.

DRY $10 AV

Jackson Estate Grey Ghost Sauvignon Blanc ★★★★

Far outside the commercial mainstream, the 2007 vintage (★★★☆) was hand-harvested in Marlborough and fermented in a 50/50 split of tanks and seasoned French oak barrels. A fully dry wine, it is mouthfilling and crisp, with ripe, gooseberryish flavours and a dry, slightly flinty finish. A cellaring style, it should be at its best during 2010 (the 2006 opened superbly in late 2008).

Vintage	08	07	06
WR	5	7	6
Drink	09-14	09-15	09-10

DRY $30 –V

Jackson Estate Stich Marlborough Sauvignon Blanc ★★★★★

Grown at a dozen sites in the Wairau Valley and its southern offshoots, this is typically a lush, ripe and rounded wine with good concentration and huge drinkability. In a vertical tasting of the 1991–2007 vintages, held in late 2007, the wine revealed excellent aging ability, especially since the introduction of screwcaps in 2001. The 2009 vintage (★★★★★) is a finely poised, immaculate wine, fresh and vibrant, with penetrating, ripe gooseberry and lime flavours threaded with racy acidity and a crisp, dry, sustained finish.

Vintage	09
WR	7
Drink	09-12

DRY $22 V+

Johanneshof Marlborough Sauvignon Blanc   ★★★☆

The 2009 vintage (★★★★) from this small producer is medium to full-bodied, with ripe passionfruit and lime flavours, showing very good depth, and a smooth finish.

Vintage	09
WR	4
Drink	09-11

 MED/DRY $23 AV

Johner Gladstone Sauvignon Blanc   ★★★☆

Grown in the Wairarapa, the 2008 (★★★☆) is a tropical fruit-flavoured wine with fresh acidity keeping things lively, mouthfilling body and some richness. The 2009 vintage (★★★☆) has good depth of ripe tropical-fruit/lime flavours, fresh and appetisingly crisp.

 DRY $21 AV

Jules Taylor Marlborough Sauvignon Blanc   ★★★★★

The 2009 vintage (★★★★☆) was grown in the Awatere and Wairau valleys. Richly scented, with a hint of 'sweaty armpit', it is concentrated and immaculate, with rich, vibrant melon/lime flavours, a minerally streak and a finely textured, long finish.

Vintage	09
WR	6
Drink	09-12

 DRY $22 V+

Julicher Martinborough Sauvignon Blanc   ★★★★

The 2008 vintage (★★★★) was estate-grown, hand-picked and mostly handled in tanks, with a small percentage of barrel fermentation. It's a stylish, instantly likeable wine, vibrantly fruity, with fresh, concentrated, ripely herbaceous flavours, a touch of complexity, crisp acidity and a lingering, fully dry finish. Fine value.

Vintage	08	07
WR	5	6
Drink	09-10	P

 DRY $19 V+

Kaimira Estate Nelson Sauvignon Blanc   ★★★☆

The 2008 vintage (★★★☆), partly (8 per cent) barrel-fermented, has fresh, lively tropical-fruit flavours woven with crisp acidity. It's a medium-bodied wine, fully dry, with a touch of passionfruit and very good balance and depth.

DRY $19 V+

Kaituna Valley Marlborough Awatere Vineyards Sauvignon Blanc   ★★★☆

Grown at three sites in the Awatere Valley, the 2008 (★★☆) is a disappointing vintage for this normally rewarding label. Ripely flavoured, with a sliver of sweetness (5 grams/litre of residual sugar), it shows a slight lack of freshness and vibrancy.

Vintage	08
WR	7
Drink	09-10

MED/DRY $19 V+

Kakapo Marlborough Sauvignon Blanc   ★★★★

This distributor's label (SANZ Global) is consistently good – and good value. The 2008 vintage (★★★★) is fleshy, ripe and punchy, with tropical-fruit and herbaceous flavours, showing excellent freshness, balance and depth.

DRY $19 V+

Kawarau Estate Central Otago Sauvignon Blanc   ★★☆

Grown organically, the 2008 vintage (★★☆) is a single-vineyard wine, hand-picked at Pisa and lees-aged in tanks. Pale, it's a crisp, citrusy and limey wine, fresh and lively, with decent flavour depth and a slightly sweet (7.2 grams/litre of residual sugar) finish.

MED/DRY $23 –V

Kemblefield The Vista Sauvignon Blanc   (★★★)

The 2008 vintage (★★★☆) of this unoaked wine, estate-grown at Mangatahi, in Hawke's Bay, has fresh, ripely herbaceous aromas. It's a vibrantly fruity wine with strong gooseberry and lime flavours, a hint of passionfruit, and a refreshingly crisp finish.

DRY $17 AV

Kennedy Point Marlborough Sauvignon Blanc   ★★★

The 2008 vintage (★★☆) from this Waiheke Island-based producer is an easy-drinking style with light, citrusy, appley, limey flavours and a smooth finish.

DRY $18 AV

Kim Crawford Marlborough Sauvignon Blanc   ★★★☆

This is a very fresh and punchy style from Constellation NZ. The 2008 vintage (★★★☆), a 'pot-pourri' of Marlborough, was blended from grapes from 65 sites and produced in hundreds of thousands of cases. It offers strong, ripe melon/capsicum flavours, crisp acidity and a dry finish (3.7 grams/litre of residual sugar).

DRY $23 AV

Kim Crawford SP Flowers Marlborough Sauvignon Blanc   ★★★★

This top-end label from Constellation NZ is sourced from various vineyards. A generous wine with a strong presence, the 2008 vintage (★★★★) has concentrated tropical-fruit and herbaceous flavours, fresh, crisp and dry.

DRY $33 –V

Kim Crawford SP Spitfire Marlborough Sauvignon Blanc   ★★★★☆

The 2008 vintage (★★★★) is ripely scented and weighty, in a fresh, tropical fruit-flavoured style with a hint of herbs and good concentration. Why is it called 'Spitfire'? The grapes were grown on the site of an old airbase.

DRY $33 –V

Kina Beach Vineyard Estuary Block Sauvignon Blanc ★★★☆

Grown at a coastal Nelson site, the 2009 vintage (★★★★) is ripely scented, with mouthfilling body, sweet-fruit characters and lively, ripe melon/lime flavours that linger well.

Vintage	09	08	DRY $20 AV
WR	7	6	
Drink	09-11	P	

Konrad Marlborough Sauvignon Blanc ★★★☆

The 2008 vintage (★★★☆), estate-grown in the Wairau and Waihopai valleys, was mostly handled in tanks; 3 per cent was barrel-fermented. It's a crisp, still fresh and lively wine with tropical-fruit and herbaceous flavours, punchy and dry (3.8 grams/litre of residual sugar).

Vintage	08	07	DRY $20 AV
WR	4	4	
Drink	09-11	09-10	

Koru Sauvignon Blanc ★★★★☆

One of the few Marlborough Sauvignon Blancs to ponder over, this rare wine (358 cases in 2007) is grown by Jasper and Sally Raats (ex Clos Henri) in a 1-hectare vineyard in the upper Wairau Valley. The 2007 vintage (★★★★☆) was partly barrel-fermented and bottled without fining and filtering. Beautifully and ripely scented, it is fleshy (over 14 per cent alcohol) and dry, with highly concentrated tropical-fruit flavours, indigenous yeast notes adding complexity, and a slightly minerally, long finish, just let down by a touch of hardness.

Vintage	07	06	05	04	DRY $44 –V
WR	7	7	7	6	
Drink	09-16	09-15	09-13	09-10	

Koura Bay Awatere Valley Sauvignon Blanc ★★★☆

The 2009 vintage (★★★☆), estate-grown, is aromatic and punchy, with strong, clearly herbaceous flavours of gooseberries and capsicums, fresh and crisp.

Vintage	09	08	DRY $19 V+
WR	7	5	
Drink	10-12	09-10	

Kumeu River Sauvignon Blanc ★★★★

The 2008 vintage (★★★★), grown in Marlborough, is drinking well now. Mouthfilling, with a 'funky' bouquet, reflecting the use of indigenous yeasts, and ripe tropical-fruit rather than herbaceous flavours, it shows good concentration, with a fully dry, slightly flinty finish.

DRY $22 V+

Kumeu River Village Sauvignon Blanc (★★★)

Grown in Marlborough, the 2009 vintage (★★★) has 'funky', indigenous yeast aromas, leading into a lively, dry and flavoursome wine with ripe citrus-fruit, lime and spice characters, showing good individuality. It's ready to roll.

DRY $18 AV

Lake Chalice Marlborough Sauvignon Blanc   ★★★★

The 2008 vintage (★★★☆) was grown at seven sites in the Wairau and Awatere valleys. Opening out well, it is mouthfilling, with very good depth of fresh, zingy gooseberry, melon and capsicum flavours, with a basically dry (4 grams/litre of residual sugar), crisply herbaceous finish.

Vintage	08	DRY $20 V+
WR	6	
Drink	P	

Lake Chalice The Raptor Marlborough Sauvignon Blanc   ★★★★

Less than 2 per cent of the winery's Sauvignon Blanc grapes go into this top label. The 2008 (★★★★☆) has lifted, 'tomato stalk' aromas, leading into a mouthfilling, intense and zingy wine with an array of fruit flavours – melon, lime and passionfruit. It shows appetising acidity, with a long finish.

Vintage	08	DRY $27 –V
WR	6	
Drink	09-10	

La Strada Marlborough Sauvignon Blanc   (★★★★)

After 16 vintages, the Fromm winery, renowned for Pinot Noir, finally made its first Sauvignon Blanc in 2008 (★★★★). Partly fermented in old French oak barrels and made in a bone-dry style, it's a fleshy, subtle wine with ripe melon/lime flavours, a touch of complexity and a smooth, finely balanced, lingering finish.

Vintage	08	DRY $26 –V
WR	6	
Drink	09-12	

Latitude 41 New Zealand Sauvignon Blanc   ★★★☆

From Spencer Hill, the 2008 vintage (★★★☆) is drinking well now. A blend of Nelson and Marlborough grapes, it has mouthfilling body, with ripe, gooseberryish, slightly toasty flavours, a touch of complexity, and a well-rounded finish.

DRY $20 AV

Lawson's Dry Hills Marlborough Sauvignon Blanc   ★★★★★

Consistently among the region's best Sauvignon Blancs, this is a stylish wine, vibrantly fruity, intense and finely structured. The grapes are grown at several sites (six in 2008) in the Wairau, Waihopai and Brancott valleys. To add a subtle extra dimension, 4 to 8 per cent of the blend is fermented with indigenous and cultured yeasts in seasoned French oak barriques, and encouraged to undergo malolactic fermentation. The wine typically has great impact in its youth, but also has a proven ability to age well, acquiring toasty, minerally complexities. The 2008 vintage (★★★★☆) is a complex, dry style (2.6 grams/litre of residual sugar) with ripe grapefruit, lime and gooseberry flavours, faintly nutty and minerally, and strong personality.

Vintage	09	08	07	06
WR	7	6	6	7
Drink	09-10	P	P	P

DRY $21 V+

Lime Rock Sauvignon Blanc   ★★★☆

Grown at 240 metres above sea level, the 2008 vintage (★★★★) is a single-vineyard wine, hand-picked, tank-fermented and briefly lees-aged. One of the finest wines yet from Central Hawke's Bay, it has a fresh, punchy bouquet and a weighty palate with an array of grapefruit, herbal and mineral flavours, fresh, crisp, dry and long.

DRY $24 –V

Lobster Reef Marlborough Sauvignon Blanc   (★★★☆)

From Cape Campbell, the 2008 vintage (★★★☆) is scented, lively and crisp, with clearly herbaceous flavours, punchy and tangy, and a basically dry finish (3.8 grams/litre of residual sugar). Good value.

DRY $16 V+

Lonestone Marlborough Sauvignon Blanc   ★★★★

From wine distributor Bennett & Deller, the 2008 vintage (★★★★) is a bone-dry style, grown in the Wairau Valley. The bouquet is punchy and herbaceous; the palate is mouthfilling, with strongly varietal, gooseberry/lime flavours, slightly minerally, tangy and long. Great value.

DRY $16 V+

Longbush Marlborough Sauvignon Blanc   (★★☆)

From a Gisborne-based producer, the 2008 vintage (★★☆) has herbaceous, gooseberry and green-capsicum flavours, with a dry, rounded finish. It's a sharply priced wine, now ready.

Vintage	08
WR	6
Drink	09-11

DRY $13 V+

Longridge Hawke's Bay Sauvignon Blanc   ★★★

From Pernod Ricard NZ, the 2008 vintage (★★★) is medium-bodied, with clearly varietal, ripely herbaceous flavours, showing good balance and depth.

Vintage	08	07
WR	7	7
Drink	P	P

DRY $18 AV

Mahi Ballot Block Marlborough Sauvignon Blanc   (★★★★★)

From a slightly elevated, relatively cool site in the Brancott Valley, the very stylish 2008 vintage (★★★★★) was hand-picked and barrel-fermented with indigenous yeasts. It has a fragrant, complex bouquet, with fresh acidity woven through its concentrated, ripe, very gently oaked flavours, which build to a sustained, fully dry finish.

Vintage	08
WR	6
Drink	09-14

DRY $27 V+

Mahi Boundary Farm Sauvignon Blanc   (★★★★☆)

Grown on the lower slopes of the Wither Hills, at an early-ripening site, the 2008 vintage (★★★★) was hand-picked, fermented with indigenous yeasts and lees-aged for nearly a year in French oak barriques (10 per cent new). The bouquet is rich and complex; the palate is almost Chardonnay-like – very weighty, ripe and rounded, with rich tropical-fruit flavours and a bone-dry finish.

Vintage	08	07
WR	6	6
Drink	09-12	09-12

DRY $27 AV

Mahi Marlborough Sauvignon Blanc   ★★★★

Full-bodied and full-flavoured, the 2008 vintage (★★★★) was hand-picked at six sites and mostly handled in tanks; 4 per cent of the final blend was barrel-fermented. Sweet-fruited, it is ripe and rich, with a touch of complexity and a lingering, crisp finish.

Vintage	08	07
WR	6	6
Drink	09-10	P

DRY $20 V+

Mahi The Alias Marlborough Sauvignon Blanc   (★★★★☆)

The 2008 vintage (★★★★☆) was made entirely from Sauvignon Blanc grapes, but it's not intended to be an intensely 'varietal' wine. Grown at Renwick, it was fermented with indigenous yeasts, initially in tanks, then transferred into seasoned French oak barrels, where it completed its fermentation and matured for 10 months. Fleshy and generous, it is sweet-fruited and finely textured, with very ripe fig, spice and subtle oak flavours, showing excellent complexity, and a dry, rounded finish.

Vintage	08
WR	6
Drink	09-13

DRY $27 AV

Main Divide Marlborough Sauvignon Blanc   ★★★☆

From Pegasus Bay. Grown in the Wairau Valley, the 2008 vintage (★★★☆) is aromatic, attractively crisp and zesty, with good body and depth of ripe melon, capsicum and lime flavours, woven with fresh acidity, and a dry finish.

Vintage	08	07	06
WR	6	6	6
Drink	09-12	09-10	P

DRY $20 AV

Man O' War Gravestone Waiheke Island Sauvignon Blanc   ★★★☆

The 2007 vintage (★★★★) was fermented and matured for a year in French oak barrels (30 per cent new). It has a nutty, creamy bouquet and substantial body (14 per cent alcohol). Concentrated, with ripe stone-fruit flavours seasoned with toasty oak, it's a world apart from the crisply herbaceous wines from the south, possessing a Chardonnay-like power and richness.

Vintage	07
WR	6
Drink	09-10

DRY $40 –V

Man O' War Waiheke Island Sauvignon Blanc ★★★★

A distinctive wine, worth discovering. Grown at the eastern end of the island, the 2008 vintage (★★★☆) was mostly handled in tanks, but 10 per cent was fermented and matured in seasoned French oak barriques. It's a refreshingly crisp wine, fresh and vibrant, with high acidity and very good depth of ripe tropical-fruit flavours.

Vintage	08	07
WR	6	6
Drink	09-10	P

DRY $24 AV

Mansion House Bay Marlborough Sauvignon Blanc (★★★★)

From Whitehaven, the 2008 vintage (★★★★) is a fresh, vibrantly fruity wine with good body and delicious, punchy gooseberry/lime flavours threaded with lively acidity.

Vintage	08
WR	6
Drink	09-10

DRY $19 V+

Manu Marlborough Sauvignon Blanc (★★★)

From winemaker Steve Bird, the 2009 vintage (★★★) is a full-bodied, dry wine, grown in the Wairau Valley. Fresh, with good balance and depth of ripe passionfruit and lime flavours, it's priced sharply.

DRY $15 V+

Map Maker Marlborough Sauvignon Blanc (★★★☆)

A 'negociant' label from Staete Landt, based on vineyards in the Rapaura district and 5 per cent barrel-fermented, the 2008 vintage (★★★☆) has a punchy, ripely herbaceous bouquet, mouthfilling body and fresh tropical-fruit and green-capsicum flavours, crisp and strong.

DRY $19 V+

Margrain Martinborough Sauvignon Blanc ★★★☆

The 2008 vintage (★★★☆) is a fresh-scented, strongly varietal, briskly herbaceous wine, slightly sweet (6.2 grams/litre of residual sugar), with very good depth of melon and green-capsicum flavours, crisp, tangy and balanced for easy drinking.

MED/DRY $24 –V

Marsden Marlborough Sauvignon Blanc (★★★☆)

Fresh, crisp and lively, the 2008 vintage (★★★☆) from this Northland-based producer is a dry style with tropical-fruit and herbaceous flavours, showing good vigour, balance and depth.

DRY $18 V+

Martinborough Vineyard Sauvignon Blanc ★★★★

The delicious 2008 vintage (★★★★☆) was hand-harvested in Martinborough and mostly handled in tanks; a small percentage of the blend was barrel-fermented. Sweet-fruited, with lovely delicacy and depth of tropical-fruit flavours, it is impressively ripe, concentrated and well-rounded.

Vintage	08	07	06
WR	7	7	7
Drink	09-11	09-10	P

DRY $26 –V

Martinborough Vineyard Te Tera Sauvignon Blanc ★★★

The 2008 vintage (★★★☆), grown in vineyards in and around the township of Martinborough, is a punchy wine with ripe passionfruit and lime flavours, appetisingly crisp and lively. It's a fresh, strongly varietal wine, with good vigour and depth.

Vintage	08	07	06
WR	6	6	6
Drink	09-11	09-10	P

DRY $25 –V

Massey Dacta Marlborough Sauvignon Blanc ★★★

From Glover Family Vineyards, who also market wine under the Zephyr brand, the 2009 vintage (★★★☆) offers fine value. Already enjoyable, it is fresh and finely balanced, with vibrant tropical-fruit and gentle herbaceous flavours, moderately concentrated, ripe and smooth.

DRY $15 V+

Matahiwi Estate Holly Wairarapa Sauvignon Blanc ★★★☆

The 2008 vintage (★★★★) was grown at Opaki, near Masterton. Fermented – mostly with indigenous yeasts – in seasoned oak barrels, it is pale yellow, with concentrated, ripe passionfruit and pineapple flavours, slightly toasty, fresh and crisp. Showing good complexity, it's drinking well now.

DRY $25 –V

Matahiwi Estate Wairarapa Sauvignon Blanc ★★★☆

The 2008 vintage (★★★☆) is fresh and zesty, with vibrant melon/lime flavours, showing very good vigour and depth.

Vintage	08
WR	7
Drink	09-10

DRY $18 V+

Matakana Estate Marlborough Sauvignon Blanc ★★★

The 2008 vintage (★★★☆) was mostly handled in tanks, but 10 per cent of the blend was lees-aged for four months in seasoned French oak barriques. A crisp, punchy, freshly herbaceous style, it is dry and nettley, with good depth and lively acidity.

DRY $22 –V

Matariki Aspire Hawke's Bay Sauvignon Blanc – see Aspire Hawke's Bay Sauvignon Blanc

Matariki Hawke's Bay Sauvignon Blanc　　　★★★☆

The 2008 vintage (★★★☆) was grown in the Gimblett Gravels, tank-fermented and lees-aged for six weeks. It's a subtle, refined wine with mouthfilling body, very good depth of ripe sweet-fruit flavours of citrus fruits and limes, and an appetisingly crisp, dry finish.

Vintage	08
WR	5
Drink	09-10

DRY $22 AV

Matariki Reserve Hawke's Bay Sauvignon Blanc　　　★★★★☆

The classy, complex 2007 vintage (★★★★★) was hand-picked in the Gimblett Gravels and partly handled in tanks, but 55 per cent of the blend was fermented in barrels (80 per cent new). Maturing very gracefully, it has concentrated, ripe flavours of peaches and nectarines, seasoned with nutty oak, a deliciously creamy texture and a dry, lingering finish.

Vintage	07
WR	6
Drink	09-11

DRY $25 AV

Matawhero Gisborne Sauvignon Blanc　　　(★★★☆)

The historic Matawhero brand has recently been revived by the Searle family, owner of Brunton Road. A good debut, the 2009 vintage (★★★☆) is a medium-bodied wine (11.5 per cent alcohol), very fresh and vibrant, with smooth, ripe citrus and tropical-fruit flavours. It's already enjoyable.

DRY $25 –V

Matua Valley Hawke's Bay Sauvignon Blanc　　　★★★

Consistently good and bargain-priced. The 2009 vintage (★★★) is fresh, ripe and rounded, with satisfying depth of tropical-fruit flavours and a bone-dry, finely balanced finish.

DRY $15 V+

Matua Valley Matua Road Sauvignon Blanc　　　(★★☆)

Grown in New Zealand, although not identified by region, the 2008 vintage (★★☆) is an easy-drinking wine with decent depth of ripe tropical-fruit rather than herbaceous flavours and a smooth finish. Fine value.

DRY $10 V+

Matua Valley Paretai Marlborough Sauvignon Blanc　　　★★★★☆

The winery's flagship Sauvignon Blanc is sometimes but not always sourced from the company-controlled Northbank Vineyard, an inland site on the north bank of the Wairau River. The 2008 vintage (★★★★☆) is very refined, with lifted, 'tomato stalk' aromas and fresh, intense flavours of passionfruit and lime, vibrant and racy.

DRY $25 AV

Matua Valley Reserve Marlborough Sauvignon Blanc ★★★★

The 2008 vintage (★★★★) is generous, with slightly nettley, 'tomato stalk' aromas leading into a fresh, punchy, clearly herbaceous palate. It's drinking well now, with excellent body and depth and a well-rounded finish.

DRY $20 V+

Matua Valley Shingle Peak Marlborough Sauvignon Blanc – see Shingle Peak Marlborough Sauvignon Blanc

Maven Marlborough Sauvignon Blanc ★★★☆

The 2008 vintage (★★★☆) is a scented, lively wine, estate-grown on the northern side of the Wairau Valley. It shows very good depth of tropical-fruit and herbaceous flavours, with a touch of complexity from some use of seasoned French oak casks.

DRY $19 V+

Metis Hawke's Bay Sauvignon Blanc (★★★★)

From a joint venture between Trinity Hill and Loire Valley producer Pascal Jolivet, the 2008 vintage (★★★★) is an export-only label, apart from cellar-door sales. Crisp, tight and youthful, with limey-grassy aromatics, it is weighty, sweet-fruited, slightly minerally and dry, with very good depth, acid spine and length. It's opening out well with bottle-age.

DRY $28 –V

Mill Road New Zealand Sauvignon Blanc ★★☆

The non-vintage wine (★★) on sale in late 2009 is plain and slightly rustic, with ripe, tropical-fruit flavours, simple and smooth.

DRY $13 V+

Mills Reef Reserve Hawke's Bay Sauvignon Blanc ★★★★

The 2008 (★★★★), grown in 'cooler, coastal vineyards', is a freshly mouthfilling wine with ripe tropical-fruit flavours woven with crisp acidity and a dry, lingering finish.

DRY $23 AV

Mills Reef Sauvignon Blanc ★★★

The lower-tier Sauvignon Blanc from Mills Reef used to be a Hawke's Bay regional wine, but the 2008 vintage (★★★) is a blend of Hawke's Bay and Marlborough grapes. Ripely scented, it is smooth and flavoursome, with tropical-fruit characters to the fore and a crisp, dry finish.

DRY $17 AV

Mission Hawke's Bay Sauvignon Blanc ★★★

The 2008 vintage (★★★) is full-bodied, fresh and finely balanced, with pleasing depth of ripely herbaceous flavours, crisp and dry.

DRY $17 AV

Mission Reserve Sauvignon Blanc   ★★★☆

The 2009 vintage (★★★★) has the word 'Reserve' only on the back label. Grown at two sites in Hawke's Bay (80 per cent Ohiti and 20 per cent Mangatahi), it was fermented and lees-aged in French oak barriques. Mouthfilling and dry, with ripe tropical-fruit and slightly nutty flavours, showing very good depth and complexity, it's a fresh, tightly structured wine, likely to open out well during 2010–11.

Vintage	09	08	07
WR	7	4	6
Drink	10-15	09-12	P

DRY $22 AV

Mission Vineyard Selection Sauvignon Blanc   ★★★★

The 2008 vintage (★★★★) was grown at Ohiti Road, in Hawke's Bay, and handled entirely in tanks. Scented, ripe-fruit aromas lead into a full-bodied, smooth wine with sweet-fruit delights and strong tropical-fruit flavours, ripe and rounded. A good example of the regional style, it's full of drink-young charm.

DRY $18 V+

Moana Park Vineyard Selection Sauvignon Blanc   ★★★☆

Grown in Hawke's Bay, the 2008 vintage (★★★☆) is dry and mouthfilling, with plenty of crisp, lively passionfruit and lime flavour, fresh and vibrant. It's bargain-priced.

DRY $15 V+

Momo Marlborough Sauvignon Blanc   ★★★☆

From Seresin, the 2009 vintage (★★★☆) is an organically certified wine, hand-picked at two sites. Mouthfilling, it's a dry wine with well-ripened tropical-fruit rather than herbaceous flavours, showing very good depth.

Vintage	09
WR	7
Drink	09-10

DRY $20 AV

Moncellier Marlborough Sauvignon Blanc   (★★★★)

The debut 2008 vintage (★★★★) was grown in the Awatere and Omaka valleys. Freshly herbaceous, with good intensity, it is crisp and dry, with pure melon and capsicum flavours, vibrant, dry and long.

Vintage	09
WR	5
Drink	10-12

DRY $24 AV

Monkey Bay Marlborough Sauvignon Blanc   ★★★

From Constellation NZ, this wine is a roaring success in the US (reflecting its effective promotion, style and modest price). It is typically gently sweet, fresh and vibrant, with medium body, ripe-fruit flavours of melons and limes, and lots of drink-young charm. The 2008 vintage (★★★) is full-bodied and lively, with crisp, ripe, non-herbaceous fruit flavours, fresh and smooth.

MED/DRY $15 V+

Monowai Crownthorpe Sauvignon Blanc ★★★★

Estate-grown at a cool, elevated, inland site in Hawke's Bay, the 2008 vintage (★★★★) was handled entirely in tanks. Medium-bodied, with slightly 'sweaty', ripe-fruit aromas, it has concentrated tropical-fruit flavours, with fresh acidity and a lingering, off-dry (6 grams/litre of residual sugar) finish. Priced sharply.

MED/DRY $18 V+

Montana 'B' Brancott Marlborough Sauvignon Blanc ★★★★★

Promoted as 'our finest expression of Marlborough's most famous variety', Pernod Ricard NZ's wine lives up to its billing. 'Palate weight, concentration and longevity' are the goal. It has traditionally been grown in the company's sweeping Brancott Estate Vineyard, on the south, slightly cooler side of the Wairau Valley, and a small portion of the blend is fermented and lees-aged in French oak barriques (new and one-year-old), to add 'some toast and spice as well as palate richness'. It matures well for several years, developing nutty, minerally, toasty flavours in the best vintages, fresh asparagus notes in others. The 2008 vintage (★★★★☆) is very ripely scented, weighty and rounded, with rich tropical-fruit flavours, tight and concentrated. Showing excellent freshness and vigour, it's a finely poised wine that should mature well.

DRY $34 AV

Montana Marlborough Sauvignon Blanc ★★★☆

This famous, bargain-priced label rests its case on the flavour explosion of slow-ripened Marlborough fruit – a breathtaking style of Sauvignon Blanc which this wine, more than any other, has introduced to wine lovers in key markets around the world. Recent vintages are less lush, more pungently herbaceous than some other Marlborough labels; 'this is the style we can sell locally and the UK wants,' reports Pernod Ricard NZ. The 2008 vintage (★★★☆), the first in which production exceeded one million cases, was mostly grown in the Wairau Valley, but the inclusion of Awatere Valley fruit (30 per cent) gives 'a more herbal note, vibrancy and aromatic lift'. Punchy and fresh, with good vigour and depth, it's highly enjoyable in its youth. The 2009 (tasted prior to bottling, and so not rated) has fresh, pure tropical-fruit and herbaceous flavours, crisp and zingy.

Vintage	09	08	07
WR	7	6	6
Drink	09-10	P	P

DRY $18 V+

Montana Reserve Marlborough Sauvignon Blanc ★★★★

This label is designed to highlight the fresh, herbaceous style of Sauvignon Blanc Pernod Ricard NZ achieves on the south side of the Wairau Valley, compared to its more tropical fruit-flavoured Stoneleigh Sauvignon Blanc, grown on the north side of the valley. The 2009 vintage (★★★★) has mouthfilling body and fresh, tight gooseberry and capsicum flavours. Finely textured, it's a classic regional style, dry and long.

Vintage	09	08	07
WR	7	6	6
Drink	09-12	09-11	P

DRY $24 AV

Montana Terroir Conders Forest Marlborough Sauvignon Blanc ★★★★

Grown in the relatively warm Rapaura district, on the northern side of the Wairau Valley, and lees-aged in tanks, the 2008 vintage (★★★★) is fresh and punchy, with smooth, ripe tropical-fruit flavours, showing excellent delicacy and length.

Vintage	08	07
WR	6	6
Drink	P	P

DRY $24 AV

Montana Terroir Festival Block Marlborough Sauvignon Blanc ★★★★

From Pernod Ricard NZ, this wine is grown on the relatively cool, southern side of the Wairau Valley. The 2008 vintage (★★★★) is fresh and punchy, with intensely varietal, clearly herbaceous flavours, crisp, dry and lingering.

Vintage	08	07
WR	6	7
Drink	P	P

DRY $24 AV

Montana Terroir Rail Bridge Marlborough Sauvignon Blanc ★★★★☆

Grown in the Awatere Valley, the 2008 vintage (★★★★☆) is intensely varietal and herbaceous, with the classic 'tomato stalk' aromas and flavours of the sub-region, and excellent body, texture and depth.

Vintage	08	07
WR	6	6
Drink	P	P

DRY $24 V+

Morton Estate Stone Creek Marlborough Sauvignon Blanc ★★★

The 2007 vintage (★★★) is punchy, with slightly herbaceous flavours, minerally, crisp and dry.

Vintage	07
WR	6
Drink	P

DRY $20 AV

Morton Estate White Label Hawke's Bay Sauvignon Blanc ★★★☆

The 2008 vintage (★★★☆) was grown in the inland, elevated Colefield and Kinross vineyards. Fresh, crisp and flavoursome, it's a lively, slightly nettley style with a sliver of sweetness balanced by appetising acidity, and good vigour and aromatic intensity.

Vintage	08
WR	5
Drink	P

MED/DRY $16 V+

Morton Estate White Label Marlborough Sauvignon Blanc ★★★

The 2008 vintage (★★★), grown mostly in the Kuranui Vineyard, in the Awatere Valley, is mouthfilling, with good depth. The 2009 (★★★) is fresh and smooth, with good depth of tropical-fruit and herbaceous flavours, balanced for easy drinking.

Vintage	09
WR	7
Drink	09-11

DRY $18 AV

Mountain Road Taranaki Sauvignon Blanc   ★★★

Grown at Brixton, just north of New Plymouth, the 2008 vintage (★★★) was made from vines planted in 2004. It's a medium-bodied, slightly sweet wine with good vivacity and depth of fresh, crisp, clearly varietal, melon/lime flavours. (Only 1420 bottles were made.)

MED/DRY $24 –V

Mount Fishtail Marlborough Sauvignon Blanc   ★★☆

From Konrad and Co, the ripely scented 2009 vintage (★★★) was grown in the Wairau and Waihopai valleys. It's a fresh, medium-bodied wine with melon, gooseberry and lime flavours, showing good depth, and a crisp, dry finish.

Vintage	09
WR	3
Drink	09-11

DRY $16 AV

Mount Nelson Marlborough Sauvignon Blanc   ★★★★

Mount Nelson is owned by Tenuta Di Biserno, itself controlled by members of the famous Tuscan wine family, Antinori. The company owns a vineyard on the south side of the Wairau Valley, from which most of the grapes are drawn. The aim is to make 'a classic Marlborough Sauvignon Blanc, with stronger emphasis on texture and length'. Crisp and dry, this is typically a full-bodied wine with very good depth of melon/lime flavours and a slightly minerally, lingering finish. Quietly classy.

DRY $21 V+

Mount Riley Marlborough Sauvignon Blanc   ★★★★

Notably fresh and full-bodied, with ripely herbaceous flavours, deep, dry and lasting, the 2008 vintage (★★★★★) shared the Best White Wine Buy of the Year award in last year's *Guide*. The 2009 (★★★☆) is mouthfilling, with fresh gooseberry/lime flavours showing very good depth and a crisp, dry (3 grams/litre of residual sugar) finish.

Vintage	09	08	07
WR	6	6	6
Drink	09-10	P	P

DRY $18 V+

Mount Riley Seventeen Valley Sauvignon Blanc   ★★★★

The 2007 vintage (★★★★) was hand-picked in the heart of the Wairau Valley and fermented with indigenous yeasts in seasoned French oak barriques. A distinctive style, it is weighty and complex, with ripe tropical-fruit aromas and flavours. Some 'funky' notes add interest, with good richness through the palate and a dry finish (2.7 grams/litre of residual sugar).

Vintage	07
WR	6
Drink	P

DRY $22 V+

Mount Vernon Marlborough Sauvignon Blanc   (★★☆)

From Lawson's Dry Hills, the 2008 vintage (★★☆) was blended with Sémillon (10 per cent). It's a smooth, ripe-tasting wine with melon and capsicum flavours, showing moderate depth.

DRY $18 –V

Mt Beautiful Cheviot Hills North Canterbury Sauvignon Blanc   (★★★★)

From a new sub-region, north of Waipara, the 2008 vintage (★★★★) is a fleshy, rich wine, ripely scented, with sweet-fruit delights, strong, dry tropical-fruit flavours and finely balanced acidity.

DRY $22 V+

Mt Difficulty Central Otago Sauvignon Blanc   ★★★☆

Grown at Bannockburn, the 2008 vintage (★★★☆) is fresh, lively, citrusy and grassy, with a slightly minerally, crisp, dry finish.

Vintage	08
WR	6
Drink	09-12

DRY $25 –V

Mt Hector Wairarapa Sauvignon Blanc   (★★☆)

From Matahiwi, the 2008 vintage (★★☆) is a medium-bodied, green-edged wine with fresh, crisp, capsicum-like flavours, showing solid depth. Fine value.

DRY $10 V+

Mt Rosa Sauvignon Blanc   ★★☆

The 2009 vintage, grown at Gibbston, in Central Otago, was bottle-shocked when tasted, so is not rated. Crisp and basically dry (4 grams/litre of residual sugar), it looked promising, with lively, gooseberry/lime, slightly minerally flavours.

DRY $22 –V

Mud House Marlborough Sauvignon Blanc   ★★★★

This is typically a strongly herbaceous style. The 2008 vintage (★★★☆) is a punchy, clearly herbaceous wine with crisp acidity and green-capsicum notes to the fore, fresh, lively and strong.

Vintage	08	07	06
WR	6	7	7
Drink	P	P	P

DRY $19 V+

Mud House Swan Marlborough Sauvignon Blanc   (★★★★☆)

The 2008 vintage (★★★★☆) is slightly 'sweaty', with excellent intensity of melon/capsicum flavours, very fresh, vibrant and crisp.

DRY $25 AV

Muddy Water Growers Series Sauvignon Blanc   (★★★★)

Grown at two sites at Waipara, the 2008 vintage (★★★★) was hand-picked, fermented with indigenous yeasts in old barrels, and lees-aged in oak for six months. Mouthfilling, it has concentrated, ripe passionfruit and lime flavours, with a hint of nutty oak adding complexity and a crisp, fully dry finish.

DRY $25 AV

Murdoch James Wairarapa Sauvignon Blanc   ★★☆

The 2008 vintage (★★☆) was grown at Martinborough and Masterton. It's a medium-bodied wine with appley, limey flavours and a sliver of sweetness (5.1 grams/litre of residual sugar) balanced by crisp, lively acidity.

Vintage	08	MED/DRY $20 –V
WR	5	
Drink	09-10	

Nautilus Marlborough Sauvignon Blanc   ★★★★

Typically a richly fragrant wine with mouthfilling body and a surge of ripe, passionfruit and lime-like flavours, enlivened by fresh acidity. Oak plays no part in the wine, but it is briefly matured on its yeast lees. The 2008 vintage (★★★★) is weighty, with fresh, finely balanced passionfruit/lime flavours, showing excellent delicacy and depth. Retasted in mid-2009, it shows impressive intensity and vigour, with a crisp, dry (2.3 grams/litre of residual sugar), lingering finish.

Vintage	08	07	06	DRY $25 AV
WR	6	7	6	
Drink	09-10	P	P	

Ned, The, Waihopai River Marlborough Sauvignon Blanc   ★★★☆

The 2009 vintage (★★★☆) is a single-vineyard wine, tight and punchy, with excellent vigour and depth of passionfruit and lime flavours. Minerally and crisp, it's a finely balanced wine, priced sharply.

DRY $18 V+

Nest, The, Marlborough Sauvignon Blanc   (★★★☆)

From Lake Chalice, the debut 2008 vintage (★★★☆) is mouthfilling, with very good depth of fresh tropical-fruit flavours and a rounded finish.

DRY $20 AV

Neudorf Nelson Sauvignon Blanc   ★★★★☆

Looking for a Sauvignon Blanc 'with texture, that is complex and satisfying', Neudorf grew the grapes for the 2008 vintage (★★★★☆) at Brightwater, on the Waimea Plains. Partly (15 per cent) fermented in old oak barrels, and bottle-aged prior to its release, it is ripely scented, with sweet-fruit delights and excellent intensity of fresh passionfruit, lime and pineapple flavours, carrying the dry style (1.7 grams/litre of residual sugar) well.

Vintage	08	07	06	05	DRY $22 V+
WR	5	6	6	5	
Drink	09-11	09-12	09-10	09-10	

Ngatarawa Silks Marlborough Sauvignon Blanc ★★★

Light and smooth, the 2008 vintage (★★★) has decent depth of citrusy, limey flavours, gentle acidity and a dry finish.

Vintage	08	07	06
WR	6	6	5
Drink	09-11	09-10	P

DRY $20 AV

Ngatarawa Stables Sauvignon Blanc ★★★

Grown in Hawke's Bay and Marlborough, the 2008 vintage (★★☆) is a solid, medium to full-bodied wine with ripe tropical-fruit flavours, ready now.

Vintage	08	07	06
WR	6	6	5
Drink	09-11	09-10	P

DRY $18 AV

Nga Waka Martinborough Sauvignon Blanc ★★★★★

Substantial in body, with concentrated, ripe, bone-dry flavours, this is a cool-climate style of Sauvignon Blanc, highly aromatic and zingy. The grapes are grown in the Home Block, on the Martinborough Terrace, planted in 1988, and the Top Block, a few kilometres away in the low hills between Martinborough and Te Muna, established in 1996. The vinification, 'very straightforward', with no use of oak, yields a wine that typically peaks at four to six years old, when it is rich, toasty, minerally and complex. The 2009 vintage (★★★★☆) is tight, crisp and dry, with good intensity of melon/lime flavours, punchy, vibrant, minerally and lingering. Best drinking 2011+.

Vintage	09	08
WR	7	7
Drink	10+	09+

DRY $25 V+

Nikau Point Hawke's Bay Sauvignon Blanc ★★☆

From One Tree Hill Vineyards (owned by Morton Estate), the 2009 vintage (★★☆) is a crisp, medium-bodied wine with melon/lime flavours, light and lively.

Vintage	09	08
WR	6	5
Drink	09-11	09-10

DRY $15 AV

Nikau Point Marlborough Reserve Sauvignon Blanc ★★★☆

This is Morton Estate's 'most minerally, acidic and grassy' Sauvignon Blanc. The 2009 vintage (★★★☆) is fresh and punchy, with vibrant melon and green-capsicum flavours, showing good balance and depth.

Vintage	09	08
WR	7	6
Drink	09-11	09-10

DRY $18 V+

Nikau Point Marlborough Sauvignon Blanc (★★☆)

The 2009 vintage (★★☆) from Morton Estate is a medium-bodied wine, freshly herbaceous, with gooseberry and lime flavours, showing solid depth.

DRY $15 AV

Nobilo Icon Marlborough Sauvignon Blanc   ★★★★

A consistently delightful wine from Constellation NZ. The 2007 vintage (★★★★) is fleshy, with an attractive marriage of fresh, vibrant, tropical-fruit and herbaceous flavours, rich and rounded.

Vintage	07	06
WR	7	7
Drink	P	P

DRY $24 AV

Nobilo Regional Collection Marlborough Sauvignon Blanc   ★★★

This is a riper style from Constellation NZ than its briskly herbaceous stablemate under the Selaks Premium Selection label (not reviewed). It is typically full-bodied, with fresh, clearly varietal gooseberry/lime flavours and a crisp, slightly off-dry finish. It no longer has a high profile in New Zealand, but recently topped the Sauvignon Blanc sales charts in the US.

MED/DRY $16 V+

Odyssey Marlborough Sauvignon Blanc   ★★★☆

The 2008 vintage (★★★☆) was estate-grown in the Brancott Valley and mostly handled in tanks; 10 per cent of the blend was matured in old oak casks. Fresh and vibrant, it has good delicacy and depth of ripe melon/lime flavours, slightly minerally and dry (3 grams/litre of residual sugar). The 2009 (★★★☆) is medium-bodied (12.5 per cent alcohol), with crisp, ripe tropical-fruit flavours in a non-herbaceous style, balanced for easy drinking.

Vintage	09	08	07	06
WR	6	6	6	6
Drink	09-11	09-10	09-10	P

DRY $19 V+

Ohinemuri Estate Wairau Valley Marlborough Sauvignon Blanc   ★★★

The 2008 vintage (★★★) was matured on its yeast lees for three months and 10 per cent barrel-fermented. It's a mouthfilling wine with strong gooseberry, melon and capsicum flavours, slight asparagus notes emerging with bottle-age, and a dry finish. Ready.

Vintage	08	07
WR	6	6
Drink	09-10	09-10

DRY $24 –V

Old Coach Road Nelson Sauvignon Blanc   ★★★

Seifried Estate's lower-tier Sauvignon. The 2009 vintage (★★★) was estate-grown, inland at Brightwater and on the coast, at Rabbit Island. An enjoyably fresh, crisp and lively wine, it is tangy, with melon and green-capsicum flavours, in a clearly herbaceous style with lots of youthful vigour.

DRY $17 AV

Olssen's Central Otago Sauvignon Blanc   ★★☆

Estate-grown at Bannockburn, the 2008 vintage (★★☆) is a mouthfilling, smooth wine (6 grams/litre of residual sugar), fresh and vibrant, with gentle apple, pear and slight spice flavours.

MED/DRY $23 –V

Omaka Springs Falveys Marlborough Sauvignon Blanc ★★★☆

This distinctive wine is made in a slightly sweet style (9.1 grams/litre of residual sugar in 2007). It typically offers melon and green-capsicum flavours, fresh and crisp, with good intensity.

MED/DRY $21 AV

Omaka Springs Marlborough Sauvignon Blanc ★★★

This wine has fresh, direct, grassy aromas in a traditional style of Marlborough Sauvignon Blanc, zesty and strongly herbaceous. It is one of the region's sweetest Sauvignon Blancs – the 2008 vintage has 8.2 grams per litre of residual sugar. The 2008 (★★★) is crisp and vibrantly fruity, with gooseberry/lime flavours and racy acidity.

MED/DRY $18 AV

One Tree Marlborough Sauvignon Blanc ★★★

Made by Capricorn, a division of Craggy Range, for sale in restaurants and supermarkets (New World, PAK'nSAVE), this is typically an aromatic wine with good depth of freshly herbaceous flavours, lively and balanced for easy drinking. The 2008 vintage (★★★☆) is mouthfilling, with strong tropical-fruit flavours, fractional sweetness (4 grams/litre of residual sugar) and fresh, lively acidity. Fine value.

Vintage	09	08
WR	7	6
Drink	09-10	09-10

DRY $15 V+

Open House Smooth Marlborough Sauvignon Blanc (★★★)

Created 'especially with women in mind', the debut 2008 vintage (★★★) was produced at Wither Hills. Offering good value, it is aromatic and lively, with plenty of fresh, herbaceous flavour and a crisp, off-dry finish.

MED/DRY $15 V+

Orinoco Nelson Sauvignon Blanc ★★★☆

Grown on the Waimea Plains, the 2008 vintage (★★★) is a crisp, full-flavoured wine with ripe tropical-fruit characters to the fore, a herbal undercurrent and firm acid spine.

DRY $19 V+

O:TU Marlborough Sauvignon Blanc ★★★★

From Otuwhero Estates, in the Awatere Valley, the 2009 vintage (★★★★) is a freshly aromatic, weighty wine with strong melon, lime and gooseberry flavours, a minerally streak, and good purity and length.

DRY $20 V+

O:TU Single Vineyard Marlborough Sauvignon Blanc ★★★★☆

The 2008 vintage (★★★★☆) is a highly aromatic, 'full-on' style from the company's original Otuwhero Vineyard in the Awatere Valley. Its intense, nettley flavours are threaded with appetising acidity, finishing fresh, crisp and long. The 2009 (★★★★☆) is weighty, with pure, penetrating melon/lime flavours, showing excellent delicacy and depth, and a long, tangy finish.

DRY $25 AV

Overstone Marlborough Sauvignon Blanc (★★☆)

From Sileni, the 2008 vintage (★★☆) is a medium-bodied style, fresh and smooth, with tropical-fruit and herbaceous flavours, showing decent depth.

DRY $14 V+

Oyster Bay Marlborough Sauvignon Blanc ★★★★

Oyster Bay is a Delegat's brand, reserved principally for Marlborough wines and enjoying huge success in international markets, especially Australia. Handled entirely in stainless steel tanks, this wine is grown at dozens of vineyards around the Wairau and Awatere valleys and made in a dry style with tropical-fruit and herbaceous flavours, crisp and punchy. The 2009 (★★★★☆) is a top vintage. Weighty and intense, it has a lovely array of fresh, dry melon, lime, passionfruit and green-capsicum flavours. Fine value.

Vintage	09	08	07
WR	6	5	6
Drink	09-13	09-11	09-11

DRY $20 V+

Palliser Estate Martinborough Sauvignon Blanc ★★★★★

At its best, this is a wholly seductive wine, one of the greatest Sauvignon Blancs in the country. A distinctly cool-climate style, it offers an exquisite harmony of crisp acidity, mouthfilling body and fresh, penetrating fruit characters. The grapes are mostly estate-grown, but are also purchased from growers on the Martinborough Terrace and a few kilometres away, at Te Muna. The fruit gives the intensity of flavour – there's no blending with Sémillon, no barrel fermentation, no oak-aging. The 2008 vintage (★★★★☆) has slightly 'sweaty' aromas. Fleshy, vibrant and sweet-fruited, it's a powerful yet very elegant style with concentrated, ripe passionfruit, citrus, lime and herb flavours, and a sustained, dry (3 grams/litre of residual sugar) finish. Great value.

DRY $18 V+

Passage Rock Waiheke Island Sauvignon Blanc ★★★

The 2009 vintage (★★★) was estate-grown at Te Matuku Bay. It's a fleshy, mouthfilling (14 per cent alcohol), well-rounded wine, sweet-fruited, with ripe, citrusy, appley flavours, creamy-textured, in a typical northern style.

DRY $23 –V

Pegasus Bay Sauvignon/Sémillon ★★★★☆

At its best, this Waipara, North Canterbury wine is lush, concentrated and complex, with loads of personality. The 2008 vintage (★★★★☆) is a youthful, slightly minerally and nutty blend of Sauvignon Blanc (70 per cent) and Sémillon (30 per cent), fermented with indigenous yeasts and lees-aged for nine months in a mix of stainless steel tanks, large oak vats and old barriques. Weighty and sweet-fruited, with ripe flavours of citrus fruits, gooseberries and lime, appetising acidity and impressive vigour, complexity and length, it's already drinking well, but worth cellaring.

Vintage	08	07
WR	6	6
Drink	09-15	09-13

DRY $28 AV

Pencarrow Sauvignon Blanc   ★★★☆

Pencarrow is the second-tier label of Palliser Estate, but this is typically a satisfying wine in its own right, bargain-priced. The 2008 vintage (★★★★), made from Martinborough grapes, is a crisp, lively wine with a 'sweaty' bouquet, mouthfilling body and tropical-fruit flavours showing excellent freshness, vigour and richness. The 2009 is a blend of Martinborough (80 per cent) and Marlborough (20 per cent) grapes.

DRY $15 V+

Penny Lane Marlborough Sauvignon Blanc   ★★☆

From Morton Estate, the 2008 vintage (★★☆) is medium-bodied, with herbaceous flavours, a suggestion of slight sweetness and a crisp, smooth finish. Ready.

Vintage	08	DRY $15 AV
WR	5	
Drink	09-10	

Peter Yealands Marlborough Sauvignon Blanc   (★★★☆)

The label on the 2009 vintage (★★★☆) makes no mention of the Awatere Valley – but it sure smells of it, with the lifted, 'tomato stalk' aromas typical of the sub-region. An intensely herbaceous style, it is vibrant, with punchy gooseberry and green-capsicum flavours, crisp and lively.

DRY $19 V+

Ra Nui Marlborough Wairau Valley Sauvignon Blanc   ★★★★

The 2009 vintage (★★★★) was mostly handled in tanks (3 per cent of the blend was barrel-fermented). It's a classic regional style, mouthfilling, crisp and finely balanced, with melon, lime and passionfruit flavours, showing good purity, delicacy and length. It's already drinking well. Fine value.

DRY $18 V+

Rapaura Road Marlborough Sauvignon Blanc –
see Boundary Vineyards Rapaura Road Marlborough Sauvignon Blanc

Rapaura Springs Marlborough Sauvignon Blanc   ★★★☆

The 2008 vintage (★★★☆) is a ripe tropical fruit-flavoured wine with mouthfilling body and very satisfying depth. An understated style, it is dry, with good purity and freshness. A top buy.

Vintage	08	DRY $15 V+
WR	6	
Drink	09-10	

Rapaura Springs Vineyard Reserve Marlborough Sauvignon Blanc   (★★★)

The 2007 vintage (★★★) was grown at Dillons Point, 30 per cent barrel-fermented and lees-aged for 11 months. Still youthful in colour, it has nettley, slightly nutty aromas, mouthfilling body and lively, herbaceous flavours, at the greener end of the ripeness spectrum.

Vintage	07	DRY $19 AV
WR	6	
Drink	09-10	

Redoubt Hill Vineyard Nelson Sauvignon Blanc   ★★☆

From 'probably the steepest vineyard in Nelson', the 2009 vintage (★★☆) was grown at Motueka, hand-picked and handled entirely in tanks. Fresh and light-bodied, it's a crisp, limey wine, attractively scented, with good delicacy and balance (4 grams/litre of residual sugar), but lacks the intensity to rate more highly.

DRY $20 –V

Redwood Pass by Vavasour Marlborough Sauvignon Blanc   ★★★★

The 2008 vintage (★★★★) is a blend of Awatere Valley (90 per cent) and Wairau Valley grapes. Freshly aromatic, it is weighty and zingy, with good intensity of melon/lime flavours, dryish (5 grams/litre of residual sugar) and delicious from the start. A good buy.

Vintage	09
WR	7
Drink	09-11

MED/DRY $18 V+

Renato Nelson Sauvignon Blanc   ★★★★

Blended from grapes grown at Kina, on the coast, and on the Waimea Plains, the 2008 (★★★☆) was tank-fermented and made in a dry style (3.5 grams/litre of residual sugar). The bouquet is slightly grassy; the palate is mouthfilling, with very good depth of freshly herbaceous, gooseberry/lime flavours and crisp, lively acidity. The 2009 vintage (★★★★) is medium-bodied, crisp and punchy, with tropical-fruit and herbaceous flavours, showing excellent balance, vigour and intensity.

Vintage	09	08
WR	6	5
Drink	10-11	09-10

DRY $19 V+

Resolute Marlborough Sauvignon Blanc   (★★★★★)

The absorbing, weighty, minerally 2007 vintage (★★★★★) was hand-picked at 23.5 brix in the heart of the Winegrowers of Ara Vineyard, near Renwick, tank-fermented and lees-aged for eight months. Much less aggressive than most of the region's Sauvignon Blancs, it is notably full-bodied, with a rich array of peach, nectarine and lime flavours, a distinctly minerally streak and a rounded, bone-dry, lasting finish. A real conversation piece.

Vintage	07
WR	7
Drink	09-10

DRY $28 V+

Ribbonwood Marlborough Sauvignon Blanc   (★★★☆)

From Framingham, the 2008 vintage (★★★☆) is an aromatic, freshly herbaceous wine with passionfruit and green-capsicum flavours, crisp and lively, a smooth finish and very good depth.

DRY $18 V+

Richmond Plains Nelson Sauvignon Blanc ★★★☆

Grown organically and certified by BioGro, the 2009 vintage (★★★☆) is lively and medium-bodied with fresh, grassy aromas leading into a tangy wine with plenty of crisp, limey flavour.

Vintage	09	08	07
WR	6	6	7
Drink	09-11	09-10	P

DRY $20 AV

Richmond Plains Whakatu Sauvignon Blanc (★★★)

The 2009 vintage (★★★) is light and lively, with lifted, herbaceous aromas and good depth of fresh, grassy flavours, enlivened with racy acidity.

DRY $20 AV

Riverby Estate Marlborough Sauvignon Blanc ★★★☆

A single-vineyard wine, grown in Jacksons Road, in the heart of the Wairau Valley, the 2008 vintage (★★★☆) is mouthfilling and gently aromatic, with ripe tropical-fruit flavours showing good depth and a dry finish.

DRY $19 V+

River Farm Ben Morven Marlborough Sauvignon Blanc (★★★☆)

The 2008 vintage (★★★☆) was sourced mostly from the Ben Morven Vineyard, on the south side of the Wairau Valley, and blended with 'some of our St Maur, hand-picked, wild yeast, barrel-fermented wine to add flavour and complexity'. It shows very good freshness, vigour and depth, with ripe, slightly nettley flavours, showing a touch of complexity, and a crisp, dry (3.6 grams/litre of residual sugar) finish.

Vintage	08
WR	5
Drink	10-11

DRY $22 AV

River Farm Saint Maur Marlborough Sauvignon Blanc (★★★★☆)

A rich and complex style, the 2008 vintage (★★★★☆) was harvested at over 25 brix in the Saint Maur Vineyard on the south side of the Wairau Valley, fermented with indigenous yeasts in older French oak barriques and oak-aged for 10 months. Freshly scented, with mouthfilling body, a strong surge of ripe tropical-fruit flavours, a gentle seasoning of oak, and a sliver of sweetness (5.2 grams/litre of residual sugar) balanced by lively acidity, it's a powerful wine with loads of personality.

Vintage	08
WR	6
Drink	10-12

MED/DRY $29

Riverstone Sauvignon Blanc (★★☆)

From Villa Maria, the non-vintage wine (★★☆) on the shelves in 2009 has decent depth of tropical-fruit flavours, fresh, vibrant and smooth.

DRY $11 V+

Rockburn Central Otago Sauvignon Blanc ★★★

The 2008 vintage (★★★☆) was mostly sourced from Gibbston and handled in tanks, but 35 per cent of the blend, grown at Parkburn, in the Cromwell Basin, was French oak-fermented. It offers strong, crisp tropical-fruit and herbal flavours, with a touch of complexity, and good freshness and vigour.

Vintage 08
WR 7
Drink 09-14

DRY $23 –V

Rochfort Rees Awatere Valley Marlborough Sauvignon Blanc (★★★★)

From an Auckland-based company, the 2008 vintage (★★★★) is a blend of Awatere Valley (95 per cent) and Wairau Valley grapes. Fresh, brisk and clearly herbaceous, with tropical-fruit flavours too, it's a lively wine with good intensity and immediacy.

DRY $20 V+

Rongopai East Coast Sauvignon Blanc ★★★

From Babich, the 2008 vintage (★★★) is an easy-drinking style, mouthfilling, with ripe tropical-fruit flavours to the fore, fresh and smooth. It's drinking well now and offers good value.

DRY $14 V+

Rua Whenua Hawke's Bay Reserve Sauvignon Blanc (★★★☆)

Still on sale, the highly distinctive 2006 vintage (★★★☆) was estate-grown at Te Awanga and harvested from 24-year-old vines at an average of 26 brix, 'with a fair amount of dry botrytis'. It is tight, very crisp, concentrated and minerally, in a dry, slightly austere style, likely to be long-lived.

DRY $19 V+

Ruben Hall Sauvignon Blanc (★★☆)

Villa Maria's non-vintage quaffer (★★☆) on sale in 2009 is a blend of New Zealand and Chilean wines. It's an easy-drinking style with tropical-fruit rather than herbaceous flavours, fresh and well-rounded.

DRY $11 V+

Ruby Bay Vineyard Sauvignon Blanc ★★★

The 2009 vintage (★★★) is a single-vineyard Nelson wine. It's a medium-bodied style (11.5 per cent alcohol), with fresh, ripe gooseberry and lime flavours, appetisingly crisp and dry.

Vintage 09
WR 5
Drink 09-12

DRY $20 AV

Sacred Hill Marlborough Vineyards Sauvignon Blanc ★★★☆

The 2009 vintage (★★★) is a fresh, medium to full-bodied wine (12.5 per cent alcohol), with tropical-fruit and herbaceous flavours, showing good but not great depth.

DRY $21 AV

Sacred Hill Sauvage Sauvignon Blanc ★★★★

One of the country's most expensive Sauvignon Blancs, at its best this is an impressively rich, complex example of the widely underrated, barrel-matured Hawke's Bay Sauvignon Blanc style. The 2007 (★★★★☆) is a distinctive wine, hand-picked, barrel-fermented with indigenous yeasts and oak-aged for 10 months. Full-bodied, with concentrated, ripe tropical-fruit flavours, enriched with French oak and a bone-dry, lingering finish, it's a top vintage, still unfolding.

Vintage	07	DRY $33 –V
WR	7	
Drink	12-14	

Saint Clair Marlborough Sauvignon Blanc ★★★★☆

This label has shown fine form lately and is a top buy. The 2009 vintage (★★★★☆), grown mostly in the lower and central Wairau Valley, was handled entirely in tanks. Strong, slightly 'sweaty armpit' aromas lead into a fresh, concentrated wine with pure tropical-fruit flavours, a herbaceous undercurrent, zingy acidity and a dry (3.1 grams/litre of residual sugar) finish.

Vintage	09	08	07	06	DRY $21 V+
WR	7	7	7	7	
Drink	09-11	09-10	P	P	

Saint Clair Pioneer Block 1 Foundation Sauvignon Blanc ★★★★☆

This single-vineyard Marlborough wine is grown east of Blenheim, in the lower Wairau Valley, at a site formerly the source of the Wairau Reserve Sauvignon Blanc. The 2009 vintage (★★★★★) is finely scented and weighty, with tropical-fruit and gently herbaceous flavours, strikingly fresh, pure, intense and racy.

Vintage	09	08	07	DRY $25 AV
WR	7	7	7	
Drink	09-10	P	P	

Saint Clair Pioneer Block 2 Swamp Block Sauvignon Blanc ★★★★

Sourced from a vineyard with a 'cooler climate', close to the coast at Dillons Point, in the lower Wairau Valley of Marlborough, the 2009 vintage (★★★★) is fresh and lively, with pungently herbaceous flavours, crisp and lingering.

Vintage	09	DRY $25 AV
WR	7	
Drink	09-10	

Saint Clair Pioneer Block 3 43 Degrees Sauvignon Blanc ★★★★

This Marlborough wine is grown in the lower Wairau Valley, at a site with rows 'running at an unusual angle of 43 degrees north-east to south-west', which gives 'a slightly more herbaceous Sauvignon Blanc'. The 2009 vintage (★★★☆) is fresh, mouthfilling, vibrant and moderately intense, with gooseberry and lime flavours showing good vigour and a crisp, green-edged finish.

Vintage	09	08	DRY $25 AV
WR	7	7	
Drink	09-10	P	

Saint Clair Pioneer Block 6 Oh! Block Sauvignon Blanc   ★★★★☆

Grown in fertile, silty soils in the lower Rapaura district of Marlborough's Wairau Valley, the 2009 vintage (★★★★) has lifted, freshly herbaceous aromas and vibrant flavours of melons, capsicums and limes, crisp and strong. If you like a 'full-on' style of Sauvignon Blanc, try this.

Vintage	09	08	07
WR	7	7	7
Drink	09-10	P	P

DRY $25 AV

Saint Clair Pioneer Block 7 Berry Block Sauvignon Blanc   ★★★☆

From Dillons Point, in the lower Wairau Valley, the 2008 vintage (★★★☆) is a scented, ripely herbaceous wine with a slightly nettley bouquet, good flavour depth and lively acidity.

DRY $25 –V

Saint Clair Pioneer Block 18 Snap Block Sauvignon Blanc   ★★★★

A classic lower Wairau Valley style, grown east of Blenheim, the 2009 vintage (★★★★☆) is mouthfilling, with rich, ripe tropical-fruit flavours, a herbal undercurrent, a hint of spice, and excellent concentration.

Vintage	09
WR	7
Drink	09-10

DRY $25 AV

Saint Clair Pioneer Block 19 Bird Block Sauvignon Blanc   (★★★★)

Grown north of Blenheim, in the lower Wairau Valley, the 2009 vintage (★★★★) is a generous, vibrantly fruity wine, with fresh, ripe passionfruit and lime flavours, punchy and smooth.

Vintage	09
WR	7
Drink	09-10

DRY $25 AV

Saint Clair Pioneer Block 20 Cash Block Sauvignon Blanc   (★★★★)

Grown close to the sea, at a relatively cool site east of Blenheim, the 2009 vintage (★★★★) is a 'full-on' style, with a blast of herbaceous aromas and penetrating gooseberry and green-capsicum flavours, crisp and long.

Vintage	09
WR	7
Drink	09-10

DRY $25 AV

Saint Clair Vicar's Choice Marlborough Sauvignon Blanc   ★★★★

Vicars, like many of us, will gladly worship a bargain – and this wine delivers the goods. The 2009 vintage (★★★☆) is smooth, with good depth of vibrant passionfruit/lime flavours, fresh, crisp and finely balanced for easy drinking.

Vintage	09	08	07
WR	7	6	6
Drink	09-10	P	P

DRY $19 V+

Saint Clair Wairau Reserve Sauvignon Blanc   ★★★★★

The 2001 and subsequent vintages have been exceptional, in a super-charged, deliciously ripe and concentrated style, lush and rounded, that has enjoyed glowing success on the show circuit, here and overseas. The vineyards vary from vintage to vintage, but all are at the cooler, lower end of the Wairau Valley. The wine is handled entirely in stainless steel tanks and drinks best in its first couple of years, while still fresh, zingy and exuberantly fruity. The 2008 vintage (★★★★★) has a punchy, slightly 'sweaty' bouquet. Mouthfilling, it is deliciously ripe and sweet-fruited, with fresh melon/lime flavours showing great delicacy and intensity, and a crisp, dry (3 grams/litre of residual sugar), lasting finish. The 2009 (★★★★★) is very weighty and sweet-fruited, with rich passionfruit and lime flavours, tight, crisp, dry and long.

Vintage	09	08	07
WR	7	7	7
Drink	09-10	P	P

DRY $33 AV

Sanctuary Marlborough Sauvignon Blanc   ★★★

Grove Mill's lower-tier label. The 2008 vintage (★★☆) is a fresh, medium-bodied wine with solid depth of melon, gooseberry and lime flavours, and a basically dry (4 grams/litre of residual sugar), crisp finish.

Vintage	09	08
WR	7	6
Drink	09-10	P

DRY $18 AV

Satellite Marlborough Sauvignon Blanc   (★★★)

From Spy Valley, the 2008 vintage (★★★) is fresh and lively, with punchy melon and green-capsicum flavours in a strongly herbaceous style, crisp and dry.

DRY $17 AV

Saveé Sea Marlborough Sauvignon Blanc   (★★★)

The 2008 vintage (★★★) is a ripely scented, full-bodied and fresh blend of Wairau Valley (70 per cent) and Awatere Valley grapes. It has tropical-fruit flavours, with a hint of lime and a crisp, lively finish. Good value.

DRY $13 V+

Sea Level Awatere Marlborough Sauvignon Blanc   (★★★★)

The 2009 vintage (★★★★) offers top value. Fresh, punchy and dry (3 grams/litre of residual sugar), it has racy melon and lime flavours, showing excellent vigour and depth.

DRY $17 V+

Secret Stone Marlborough Sauvignon Blanc   ★★★☆

From Matua Valley, the 2008 vintage (★★★★) has a real touch of class. Fresh, lifted, ripely herbaceous aromas lead into a crisp, lively wine with passionfruit, lime and green-capsicum flavours, showing excellent delicacy and depth.

DRY $18 V+

Seifried Nelson Sauvignon Blanc   ★★★★

Typically a good buy. The 2009 vintage (★★★★), mostly grown in the Cornfield Vineyard, adjacent to the winery, has slightly 'sweaty' aromas leading into a punchy wine with vibrant gooseberry and lime flavours, showing good fruit sweetness, and a fully dry, mouth-wateringly crisp finish.

Vintage	09
WR	6
Drink	09-11

DRY $19 V+

Seifried Winemakers Collection Nelson Sauvignon Blanc   ★★★★

The 2009 vintage (★★★★) is mouthfilling and punchy, with fresh, lively, ripely herbaceous gooseberry/lime flavours and a long, dry (1.7 grams/litre of residual sugar) finish.

Vintage	09	08
WR	6	7
Drink	09-11	09-10

DRY $23 AV

Selaks The Favourite Marlborough Sauvignon Blanc   ★★★★

The powerful, punchy 2008 vintage (★★★★) from Constellation NZ is a full-on style, grown in the Awatere Valley. It has fresh, 'tomato stalk' aromas, with excellent body and depth of strongly herbaceous flavours, crisp and lively.

DRY $21 V+

Sentinel Vineyard Marlborough Sauvignon Blanc   ★★★☆

A single-vineyard, Brancott Valley wine, the 2008 vintage (★★★☆) is medium-bodied, fresh, crisp, dry and lively, with good intensity of ripe gooseberry and lime flavours.

DRY $28 –V

Seresin Marama Sauvignon Blanc   ★★★★☆

This complex style of Sauvignon Blanc is hand-picked from the oldest vines in the estate vineyard at Renwick, in Marlborough, fermented with indigenous yeasts in French oak barriques (25 per cent new in 2007), and wood-matured for well over a year. The 2007 vintage (★★★★★) has a scented, ripely herbal, complex bouquet. Sturdy (14.5 per cent alcohol) and rich, it's a very powerful, sweet-fruited wine with highly concentrated stone-fruit flavours, slightly nutty, dry and long.

Vintage	07
WR	7
Drink	09-15

DRY $38 –V

Seresin Marlborough Sauvignon Blanc ★★★★★

One of the region's most sophisticated, subtle and satisfying Sauvignons. The grapes are grown in the original estate vineyard near Renwick, and in the company's two younger vineyards – Tatou, further inland, and Raupo Creek, on an elevated slope in the Omaka Valley. The wine (which includes 6 to 9 per cent Sémillon) is mostly fermented in tanks (40 per cent with indigenous yeasts in 2008), but 15 per cent of the blend is fermented and lees-aged in seasoned French oak casks. The 2008 vintage (★★★★☆) is weighty and complex, sweet-fruited and concentrated, with ripe, limey, slightly minerally flavours, showing good complexity and texture, fresh acidity and a dry finish (2 grams/litre of residual sugar). Full of personality, it's already delicious.

Vintage	08	07	DRY $25 V+
WR	6	7	
Drink	09-15	09-12	

Seresin Reserve Marlborough Sauvignon Blanc ★★★★★

Grown organically, the 2008 vintage (★★★★★) was hand-picked from 18-year-old vines in the Home Vineyard at Renwick, 'pruned to less than half their normal crop'. Fermented with indigenous yeasts in a 50/50 split of tanks and seasoned French oak barriques, it's a beauty – very ripely scented, with notable body, delicacy and depth. Fresh and vibrant, with passionfruit, pear and spice flavours, it is complex and finely textured, with great personality.

Vintage	08	07	DRY $50 AV
WR	6	7	
Drink	09-18	09-18	

Seven Terraces Marlborough Sauvignon Blanc ★★★☆

From Foxes Island, the 2008 vintage (★★★) was tank-fermented and lees-aged for three months. Mouthfilling, it has good depth of ripe grapefruit and lime flavours, fresh and vibrant, and a smooth finish.

DRY $22 AV

Shepherds Ridge Vineyard Marlborough Sauvignon Blanc ★★★☆

From Wither Hills, the 2009 vintage (★★★☆) is a fresh, medium to full-bodied wine with crisp, lively gooseberry and lime flavours, showing very good delicacy and depth.

Vintage	09	08	DRY $20 AV
WR	6	6	
Drink	09-11	09-10	

Shingle Peak Marlborough Sauvignon Blanc ★★★☆

From Matua Valley, the 2009 vintage (★★★☆) is punchy, with clearly herbaceous, gooseberry and lime flavours, fresh, vibrant and strong, and an appetisingly crisp, dry finish. As usual, it's a good buy.

DRY $16 V+

Shingle Peak Reserve Marlborough Sauvignon Blanc ★★★☆

The 2008 vintage (★★★☆) is mouthfilling and smooth, with ripe tropical-fruit flavours to the fore, some distinctly herbaceous notes, very good depth, and crisp acidity on the finish.

DRY $20 AV

Shipwreck Bay Sauvignon Blanc   (★★☆)

From Okahu Estate, the 2008 vintage (★★☆) is an easy-drinking Marlborough wine, medium-bodied, with gooseberry/lime flavours showing decent depth and a smooth finish.

DRY $18 –V

Sileni Benchmark Block Three Thirteen Rows Marlborough Sauvignon Blanc   (★★★☆)

The 2008 vintage (★★★☆) is a single-vineyard wine, grown on the floor of the Wairau Valley, in a band of shingly soil that gives early-ripening fruit. It's a medium to full-bodied, well-rounded wine with very good depth of ripe, gently herbaceous flavours, fresh acidity and a smooth finish.

DRY $25 –V

Sileni Benchmark Block Two Omaka Slopes Marlborough Sauvignon Blanc   (★★★★)

From two north-facing hillside vineyards, the 2008 vintage (★★★★) is a highly aromatic, fleshy wine with pure, ripe flavours of passionfruit, melon and capsicum, fresh acidity and a long, dry finish.

DRY $25 AV

Sileni Cellar Selection Marlborough Sauvignon Blanc   ★★★☆

The 2009 vintage (★★★★) is the best yet. Highly aromatic, it is a medium-bodied style with fresh tropical-fruit and herbaceous flavours, finely balanced and deliciously vibrant and punchy. Enjoyable from the start.

Vintage	09	08	07
WR	6	5	6
Drink	09-10	P	P

DRY $20 AV

Sileni The Cape Hawke's Bay Sauvignon Blanc   ★★★★

The 2009 vintage (★★★★) is mouthfilling, with strong tropical-fruit flavours, hints of pears and spices, lively acidity, and good freshness and length. It's a top example of the regional style, for drinking now to 2011.

DRY $25 AV

Sileni The Straits Marlborough Sauvignon Blanc   ★★★★☆

The 2009 vintage (★★★★☆) is very aromatic, crisp and punchy, with excellent weight and intensity of fresh gooseberry, lime and capsicum flavours.

Vintage	09	08	07
WR	7	5	6
Drink	09-11	09-10	P

DRY $25 AV

Sisters, The, Single Vineyard Marlborough Sauvignon Blanc   (★★★☆)

Grown in the Awatere Valley, the 2008 vintage (★★★☆) is mouthfilling, with a scented, ripely herbaceous bouquet, punchy flavours, balanced acidity and a lingering finish. Good value.

DRY $19 V+

Sliding Hill Marlborough Sauvignon Blanc   (★★★★)

From Kesbury Estate, the 2008 vintage (★★★★) is mouthfilling and dry, with ripe tropical-fruit flavours showing excellent freshness and depth. Tasted in late 2009, it's maturing well.

DRY $19 V+

Soho Marlborough Sauvignon Blanc   ★★★☆

From an Auckland-based company, the 2009 vintage (★★★★) is full of youthful vigour. Aromatic and punchy, it is fresh, full-flavoured and ripely herbaceous, with a crisp, minerally, dry finish.

DRY $22 AV

Soljans Marlborough Sauvignon Blanc   ★★☆

The 2008 vintage (★★☆) is a single-vineyard wine, medium-bodied, with moderate depth of gooseberry and lime flavours and a dry (2 grams/litre of residual sugar) finish.

DRY $20 –V

Southbank Estate Marlborough Sauvignon Blanc   ★★★☆

The 2008 vintage (★★☆), grown in the Wairau Valley, is fresh, crisp and limey, in a medium-bodied, clearly varietal style that lacks real richness.

Vintage	08	07
WR	6	7
Drink	P	09-10

DRY $20 AV

Southern Cross Marlborough Sauvignon Blanc   (★★★)

From One Tree Hill Vineyards, a division of Morton Estate, the 2008 vintage (★★★) is an aromatic, easy-drinking wine with good depth of fresh, lively tropical-fruit and herbaceous flavours and a rounded finish. Fine value.

DRY $13 V+

Spinyback Nelson Sauvignon Blanc   ★★★★

From Waimea Estates, this is a great buy. The 2008 (★★★☆) is mouthfilling, with very good depth of passionfruit/lime flavours and a hint of sweetness (6 grams/litre of residual sugar) balanced by fresh, crisp acidity. The 2009 vintage (★★★☆) is a crisp, medium-bodied wine with strong gooseberry, capsicum and lime flavours, fresh and tangy.

Vintage	09
WR	6
Drink	09-10

MED/DRY $15 V+

Springwood Marlborough Sauvignon Blanc   (★★☆)

The low-priced, easy-drinking 2008 vintage (★★☆) was made by Ager Sectus, owner of the Southbank, The Crossings and Crossroads brands. It's a tangy, medium-bodied wine with decent depth of gooseberry, melon and capsicum flavours, crisp and still fresh.

DRY $10 V+

Spy Valley Marlborough Sauvignon Blanc   ★★★★

Always a good buy. The 2008 vintage (★★★★) was harvested at 21 to 23.6 brix, tank-fermented (partly with indigenous yeasts) and lees-aged for several months. It's a mouthfilling, ripely scented wine with generous pineapple, melon and green-capsicum flavours and a crisp, fully dry finish.

Vintage	09	08	07	DRY $20 V+
WR	6	6	6	
Drink	10-11	09-10	P	

Squawking Magpie Reserve Marlborough Sauvignon Blanc   ★★★

The 2008 vintage (★★★) has ripe tropical-fruit flavours, fresh, finely balanced and smooth.

DRY $20 AV

Staete Landt Marlborough Sauvignon Blanc   ★★★★★

Ripely scented, rich and zingy, this single-vineyard wine is grown at Rapaura and mostly handled in tanks, with some fermentation and lees-aging in seasoned French oak casks (10 per cent in 2008). The 2008 vintage (★★★★☆) is a powerful wine, delicious now, with excellent depth of tropical, sweet-fruit flavours. Full-bodied and dry, with a faint suggestion of oak, it has impressive weight, texture and richness.

Vintage	08	07	06	05	DRY $23 V+
WR	7	6	6	6	
Drink	09-13	09-12	P	P	🍇

Stafford Lane Estate Nelson Sauvignon Blanc   ★★☆

Grown on the Waimea Plains, the 2009 vintage (★★☆) is light and crisp, with moderate depth of citrusy, limey, appley flavours, fresh and tangy. Priced right.

DRY $15 AV

Starborough Marlborough Sauvignon Blanc   ★★★★

The 2009 vintage (★★★★☆) is a classy young wine, based on Wairau Valley (60 per cent) and Awatere Valley (40 per cent) grapes and mostly handled in tanks; 3 per cent of the blend was barrel-fermented. Punchy and pure, with sweet-fruit delights, it has intense, vibrant gooseberry, melon and lime flavours that linger well.

DRY $21 V+

Stonecroft Sauvignon Blanc   ★★★☆

This Hawke's Bay winery uprooted its own Sauvignon Blanc vines after the 2001 vintage, but now sources grapes from Te Mata Estate's Woodthorpe Vineyard, in the Dartmoor Valley. The 2008 vintage (★★★☆) is full-bodied and lively, with good depth of fresh, ripe melon and lime flavours, and a dry, crisp finish.

DRY $20 AV

Stoneleigh Marlborough Sauvignon Blanc   ★★★★

From Pernod Ricard NZ, this consistently good wine flows from the stony and relatively warm Rapaura district of the Wairau Valley, which produces a ripe style of Sauvignon Blanc, yet retains good acidity and vigour. The 2008 vintage (★★★★) wasn't hard to find – over 300,000 cases were produced. It's a ripely scented and mouthfilling wine, with tropical-fruit flavours showing excellent depth and fresh, lively acidity. The 2009 (★★★★) is mouthfilling, with strong, pure flavours of passionfruit, melon and lime, showing excellent freshness, delicacy and depth.

Vintage	09	08	07	06
WR	7	6	6	6
Drink	09-10	P	P	P

DRY $23 AV

Stoneleigh Vineyards Rapaura Series Marlborough Sauvignon Blanc   ★★★★☆

This richly flavoured wine is grown in the warm, shingly soils of the Rapaura district and lees-aged for two months, with regular stirring. The 2008 (★★★★) is medium-bodied (12.5 per cent alcohol), with good intensity of ripely herbaceous flavours, fresh and tight. The 2009 vintage (★★★★☆) is more full-bodied, with a strong surge of fresh, ripe tropical-fruit flavours, pure, dry and lingering.

Vintage	09	08	07
WR	7	6	7
Drink	09-10	P	P

DRY $27 AV

Stone Paddock Hawke's Bay Sauvignon Blanc   ★★★

From Paritua Vineyards, the 2008 vintage (★★★) was mostly handled in tanks, but 10 per cent of the blend was fermented and matured for two months in seasoned French oak casks. It's a medium-bodied wine with ripe tropical-fruit flavours, fresh, crisp, slightly spicy and dry.

Vintage	08
WR	6
Drink	09-12

DRY $20 AV

Stonewall Marlborough Sauvignon Blanc   ★★☆

The 2009 vintage (★★☆) is a solid, no-fuss wine from Forrest, medium-bodied, with citrusy, appley, limey flavours, crisp and dry.

DRY $17 AV

Stop Banks Marlborough Sauvignon Blanc   (★★★★)

The 2008 vintage (★★★★) is worth buying, with a freshly herbaceous bouquet leading into a mouthfilling, punchy, intensely varietal wine with good intensity of gooseberry/lime flavours.

DRY $18 V+

Summerhouse Marlborough Sauvignon Blanc   ★★★★

This single-vineyard, Wairau Valley wine is consistently impressive. The 2009 vintage (★★★★☆) has an array of fresh, pure fruit flavours – passionfruit, melon, capsicum and lime. It's a very youthful, slightly minerally wine with good intensity and a lingering, finely balanced finish.

DRY $22 V+

Tasman Bay New Zealand Sauvignon Blanc   ★★★

The 2008 vintage (★★★) is a fresh, vibrantly fruity blend of Nelson and Marlborough fruit, oak-aged for three months. It's a ripely herbaceous style, clearly varietal, with plenty of flavour and a smooth, well-balanced finish.

DRY $19 AV

Te Awa Sauvignon Blanc   ★★★★

This is a rich, complex Hawke's Bay Sauvignon Blanc, grown in the Gimblett Gravels. The 2007 vintage (★★★★), 30 per cent barrel-fermented, is an elegant, tightly structured wine with ripe tropical-fruit flavours, a twist of oak, and a crisp, dry finish. It should mature well.

DRY $22 V+

Te Kairanga Martinborough Sauvignon Blanc   ★★★☆

The 2008 vintage (★★★☆) is a mouthfilling, fleshy wine with strong, ripe flavours that linger well. Entirely estate-grown, it is finely balanced, with good acidity and a dry finish.

Vintage	08	07
WR	6	6
Drink	09-12	09-11

DRY $21 AV

Te Mania Nelson Sauvignon Blanc   ★★★☆

The 2008 vintage (★★★☆) is ripely scented and fleshy, with good depth of tropical, sweet-fruit flavours, fresh acidity and a well-rounded finish.

Vintage	09	08	07
WR	6	5	6
Drink	09-11	P	P

DRY $19 V+

Te Mania Reserve Nelson Sauvignon Blanc   ★★★☆

Packed with flavour, the characterful 2008 vintage (★★★★) was tank-fermented, then matured in a 50/50 split of tanks and seasoned oak barrels. Clearly herbaceous, it is fleshy and rich, with strong gooseberry, herb, fig and spice flavours, a slightly nutty twist and considerable complexity.

Vintage	08	07
WR	6	6
Drink	09-12	09-11

DRY $25 –V

Te Mata Cape Crest Sauvignon Blanc   ★★★★★

This oak-aged Hawke's Bay label is impressive for its ripely herbal, complex, sustained flavours. Most of the grapes come from the company's relatively warm Bullnose Vineyard, inland from Hastings (the rest is grown at Woodthorpe, in the Dartmoor Valley), and the blend includes small proportions of Sémillon (to add longevity) and Sauvignon Gris (which contributes weight and mouthfeel). The wine is fully fermented and lees-aged for eight months in French oak barriques (30 per cent new). In a vertical tasting, the two to four-year-old wines look best – still fresh, but very harmonious. The 2008 vintage (★★★★★) is richly and ripely scented, with mouthfilling body, lovely sweet-fruit flavours of guava, grapefruit, passionfruit and lime, slightly mealy, biscuity notes adding complexity and a rich, rounded, dry finish. It's a highly concentrated wine, already delicious.

Vintage	08	07	06	05	04
WR	7	7	7	7	7
Drink	09-12	09-12	09-11	P	P

DRY $28 V+

Te Mata Estate Woodthorpe Vineyard Sauvignon Blanc   ★★★★

Estate-grown at an inland site in the Dartmoor Valley of Hawke's Bay, the 2009 vintage (★★★★☆) was handled entirely in tanks. Highly aromatic, it is weighty, with punchy, ripe tropical-fruit flavours, crisp and zesty, a slightly minerally streak and a long, dry finish. Notably fresh, vibrant and intense, it's already delicious. A top buy.

Vintage	09	08	07	06
WR	7	7	7	7
Drink	09-11	09-10	P	P

 DRY $19 V+

Terrain Marlborough Sauvignon Blanc   ★★★

Sold in supermarkets, the 2008 vintage (★★★) is a full-bodied style, fresh and lively, with good depth of tropical-fruit flavours, a herbal undercurrent and a crisp finish.

 DRY $14 V+

Terravin Marlborough Sauvignon Blanc   ★★★★☆

The 2008 vintage (★★★★☆) is a single-vineyard wine, mostly handled in tanks, but 7 per cent barrel-fermented. It is ripely scented and mouthfilling, with highly concentrated, very ripe flavours of tropical fruit, pears and spices, smooth and rich. Powerful and tightly structured, it should mature well.

DRY $23 V+

Te Whare Ra Marlborough Sauvignon Blanc   ★★★☆

Grown in the Awatere Valley, this single-vineyard wine is typically dry and fresh, with moderately intense melon/lime flavours, ripe and rounded.

DRY $22 AV

The Ned Marlborough Sauvignon Blanc — see Ned, The, Waihopai River Marlborough Sauvignon Blanc

Thornbury Marlborough Sauvignon Blanc   ★★★★☆

The 2009 vintage (★★★★☆) from Villa Maria, grown in the Awatere and Wairau valleys, is full-bodied, with deep, dry gooseberry and lime flavours. Aromatic and punchy, it shows excellent intensity, with a rounded, lingering finish.

Vintage	09	08
WR	7	6
Drink	09-11	09-10

DRY $21 V+

Three Stones Marlborough Sauvignon Blanc —
see 3 Stones Marlborough Sauvignon Blanc (at the start of this section)

Three Paddles Martinborough Sauvignon Blanc   ★★★★

A top buy. From Nga Waka, the 2009 vintage (★★★★) is crisp and dry, with vibrant melon, lime and passionfruit flavours showing excellent freshness, delicacy and depth. Fleshy and finely balanced, it's already delicious.

Vintage	09	08
WR	7	7
Drink	10+	09+

DRY $18 V+

Tiki Single Vineyard Marlborough Sauvignon Blanc   (★★★★)

Grown in the Wairau Valley, the 2009 vintage (★★★★) is a finely textured wine from McKean Estates, fresh and full-bodied, with excellent delicacy and depth of ripe gooseberry and lime flavours and a well-rounded finish.

DRY $25 AV

Timara Sauvignon Blanc   (★★★)

From Pernod Ricard NZ, the 2008 vintage (★★★) is not labelled by region, but was made from New Zealand grapes. Fresh, crisp, lively and smooth, with punchy, tropical-fruit flavours, it offers top value.

DRY $12 V+

Tinpot Hut Marlborough Sauvignon Blanc   ★★★★

A blend of Awatere Valley (two-thirds) and Wairau Valley grapes, the 2008 vintage (★★★★) is crisp and very punchy, with fresh melon, gooseberry and capsicum flavours, showing excellent vibrancy and length.

DRY $21 V+

Ti Point Marlborough Sauvignon Blanc   ★★★★

The fresh, refined 2008 vintage (★★★★) has ripe melon/lime flavours showing excellent delicacy and drinkability. It's a finely textured wine with a touch of class and a crisp, lingering finish.

DRY $21 V+

Tohu Marlborough Sauvignon Blanc   ★★★★☆

Tohu is a joint venture between three Maori land incorporations. This is a consistently excellent wine and the 2009 vintage (★★★★☆) offers outstanding value. A single-vineyard wine, grown in the Awatere Valley, it is weighty and sweet-fruited, with strong, ripe passionfruit-like flavours to the fore, some of the herbaceous, 'tomato stalk' notes typical of the valley, excellent concentration and a crisp, dry (3 grams/litre of residual sugar), racy finish.

DRY $19 V+

Tohu Mugwi Marlborough Sauvignon Blanc   ★★★★

Named after a Blenheim kaumatua, the 2008 vintage (★★★☆) has pungent aromatics, with a soft, rounded, clearly herbaceous palate, showing good but not great depth.

DRY $23 AV

Torea Marlborough Sauvignon Blanc   (★★★★)

From Fairhall Downs, the 2009 vintage (★★★★) is full-bodied and dry, with fresh, vibrant, ripely herbaceous flavours, finely balanced, crisp, pure and lingering. A top buy.

DRY $19 V+

Torlesse Waipara Sauvignon Blanc   ★★★☆

The 2008 vintage (★★★★), 10 per cent barrel-fermented, is a freshly scented, refined wine with good body, vibrant, ripe-fruit flavours with a hint of 'tomato stalk' and a well-rounded (5 grams/ litre of residual sugar) finish.

Vintage	08
WR	5
Drink	P

MED/DRY $17 V+

Torrent Bay Nelson Sauvignon Blanc   ★★★

From Anchorage Wines, the 2008 vintage (★★★) is a single-vineyard wine, medium-bodied, with a sliver of sweetness (4.5 grams/litre of residual sugar) amid its fresh, lively melon and green-capsicum flavours.

DRY $19 AV

Tranquil Valley Marlborough Sauvignon Blanc   ★★☆

From Huasheng Wines, based at Matakana, the 2008 vintage (★★☆) is a dry wine with moderate depth of melon and green-capsicum flavours, crisp and lively.

DRY $20 –V

Trinity Hill Hawke's Bay Sauvignon Blanc   ★★★☆

The 2008 vintage (★★★☆), grown in seven vineyards, coastal and inland, was harvested at 17.6 to 23.6 brix and tank-fermented to near dryness (4 grams/litre of residual sugar). A crisp, medium-bodied style with an array of fruit flavours, it is ripely scented and fleshy, with very good vigour, depth and harmony.

DRY $20 AV

Triplebank Awatere Valley Marlborough Sauvignon Blanc   ★★★★

From Pernod Ricard NZ, the 2008 vintage (★★★★) is ripely scented and fleshy, with strong, tropical-fruit flavours and a herbal undercurrent. Crisp and dry, it shows good intensity. The 2009 (★★★★) is mouthfilling, with vibrant, ripely herbaceous flavours, slightly nettley, minerally and dry.

Vintage	09	08	07
WR	7	6	6
Drink	09-10	P	P

DRY $24 AV

Tupari Marlborough Sauvignon Blanc   ★★★★☆

Grown in the upper Awatere Valley, the 2008 vintage (★★★★) is a single-vineyard wine. Made by Glenn Thomas, of Vavasour, who is a shareholder in Tupari, handled in tanks and lees-aged for five months, it's a fleshy, ripely scented and rounded wine with tropical-fruit flavours, showing a slightly creamy texture. It's delicious now.

DRY $26 AV

Turning Point New Style Sauvignon Blanc   (★★★)

From Spencer Hill, the 2008 vintage (★★★) is a blend of Marlborough and Nelson grapes, based mostly on Sauvignon Blanc, supplemented by five other 'aromatic' varieties, accounting for 15 per cent of the blend. The bouquet is clearly herbaceous, with fresh gooseberry and green-capsicum flavours, some peachy and spicy notes, a hint of toasty oak, and a crisp, dry finish.

DRY $16 V+

Tussock Nelson Sauvignon Blanc ★★☆

From Woollaston, the 2009 vintage (★★☆) is smooth (5.1 grams/litre of residual sugar), with limey, appley flavours, showing solid depth.

MED/DRY $17 AV

Twin Islands Marlborough Sauvignon Blanc ★★★

Negociants' wine is finely balanced for easy drinking. The 2008 vintage (★★★) is smooth, with ripe tropical-fruit flavours, fresh, vibrant and enjoyable from the start.

DRY $19 AV

Two Rivers of Marlborough Convergence Sauvignon Blanc ★★★★☆

The 2008 vintage (★★★★☆) is a skilfully crafted blend of equal parts of Awatere Valley and Wairau Valley grapes, 10 per cent barrel-fermented. It has a grassy bouquet, with mouthfilling body, some tropical-fruit influence, excellent delicacy and intensity, and a fresh, crisp, slightly minerally finish.

DRY $22 V+

Two Tails Marlborough Sauvignon Blanc (★★★☆)

From Fairbourne, the 2008 vintage (★★★☆) is a bone-dry wine, grown in the Wairau Valley. It's a medium-bodied style with good depth of tropical-fruit and herbaceous flavours, fresh and lively.

Vintage	08
WR	4
Drink	09-10

DRY $18 V+

Two Tracks Marlborough Sauvignon Blanc ★★★

From Wither Hills, the debut 2008 vintage (★★★) is mouthfilling and smooth, with crisp, lively melon/lime flavours, showing good vibrancy and immediacy.

DRY $17 AV

Tylers Stream East Coast Sauvignon Blanc (★★☆)

Tylers Stream is in the Wairau Valley, but the 2007 vintage (★★☆) from Pernod Ricard NZ is not labelled as being of Marlborough origin. It's a solid but slightly plain wine with tropical-fruit and herbaceous flavours, crisp and dry.

DRY $15 AV

Urlar Gladstone Sauvignon Blanc (★★★☆)

Fermented in tanks (90 per cent) and seasoned oak barrels (10 per cent), the 2008 vintage (★★★☆) is a briskly herbaceous wine with fresh, vibrant melon and green-capsicum flavours. It's highly aromatic, with cool-climate immediacy and appetising acidity.

DRY $22 AV

Vavasour Awatere Valley Sauvignon Blanc   ★★★★☆

A consistently classy wine. The 2008 vintage (★★★★☆) is aromatic, intense and tangy, with a hint of 'sweaty armpit'. Vibrant, with mouthfilling body and fresh, pure tropical-fruit and herbaceous flavours, it shows excellent depth, delicacy and length.

Vintage	09	08	07	06
WR	7	6	6	6
Drink	09-12	09-11	P	P

DRY $21 V+

Vidal Marlborough Sauvignon Blanc   ★★★★

The 2009 vintage (★★★★) is a mouthfilling wine with strong melon and green-capsicum flavours, fresh, ripe and smooth. Finely balanced, with appetising acidity and slight minerally touches, it shows excellent delicacy, purity and length.

Vintage	09	08	07
WR	7	6	7
Drink	09-11	09-10	P

DRY $20 V+

Villa Maria Cellar Selection Marlborough Sauvignon Blanc   ★★★★☆

An intensely flavoured wine, typically of a very high standard. Grown in the Wairau and Awatere valleys and tank-fermented, the 2009 vintage (★★★★☆) is freshly aromatic and zingy, with vibrant, ripe melon and lime flavours, showing excellent delicacy and concentration, and a long, dry (2 grams/litre of residual sugar) finish.

Vintage	09	08	07
WR	7	6	7
Drink	09-11	P	P

DRY $23 V+

Villa Maria Private Bin Marlborough Sauvignon Blanc   ★★★★

Villa Maria's large-volume label offers impressive quality and consistently good value. The 2009 vintage (★★★★) was tasted as a vivacious early release, identified on the back label by the words 'First bottling May 2009'. Scented, with punchy, ripe tropical-fruit flavours, a herbal undercurrent and fresh, appetising acidity, it is vibrant, zingy and delicious from the start.

Vintage	09	08	07
WR	7	6	7
Drink	09-11	09-10	P

DRY $20 V+

Villa Maria Reserve Clifford Bay Sauvignon Blanc   ★★★★★

Grown in the Awatere Valley (although the label refers only to 'Clifford Bay', into which the Awatere River empties), this is an exceptional Marlborough wine. Seddon Vineyards and the Taylors Pass Vineyard – both managed but not owned by Villa Maria – are the key sources of fruit. Handled entirely in stainless steel tanks and aged on its light yeast lees for two months, the wine typically exhibits the leap-out-of-the-glass fragrance and zingy, explosive flavour of Marlborough Sauvignon Blanc at its inimitable best. The 2009 vintage (★★★★★) is a classic sub-regional style, with intense, 'tomato stalk' aromas. Rich and vibrantly fruity, it has intense melon, lime and capsicum flavours, and a long, bone-dry, racy finish.

Vintage	09	08	07	06
WR	7	6	7	7
Drink	09-11	09-10	P	P

DRY $26 V+

Villa Maria Reserve Wairau Valley Sauvignon Blanc ★★★★★

An authoritative wine, it is typically ripe and zingy, with impressive weight and length of flavour, and tends to be fuller in body, less herbaceous and rounder than its Clifford Bay stablemate (above). The contributing vineyards vary from vintage to vintage, but Peter and Deborah Jackson's warm, stony vineyard in the heart of the valley has long been a key source of grapes, and sometimes a small part of the blend is barrel-fermented, to enhance its complexity and texture. The 2009 vintage (★★★★★) is highly scented, with slight 'armpit' aromas and fresh, finely poised passionfruit, melon and lime flavours that build across the palate to a long, dry finish. It's a sweet-fruited wine, very refined and vivacious.

Vintage	09	08	07
WR	7	7	7
Drink	09-11	09-10	P

DRY $26 V+

Villa Maria Single Vineyard Graham Marlborough Sauvignon Blanc ★★★★

Grown in the Awatere Valley, near the coast, the 2009 vintage was tasted prior to bottling, so is not rated. It looked highly promising, with nettley aromas and crisp, dry gooseberry and lime flavours, fresh, strong and zingy.

Vintage	09
WR	7
Drink	09-11

DRY $26 –V

Villa Maria Single Vineyard Southern Clays Marlborough Sauvignon Blanc (★★★★)

Grown in the foothills of the Wither Hills, on the south side of the Wairau Valley, this wine was formerly labelled 'Single Vineyard Maxwell'. The 2009 vintage, tasted prior to bottling, and so not rated, is a bone-dry wine with strong, ripe tropical-fruit flavours, threaded with mouth-watering acidity.

DRY $26 –V

Villa Maria Single Vineyard Taylors Pass Marlborough Sauvignon Blanc ★★★★★

Taylors Pass vineyard lies 100 metres above sea level in the Awatere Valley. The 2008 vintage (★★★★★) has fresh, inviting aromas and lovely intensity on the palate. It has delicate, green capsicum-like flavours, very elegant and lively, with tight acidity and impressive length. Tasted prior to bottling, and so not rated, the 2009 vintage is minerally, with intense melon/lime flavours, dry and zingy.

Vintage	09
WR	7
Drink	09-11

DRY $26 V+

W5 Marlborough Sauvignon Blanc (★★★)

Top value from Mt Olympus, the 2008 vintage (★★★) is light and lively, with ripe tropical-fruit and green-capsicum flavours and a crisp finish.

DRY $13 V+

Waimea Barrel Fermented Nelson Sauvignon Blanc   (★★★★)

The full-bodied 2008 vintage (★★★★) was grown on the Waimea Plains and fermented and matured for four months in seasoned oak barrels. It's a fleshy, ripely flavoured wine, nutty, dry, slightly creamy and rounded. Still fresh and youthful, it should be at its best during 2010.

Vintage	08
WR	6
Drink	09-13

DRY $22 V+

Waimea Bolitho SV Nelson Sauvignon Blanc   ★★★☆

'SV' means Signature Vineyard. Weighty, with ripe tropical-fruit flavours, some cut-grass notes and a dry, mouth-wateringly crisp finish, the 2008 vintage (★★★☆) is very fresh, lively and zingy.

DRY $22 AV

Waimea Nelson Sauvignon Blanc   ★★★★

A great buy. The 2009 vintage (★★★★), estate-grown on the Waimea Plains, is a medium-bodied wine (12.5 per cent alcohol), punchy and vibrant, with penetrating gooseberry, lime and passionfruit flavours, very fresh, lively, crisp and finely balanced (4.6 grams/litre of residual sugar).

Vintage	09
WR	6
Drink	09-12

DRY $18 V+

Waipara Hills Southern Cross Selection Waipara Sauvignon Blanc   (★★★☆)

The 2008 vintage (★★★☆) is fresh and vibrantly fruity, with ripely herbaceous flavours, showing very good depth and vigour.

DRY $30 –V

Waipara Springs Waipara Sauvignon Blanc   ★★★★

The 2008 vintage (★★★★) was estate-grown, from vines ranging up to 20 years old. Fresh, vibrant and punchy, it shows good intensity of ripe melon/lime flavours, crisp, dry (4 grams/litre of residual sugar) and lively.

Vintage	08	07
WR	6	6
Drink	P	P

DRY $19 V+

Waipara West Sauvignon Blanc   ★★★☆

The 2008 vintage (★★★☆) is a fresh, vibrant wine with strong, crisp, limey flavours, flinty, dry and lingering.

DRY $20 AV

Waipipi Wairarapa Sauvignon Blanc   ★★☆

The 2009 vintage (★★☆) is a solid, moderately varietal wine with fresh, crisp pear and lime flavours.

Vintage	09
WR	5
Drink	09-10

DRY $21 –V

Wairau River Home Block Marlborough Sauvignon Blanc   (★★★★)

Maturing gracefully, the 2007 vintage (★★★★) was mostly handled in tanks, but 10 per cent of the blend was matured in new oak casks. It's a dry, minerally, complex style, slightly funky, with strong, crisp flavours, showing a subtle wood influence. It's drinking well now.

Vintage	07
WR	6
Drink	09-11

`DRY $24 AV`

Wairau River Marlborough Sauvignon Blanc   ★★★☆

The 2009 vintage (★★★★) has a freshly aromatic, limey bouquet. Full-bodied, fresh and dry (4.3 grams/litre of residual sugar), it shows good intensity of melon and green-capsicum flavours, vibrant and zingy. A top year.

Vintage	09	08
WR	6	5
Drink	09-10	P

`DRY $20 AV`

Wairau River Reserve Marlborough Sauvignon Blanc   (★★★★)

The 2009 vintage (★★★★) is a single-vineyard wine, grown alongside the Opawa River and made in a slightly off-dry (5.6 grams/litre of residual sugar) style. It's a classy, weighty wine with strong, fresh tropical-fruit flavours, rich, ripe and rounded.

Vintage	09
WR	6
Drink	09-12

`MED/DRY $23 AV`

Walnut Block Collectables Marlborough Sauvignon Blanc   (★★☆)

The 2008 vintage (★★☆) is a mouthfilling, dry wine with restrained, citrusy, limey flavours.

`DRY $18 –V`

Walnut Block Marlborough Sauvignon Blanc   ★★★☆

The 2008 vintage (★★★☆) is a single-vineyard, Wairau Valley wine, mostly handled in tanks, but 15 per cent was fermented in old French oak casks. Fresh and smooth, it has ripe tropical-fruit flavours, showing good texture and depth.

`DRY $22 AV`

Weka River Waipara Valley Sauvignon Blanc   (★★★★)

From a single vineyard, 'approximately two rugby fields in size', the 2008 vintage (★★★★) is dry and minerally, with citrusy, limey flavours that linger well. A distinctive wine, it is tightly structured and should mature well.

`DRY $20 V+`

West Brook Blue Ridge Marlborough Sauvignon Blanc – see Blue Ridge Marlborough Sauvignon Blanc

West Brook Marlborough Sauvignon Blanc   ★★★★

The 2008 vintage (★★★★) is very fresh, vibrant and pure, with ripe tropical-fruit flavours, finely balanced (3 grams/litre of residual sugar) and long. The 2009 is fresh and crisp, with lively acidity and vibrant gooseberry, lime and herb flavours showing very good depth.

DRY $20 V+

Whalesback Marlborough Sauvignon Blanc   ★★★

From Koura Bay, the 2009 vintage (★★★) has good depth of tropical-fruit and herbaceous flavours, threaded with fresh, lively acidity.

Vintage	09	08
WR	6	6
Drink	10-11	09-10

DRY $16 V+

Whitecaps Marlborough Sauvignon Blanc   (★★☆)

From Whitehaven, the 2008 vintage (★★☆) doesn't set the world on fire – but it's a top buy at $10. Fresh and crisp, it has citrusy and appley flavours, only moderately varietal. A good, drink-young quaffer.

DRY $10 V+

Whitehaven Greg Marlborough Sauvignon Blanc   (★★★★★)

Dedicated to founder Greg White (1952–2007), the 2009 (★★★★★) is a single-vineyard wine, grown in the Awatere Valley. A shining example of the vintage, it offers very rich gooseberry, melon and lime flavours, showing excellent purity, delicacy and length.

Vintage	09
WR	7
Drink	09-11

DRY $25 V+

Whitehaven Marlborough Sauvignon Blanc   ★★★★★

Whitehaven adopts a low profile in New Zealand, but this consistently impressive wine is a big seller in the US, where it is distributed by one of its shareholders, global wine giant E & J Gallo. The grapes are grown at dozens of sites in the Wairau and Awatere valleys, and the wine is handled entirely in tanks. At its best within two years, it offers beautifully fresh, deep and delicate flavours of passionfruit and limes, pure and smooth. The 2008 vintage (★★★★) is a tropical-fruit style, ripe, dry and flavoursome, with fresh, lifted aromas and good balance and freshness.

Vintage	09
WR	7
Drink	09-11

DRY $20 V+

Wild Rock Elevation Marlborough Sauvignon Blanc   (★★★☆)

The mouthfilling and smooth 2008 vintage (★★★☆) was grown in the Wairau Valley and blended with 5 per cent Viognier and 4 per cent Riesling. Dry and lively, it has ripely herbaceous flavours, slightly peachy and spicy, and a fresh, crisp finish.

Vintage	09	08
WR	6	6
Drink	09-11	09-10

DRY $19 V+

Wild Rock Marlborough Sauvignon Blanc   (★★★☆)

Sold only in supermarkets, the 2008 vintage (★★★☆) is aromatic, with fresh, vibrant tropical-fruit and capsicum flavours, crisp and strong.

DRY $19 V+

Wild Rock The Infamous Goose Marlborough Sauvignon Blanc   ★★★

From Wild Rock, a division of Craggy Range, the 2008 vintage (★★★) is fresh, crisp and dry, with ripe melon and capsicum flavours, showing good depth.

Vintage	09	08
WR	6	7
Drink	09-11	09-10

DRY $19 −V

Wild South Marlborough Sauvignon Blanc   ★★★☆

From Sacred Hill, the 2008 vintage (★★★) was mostly estate-grown in the Waihopai Valley. It is fresh and smooth, with good but not great depth of lively, ripely herbaceous flavours and tangy acidity enlivening the finish.

DRY $19 V+

William Thomas Marlborough Sauvignon Blanc   ★★★★

(Now a brand owned by Fromm.) The 2008 vintage (★★★★) was grown at the base of the Brancott Valley and a small portion was matured in old barrels. It's a crisp, medium-bodied wine, dry, with sweet-fruit characters and very good depth of fresh, ripe melon/lime flavours, tight and youthful.

Vintage	09	08	07
WR	6	6	6
Drink	09-13	09-12	09-11

DRY $20 V+

Wingspan Nelson Sauvignon Blanc   (★★★☆)

From Woollaston, the 2008 vintage (★★★☆) is fresh and vibrant, with strong melon and lime flavours, balanced for easy drinking (5 grams/litre of residual sugar). Fine value.

MED/DRY $17 V+

Wither Hills Single Vineyard Rarangi Sauvignon Blanc   ★★★★★

Grown at Rarangi, on the Wairau Valley coast, the 2008 vintage (★★★★★) is a striking wine. Fleshy and very punchy, it is weighty, with highly concentrated gooseberry/lime flavours woven with crisp, minerally acidity, and a deliciously long finish. The 2007 (★★★★★) is equally memorable.

Vintage	09	08	07
WR	7	7	7
Drink	10-13	09-10	P

DRY $25 V+

Wither Hills Wairau Valley Marlborough Sauvignon Blanc   ★★★☆

This huge-selling wine is sourced mostly (80 per cent) from company-owned vineyards, planted since 1993 in the Wairau Valley. Oak plays no part in the recipe: 'The vines are old enough to offer weight, texture and length,' says winemaker Ben Glover, who matures part of the final blend on yeast lees, to add palate weight, but avoids lees-stirring. The 2009 vintage (★★★★) is sweet-fruited, with strong, fresh, tropical-fruit and gently herbaceous flavours. It's an instantly appealing, finely balanced wine, vibrant, crisp and lingering.

Vintage	09	08
WR	5	6
Drink	09-11	P

DRY $20 AV

Woodman's Bend Classic Marlborough Sauvignon Blanc   (★★★)

Sold in supermarkets in mid to late 2009, the 2008 vintage (★★★) is a brilliant buy. Crisp, lively and freshly herbaceous, it's a medium-bodied style with plenty of gooseberryish, limey flavour, enjoyable now. It's a surprisingly good wine for $5.99.

DRY $6 V+

Woollaston Nelson Sauvignon Blanc   ★★★

The 2008 vintage (★★★) was grown on the Waimea Plains. It's a mouthfilling wine with melon/capsicum flavours and a dryish (5 grams/litre of residual sugar), crisp finish. The 2009 (★★★) is medium-bodied (12.5 per cent alcohol), with tropical-fruit and gentle herbaceous flavours, finely balanced and crisp.

MED/DRY $18 AV

Yealands Estate Marlborough Sauvignon Blanc   ★★★★

Estate-grown at Seaview, in the lower Awatere Valley, the 2008 vintage (★★★★) is an auspicious debut. It's a punchy, intensely varietal wine with 'tomato stalk' aromas and good intensity of melon and green-capsicum flavours, very fresh and racy. The 2009 (★★★★☆) is even better, with a pungent, aromatic bouquet, incisive gooseberry/lime flavours, very crisp, vibrant and punchy, and a long, dry finish.

DRY $24 AV

Yealands Marlborough Sauvignon Blanc   (★★★☆)

The debut 2008 vintage (★★★☆) of this regional blend has a punchy, herbaceous bouquet and fresh, vibrant, green-capsicum and lime flavours, showing good depth.

DRY $19 V+

Sémillon

You'd never guess it from the tiny selection of labels on the shelves, but Sémillon is New Zealand's sixth most widely planted white-wine variety – ahead of Viognier. The few winemakers who 20 years ago played around with Sémillon could hardly give it away, so aggressively stemmy and spiky was its flavour. Now, there is a new breed of riper, richer, rounder Sémillons emerging – and they are 10 times more enjoyable to drink.

The Sémillon variety is beset by a similar problem to Chenin Blanc. Despite being the foundation of outstanding white wines in Bordeaux and Australia, Sémillon is out of fashion in the rest of the world, and in New Zealand its potential is still largely untapped. The area of bearing Sémillon vines has contracted markedly between 2007 and 2010, from 230 to 181 hectares.

Sémillon is highly prized in Bordeaux, where as one of the two key varieties both in dry wines, most notably white Graves, and the inimitable sweet Sauternes, its high levels of alcohol and extract are perfect foils for Sauvignon Blanc's verdant aroma and tartness. With its propensity to rot 'nobly', Sémillon forms about 80 per cent of a classic Sauternes.

Cooler climates like those of New Zealand's South Island, however, bring out a grassy-green character in Sémillon which, coupled with its higher acidity in these regions, can give the variety strikingly Sauvignon-like characteristics.

Grown principally in Marlborough (43 per cent of the country's plantings), Gisborne (32 per cent) and Hawke's Bay (22 per cent), Sémillon is mostly used in New Zealand not as a varietal wine but as a minor (and anonymous) partner in wines labelled Sauvignon Blanc, contributing complexity and aging potential. By curbing the variety's natural tendency to grow vigorously and crop bountifully, winemakers are now overcoming the aggressive cut-grass characters that in the past plagued the majority of New Zealand's unblended Sémillons. The spread of clones capable of giving riper fruit characters (notably BVRC-14 from the Barossa Valley) has also contributed to quality advances. However, very few wineries in New Zealand are exploring Sémillon's potential to produce complex, long-lived dry whites.

Askerne Hawke's Bay Sémillon   ★★☆

Estate-grown near Havelock North, the 2009 vintage (★★☆) was matured in tanks (67 per cent) and old oak casks (33 per cent). It has tropical-fruit and slight nut flavours, crisp and fully dry, but lacks real charm.

Vintage	09
WR	6
Drink	09-12

DRY $16 AV

Clearview Hawke's Bay Sémillon   ★★★★

Tightly structured, very fresh and lively, the 2008 vintage (★★★★) was hand-harvested at Te Awanga and fermented in new American and one-year-old French oak barriques. Youthful, with strong tropical-fruit flavours, a slight herbal undercurrent, oak-derived richness and complexity, and a crisp, lingering finish, it's well worth cellaring.

Vintage	08
WR	6
Drink	09-18

DRY $25 AV

Kaimira Estate Brightwater Sémillon   ★★★☆

Grown in Nelson, the 2008 vintage (★★★☆) is a mouthfilling, virtually dry wine (4.6 grams/litre of residual sugar), with very good depth of ripe melon, lime and faintly nutty flavours, fresh and smooth. Worth cellaring.

Vintage	08	07
WR	6	5
Drink	09-15	09-12

DRY $20 AV

Verdelho

Verdelho, a Portuguese variety traditionally grown on the island of Madeira, preserves its acidity well in hot regions, yielding enjoyably full-bodied, lively, lemony table wines in Australia. It is still extremely rare in New Zealand, with only 2 hectares of bearing Verdelho vines in 2010, mostly in Hawke's Bay.

Esk Valley Hawke's Bay Verdelho   ★★★★

Hand-picked and 50 per cent barrel-fermented with indigenous yeasts, the 2009 vintage (★★★★) is a full-bodied wine with excellent freshness and depth of ripe pear, spice and apricot flavours, dryish (6 grams/litre of residual sugar), crisp and finely balanced. It should open out well from mid-2010+.

Vintage	09	08	07
WR	7	7	7
Drink	09-11	09-10	09-10

MED/DRY $23 AV

Villa Maria Single Vineyard Ihumatao Vineyard Auckland Verdelho   (★★★★☆)

The debut 2008 vintage (★★★★☆) is classy. Estate-grown at Mangere, in South Auckland, it was partly (55 per cent) fermented with indigenous yeasts in two-year-old French oak barriques; the rest was handled in tanks. Sturdy (14.5 per cent alcohol), it has excellent delicacy and depth of tropical-fruit flavours, a subtle seasoning of oak, balanced acidity and a dry, finely poised, long finish.

Vintage	08
WR	7
Drink	09-12

DRY $26 AV

Viognier

Viognier is a classic grape of the Rhône Valley, in France, where it is renowned for its exotically perfumed, substantial, peach and apricot-flavoured dry whites. A delicious alternative to Chardonnay, Viognier (pronounced *Vee-yon-yay*) is an internationally modish variety, popping up with increasing frequency in shops and restaurants here.

Viognier accounts for only 0.5 per cent of the national vineyard, but the area of bearing vines is expanding steadily, from 15 hectares in 2002 to 174 hectares in 2010. Almost 80 per cent of the vines are clustered in Gisborne and Hawke's Bay.

As in the Rhône, Viognier's flowering and fruit set have been highly variable here. The deeply coloured grapes go through bud-burst, flowering and *veraison* (the start of the final stage of ripening) slightly behind Chardonnay and are harvested about the same time as Pinot Noir.

The wine is often fermented in seasoned oak barrels, yielding scented, substantial, richly alcoholic wines with gentle acidity and subtle flavours. If you enjoy mouthfilling, softly textured, dry or dryish white wines, but feel like a change from Chardonnay and Pinot Gris, try Viognier. You won't be disappointed.

Alpha Domus Hawke's Bay Viognier ★★★★

Floral and creamy-textured, the 2007 vintage (★★★★) was fermented in tanks (65 per cent) and barrels (35 per cent). Mouthfilling, it has ripe, peachy, slightly toasty flavours, showing barrel-ferment complexity and very good depth, and an off-dry finish (6 grams/litre of residual sugar), giving wide appeal.

Vintage	08	07	06
WR	7	5	6
Drink	09-13	09-10	P

MED/DRY $27 AV

Anchorage Nelson Viognier (★★☆)

The 2008 vintage (★★☆), from first-crop vines, is fresh, citrusy and appley, with a very crisp, dry finish.

DRY $19 –V

Ascension The Apogee Matakana Viognier ★★★☆

The 2008 vintage (★★★) was hand-picked at 24 brix and mostly tank-fermented; 20 per cent of the blend was fermented in seasoned French oak barriques. It's a fleshy wine, peachy and slightly toasty, with a tight, dry finish. Worth cellaring.

MED/DRY $30 –V

Babich Hawke's Bay Viognier ★★★

The 2007 vintage (★★★) was fermented and lees-aged in a mix of tanks (70 per cent) and old French oak casks. It's a full-bodied wine with attractive, citrusy, slightly appley flavours and a crisp, dry finish. The 2008 (★★★) is an enjoyable, drink-young style – mouthfilling, fruity, lemony, slightly spicy and crisp.

DRY $20 AV

Bilancia Hawke's Bay Viognier   ★★★★☆

The 2007 vintage (★★★★) was grown at the base of the *la collina* vineyard at Roy's Hill, in the Gimblett Gravels, hand-picked and fermented in a 50/50 split of tanks and seasoned oak barrels. Less lush in its youth than the striking 2006 (★★★★★), it is full-bodied (14 per cent alcohol), with vibrant melon, citrus-fruit and spice flavours, showing excellent delicacy and depth. A youthful, fully dry wine, it's a cellaring style.

Vintage	07	06	05	04
WR	6	7	7	6
Drink	09-11	09-10	P	P

DRY $34 AV

Brookfields Milestone Viognier   ★★★★

Grown in Hawke's Bay and fermented in tanks and barrels, the 2009 vintage (★★★★) is weighty (14.5 per cent alcohol) and rounded, with peachy, slightly spicy flavours, dry and creamy-textured. Fleshy and forward, with considerable complexity, it's a good buy.

DRY $22 V+

Bushmere Estate Gisborne Viognier   (★★★★)

Already highly enjoyable, the 2008 vintage (★★★★) was hand-picked at over 25 brix and the fermentation was finished in seasoned French oak barriques. Fleshy and vibrantly fruity, it's a mouthfilling wine (14.5 per cent alcohol), with rich stone-fruit flavours, a slightly oily texture and a smooth, dryish finish.

MED/DRY $23 V+

Butterfish Bay Northland Viognier   (★★★★)

Grown in the Far North on Paewhenua Island – a small peninsula reaching into Mangonui Harbour – the 2009 vintage (★★★★) is an impressive debut. Robust (14.5 per cent alcohol), it is very fresh and vibrant, with a deliciously soft, slightly oily texture, ripe citrus-fruit, pear and spice flavours, and a rounded, fully dry finish.

Vintage	09
WR	6
Drink	09-11

DRY $28 AV

Church Road Reserve Hawke's Bay Viognier   ★★★★☆

Delicious now, the 2007 vintage (★★★★☆) was hand-harvested in Pernod Ricard NZ's Redstone Vineyard and fermented in seasoned French oak barriques. Weighty (with a noticeably high alcohol level of 14.5 per cent), it is intensely varietal, with peach, grapefruit and apricot flavours, creamy-textured and rich.

Vintage	07	06
WR	6	6
Drink	P	P

DRY $36 –V

Clos de Ste Anne Viognier Les Arbres   ★★★★★

An organic Gisborne wine of arresting richness and complexity. The 2007 vintage (★★★★★) from Millton was hill-grown, hand-picked and fermented with indigenous yeasts in large, 600-litre barrels. Weighty and complex, with a hint of honey and a slightly oily texture, it has deep, beautifully ripe flavours of stone-fruit and spice and a subtle seasoning of oak. An authoritative wine, it's still unfolding.

Vintage	07	06	05
WR	7	6	7
Drink	09-12	09-10	09-10

DRY $54 AV

Coopers Creek Gisborne Viognier   ★★★☆

The easy-drinking 2008 vintage (★★★) is mouthfilling, with decent depth of fresh peach, pear and spice flavours and a rounded finish.

Vintage	08	07	06
WR	5	6	6
Drink	09-10	P	P

DRY $20 AV

Coopers Creek SV Chalk Ridge Hawke's Bay Viognier   ★★★☆

Grown on a steep, north-facing slope and fermented and French oak-fermented, the 2008 vintage (★★★) is a soft, creamy-textured wine with citrus, peach and spice flavours, a touch of toasty oak, and substantial body (14.5 per cent alcohol). A drink-young style.

Vintage	08	07
WR	6	5
Drink	09-10	09-10

DRY $24 AV

Craggy Range Gimblett Gravels Vineyard Viognier   ★★★★☆

The 2008 vintage (★★★★★) is an authoritative Hawke's Bay wine, weighty and lush. Finely scented, with fresh, rich flavours of peaches and apricots, very pure and soft, enriched by a subtle seasoning of French oak, it is powerful but finely balanced, allowing Viognier's delicate, floral notes to shine through.

Vintage	08
WR	6
Drink	09-12

DRY $38 –V

Cypress Terraces Viognier   ★★★★

From a steep, terraced site at Roy's Hill, in Hawke's Bay, the 2008 vintage (★★★★) is a powerful (14.5 per cent alcohol) dry wine, barrel-fermented. It's creamy-textured with a subtle oak influence, concentrated, ripe, peachy, slightly spicy flavours, an oily texture and a rich, rounded finish.

Vintage	08	07
WR	6	5
Drink	09-12	09-11

DRY $29 AV

Dry River Estate Martinborough Viognier   ★★★★☆

Estate-grown and not oak-aged, the 2009 vintage (★★★★☆) is a fully dry style, sturdy (14 per cent alcohol) and still very youthful, with substantial body (14 per cent alcohol), gentle acidity and rich, vibrant stone-fruit and spice flavours. It shows excellent texture, delicacy and richness; open mid-2010+.

Vintage	09	08
WR	7	7
Drink	10-14	09-13

DRY $42 –V

Edge, The, Gisborne Viognier   (★★★)

From Escarpment, the 2008 vintage (★★★) is a softly mouthfilling wine with good body and
depth of peach, pear and apple flavours and a rounded, dry finish.

DRY $22 –V

Elephant Hill Hawke's Bay Viognier   ★★★☆

Grown at Te Awanga and made without oak, the 2008 (★★★) is a vibrantly fruity wine with
citrusy, appley, limey flavours, fresh and aromatic. The 2009 vintage (★★★☆) is fleshy and
rounded, with stone-fruit and spice flavours, gentle acidity, and good texture and depth.

DRY $28 –V

Gladstone Wairarapa Viognier   ★★★☆

The 2008 vintage (★★★☆), grown in the Home Block, was hand-picked at 23 brix and
fermented in tanks and old French oak barrels. It's a fully dry wine, mouthfilling, with peach,
lychee and spice flavours, a hint of oak and a slightly creamy texture. Best drinking 2010+.

DRY $28 –V

Glazebrook Regional Reserve Hawke's Bay Viognier   (★★★★)

From the Ngatarawa winery, the 2008 vintage (★★★☆) was grown in The Triangle and Moteo
districts. Mouthfilling, with complexity from full barrel fermentation (French, one-third new),
it has moderately concentrated stone-fruit and spice flavours, with a creamy texture, and a
rounded, dry finish.

Vintage	08
WR	6
Drink	09-11

DRY $27 AV

Hans Herzog Marlborough Viognier   ★★★★★

This dry wine is a cellaring style. The 2008 vintage (★★★★) was hand-picked, fermented with
indigenous yeasts and lees-aged for a year in French oak puncheons. It's a fleshy wine with some
'funky' notes on the nose and a fleshy, rich palate, sweet-fruited, dry and rounded. It needs time;
open mid-2010+.

Vintage	08
WR	7
Drink	09-14

DRY $45 AV

Huntaway Reserve Gisborne Viognier   ★★★

The 2007 vintage (★★★★) from Pernod Ricard NZ was handled in a mix of tanks and old
barrels. It's an elegant wine, maturing well, with fresh, vibrant pear, lychee and spice flavours, a
subtle oak influence and a rounded finish. Good now.

Vintage	07	06	05
WR	7	6	5
Drink	09-10	P	P

DRY $24 –V

Karikari Estate Viognier/Chardonnay   (★★★)

The flavoursome 2007 vintage (★★★) is a Northland blend of Viognier (68 per cent) and Chardonnay (32 per cent), handled entirely in tanks. It's a ripe, fruity wine with lees-aging notes adding a touch of complexity and a rounded, dryish finish (7 grams/litre of residual sugar).

MED/DRY $34 –V

Kim Crawford SP Moteo Vineyard Hawke's Bay Viognier   (★★★★)

Attractively scented, the 2008 vintage (★★★★) is full-bodied, with rich, dry flavours of peaches and melons. French oak-aged, it's a vibrant, fruit-driven style with good immediacy, drinking well in its youth.

DRY $33 –V

Longbush Viognier   (★★★)

The 2007 (★★★) 'bird series' wine was French oak-aged for 10 months. Fleshy, with peachy, slightly spicy and buttery flavours and a dry, rounded finish, it's maturing solidly.

Vintage	07
WR	6
Drink	09-12

DRY $18 AV

Matua Valley Innovator Hawke's Bay Viognier   (★★★)

The 2007 vintage (★★★) was mostly handled in tanks, but 20 per cent of the blend was fermented and matured for six months in old French oak casks. It's a fully dry style with mouthfilling body and lemon, pear, apple and spice flavours, showing some complexity, but lacks real richness and roundness.

DRY $25 –V

Mills Reef Hawke's Bay Viognier   (★★★)

The bargain-priced 2007 vintage (★★★) is a single-vineyard Hawke's Bay wine, grown at Meeanee and fermented and matured for two months in seasoned French oak barrels. Full-bodied and smooth, it's a slightly Chardonnay-like wine with plenty of peachy, creamy flavour.

MED/DRY $17 V+

Millton Clos de Ste Anne Viognier Les Arbres — see Clos de Ste Anne Viognier Les Arbres

Millton Riverpoint Vineyard Gisborne Viognier   ★★★★

Drinking well now, the organically grown, gently oaked 2008 vintage (★★★☆) is floral and fruity, with mouthfilling body and very good depth of smooth, peachy flavours, slightly sweet, spicy and honeyed.

Vintage	08	07
WR	6	7
Drink	09-10	09-10

MED/DRY $28 AV

Mission Reserve Hawke's Bay Viognier   ★★★☆

The 2008 vintage (★★★☆) is a single-vineyard wine, fermented and matured in French oak casks (10 per cent new). Medium-bodied, with peachy, faintly buttery and toasty flavours and a dry, finely balanced finish, it is floral, with a hint of apricots.

DRY $23 AV

Moana Park Vineyard Tribute Viognier   (★★★☆)

Grown in the Gimblett Gravels of Hawke's Bay and partly barrel-fermented, the 2008 vintage (★★★☆) is peachy, slightly creamy and toasty, with vibrant fruit characters, a touch of complexity, and very good depth.

Vintage 08
WR   5
Drink   09-11

DRY $20 AV

Morton Estate White Label Hawke's Bay Viognier   ★★★☆

The 2009 vintage (★★★☆) is a full-bodied (14 per cent alcohol), fruity wine with ripe stone-fruit and spice flavours, showing good depth, and a soft, well-rounded finish. It's already drinking well.

Vintage 09
WR   7
Drink   09-12

DRY $19 V+

Morton Estate White Label Private Reserve Hawke's Bay Viognier   (★★★★)

Weighty and fleshy, the 2007 vintage (★★★★) has peachy, spicy, faintly honeyed flavours showing good intensity. It's a slightly creamy and leesy wine, with some complexity and a dry, well-rounded finish.

Vintage 07
WR   7
Drink   09-10

DRY $23 V+

Obsidian Waiheke Island Viognier   ★★★★

The 2008 vintage (★★★★) was mostly handled in tanks, but 40 per cent was fermented and lees-aged for six months in old French oak casks. It's a very youthful wine with generous, ripe stone-fruit flavours, gently seasoned with toasty oak. Fleshy, with good complexity and a rounded finish, it's still unfolding; drink mid-2010+.

Vintage 08   07
WR   7   6
Drink   09-11 09-10

DRY $33 –V

Passage Rock Viognier   ★★★★

Grown on Waiheke Island, the barrel-fermented 2008 vintage (★★★★) is powerful, rich and oily, with concentrated stone-fruit flavours, fresh, ripe and slightly creamy. Still youthful, it's developing well.

DRY $30 AV

Riverside Stirling Reserve Viognier   (★★★★)

The stylish 2007 vintage (★★★★) was hand-picked in the Dartmoor Valley, Hawke's Bay, and fermented and matured for a year in French oak barriques (new and one-year-old). It's a rich, sweet-fruited wine, fully dry, with vibrant stone-fruit and slight spice flavours, hints of pears and lychees, a subtle oak influence, and impressive depth.

DRY $25 AV

Saint Clair East Coast Viognier   (★★★)

Floral and scented, the 2007 vintage (★★★) is a blend of Gisborne (mostly) and Marlborough grapes. Crisp and slightly oily, it is ripe, peachy and spicy, in a clearly varietal style with good body and a dry finish.

Vintage	07
WR	6
Drink	09-10

DRY $20 AV

Salvare Hawke's Bay Viognier   (★★★)

The 2008 (★★★) is vibrant and mouthfilling, with dry, citrusy, slightly spicy flavours.

DRY $25 –V

Selaks The Favourite Gisborne Viognier   (★★★★)

Grown at Hexton and made in a fully dry style, the 2007 vintage (★★★★) from Constellation NZ has vibrant peach/melon flavours, showing excellent purity, delicacy and softness.

DRY $21 V+

Staete Landt Marlborough Viognier   ★★★★

Estate-grown at Rapaura, the 2008 vintage (★★★★) was hand-harvested at 25.6 brix, fermented in seasoned French oak puncheons, and then lees-aged for nine months in tanks, prior to bottling. It's a full-bodied, dryish wine (6.3 grams/litre of residual sugar), sweet-fruited and finely textured, with good weight and concentrated, peachy, slightly spicy and buttery flavours. Drink now onwards.

Vintage	08	07
WR	6	5
Drink	09-13	09-12

MED/DRY $45 –V

Stone Bridge Viognier   (★★★☆)

The 2007 vintage (★★★☆) was grown in Gisborne, harvested at 25.8 brix and fermented in three-year-old French oak casks. Developing well, it's a robust wine (14.8 per cent alcohol), with strong, ripe, peachy flavours and nutty, creamy notes.

DRY $22 AV

Te Mata Zara Viognier   ★★★★☆

Until recently labelled as 'Te Mata Woodthorpe Viognier', this estate-grown wine is from the Woodthorpe Terraces vineyard, on the south side of the Dartmoor Valley in Hawke's Bay. Hand-harvested, it is mostly (70 per cent in 2008) fermented and lees-aged for eight months in seasoned French oak barriques. The 2008 vintage (★★★★☆) is mouthfilling, fresh and sweet-fruited, with strong, vibrant peach, pear and slight apricot flavours, mealy, biscuity notes adding complexity, a slightly oily texture and a finely balanced, bone-dry finish.

Vintage	08	07	06	05	04
WR	7	7	7	7	7
Drink	09-12	09-12	09-11	P	P

DRY $28 V+

Trinity Hill Gimblett Gravels Hawke's Bay Viognier   ★★★★★

An emerging star. Peachy, slightly nutty and full-flavoured, the 2008 vintage (★★★★) was hand-picked and fermented in a mix of tanks and seasoned French oak barrels. It's a complex, fully dry wine with an oily texture and impressive harmony.

Vintage	08	07	06
WR	5	6	6
Drink	09-12	09-12	09-11

DRY $30 V+

Trinity Hill Hawke's Bay Viognier   (★★★)

Hand-picked in the Gimblett Gravels and partly barrel-fermented, the 2007 vintage (★★★) is full-bodied (14.5 per cent alcohol), with a floral bouquet and decent depth of citrusy, peachy flavours, dry (4 grams/litre of residual sugar), still fresh and lively.

DRY $19 AV

TW Estate Gisborne Viognier   ★★★☆

Past vintages have been attractive and sometimes – notably in 2007 (★★★★★) – outstanding. However, the 2008 vintage (★) is disappointing. Hand-picked and barrel-fermented, it is peachy and soft, but lacks freshness and vibrancy.

DRY $25 –V

Vidal East Coast Viognier   ★★★★

A good, well-priced introduction to Viognier. The 2009 vintage (★★★☆) is a blend of Gisborne (59 per cent), Hawke's Bay and Marlborough grapes, partly handled in tanks, but 60 per cent of the blend was fermented and lees-aged for four months in seasoned French oak barriques. A bone-dry style, it's full-bodied (14.5 per cent alcohol), with gentle acidity, a touch of complexity and good depth of pear and spice flavours, fresh and well-rounded.

Vintage	09	08	07
WR	6	7	7
Drink	09-11	09-10	P

DRY $20 V+

Vidal Reserve Hawke's Bay Viognier   (★★★★☆)

Grown mostly in the Gimblett Gravels (84 per cent), supplemented by fruit from the Tukituki Valley, the 2007 vintage (★★★★☆) was fermented and lees-aged for six months in seasoned French oak barriques. Maturing well, it's a sturdy, fully dry wine with rich stone-fruit and spice flavours, slightly nutty, complex and rounded.

Vintage	08	07
WR	NM	6
Drink	NM	09-11

DRY $30 AV

Villa Maria Cellar Selection Hawke's Bay Viognier   ★★★★☆

The 2009 vintage (★★★★) was hand-picked, fermented (15 per cent with indigenous yeasts) in French oak barriques (23 per cent new), and oak-aged for four months. It's a fleshy (14.5 per cent alcohol), rich wine with generous tropical-fruit flavours and a dry (3.7 grams/litre of residual sugar) finish.

Vintage	09
WR	7
Drink	09-14

`DRY $23 V+`

Villa Maria Private Bin East Coast Viognier   (★★★☆)

The fine-value 2008 vintage (★★★☆) is a blend of Hawke's Bay and Gisborne fruit, fermented in tanks and seasoned oak barrels. Fleshy and soft, with strong, ripe, peachy, clearly varietal flavours and a fully dry, slightly spicy and creamy finish, it's enjoyable now.

Vintage	08
WR	6
Drink	09-11

`DRY $19 V+`

Villa Maria Single Vineyard Omahu Gravels Vineyard Hawke's Bay Viognier

★★★★★

Weighty, fleshy and soft, the 2008 vintage (★★★★★) was fermented in French oak barrels (48 per cent new), with extensive use of indigenous yeasts and malolactic fermentation also adding complexity. Richly floral, with hints of apricots, it is very full-bodied and finely textured, with concentrated stone-fruit and slight spice flavours, and a bone-dry, well-rounded finish.

Vintage	08	07	06	05
WR	7	7	6	6
Drink	09-14	09-12	09-12	09-11

`DRY $30 V+`

Waimea Nelson Viognier   ★★★☆

Hand-picked at 23 brix and mostly handled in tanks, with a small percentage of barrel fermentation, the 2008 vintage (★★★★) is a refined, vibrantly fruity wine with mouthfilling body and fresh, rich stone-fruit and spice flavours. Dry, with lively acidity, it's an elegant wine, worth cellaring.

Vintage	08	07	06
WR	7	6	5
Drink	09-12	09-10	P

`DRY $24 AV`

Wairau River Marlborough Viognier   (★★★★)

Enjoyable from the start, the 2009 vintage (★★★★) is weighty (14.5 per cent alcohol), with fresh, pure peach and apricot flavours, showing excellent depth. Partly (10 per cent) oak-aged, with an off-dry (6.5 grams/litre of residual sugar) finish, it's a deliciously vibrant and harmonious wine.

Vintage	09
WR	6
Drink	09-12

`MED/DRY $23 V+`

Yealands Estate Marlborough Viognier   (★★★)

The fresh, vibrant 2008 vintage (★★★) is an Awatere Valley wine with mouthfilling body, good depth of citrusy, peachy, slightly spicy flavours and a dry (4 grams/litre of residual sugar) finish. Handled without oak and balanced for easy drinking, it's a promising debut.

`DRY $23 –V`

Würzer

A German crossing of Gewürztraminer and Müller-Thurgau, Würzer is extremely rare in New Zealand, with 1 hectare of bearing vines in 2010. Seifried has 'a few rows' at its Redwood Valley Vineyard, in Nelson.

Seifried Nelson Würzer   ★★★☆

The finely scented, gently sweet 2008 (★★★★) is vibrantly fruity and lightly spicy, with hints of ginger and apricots, gentle acidity and excellent depth and harmony. The fresh, slightly sweet 2009 vintage (★★★☆) is very undemanding, with pear, spice and slight apricot flavours, a splash of sweetness (14 grams/litre of residual sugar) and enough acidity to keep things lively. Best drinking mid-2010+.

Vintage	09	08
WR	6	6
Drink	09-11	09-11

MED/DRY $19 AV

Sweet White Wines

New Zealand's sweet white wines (often called dessert wines) are not taking the world by storm, accounting for just 0.03 per cent of our wine exports. Yet around the country, winemakers work hard to produce some ravishingly beautiful, honey-sweet white wines that are worth discovering and can certainly hold their own internationally. Seifried Winemakers Collection Sweet Agnes Riesling Ice Wine 2008 won the trophy for 'Best Sweet White Over Ten Pounds' at the 2009 *Decanter* World Wine Awards, judged in London.

New Zealand's most luscious, concentrated and honeyish sweet whites are made from grapes which have been shrivelled and dehydrated on the vines by 'noble rot', the dry form of the *Botrytis cinerea* mould. Misty mornings, followed by clear, fine days with light winds and low humidity, are ideal conditions for the spread of noble rot, but in New Zealand this favourable interplay of weather factors occurs irregularly.

Some enjoyable but rarely exciting dessert wines (often labelled Ice Wine) are made by the freeze-concentration method, whereby a proportion of the natural water content in the grape juice is frozen out, leaving a sweet, concentrated juice to be fermented.

Marlborough has so far yielded a majority of the finest sweet whites. Most of the other wine regions, however – except Auckland (too wet) and Central Otago (usually too dry and cool) – can also point to the successful production of botrytised sweet whites in favourable vintages.

Riesling has been the foundation of the majority of New Zealand's most opulent sweet whites, but Sauvignon Blanc, Sémillon, Gewürztraminer, Pinot Gris, Müller-Thurgau, Chenin Blanc, Viognier and Chardonnay have all yielded fine dessert styles. With their high levels of extract and firm acidity, most of these wines mature well for two to three years, although few are very long-lived.

Alana Estate Martinborough L'Apéritif ★★★★

The 2008 vintage (★★★★) is a perfumed, musky Riesling with concentrated, citrusy, limey flavours and a sweet (100 grams/litre of residual sugar), crisp finish. It's a lovely, late-harvest style, designed as an apéritif rather than a dessert wine.

Vintage	08
WR	6
Drink	09-18

SW $35 (375ML) –V

Allan Scott Late Harvest Marlborough Riesling (★★★★)

The 2007 vintage (★★★★) is an elegant wine with ripe, citrusy flavours and hints of honey. A gently botrytised style, matured in old oak barrels, it is sweet (144 grams/litre of residual sugar), with lovely lightness (10.5 per cent alcohol) and vivacity.

SW $27 (375ML) AV

Allan Scott Late Harvest Marlborough Sauvignon Blanc (★★★★☆)

The pale gold 2008 vintage (★★★★☆) is a rich, complex style, hand-picked and fermented and matured for six months in old French oak barriques. Mouthfilling (although only 9 per cent alcohol), with a fragrant, honeyed bouquet, it has an oily texture and lovely depth and freshness of very ripe tropical-fruit flavours, enriched by noble rot.

SW $29 (375ML) V+

Alluviale Anobli   (★★★★★)

The light gold, Sauternes-style 2008 vintage (★★★★★) was made from botrytised Sauvignon Blanc grapes, harvested at Mangatahi, in Hawke's Bay, at 52 brix. French oak-aged, with a beautiful, richly honeyed fragrance, it is a flawless wine, concentrated and sweet (270 grams/litre of residual sugar), with an oily texture and lovely ripeness, richness and roundness.

SW $40 (375ML) AV

Alpha Domus The Pilot Leonarda Late Harvest Sémillon   ★★★☆

Made without oak, the 2007 vintage (★★★☆) is a slightly honeyed wine with grapefruit and peach flavours, mouthfilling, ripe, sweet (100 grams/litre of residual sugar) and smooth, in a gentle Sauternes style from Hawke's Bay.

Vintage	08	07
WR	6	6
Drink	09-11	09-11

SW $19 (375ML) V+

Askerne Late Harvest Sémillon   ★★☆

The golden, treacly 2008 vintage (★★☆) was harvested in Hawke's Bay at 36 brix. It has strong, sweet (160 grams/litre of residual sugar) flavours of peaches, apricots and honey, but lacks a bit of freshness.

SW $20 (375ML) –V

Askerne Noble Sémillon   ★★★★

At its best, this is a ravishing Hawke's Bay beauty in the mould of classic Sauternes. The 2007 vintage (★★★★) was fermented in French oak barrels (25 per cent new). Deep amber, it's an oily, treacly wine with highly concentrated flavours of honey and apricots, soaring sweetness (350 grams/litre of residual sugar) and a powerful botrytis influence. Drink now.

Vintage	07	06	05	04
WR	6	6	6	7
Drink	10-15	09-12	09-11	09-10

SW $30 (375ML) AV

Astrolabe Experience Noble Riesling   (★★★★)

Grown at Astrolabe Farm, in the lower Wairau Valley of Marlborough, the 2007 vintage (★★★★) is light gold, with concentrated, citrusy, honeyed flavours, sweet (214 grams/litre of residual sugar) and crisp, and an oily richness. Drink now onwards.

Vintage	07
WR	6
Drink	09-10

SW $24 (375ML) V+

Ata Rangi Kahu Botrytis Riesling   ★★★★

Grown in the Kahu Vineyard, neighbouring the Ata Rangi winery in Martinborough, the 2008 vintage (★★★☆) is a late-harvest style with a gentle botrytis influence. Fresh and youthful, with ripe citrus-fruit and passionfruit flavours, it should reward cellaring.

Vintage	08
WR	6
Drink	09-12

SW $32 (375 ML) –V

Aurora Vineyard Late Harvest Riesling

(★★★☆)

Light and lively, the bargain-priced 2008 vintage (★★★☆) is a Central Otago wine with plentiful sweetness (95–100 grams/litre of residual sugar). Scented, with a citrusy, slightly honeyed fragrance, it has lemony flavours showing very good delicacy and purity.

SW $16 (375ML) V+

Aurum Pinot Gris 18 Carat

(★★★★)

Estate-grown at Lowburn, in Central Otago, the 2009 vintage (★★★★) was made only from bunches with at least a 50 per cent 'noble rot' infection and not oak-aged. Pale straw, it is already delicious, with good weight, abundant sweetness (170 grams/litre of residual sugar) and strong, pure, pear and spice flavours, faintly honeyed, very smooth and harmonious.

Vintage	09
WR	6
Drink	10-20

SW $28 (375ML) AV

Aurum Pinot Gris 24 Carat

(★★★★)

Sweeter and more youthful than its stablemate (above), the 2008 vintage (★★★★) was made from botrytised grapes, estate-grown at Lowburn, in Central Otago. Barrel-fermented, it's a gently honeyed wine with fresh, vibrant pear and lychee flavours, sweet (220 grams/litre of residual sugar) and rich. Best drinking 2011+.

Vintage	09
WR	7
Drink	10-20

SW $55 (375ML) –V

Bilancia la collina Viognier Tardi

(★★★★★)

When darkness fell, the vineyard crew were unable to pick the last of Bilancia's Viognier crop. Several weeks later, the bunches were finally harvested, at a super-ripe 38 brix, and the wine was fermented in old oak barrels. The 2007 vintage (★★★★★) is rare – just 50 cases. Light gold, with a fragrant, richly honeyed bouquet, it is full-bodied, with lush pear, spice and honey flavours, plentiful sweetness (180 grams/litre of residual sugar) and a deliciously soft finish.

SW $33 (375ML) V+

Brightwater Riesling Ice Wine

★★★

Grown at Nelson and freeze-concentrated in the winery, the 2008 vintage (★★★) is sweet (85 grams/litre of residual sugar) and light (9 per cent alcohol), with fresh lemon/lime flavours and a hint of sherbet. It tasted fairly simple in its infancy, but should develop greater richness with bottle-age.

Vintage	08
WR	5
Drink	09-11

SW $24 (375ML) –V

Brookfields Indulgence   ★★★☆

Delicious now, the 2007 vintage (★★★☆) is a botrytis-affected Sauvignon Blanc, grown in Hawke's Bay. Attractively scented, it's a medium-bodied style (10 per cent alcohol) with ripe, late-harvest fruit flavours to the fore, very non-herbaceous and sweet, and a smooth finish. The 2008 (★★★☆) is similar – a late-harvest style, with fresh, ripe fruit flavours, gently honeyed and delicious young.

Vintage	08
WR	7
Drink	09-13

SW $25 (375ML) AV

Charles Wiffen Late Harvest Riesling   (★★★☆)

Grown in Marlborough, the light gold 2007 vintage (★★★☆) has a honeyed bouquet and a crisp, sweet palate (120 grams/litre of residual sugar), with strong, citrusy, honeyed, slightly limey flavours and firm acid spine. Drink now or cellar.

SW $35 (500ML) AV

Church Road Reserve Noble Viognier   (★★★★☆)

The 2008 vintage (★★★★☆) from Pernod Ricard NZ is classy. Grown in Hawke's Bay, it's a deliciously soft wine with a subtle oak influence and lush, ripe stone-fruit, pear and spice flavours, concentrated, sweet and complex.

SW $36 (375 ML) –V

Clearview Noble Harvest Chardonnay   ★★★★☆

From hand-picked, botrytised Chardonnay grapes, left on the vines to raisin, the 2007 vintage (★★★★) of this Hawke's Bay wine is light green/gold, with rich, peachy, honey-sweet flavours (130 grams/litre of residual sugar). Barrel-fermented, it has hints of tea and spice, and good complexity. Drink now or cellar.

Vintage	07	06	05	04
WR	7	6	NM	6
Drink	09-12	09-10	09-10	09-10

SW $65 (375 ML) –V

Cloudy Bay Late Harvest Riesling   ★★★★★

Cloudy Bay only makes this Marlborough wine about every second year, on average, but it's usually worth waiting for. The 2004 vintage (★★★★☆) was harvested in the Ashmore Vineyard at Fairhall, when the grape sugar levels had reached an average of 30 brix and over half of the berries were botrytis-affected. Fermented in a mix of tanks and barrels, then matured on its yeast lees in old French oak casks for 18 months, it's a lemon-hued, citrusy, honeyed wine with a scented, complex bouquet. Rich and refined, with greater complexity than most New Zealand dessert wines, it offers lovely drinking from now onwards.

Vintage	04	03	02	01	00
WR	6	NM	6	NM	6
Drink	09-10	NM	P	NM	P

SW $33 (375ML) V+

Corbans Cottage Block Hawke's Bay Cut Cane Pinot Gris   (★★★★★)

The enticingly scented 2008 vintage (★★★★★) was hand-picked at 34 to 38 brix at Matapiro, fermented in stainless steel barrels and lees-aged for 10 months. The grapes, shrivelled but not botrytis-affected, have yielded a lovely late-harvest style, weighty and rounded, with ripe stone-fruit and spice flavours showing notable delicacy and depth, plentiful sweetness (130 grams/litre of residual sugar), gentle acidity and a long finish.

SW $32 (375ML) V+

Craggy Range Noble   (★★★★)

The 2006 vintage (★★★★) is a sweet, late-harvest blend of Sauvignon Blanc (66 per cent) and Riesling (34 per cent), grown in Martinborough. Attractively scented, it has a subtle botrytis influence, with fresh, beautifully ripe pear and citrus-fruit flavours, a hint of honey and gentle acidity.

SW $37 (375ML) –V

Crater Rim, The, Dr Kohl's Riesling   (NR)

Tasted prior to bottling, and so not rated, the 2008 vintage looked full of promise. It's a low-alcohol (7 per cent), sweet wine (100 grams/litre of residual sugar), lemon-scented and intensely flavoured.

SW $30 (750ML) V?

Doctors', The, Noble Chenin Blanc   (★★★★★)

From Forrest Estate, in Marlborough, the 2008 vintage (★★★★★) is a gorgeous sweet wine (220 grams/litre of residual sugar) with a richly honeyed fragrance. Concentrated, with an oily texture, it has beautifully ripe peach and apricot flavours, enriched but not swamped by noble rot, good acid spine and lovely freshness and harmony. Drink now or cellar.

Vintage   08
WR   6
Drink   09-20

SW $30 (375 ML) V+

Domaine Georges Michel Autumn Folly   ★★

The 2006 vintage (★★) is a blend of Marlborough Sauvignon Blanc and Sémillon, stop-fermented by the addition of grape spirit (creating a high alcohol content of 14.5 per cent). Sweet (106 grams/litre of residual sugar) and smooth, it has a spirity rather than grapey bouquet, with strong, lemony flavours. I rated it higher in 2008 than in 2009, when it seemed to be losing freshness.

Vintage   06
WR   6
Drink   09-10

SW $29 (375ML) –V

Dry River Late Harvest Craighall Riesling   ★★★★★

Dry River produces beautiful botrytised sweet wines in Martinborough – sometimes light and fragile, sometimes high in alcohol and very powerful – from a range of varieties, but for winemaker Neil McCallum, Riesling is the queen of dessert wines. Grown in the Craighall Vineyard, 500 metres from the winery, the grapes are hand-selected over a one-month period, extending into late May. The 2008 vintage (★★★★★) is scented, with a ripe bouquet of citrus fruits and a hint of marmalade. Showing lovely lightness (10 per cent alcohol), freshness and purity, and a delightful interplay of sweetness (60 grams/litre of residual sugar) and crispness, it's an intense, citrusy and slightly minerally wine, for drinking now or cellaring.

Vintage	07	06	05	04	03	02
WR	7	7	7	7	NM	7
Drink	09-14	09-14	09-10	09-10	NM	09-10

SW $51 (750 ML) V+

Escarpment Martinborough Hinemoa Riesling   (★★★★☆)

Estate-grown at Te Muna, the 2006 vintage (★★★★☆) is full of personality. Pale gold, with a honeyed, slightly minerally bouquet, it is tight and elegant, with excellent intensity of citrusy, honeyed flavour, in a sweet but not super-sweet (120 grams/litre of residual sugar) style with fresh acidity and a finely poised, long finish.

SW $27 (375ML) V+

Farmgate Noble Harvest Riesling   (★★★★★)

Lovely now, the 2007 vintage (★★★★★) from Ngatarawa was hand-picked in Hawke's Bay and stop-fermented with 10 per cent alcohol and 279 grams per litre of residual sugar. Golden, it's a strongly botrytised style with an oily texture and fresh, concentrated peach, apricot and honey flavours, showing beautiful poise and richness.

Vintage	07
WR	7
Drink	09-11

SW $40 (375ML) AV

Felton Road Block 1 Riesling   ★★★★☆

Grown on a 'steeper slope' which yields 'riper fruit' without noble rot, this Bannockburn, Central Otago wine is made in a style 'similar to a late-harvest, Mosel spätlese', says winemaker Blair Walter. Light lemon/green, the 2009 vintage (★★★★★) is deliciously light (9.5 per cent alcohol) and lively, with very incisive lemon/lime flavours, minerally and racy. Approachable now, it should flourish with cellaring.

Vintage	09	08	07	06
WR	7	6	7	6
Drink	09-29	09-28	09-27	09-26

SW $34 (750 ML) V+

Forrest Estate Botrytised Riesling   ★★★★★

Since 2001, this Marlborough beauty has been outstanding. Luscious, ripe and oily, the 2008 vintage (★★★★☆) is very honeyed, with a powerful botrytis influence and sweet (220 grams/litre of residual sugar), concentrated, apricot-like flavours.

Vintage	08	07	06	05	04	03	02
WR	6	6	6	4	6	7	6
Drink	09-20	09-12	09-12	09-10	09-10	P	P

SW $35 (375ML) AV

Forrest Late Harvest Gewürztraminer   (★★★☆)

The scented 2007 vintage (★★★☆), grown in Marlborough, is a sweet wine (90 grams/litre of residual sugar) with pear, lemon, apple and spice flavours, showing some richness. There's an intriguing back-label reference to 'hokey pokey ice cream' characters – and it's true. Ready; no rush.

Vintage	07
WR	4
Drink	09-11

SWEET $20 (375ML) AV

Forrest Late Harvest Riesling   ★★★☆

The 2007 vintage (★★★), grown in Marlborough, is light in body (9.5 per cent alcohol) and gently sweet (70 grams/litre of residual sugar), with pure, ripe, lemon/lime flavours and a floral bouquet.

Vintage	07
WR	4
Drink	09-11

SW $20 (375 ML) AV

Framingham Gewürztraminer SGN   (★★★★☆)

Estate-grown in Marlborough, the 2008 vintage (★★★★☆) is pale gold, with a distinctly spicy, exotically perfumed bouquet. Light (8 per cent alcohol), sweet and rich, it has concentrated, spicy, honeyed flavours, showing a lovely harmony of fruit and botrytis. It's already drinking well.

SW $40 (375 ML) –V

Framingham Noble Riesling   ★★★★

From two blocks of 28-year-old vines on the estate in Marlborough, the 2008 vintage (★★★★) is an elegant, gently honeyed wine with youthful, citrus-fruit and pear flavours, fresh acidity and good richness. Open 2010+.

Vintage	08	07	06	05	04
WR	6	6	7	6	7
Drink	09-13	09-12	09-11	09-10	P

SW $30 (375 ML) AV

Framingham Riesling Auslese   ★★★★★

Based on 28-year-old vines in the Wairau Valley, Marlborough, the 2008 vintage (★★★★★) yielded three slightly different wines, normally components of the Noble Riesling (above), but this year bottled separately as #1, #2 and #3. Harvested at slightly different brix levels (34 to 40) and varying slightly in alcohol (7 to 8 per cent), they show lovely poise and intensity. Light gold, oily and lush, #3 (★★★★★) is the hardest to resist right now, but #1 (★★★★★) is my pick for the long haul.

SW $40 (375ML) AV

Framingham Select Riesling   ★★★★☆

The 2008 vintage (★★★★☆), grown in Marlborough and late-picked by hand, was inspired by the German *spätlese* style. Pale and light (7.5 per cent alcohol), it has a limey and minerally, complex bouquet. Finely poised and intense, it is pure, lemony and appley, with a lovely harmony of sweetness (60 grams/litre of residual sugar) and acidity. Best drinking 2011+.

Vintage	08	07	06	05	04
WR	6	7	6	6	7
Drink	10-17	09-14	09-12	09-12	09-10

SW $31 (750ML) V+

Fromm Gewürztraminer Late Harvest   ★★★★

The 2008 vintage (★★★★) is the Marlborough winery's second late-harvest Gewürztraminer. Already drinking well, it's a medium-bodied wine (12 per cent alcohol), soft and peachy, slightly spicy and gingery, with excellent delicacy and complexity.

Vintage	09	08	07	06	05
WR	6	6	6	6	6
Drink	10-15	09-14	09-13	09-12	09-11

SW $24 (375ML) V+

Fromm Riesling Spätlese   ★★★★☆

This vivacious Marlborough wine is made from the ripest hand-harvested grapes with no botrytis infection, in an intense, low-alcohol style with plentiful sweetness and incisive, lemony, limey, minerally flavours. The 2008 vintage (★★★★★) is one of the lowest-alcohol (7 per cent) New Zealand wines I've ever encountered – but it's definitely a wine! Offering lovely richness of fresh, lemony, appley, spicy flavour, it's a finely poised wine, sweet, minerally and racy. Drink now or cellar.

Vintage	09	08	07	06	05	04
WR	7	6	6	7	6	6
Drink	10-19	09-16	09-15	09-16	09-15	09-14

SW $28 (750ML) V+

Gibbston Valley Late Harvest Riesling   ★★★☆

The 2008 vintage (★★★☆) was grown in the Mondillo Vineyard at Bendigo, in Central Otago. It's a light (10 per cent alcohol) wine with an array of fresh, ripe-fruit flavours (lemon, apple, pear), abundant sweetness (120 grams/litre of residual sugar), gentle acidity and good harmony. Drink now or cellar.

Vintage	08
WR	7
Drink	12-20

SW $26 (375ML) –V

Gibbston Valley Noble Riesling   (★★★★)

The tight, youthful 2008 vintage (★★★★) was grown at Bendigo, in the Mondillo Vineyard. Bright, light lemon/green, it is mouthfilling (12.5 per cent alcohol), rich, peachy and honeyed, with plentiful sweetness (120 grams/litre of residual sugar) and good acid spine. Open 2011+.

Vintage	08
WR	7
Drink	12-20

SW $40 (375ML) –V

Glazebrook Regional Reserve Noble Harvest Riesling   ★★★★★

From Ngatarawa, this classic Hawke's Bay wine is typically richly botrytised and honey-sweet, concentrated and treacly, in top vintages dripping with honey, apricot and raisin flavours. The 2006 (★★★★★) was harvested from five-year-old vines in The Triangle district and not oak-aged. The floral bouquet leads into a very elegant, sweet (155 grams/litre of residual sugar) and concentrated wine with pristine, late-harvest fruit flavours woven with fresh acidity. It's a less botrytis-influenced wine than its predecessors, but equally compelling.

Vintage	07	06	05	04	03	02	01	00
WR	NM	7	7	NM	NM	7	NM	6
Drink	NM	09-11	09-10	NM	NM	09-10	NM	P

SW $32 (375ML) V+

Gravitas Hugo's Delight Late Harvest Riesling   ★★★☆

Named after one of the proprietor's sons, the 2007 vintage (★★★★) was picked in Marlborough at 34 brix and stop-fermented with 150 grams/litre of residual sugar. Golden, with a strongly botrytised bouquet, it is rich, peachy and honeyed, with crisp acidity keeping things lively. Drink now or cellar.

SW $25 (375ML) AV

Gravitas Marlborough Noble Riesling   (★★★★)

The 2007 vintage (★★★★) was harvested at 33 brix, when 60 per cent of the berries were shrivelled and 30 per cent were nobly rotten. It's a strongly botrytised wine, golden, with a honeyed bouquet and intense, citrusy, peachy flavours, sweet (150 grams/litre of residual sugar) and crisp, with an oily richness. Drink now onwards.

Vintage	07
WR	6
Drink	09-12

SW $27 (375ML) AV

Greystone Waipara Late Harvest Riesling   (★★★★)

The debut 2009 vintage (★★★★) is light (only 9 per cent alcohol) and sweet (102 grams/litre of residual sugar), with strong, ripe, lemony, appley flavours, gentle acidity and a well-rounded finish. It's already delicious.

SW $34 (750ML) V+

Hans Herzog Marlborough Botrytis Pinot Gris   (★★★★☆)

The 2006 vintage (★★★★☆) was hand-picked in May and matured for 10 months in new French oak barriques. It's a slightly Sauternes-like wine, full-bodied, rich, honeyed and smooth, with sweet, peachy, spicy flavours showing good complexity.

SW $85 (750ML) –V

Hunter's Hukapapa Riesling Dessert Wine   ★★★

Hukapapa means 'frost, ice'. The 2006 vintage (★★★), a freeze-concentrated Marlborough wine, has sweet, lemony, limey flavours and a hint of sherbet. Simple and smooth, it shows some richness.

Vintage	07	06	05	04
WR	5	5	NM	5
Drink	10-12	P	NM	P

SW $25 (375ML) –V

Isabel Marlborough Noble Sauvage   ★★★★

The 2006 vintage (★★★★) had a 'painfully slow' fermentation, lasting 10 months, in French oak barriques. Golden, with oak complexity, it is sweet (170 grams/litre of residual sugar), crisp and honeyed, with excellent depth.

Vintage	06
WR	7
Drink	09-16

SW $39 (375ML) –V

Jackson Estate Botrytis Riesling   ★★★★☆

The golden 2006 vintage (★★★★☆) is an unabashedly sweet wine (250 grams/litre of residual sugar), handled entirely in tanks. Richly honeyed, with a powerful botrytis influence, it has concentrated ripe-fruit flavours of citrus fruits and apricots, with good acid spine. Drink now or cellar.

Vintage	06
WR	7
Drink	09-20

SW $35 (375ML) AV

Johanneshof Noble Late Harvest Riesling   ★★★★☆

The 2006 vintage (★★★★), picked in Marlborough at 40 brix, has 188 grams/litre of residual sugar. Honey-sweet on the nose, it's a weighty (although only 9.5 per cent alcohol) wine, with rich, liquid honey flavours, a slightly oily texture and rounded finish. The 2007 (★★★★★), made from fully botrytised grapes, is golden, oily and complex, with citrusy, richly honeyed flavours, a hint of apricots, and lovely poise and intensity.

Vintage	07	06
WR	5	5
Drink	09+	09-12

SW $34 (375ML) AV

Johner Noble Sauvignon Blanc   (★★★☆)

Estate-grown at Gladstone, in the Wairarapa, the 2009 vintage (★★★☆) is vibrant, sweet and peachy, with firm acidity and a hint of honey. (There is also a strawberryish, slightly spicy, sweet and crisp Noble Syrah 2008 (★★★☆), well worth trying.)

SW $22 (375ML) –V

John Forrest Collection Noble Riesling   (★★★★★)

Launched from the 2005 vintage (★★★★★), this delectable Marlborough wine was grown on an elevated, relatively cool site in the Brancott Valley. The bouquet is ravishingly beautiful, with rich aromas of citrus fruits and honey. Golden, it is low in alcohol (9 per cent), with plentiful sweetness (220 grams/litre of residual sugar) and intense lemon, honey and apricot flavours, very fresh, pure, oily and long. It's drinking well now.

Vintage	05
WR	7
Drink	09-20

SW $45 (375ML) AV

Kim Crawford SP Noble Reka Marlborough Riesling   ★★★★

Reka means 'sweet'. The 2007 vintage (★★★★) was harvested at an average of 36 brix and stop-fermented with 10 per cent alcohol and 161 grams per litre of residual sugar. Light-bodied, with rich, soft flavours of apricots, pears and honey, it's drinking well now.

SW $34 (375ML) –V

Konrad Bunch Selection Marlborough Riesling   ★★★★

The 2008 vintage (★★★★) was estate-grown in the Waihopai Valley and stop-fermented with low alcohol (8 per cent) and abundant sweetness (57 grams/litre of residual sugar). It has firm acidity, a hint of sherbet and very good intensity of lemony, appley flavours.

Vintage	08
WR	5
Drink	09-19

SW $27 (750ML) V+

Konrad Sigrun Noble Two   ★★★★

Showing a Sauternes-style richness, the 2008 vintage (★★★★☆) of this estate-grown, Waihopai Valley beauty is a blend of 58 per cent tank-fermented Riesling and 42 per cent barrel-fermented Sauvignon Blanc, hand-picked between early May and mid-June at an average of 45 brix. Pale gold, it is very fresh and vibrant, with impressively concentrated, honey-sweet flavours, showing lovely harmony and depth.

Vintage	08	07
WR	6	5
Drink	09-18	09-17

SW $27 (375ML) AV

Lake Chalice The Tiercel Marlborough Botrytised Riesling   (★★★☆)

The 2007 vintage (★★★☆) was harvested at 39 brix in the company's Falcon Vineyard at Rapaura. It is weighty (13.5 per cent alcohol), ripe and sweet, with rich grapefruit and lime flavours, enhanced by honeyed, botrytis notes. Drink now or cellar.

SW $27 (375ML) –V

Lawson's Dry Hills Late Harvest Gewürztraminer   (★★★)

Grown at two sites – the home block near Blenheim and in the Waihopai Valley – the 2004 vintage (★★★) is a sweet but not super-sweet style (60 grams/litre of residual sugar). Light yellow/green, it is mouthfilling, spicy and gingery, in a developed style with some bottle-aged complexity. Ready.

SW $26 (375ML) –V

Lincoln Ice Wine   ★★★

The 2009 vintage (★★★) is a freeze-concentrated Riesling, light (10 per cent alcohol) and lively, with ripe, citrusy, limey, spicy flavours, sweet, crisp and already drinking well.

SW $20 (375ML) AV

Margrain Botrytis Selection Chenin Blanc   ★★★★☆

The 2008 vintage (★★★★★) is a rare Martinborough beauty, picked from 25-year-old vines in early June and stop-fermented at 240 grams per litre of residual sugar. Light gold, with an enticing, honeyed fragrance and concentrated, ripe flavours of citrus fruits and honey, it is notably pure and vibrant, with good acid spine, and should be long-lived.

Vintage	08
WR	7
Drink	09-19

SW $38 (375 ML) –V

Margrain Botrytis Selection Sauvignon Blanc   (★★★★☆)

Harvested from a neighbouring vineyard in Martinborough at 46.8 brix, the 2008 vintage (★★★★☆) is a golden, Sauternes-style wine, with a richly honeyed bouquet. It's a highly concentrated wine, super-sweet (286 grams/litre of residual sugar), with stone-fruit and honey flavours that retain firm acidity. Delicious drinking now onwards.

Vintage	08
WR	7
Drink	09-19

SW $28 (375ML) V+

Matariki Late Harvest Riesling   ★★★☆

The 2007 vintage (★★★☆) was hand-picked in the Gimblett Gravels district of Hawke's Bay, with a 'significant' proportion of noble rot. A medium-bodied wine (11.5 per cent alcohol), with ripe citrus-fruit characters, hints of honey and marmalade, plentiful sweetness (100 grams/litre of residual sugar) and very good depth, it's a drink-now or cellaring proposition.

Vintage	07	06	05	04
WR	6	6	NM	7
Drink	09-11	09-10	NM	P

SW $30 (375ML) –V

Matua Valley Shingle Peak Late Harvest Riesling   (★★★)

From grapes hand-harvested from a single vineyard in early June, the 2007 vintage (★★★) is a citrusy, gently sweet (67 grams/litre of residual sugar) but not botrytised Marlborough wine with crisp acidity to keep things lively. Simple but attractive.

Vintage	07
WR	5
Drink	09-13

SW $18 (375ML) AV

Matua Valley Shingle Peak Reserve Botrytis Riesling   (★★★★)

From an early June harvest of botrytised grapes, the 2007 vintage (★★★★) is a rich, oily, single-vineyard Marlborough wine with strong, citrusy, slightly spicy, honeyed flavours. It's a very elegant wine with a rich but not overwhelming botrytis influence.

Vintage	07
WR	6
Drink	09-13

SW $25 (375ML) AV

Millton Clos Samuel Viognier Special Bunch Selection   (★★★★★)

The hedonistic 2007 vintage (★★★★★) was grown biodynamically in Gisborne. Golden, it is lush and sweet (250 grams/litre of residual sugar), with super-rich flavours of peaches, apricots and honey, showing good complexity. Very oily and concentrated, with underlying acidity, it's delicious now but also worth cellaring.

Vintage	07
WR	7
Drink	09-15

SW $43 (375ML) AV

Millton Muskats @ Dawn – see the Muscat section

Moana Park Vineyard Tribute Ice Wine   ★★☆

The 2007 vintage (★★★), grown in the Dartmoor Valley, Hawke's Bay, is pink/orange, sweet

(231 grams/litre of residual sugar) and crisp, with strawberry, orange and spice flavours and a Muscat-like, floral bouquet. Ready.

Vintage	07
WR	4
Drink	09-15

SW $25 (375 ML) –V

Morton Estate Black Label Late Harvest Sémillon   (★★★☆)

Grown in Hawke's Bay and oak-aged, the 2006 vintage (★★★☆) is amber-hued, with a bouquet of honey and tea. A strongly botrytised wine, with apricot and honey flavours, firm acidity and very good depth, it's ready now.

Vintage	06
WR	6
Drink	P

SW $32 (375ML) –V

Muddy Water Growers' Series Unplugged Riesling   ★★★★

The 2008 vintage (★★★★) was hand-harvested in Waipara at 28 to 32 brix. Based solely on 'clusters infected with noble rot', it was tank-fermented with indigenous yeasts and lees-aged for seven months. Bright, light yellow/green, with honeyed aromas and flavours, it's a sweet (73 grams/litre of residual sugar) but not cloying wine, with rich grapefruit and lime flavours, balanced acidity and strong drink-young appeal.

Vintage	08
WR	6
Drink	09-20

SW $26 (750ML) V+

Muddy Water Sugar Daddy Riesling   (★★★★★)

'Controlled decadence', I jotted down after tasting the 2008 vintage (★★★★★) of the Waipara winery's first 'fully botrytised' sweet wine. Hand-picked at 47 brix and fermented with indigenous yeasts for over 10 months, it has just 6.6 per cent alcohol. Pale gold/slight amber, with a richly honeyed bouquet and intense, apricot-like flavours, it has a powerful botrytis influence and enough acidity to balance its advanced level of sweetness (306 grams/litre of residual sugar). Already delicious, it should be long-lived.

Vintage	08
WR	7
Drink	09-20

SW $50 (375ML) AV

Ngatarawa Alwyn Winemaker's Reserve Noble Harvest Riesling   ★★★★★

'Botrytis plays a huge part in this wine,' says Hawke's Bay winemaker Alwyn Corban. The 2006 vintage (★★★★★) was hand-harvested at 44 brix and fermented and matured for five months in French oak barriques (one and two years old). A golden, abundantly sweet wine (220 grams/litre of residual sugar), with beautifully ripe pear, spice and honey flavours, enriched but not overwhelmed by botrytis, it's the most finely balanced, exquisite wine yet under this label.

Vintage	07	06	05
WR	NM	7	NM
Drink	NM	09-11	NM

SW $60 (375ML) –V

Ngatarawa Glazebrook Noble Harvest Riesling – see Glazebrook Regional Reserve Noble Harvest Riesling

Ngatarawa Stables Late Harvest ★★★☆

This Hawke's Bay wine is called 'a fruit style' by winemaker Alwyn Corban, meaning it doesn't possess the qualities of a fully botrytised wine. The 2009 vintage (★★★☆) is a blend of Gewürztraminer (87 per cent) and Riesling (13 per cent). Full-bodied (13.5 per cent alcohol), it's a gently sweet wine (60 grams/litre of residual sugar) with generous, peachy, citrusy, slightly spicy flavours and a slightly honeyed bouquet. Drink now or cellar.

Vintage	09
WR	6
Drink	09-14

SW $17 (375ML) V+

Palliser Estate Noble Riesling (★★★★)

The 2008 vintage (★★★★), grown in Martinborough, is a late-harvest style with lemony, appley, slightly honeyed aromas and flavours, abundant sweetness (111 grams/litre of residual sugar) and gentle acidity. It's a light wine, fresh and elegant, with aging potential.

SW $24 (375ML) V+

Paritua Dinah Noble Harvest Sémillon ★★★☆

Grown in Hawke's Bay, barrel-fermented and oak-aged for five months, the 2008 vintage (★★★★) is a weighty, Sauternes-style wine, rich and honeyed. Sweet (184 grams/litre of residual sugar), with ripe-fruit flavours enriched by noble rot, it has an oily texture and considerable complexity.

Vintage	08
WR	5
Drink	09-20

SW $37 (375ML) –V

Pegasus Bay Aria Late Harvest Riesling ★★★★☆

The 2008 vintage (★★★★★) is a classy, very elegant Waipara wine, made from ripe bunches in which at least a third of the berries were nobly rotten. It has a floral, gently honeyed bouquet and fresh, pure, late-harvest fruit flavours, showing excellent richness. Finely focused, with a luscious sweetness (100 grams/litre of residual sugar) coupled with mouth-watering acidity, it's a beauty.

Vintage	08	07	06	05	04	03	02
WR	7	7	7	NM	6	NM	5
Drink	09-20	09-18	09-15	NM	09-14	NM	09-15

SW $37 (750ML) V+

Pegasus Bay Encore Noble Riesling ★★★★☆

The honeyed 2007 vintage (★★★★) is a Waipara wine with vibrant lemon, lime and apricot flavours, sweet (150 grams/litre of residual sugar) and rich, with balanced acidity. It's a concentrated wine, still youthful.

Vintage	08	07
WR	6	5
Drink	09-18	09-19

SW $37 (375ML) –V

Pegasus Bay Finale Noble Sémillon (★★★★☆)

The deliciously rich, honey-sweet 2007 vintage (★★★★☆) was harvested at Waipara during late autumn and early winter (with a final pick in late June), barrel-fermented and oak-aged for two years. Light gold, with a full-bloomed, honeyed bouquet, revealing a strong noble rot influence, it is full-bodied and sweet (140 grams/litre of residual sugar), with concentrated, ripe tropical-fruit and honey flavours, and mouth-watering acidity. It's still youthful.

Vintage	07
WR	6
Drink	09-16

SW $37 (375ML) –V

Peregrine Charcoal Creek Riesling ★★★★

Ensconced in a full bottle, the 2007 vintage (★★★★) is a good buy. Late-harvested at Lowburn, in the Cromwell Basin, it has a gently honeyed bouquet, plentiful sweetness (109 grams/litre of residual sugar) and lovely depth of ripe, citrusy flavours, finely balanced and long.

SW $25 (750ML) V+

Pyramid Valley Vineyards Growers Collection
Lebecca Vineyard Marlborough Riesling ★★★★☆

Hand-picked at Rapaura, tank-fermented with indigenous yeasts and lees-aged, this is typically a poised, intense wine, made in a light, low-alcohol style (around 8.5 per cent) with sweet but not super-sweet flavours, showing impressive complexity and richness.

SW $29 (750ML) V+

Richmond Plains Nelson Aries (★★★★)

The first New Zealand wine made from certified biodynamic grapes, the 2008 vintage (★★★★) was grown in the same vineyard that produced the country's first certified organic Sauvignon Blanc and Pinot Noir. A late-harvest Pinot Noir, hand-picked on 1 June, 'as the moon moved through the constellation of Aries', it is very rare – only 300 bottles were produced. Delicious now, it is sweet and smooth, with plum and strawberry flavours, showing excellent harmony and depth.

SW $30 (375ML) AV

Riverby Estate Marlborough Noble Riesling (★★★★★)

Light gold, the bargain-priced 2008 vintage (★★★★★) has a richly scented, honeyed bouquet and intense, late-harvest fruit flavours, very pure, rich, sweet (165 grams/litre of residual sugar) and luscious.

Vintage	08
WR	7
Drink	09-12

SW $25 (375 ML) V+

Rose Tree Cottage Noble Riesling ★★★★

From Constellation NZ, the 2007 vintage (★★★★) was grown at the Matador Estate in Marlborough. Light gold, it's an elegant wine with rich, citrusy, slightly honeyed flavours, sweet (150 grams/litre of residual sugar) and youthful.

SW $24 (375 ML) V+

Rose Tree Cottage Noble Sémillon (★★)

The 2007 vintage (★★) from Constellation NZ was grown in Marlborough. It's a peachy, sweet wine (150 grams/litre of residual sugar), but shows a slight lack of freshness and vibrancy.

SW $24 (375ML) –V

Saint Clair Doctor's Creek Reserve Noble Riesling ★★★★

The 2007 vintage (★★★★), hand-picked in the company's Doctor's Creek Vineyard, is lovely now, with fresh, rich flavours enriched but not dominated by noble rot. Scented, sweet (156 grams/litre of residual sugar) and smooth, with citrus-fruit, apricot and honey notes in a very harmonious style, it's very open and expressive.

Vintage	07	06	05	04
WR	6	NM	NM	6
Drink	09-10	NM	NM	P

SW $27 (375ML) AV

Saints Gisborne Noble Sémillon ★★★☆

The fine-value 2004 vintage (★★★★) from Pernod Ricard NZ is a Sauternes style, fermented in a mix of tanks and French and American oak barriques. Mouthfilling, ripe, sweet (157 grams/litre of residual sugar) and concentrated, it has peach and marmalade flavours, slightly oily, rich and rounded.

Vintage	04
WR	6
DRINK	P

SW $20 (375ML) AV

Seifried Winemakers Collection Sweet Agnes Riesling Ice Wine ★★★★

A popular wine, priced sharply. The 2009 vintage (★★★☆) was grown at Brightwater, freeze-concentrated to 38 brix and stop-fermented with 10 per cent alcohol and 200 grams per litre of residual sugar. The bouquet is fresh and slightly spicy; the palate is light, with vibrant peach, apricot and spice flavours, abundant sweetness balanced by appetising acidity, and a hint of sherbet.

Vintage	09
WR	7
Drink	09-17

 SW $19 (375ML) V+

Selaks Premium Selection East Coast Ice ★★★☆

This low-priced, freeze-concentrated wine is popular in supermarkets. The 2007 vintage (★★★), blended from Gewürztraminer and Riesling, is light-bodied, with enjoyable but straightforward, lemony, slightly spicy flavours, sweet and fresh.

 SW $17 (375ML) V+

Sileni Estate Selection Late Harvest Sémillon ★★★

The 2008 vintage (★★★) is a gently sweet style (92 grams/litre of residual sugar) from Hawke's Bay with strong, lemony, slightly limey flavours, fresh and crisp, and an attractive, floral bouquet.

SW $20 (375 ML) AV

Sileni Exceptional Vintage Pourriture Noble ★★★★

The 2006 vintage (★★★★) is a golden, honeyed Hawke's Bay Sémillon, picked at 42 brix and tank-fermented over a period of five months. It's only 10 per cent alcohol, yet still mouthfilling and impressively concentrated, with an oily texture and generous, sweet, apricot-like flavours.

Vintage 06
WR   5
Drink   09-10

SW $32 (375ML) –V

Spy Valley Envoy Marlborough Riesling   ★★★★★

The 2007 vintage (★★★★☆) was hand-picked from mature vines, tank-fermented and matured for six months in a large oak cuve. Still youthful, it is light (9 per cent alcohol) and gently sweet (56 grams/litre of residual sugar), with good intensity of citrusy, appley flavours, a minerally streak and a lingering finish.

Vintage 08
WR   7
Drink   10-16

SW $29 (375ML) V+

Spy Valley Marlborough Noble Riesling   ★★★★

The attractively scented 2008 vintage (★★★★) was hand-picked at 36.6 brix, tank-fermented and matured for three months in small oak barrels. Already delicious, it has a citrusy, gently honeyed bouquet, generous depth of ripe, citrusy, honeyed flavours, hints of lime and marmalade, and a sweet, smooth finish.

SW $23 (375 ML) V+

Spy Valley Marlborough Noble Sauvignon Blanc   (★★★★)

Delicious young, the 2008 vintage (★★★★) was harvested at 31.6 brix from mature vines and fermented and matured for four months in old French oak barrels. A very harmonious wine, it offers concentrated, very ripe peach and passionfruit flavours, a hint of honey and a well-rounded finish.

SW $23 (375ML) V+

Staete Landt Marlborough Riesling Auslese   ★★★☆

Estate-grown and hand-picked at Rapaura, the 2008 vintage (★★★★) stop-fermented of its own accord with 8.5 per cent alcohol, leaving 67 grams per litre of residual sugar. Matured for five months in old oak casks, it is ripely flavoured, lemony, appley and spicy, with a lovely interplay of sweetness and crispness and good intensity.

Vintage 08 07
WR   7   5
Drink   09-15 09-15

SW $32 (750ML) V+

Stone Paddock Isabella Late Harvest Sémillon   ★★★★

From Paritua Vineyards, in Hawke's Bay, the 2008 vintage (★★★★) is a pale gold, Sauternes-style dessert wine, rich, peachy and honeyed, with plentiful sweetness (158 grams/litre of residual sugar), a slightly oily texture, and good concentration.

Vintage 08
WR   5
Drink   09-15

SW $25 (375ML) AV

Te Mania Nelson Koha Ice Wine   ★★★☆

From hand-picked Riesling grapes, freeze-concentrated in tanks, the 2009 vintage (★★★★) is a pale, low-alcohol style (8.5 per cent), lemony and sweet (120 grams/litre of residual sugar), with good sugar/acid balance and lovely lightness, delicacy and harmony. It's well worth cellaring.

Vintage	09
WR	5
Drink	09-14

SW $25 (375ML) AV

Terravin Noble Sauvignon   (★★★★★)

Light yellow, the rare 2006 vintage (★★★★★) was harvested at 39.8 brix in the upper Brancott Valley of Marlborough, French oak-fermented with indigenous yeasts and barrel-aged for nearly two years. Mouthfilling, sweet and honeyed, it's exceptionally rich, in a Sauternes style, complex and youthful. It should be very long-lived.

SW $48 (375ML) AV

Trinity Hill Gimblett Gravels Hawke's Bay Noble Viognier   ★★★★☆

The honeyed, rich 2008 vintage (★★★★) was made from hand-picked, botrytised grapes and partly barrel-fermented. 'Suited to the most decadent of occasions', it is sweet (200 grams/litre of residual sugar) and concentrated, with strong, ripe flavours of citrus fruits, apricots and honey and gentle acidity giving a rounded finish. It's already delicious.

Vintage	08	07	06	05
WR	6	6	4	6
Drink	10-17	09-15	09-10	09-12

SW $30 (375ML) AV

Turanga Creek New Zealand Late Harvest Viognier   (★★★)

Grown at Whitford, in South Auckland, the 2008 vintage (★★★) isn't quite sweet enough (43 grams/litre of residual sugar) to qualify for the Sweet White Wines chapter, but it's reviewed here due to its Late Harvest designation and small bottle. Drinking well now, it's a peach, medium-sweet wine, pale straw, with soft acidity and gentle stone-fruit flavours.

SW $30 (375ML) –V

TW Grower's Selection Botrytis Viognier   ★★★★

Gold/amber, with tea and honey aromas, the 2008 vintage (★★★☆) shows considerable early development. Rich, oily and sweet, with strong apricot and honey flavours, it's probably at its best now.

SW $32 (375ML) –V

Villa Maria Reserve Noble Riesling   ★★★★★

One of New Zealand's top sweet wines on the show circuit. It is typically stunningly perfumed, weighty and oily, with intense, very sweet honey/citrus flavours and a lush, long finish. The grapes are grown mainly in the Fletcher Vineyard, in the centre of Marlborough's Wairau Plains, where trees create a 'humidity crib' around the vines and sprinklers along the vines' fruit zone create ideal conditions for the spread of noble rot. The 2007 vintage (★★★★★) is outstanding. Deep yellow, with a richly honeyed bouquet, it is very refined and youthful, with concentrated, citrusy, honeyed flavours, enriched but not overpowered by botrytis, and lovely balance of sweetness and acidity.

Vintage 07	SW $50 (375ML) AV
WR 7	
DRINK 09-18	

Vin Alto Vin Santo   (★★★☆)

Still on sale, the 2004 vintage (★★★☆), grown at Clevedon, in South Auckland, is a blend of Pinot Gris and Chardonnay grapes, dried on racks for up to three months to concentrate their flavours. Light gold, it's a weighty, oak-matured wine with smooth, peachy, honeyed flavours, showing good complexity and richness.

Vintage 04	SW $33 (375ML) –V
WR 7	
Drink 09-20	

Waimea Bolitho SV Noble Chardonnay   ★★★★☆

The 2006 vintage (★★★★☆) is a richly botrytised Nelson wine, hand-picked at 44.7 brix and barrel-fermented. Golden, with abundant sweetness (217 grams/litre of residual sugar), it has excellent depth and complexity of honey and toast flavours, fresh acidity and a long finish.

Vintage 06	SW $30 (375ML) AV
WR 6	
Drink 09-11	

Waimea Bolitho SV Noble Riesling   ★★★★☆

The gold/amber, very rich ,and treacly 2004 vintage (★★★★☆) was estate-grown in the Annabrook Vineyard, in Nelson, harvested in mid-June at 50 brix and aged in seasoned French oak casks. Highly concentrated, with low alcohol (7.5 per cent) and a soaring level of sweetness (310 grams/litre of residual sugar), it has softening, toffee and marmalade flavours, ready now. The 2005 (★★★★), harvested at 44.4 brix, is a deep amber, treacly wine with sweet (200 grams/litre of residual sugar) apricot, tea and honey flavours, showing some maturity.

Vintage 04	SW $30 (375ML) AV
WR 7	
Drink 09-14	

Waimea Late Harvest Riesling   ★★★★

The 2006 vintage (★★★★) is an absolute steal. A Nelson wine made from fully botrytised grapes, hand-picked at 32 brix, it is intense, citrusy and gently honeyed, in a sweet (84 grams/litre of residual sugar) but not super-sweet style with a creamy, oily richness.

Vintage 06	SW $14 (375ML) V+
WR 6	
Drink 09-11	

Waipara Downs Late Harvest Riesling   (★★☆)

The pale gold 2008 vintage (★★☆) was fermented with indigenous yeasts in seasoned French oak puncheons. It's a citrusy, sweet, honeyed wine, showing some early development and probably best drunk young.

SW $22 (375ML) –V

Wishart Late Harvest Chardonnay   (★★☆)

Still on sale, the 2003 vintage (★★☆) of this Hawke's Bay wine doesn't really qualify for the sweet wine section of the *Guide*, as it only has 38 grams per litre of residual sugar, making it a medium-sweet style, but this is where you'd expect to find it, given its name and half bottle size. Light gold, it's peachy and rounded, but shows a slight loss of freshness. Ready.

Vintage	03
WR	4
Drink	P

SW $20 (375ML) –V

Sparkling Wines

Fizz, bubbly, *méthode traditionnelle*, sparkling – whatever name you call it by (the word Champagne is reserved for the wines of that most famous of all wine regions), wine with bubbles in it is universally adored.

How good are Kiwi bubblies? Good enough for the local industry to ship 219,556 cases of bubbly in the year to June 2009 – mostly to Australia and the UK. In the past year, sparkling wine accounted for 1.7 per cent of New Zealand's wine exports.

Yet the selection of New Zealand sparklings is not wide. Most small wineries find the production of bottle-fermented sparkling wine too time-consuming and costly, and the domestic demand for premium bubbly is limited. About 12 per cent of the wine we drink is sparkling, but the vast majority of purchases are under $15.

New Zealand's sparkling wines can be divided into two key classes. The bottom end of the market is dominated by extremely sweet, simple wines which acquire their bubbles by simply having carbon dioxide pumped into them. Upon pouring, the bubbles race out of the glass.

At the middle and top end of the market are the much drier, bottle-fermented, *méthode traditionnelle* (formerly *méthode Champenoise*, until the French got upset) labels, in which the wine undergoes its secondary, bubble-creating fermentation not in a tank but in the bottle, as in Champagne itself. Ultimately, the quality of any fine sparkling wine is a reflection both of the standard of its base wine, and of its later period of maturation in the bottle in contact with its yeast lees. Only bottle-fermented sparkling wines possess the additional flavour richness and complexity derived from extended lees-aging.

Pinot Noir and Chardonnay, both varieties of key importance in Champagne, are also the foundation of New Zealand's top sparkling wines. Pinot Meunier, also extensively planted in Champagne, is still rare here, with 19 hectares planted.

Two-thirds of the grapes for the country's most popular bubbly, Lindauer, are grown in Gisborne, where grape yields are high (necessary for such a low-priced wine) and the fruit is harvested early to retain the desired high levels of acidity. However, Marlborough, with its cool nights preserving the grapes' fresh natural acidity, has emerged as the country's premier region for bottle-fermented sparkling wines (8 per cent of the region's Pinot Noir is cultivated specifically for sparkling – rather than red – wine).

The vast majority of sparkling wines are ready to drink when marketed, and need no extra maturation. A short spell in the cellar, however, can benefit the very best bottle-fermented sparklings.

Allan Scott Blanc de Blancs NV   ★★★★

This refreshing Marlborough bubbly is based entirely on Chardonnay. The batch on sale in 2009 (★★★★), 5 per cent oak-aged, is an elegant, dry wine with crisp, citrusy flavours, showing good delicacy and yeast-derived complexity. It's a vivacious wine, very fresh, light and lively.

DRY $28 AV

Aquila Sparkling Wine   ★★☆

This low-priced bubbly is fresh and fruity, with a sweetish finish. Within Pernod Ricard NZ's range of sparklings, in terms of sweetness Aquila (which has 50 grams/litre of residual sugar) sits between the medium Lindauer Sec and the unabashedly sweet Bernadino Spumante. The non-vintage wine I tasted in mid-2009 (★★☆) was perfumed and light, with simple, lemony, appley flavours, fresh, lively and smooth.

SW $10 AV

Arcadia NV Brut   ★★★☆

This bottle-fermented bubbly is produced by Amisfield in Central Otago from Pinot Noir and Chardonnay. The non-vintage wine I tasted in mid-2009 (★★★☆) was pale straw, with a hint of pink, with peachy, strawberryish, yeasty flavours, showing good complexity, and a slightly buttery, softening finish.

MED/DRY $22 AV

Bernadino Spumante   ★★★

What great value! Pernod Ricard NZ's popular Asti-style wine is an uncomplicated style, based on Muscat grapes grown in Gisborne. A slightly higher-alcohol wine (9.5 per cent) than most true Asti Spumantes (which average around 7.5 per cent) and less ravishingly perfumed, it's still delicious, with grapey flavours and distinct sweetness (75 grams/litre of residual sugar). The non-vintage wine I tasted in mid-2009 (★★★) was finely balanced, with fresh, vibrant flavours of lemons and oranges and a sweet, crisp finish.

SW $8 V+

Chardon Medium Sparkling White Wine   ★★

Frothy and simple, the non-vintage wine on sale in 2009 (★★) from Pernod Ricard NZ is pale and very light (only 5.8 per cent alcohol). It offers pleasant, lemony, appley flavours, sweet and crisp.

MED $8 AV

Corbans Verde – see Verde

Cuvée No. 1   ★★★★

This is a non-vintage *blanc de blancs* style, based entirely on Marlborough Chardonnay. Made by Daniel Le Brun (in his family company) and matured for two years on its yeast lees, the wine I tasted in 2009 (★★★★) was floral, fresh and vivacious, with crisp, lemony, lively flavours, good yeast autolysis and a hint of sweetness giving an easy-drinking charm.

MED/DRY $35 –V

Cuvée No. 1 [Rosé]   (★★★★☆)

Just labelled as Cuvée No. 1, but made in a rosé style, this non-vintage wine (★★★★☆) is pale pink, scented, vibrant and smooth, with strawberryish, yeasty flavours, showing excellent delicacy and complexity, and a crisp, dryish finish.

MED/DRY $50 –V

Cuvée Number Eight   ★★★

An 'apéritif style' from Daniel Le Brun's family company, this is a non-vintage blend of Marlborough Pinot Noir and Chardonnay. The batch on the market in late 2009 (★★★★) is one of the best yet – pale straw, creamy and smooth, with strong, yeasty flavours showing good complexity and harmony.

MED/DRY $30 –V

Daniel Le Brun Brut NV   ★★★★

After buying Cellier Le Brun, Mahi sold the Daniel Le Brun brand to Lion Nathan. A Marlborough blend of Pinot Noir (60 per cent), Chardonnay (30 per cent) and Pinot Meunier (10 per cent), it is typically rich and toasty, in a high-flavoured style, crisp and yeasty, with good vigour and freshness.

MED/DRY $29 AV

Deutz Marlborough Cuvée   ★★★★★

The marriage of Pernod Ricard NZ's fruit at Marlborough with the Champagne house of Deutz's 150 years of experience created an instant winner. Bottled-fermented and matured on its yeast lees for two to three years, this non-vintage wine has evolved over the past decade into a less overtly fruity, more delicate and flinty style. The Pinot Noir grapes are drawn principally from Kaituna Estate, on the north side of the Wairau Valley; the Chardonnay comes mostly from Renwick Estate, in the middle of the valley. Before being bottled, the base wine is lees-aged for up to three months and given a full malolactic fermentation. Reserve wines, a year or two older than the rest, are added to each batch, contributing consistency and complexity to the final blend. The wine I tasted in late 2008 (★★★★☆) was pale and finely scented, with citrusy, slightly biscuity flavours that linger well. It's an elegant, subtle wine, beautifully fresh, crisp and harmonious.

MED/DRY $35 V+

Deutz Marlborough Cuvée Blanc de Blancs   ★★★★★

This Chardonnay-predominant blend is hand-harvested on the south side of the Wairau Valley, mostly at Renwick Estate, and matured for '3 to 5 years' on its yeast lees. It is typically a very classy wine with delicate, piercing, lemony, appley flavours, well-integrated yeastiness and a slightly creamy finish. The 2005 vintage (★★★★★) is refined and tightly structured, with lovely delicacy and rich, citrusy flavours, intensely yeasty and nutty. It's a very elegant and harmonious wine, intense, tight-knit, long and refined. The 2006 (★★★★★) is similar – very refined and finely balanced, with intense, citrusy, yeasty flavours, crisp and lingering.

MED/DRY $39 AV

Deutz Marlborough Cuvée Rosé   ★★★★☆

The non-vintage wine (★★★★☆) on the market in 2009 – made predominantly from Pinot Noir – is salmon pink, floral, fresh and finely textured, with crisp, strawberryish, yeasty flavours showing excellent vigour and complexity.

MED/DRY $39 –V

Doctors', The, Bubbles for Beth   (★★★☆)

The 2005 vintage (★★★☆) from Forrest is a sparkling red, made from Marlborough Syrah and Malbec and bottle-fermented. Full-coloured, it is berryish and gently yeasty, with a hint of dark chocolate and a smooth, lively finish. Worth trying.

MED/DRY $30 –V

Doctors', The, Remedy   (★★★☆)

Made by Forrest, the 2005 vintage (★★★☆) is a bottle-fermented Marlborough sparkling, based on Pinot Noir and Chardonnay. Light, crisp and elegant, with gentle yeastiness, it's a delicate, slightly nutty wine, showing good freshness and vigour.

MED/DRY $30 –V

Elstree Marlborough Cuvée Brut   ★★★★

The 2005 vintage (★★★★☆) from Highfield is a blend of Pinot Noir and Chardonnay, hand-picked and disgorged after three years on its yeast lees. Pale straw-coloured, it's a concentrated, complex wine with crisp, biscuity, yeasty, nutty flavours, showing excellent intensity and vigour, and a basically dry finish.

Vintage	05	04
WR	6	5
Drink	09-11	09-10

MED/DRY $37 –V

Flirt 'N Frolic Matakana Sparkling Rosé   (★★)

The rust-coloured non-vintage wine (★★) on sale in 2009, made by Hinchco, has crisp, dryish strawberry, spice and slight herb flavours, but lacks a bit of freshness and charm.

MED/DRY $20 –V

Forrest Estate Bubbles for Brigid   ★★★★

Bottled with a crown seal, rather than a cork, the 2005 vintage (★★★★) is a bottle-fermented Marlborough blend of Pinot Noir and Chardonnay. Pale straw, with an eruption of tiny bubbles, it is elegant and light, lemony and biscuity, with good yeast-derived complexity and a tight-knit, unusually dry (3 grams/litre of residual sugar) but very harmonious finish.

Vintage	05
WR	6
Drink	09-11

DRY $30 AV

Fusion Sparkling Muscat – see Soljans Fusion Sparkling Muscat

Hinchco Sparkling Merlot Rosé   (★★)

From Matakana, the 2008 vintage (★★) is rust-coloured, crisp and dryish, with strawberry and spice flavours that lack a bit of freshness and charm.

MED/DRY $25 –V

Huia Marlborough Brut   ★★★☆

The 2004 vintage (★★★★), a blend of Chardonnay (55 per cent), Pinot Noir (41 per cent) and Pinot Meunier (4 per cent), was fermented in old barrels prior to its secondary fermentation in the bottle, and disgorged after several years on its yeast lees. Straw-coloured, with a toasty, yeasty bouquet, it's a rich style with lively, nutty, yeasty, smooth flavours, showing good complexity. Delicious now.

Vintage	04	02
WR	6	6
Drink	09-12	09-10

MED/DRY $39 –V

Hunter's Miru Miru   ★★★☆

'Miru Miru' means bubbles. A stimulating apéritif, this wine is disgorged a year earlier than
its Reserve stablemate (below), has a lower Pinot Noir content and a crisper finish. The straw-
coloured 2006 vintage (★★★☆), blended from Chardonnay (55 per cent), Pinot Noir (41 per
cent) and Pinot Meunier (4 per cent) is smooth, with strong, citrusy, peachy flavours and good
yeast-derived complexity.

MED/DRY $26 –V

Hunter's Miru Miru Reserve   ★★★★

This has been one of Marlborough' finest sparklings, full and lively, with loads of citrusy, yeasty,
nutty flavour and a creamy, long finish. It is matured on its yeast lees for an average of three and
a half years. The 2004 vintage (★★★★) is a blend of Pinot Noir (63 per cent), Chardonnay (29
per cent) and Pinot Meunier (8 per cent). Straw-hued, it is crisp, toasty and yeasty, in a high-
flavoured style with excellent vigour, richness and harmony.

Vintage	06
WR	6
Drink	10-13

MED/DRY $32 –V

Italiano Bianco Spumante   (★★★)

From Pernod Ricard NZ, the non-vintage bubbly on sale in 2009 (★★★) offers great value.
Muscat-scented, it is light and lively, sweet and soft, with a steady stream of bubbles, good
freshness and vivacity, and lots of charm. Easy to underestimate!

SW $9 V+

Johanneshof Emmi   ★★★★

The non-vintage wine (★★★★) on sale in 2009 is a Marlborough blend of Pinot Noir and
Chardonnay, disgorged after 'several' years on its yeast lees. Bright, light yellow/green, it shows
excellent vigour and freshness, with strong, crisp, nutty flavours, dryish, lemony and long.

MED/DRY $35 –V

Lake Chalice Cracklin' Rosie   (★★☆)

The non-vintage, crown-sealed wine on the market in late 2008 (★★☆) was made from 2007
Marlborough Pinot Noir, with the 'added excitement of a little spritz'. Pink-hued, with a hint of
orange and gentle bubbles, it is light and crisp, in a very easy-drinking style with fresh, simple,
strawberryish flavours, slightly sweet (8 grams/litre of residual sugar) and smooth. Priced right.

MED/DRY $15 AV

La Michelle   (★★★★)

Classy, new sparkling wines are a rare breed in New Zealand, so the 2006 vintage (★★★★)
blend of Martinborough Pinot Noir (two-thirds) and Chardonnay from Margrain is welcome. A
notably dry style (5 grams/litre of residual sugar), lees-aged for two years, it is pale, smooth and
lively, with delicate, citrusy, appley, slightly nutty flavours and good yeast-derived complexity.
Finely textured and not at all austere, it carries the dry style well.

MED/DRY $38 –V

Lindauer Brut   ★★★

Given its good quality, low price and huge volumes, this non-vintage bubbly from Pernod Ricard NZ is one of the miracles of modern winemaking. It is blended from Pinot Noir and Chardonnay, grown in Gisborne and Hawke's Bay, and matured for a year on its yeast lees. Fractionally sweet (12 grams/litre of residual sugar), it generally shows good vigour and depth in a refined style, crisp and finely balanced, with lively, lemony, slightly nutty and yeasty flavours.

MED/DRY $16 V+

Lindauer Fraise   ★★☆

Pronounced 'Frez', the strawberry-flavoured Lindauer is 'aimed at the RTD [ready-mixed drinks] market', according to a major wine retailer. Made 'with an added touch of natural strawberry', the non-vintage wine on sale in 2009 (★★☆) is bright pink, with flavours that are very smooth and – well – strawberryish, in a fresh, light and lively, simple style with gentle sweetness. It's unlikely to appeal to regular wine drinkers, but we are obviously not the target market.

MED $16 AV

Lindauer Rosé   ★★★

Pernod Ricard NZ's bottle-fermented rosé is blended from Chardonnay and Pinot Noir, grown in Gisborne and Hawke's Bay. It is typically pink, with strawberryish, moderately yeasty aromas and flavours, fresh and lively, and a crisp, gently sweet (16 grams/litre of residual sugar) finish.

MED $16 V+

Lindauer Sauvignon   (★★★)

The only Lindauer-branded bubbly that is not bottle-fermented, this is a 'spritzig' (gently sparkling) blend of Marlborough Sauvignon Blanc (85 per cent), Chardonnay (14 per cent) and Pinot Noir (1 per cent). It's an easy summer sipper – refreshing, with lively, limey flavours and a slightly sweet (16 grams/litre of residual sugar), appetisingly crisp finish.

MED $15 V+

Lindauer Sec   ★★★

The medium version of Pernod Ricard NZ's best-seller is twice as sweet (24 grams/litre of residual sugar) as its Brut stablemate (which has 12 grams/litre). A bottle-fermented blend of Chardonnay and Pinot Noir, grown in Gisborne and Hawke's Bay, it is typically fresh and vivacious, with moderately yeasty flavours and a crisp, gently sweet finish.

MED $16 V+

Lindauer Special Reserve   ★★★☆

Pernod Ricard NZ's immensely drinkable bubbly is a non-vintage blend of Pinot Noir (60 per cent) and Chardonnay (40 per cent), grown in Gisborne and Hawke's Bay, and matured on its yeast lees for two years. Retasted in mid-2009 (★★★☆), it is pale pink, with very good depth of strawberryish, yeasty flavour and a dryish (12 grams/litre of residual sugar), crisp and vivacious finish.

MED/DRY $20 AV

Lindauer Special Reserve Blanc de Blancs   ★★★★

This non-vintage wine (★★★★), based entirely on Chardonnay grown in Gisborne (mostly) and Hawke's Bay, is disgorged after two years on its yeast lees. It's a deliciously well-balanced wine, lemony and nutty, with gentle yeast autolysis characters and a slightly creamy, dryish (12 grams/litre of residual sugar) finish.

MED/DRY $21 V+

Lindauer Special Reserve Cuvée Riche   ★★★☆

This non-vintage wine is a blend of Pinot Noir and Chardonnay, grown in Gisborne and Hawke's Bay. Pink/straw in hue, it shows good complexity and richness, with delicious peach, orange and slight honey flavours, abundantly sweet (40 grams/litre of residual sugar) and crisp.

MED $20 AV

Lindauer Special Reserve Vintage   (★★★★)

The 2004 (★★★★) is the first bubbly under the Lindauer brand from Pernod Ricard NZ to be vintage-dated. A blend of Chardonnay (70 per cent) and Pinot Noir (30 per cent), grown in Marlborough and Gisborne, and disgorged after two years on its yeast lees, it's fresh, intense, citrusy and yeasty, with excellent delicacy and depth.

MED/DRY $25 AV

Matua Valley Bubbly   (★★☆)

Launched in 2006, this non-vintage wine is a Gisborne-grown blend of Chardonnay (90 per cent) and Muscat. Pale, with fresh aromas, it's an appley, gently perfumed wine, crisp, simple and lively.

MED $16 AV

Matua Valley Reserve Release Méthode Traditionnelle   (★★★★)

Released in 2009, the 2004 vintage (★★★★) is a blend of Pinot Noir, Chardonnay and Pinot Meunier, grown in Marlborough and disgorged after more than four years on its yeast lees. Light straw, with slightly biscuity aromas, it is crisp and lively, with lemony, slightly nutty flavours, showing good yeast-derived complexity, and a finely balanced, smooth finish.

MED/DRY $23 V+

Montana Chardonnay/Pinot Noir Brut Cuveé NV   ★★★★

This deliciously easy-drinking wine was the first-ever bottle-fermented bubbly under the Montana label when it was launched in 2006. Unexpectedly stylish (for the price), it is based mostly on Gisborne Chardonnay, with 30 per cent Pinot Noir (mostly from Hawke's Bay), and disgorged after a year of lees-aging in the bottle. It is crisp and lively, with elegant fruit flavours, biscuity, nutty, yeasty notes adding complexity, and a dryish (12 grams/litre of residual sugar), lingering finish.

MED/DRY $22 V+

Montana Chardonnay/Pinot Noir Rosé   (★★★☆)

This non-vintage wine (★★★☆) is light and lively, with bright pink colour, fresh, berryish aromas and attractive, slightly sweet (12 grams/litre of residual sugar), gently yeasty flavours.

MED/DRY $22 AV

Montana Reserve Chardonnay/Pinot Noir Brut Cuvée Rosé   ★★★★

This non-vintage, bottle-fermented sparkling is pale pink, with considerable elegance and complexity. Crisp and lively, with strawberryish, yeasty flavours, showing good delicacy, it's a vivacious, dryish wine, priced sharply.

MED/DRY $22 V+

Morton Black Label Méthode Traditionnelle   ★★★★

The 2002 vintage (★★★★), grown mostly at the Riverview Vineyard in Hawke's Bay, is a blend of Pinot Meunier (62 per cent), Pinot Noir (33 per cent) and Chardonnay (5 per cent). Disgorged after over five years on its yeast lees, it is pale straw, with complex, very biscuity and nutty flavours, crisp and dry.

Vintage	02
WR	7
Drink	09-12

MED/DRY $35 –V

Morton Blanc de Blancs   ★★★★

Still on the market, the 2000 vintage (★★★★) was made solely from Chardonnay, grown in Hawke's Bay and Marlborough, and disgorged after seven years on its yeast lees. The bouquet is very yeasty; the palate is crisp, citrusy and bready, with good vigour and intensity and a long, nutty, dryish finish.

Vintage	00
WR	6
Drink	09-12

MED/DRY $28 AV

Morton IQ3   (★★★★)

'IQ3' stands for 'improving quietly for three years'. A blend of Chardonnay, Pinot Noir and Pinot Meunier, grown in Hawke's Bay and Marlborough, it started life as Morton Premium Brut, then spent three years on its yeast lees. Pale straw, it is an elegant, still youthful wine, lemony, appley, nutty and yeasty, with excellent freshness, vigour and crispness.

MED/DRY $25 AV

Morton Premium Brut   ★★★☆

This has long been popular as an easy-drinking, creamy-smooth, bottle-fermented bubbly. Blended from Pinot Noir, Chardonnay and Pinot Meunier, grown in Marlborough and Hawke's Bay, and given a full, softening malolactic fermentation, it is disgorged on demand after a minimum of 18 months on its yeast lees, and includes base wine from earlier vintages. It typically shows some elegance and lovely harmony, with crisp, citrusy, appley flavours, very fresh, delicate and lively, and a moderately yeasty finish. The sample I tasted in mid to late 2009 (★★★☆) was fresh, crisp and vigorous, with citrusy, gently yeasty flavours.

MED/DRY $21 AV

Morton Reserve Sec   ★★★☆

This pale straw, non-vintage wine is a bottle-fermented blend of Chardonnay, Pinot Noir and Pinot Meunier, grown in Hawke's Bay and disgorged after a minimum of 18 months on its yeast lees. The wine I tasted in mid to late 2009 (★★★☆) is a slightly sweet style with lively, lemony, appley, crisp flavours, a hint of cashew nuts, and good vivacity.

MED/DRY $20 AV

Mount Riley Savée Sparkling Sauvignon Blanc   ★★★

This distinctive Marlborough bubbly is bottle-fermented and then removed swiftly from its lees to retain its fresh, tangy varietal characters. The 2008 vintage (★★★☆) is tropical-fruit flavoured, in a ripely herbaceous style, slightly sweet (7 grams/litre of residual sugar), crisp and lively, with a steady 'bead' and gently yeasty finish.

MED/DRY $21 –V

Nautilus Cuvée Marlborough   ★★★★★

Recent releases of this non-vintage, bottle-fermented sparkling have generally revealed an intensity and refinement that positions the label among the finest in the country. A blend of Pinot Noir (75 per cent) and Chardonnay (25 per cent), it is blended with older, reserve stocks held in old oak barriques and disgorged after a minimum of three years aging on its yeast lees. Lean and crisp, piercing and long, it's a beautifully tight, vivacious and refined wine, its Marlborough fruit characters enriched with intense, bready aromas and flavours.

MED/DRY $39 AV

No. 1 Family Estate Limited Edition Marlborough Reserve Cuvée 10   ★★★★☆

Celebrating the first decade of Daniel and Adele Le Brun's No. 1 Family Estate, this wine varies in terms of its varietal blend. The current release (★★★★☆), based on Pinot Noir (80 per cent) and Chardonnay (20 per cent), was disgorged after four years on its yeast lees. The back label describes it as 'generous, rich, creamy and full-bodied' – and it's right. Finely fragrant, with a nutty, yeasty bouquet, it's a straw-hued wine with a steady 'bead' and citrus-fruit, bread and cashew nut flavours, showing excellent richness, complexity and smoothness. It's now mature, but still very lively.

MED/DRY $50 –V

Nobilo Méthode Traditionnelle   ★★★☆

The classy 2005 vintage (★★★★) from Constellation NZ is a bottle-fermented blend based on Pinot Noir (46 per cent) and Chardonnay (43 per cent), plus 11 per cent Pinot Meunier. The bouquet is stylish, fresh and slightly nutty; the palate is lean and lively, with good vigour and delicacy and lemony, nutty, yeasty flavours that linger well.

MED/DRY $23 AV

Palliser Estate Martinborough Méthode Traditionnelle   ★★★★

This is Martinborough's finest sparkling (although few have been produced). The 2005 vintage (★★★★), made from Pinot Noir and Chardonnay, is very elegant and harmonious, with good intensity of citrusy, appley, yeasty, nutty flavours, crisp and lively.

MED/DRY $34 –V

Pelorus
★★★★★

Cloudy Bay's bottle-fermented sparkling is typically a powerful wine, creamy, nutty and full-flavoured. A blend of Pinot Noir and Chardonnay – with always a higher proportion of Pinot Noir – it is given its primary alcoholic fermentation (partly with indigenous yeasts) in a mixture of stainless steel tanks, large oak vats and French oak barriques, followed by malolactic fermentation and lengthy lees-aging of the base wines prior to blending, and once bottled it is matured for three years on its yeast lees before it is disgorged. The 2005 vintage (★★★★☆) is rich and refined, with a steady stream of tiny bubbles and very vibrant, ripe, peachy and yeasty flavours, fresh, vivacious and long.

MED/DRY $48 AV

Pelorus NV
★★★★

Cloudy Bay's non-vintage Marlborough bubbly is a Chardonnay-dominant style, with 20 per cent Pinot Noir, matured for at least two years on its yeast lees (a year less than for the vintage). It is made in a more fruit-driven style than the vintage, but still very refined and refreshing. The batch on sale in 2009 (★★★★★) is the best I've tasted. Very elegant, crisp and lively, it is citrusy and slightly nutty, vivacious and racy, with a Champagne-like complexity and immediacy.

MED/DRY $35 –V

Quartz Reef Méthode Traditionnelle NV
★★★★

This increasingly Champagne-like, non-vintage bubbly is from a small Central Otago company. The batches vary in varietal composition, but the latest release (★★★★) in mid to late 2009 is a blend of Chardonnay (57 per cent) and Pinot Noir (43 per cent), grown at Bendigo. It's a distinctly cool-climate style, crisp, lively and yeasty, with good delicacy and intensity of lemony, appley, slightly nutty flavours.

MED/DRY $29 AV

Quartz Reef Méthode Traditionnelle Vintage
★★★★★

The 2000–2002 vintages have all been outstanding. The aristocratic 2002 (★★★★★) is the finest Central Otago bubbly yet. A blend of Pinot Noir (55 per cent) and Chardonnay (45 per cent), it was disgorged in September 2006 after nearly four years of lees-aging. Very pale straw in colour, it is beautifully scented, with tight-knit, citrusy, very yeasty and nutty flavours, poised and lingering. Showing great vigour and complexity, it's a distinctly Champagne-like wine, intense and highly refined. The 2006 vintage (which has also yielded a rosé version) will be released in late 2010.

MED/DRY $39 AV

Selaks Winemaker's Favourite Méthode Traditionnelle
(★★★★)

The stylish 2006 vintage (★★★★) is a Marlborough blend of Pinot Noir (78 per cent) and Chardonnay (22 per cent). Disgorged after two years on its yeast lees, it is pale straw, very fresh and lively, with tight, citrusy, slightly nutty flavours, showing good delicacy and immediacy.

MED/DRY $25 AV

Soljans Fusion Sparkling Muscat ★★★★

Soljans produces this delicious bubbly from Muscat grapes grown in Gisborne. It is fresh and vivacious, perfumed and sweetly seductive (80 grams/litre of residual sugar), with low alcohol (8 per cent), a steady stream of bubbles and rich, lemony, appley flavours, ripe and smooth. An excellent Asti Spumante copy, it's full of easy-drinking charm and bargain-priced. When retasted in 2009, it was right on form.

SW $16 V+

Soljans Fusion Sparkling Rosé (★★★☆)

The pale red, non-vintage wine on sale in 2009 (★★★☆) is a Gisborne blend of Pinotage and Muscat. Buoyantly fruity and slightly sweetish, it is crisp and lively, with strawberryish flavours and instant appeal.

MED $18 V+

Soljans Legacy Méthode Traditionnelle ★★★☆

Still on sale, the stylish 2004 vintage (★★★★) is a blend of Chardonnay (60 per cent) and Pinot Noir (40 per cent), grown in Hawke's Bay and Marlborough. Tight and elegant, it's a skilfully crafted wine, citrusy and appley, with good vigour and yeasty, nutty characters adding complexity.

MED/DRY $32 –V

Spy Valley Echelon ★★★☆

The 2005 vintage (★★★☆) of this bottle-fermented bubbly is a blend of Marlborough Pinot Noir (60 per cent), Chardonnay (32 per cent) and Pinot Meunier (8 per cent), disgorged after 18 months on its yeast lees. Pale pink, it is an exuberantly fruity style with smooth, strawberryish, peachy flavours, lively and gently yeasty, and a crisp, dryish finish.

MED/DRY $29 –V

Summerhouse Marlborough Blanc de Blancs (★★★★)

Made from estate-grown Chardonnay and lees-aged for two years, this non-vintage wine (★★★★) is attractively scented, lively and crisp, with citrusy, nutty and yeasty flavours, showing good complexity and intensity, and a dryish finish.

MED/DRY $32 –V

Twin Islands Chardonnay/Pinot Noir Brut NV ★★★★

'A great bottle to be seen with in some of the classiest bars and restaurants', Nautilus's lower-priced bubbly sold for $17 a few years ago, then vanished for a while, until its relaunch in late 2009. The price is now $25, but it's worth it. Very fresh, delicate and lively, it's a refined Marlborough wine, lemony and slightly nutty, that floats very smoothly across the palate.

MED/DRY $25 AV

Verde NV   ★★★☆

Popular as 'a wedding wine, upmarket from Lindauer', this Hawke's Bay sparkling from Pernod Ricard NZ is based on Chardonnay (60 per cent) and Pinot Noir (to provide a style contrast to the Pinot Noir-dominant Lindauer Special Reserve). Matured on its yeast lees for 18 months, it is typically very lively, with lemony, slightly sweet (12 grams/litre of residual sugar) flavours showing good, yeast-derived complexity.

MED/DRY $21 AV

Villa Maria Méthode Traditionnelle NV   (★★★★)

Launched in 2009, this is a rich, mature style, based on 68 per cent Pinot Noir (grown in Hawke's Bay and Auckland) and 32 per cent Chardonnay (Marlborough), with base wines dating back to 2003. Disgorged after three years on its yeast lees (and closed with a crown seal, rather than a cork), it's pale yellow, citrusy, yeasty and nutty, with a crisp, almost bone-dry finish (3.5 grams/litre of residual sugar), and excellent complexity and harmony.

DRY $35 –V

Waipipi Chenin Blanc Brut Méthode Traditionnelle   ★★★★

Disgorged from its yeast lees in mid 2009, the 2007 vintage (★★★★) was made from Chenin Blanc grapes, grown at Opaki, north of Masterton, in the Wairarapa. Very fresh and lively, it is light (11 per cent alcohol), with strong, lemony, appley and nutty, gently sweet flavours, fresh, vivacious and racy, with good yeast-derived complexity. Well worth discovering.

Vintage	07	06	05
WR	6	6	6
Drink	09-15	09-13	09-10

MED/DRY $33 –V

Rosé Wines

The number of rosé labels on the market has exploded recently, as drinkers discover that rosé is not an inherently inferior lolly water, but a worthwhile and delicious wine style in its own right. New Zealand rosé is even finding offshore markets (78,222 cases shipped in the year to June 2009, a steep rise from 905 cases in 2003) and collecting overseas awards.

In Europe many pink or copper-coloured wines, such as the rosés of Provence, Anjou and Tavel, are produced from red-wine varieties. (Dark-skinned grapes are even used to make white wines: Champagne, heavily based on Pinot Meunier and Pinot Noir, is a classic case.) To make a rosé, after the grapes are crushed, the time the juice spends in contact with its skins is crucial; the longer the contact, the greater the diffusion of colour, tannin and flavour from the skins into the juice.

'Saignée' (bled) is a French term that is seen occasionally on rosé labels. A technique designed to produce a pink wine or a more concentrated red wine – or both – it involves running off or 'bleeding' free-run juice from crushed, dark-skinned grapes after a brief, pre-ferment maceration on skins. An alternative is to commence the fermentation as for a red wine, then after 12 or 24 hours, when its colour starts to deepen, drain part of the juice for rosé production and vinify the rest as a red wine.

Pinot Noir and Merlot are the grape varieties most commonly used in New Zealand to produce rosé wines. Regional differences are emerging: South Island and Wairarapa rosés, usually made from Pinot Noir, are typically fresh, slightly sweet and crisp, while those from the middle and upper North Island – Hawke's Bay, Gisborne and Auckland – tend to be Merlot-based, fuller-bodied and drier.

These are typically charming, 'now-or-never' wines, peaking in their first six to 18 months with seductive strawberry/raspberry-like fruit flavours. Freshness is the essence of the wines' appeal.

25 Steps Central Otago Pinot Noir Rosé   (★★★★)

Estate-grown at Lowburn, the delicious 2008 vintage (★★★★) was harvested at 24.8 brix, held on its skins for 24 hours and tank-fermented. Bright pink, it is fruity, strawberryish and spicy, with a sliver of sweetness, fresh, lively acidity and good richness and roundness.

MED/DRY $25 –V

Akarua Pinot Rosé   ★★★☆

Grown at Bannockburn, in Central Otago, and made from Pinot Noir, this is typically a charming, bright pink/light red wine, attractively scented, with vibrant, berryish, gently sweet flavours, enlivened with fresh acidity.

MED/DRY $21 –V

Alexia Hawke's Bay Rosé   (★★★★)

The very finely balanced 2008 vintage (★★★★) was made from Merlot grapes, grown in The Triangle district. Bright pink/pale red, it is lively and smooth, with fresh acidity, faint sweetness and strong plum, red-berry and spice flavours, all in lovely harmony.

MED/DRY $20 AV

Amisfield Saignée Rosé   ★★★☆

Made from Pinot Noir, estate-grown in the Cromwell Basin and tank-fermented, the 2009 vintage (★★★☆) of this Central Otago wine is pink/pale red, mouthfilling (13.8 per cent alcohol) and slightly sweet (7 grams/litres of residual sugar), with strawberry and spice flavours showing very good freshness, delicacy and depth. It's ready to roll.

Vintage	09	08
WR	5	6
Drink	09-11	09-12

MED/DRY $25 –V

Ascension The Rosarian Matakana Rosé   ★★★

The 2008 vintage (★★★) is a pink, lively blend of Merlot (50 per cent) with smaller portions of Malbec, Pinotage and Cabernet Franc. It is fresh and vibrant, with crisp, strawberryish, spicy flavours.

MED/DRY $24 –V

Askerne Hawke's Bay Rosé   ★★★

The 2009 vintage (★★★☆) is a full-bodied Hawke's Bay wine (14.5 per cent alcohol), almost fully dry (4 grams/litre of residual sugar), with an inviting, bright pink/pale red colour, fresh, ripe berry and plum flavours, showing good depth, and a well-rounded finish.

Vintage	09
WR	6
Drink	09-10

DRY $16 AV

Ata Rangi Summer Rosé   ★★★★

Typically made from Hawke's Bay Merlot at the Ata Rangi winery in Martinborough, this is a vivacious, bright pink/light red wine, floral and fresh, with plum and red-berry flavours, generous and smooth.

MED/DRY $18 V+

Auntsfield Pretty Horses Marlborough Rosé   ★★★★

Made from Pinot Noir and 10 per cent barrel-fermented, the 2008 vintage (★★★★) is bright pink, with substantial body, excellent depth of fresh, strawberry and spice flavours, a touch of complexity and a dry finish.

DRY $25 –V

Bald Hills Friends and Lovers Rosé   (★★★★)

Full of appeal, the 2008 vintage (★★★★) was made from Pinot Noir, estate-grown at Bannockburn, in Central Otago. Bright pink, it is very floral and fresh, with strong, buoyant, cherry and plum flavours, slightly spicy and smooth.

Vintage	08
WR	6
Drink	10-12

DRY $20 AV

Bannock Brae Cathy's Rosé   ★★★☆

Named after the partnership's 'better-looking half', the 2008 vintage (★★★☆) was made from estate-grown Central Otago Pinot Noir. Bright pink, it is still very fresh and lively, with red-berry and spice flavours, showing good depth, and a well-rounded finish.

MED/DRY $24 –V

Bell Bird Bay Hawke's Bay Rosé   (★★★★)

Made at the Alpha Domus winery, the 2008 vintage (★★★★) is an excellent buy. Its bright pink colour is enticing; so are the floral bouquet and strong, smooth, strawberryish flavours, fresh and dryish.

MED/DRY $15 V+

Black Barn Hawke's Bay Rosé   (★★☆)

The 2008 vintage (★★☆) has a light red, slight orange colour and berry and spice flavours, dry and mellow. It's a solid wine, but lacks a bit of softness and charm.

DRY $18 –V

Bracken's Order Blanc de Pinot Noir   (★★★★)

Estate-grown at Gibbston, in Central Otago, the 2008 vintage (★★★★) was fermented in small stainless steel 'barrels'. Pink/red, with attractive, berryish scents, it is mouthfilling (14 per cent alcohol), with fresh, strong flavours of red berries, plums and spices in a crisp, slightly sweet style, very lively and harmonious.

MED/DRY $20 AV

Brick Bay Matakana Rosé   ★★★

The bright pink 2008 vintage (★★★) is a blend of Cabernet Sauvignon (41 per cent), Malbec (30 per cent) and Merlot (29 per cent). Made in a slightly sweet style (9 grams/litre of residual sugar), it has strawberryish, spicy flavours, vibrant and refreshing.

MED/DRY $22 –V

Brightside Nelson Rosé   (★★☆)

From Kaimira, the 2008 vintage (★★☆) was made from Pinot Noir and fermented to full dryness. It's a pink, mouthfilling wine (14 per cent alcohol), with solid depth of strawberry and spice flavour.

DRY $15 AV

Butterfish Bay Northland Paewhenua Rosé   (★★★☆)

Grown on a peninsula extending into Mangonui Harbour, the 2009 vintage (★★★☆) is a good debut. Bright pink/pale red, with fresh, red-berry aromas, it's a medium-bodied wine, vibrantly fruity, with plenty of slightly sweet (7 grams/litre of residual sugar), plummy flavour.

MED/DRY $19 AV

Cable Bay Waiheke Island Rosé   ★★★★

Waiheke Island is producing some excellent rosés, such as the 2008 vintage (★★★★) from Cable Bay. Made from Merlot and Malbec grapes, grown at Church Bay, it is bright pink/red, full-bodied, with fresh, vibrant, berryish, spicy flavours and a smooth (6 grams/litre of residual sugar) finish. It's already delicious.

Vintage	08
WR	7
Drink	P

MED/DRY $20 AV

Clearview Estate Black Reef Blush   ★★★★

A top buy. Delicious in its youth, the 2009 vintage (★★★★) is a full-bodied wine, grown at Te Awanga, in Hawke's Bay. Based on the French hybrid, Chambourcin, it is bright pink/pale red, with a floral bouquet and strong red-berry and plum flavours, refreshingly crisp and dry (3 grams/litre of residual sugar).

Vintage	09	08	07
WR	7	6	6
Drink	09-11	09-10	P

DRY $16 V+

Coal Pit Central Otago Rosé   (★★★)

Estate-grown at Gibbston, the 2009 vintage (★★★) was made from Pinot Noir. Pink/pale red, it has fresh, berryish aromas, mouthfilling body and good depth of berryish, slightly spicy and herbal flavour, crisp and lively.

Vintage	09
WR	7
Drink	09-11

MED/ DRY $20 –V

Coney Ramblin' Rosé   (★★★)

Made from Martinborough Pinot Noir, the 2008 vintage (★★★) is pale pink, smooth and slightly sweet, with strawberryish, slightly spicy flavours, showing good body and depth.

MED/DRY $22 –V

Coopers Creek Huapai Rosé   (★★★★)

Enjoyable from the start, the 2008 vintage (★★★★) is an estate-grown blend of Merlot (82 per cent) and Malbec. Bright pink, with invitingly fresh, ripe, plummy, spicy aromas, it is mouthfilling and smooth, with gentle acidity and smooth, strawberryish flavours, instantly appealing.

MED/DRY $18 V+

Corazon Single Vineyard Rosé   (★★★)

Grown at Mangatawhiri, in the Waikato, the 2008 vintage (★★★) is a basically dry style (4.5 grams/litre of residual sugar), made from Syrah. Bright pink, it's a mouthfilling wine with fresh, vibrant berry and spice flavours, showing crisp acidity and good depth.

Vintage	08
WR	5
Drink	09-10

DRY $18 –V

Crawford Farm Rosé   (★★☆)

From Constellation NZ, the 2007 vintage (★★☆) offers no information about its varietal or regional origins. Tasted in mid-2009, it has a pale red, slightly developed colour, mouthfilling body (14.5 per cent alcohol) and dryish strawberry, herb and spice flavours that taste mature. Ready.

DRY $22 –V

Desert Heart Rosé   ★★★

The salmon pink 2008 vintage (★★★☆) is a 'serious' style of rosé, best served with food. Made from Pinot Noir, grown at Bannockburn, in Central Otago, it was lees-aged for five months in seasoned French oak casks. Full-bodied, it has strawberry and spice flavours, showing a touch of complexity, and a dry finish.

Vintage	08
WR	6
Drink	09-12

DRY $23 –V

Dolbel Estate Hawke's Bay Rosé   (★★★☆)

Made from Merlot and briefly oak-aged, the pale pink 2008 vintage (★★★☆) is a dry style, designed for the table rather than as an apéritif. Mouthfilling, with gentle strawberry and spice flavours, it shows greater complexity than most rosés.

DRY $20 AV

Domaine Georges Michel Summer Folly Rosé Pinot Noir   ★★☆

Grown in Marlborough, the 2009 vintage (★★★) has a bright, light red colour, with berry and spice aromas and flavours, fresh, lively and smooth.

DRY $15 AV

Domain Road Central Otago Pinot Noir Rosé   (★★★★)

Full of drink-young charm, the 2009 vintage (★★★★) is scented and pink, with fresh, lively raspberry, strawberry and spice flavours, dryish, finely balanced and lingering. The 2008 (★★★★) is also very pretty, with an enticing floral bouquet, delicious strawberry and spice flavours and a well-rounded finish.

MED/DRY $22 AV

Elephant Hill Rosé   (★★★☆)

Made from Central Otago Pinot Noir, the 2009 vintage (★★★☆) is bright pink, floral and fresh, with attractive strawberryish flavours, showing good delicacy and depth. Vibrantly fruity and soft, it's a drink-young charmer.

MED/DRY $20 AV

Esk Valley Merlot/Malbec Rosé

★★★★★

This is clearly New Zealand's best rosé, with several trophies to prove it. The skilfully balanced and vivacious 2008 vintage (★★★★) is a Hawke's Bay blend, Merlot-based (93 per cent), with a splash of Malbec. Handled without oak, it's a mouthfilling, dryish wine (5.5 grams/litre of residual sugar), pink/pale red, with attractively scented, berryish aromas and an abundance of cherryish, plummy flavour, deliciously fresh and smooth. (There is no 2009.)

Vintage	09	08	07
WR	NM	6	6
DRINK	NM	09-10	P

MED/DRY $23 V+

Forrest Estate Marlborough Rosé

★★★★

The 2008 vintage (★★★☆) is a freshly scented blend of Merlot, Pinot Noir, Malbec and Syrah. Pink/red, it has plummy, slightly spicy flavours, with a sliver of sweetness (7 grams/litre of residual sugar) and a crisp, vibrant, lingering finish.

Vintage	08
WR	4
Drink	09-10

MED/DRY $17 V+

Fossil Ridge Rosé

★★★

Pale pink, the easy-drinking 2009 vintage (★★★) is a hand-picked, single-vineyard Nelson Pinot Noir, gently sweet (10 grams/litre of residual sugar), with strawberryish, slightly spicy flavours, fresh and smooth.

MED/DRY $20 –V

Gibbston Valley Blanc de Pinot Noir

★★★☆

This Central Otago wine 'will make truck drivers weep for the agonising beauty of the world'. The 2009 vintage (★★★☆) is bright pink/pale red, floral and charming, with good body and depth of fresh, vibrant, berryish flavours, crisp, slightly sweet and smooth.

MED/DRY $28 –V

Gladstone Wairarapa Rosé

★★★

The 2008 vintage (★★★) is a blend of Cabernet Franc, Merlot and Malbec, grown near Masterton, in the Wairarapa. Pink/slight orange, it's a soft, forward wine, berryish, slightly spicy, smooth and ready for drinking.

MED/DRY $21 –V

Greystone Waipara Rosé Pinot Noir

(★★★☆)

Full of drink-young appeal, the 2009 vintage (★★★☆) is bright pink/red, mouthfilling and smooth, with berryish, slightly spicy flavours, showing good depth. It's an easy-drinking, slightly sweet style (14 grams/litre of residual sugar).

MED/DRY $19 AV

Hincho Matakana Merlot Rosé

(★★)

Created 'to enhance the foods of a Matakana long lunch', the 2008 vintage (★★) is an off-dry style with slightly developed colour and simple berry, spice and herb flavours.

MED/DRY $20 –V

Hitchen Road Rosé   (★★★☆)

Estate-grown at Pokeno, in North Waikato, the salmon pink 2009 vintage (★★★☆) was made from hand-picked Pinotage. A good 'food' wine, it's bone-dry, mouthfilling and smooth, with strawberry and spice flavours, a hint of oranges and gentle tannins.

DRY $18 AV

Huia Marlborough Rosé   (★★★)

Grown in the Brancott Valley, the 2009 vintage (★★★) is a blend of Merlot and Malbec. Pale pink, it's a dryish style (5.5 grams/litre of residual sugar), mouthfilling, berryish, slightly savoury and spicy.

Vintage	09
WR	7
Drink	09-12

MED/DRY $23 –V

Jules Taylor Rosé   (★★★★)

Not identified by region, the charming 2009 vintage (★★★★) from this Marlborough-based producer is bright pink/pale red, floral and fruity, with vibrant, ripe plum and red-berry flavours. A very pretty wine, slightly sweet (10.5 grams/litre of residual sugar) and smooth, it's delicious from the start.

Vintage	09
WR	5
Drink	09-12

MED/DRY $22 AV

Julicher Rosé   (★★★)

The floral, fresh 2008 vintage (★★★) is a Martinborough wine, based entirely on Pinot Noir. Strawberryish, spicy and smooth, it has a hint of sweetness and plenty of drink-young charm.

MED/DRY $20 –V

Jurassic Ridge Waiheke Island Syrah Rosé   (★★★★★)

The 2009 vintage (★★★★★) is fleshy, dry and rich, with sweet-fruit characters and strong, vibrant, berry and spice flavours. It's a serious yet charming wine, already delicious.

DRY $29 AV

Kina Beach Vineyard Nelson Merlot Rosé   ★★★☆

Ready to roll, the 2009 vintage (★★★) includes 15 per cent Cabernet Franc. Pink/pale red, it's a medium-bodied wine with fresh acidity, gentle strawberry and spice flavours and a rounded (5 grams/litre of residual sugar) finish.

Vintage	09	08
WR	6	6
Drink	09-11	P

MED/DRY $20 AV

Kumeu River Village Pinot Rosé   (★★☆)

The 2009 vintage (★★☆) was made from Pinot Noir grown at Kumeu, in West Auckland. Pink/pale red, with earthy aromas, it is light to medium-bodied, with strawberry and spice flavours, gentle tannins and a dry finish.

DRY $18 –V

Lawson's Dry Hills Pinot Rosé   ★★★

The pink/red 2008 vintage (★★★) of this Marlborough wine is juicy and berryish, with crisp, vibrant, slightly sweet flavours.

Vintage	09	08	07
WR	7	6	7
Drink	09-10	P	P

MED/DRY $20 –V

Locharburn Central Otago Pinot Rosé   (★★★)

Grown at Lowburn, the 2008 vintage (★★★) is salmon pink, with scented, strawberry and spice aromas and flavours. It's a harmonious, slightly sweet style (7 grams/litre of residual sugar) with a hint of apricots and a slightly creamy mouthfeel.

Vintage	08
WR	5
Drink	09-10

MED/DRY $22 –V

Lowburn Ferry Central Otago Pinot Rosé   (★★★★)

Delicious from the start, the 2009 vintage (★★★★) is a vibrantly fruity, crisp, dry style (3 grams/litre of residual sugar), bright pink, with mouthfilling body (14 per cent alcohol) and fresh, strong berry and spice flavours, showing excellent delicacy and immediacy.

DRY $24 –V

Maori Point Central Otago Pinot Noir Rosé   (★★★☆)

Grown at Tarras, the pale pink 2008 vintage (★★★☆) is a mouthfilling, dryish style (5.5 grams/litre of residual sugar) with strong, smooth berry and spice flavours, hints of apricots and peaches, and a lingering finish.

Vintage	08
WR	6
Drink	09-12

MED/DRY $19 AV

Margrain Pinot Rosé   ★★★☆

The 2008 vintage (★★★☆), grown in Martinborough, is bright pink/light red, with good depth and delicacy of berry, plum and spice flavours, crisp, slightly sweet (11.8 grams/litre of residual sugar) and lively.

Vintage	09
WR	6
Drink	09-10

MED/DRY $24 –V

Marsden Bay of Islands Rosé   ★★☆

Blended from Northland grapes, the 2008 vintage (★★☆) is slightly sweet (7 grams/litre of residual sugar), with pink/orange colour, showing some development, and smooth, berryish, slightly leafy flavours. Ready.

MED/DRY $18 –V

Martinborough Vineyard Rosé   ★★★☆

Made from Pinot Noir, the 2008 vintage (★★★☆) is ruby-hued, fleshy and smooth, with satisfying body, fresh, strong, berryish, plummy flavours and an off-dry (6 grams/litre of residual sugar) finish.

MED/DRY $20 (375ML) –V

Matua Valley North Island Rosé   ★★★

Designed to go 'with a bit of shade from the sun, a book and the cricket on the radio', the 2009 vintage (★★★☆) was made in a gently sweet style (6 grams/litre of residual sugar). Bright pink/red, with fresh, raspberryish aromas, it's a full-bodied wine with strong red-berry and plum flavours, very smooth and harmonious.

MED/DRY $15 AV

Millton Te Arai Vineyard Merlot Rosé   ★★★★

Enjoyed during summer in 'bars, cafés and back gardens all around the country', this very easy-drinking wine is grown in Gisborne and stop-fermented in a slightly sweet style (10 grams/litre of residual sugar in 2008). The 2008 vintage (★★★★) is pink/red, fleshy and vibrantly fruity, with berry, plum and spice flavours, fresh acidity and an attractively scented bouquet.

Vintage	08	07
WR	7	6
Drink	P	P

MED $21 AV

Miro Vineyard Rosé NV   (★★★)

Grown at Onetangi, on Waiheke Island, the non-vintage wine (★★★) on sale in 2009 is light (11.5 per cent alcohol) and pleasant, with bright, light pink colour and gently sweet strawberry and spice flavours.

MED/DRY $25 –V

Mission Hawke's Bay Rosé   ★★☆

The 2009 vintage (★★★) is pink/slight orange, with high alcohol (14.5 per cent) and generous, berryish, spicy flavours, dry and smooth. Ready.

DRY $16 –V

Montana East Coast Rosé   ★★★

This easy-drinking wine from Pernod Ricard NZ is medium-bodied, with Merlot as the key variety, blended with such grapes as Pinotage, Pinot Noir and Cabernet Franc. The 2008 vintage (★★★) is fresh and crisp, with raspberry and spice flavours, slightly sweet and smooth.

MED/DRY $18 –V

Morton Estate Musetta Hawke's Bay Rosé   (★★★☆)

The 2007 vintage (★★★☆) is a blend of Merlot and Malbec. It was very charming in its youth, with an inviting, bright pink/light red colour and vibrant berry and plum flavours, deliciously rich, ripe and rounded. However, it is now a bit past its best.

Vintage	07
WR	7
Drink	P

DRY $18 AV

Mount Dottrel Central Otago Saignée Rosé   ★★★☆

Made from Pinot Noir, the charming 2009 vintage (★★★☆) is bright pink, crisp and dry, with vibrant flavours of strawberries, spices and herbs, fresh and crisp.

Vintage	09	08
WR	6	7
Drink	09-11	09-10

DRY $23 –V

Mt Difficulty Central Otago Pinot Noir Rosé   ★★★★☆

The 2008 vintage (★★★★☆) is more full-bodied, complex and downright satisfying than most rosés. Partly barrel-fermented, it is bright pink and mouthfilling, with a strong surge of berryish, spicy flavours, deliciously fresh, smooth and lingering.

MED/DRY $25 AV

Mt Rosa Rosé   ★★☆

The 2009 vintage (★★☆) is a Central Otago wine, bright pink, with fresh, smooth berry, plum and herb flavours, a slightly earthy streak and a crisp, dry finish (4 grams/litre of residual sugar).

DRY $22 –V

Muddy Water Growers' Series Waipara Rosé   ★★★★

The 2009 vintage (★★★☆) was made from Pinot Noir. Bright pink, it has vibrant strawberry and spice flavours, fresh and strong, and a finely balanced, dry (4 grams/litre of residual sugar) finish.

Vintage	09
WR	7
Drink	09-11

DRY $23 AV

Mud House Central Otago Rosé   (★★★★)

Full of charm, the 2008 vintage (★★★★) is a Bendigo wine, bright pink, with floral, berryish scents. Full-bodied and very smooth, with strong strawberry and spice flavours and a sliver of sweetness (10 grams/litre of residual sugar), it is deliciously fresh and vibrant.

MED/DRY $21 AV

Neudorf Kina Pinot Rosé   (★★★★)

A dry style (4 grams/litre of residual sugar), the 2008 vintage (★★★★) was harvested at over 24 brix and held overnight on its skins. Pale pink, it is mouthfilling (14 per cent alcohol), with youthful berry and spice flavours, showing good delicacy, and a smooth, finely balanced finish.

DRY $22 AV

Odyssey Marlborough Rosé   ★★★☆

Made from estate-grown Pinot Noir, the thirst-quenching 2009 vintage (★★★☆) is bright pink/pale red, with good body and depth of berryish flavours, fresh and vibrant, and a crisp, dry finish.

DRY $19 AV

Olssen's Summer Dreaming Pinot Noir Rosé   (★★★)

Grown at Bannockburn, in Central Otago, the 2008 vintage (★★★) is still lively – bright pink, mouthfilling and smooth, with vibrant plum, spice and herb flavours, crisp and fresh, and an off-dry (7 grams/litre of residual sugar) finish.

MED/DRY $24 –V

Omaha Bay Vineyard Matakana Rosé   (★★★★)

Made from Syrah, the 2009 vintage (★★★★) has an inviting, bright pink colour. It's a very attractive wine, softly mouthfilling, very fresh and delicate, with an array of plum, spice and strawberry flavours, showing lovely harmony.

Vintage	09	MED/DRY $20 AV
WR	6	
Drink	09-12	

Omori Estate Rosé   (★★☆)

Grown at Lake Taupo, the 2008 vintage (★★☆) was made from Pinot Noir. Salmon pink, it is mouthfilling and smooth, with berryish, spicy, slightly herbal flavours, balanced for easy drinking.

MED/DRY $25 –V

Passage Rock Waiheke Island Rosé   ★★★☆

The 2009 vintage (★★★☆) is a blend of Malbec, Merlot and Syrah. 'Best consumed within 24 hours of purchase', it is pink/red, fleshy and smooth, with good depth of berry, plum and spice flavours, fresh, slightly sweet, and finely balanced for easy, summer drinking.

MED/DRY $22 –V

Poderi Crisci Rosé   (★★☆)

The 2009 vintage (★★☆) was grown on Waiheke Island and made from Merlot. Pale pink, it has ripe, berryish, spicy, slightly peachy flavours, showing decent depth, and a fully dry finish.

Vintage	09	DRY $20 –V
WR	5	
Drink	09-11	

Puriri Hills Clevedon Rosé   ★★★★

Still on sale and more 'red winey' than most New Zealand rosés, the 2007 vintage (★★★★) was grown in South Auckland and made entirely from Merlot. Pale red in colour, it is mouthfilling, with fresh, berryish, spicy, fully dry flavours, a touch of complexity, and very satisfying depth.

Vintage	07	DRY $25 –V
WR	5	
Drink	09-10	

Rannach Rosé   ★★★

Grown at Clevedon, in South Auckland, and made from Merlot, the 2008 vintage (★★★★) is the best yet. Still very fresh and lively, it is bright pink/light red, with strong berry, plum and spice flavours, dry and refreshing.

Vintage	08	DRY $18 –V
WR	6	
Drink	09-11	

Richmond Plains Nelson Blanc de Noir   ★★★

Made from organically grown, hand-picked Pinot Noir, the 2008 vintage (★★☆) is faintly pink, with medium body and slightly sweet (9 grams/litre of residual sugar), smooth, light flavours of strawberries, spices and peaches.

Vintage	08	MED/DRY $20 –V
WR	6	
Drink	09-10	

Rockburn Stolen Kiss   ★★★☆

The very easy-drinking 2008 vintage (★★★☆) was made from Central Otago Pinot Noir. Light pink, it's a mouthfilling wine (over 14 per cent alcohol), with strawberryish, spicy flavours, very harmonious, slightly sweet and smooth.

MED/DRY $20 AV

Saint Clair Marlborough Pinot Rosé   (★★★)

The bright pink 2008 vintage (★★★), made from Pinot Noir, offers refreshing red-berry, cherry and spice flavours, dryish (5 grams/litre of residual sugar), fresh and crisp.

Vintage	08	MED/DRY $21 –V
WR	6	
Drink	P	

Shipwreck Bay Rosé   ★★☆

From Okahu Estate, but not labelled by any region, the 2008 vintage (★★☆) was made from Merlot, Cabernet Franc and Syrah, grown in Northland and Waikato. Pink/pale red, it is light and lively, with slightly sweet berry, spice and herb flavours, fruity, fresh and smooth.

MED/DRY $18 –V

Sileni Cellar Selection Cabernet Franc Rosé   ★★★☆

The 2008 vintage (★★★☆), grown in Hawke's Bay, is a basically dry style (4.4 grams/litre of residual sugar). Bright pink/red, it is mouthfilling (14 per cent alcohol) and smooth, with very good delicacy and depth of fresh, vibrant, berryish flavours.

Vintage	08	07	DRY $19 AV
WR	6	6	
Drink	09-10	P	

Soho Hawke's Bay Rosé   (★★★☆)

Made from Merlot, the 2008 vintage (★★★☆) is bright pink, full-bodied and smooth, with very good depth of strawberry and spice flavours, well balanced for easy drinking.

MED/DRY $22 –V

Soho Waiheke Island Rosé   (★★★)

Pleasantly fruity, the 2009 vintage (★★★) is mouthfilling, with bright pink, light red colour and raspberry and spice flavours, off-dry and smooth.

MED/DRY $22 –V

Soland Runty Rosé   ★★★☆

Grown at Kerikeri, in Northland, the 2008 vintage (★★★☆) was made from Syrah. Bright pink/red, it is fleshy, with slightly sweet, berryish, spicy flavours, attractively ripe and rounded.

MED/DRY $16 V+

Soljans Two Sisters Rosé   ★★★☆

The 2008 vintage (★★★) is a Gisborne blend of Pinotage (76 per cent) and Muscat (24 per cent). Pink/pale red, it's a medium-dry style, vibrantly fruity, with fresh, smooth, berryish flavours.

MED/DRY $18 AV

Southbank Estate Marlborough Sauvignon Pink   (★★☆)

It's not labelled as a rosé, but the 2008 vintage (★★☆) looks and tastes like one. A blend of Sauvignon Blanc (96 per cent) and Syrah (4 per cent), it's a medium-bodied wine, salmon pink, fresh and crisp, with gently herbaceous, berryish flavours, lively and dry (3.6 grams/litre of residual sugar).

DRY $20 –V

Stoneleigh Marlborough Pinot Noir Rosé   ★★★☆

Grown principally at Kaituna, in the Wairau Valley, the 2008 vintage (★★★☆) is an off-dry style (6.5 grams/litre of residual sugar). Bright pink, it is vibrantly fruity, with berry, plum and spice flavours, showing very good freshness and depth.

MED/DRY $21 –V

Tarras Vineyards Florian Pinot Noir Rosé   (★★★☆)

A dry style, the 2008 vintage (★★★☆) is a bright pink, mouthfilling Central Otago wine, fully barrel-fermented. It's a full-bodied wine, with plenty of plummy, spicy flavour and a creamy-smooth finish.

Vintage	08
WR	7
Drink	09-12

DRY $28 –V

Tarras Vineyards Rosé   (★★★☆)

The bright pink 2008 vintage (★★★☆) is a Central Otago wine, made from Pinot Noir and 20 per cent barrel-fermented. It shows very good body and depth of fresh berry/spice flavours and a crisp, dry finish.

DRY $20 AV

Te Kairanga East Coast Rosé   (★★★)

The 2008 vintage (★★★) is pink/pale red, with satisfying body, good depth of strawberry and spice flavours and a smooth, dryish finish.

MED/DRY $17 AV

To Mania Nelson Pinot Noir Rosé   ★★★

A drier style than most, the 2008 vintage (★★★) is pale pink, with good body and depth of strawberry and spice flavours.

Vintage	08
WR	6
Drink	P

DRY $18 –V

Trinity Hill Hawke's Bay Rosé   ★★★

The 2008 vintage (★★★) is a blend of Merlot (56 per cent) and Cabernet Franc (44 per cent). Bright pink, it is light-bodied (11.5 per cent), with fresh, lively strawberry and spice flavours and a dryish finish.

MED/DRY $20 –V

True North Rosé   (★★★)

Grown at Doubtless Bay, in Northland, the 2007 vintage (★★★) is a Merlot-based blend, with youthful colour. Medium-bodied, it is berryish and smooth, with some plum and spice notes, and good freshness.

DRY $16 AV

Tussock Nelson Pinot Noir Rosé   ★★☆

From Woollaston, the 2009 vintage (★★★) is pale pink, light and lively, with gently sweet strawberry and spice flavours, a hint of apricots and mouth-watering acidity.

MED $15 AV

TW Lilly   ★★★

From Gisborne, the 2007 vintage (★★★★) was a blend of Malbec and Merlot, with excellent body and depth. However, the 2008 (★☆) is light, mellow and past its best.

MED/DRY $16 AV

Vavasour Awatere Valley Rosé   ★★★★

Made from Cabernet Franc, this is typically a deep pink, full-bodied Marlborough wine, buoyantly fruity and smooth, with slightly sweet plum, raspberry and spice flavours showing very good delicacy and freshness.

Vintage	08
WR	6
Drink	09-10

MED/DRY $25 –V

Villa Maria Private Bin East Coast Rosé   ★★★☆

A pink/pale red blend of Hawke's Bay and Gisborne fruit, the 2008 vintage (★★★☆) is based mostly on Merlot (82 per cent). It has fresh, berry and spice aromas and flavours, with good body, gentle tannins and a smooth, fully dry finish.

Vintage	08	07	06
WR	6	6	
Drink	09-11	P	P

DRY $20 AV

Vynfields Blanc de Noir   (★★★☆)

Certified organic, the 2008 vintage (★★★☆) is a faintly pink Martinborough wine with good depth of dry, spicy, slightly strawberryish flavours.

DRY $25 –V

Vynfields Pinot Rosé   ★★★★

The pale pink 2008 vintage (★★★★), grown organically in Martinborough, is a softly mouthfilling wine with vibrant strawberry and spice flavours, a hint of apricots, and good complexity and richness.

DRY $27 –V

Waimea Pinot Rosé   ★★★☆

The charming 2009 vintage (★★★☆), made from Nelson Pinot Noir, was partly (17 per cent) fermented in one-year-old American oak barrels; the rest was handled in tanks. Bright, light pink, it is fruity, plummy and slightly spicy, with fresh acidity and a slightly sweet (7.5 grams/litre of residual sugar) finish.

Vintage	09	08
WR	7	6
Drink	09-10	P

MED/DRY $18 AV

Weeping Sands Waiheke Island Rosé   ★★★☆

The rosés from the Obsidian Vineyard at Onetangi are full of interest. The 2009 vintage (★★★★), made with 'brief barrel time of one component', is a dry (4 grams/litre of residual sugar), Merlot-based wine, with splashes of Malbec (4 per cent) and Montepulciano (4 per cent). Bright pink, with fresh, generous strawberry/spice flavours, it shows greater complexity than most rosés, and good liveliness.

DRY $22 –V

Wild Earth Central Otago Pinot Noir Rosé   (★★★☆)

Pink-hued, the 2008 vintage (★★★☆) was grown at Bannockburn and Lowburn. Full of charm, it has very good depth of fresh, soft, strawberryish, spicy flavours and a distinct splash of sweetness (13 grams/litre of residual sugar).

MED/DRY $21 –V

Wild Rock Vin Gris Hawke's Bay Rosé ★★★☆

The 2008 vintage (★★★☆) from Wild Rock (a division of Craggy Range) is a pink/pale red blend of Merlot (81 per cent), Syrah and Pinot Noir. It is fresh, with strong red-berry, strawberry and spice flavours, good body and a smooth, off-dry (6 grams/litre of residual sugar) finish.

Vintage	09	08
WR	6	6
Drink	09-11	09-11

 MED/DRY $19 AV

Wooing Tree Rosé ★★★★

The 2009 vintage (★★★★) was made from Pinot Noir, estate-grown and hand-picked in the Cromwell Basin, Central Otago. Bright pink, it is fresh, buoyantly fruity and smooth, with plum, strawberry and spice flavours, showing excellent delicacy and length. It's already delicious.

DRY $23 AV

Red Wines

Branded and Other Red Wines

The majority of New Zealand red wines carry a varietal label, such as Pinot Noir, Merlot or Cabernet Sauvignon (or blends of the last two). Those not labelled prominently by their principal grape varieties – often prestigious wines such as Tom, Esk Valley The Terraces, Mills Reef Elspeth One or Unison Selection – can be found here. Although not varietally labelled, these wines are mostly of high quality and sometimes outstanding.

Alluviale ★★★★☆

The 2007 vintage (★★★★★), blended from Merlot (62 per cent) and Cabernet Franc (38 per cent), was grown in Gimblett Road, Hawke's Bay, and matured for 16 months in French oak barriques (90 per cent new). Boldly coloured, it is full-bodied (14.5 per cent alcohol), with dense, warm blackcurrant, spice and slight coffee flavours, showing excellent concentration and suppleness. It should be long-lived.

DRY $30 AV

Alpha Domus AD The Aviator ★★★★☆

Still on sale, the 2002 vintage (★★★★☆), grown at Maraekakaho, is a blend of Cabernet Sauvignon, Merlot, Malbec and Cabernet Franc, matured for 22 months in French oak barriques (75 per cent new). Dark, with maturing colour, it reveals highly concentrated cassis, plum, spice, herb and nut flavours, showing impressive complexity. Now starting to soften, it's at its peak. (The next release is from 2007.)

Vintage	07
WR	6
Drink	10-20

DRY $65 –V

Alpha Domus AD The Navigator ★★★★

The 2004 vintage (★★★★) is drinking well now. A blend of Merlot (42 per cent), Cabernet Sauvignon (30 per cent), Cabernet Franc (20 per cent) and Malbec (8 per cent), it was grown at Maraekakaho, in Hawke's Bay, and matured for 20 months in French (70 per cent) and American oak barriques (40 per cent new). Deeply coloured, it's a classic claret-style red, savoury and smooth, with blackcurrant and herb flavours showing excellent depth and harmony. (The next release is from 2007.)

Vintage	07
WR	6
Drink	09-17

DRY $25 AV

Ata Rangi Célèbre ★★★★☆

Pronounced *say-lebr*, this regional blend is made from Merlot, Cabernet Sauvignon and Syrah. Robust and vibrantly fruity, it has impressive weight and depth of plummy, spicy flavour in a complex style that matures well. The excellent 2006 vintage (★★★★☆) is a blend of Martinborough Merlot (50 per cent), Hawke's Bay Syrah (30 per cent) and Martinborough Cabernet Sauvignon (20 per cent). Deep and youthful in colour, it is mouthfilling, rich and flowing, with a distinctly spicy bouquet, concentrated flavours of blackcurrants, herbs, spices and plums, and a backbone of ripe, supple tannins. Drink now or cellar.

Vintage	06	05	04	03	02
WR	7	7	6	7	6
Drink	09-18	09-10	P	09-10	P

DRY $32 AV

Babich The Patriarch   ★★★★★

This is Babich's best red, regardless of the variety or vineyard, but all vintages have been grown in the company's shingly vineyards in Gimblett Road, Hawke's Bay. It is typically a dark, ripe and complex, deliciously rich red, matured for 15 to 22 months in mostly French oak barriques (30 to 35 per cent new). The 2005 vintage (★★★★☆), a 2:1 blend of Merlot and Cabernet Sauvignon, is still fairly youthful, with excellent complexity, depth and harmony. However, the 2006 (★★★) is disappointing, showing considerable early development. The 2007 vintage (★★★★★) brings a return to form. Dense and youthful in colour, it is powerful, with very concentrated blackcurrant and spice flavours, hints of coffee and dark chocolate, firm tannins, and obvious potential. Open 2011+.

> **DRY $60 AV**
>

Benfield & Delamare   ★★★★★

Bill Benfield and Sue Delamare specialise in claret-style reds of exceptional quality and impressive longevity at their tiny Martinborough winery. Benfield & Delamare is typically slightly leaner than the leading Hawke's Bay reds, yet very elegant, intensely flavoured and complex. Estate-grown, it is produced from ultra-low-yielding vines (2.4 tonnes/hectare), and the wine is matured in French oak barriques (up to two-thirds new) for about 20 months. The 2006 vintage (★★★★) is a youthful blend of Merlot, Cabernet Sauvignon and Cabernet Franc. Densely coloured, with a bouquet of raspberries and pencil shavings, it is fresh and vibrant, with concentrated blackcurrant and plum flavours and a firm backbone of tannin. It's an elegant, structured wine for cellaring.

Vintage	06	05	04	03	02
WR	6	6	NM	7	6
Drink	10-25	09-20	NM	09-20	09-20

> **DRY $58 AV**
>

Benfield & Delamare A Song For Osiris   ★★★☆

Dedicated to Osiris, an ancient patron of the grape and wine, this Martinborough red is designed as a 'lively, fruit-driven style, suitable for early drinking'. Made from barrels excluded from the premium blend (above), it is typically vibrantly fruity, with strong, fresh, plummy, spicy flavours, gently oaked and smooth. Blended from Cabernet Sauvignon, Merlot and Cabernet Franc, the 2006 vintage (★★★☆) has full, bright colour and a bouquet of red berries and pencil shavings. It's a full-bodied, moderately complex wine with fresh, vibrant, red-berry and plum flavours.

> **DRY $25 AV**

Brick Bay Pharos   ★★★★

Brick Bay's top red (pronounced *fair-ross*) is named after the famous lighthouse off the coast of Alexandria. A blend of Cabernet Sauvignon (42 per cent), Cabernet Franc (30 per cent), Malbec (17 per cent) and Merlot (11 per cent), the 2005 vintage (★★★★☆) was grown at Sandspit, near Matakana, and matured in new French oak barriques. Deeply coloured, it's a delicious red – the best Pharos yet – with excellent body and depth of fresh blackcurrant, plum, herb and spice flavours, finely textured, savoury and supple.

Vintage	05	04	03	02
WR	7	7	NM	7
Drink	09-13	09-12	NM	P

> **DRY $29 AV**

Cheeky Little Red   ★★☆

Created by Babich for supermarkets owned by Foodstuffs, the 2007 vintage (★★☆) is an easy-drinking blend, grown on the East Coast. Full-coloured, with a slightly earthy bouquet, suggestive of Pinotage, it is fresh, plummy and spicy, with gentle tannins and satisfying depth. Fine value.

DRY $10 V+

Clearview Basket Press   ★★★★★

The rare 2004 vintage (★★★★★) is a Cabernet Sauvignon-predominant blend, matured for 30 months in new French oak barriques. Boldly coloured, it's a powerful Hawke's Bay wine with dense blackcurrant and plum flavours, very ripe and concentrated, and a lasting, silky-smooth finish. The 2007 (tasted in mid-2009, still prior to bottling, and so not rated) is densely coloured, with highly concentrated blackcurrant, plum and spice flavours in the classic Bordeaux style. Very generous and complex, ripe and supple, it looks outstanding.

Vintage	07
WR	6
Drink	09-18

DRY $120 –V

Clearview Enigma   ★★★★★

This consistently distinguished Hawke's Bay red is a Merlot-predominant blend, grown near the sea at Te Awanga. Typically dark and flavour-crammed, it ages well and is matured for about 18 months in French oak barriques (predominantly new). The 2007 vintage (★★★★★) is a powerful blend of Merlot (76 per cent), Cabernet Franc, Cabernet Sauvignon and Malbec. Densely coloured, with notably concentrated flavours of plums, spices, coffee and nuts, it is still unfolding, with excellent complexity and long-term potential.

Vintage	07	06	05	04
WR	7	6	7	7
Drink	09-18	09-15	09-14	09-15

DRY $40 AV

Clearview Old Olive Block   ★★★★★

This Hawke's Bay red, Cabernet Sauvignon-dominant, is grown in the estate vineyard at Te Awanga, which has a very old olive tree in the centre, and Gimblett Road. The 2007 vintage (★★★★★) is a dark, complex blend of Cabernet Sauvignon (48 per cent), Cabernet Franc (25 per cent), Merlot (14 per cent) and Malbec (13 per cent), matured for 18 months in predominantly French oak barriques. Vibrant and very youthful, it has strong blackcurrant, plum, olive and spice flavours, with a strong, nutty oak influence and firm tannins. It should mature well.

Vintage	07	06	05	04	03
WR	7	6	7	7	5
Drink	09-17	09-14	09-14	09-10+	P

DRY $35 V+

Clearview Two Pinnacles   ★★★☆

Estate-grown at Te Awanga, in Hawke's Bay, the gutsy 2007 vintage (★★★★) is a densely coloured blend of Malbec (85 per cent) and Cabernet Sauvignon (15 per cent), matured for 17 months in mostly French oak barriques and bottled unfiltered. It's a real fruit bomb, with dense, ripe, plummy, slightly chocolatey flavours and bold tannins.

Vintage	07	06	05	04
WR	7	6	7	6
Drink	09-17	09-12	09-12	09-10

DRY $25 AV

Coopers Creek Four Daughters Hawke's Bay Red   (★★★)

The 2005 vintage (★★★) is a full-flavoured blend of Cabernet Franc (36 per cent) and Malbec (35 per cent), with smaller proportions of Syrah and Merlot. Slightly developed in colour, it has some leafy notes, but also leather, spice and coffee elements adding complexity.

Vintage	05
WR	6
Drink	09-11

DRY $18 AV

Cottle Hill Pheasant's Walk   (★☆)

This non-vintage red is described by the producer as a 'sweet soft red wine', made 'for entry level red wine drinkers'. It is typically slightly sweet, light and mellow.

MED $18 –V

Craggy Range Aroha   (★★★★★)

The powerful, lush, finely textured 2007 vintage (★★★★★) was made from the company's best Pinot Noir, grown at Te Muna, just south of Martinborough. Deeply coloured, it is very refined, concentrated and supple, with gentle acidity and a strong surge of cherry, plum and slight herb flavours. A generous, youthful wine, with cool-climate vibrancy, it's well worth cellaring.

Vintage	07
WR	7
Drink	10-18

DRY $80 AV

Craggy Range Le Sol   ★★★★★

This super-charged Syrah has pushed the boundaries in terms of its enormous scale – and succeeded brilliantly. Grown in the Gimblett Gravels district of Hawke's Bay, it is hand-harvested when the grapes are 'supremely ripe', in several 'passes' through the vineyard, fermented with indigenous yeasts, and bottled without fining or filtering. Craggy Range views the 2007 vintage (★★★★★) as its greatest Syrah yet – and it's hard to argue. Matured for 20 months in French oak barriques (42 per cent new), it is purple/black, with a voluminous bouquet of cassis, spice and black pepper. Full-bodied and supple, it has concentrated, ripe, spicy, nutty flavours, showing superb density, elegance and length.

Vintage	07	06	05	04	03	02
WR	7	6	7	7	NM	7
Drink	10-22	09-20	09-15	09-13	NM	09-12

DRY $90 AV

Craggy Range Sophia   ★★★★★

Likely to be long-lived, the 2007 vintage (★★★★☆) is a Gimblett Gravels, Hawke's Bay blend of Merlot (81 per cent), Cabernet Franc (10 per cent), Cabernet Sauvignon (7 per cent) and Malbec (2 per cent), harvested at an average of 24.1 brix and matured for 18 months in French oak barriques (50 per cent new). The colour is dark and youthful; the flavours are concentrated, with blackcurrant, plum and spice characters, and fine-grained tannins. Sweet-fruited and supple, with underlying power, it's a strong candidate for cellaring.

Vintage	07	06	05	04	03	02	01
WR	7	7	7	6	6	7	6
Drink	10-27	10-26	09-20	09-15	09-13	09-12	09-11

DRY $50 AV

Craggy Range Te Kahu ★★★★☆

The powerful but very approachable 2007 vintage (★★★★☆) is a Merlot-dominant blend (55 per cent), with smaller portions of Cabernet Franc (17 per cent), Malbec (14 per cent), Cabernet Sauvignon (13 per cent) and Petit Verdot (1 per cent). Grown in the Gimblett Gravels, Hawke's Bay, and matured for 20 months in French oak barriques (20 per cent new), it is dark and fragrant, with a generous, silky-smooth palate showing excellent concentration of cassis, plum and spice flavours and supple, ripe tannins. Drink now or cellar.

Vintage	07	06
WR	7	6
Drink	10-22	09-20

DRY $23 V+

Craggy Range The Quarry ★★★★★

Youthful yet approachable, the 2007 vintage (★★★★★) of this Cabernet Sauvignon-based (83 per cent) red was grown in the Gimblett Gravels of Hawke's Bay and matured for 20 months in French oak barriques (64 per cent new). It also has a splash of Merlot (9 per cent) and Cabernet Franc (8 per cent) in the blend. Deeply coloured, it is mouthfilling (14.5 per cent alcohol) and supple, with powerful blackcurrant, plum and spice flavours, dense, savoury, nutty and long. Open 2012+.

Vintage	07	06	05	04	03	02	01
WR	7	7	7	6	NM	6	6
Drink	10-27	10-26	09-17	09-14	NM	09-12	09-13

DRY $60 AV

Crossroads Talisman ★★★★☆

A blend of six red grapes whose identities the winery delights in concealing (I see Malbec as a prime suspect), Talisman has long been estate-grown in the Origin Vineyard at Fernhill, in Hawke's Bay, but now also includes fruit from the Gimblett Gravels. The 2005 (★★★★) is a fleshy red with rich blackcurrant, olive, plum and spice flavours, savoury notes adding complexity, silky tannins and youthful colour. The 2007 vintage (★★★★☆) was matured for a year in French (principally) and American oak barriques (partly new). Dark, rich and flowing, it has bold, berryish flavours, very spicy and smooth. Delicious young.

Vintage	07	06	05	04	03	02	01	00
WR	7	NM	6	NM	NM	6	NM	6
Drink	09-13	NM	09-10	NM	NM	P	NM	P

DRY $40 AV

Destiny Bay Destinae ★★★★☆

Grown on Waiheke Island, the 2006 vintage (★★★★★) is a classy, Cabernet Sauvignon-based blend (46 per cent), with Merlot (22 per cent), Cabernet Franc (16 per cent) and Malbec (16 per cent). Harvested at 23.6 to 26.1 brix, and matured in American (60 per cent) and French oak barriques (half new), it has bright, rich colour, a fragrant, nutty bouquet, and highly concentrated, ripe berry fruit and spice flavours. Sweet-fruited, with firm tannins and impressive complexity, it's still youthful, with the power and structure to age. The 2007 (★★★★), to be released in 2010, is berryish, plummy, ripe and silky, but less intense than the 2006. It's already enjoyable.

Vintage	06
WR	6
Drink	10-16

DRY $75 −V

Destiny Bay Magna Praemia   ★★★★★

The very high-priced 2006 vintage (★★★★★) of this Waiheke Island producer's flagship red is a Cabernet Sauvignon-based blend (74 per cent), with smaller portions of Merlot (14 per cent), Malbec (7 per cent) and Cabernet Franc (5 per cent). Matured in a 60/40 split of French and American oak casks (new and one-year-old), it is deeply coloured, lush and silky, with gentle tannins and lovely depth, complexity, harmony and length. The 2007 (★★★★★), to be released in 2010, is also Cabernet Sauvignon-based (69 per cent). Invitingly fragrant, it has substantial body, sweet-fruit delights and deep blackcurrant and nut flavours, complex, savoury and supple. Drink now or cellar.

Vintage	06	05	DRY $275 –V
WR	7	7	
Drink	12-16	09-15	

Destiny Bay Mystae   ★★★★☆

Lovely now, the 2005 vintage (★★★★★) of this Waiheke Island red is a blend of Merlot (49 per cent), Cabernet Sauvignon (35 per cent), Cabernet Franc (12 per cent) and Malbec (4 per cent), matured in French and American oak barriques (60 per cent new). It's a very Bordeaux-like wine, highly fragrant, complex, spicy and leathery, with good tannin support. The 2006 (★★★★) is vibrant and supple, with fruity, spicy flavours showing good concentration and complexity. The 2007 vintage (★★★★☆), to be released in 2010, is Cabernet Sauvignon-based (55 per cent). Very finely textured, it has impressive depth of plum, berry, spice and herb flavours, seasoned with nutty oak, and good complexity. Already approachable, it should also cellar well.

Vintage	06	DRY $115 –V
WR	6	
Drink	10-16	

Esk Valley The Terraces   ★★★★★

Grown on the steep, terraced, north-facing hillside flanking the winery at Bay View, Hawke's Bay, this is a strikingly bold, dark wine with bottomless depth of blackcurrant, plum and strongly spicy flavour. Malbec (43 per cent of the vines) and Merlot (35 per cent) are typically the major ingredients, supplemented by Cabernet Franc; the Malbec gives 'perfume, spice, tannin and brilliant colour'. Yields in the 1-hectare vineyard are very low, and the wine is matured for 17 to 22 months in all-new French oak barriques. *En primeur* (payment at a reduced price of $98, in advance of delivery) is the best way to buy. It typically matures well, developing a beautiful fragrance and spicy, Rhône-like complexity. The 2006 vintage (★★★★★) is tightly structured and harmonious, with lovely ripeness and density of berry and spice flavours. You can drink it now, with pleasure, but it should flourish for a decade.

Vintage	06	05	04	03	02	01	00	99	98	DRY $125 AV
WR	7	NM	7	NM	7	NM	7	NM	7	ᒷᒷᒷ
Drink	09-18	NM	09-16	NM	09-17	NM	09-12	NM	09-13	

Gillman   ★★★★☆

This rare Matakana red is blended from Cabernet Franc, Merlot and Malbec, and matured for two years in all-new French oak barriques. In a vertical tasting in mid-2009, the star was the finely scented, deeply coloured 2004 vintage (★★★★★), which shows lovely concentration and complexity. It's maturing superbly. The 2005 (★★★★☆) is full-bodied and supple, with generous blackcurrant and herb flavours, still vibrant and youthful. The 2006 (★★★★☆) is an elegant wine, medium to full-bodied, with youthful cassis, plum, herb and spice flavours, showing good complexity and depth. These are classy wines.

Vintage	06	05	04	03
WR	5	7	7	7
Drink	10-16	09-17	09-16	09-14

DRY $56 –V

Gladstone Auld Alliance ★★★

The 'premier Bordeaux-style' from this Wairarapa winery can be light and leafy, but the 2006 vintage (★★★★) is the best yet. A blend of Cabernet Franc (55 per cent), Merlot (25 per cent) and Malbec (20 per cent), it was matured for a year in French (95 per cent) and American oak casks. It's a full-coloured, fleshy wine with generous, plummy flavours, oak complexity and a smooth, rich finish.

Vintage	06
WR	5
Drink	09-16

DRY $28 –V

Goldwater Goldie ★★★★★

This Waiheke Island wine is one of New Zealand's top claret-style reds. For many years called Goldwater Cabernet Sauvignon & Merlot, since the 2002 vintage it has been renamed as Goldwater Goldie. The vineyard (recently extensively replanted) lies on sandy clay soils on the hillside overlooking Putiki Bay, and the vinification is based on classic Bordeaux techniques, including maturation for 14 to 18 months in French oak barriques (typically half new). The wine generally matures well for 10–12 years, gaining in complexity and personality. The 2005 (★★★★★) is a blend of Cabernet Sauvignon (60 per cent) and Merlot (40 per cent). A star vintage, it is dark and highly fragrant, with lovely richness of blackcurrant, plum and spice flavours. Very generous, sweet-fruited and supple, it's already a delight to drink.

Vintage	05	04	03	02	01	00	99	98
WR	7	7	NM	7	NM	7	7	7
Drink	09-15	09-12	NM	09-12	NM	09-10	09-11	P

DRY $55 AV

Great Red (★★☆)

A Merlot-based blend from Preston Wine Group (owner of Mills Reef), the 2008 vintage (★★☆) is a good quaffer. Grown in Hawke's Bay, it is full-coloured and gutsy, with smooth, plummy, slightly spicy flavours.

DRY $10 V+

Hay Paddock, The (★★★★)

The debut 2006 vintage (★★★★) of this Waiheke Island red is an Onetangi blend of Syrah (88 per cent) and Petit Verdot (12 per cent). Harvested at 24 brix from young vines and matured for over a year in French oak barriques (75 per cent new), it is deeply coloured and finely textured, with an array of plum, pepper, herb and nut flavours, silky-smooth and rich. Drink now to 2011.

DRY $65 –V

Hihi Lock Stock and Many Barrels ★★★☆

The 2007 vintage (★★★☆) is a very hearty Gisborne red, blended from equal portions of Cabernet Franc, Pinotage, Merlot and Malbec. Grown at Patutahi and Manutuke, and matured for 10 months in seasoned American and French oak barrels, it is fruity, with strong, ripe, berryish, spicy flavours, showing considerable complexity. Good value.

DRY $18 V+

Hinchco Hinch   (★★☆)

A Matakana Merlot, matured in predominantly French oak, the 2004 vintage (★★☆) has fullish, slightly developed colour. Ready now, it is mouthfilling and flavoursome, but also shows a slight lack of full ripeness, with a distinct leafiness.

DRY $40 –V

Hopsbarn Dry Red   (★★☆)

From Moutere Hills Vineyard, the 2007 vintage (★★☆) is a Nelson blend of Cabernet Sauvignon (95 per cent) and a splash of Pinot Noir. A ruby-hued, medium-bodied wine with berry, plum and spice flavours, a hint of herbs and gentle tannins, it's a pleasant drink-young style, but pricey.

DRY $28 –V

Karikari Estate Toa Iti   (★★★☆)

Estate-grown on the Karikari Peninsula, in the Far North, the 2006 vintage (★★★☆) is a Cabernet Sauvignon-based red (44 per cent), with Merlot (30 per cent), Cabernet Franc (16 per cent), and minor portions of Malbec, Syrah and Pinotage. Full-coloured, it is flavoursome and spicy, although slightly leafy, with good complexity and a firm backbone of tannin. Worth cellaring.

DRY $29 –V

Kumeu River Melba   ★★★★

Kumeu River's top claret-style red is named in honour of the company matriarch, Melba Brajkovich. Delicious now and still on sale in 2009, the 2000 vintage (★★★★☆), blended from Merlot (70 per cent) and Malbec (30 per cent) and matured for 20 months in French oak barriques (25 per cent new), is a richly coloured, beautifully fragrant wine with concentrated spice, leather and chocolate characters and warm, ripe tannins. (There are no 2002–2005 vintages, but a Melba's Vineyard Merlot, made entirely from Merlot, will be released from 2006.)

Vintage	06	05	04	03	02	01	00
WR	7	NM	NM	NM	NM	5	7
Drink	09-16	NM	NM	NM	NM	P	09-10

DRY $30 AV

Kupe by Escarpment   ★★★★★

This estate-grown Pinot Noir, based on closely planted vines at Te Muna, in Martinborough, is fermented in French cuves and matured in French oak barriques (50 per cent new). The 2006 vintage (★★★★★) is deep and youthful in colour, rich and ripe, in a mouthfilling, impressively concentrated style with lovely texture and length. Very finely structured, powerful but not heavy, it's a densely packed, complex, supple wine, with obvious potential for long-term cellaring.

Vintage	06	05	04	03
WR	7	7	NM	7
Drink	09-16	09-15	NM	09-15

DRY $85 AV

Man O' War Ironclad   ★★★☆

The 2007 vintage (★★★★), from the eastern end of Waiheke Island, is a blend of Cabernet Sauvignon (54 per cent) and Cabernet Franc (34 per cent), with splashes of Merlot and Petit Verdot. Matured for a year in French (mostly) and American oak casks (25 per cent new), it is dark and youthful in colour, mouthfilling and firm, with rich blackcurrant and spice flavours, seasoned with fine-quality oak. One for the cellar.

Vintage	08	07
WR	7	6
Drink	10-18	09-12

DRY $46 –V

Matariki Quintology   ★★★★

This Gimblett Gravels, Hawke's Bay red is a blend of five varieties, in 2005 (★★★★) Merlot (41 per cent), Cabernet Sauvignon (30 per cent), Malbec (12 per cent), Cabernet Franc (10 per cent) and Syrah (7 per cent). Matured for 17 months in French oak casks (50 per cent new), it is full-flavoured, with blackcurrant and spice notes, and savoury, nutty characters adding complexity. Showing some development, it's drinking well now.

Vintage	04	03	02
WR	7	NM	7
Drink	09-14	NM	09-12

DRY $45 –V

Matua Valley Innovator GSM   (★★★☆)

The easy-drinking 2007 vintage (★★★☆) adds a new twist to the term GSM, in Australia used commonly for blends of Grenache, Shiraz and Mourvedre – in this case, the blend is Grenache, Syrah and Merlot. Grown in the Bullrush Vineyard in Hawke's Bay, it's a full-coloured red with vibrant plum and spice flavours, showing some savoury, leathery complexity, and a hint of oak (French, 18 per cent new).

DRY $25 AV

Matua Valley Matua Road Vintage Red   (★★)

The 2007 vintage (★★) is a light quaffer with moderate depth of berryish, slightly spicy flavour and a fairly firm finish. The 2008 was made from Gisborne grapes – a long way from Matua Road, in West Auckland.

DRY $10 AV

Mills Reef Elspeth One   ★★★★★

Named after Elspeth Preston (mother of founder Paddy Preston), and designed as the peak of the Mills Reef range, this distinguished Hawke's Bay red is a blend of Merlot, Cabernet Franc, Malbec, Syrah and Cabernet Sauvignon, grown in the company's Mere Road Vineyard, in the Gimblett Gravels. The very savoury 2005 vintage (★★★★★) was matured for 17 months in French oak barriques (60 per cent new). Deeply coloured, with a fragrant, spicy, complex bouquet, it shows lovely concentration and texture, with mouthfilling body, warm blackcurrant, spice, plum and nut flavours, and velvety tannins. It's a multi-faceted, very 'complete' wine (although the price soared from $50 for the 2004 to $80 for the 2005).

Vintage	05	04	03	02
WR	7	7	NM	7
Drink	09-16	09-15	NM	09-16

DRY $80 –V

Millton Cosmo   (★★★)

Priced right, the 2007 vintage (★★★) is a Gisborne blend of Malbec, Merlot, Syrah and Pinot Noir, grown organically. Full-coloured, it is plummy, spicy, minty and flavoursome, with some savoury complexity.

DRY $20 AV

Miro   ★★★

The 2005 vintage (★★☆) of this Waiheke Island red, grown at Onetangi, is a blend of Cabernet Sauvignon, Merlot, Cabernet Franc and Malbec, matured for a year in French oak barriques (half new). Medium-bodied, it's a slightly rustic wine, spicy and leafy.

DRY $35 –V

Miro Vineyard Summer Aphrodisiac   (★★★)

'Pour yourself a stiff one', invites the label on this Waiheke Island red. The non-vintage wine (★★★) on sale in 2009 (previously sold as Archipelago Cabernets) has fresh berry and spice, green-edged flavours, showing decent depth.

DRY $18 AV

Moana by Escarpment   (★★★★☆)

The 2006 vintage (★★★★☆) from Escarpment is based on 25-year-old Pinot Noir vines in the Cleland Vineyard, in Martinborough. Matured for a year in French oak barriques (30 per cent new) and seen by winemaker Larry McKenna as 'an old world, savoury style', it's a deeply coloured and generous wine, full of personality, with concentrated plum, spice and slight herb flavours, gentle tannins and a rich, rounded finish.

DRY $65 –V

Morton Estate The Regent of Morton   ★★★

Still on sale, the 2004 vintage (★★☆) is a Merlot-based blend, with Cabernet Sauvignon and Cabernet Franc. A mouthfilling Hawke's Bay wine with full, developed colour, it is spicy and savoury, but now past its best.

Vintage	04
WR	6
Drink	09-12

DRY $55 –V

Morton Estate White Label The Mercure   ★★★

The 2007 vintage (★★★) is a Hawke's Bay, Merlot-based blend with mouthfilling body and plenty of brambly flavour, showing a touch of complexity.

Vintage	07	06
WR	6	6
Drink	09-15	09-15

DRY $19 AV

Muddy Water Deliverance   (★★★)

The 2008 vintage (★★★) is a blend of Pinotage and Syrah, grown at Waipara. Fullish in colour, with a gamey, earthy, spicy bouquet, it has plum, herb and spice flavours, not concentrated but smooth, with drink-young appeal.

DRY $16 AV

Newton Forrest Estate Cornerstone   ★★★★★

Grown in the Cornerstone Vineyard, on the corner of Gimblett Road and State Highway 50 – where the first vines were planted in 1989 – this is a consistently distinguished Hawke's Bay blend of Cabernet Sauvignon, Merlot and Malbec, matured in French (principally) and American oak barriques. The 2006 vintage (★★★★★) is a stylish, dark wine with dense flavours of blackcurrants, plums and spices, showing lovely concentration, warmth, complexity and harmony. It's still youthful, but already delicious.

Vintage	06	05	04	03	02	01	00
WR	6	7	5	NM	6	4	7
Drink	09-20	15-25	09-12	NM	09-10	09-12	09-10

DRY $50 AV

Newton Forrest Estate Stony Corner   (★★★★☆)

A bold, upfront style, the 2007 vintage (★★★★☆) is a Gimblett Gravels, Hawke's Bay blend of Cabernet Sauvignon, Merlot and Malbec, matured in French (60 per cent) and American (40 per cent) oak. Deeply coloured, with a fragrant, spicy, sweetly oaked bouquet, it is powerful, with cassis, plum and spice flavours, a hint of coffee and excellent concentration.

Vintage	07
WR	5
Drink	09-11

DRY $30 AV

Obsidian   ★★★★☆

The Obsidian Vineyard at Onetangi produces one of the most stylish claret-style reds on Waiheke Island. Matured in French oak barriques (40 per cent new), the 2007 vintage (★★★★☆) is a blend dominated by Cabernet Sauvignon (39.5 per cent), Merlot (24 per cent) and Cabernet Franc (24 per cent), with Petit Verdot (12 per cent) and Malbec (0.5 per cent). It's a supple, mouthfilling wine with generous blackcurrant, plum, spice and herb flavours, showing good complexity and already drinking well. The 2008 (★★★★★), not yet released, is a stunner – fragrant, dark and very Bordeaux-like, with ripe, dense flavours.

Vintage	07	06	05	04	03	02	01	00
WR	5	NM	7	6	NM	7	NM	7
Drink	10-19	NM	09-15	09-14	NM	09-12	NM	09-12

DRY $46 –V

Olssen's Robert the Bruce A Bannockburn Red   ★★★

The 2008 vintage (★★★) is a Central Otago blend of Pinotage, Cabernet Sauvignon and Syrah, French and American oak-aged. Brightly coloured and floral, it's an easy-drinking style, vibrantly fruity and supple, with a hint of sweet oak and drink-young appeal.

DRY $28 –V

Paritua Red   (★★★★)

Grown in The Triangle district, Hawke's Bay, the powerful 2007 vintage (★★★★) is a blend of Cabernet Sauvignon (54 per cent), Merlot (32 per cent), Cabernet Franc (9 per cent) and Malbec (5 per cent), French oak-matured (60 per cent new). Boldly coloured, it is concentrated, with cassis, spice, herb and nut flavours, showing considerable complexity.

Vintage	07
WR	7
Drink	10-20

DRY $37 –V

Paritua Twenty One-Twelve   (★★★★★)

The commanding 2007 vintage (★★★★★) was grown in Hawke's Bay and matured for 18 months in French oak barriques (half new). Dense and youthful in colour, it is very powerful and concentrated, with layers of blackcurrant, plum, herb, spice and nut flavours, buried tannins, and loads of cellaring potential.

Vintage	07	DRY $50 AV
WR	7	
Drink	10-20	

Passage Rock Sisters   ★★★☆

The Waiheke Island winery's 'earlier drinking style of Bordeaux wine' from 2008 (★★★★) is the best yet. A blend of Merlot (50 per cent), Syrah (30 per cent), Cabernet Franc (10 per cent) and Malbec (10 per cent), it is full-coloured, with generous blackcurrant, plum and spice flavours, seasoned with sweet oak, good ripeness and complexity, gentle tannins and strong, drink-young appeal.

DRY $23 AV

Pegasus Bay Maestro   ★★★★

The 2005 vintage (★★★★☆) is a Waipara blend of Merlot (85 per cent) and Malbec (15 per cent). Matured for two years in barriques, followed by nine months in larger barrels, it has substantial body (14.5 per cent alcohol) and rich colour, in a fragrant, highly concentrated style with blackcurrant and herb flavours, nutty, leathery notes adding complexity, and a firm foundation of tannin.

Vintage	06	05	DRY $45 –V
WR	6	7	
Drink	09-17	09-16	

Providence – see Providence Private Reserve Merlot/Cabernet Franc/Malbec in the Merlot section

Puriri Hills Estate   ★★★★

The 2005 vintage (★★★★☆) of this impressive Clevedon, South Auckland red is the finest yet. A blend of Merlot (63 per cent), Cabernet Sauvignon (17 per cent) and Cabernet Franc (11 per cent), with smaller amounts of Carmenère and Malbec, it is deep, youthful in colour. The bouquet is perfumed; the palate is rich and welcoming, with concentrated blackcurrant, plum, herb and spice flavours, seasoned with quality French oak, and silky tannins. It's a very refined, harmonious and supple wine, offering delicious drinking from now onwards. The 2004 (★★★★), released after the 2005, has deep, fairly mature colour. Still fresh, it's a generous wine, fleshy, savoury and complex, probably nearing its peak and delicious now.

Vintage	05	04	03	02	01	DRY $36 –V
WR	7	7	6	6	5	
Drink	09-20	09-15	P	P	P	

Puriri Hills Pope   (★★★★★)

The very classy debut 2005 vintage (★★★★★) was named after Ivan Pope, who planted and tended the vines at this Clevedon, South Auckland vineyard. Blended from Merlot (47 per cent), Carmenère (33 per cent), Cabernet Franc (10 per cent) and Malbec (10 per cent), it has dark colour and a brambly, slightly toasty bouquet. Youthful, with obvious potential, it is rich, ripe and highly concentrated, with hints of coffee and spices, and notable power, complexity and density.

Vintage	06	05
WR	6	7
Drink	09-18	09-20

DRY $120 –V

Puriri Hills Reserve   ★★★★★

A regional classic. Grown at Clevedon, in South Auckland, the 2004 vintage (★★★★★) was released in 2008 – after the 2005 (★★★★★). Deep and still fairly youthful in colour, it is deliciously harmonious, rich and silky, with vibrant blackcurrant, herb and spice flavours, nutty, savoury, generous and long. The 2006 (★★★★★), a blend of Merlot (53 per cent), Carmenère (33 per cent) and Cabernet Franc (14 per cent), was matured in French oak barrels (60 per cent new), and bottled unfined and unfiltered. Dark, rich and supple, it is lush and finely textured, with blackcurrant, spice, herb and plum flavours, showing lovely richness and roundness.

Vintage	06	05	04	03	02
WR	6	7	7	NM	6
Drink	09-20	09-20	09-20	NM	09-10

DRY $70 AV

Ransom Dark Summit   ★★★☆

Still on sale, the 2005 vintage (★★★★), grown at Matakana, is a Cabernet Sauvignon and Carmenère-based blend, with smaller portions of Cabernet Franc, Merlot and Malbec. Barrel-aged for a year, it has deep, fairly youthful colour, a slightly leafy bouquet and generous, brambly, plummy flavours, savoury and complex, with a strong finish. It shows good personality; drink 2009–11.

DRY $35 –V

Recession Red   (★★★)

From Unison, in Hawke's Bay, the 2008 vintage (★★★) is a barrel-aged blend of Cabernet Sauvignon and Syrah, released as a one-year-old 'fun wine'. Ruby-hued, it's medium-bodied (12.5 per cent alcohol), with decent depth of fresh berry and spice flavours, slightly peppery and lightly oaked, in a supple, easy-drinking style.

DRY $15 AV

Redd Gravels   ★★★★★

The 2006 vintage (★★★★★) is the third release of the highly acclaimed, top red from Blake Family Vineyard, the source of Alluviale (see above). Grown in Gimblett Road, Hawke's Bay, it was fermented with indigenous yeasts and matured for 18 months in French oak barriques (92 per cent new). A blend of Merlot (84 per cent) and Cabernet Franc (16 per cent), it is deep and youthful in colour, with a highly fragrant bouquet of ripe berry fruit and spices. A generous and silky-textured wine, it is ripe, concentrated and complex, with deep plum, coffee and dark chocolate flavours. Delicious drinking now onwards.

DRY $80 AV

Red Wire ★★★☆

From Mount George, owned by Paritua, the 2008 vintage (★★★) is a Hawke's Bay blend of Merlot, Malbec, Cabernet Franc and Cabernet Sauvignon, partly barrel-aged. It's a full-coloured wine, fresh and vibrantly fruity, with plenty of plummy, berryish flavour and gentle tannins, in an easy-drinking style.

Vintage	08	DRY $15 V+
WR	6	
Drink	09-13	

San Hill The Benches Red ★★★

Still unfolding, the 2007 vintage (★★★☆) of this Central Hawke's Bay red from Pukeora Estate is a deeply coloured, Merlot-predominant blend, with smaller portions of Cabernet Sauvignon, Syrah and Malbec. Matured for 20 months in barriques (half new), it has a fragrant, berryish, spicy bouquet, tinged with sweet oak. Mouthfilling and vibrantly fruity, it is plummy, spicy and oaky, with some savoury complexity, very good depth and obvious cellaring potential.

Vintage	07	06	DRY $25 –V
WR	6	6	
Drink	09-12	09-10	

Seifried Sylvia ★★☆

Named after Agnes Seifried's late mother, this Nelson red is made from an Austrian variety, Zweigelt, which the Seifrieds have pioneered here. Grown at Brightwater and French oak-aged, the 2008 vintage (★★☆) is an easy-drinking quaffer, simple and smooth.

DRY $19 –V

Soho Revolver ★★★★

The 2008 vintage (★★★★) is a Waiheke Island blend of Merlot (46 per cent), Malbec (31 per cent), Cabernet Sauvignon (17 per cent) and Cabernet Franc (6 per cent), matured in French oak casks (20 per cent new). It's a full-coloured wine, fragrant and ripe, with strong, plummy, spicy flavours, showing good concentration and complexity.

DRY $38 –V

Stone Paddock Scarlet (★★★☆)

Estate-grown by Paritua in The Triangle district of Hawke's Bay, the 2007 vintage (★★★☆) is a fragrant blend of Merlot (37 per cent), Cabernet Sauvignon (35 per cent), Cabernet Franc (16 per cent) and Malbec (12 per cent). Barrel-aged for a year, it's a gutsy, full-coloured wine with strong blackcurrant, mint and nut flavours and firm, youthful tannins.

Vintage	07	DRY $25 AV
WR	7	
Drink	09-16	

Stonyridge Airfield ★★★★

The 2008 vintage (★★★★) is a blend of Cabernet Sauvignon (61 per cent), Merlot (28 per cent) and Cabernet Franc (11 per cent), grown at Onetangi, on Waiheke Island, and matured for a year in French oak casks (40 per cent new). It's a deeply coloured, mouthfilling wine, firmly structured, with strong, youthful plum and spice flavours, showing good ripeness and complexity. Worth cellaring to 2011+.

DRY $45 –V

Stonyridge Luna Negra – see Luna Negra Waiheke Island Hillside Malbec in the Malbec section

Te Awa Boundary   ★★★★★

This very stylish Hawke's Bay red is blended from Merlot (80 to 85 per cent), Cabernet Sauvignon (10 to 15 per cent), Cabernet Franc (3 to 5 per cent), and sometimes a splash of Malbec. Based on low-yielding 10 to 13-year-old vines in the Gimblett Gravels and matured for 15 to 18 months in French oak barriques (50 per cent new), it was made until recently by Jenny Dobson, who was once *maître d'chais* at a respected Haut-Médoc *cru bourgeois*, Château Senejac. Subtle, multi-faceted and beautifully harmonious, it is more complex and savoury than most New Zealand reds. Still on sale, the 2004 vintage (★★★☆) has deep, slightly developed colour. It's a fleshy and supple wine with highly concentrated blackcurrant and spice flavours, drinking well now.

Vintage	04	03	02	01	00
WR	7	NM	7	6	7
Drink	09-14	NM	09-12	P	P

DRY $40 AV

Te Mata Coleraine   ★★★★★

Breed, rather than brute power, is the hallmark of Coleraine, which since its first vintage in 1982 has carved out an illustrious reputation among New Zealand's claret-style reds. Since the 2005 vintage (★★★★★), it is no longer labelled as a Cabernet/Merlot, but simply as Coleraine (and in some recent vintages has contained more Merlot than Cabernet Sauvignon). At its best, it is a magical Hawke's Bay wine, with a depth, complexity and subtlety on the level of a top-class Bordeaux. The grapes are grown in the Havelock North hills, in the company's warm, north-facing Buck and 1892 vineyards, and the wine is matured for 18 to 20 months in French oak barriques, predominantly new. Cabernet Sauvignon in 2007 accounted for 52 per cent of the blend, Merlot 34 per cent and Cabernet Franc 14 per cent (Malbec is definitely not in the recipe). A complete vertical tasting of Coleraine (1982 to 2006), held in mid-2008, showed that all vintages since 1989 are still drinking well and the 2004 to 2006 vintages have scaled new heights (surpassing the great trio of 1989–1991). The 2007 vintage (★★★★★) is deeply coloured, tightly structured and youthful, with mouthfilling body (14 per cent alcohol) and notably concentrated blackcurrant, spice and new oak flavours. Powerful yet highly refined, it should flourish for 20 years.

Vintage	07	06	05	04	03	02	01	00	99	98
WR	7	7	7	7	7	7	6	7	6	7
Drink	11-27	10-26	09-25	09-16	09-18	09-15	09-13	09-15	P	09-20

DRY $70 AV

Te Rehua by Escarpment   (★★★★)

Grown in the Barton Vineyard in Huangarua Road, Martinborough, where the Pinot Noir vines are over 20 years old, the 2006 vintage (★★★★) was matured for a year in French oak barriques (30 per cent new). Fragrant, berry and herb aromas lead into a firm, rich palate with plenty of 'forest floor' complexity.

DRY $65 –V

Te Whau The Point
★★★★☆

This classy Waiheke Island red flows from a steeply sloping vineyard at Putiki Bay. The 2007 vintage (★★★★☆) is a Cabernet Sauvignon-based blend (55 per cent), with Merlot (31 per cent), Cabernet Franc (10 per cent) and Malbec (4 per cent). Fermented with indigenous yeasts and matured in French oak barriques, it is deeply coloured, with generous blackcurrant, plum, herb and spice flavours, showing excellent density, complexity and structure. (The 2008 vintage is described by Te Whau as 'the most profound red wine that we have produced . . .')

DRY $70 –V

Ti Point One
★★★★

Grown at Leigh, near Matakana, north of Auckland, this Merlot-based red is consistently classy. Still on sale, the 2005 vintage (★★★★☆) is deeply coloured, highly fragrant and mouthfilling, with concentrated, slightly nutty flavours and silky tannins. It's an impressively rich, ripe and complex wine, for drinking now or cellaring.

Vintage	06	05	04
WR	6	7	6
Drink	09-12	09-15	09-10

DRY $38 –V

Tom
★★★★★

Pernod Ricard NZ's Hawke's Bay claret-style red, once promoted as 'the New Zealand equivalent of Grange', honours pioneer winemaker Tom McDonald, the driving force behind New Zealand's first prestige red, McWilliam's Cabernet Sauvignon. The early vintages in the mid-1990s were Cabernet Sauvignon-predominant, whereas the 1998, 2000 and 2002 have Merlot as the principal variety. It is typically a wine of great finesse, savoury, complex and more akin to a quality Bordeaux than other New World reds. The 2002 vintage (★★★★★) is a blend of Merlot (48 per cent), Cabernet Sauvignon (47 per cent) and Malbec (5 per cent). Matured for 18 months in French oak barriques (52 per cent new), it is extremely refined – dark, fleshy, savoury and silky, with lovely complexity and length. Best drinking 2010+.

Vintage	02	01	00	99	98
WR	7	NM	6	NM	7
Drink	09-12	NM	09-10	NM	09-15

DRY $135 –V

Trinity Hill The Gimblett
★★★★★

A great buy, the 2007 vintage (★★★★★) is a refined, youthful blend of Merlot (51 per cent) with Cabernet Sauvignon (17 per cent), Petit Verdot (12 per cent), Cabernet Franc (11 per cent) and Malbec (9 per cent), hand-picked in the Gimblett Gravels, Hawke's Bay, and matured for 18 months in principally French oak barrels (40 per cent new). Deeply coloured and fragrant, with fresh blackcurrant, plum, spice and slight coffee flavours, it has a subtle seasoning of oak and a rich, lingering finish.

Vintage	07	06	05
WR	5	6	5
Drink	09-15	09-15	09-12

DRY $30 V+

Trinity Hill The Trinity
★★★

The easy-drinking 2006 vintage (★★★) is a Gimblett Gravels, Hawke's Bay red, blended from Merlot (52 per cent), Cabernet Sauvignon (26 per cent), Cabernet Franc (17 per cent) and Syrah (5 per cent), and matured in tanks and French and American oak barrels. Ruby-hued, it has blackcurrant, herb and spice flavours in a pleasant, fruit-driven style.

DRY $20 AV

TW Makauri   ★★★☆

Still on sale, the sturdy 2004 vintage (★★★☆) is a 50/50 Gisborne blend of Merlot and Malbec, American oak-aged. Deep and still bright in colour, it is maturing well, with fresh, vibrant flavours of plums, spices and dark chocolate, the earthy notes typical of Malbec and a well-rounded finish.

Vintage	04
WR	6
Drink	09-15

DRY $26 –V

Unison Classic Blend   ★★★★☆

Based on a block of densely planted vines in an old river bed near Hastings, this blend of Merlot, Cabernet Sauvignon and Syrah is typically dark, with concentrated flavours of cassis, plum and spice and a long finish. The 2007 vintage (★★★★☆) is deeply coloured, with fresh, strong blackcurrant, plum and spice flavours, hints of nuts and coffee, and excellent complexity and harmony. Savoury and supple, it's a refined wine, drinking well from now onwards.

Vintage	07	06	05	04	03	02	01	00
WR	7	6	6	7	NM	7	6	7
Drink	09-17	09-15	09-14	09-14	NM	09-12	P	P

DRY $28 V+

Unison Selection   ★★★★★

Designed for cellaring and oak-matured longer than the above wine, this is a consistently outstanding Hawke's Bay red. The Gimblett Gravels vines, more than a decade old, are densely planted and cropped lightly. A vineyard (rather than barrel) selection of Merlot, Cabernet Sauvignon and Syrah, it is matured initially for 20 months in French and American oak barriques (half new), then (for 'harmonising') for a further five months in large Italian casks of French and Slavonian oak. The 2006 vintage (★★★★★) is dark and still youthful in colour. Rich and silky, it has sweet-fruit delights, concentrated blackcurrant, plum and spice flavours, and ripe, supple tannins. Drink now and over the next few years.

Vintage	06	05	04	03	02	01	00	99	98
WR	6	6	7	NM	7	6	7	6	6
Drink	09-17	09-16	09-16	NM	09-15	09-13	09-13	09-10	09-10

DRY $48 AV

Vin Alto Celaio   ★★★☆

This Clevedon, South Auckland red was blended from traditional French and Italian grape varieties, such as Merlot, Sangiovese, Cabernet Franc and Montepulciano, and given a lengthy spell in oak barrels. Still on sale, the ruby-hued 2004 (★★★☆) is plummy, vibrantly fruity, flavoursome and supple.

Vintage	04
WR	6
Drink	09-12

DRY $39 –V

Vin Alto Retico   ★★★★☆

On a relatively cool, elevated site at Clevedon, in South Auckland, Enzo Bettio set out 'to make traditional Italian-style wines in New Zealand'. His most prized wine, Retico, based on air-dried, highly concentrated grapes, is Clevedon's equivalent of the prized *amarones* of Verona. Based on traditional French and Italian grape varieties (such as Cabernet Franc, Merlot and Montepulciano), it is barrique-aged for two years. Still on sale, the 2003 vintage (★★★★☆) is a strapping wine (15.5 per cent alcohol), with full colour and rich, spicy, raisiny flavours. A muscular, concentrated and complex wine, it's best served at the end of a meal, 'with cheese, in front of the fire'.

Vintage	03
WR	7
Drink	09-17

DRY $85 –V

Vin Alto Ritorno   ★★★★

Created in the Veronese *ripasso* tradition, this Clevedon, South Auckland red is a blend of traditional French and Italian grape varieties (such as Merlot, Cabernet Franc and Montepulciano), fermented on the skins of the air-dried Retico grapes (above) and oak-matured for two years. Still on sale, the 2000 vintage (★★★★) is fragrant and leathery, concentrated and slightly raisiny, in a style that *demands* food.

Vintage	00	99
WR	7	7
Drink	09-10	09-10

DRY $59 –V

Voyager by Escarpment   (★★★★★)

The debut 2006 vintage (★★★★★) was made in an 'exceedingly New World style' by Larry McKenna from 25-year-old vines (clone 10/5) in the McCreanor Vineyard, in Princess Street, Martinborough. Matured for a year in French oak barriques (30 per cent new), it has beautifully rich, ripe cherry/plum flavours and silky tannins. A notably graceful, highly concentrated red, it's delicious now.

DRY $65 AV

Waipipi Hawke's Bay/Wairarapa Waipipi Red   (★★★)

The 2007 vintage (★★★) is a blend of Merlot (53 per cent) and Cabernet Sauvignon (47 per cent), grown in Hawke's Bay and the Wairarapa, and matured in French oak barriques. Fullish in colour, it is mouthfilling, fresh and smooth, with blackcurrant, plum, herb and spice flavours, a hint of sweet oak, and good depth. It's drinking well now.

DRY $22 –V

Wishart Legend   ★★★☆

The rich, mature 2005 vintage (★★★★) is a Bay View, Hawke's Bay blend of Merlot (50 per cent), Malbec, Cabernet Franc and Syrah, barrel-aged for 20 months. It has a fragrant, complex bouquet, leading into a savoury wine with deep blackcurrant, spice and coffee flavours and firm, ripe tannins. Ready.

DRY $35 –V

Cabernet Franc

New Zealand's fifth most widely planted red-wine variety – just ahead of Malbec – Cabernet Franc is probably a mutation of Cabernet Sauvignon, the much higher-profile variety with which it is so often blended. Jancis Robinson's phrase, 'a sort of claret Beaujolais', aptly sums up the nature of this versatile and underrated red-wine grape.

As a minority ingredient in the recipe of many of New Zealand's top reds, Cabernet Franc lends a delicious softness and concentrated fruitiness to its blends with Cabernet Sauvignon and Merlot. However, admirers of Château Cheval Blanc, the illustrious St Émilion (which is two-thirds planted in Cabernet Franc), have long appreciated that Cabernet Franc need not always be Cabernet Sauvignon's bridesmaid, but can yield fine red wines in its own right. The supple, fruity wines of Chinon and Bourgueil, in the Loire Valley, have also proved Cabernet Franc's ability to produce highly attractive, soft, light reds.

According to the latest national vineyard survey, the bearing area of Cabernet Franc will be 166 hectares in 2010 – well below the 213 hectares in 2004. Two-thirds of the vines are clustered in Hawke's Bay. As a varietal red, Cabernet Franc is lower in tannin and acid than Cabernet Sauvignon; or as Michael Brajkovich of Kumeu River puts it: 'more approachable and easy'.

Abbey Cellars Cabernets/Merlot (★★☆)

Still on sale, the 2005 vintage (★★☆) was grown at Bridge Pa, in Hawke's Bay. It's a full-coloured blend of Cabernet Franc (50 per cent) and Merlot (41 per cent), with splashes of Cabernet Sauvignon and Malbec. Matured in '100 per cent new French oak and a little American', it's a lean, slightly rustic wine with some complexity, but lacks real richness and finesse.

DRY $26 –V

Artisan Kauri Ridge Cabernet/Merlot (★★★★)

The densely coloured 2006 vintage (★★★★) is a generous, supple, West Auckland blend of Cabernet Franc (60 per cent) and Merlot (40 per cent). It offers blackcurrant, spice and green-olive flavours, showing excellent concentration.

Vintage	06
WR	5
Drink	09-12

DRY $29 AV

Ascension The Benediction Reserve Cabernet Franc (★★★☆)

Grown at Matakana, the 2007 vintage (★★★☆) is a blend of Cabernet Franc (82 per cent) and Merlot (18 per cent), matured for 14 months in French and American oak barriques (a third new). It's a medium to full-bodied wine with plum, berry, herb and spice flavours, showing very good complexity and length, firm tannins, and more than a hint of red Bordeaux.

DRY $35 –V

Beach House Hawke's Bay Cabernet Franc (★★★★☆)

Grown in The Track Vineyard, in the Gimblett Gravels, the 2007 vintage (★★★★☆) was matured for a year in French and American oak casks. Deeply coloured, with a fresh, spicy fragrance, it's full-bodied, with strong, youthful flavours of blackcurrants, plums and spices, hints of dark chocolate and sweet oak, and a rich, smooth finish. Enjoyable now, it should also be long-lived.

Vintage	07
WR	7
Drink	09-30

DRY $25 V+

Clearview Reserve Cabernet Franc   ★★★★☆

The classy, very elegant 2007 vintage (★★★★★) was hand-harvested from 21-year-old vines at Te Awanga, in Hawke's Bay, blended with Merlot (7 per cent) and Cabernet Sauvignon (2 per cent), and matured for 16 months in French oak barriques (predominantly new). Deep and youthful in colour, with a floral bouquet and rich blackcurrant, plum, herb and nut flavours, it's a complex, age-worthy, distinctly Bordeaux-like style.

Vintage	07	06
WR	7	6
Drink	09-17	09-12

DRY $40 AV

Crossroads Hawke's Bay Cabernet Franc   (★★★☆)

The deeply coloured 2007 vintage (★★★ ☆) was hand-picked and matured for over a year in French oak. Mouthfilling and smooth, it has strong, slightly earthy plum/spice flavours and plenty of drink-young appeal.

DRY $20 AV

Hawk's Nest Back Paddock Cabernet Franc/Malbec   (★★☆)

The 2006 vintage (★★☆) was grown at Matakana and matured in French oak casks (25 per cent new). It's a medium-bodied red, fruity and slightly leafy, with some savoury complexity and solid depth.

Vintage	06	05
WR	5	7
Drink	09-11	09-10

DRY $19 –V

Judge Valley Four Daughters Cabernet Franc/Merlot/Malbec   (★★★☆)

Still on sale, the 2005 vintage (★★★☆) is a full-coloured Waikato wine with good body and depth of cassis, plum and spice flavours. Sweetly oaked, it has a minty, herbal thread and a slight lack of warmth on the finish, but past vintages have flourished with bottle-age, typically breaking into full stride after two or three years.

Vintage	05
WR	5
Drink	09-12

DRY $60 –V

Jurassic Ridge Cabernet Franc   ★★★☆

Grown at Church Bay, on Waiheke Island, the 2006 (★★★☆) was matured for nine months in French oak casks. Drinking well now, it's vibrantly fruity, with good depth of plum and spice flavours, showing considerable complexity. The 2007 vintage (★★★★), which includes 14 per cent Merlot, has very attractive berry, plum and spice flavours, showing good freshness, ripeness and complexity.

Vintage	08
WR	7
Drink	09-14

DRY $29 –V

Man O' War Cabernet Franc/Merlot   (★★★☆)

From the eastern end of Waiheke Island, the 2007 vintage (★★★☆) is a blend of Cabernet Franc (68 per cent), Merlot (24 per cent), Cabernet Sauvignon (5 per cent) and Petit Verdot (3 per cent), matured for 10 months in French and American oak casks. Full-coloured, fresh and vibrantly fruity, with cassis, plum and spice flavours, gently seasoned with oak, it's a mouthfilling, flavoursome wine, drinking well now.

`DRY $28 –V`

Matakana Estate Cabernet Franc/Merlot   (★★☆)

Verging on three-star quality, the 2006 vintage (★★☆) is a blend of Cabernet Franc (61 per cent) and Merlot (39 per cent), grown in Hawke's Bay and French oak-aged for a year. Fullish in colour, it's a reasonably generous wine with some complexity, but green-edged, showing a slight lack of ripeness and roundness.

`DRY $28 –V`

Mills Reef Elspeth Cabernet Franc   ★★★★

This single-vineyard wine is grown in Mere Road, on the edge of the Gimblett Gravels district in Hawke's Bay, and French oak-matured for 18 months. The deeply coloured, floral 2005 vintage (★★★★☆) was hand-picked at 24.4 brix. Concentrated, with ripe, sweet-fruit characters and blackcurrant, red-berry and plum flavours showing excellent complexity, it has supple tannins and a rich finish. Maturing very gracefully, it's a classy wine, for drinking now or cellaring.

Vintage	06	05	04	03	02	01	00
WR	NM	7	7	NM	7	NM	7
Drink	NM	09-16	09-15	NM	09-14	NM	P

`DRY $40 –V`

Murdoch James Martinborough/Hawke's Bay Cabernet Franc/Cabernet Sauvignon   (★★☆)

The 2007 vintage (★★☆) of this varietal and regional blend was matured for 10 months in French oak barriques. Lightish and fairly youthful in colour, it's a pleasant, light red, plummy, slightly spicy and smooth.

Vintage	07
WR	5
Drink	09-11

`DRY $20 –V`

Omaha Bay Vineyard Matakana Cabernet Franc/Malbec/Petit Verdot   ★★★☆

The 2007 vintage (★★★★), the best yet, is dark, brambly, concentrated and supple, in a very generous style, maturing well. The 2008 (★★★☆) is full-coloured, with good depth of vibrant, plummy, slightly herbal flavour, seasoned with sweet oak, and a smooth finish.

Vintage	08	07	06
WR	6	7	5
Drink	09-15	09-19	09-12

`DRY $40 –V`

Te Kairanga Jack's Union Cabernet Franc/Cabernet Sauvignon   ★★★☆

The 2005, 2006 and 2007 vintages of Te Kairanga's Cabernet Franc-based reds, grown in Hawke's Bay, are all on sale now. Based on different varietal proportions (and labelled accordingly), they are all of very good quality. My pick is the 2006 (★★★★), a blend of 76 per cent Cabernet Franc and 24 per cent Cabernet Sauvignon. Deeply coloured, it is rich and ripe, vibrantly fruity and concentrated, with good complexity and harmony.

Vintage	07	06	05
WR	6	6	6
Drink	09-15	09-14	09-13

`DRY $22 AV`

Cabernet Sauvignon and Cabernet-predominant Blends

Cabernet Sauvignon has proved a tough nut to crack in New Zealand. Mid-priced models were – until recently – usually of lower quality than a comparable offering from Australia, where the relative warmth suits the late-ripening Cabernet Sauvignon variety. Yet a top New Zealand Cabernet-based red from a favourable vintage can hold its own in illustrious company, and the overall standard of today's offerings is far higher than many wine lovers realise – which makes for some great bargains.

Cabernet Sauvignon was widely planted here in the nineteenth century. The modern resurgence of interest in the great Bordeaux variety was led by Tom McDonald, the legendary Hawke's Bay winemaker, whose string of elegant (though, by today's standards, light) Cabernet Sauvignons under the McWilliam's label, from the much-acclaimed 1965 vintage to the gold-medal winning 1975, proved beyond all doubt that fine-quality red wines could be produced in New Zealand.

During the 1970s and 1980s, Cabernet Sauvignon ruled the red wine roost in New Zealand. Since then, as winemakers – especially in the South Island, but also Hawke's Bay – searched for red-wine varieties that would ripen more fully and consistently in our relatively cool grape-growing climate than Cabernet Sauvignon, it has been pushed out of the limelight by Merlot, Pinot Noir and Syrah. According to the latest national vineyard survey, between 2003 and 2010, the country's total area of bearing Cabernet Sauvignon vines will contract from 741 to 517 hectares. Growers with suitably warm sites have often retained faith in Cabernet Sauvignon, but others have moved on to less challenging varieties.

Three-quarters of the country's Cabernet Sauvignon vines are clustered in Hawke's Bay, and Auckland also has significant plantings. In the South Island, where only 7 per cent of the vines are planted, Cabernet-based reds have typically lacked warmth and richness. This magnificent but late-ripening variety's future in New Zealand clearly lies in the warmer vineyard sites of the north.

What is the flavour of Cabernet Sauvignon? When newly fermented a herbal character is common, intertwined with blackcurrant-like fruit aromas. New oak flavours, firm acidity and taut tannins are other hallmarks of young, fine Cabernet Sauvignon. With maturity the flavour loses its aggression and the wine develops roundness and complexity, with assorted cigar-box, minty and floral scents emerging. It is infanticide to broach a Cabernet Sauvignon-based red with any pretensions to quality at less than two years old; at about four years old the rewards of cellaring really start to flow.

Abbey Cellars Cabernets/Merlot – see the Cabernet Franc section

Abbey Cellars Cardinal Cabernet Sauvignon ★★★

The 2006 vintage (★★★), grown at Bridge Pa, in Hawke's Bay, is a blend of Cabernet Sauvignon (87 per cent) with minor amounts of Cabernet Franc, Merlot and Malbec. Matured for a year in new French oak, it is medium to full-bodied, with blackcurrant, plum and slight chocolate flavours, an earthy streak and a smooth finish. A mellow style, it's ready for drinking now onwards.

DRY $25 –V

Artisan Kauri Ridge Vineyard Cabernet/Merlot – see the Cabernet Franc section

---

Ashwell Martinborough Cabernet Sauvignon ★★★

The 2008 vintage (★★★), matured in French oak barriques, has deep, youthful colour. It's a medium-bodied style (12.5 per cent alcohol), fruity, flavoursome and supple, with fresh acidity, and should mature solidly.

Vintage	08
WR	5
Drink	09-14

DRY $26 –V

Aspire Cabernet Sauvignon/Merlot (★★★)

From Matariki, the 2006 vintage (★★★) is a Hawke's Bay red, grown in the Gimblett Gravels and barrel-aged for a year. Full-coloured, with a slightly leafy bouquet, it's a fruit-driven style with fresh berry, plum and spice flavours and a very restrained oak influence. It's enjoyable now.

Vintage	06
WR	5
Drink	09-11

DRY $20 AV

Awaroa Waiheke Island Cabernet/Merlot/Malbec ★★★☆

The 2006 vintage (★★★★) was handpicked from 'organic' vineyards and matured in French oak casks (50 per cent new). Deep and youthful in colour, with lots of spicy French oak on the nose, it has good density of fresh, vibrant, blackcurrant-like flavours and a hint of herbs, in a savoury, firm style. The 2007 (★★★) has solid depth of plum, spice and herb flavours, showing some complexity.

Vintage	06	05	04
WR	6	7	5
Drink	10-14	10-14	09-10

DRY $30 –V

Babich Irongate Cabernet/Merlot/Franc ★★★★☆

Grown in the Irongate Vineyard in Gimblett Road, Hawke's Bay and matured in French oak barriques (30 per cent new), this elegant, complex, firmly structured red is designed for cellaring. The 2005 vintage (★★★★★) is a classic – classy and refined. Deeply coloured, it has pure, blackcurrant-like flavours to the fore, rich and ripe, but not heavy, in a subtle style that will appeal strongly to Bordeaux lovers. The 2006 (★★★☆) is not a great year. Full and slightly advanced in colour, it has leathery, spicy flavours, showing complexity and depth, but also a lack of optimal ripeness, with leafy notes and considerable development.

DRY $35 AV

Babich The Patriarch – see the Branded and Other Reds section

Balthazar Magi Cabernet Sauvignon/Merlot/Cabernet Franc (★★★☆)

Grown in the Gimblett Gravels, Hawke's Bay, the 2004 vintage (★★★☆) is a blend of Cabernet Sauvignon (75 per cent), Merlot (18 per cent) and Cabernet Franc (7 per cent). Full and mature in colour, it is mouthfilling and moderately ripe-tasting, with developed flavours of spices, herbs, coffee and nuts, showing some richness and savoury complexity. Ready.

DRY $35 –V

Beach House Hawke's Bay Cabernet/Malbec   (★★★★)

The 2007 vintage (★★★★) is a 60/40 blend of Cabernet Sauvignon and Malbec, grown in The Track Vineyard in Mere Road, in the Gimblett Gravels, and matured for a year in French and American oak casks. Boldly coloured, it is youthful and concentrated, with fresh, vibrant blackcurrant, plum and spice flavours, tinged with sweet oak, a hint of coffee, and good tannin support. Fine value.

Vintage	07
WR	7
Drink	09-30

DRY $20 V+

Brick Bay Cabernet/Merlot/Franc   ★★☆

The 2005 vintage (★★★) was blended from Cabernet Sauvignon (45 per cent), Merlot (36 per cent), Cabernet Franc (17 per cent) and Malbec (2 per cent), grown at Matakana and French oak-aged for a year. Fullish in colour, it is berryish, spicy and flavoursome, with some savoury, nutty complexity.

Vintage	05	04	03
WR	7	7	6
Drink	09-11	09-10	P

DRY $22 –V

Brookfields Ohiti Estate Cabernet Sauvignon   ★★★☆

Hawke's Bay winemaker Peter Robertson believes that Ohiti Estate produces 'sound Cabernet Sauvignon year after year – which is a major challenge to any vineyard'. The 2007 vintage (★★★★), matured for a year in French and American oak casks, is one of the best. Dark, with the distinctive aromas of Cabernet Sauvignon and mouthfilling body, it has strong, youthful blackcurrant, plum, spice and herb flavours, showing good concentration. Drink now or cellar.

Vintage	07	06
WR	7	7
Drink	10-17	09-13

DRY $19 V+

Brookfields Reserve Vintage ['Gold Label'] Cabernet/Merlot   ★★★★★

Brookfields' 'gold label' red is one of the most powerful and long-lived reds in Hawke's Bay. At its best, it is a thrilling wine – robust, tannin-laden and overflowing with very rich cassis, plum and mint flavours. Since 2000, the grapes have been sourced from the Lyons family's sloping, north-facing vineyard at Bridge Pa, and the wine is matured for 18 months in French oak barriques (95 to 100 per cent new). The 2007 vintage (★★★★★) is dark and youthful in colour, with a fragrant bouquet of blackcurrants and herbs. Highly concentrated, yet supple, it has deep cassis, herb and spice flavours, in a serious, complex yet approachable style, that reminded me of a good St Estephe. Drink now or cellar.

Vintage	07	06	05	04	03	02	01	00
WR	7	7	NM	7	NM	7	NM	7
Drink	10-19	09-16	NM	10-12	NM	09-10	NM	09-12

DRY $55 AV

Canadoro Cabernet Sauvignon   ★★★☆

Dark and still youthful in colour, the 2006 vintage (★★★★) of this Martinborough red should be long-lived. Matured for 18 months in French oak barriques (new and seasoned), it's a stylish, finely textured wine with highly concentrated, well-ripened blackcurrant, herb and nut flavours.

DRY $30 –V

Church Road Cabernet/Merlot — see Church Road Merlot/Cabernet

Church Road Cuve Series Hawke's Bay Cabernet Sauvignon   (★★★★★)

The 2007 vintage (★★★★★) from Pernod Ricard NZ is dark, with blackcurrant, plum, herb and spice flavours, supple, ripe and highly concentrated. Finely textured, it's an approachable wine with gentle tannins and impressive density. A top buy.

DRY $26 V+

Church Road Reserve Cabernet/Merlot   ★★★★★

The dark, flavour-drenched 2007 vintage (★★★★★) shows just what Hawke's Bay can do in a favourable season with Cabernet Sauvignon-predominant reds. Hand-picked and matured for 21 months in French oak barriques, it is dense and boldly coloured, with concentrated blackcurrant, herb and nut flavours, showing good, savoury complexity, and a firm underlay of tannin.

Vintage	07
WR	7
Drink	09-15

DRY $36 V+

C.J. Pask Declaration Cabernet/Merlot/Malbec   ★★★★

Refined, with deep, youthful colour, the 2005 vintage (★★★★) is a Gimblett Gravels blend of Cabernet Sauvignon (48 per cent), Merlot (35 per cent) and Malbec (17 per cent), matured for 18 months in French and American oak. Warm, savoury and tightly structured, it offers excellent concentration of brambly, herbal, spicy flavours.

DRY $45 –V

C.J. Pask Gimblett Road Cabernet/Merlot/Malbec   ★★★★

The 2007 vintage (★★★☆) is a blend of Cabernet Sauvignon (56 per cent), Merlot (27 per cent) and Malbec (17 per cent), barrel-aged for 16 to 18 months. Dark, it has concentrated plum and spice flavours, the herbal, leafy notes typical of Cabernet Sauvignon, and good structure and complexity.

DRY $20 V+

Clearview Cape Kidnappers Cabernet/Merlot   ★★★☆

Grown in Hawke's Bay and matured for a year in French and American oak casks (mostly seasoned), this is typically a sturdy red with sweet-fruit characters and plenty of savoury, spicy flavour. The 2007 vintage (★★★☆) is a blend of estate-grown, hand-picked Cabernet Sauvignon (44 per cent) with Merlot (42 per cent) and Malbec (14 per cent). Made for early drinking, it's a vibrantly fruity, deeply coloured red with good depth of berryish, slightly minty flavour, a hint of sweet oak and a smooth finish.

Vintage	07
WR	7
Drink	09-14

DRY $21 AV

Coopers Creek SV Gimblett Gravels Hawke's Bay Cabernet/Merlot ★★★★

The 2006 vintage (★★★★) is a blend of Cabernet Sauvignon (52 per cent) and Merlot (48 per cent), full-coloured, with generous, youthful blackcurrant, herb and plum flavours, showing excellent complexity and density.

Vintage	06	05
WR	6	6
Drink	09-12	09-11

DRY $28 AV

Corbans Cottage Block Hawke's Bay Cabernet/Merlot (★★★★★)

The 2007 vintage (★★★★★) is a majestic red. Matured for two years in French oak barriques (new and one-year-old), it is densely coloured, with layers of blackcurrant, plum and spice flavours, complex and concentrated, and ripe, supple tannins. It should flourish for a decade.

DRY $35 V+

Corbans Homestead Hawke's Bay Cabernet Sauvignon/Merlot ★★★

From Pernod Ricard NZ, the 2008 vintage (★★★) is deeply coloured, with good body, satisfying depth of blackcurrant and herb flavours and a smooth finish.

DRY $17 AV

Cornerstone Cabernet/Merlot/Malbec –
see Newton/Forrest Estate Cornerstone in the Branded and Other Red Wines section

Delegat's Hawke's Bay Cabernet/Merlot ★★★☆

The bargain-priced 2008 vintage (★★★☆) is dark and youthful in colour, with generous blackcurrant, plum and spice flavours. Fruity and supple, with a gentle seasoning of oak, it shows very good ripeness, balance and depth.

Vintage	08	07	06	05
WR	7	6	6	6
Drink	09-14	09-13	09-12	09-12

DRY $17 V+

Delegat's Reserve Hawke's Bay Cabernet Sauvignon/Merlot ★★★★

Top vintages offer great value. The 2007 (★★★★) is a 50/50 blend of Cabernet Sauvignon and Merlot, grown in the Gimblett Gravels and barrel-aged for a year. Dark, with cedary, spicy oak seasoning blackberry and green-olive flavours, it shows good richness and complexity.

Vintage	07	06
WR	6	5
Drink	09-13	09-13

DRY $20 V+

Distant Land Hawke's Bay Cabernet/Merlot (★★★★)

From Lincoln, the black label 'reserve' 2006 vintage (★★★★) is a dark, Cabernet Sauvignon-based red (71 per cent), with Merlot (20 per cent) and Cabernet Franc (9 per cent). Grown in the Gimblett Gravels and matured for 16 months in French oak barrels (half new), it's vibrant, with excellent concentration of cassis, plum and spice flavours, ripe and firm. A tightly structured wine, it should reward cellaring.

DRY $34 –V

Doubtless Cabernet Sauvignon   ★★★

Estate-grown at Doubtless Bay, in Northland, the 2004 vintage (★★★) includes 5 per cent Merlot and was matured for 22 months in new French oak barriques. Maturing well, it's a full-coloured wine with good varietal character and plenty of blackcurrant-like flavour, firm and moderately complex. The 2005 (★★★) is full-coloured, with blackcurrant and spice flavours, still youthful, showing some depth and complexity.

Vintage	04	03	02
WR	5	4	2
Drink	09-12	09-10	P

 DRY $20 AV

Dunleavy Cabernet/Merlot   ★★★☆

The second-tier red from Waiheke Vineyards, best known for Te Motu Cabernet/Merlot. It is typically like a minor Bordeaux – savoury and leafy, with plummy, spicy flavours, balanced for early consumption. Drinking well now, the 2006 vintage (★★★☆) is medium-bodied, with vibrant blackcurrant, herb and spice flavours, showing some savoury complexity.

DRY $45 –V

Fall Harvest Cabernet/Merlot   (★★)

The 2005 vintage (★★), still on sale in 2009, is a blend of Australian and New Zealand wines. The colour is fullish and developed; the flavours are simple, slightly under-ripe and leafy. Ready.

DRY $13 –V

Goldwater Cabernet Sauvignon & Merlot –
see Goldwater Goldie in the Branded and Other Reds section

Hatton Estate Gimblett Road Reserve Cabernet/Merlot/Franc   ★★★★

The 2005 vintage (★★★★) of this Hawke's Bay red is dark, rich and supple, with powerful blackcurrant, spice and dark chocolate flavours, and gentle tannins.

DRY $29 AV

Heart of Stone Gimblett Gravels Cabernet/Merlot   (★★★)

The 2005 vintage (★★★) is a sturdy, flavoursome red, blended by Forrest Estate from equal portions of Hawke's Bay Cabernet Sauvignon and Merlot (plus a splash of Malbec). Full-coloured, with a touch of savoury complexity, it has Cabernet Sauvignon's blackcurrant and herb characters to the fore, and a fresh, smooth finish.

DRY $20 AV

Himmelsfeld Moutere Cabernet Sauvignon   ★★★☆

Still on sale, the 2003 vintage (★★★☆) has full, moderately developed colour and a spicy, leafy fragrance. Mouthfilling, it's a firm, sturdy wine with lots of colour, body and flavour, some leafy notes and plenty of personality.

 DRY $36 –V

Hyperion Kronos Cabernet/Merlot/Malbec   ★★★☆

Grown at Matakana, north of Auckland, the 2005 vintage (★★★☆) is a blend of Cabernet
Sauvignon (60 per cent), Merlot (30 per cent) and Malbec (10 per cent), matured for a year in
French and American oak casks. Fullish and bright in colour, it is berryish, plummy, fruity and
smooth, with gentle tannins and drink-young charm.

Vintage	05	04
WR	5	6
Drink	09-14	09-14

DRY $31 –V

Hyperion The Titan Cabernet Sauvignon   ★★★☆

This Matakana red is very good, but not as gigantic as the term 'titan' suggests. The 2006 vintage
(★★★☆), based on some of the oldest vines in Matakana and oak-matured for 18 months, has
plenty of personality. Full-coloured, it offers very good depth of spicy, slightly herbal and earthy
flavours, showing some leathery, nutty complexity. The 2007 (★★★☆) is full-coloured, with
perfumed, sweet oak aromas. Mouthfilling and smooth, with blackcurrant-like flavours tinged
with sweet oak, it is savoury and complex, and drinking well now.

Vintage	06	05	04
WR	6	4	6
Drink	09-16	09-14	09-14

DRY $42 –V

Isola Estate Cabernet/Merlot   (★★★★)

Grown on Waiheke Island, the 2008 vintage (★★★★) is an impressive blend of Cabernet
Sauvignon (52 per cent), Merlot (42 per cent), Cabernet Franc (5 per cent) and Malbec (1 per
cent). Deeply coloured, it offers fresh, youthful, generous berry and plum flavours, showing
excellent concentration. Drink 2011+.

DRY $37 –V

John Forrest Collection Cabernet Sauvignon   (★★★★★)

A star label on the rise. The authoritative 2005 vintage (★★★★★) is based on mature, low-
cropped (4 to 5.6 tonnes/hectare) vines in the Gimblett Gravels district of Hawke's Bay, and
matured in French oak barriques (one-third new). Notably concentrated, complex and well-
structured, with bold, youthful colour, it is dense, warm, spicy, nutty and layered, with firm,
ripe tannins and great potential.

Vintage	05
WR	6
Drink	12-20

DRY $65 AV

Johner Cabernet/Merlot/Malbec   ★★★★

The classy, deeply coloured 2007 vintage (★★★★) is a Wairarapa blend of Cabernet Sauvignon,
Merlot, Cabernet Franc and Malbec, grown in the Gladstone and Martinborough districts.
Fragrant, it has strong, ripe, brambly and spicy flavours, complex and concentrated.

Vintage	07
WR	5
Drink	09-11

DRY $39 –V

Karikari Estate Cabernet Sauvignon/Merlot/Cabernet Franc   ★★★★

Estate-grown on the Karikari Peninsula, in the Far North, the 2005 vintage (★★★★☆) is a blend of Cabernet Sauvignon (60 per cent), Merlot (30 per cent) and Cabernet Franc (10 per cent), matured for 11 months in French (90 per cent) and American oak casks (45 per cent new). Deeply coloured, it is full-bodied, with firmly structured blackcurrant, plum, herb and spice flavours, showing excellent density and complexity. Maturing well, it should be very long-lived.

Vintage	05	04
WR	6	6
Drink	09-10	P

DRY $28 AV

Kemp Road Gimblett Gravels Cabernet/Merlot/Syrah   (★★★★☆)

From wine distributor Kemp Fine Wines, the 2002 vintage (★★★★☆) is dark and still youthful in colour, with generous, spicy, slightly chocolatey flavours, concentrated, savoury and complex. Drink now to 2012.

DRY $60 –V

Kennedy Point Reserve Cabernet Sauvignon   (★★★☆)

The 2004 vintage (★★★☆) was grown on Waiheke Island, in Auckland, and oak-aged for 18 months. A full-bodied wine with fullish, slightly developed colour and spicy, slightly leafy flavours, showing good complexity, it is savoury and mellow, offering good drinking now.

Vintage	04
WR	6
Drink	10-15

DRY $45 –V

Longview Estate Gumdiggers Reserve Cabernet Sauvignon   (★★★)

The 2005 vintage (★★★) is a Northland red, estate-grown south of Whangarei and French oak-aged for 18 months. It's an honest, mellow red with fullish, slightly developed colour and moderately concentrated, spicy, herbal flavours.

DRY 28 –V

Man O' War Cabernet Sauvignon/Cabernet Franc/Merlot   (★★★★)

Grown on Waiheke Island, the 2007 vintage (★★★★) was matured for 10 months in French and American oak casks. Full-coloured, with a fragrant, spicy bouquet, it has good concentration of blackcurrant, spice and plum flavours, finely integrated oak and firm, ripe tannins. Already highly approachable, it should mature well.

Vintage	07
WR	5
Drink	09-12

DRY $28 AV

Matariki Hawke's Bay Cabernet Sauvignon/Merlot   (★★★★)

The sturdy, rich 2007 vintage (★★★★) is a blend of Cabernet Sauvignon (57 per cent), Merlot (28 per cent), Cabernet Franc (10 per cent) and Syrah (5 per cent), grown in the Gimblett Gravels, Hawke's Bay, and matured for 21 months in French oak barriques (20 per cent new). Still fresh and youthful, it is boldly coloured, with deep blackcurrant, plum, mint and spice flavours, vibrant and supple. Worth cellaring.

Vintage	07
WR	6
Drink	09-14

DRY $27 AV

Matariki Reserve Cabernet Sauvignon   (★★★★★)

Showing power and elegance, the outstanding 2007 vintage (★★★★ ★) is a hand-picked blend of Cabernet Sauvignon (90 per cent), Merlot (5 per cent) and Cabernet Franc (5 per cent), grown in the Gimblett Gravels, Hawke's Bay, and matured for 22 months in oak casks (58 per cent new). Deeply coloured, it is fleshy and ripe, with concentrated blackcurrant, plum and spice flavours, a hint of mint, and fine-grained tannins giving a lovely texture.

Vintage	07
WR	7
Drink	09-15

DRY $40 AV

Maximus Mahurangi River Matakana Cabernet Sauvignon/Merlot/Malbec   (★★☆)

Estate-grown, hand-picked and matured in French oak barriques, the 2006 vintage (★★☆) has lightish, slightly developed colour. It's a medium-bodied wine (11.5 per cent alcohol) with moderate depth of green-edged flavours that lack real ripeness, roundness and richness.

DRY $30 –V

Mebus Dakins Road Wairarapa Cabernet/Merlot/Malbec   (★★☆)

The 2007 vintage (★★☆) is flavoursome and spicy, with some complexity, but also lacks full ripeness, with green, leafy notes detracting.

DRY $18 –V

Mills Reef Elspeth Cabernet/Merlot   ★★★★★

Grown at the company's close-planted Mere Road site in the Gimblett Gravels, this is a consistently impressive Hawke's Bay red. The 2007 vintage (★★★★☆), harvested at 24 brix, is a blend of Cabernet Sauvignon (70 per cent) and Merlot (30 per cent), matured for over a year in French oak barriques (20 per cent new). It's a full-bodied wine with strong blackcurrant, plum and spice flavours, ripe, supple tannins and good length.

Vintage	07	06	05	04	03	02
WR	7	7	7	7	NM	7
Drink	09-17	09-16	09-15	09-15	NM	09-10

DRY $40 AV

Mills Reef Elspeth Cabernet Sauvignon   ★★★★★

The 2007 vintage (★★★★☆) was hand-picked in the company's Mere Road Vineyard, in the Gimblett Gravels of Hawke's Bay, fermented partly with indigenous yeasts, and matured for 16 months in French oak barrels (60 per cent new). Rich, sweet-fruited and smooth, it has very ripe blackcurrant, plum, spice and liquorice flavours, showing good density and complexity, and gentle, silky tannins.

Vintage	07	06	05	04
WR	7	7	7	7
Drink	09-18	09-17	09-16	09-15

DRY $40 AV

Mills Reef Elspeth Trust Vineyard Cabernet Sauvignon ★★★★☆

The elegant 2007 vintage (★★★★☆) is a blend of Cabernet Sauvignon (85 per cent) and Cabernet Franc (15 per cent), harvested at 24.2 brix in Mere Road, in the Gimblett Gravels of Hawke's Bay, and matured for over a year in French oak casks (60 per cent new). Fragrant and boldly coloured, with a distinct but attractive herbal element, it has rich blackcurrant, green-olive and nut flavours, and fine, supple tannins.

Vintage	07	06
WR	7	6
Drink	09-17	09-16

DRY $40 AV

Mills Reef Reserve Cabernet/Merlot ★★★★☆

The latest releases of this Hawke's Bay red have delivered fine value. The 2007 vintage (★★★★), blended from Cabernet Sauvignon (65 per cent) and Merlot (35 per cent), is dark, fragrant and full, with the lovely, blackcurrant-like flavours of ripe Cabernet Sauvignon to the fore, a subtle oak influence – six months in French (70 per cent) and American (30 per cent) casks (35 per cent new) – and the underlying structure to age.

Vintage	07	06	05	04	03	02
WR	7	7	7	7	6	7
Drink	09-12	09-11	09-10	P	P	P

DRY $25 V+

Mission Hawke's Bay Cabernet/Merlot ★★★

The 2007 vintage (★★★★) is a top buy. A blend of Cabernet Sauvignon (43 per cent), Merlot (42 per cent), Cabernet Franc (10 per cent) and Malbec (5 per cent), it is deeply coloured, with strong blackcurrant, spice and coffee flavours, brambly, ripe and supple. The 2008 (★★★) is a mouthfilling, lightly oaked style with plenty of blackcurrant, red-berry and spice flavour, fruity and smooth.

DRY $17 AV

Mission Hawke's Bay Cabernet Sauvignon ★★★

In favourable vintages, this red offers good value. The 2007 (★★★☆) includes 10 per cent Cabernet Franc and 5 per cent Malbec. Deeply coloured, it has very good depth of berry and green-olive flavours, tinged with sweet oak, and silky tannins. The 2008 (★★☆) is dark and flavoursome, but distinctly leafy, with a smooth finish.

DRY $17 AV

Mission Hawke's Bay Reserve Cabernet Sauvignon ★★★☆

Grown at Moteo and in the Gimblett Gravels, and matured for over a year in French oak barriques (20 per cent new), the 2007 vintage (★★★☆) includes minor portions of Cabernet Franc (8 per cent) and Merlot (7 per cent). It's a generous, slightly leafy wine, concentrated and finely textured, with some coffee notes and supple tannins.

Vintage	07	06
WR	7	5
Drink	07-19	09-12

DRY $23 AV

Mission Jewelstone Hawke's Bay Cabernet/Merlot/Franc   ★★★★

The 2007 vintage (★★★★) is a Gimblett Gravels blend of Cabernet Sauvignon (46 per cent), Merlot (31 per cent), Cabernet Franc (19 per cent) and Petit Verdot (4 per cent), matured in French oak barrels (73 per cent new). Dark, it is sweet-fruited and complex, with rich flavours of blackcurrants, spices and herbs, a hint of coffee, and firm tannins.

Vintage	07
WR	7
Drink	09-20

DRY $35 –V

Mission Reserve Hawke's Bay Cabernet/Merlot   ★★★★

Blended from four grape varieties – mostly Cabernet Sauvignon (48 per cent), Merlot (40 per cent) and Cabernet Franc (9 per cent) – with a splash of Petit Verdot, the 2007 vintage (★★★★) was grown in the Gimblett Gravels and matured in French oak casks (20 per cent new). Deep and youthful in colour, it is mouthfilling, with concentrated blackcurrant, plum, spice and nut flavours, and supple tannins. Already enjoyable, it should cellar well.

Vintage	07	06
WR	7	5
Drink	09-16	09-12

DRY $23 V+

Moana Park Vineyard Tribute Cabernet Sauvignon   (★★★☆)

Deep and youthful in colour, the 2007 vintage (★★★☆) was hand-picked in the Gimblett Gravels, fermented with indigenous yeasts, and bottled unfined and unfiltered. It's a mouthfilling wine (14 per cent alcohol) with ripe berry and spice flavours, a hint of olives, and a smooth, well-rounded finish.

DRY $20 AV

Monkey Bay Cabernet/Merlot   ★★★

Grown in Hawke's Bay, the 2007 vintage (★★★) from Constellation NZ is a vibrantly fruity blend of Cabernet Sauvignon (54 per cent) and Merlot (46 per cent), partly oak-aged. It's a medium-bodied style with full, youthful colour and good depth of smooth plum, herb and spice flavours.

MED/DRY $16 AV

Mudbrick Vineyard Cabernet Sauvignon/Merlot   (★★★★)

Grown at Church Bay and Onetangi, on Waiheke Island, the 2008 vintage (★★★★) is deeply coloured and sturdy (14.2 per cent alcohol), with fresh, strong cassis, plum and spice flavours and ripe, supple tannins. Best drinking 2011+.

DRY $29 AV

Mudbrick Vineyard Cabernet Sauvignon/Merlot/Cabernet Franc/Malbec   (★★★☆)

The 2007 vintage (★★★☆) was grown on Waiheke Island. Richly coloured, it's a generous red, distinctly herbal, with very good complexity and depth. It's drinking well now.

DRY $26 –V

Newton/Forrest Cornerstone Cabernet/Merlot/Malbec –
see Newton/Forrest Estate Cornerstone in the Branded and Other Red Wines section

Newton/Forrest Estate Gimblett Gravels Hawke's Bay Cabernet Sauvignon   ★★★★☆

Grown in the Cornerstone Vineyard, the 2007 vintage (★★★★☆) was matured in French (60 per cent) and American oak casks. Boldly coloured, it's a powerful wine (14.4 per cent alcohol), brambly, plummy and spicy, with hints of coffee and nuts, and firm, slightly chewy tannins. Open mid-2010+.

Vintage	07	06
WR	5	5
Drink	09-15	09-12

DRY $40 AV

Ngatarawa Stables Cabernet/Merlot   ★★★

Typically a sturdy Hawke's Bay red with drink-young appeal. The 2008 vintage (★★★) is full-coloured, with good depth of plum, berry and herb flavours, smooth and finely balanced for current drinking.

Vintage	08	07	06
WR	6	6	6
Drink	09-13	09-12	09-12

DRY $17 AV

Passage Rock Reserve Cabernet Sauvignon/Merlot   ★★★★☆

The 2008 vintage (★★★★) is a classy young red with deep, bright colour, good weight and strong blackcurrant, berry, spice and nut flavours, showing good density and complexity. Finely balanced and supple, it shows impressive ripeness and richness.

DRY $40 AV

Peacock Ridge Cabernet/Merlot   ★★★

The 2005 vintage (★★★) is a Waiheke Island red, blended from Cabernet Sauvignon (50 per cent), Merlot (35 per cent), Cabernet Franc (10 per cent) and Malbec (5 per cent). French and American oak-aged for a year, it's a full-coloured wine with plummy, spicy, distinctly herbal flavours, showing some density and complexity.

Vintage	05
WR	6
Drink	P

DRY $25 –V

Riverside Cabernet/Merlot   (★★★)

Grown in the Dartmoor Valley, Hawke's Bay, the 2006 vintage (★★★) was matured for 18 months in new and seasoned oak casks. It's a full-coloured, very smooth and fruity red, plummy, spicy and flavoursome, offering enjoyable, easy drinking.

DRY $25 –V

St Jerome Matuka Cabernet Sauvignon/Merlot   ★★★☆

Grown and hand-harvested on a north-facing clay slope in Henderson, West Auckland, the 1999 vintage (★★★☆) was French oak-aged for two years. Spicy, slightly herbal, nutty and savoury, with fullish, mature colour, it has good complexity and depth, and is drinking well now. (Also tasted in mid to late 2008, the 1989 vintage is nutty, leafy and mellow, while the 1993 is probably at its peak, with lots of spicy, herbal, nutty flavour, firm and deep.)

Vintage	99
WR	5
Drink	09+

DRY $43 –V

Sacred Hill Helmsman Cabernet/Merlot   ★★★★★

The outstanding 2006 vintage (★★★★★) was open and expressive in its youth, but the 2007 (★★★★★) is crying out for cellaring. A powerful Hawke's Bay blend of Cabernet Sauvignon (53 per cent), Merlot (42 per cent) and Cabernet Franc (5 per cent), it was hand-picked in the Deerstalkers Vineyard, in the Gimblett Gravels, and French oak-matured for 18 months. Dark and fleshy, with a strong surge of blackcurrant, plum and spice flavours, showing excellent complexity, and fine-grained tannins, it's a bold, youthful red with obvious, long-term potential.

Vintage	07	06
WR	7	7
Drink	09-25	09-23

DRY $65 AV

Saints Hawke's Bay Cabernet/Merlot   ★★★☆

The 2008 vintage (★★★☆) from Pernod Ricard NZ is dark, with strong blackcurrant and plum flavours, some savoury complexity, and a smooth finish.

Vintage	08	07	06
WR	5	6	5
Drink	09-11	09-10	P

DRY $20 AV

Saratoga Estate Bell Tower Cabernets   (★★☆)

The 2004 vintage (★★☆) of this Waiheke Island red has moderate colour depth and green, leafy flavours that lack ripeness and roundness.

DRY $16 –V

Seifried Nelson Cabernet/Merlot   ★★☆

Typically a medium-bodied red with lightish colour and berryish, leafy flavours, offering easy drinking. The 2007 vintage (★★☆) is a blend of Cabernet Sauvignon (85 per cent), Merlot (12 per cent) and Cabernet Franc (3 per cent), grown at Brightwater and matured in French oak barriques. Full-coloured, it is mouthfilling and generous, with plenty of smooth, leafy flavour.

Vintage	08
WR	7
Drink	09-15

DRY $19 –V

Stone Paddock Hawke's Bay Cabernet Sauvignon   ★★★

The 2006 vintage (★★★☆) from Paritua is a blend of Gimblett Gravels Cabernet Sauvignon (85 per cent) and Merlot from The Triangle (15 per cent), matured for 18 months in barrels (60 per cent new). It's a mouthfilling, full-coloured wine with generous blackcurrant and green-leaf flavours, smooth and well balanced for early drinking.

DRY $23 –V

Stonyridge Larose Cabernets   ★★★★★

Typically a stunning Waiheke wine. Dark and seductively perfumed, with smashing fruit flavours, at its best it is a magnificently concentrated red that matures superbly for a decade or longer, acquiring great complexity. The vines – Cabernet Sauvignon, Merlot, Cabernet Franc, Malbec and Petit Verdot, ranging up to 27 years old – are grown in free-draining clay soils on a north-facing slope, a kilometre from the sea at Onetangi, and are very low-yielding (4 tonnes/hectare). The wine is matured for a year in French (80–90 per cent) and American oak barriques (70–90 per cent new or freshly shaved), and is sold largely on an *en primeur* basis, whereby the customers, in return for paying for their wine about nine months in advance of its delivery, secure a substantial price reduction. The 2008 vintage (★★★★★) is boldly coloured and youthful, with dense cassis, plum, coffee and spice flavours, brambly, savoury and tautly structured. From a very ripe year, it is highly concentrated and muscular (although not especially high in alcohol at 13.5 per cent), and likely to flourish for many years; best drinking 2012+.

Vintage	08	07	06	05	04	03	02	01	00
WR	7	7	7	7	7	7	7	6	7
Drink	14-25	09-17	09-17	11-22	09-17	09-14	09-15	09-10	09-13

DRY $220 –V

Te Awa Zone 10 Cabernet Sauvignon   ★★★★☆

Straight (unblended) Cabernet Sauvignon is out of fashion in New Zealand, but this wine works well. Grown in the Gimblett Gravels of Hawke's Bay, it comes from part of the vineyard that 'ripens behind other zones', giving grapes 'with more generosity and less austerity than other Cabernet Sauvignon plantings'. The 2003 vintage (★★★★) was matured for 17 months in French oak barriques (half new). Dark and still youthful in colour, it's a medium to full-bodied wine (12 per cent alcohol), not especially powerful or complex, but still a lovely expression of the variety, with fresh, pure, blackcurrant-like flavours, showing good ripeness and roundness.

Vintage	03	02	01	00	99	98
WR	6	7	NM	6	NM	6
Drink	09-12	09-12	NM	09-10	NM	P

DRY $40 AV

Te Kairanga Jack's Union Hawke's Bay Cabernet Sauvignon/Merlot   (★★★★)

Bargain-priced, the 2005 vintage (★★★★) is a blend of Cabernet Sauvignon (68 per cent) and Merlot (32 per cent), grown in the Gimblett Gravels and oak-aged. Deep and still fairly youthful in colour, it is full-bodied, with excellent depth of cassis, plum, herb and spice flavours, oak complexity and good tannin support. Starting to round out, it's drinking well now.

Vintage	05
WR	6
Drink	09-12

DRY $22 V+

Te Mata Awatea Cabernets/Merlot   ★★★★★

Positioned below its Coleraine stablemate in Te Mata's hierarchy of Hawke's Bay, claret-style reds, since 1995 Awatea has been grown at Havelock North and in the Bullnose Vineyard, inland from Hastings. The vines are up to 19 years old. A blend of Cabernet Sauvignon, Merlot and Cabernet Franc – with a splash of Petit Verdot since 2001 – it is matured for 18 months in French oak barriques (50 per cent new). Compared to Coleraine, in its youth Awatea is more seductive, more perfumed, and tastes more of sweet, ripe fruit, but is more forward and slightly less concentrated. The wine can mature gracefully for many years, but is also typically delicious at two years old. From a top vintage, the 2007 (★★★★★) is a blend of Cabernet Sauvignon (40 per cent) and Cabernet Franc (17 per cent), with Merlot (38 per cent) and Petit Verdot (5 per cent). Deeply coloured, it is perfumed, rich and flowing, with fresh, strong blackcurrant, plum and slight dark chocolate flavours, earthy, savoury notes adding complexity, and great harmony. Best drinking 2012+.

Vintage	07	06	05	04	03	02	01	00
WR	7	7	7	7	6	7	6	7
Drink	10-20	09-16	09-15	09-12	09-10	09-10	P	09-10

DRY $34 V+

Te Mata Coleraine – see the Branded and Other Red Wines section

---

Te Mata Estate Woodthorpe Vineyard Cabernet/Merlot – see Te Mata Estate Woodthorpe Vineyard Merlot/Cabernet in the Merlot section

Te Motu Cabernet/Merlot   ★★★★

The Dunleavy family's flagship Waiheke Island red is grown at Onetangi – over the fence from Stonyridge – and matured for three winters (about 28 months) in French (mostly), American and Hungarian barrels. Compared to its neighbour, it is less ripe and opulent than Stonyridge Larose, in a more earthy, leafy and savoury style. The disappointing 2004 vintage (★★★) is green-edged, showing some savoury complexity, but also a lack of real ripeness and richness. The 2005 (★★★★☆) is markedly better. Fragrant, it is full-coloured, with rich, complex, spicy flavours, hints of herbs and leather, and a good foundation of tannin. Drink now or cellar.

DRY $89 –V

Terravin J Cabernet/Merlot/Malbec   ★★★★

Grown in the Omaka Valley, this is a dark, richly flavoured Marlborough red. The 2006 vintage (★★★★), made principally from Cabernet Sauvignon (85 per cent), with 10 per cent Merlot and 5 per cent Malbec, was matured for 18 months in French oak barriques (35 per cent new) and bottled unfined and unfiltered. Deeply coloured, it is fresh, full-bodied and flowing, with concentrated blackcurrant and herb flavours showing good complexity and harmony. The 2007 (★★★★) will be sold only in magnums. Dark and youthful in colour, it is concentrated and complex, with blackcurrant, herb and nut flavours, generous and finely textured. Drink now or cellar.

Vintage	07	06	05	04	03	02
WR	7	7	7	7	6	5
Drink	09-16	09-15	09-15	09-12	09-10	P

DRY $44 –V

Tiwaiwaka Lucinda Martinborough Cabernet/Merlot/Franc   (★★★☆)

Based on 12 to 20-year-old vines, the 2006 vintage (★★★☆) is unfolding well. A blend of Cabernet Sauvignon (61 per cent), Merlot (27 per cent) and Cabernet Franc (12 per cent), it was matured for 10 months in oak barrels (30 per cent new). Deeply coloured, it is vibrantly fruity and supple, with generous plum, herb and spice flavours, seasoned with quality oak.

DRY $30 –V

Torlesse Waipara Cabernet/Merlot   (★★★☆)

Drinking well now, the 2006 vintage (★★★☆) was made from equal portions of Cabernet Sauvignon and Merlot, plus a splash of Cabernet Franc. Fragrant, with a spicy, slightly leafy bouquet, it is mouthfilling and smooth, with blackcurrant, spice and green-olive flavours, showing considerable complexity.

DRY $20 AV

Trinity Hill Gimblett Road Cabernet Sauvignon   (★★★★)

Still on sale in 2008, the 2002 vintage (★★★★) has deep, moderately youthful colour, substantial body and concentrated blackcurrant and olive flavours, savoury and lingering.

DRY $29 AV

Trinity Hill Gimblett Road Cabernet Sauvignon/Merlot   ★★★★

The full-coloured 2004 (★★★☆) shows good complexity and some development, offering strong blackcurrant and nut flavours, slightly leafy and firm. This is the last vintage of this label, now replaced by The Gimblett.

Vintage	04	03	02
WR	5	4	6
Drink	09-11	09-10	09-15

DRY $29 AV

Villa Maria Reserve Hawke's Bay Cabernet Sauvignon/Merlot   ★★★★★

The beautifully fragrant, inky-hued 2007 vintage (★★★★★) is a blend of Cabernet Sauvignon (69 per cent), Merlot (29 per cent) and Malbec (2 per cent), grown in the Gimblett Gravels and matured for 20 months in French oak barriques (46 per cent new). It offers rich, ripe blackcurrant-like flavours, with hints of tar and liquorice, firm, fine-grained tannins and lovely length.

Vintage	07	06	05	04	03	02
WR	7	7	6	7	NM	7
Drink	09-22	09-19	09-20	09-14	NM	09-11

DRY $51 AV

Weeping Sands Waiheke Cabernet/Merlot   ★★★★

This is the second label of Obsidian, grown at Onetangi ('weeping sands'). The skilfully crafted 2006 vintage (★★★★) is a blend of Cabernet Sauvignon (60 per cent), Merlot (35 per cent), and splashes of Cabernet Franc and Malbec, matured for 12 months in mostly seasoned French and American oak barriques. Deeply coloured, with a spicy bouquet and firm blackcurrant and spice flavours, it's an age-worthy wine with savoury, earthy notes adding complexity. Compared to most of the island's reds, this is well-priced.

Vintage	07	06	05	04	03	02
WR	5	6	6	6	4	7
Drink	10-15	09-14	09-14	P	P	P

DRY $26 AV

Zepelin Cabernet/Merlot   (★★★)

Grown in Hawke's Bay, the 2005 vintage (★★★) is a blend of Cabernet Sauvignon (85 per cent) and Merlot (15 per cent), French oak-aged. Full and slightly developed in colour, it has concentrated, spicy, herbal flavours and a firm tannin grip. It's a slightly austere wine, but should repay further cellaring.

DRY $25 –V

Carmenère

Ransom, at Matakana, in 2007 released New Zealand's first Carmenère. Now virtually extinct in France, Carmenère was once widely grown in Bordeaux and still is in Chile, where, until the 1990s, it was often mistaken for Merlot. In Italy it was long thought to be Cabernet Franc.

In 1988, viticulturist Alan Clarke imported Cabernet Franc cuttings here from Italy. Planted by Robin Ransom in 1997, the grapes ripened about the same time as the rest of his Cabernet Franc, but the look of the fruit and the taste of the wine were 'totally different'. So Ransom arranged DNA testing at the University of Adelaide. The result? His Cabernet Franc vines are in fact Carmenère.

The latest national vineyard survey records just 1 hectare of Carmenère in New Zealand.

Ransom Carmenère (★★★)

Grown at Matakana, the 2006 vintage (★★★) is deeply coloured, with a berryish, spicy, sweetly oaked bouquet. It's a medium to full bodied wine (12 per cent alcohol) with blackcurrant and herb flavours and fresh acidity.

DRY $28 –V

Chambourcin

Chambourcin is one of the more highly rated French hybrids, well known in Muscadet for its good disease-resistance and bold, crimson hue. Rare in New Zealand (with only 4 hectares planted), it is most often found as a varietal red in Northland.

Ake Ake Chambourcin ★★★★

Grown near Kerikeri, in the Bay of Islands, the 2008 vintage (★★★★) is a fine example of the variety. Matured for a year in American and French barrels, it is deeply coloured, with sweet oak aromas and rich berry and spice flavours, ripe and slightly earthy. A skilfully made wine with gentle tannins, it offers very easy drinking.

Vintage	08
WR	5
Drink	09-12

DRY $24 V+

Marsden Bay of Islands Chambourcin ★★★

The 2007 vintage (★★☆) is a Northland red, barrel-aged for 16 months. Brightly coloured, it is plummy, smooth and flavoursome, but also a bit rustic.

Vintage	07	06	05	04	03	02
WR	4	6	6	6	4	5
Drink	09-10	09-11	09-10	P	P	P

DRY $24 –V

Okahu Chambourcin ★★★☆

The 2007 vintage (★★★) is an estate-grown Northland red, aged in American and French oak casks. It's a deeply coloured wine with fresh acidity, strong, fruity, plummy flavours and the sweet, coconutty aromas of American oak.

DRY $30 –V

Rushbrook Chambourcin (★★★☆)

Grown at the Bay of Islands, in Northland, and American oak-aged, the 2005 vintage (★★★☆) is deep in colour, with a fragrant, slightly gamey bouquet. It's a berryish, spicy, sweetly oaked wine, vibrantly fruity and full-flavoured.

DRY $24 AV

Dolcetto

Grown in the north of Italy, where it produces purple-flushed, fruity, supple reds, usually enjoyed young, Dolcetto is extremely rare in New Zealand, with 2 hectares of bearing vines in 2010.

Hitchen Road Dolcetto ★★★

Grown at Pokeno, in North Waikato, the 2008 vintage (★★★☆) was barrel-matured for 10 months. Deep and youthful in colour, it's a medium to full-bodied wine with plummy, spicy flavours, showing very good depth. Worth cellaring.

DRY $18 AV

Waimea Nelson Dolcetto ★★★

The 2008 vintage (★★★) is a single-vineyard red, picked at 24 brix and matured for eight months in American oak barrels (25 per cent new). Ruby-hued, it is distinctly spicy, in a moderately ripe style with tight plum and spice flavours, fresh acidity, and some savoury complexity.

Vintage	08
WR	6
Drink	09-12

DRY $22 –V

Gamay Noir

Gamay Noir is single-handedly responsible for the seductively scented and soft red wines of Beaujolais. The grape is still rare in New Zealand, although the area of bearing vines will rise between 2005 and 2010 from 9 to 12 hectares. At Omaka Springs in Marlborough, Gamay ripened later than Cabernet Sauvignon (itself an end-of-season ripener), with higher levels of acidity than in Beaujolais, but at Te Mata's Woodthorpe Terraces Vineyard in Hawke's Bay, the crop is harvested as early as mid-March.

Te Mata Estate Woodthorpe Vineyard Gamay Noir ★★★★

The 2009 vintage (★★★★) is a single-vineyard Hawke's Bay red, whole-bunch fermented (in the traditional Beaujolais manner) and matured for four months in seasoned French oak casks. Floral and ruby-hued, it's a delicious drink-young style, charming and supple, with cherry, red-berry and slight spice flavours, vibrantly fruity, light and smooth.

Vintage	09	08	07	06
WR	7	7	7	7
Drink	09-10	09-10	P	P

DRY $19 V+

Malbec

With a leap from 25 hectares of bearing vines in 1998 to 157 hectares in 2010, this old Bordeaux variety is starting to make its presence felt in New Zealand, where two-thirds of all plantings are clustered in Hawke's Bay. It is often used as a blending variety, adding brilliant colour and rich, sweet-fruit flavours to its blends with Merlot, Cabernet Sauvignon and Cabernet Franc. Numerous unblended Malbecs have also been released recently, possessing loads of flavour and often the slight rusticity typical of the variety.

C.J. Pask Declaration Malbec (★★★☆)

Still on sale, the 2005 vintage (★★★☆) was grown in Gimblett Road, Hawke's Bay, and matured for 16 months in new barrels. Full but not dense in colour, it's a medium-bodied style (12 per cent alcohol), with vibrant, plummy, sweetly oaked flavours, fruity and smooth.

DRY $48 –V

Coopers Creek SV Huapui Malbec The Clays (★★★★)

The soft, rich 2006 vintage (★★★★), grown in West Auckland, has bold, purple-flushed colour. It's a seductively smooth wine with sweet-fruit delights and strong, plummy, spicy flavours, with hints of red berries, chocolate and liquorice.

Vintage	07	06
WR	NM	6
Drink	NM	09-12

DRY $26 AV

Fromm Malbec Fromm Vineyard ★★★★☆

Grown in Marlborough and matured for 16–18 months in French oak casks, the 2005 vintage (★★★★☆) is a classy red. Deeply coloured, with coffee and spice aromas, it is youthful, firm and highly concentrated, with cool-climate freshness and an almost Syrah-like spiciness. Winemaker Hätsch Kalberer suggests drinking it with 'a large piece of wild venison'.

Vintage	08	07	06	05	04	03	02
WR	6	6	6	6	6	NM	6
Drink	13-23	12-22	09-18	09-17	09-16	NM	09-12

DRY $45 –V

Hawkesby Waiheke Island Coastal Malbec (★★★★☆)

From Stonyridge, the densely coloured and bold 2008 vintage (★★★★☆) is a single-vineyard red, grown at Church Bay. Matured for a year in one-year-old French oak barrels, it is very fresh and youthful, with highly concentrated plum, spice and liquorice flavours, good tannin backbone, and the power to be long-lived. Open 2011+.

DRY $80 –V

Hitchen Road Malbec ★★★

The mouthfilling 2008 vintage (★★★☆) was grown at Pokeno, in North Waikato. Barrique-aged for 10 months, it is deeply coloured, with fresh, strong, vibrant, plummy flavours and gentle tannins.

DRY $17 AV

Hyperion Midas Malbec   (★★★★)

If you like Aussie reds, you'll enjoy the 2007 vintage (★★★★) of this Matakana red. Full-coloured, with a perfumed, sweetly oaked bouquet, it is plummy and spicy, with mouthfilling body and fresh, strong flavours, seasoned with toasty oak.

Vintage	08	07
WR	7	7
Drink	09-14	09-15

DRY $36 –V

Kennedy Point Reserve Malbec   ★★★☆

Grown on Waiheke Island and oak-aged for up to 18 months, this is typically a boldly coloured red, with oodles of firm, ripe, plummy, spicy, slightly chocolatey flavour. The 2006 vintage (★★★) is dark, gutsy and flavour-crammed, but rustic notes detract.

Vintage	07
WR	5
Drink	12-15

DRY $34 –V

Luna Negra Waiheke Island Hillside Malbec   ★★★★★

From Stonyridge, this is a consistently bold and classy red. Grown in the company's Vina del Mar Vineyard at Onetangi, it is matured for a year in American oak barriques (50 per cent new). The 2007 (★★★★★) is dark and purple-flushed, with a perfumed, sweetly oaked bouquet, sweet-fruit characters and rich, smooth, brambly flavours. Highly concentrated, it is plummy and spicy, with supple tannins giving early approachability. The 2008 (★★★★★) couples full-throttle power with complexity and the structure to age. Densely coloured, it's a powerful, fruit-packed wine, very youthful, with layers of blackcurrant, plum, spice and coffee flavours, needing another two or three years to round out.

Vintage	08	07	06
WR	7	7	7
Drink	09-15	09-13	09-12

DRY $75 AV

Mills Reef Elspeth Malbec   ★★★★☆

Grown in the Gimblett Gravels district of Hawke's Bay, hand-picked at 24.5 brix and matured for 18 months in French oak barriques, the 2005 vintage (★★★★☆) is a sturdy, dark red with bold, purple-flushed colour, floral, berryish aromas, and concentrated, plummy, spicy, slightly earthy flavours, ripe and supple. It's a vibrantly fruity, youthful wine, with the power and structure to age well. There is no 2006.

Vintage	06	05	04	03	02
WR	NM	7	7	NM	7
Drink	NM	09-16	09-15	NM	09-14

DRY $40 AV

Mills Reef Reserve Hawke's Bay Malbec   ★★★★

The 2006 vintage (★★★★) was harvested at 23.8 brix in the Gimblett Gravels, and matured for 15 months in French oak barriques (new and one-year-old). Inky-hued, it is smooth and rich, with concentrated flavours of blackcurrants, plums, spices and chocolate, and plenty of drink-young appeal.

DRY $25 AV

Newton/Forrest Gimblett Gravels Hawke's Bay Malbec   ★★★★☆

The 2006 vintage (★★★★☆) has dense, purple-flushed colour and a fragrant bouquet of spices, dark chocolate and sweet oak. Sturdy (14 per cent alcohol), it's a full-on style for those who enjoy super-charged reds. The 2007 (★★★★☆), matured in French (80 per cent) and American (20 per cent) oak casks, is dark, with a spicy, sweetly oaked, fragrant bouquet. It's a gutsy, concentrated wine, spicy, nutty, bold and firm, with plenty of life ahead.

Vintage	07	06
WR	5	5
Drink	09-12	09-12

DRY $40 AV

Saltings Estate Vineyard Matakana Malbec   (★★★★)

The gutsy 2006 vintage (★★★★) was hand-picked and matured for 16 months in French oak casks. Full-coloured, it is gutsy and generous, with plum, spice and slight herb flavours showing excellent concentration and some earthy complexity.

DRY $28 AV

TW Gisborne Malbec   (★★★☆)

Enjoyable now, the 2007 vintage (★★★☆) is a full-coloured, American oak-aged red with good depth of plum and spice flavours, sweetly wooded and smooth.

Vintage	07
WR	7
Drink	09-15

DRY $24 AV

West Brook Waimauku Estate Malbec   (★★★☆)

Deeply coloured, the 2008 vintage (★★★☆) was estate-grown in West Auckland. It has a floral, berryish bouquet, with the slight medicinal notes typical of Malbec, leading into a fresh, sweet-fruited wine, plummy and smooth, with plenty of flavour and drink-young appeal.

DRY $20 AV

Merlot

Pinot Noir is New Zealand's red-wine calling card on the world stage, but our Merlots are also proving competitive. In the year to June 2009, New Zealand exported over 214,000 cases of Merlot – a steep rise from only 24,194 cases in 2003.

Interest in this most extensively cultivated red-wine grape in Bordeaux is especially strong in Hawke's Bay (although Syrah has recently become the region's hottest red-wine variety). Everywhere in Bordeaux – the world's greatest red-wine region – except in the Médoc and Graves districts, the internationally higher-profile Cabernet Sauvignon variety plays second fiddle to Merlot. The elegant, fleshy wines of Pomerol and St Émilion bear delicious testimony to Merlot's capacity to produce great, yet relatively early-maturing, reds.

In New Zealand, after initial preoccupation with the more austere and slowly evolving Cabernet Sauvignon, the rich, rounded flavours and (more practically) earlier-ripening ability of Merlot are now fully appreciated. Poor set can be a major drawback with the older clones, reducing yields, but Merlot ripens ahead of Cabernet Sauvignon, a major asset in cooler wine regions, especially in vineyards with colder clay soils. Merlot grapes are typically lower in tannin and higher in sugar than Cabernet Sauvignon's; its wines are thus silkier and a shade stronger in alcohol.

Hawke's Bay has almost three-quarters of New Zealand's Merlot vines; the rest are clustered in Marlborough, Auckland and Gisborne. The country's fifth most widely planted variety (now trailing Pinot Gris), Merlot covers more than two and a half times the area of Cabernet Sauvignon. Between 2003 and 2010, the total area of bearing Merlot vines is expanding at a very moderate pace, from 1249 to 1371 hectares, but in top vintages, such as 2007, the wines offer wonderful value.

Merlot's key role in New Zealand was traditionally that of a minority blending variety, bringing a soft, mouthfilling richness and floral, plummy fruitiness to its marriages with the predominant Cabernet Sauvignon. Now, with a host of straight Merlots and Merlot-predominant blends on the market, this aristocratic grape is fully recognised as a top-flight wine in its own right.

Abbey Cellars Graduate Merlot/Cabernets ★★★☆

The 2006 vintage (★★★☆) is a full-coloured Hawke's Bay blend of Merlot (72 per cent) with smaller portions of Cabernet Franc, Malbec and Cabernet Sauvignon. Estate-grown at Bridge Pa and French oak-aged for a year, it is a distinctly earthy style with good body, strong, ripe, sweet-fruit flavours of plums and spices, and a rounded finish.

DRY $25 AV

Alexander Martinborough Merlot (★★★)

The 2006 vintage (★★★) was estate-grown and matured for 17 months in seasoned French oak barrels. Full-coloured, with a slightly herbaceous bouquet, it's a fleshy, smooth wine with generous flavour and gentle tannins. Drink now.

Vintage	06
WR	5
Drink	09-10

DRY $26 –V

Alexia Hawke's Bay Merlot (★★★☆)

The 2007 vintage (★★★☆) from Jane Cooper is dark and mouthfilling, with strong blackcurrant and plum flavours and a hint of herbs. It's a gutsy, fairly smooth red with very good depth, for drinking now onwards.

DRY $20 AV

Alpha Domus The Pilot Hawke's Bay Merlot ★★★

The full-coloured 2004 vintage (★★★) is a blend of Merlot (78 per cent), Malbec (9 per cent), Cabernet Sauvignon (7 per cent) and Cabernet Franc (6 per cent), matured for seven months in seasoned French and American oak barriques. It offers berry, plum, herb and spice flavours, slightly toasty and savoury, in a sweetly oaked style with satisfying depth, now ready. The 2005 (★★★) is a medium-bodied wine with plenty of plummy, spicy, fairly firm flavour.

DRY $20 AV

Ascension The Twelve Apostles Matakana Merlot/Malbec ★★☆

Made from 'twelve special rows of vines we call "The Twelve Apostles"', this American oak-aged blend is typically berryish, plummy and slightly herbal. The 2007 vintage (★★), which includes 20 per cent Malbec, is fullish in colour, with a leafy bouquet and crisp, green-edged flavours that lack ripeness and roundness.

DRY $24 –V

Askerne Hawke's Bay Merlot/Franc/Malbec ★★★

The 2007 vintage (★★★) is a blend of Merlot (67 per cent), Cabernet Franc (20 per cent) and Malbec (13 per cent), matured in French oak casks (22 per cent new). Estate-grown, it is deeply coloured and full-bodied, with strong plum, spice and herb flavours. It's green-edged, but also shows some complexity and generosity.

Vintage	07	06	05
WR	6	5	6
Drink	09-14	09-11	09-10

DRY $20 AV

Askerne Reserve Hawke's Bay Merlot ★★★☆

The 2007 vintage (★★★★) was estate-grown near Havelock North and matured in French oak casks (62 per cent new). Deep and youthful in colour, it is fleshy, with generous blackcurrant, spice and plum flavours, seasoned with quality oak, and ripe, supple tannins. Drink now or cellar.

Vintage	07	06
WR	6	6
Drink	12-15	09-12

DRY $30 –V

Awaroa Stell Hawke's Bay Merlot ★★★

From a Waiheke Island-based winery, the 2007 vintage (★★★) was grown at Te Awanga and matured in seasoned French oak casks. It's a full-bodied red with berry and plum flavours, slightly spicy and nutty, and a firm backbone of tannin.

DRY $20 AV

Awa Valley Merlot/Malbec ★★★

Grown at Kumeu, in West Auckland, the 2007 vintage (★★☆) was blended from Merlot and Malbec and barrel-aged for a year. It's a medium-bodied, fruity, slightly rustic wine with fresh plum/spice flavours, showing moderate depth.

Vintage	07
WR	6
Drink	09

DRY $20 AV

Babich Lone Tree Hawke's Bay Merlot/Cabernet   ★★★

The 2007 vintage (★★★) is full-coloured, with good depth of berry, plum, herb and spice flavours and a well-rounded finish.

DRY $16 AV

Babich Winemakers Reserve Merlot   ★★★☆

Grown in the Gimblett Gravels, Hawke's Bay, and matured in French oak casks, the 2007 vintage (★★★☆) is mouthfilling, with good depth of colour and flavour. Still youthful, it has a slightly minty bouquet, with a dash of coffee, and some richness and roundness on the palate.

Vintage	07	06	05	04	03	02
WR	7	6	7	6	5	7
Drink	09-16	09-15	09-15	09-14	09-10	P

DRY $25 AV

Bach 22 Merlot   ★★☆

From Constellation NZ, the 2006 vintage (★★★) is a Hawke's Bay red, fullish in colour, with a spicy bouquet. Enjoyable young, it is fresh and vibrant, with plummy, distinctly spicy flavour.

DRY $12 V+

Beach House Reserve Merlot   ★★★☆

Grown at The Track Vineyard in Mere Road, in the Gimblett Gravels of Hawke's Bay, the 2007 vintage (★★★☆) was matured for a year in French (25 per cent new) and seasoned American oak casks. Deep and youthful in colour, it is plummy and spicy, with ripe, sweet-fruit flavours and very good depth.

Vintage	07
WR	7
Drink	09-30

DRY $25 AV

Bell Bird Bay Hawke's Bay Merlot   ★★★☆

A great buy. Made at Alpha Domus, the full-bodied 2007 vintage (★★★☆) has plenty of fresh, plummy, spicy flavour, a hint of dark chocolate, and gentle tannins. As a low-priced, drink-young style, this is hard to beat.

DRY $15 V+

Bensen Block Merlot   ★★★

From Pernod Ricard NZ, the 2008 vintage (★★★☆) makes no claims about region of origin. It's a spicy red with good depth of ripe-fruit flavours and some savoury complexity.

DRY $17 AV

Black Barn Hawke's Bay Merlot/Cabernet Franc   ★★★

The 2005 vintage (★★★☆) is a blend of Merlot (75 per cent), Cabernet Franc (23 per cent) and Malbec (2 per cent). It's a Bordeaux-like red with full, maturing colour and very good depth of spice, herb and nut flavours, green-edged, but savoury and complex. Ready.

Vintage	05
WR	6
Drink	09-12

DRY $25 –V

Bladen Marlborough Merlot/Malbec   ★★★

The 2007 vintage (★★☆) is a blend of Merlot (75 per cent) and Malbec (25 per cent), matured in French oak casks (50 per cent new). Full and bright in colour, it is fresh and fruity, but lacks real complexity and depth.

DRY $33 –V

Brookfields Burnfoot Merlot   ★★★☆

The 2008 vintage (★★★☆) was grown in Hawke's Bay and barrel-aged for a year. Full-coloured, it is mouthfilling, with good depth of smooth, ripe berry and plum flavours, showing some complexity.

Vintage	08	07
WR	7	7
Drink	10-16	09-14

DRY $19 V+

Brunton Road Gisborne Merlot   ★★★☆

Enjoyable young, the 2008 vintage (★★★) was estate-grown at Patutahi and matured for seven months in old French and American oak barrels. It's a smooth wine with fullish colour and good depth of fresh, ripe plum and spice flavours, showing some savoury complexity.

Vintage	08	07
WR	5	6
Drink	09-11	09-11

DRY $21 AV

Bushmere Estate Gisborne Merlot   ★★★

The 2006 vintage (★★★) was hand-picked at 23 brix and matured in French oak barrels, partly new. Ruby-hued, it's a medium-bodied wine with berry, plum, nut and herb flavours, showing some savoury complexity. It's enjoyable now.

DRY $22 –V

Cable Bay Five Hills Merlot/Malbec/Cabernet Sauvignon   ★★★★

Grown at several sites on Waiheke Island and matured in French oak barriques for a year, the 2006 vintage (★★★★) is a blend of Merlot (39 per cent), Malbec (29 per cent), Cabernet Sauvignon (26 per cent) and Cabernet Franc (6 per cent). Drinking well now, it is mouthfilling and elegant, with fresh, plum/spice flavours, gently seasoned with oak, and good, savoury complexity. A skilfully crafted wine, it's likely to mature well.

Vintage	06	05	04
WR	6	7	6
Drink	09-13	09-11	09-10

DRY $34 –V

Charles Wiffen Marlborough Merlot   ★★☆

The 2007 vintage (★★☆), French oak-aged for 10 months, is a pleasant, drink-young style with fullish colour, berryish aromas and fruity, slightly leafy flavours.

DRY $24 –V

Church Road Cuve Series Hawke's Bay Merlot   ★★★★★

The great-value 2007 (★★★★★) from Pernod Ricard NZ is a powerful, richly fragrant and concentrated red with bold, bright colour and dense cassis, plum and spice flavours. A strong oak influence combines well with concentrated, sweet-fruit characters, a creamy-smooth texture and impressive length. Hand-picked in the Gimblett Gravels and matured for 20 months in French oak barriques (mostly new), the seductively fragrant, densely packed and supple debut 2005 vintage (★★★★★) is equally impressive.

 DRY $26 V+

Church Road Hawke's Bay Merlot/Cabernet Sauvignon   ★★★★☆

This is typically a full-flavoured and complex, distinctly Bordeaux-like red from Pernod Ricard NZ. The 2007 vintage (★★★★☆) is a blend of Merlot (57 per cent), Cabernet Sauvignon (30 per cent), Malbec (5 per cent), Syrah (6 per cent) and Cabernet Franc (2 per cent). It was mostly (63 per cent) grown in the company's Redstone Vineyard, in The Triangle, with smaller components from the Gimblett Gravels (22 per cent) and Havelock North (15 per cent). Matured for a year in French and Hungarian oak barrels (30 per cent new), it's a top buy, dark and generous, with ripe blackcurrant, plum and spice flavours, finely integrated oak and a rich, lingering finish. The 2008 (tasted prior to bottling, and so not rated) is deeply coloured, savoury and supple, with generous, ripe plum and spice flavours.

Vintage	08	07	06
WR	6	7	6
Drink	09-14	09-14	P

 DRY $26 V+

C.J. Pask Declaration Merlot   ★★★★

The 2006 vintage (★★★★) was grown in the Gimblett Gravels and matured for 18 months in new French and American oak barriques. Fragrant, firm and youthful, it has a smoky bouquet, with good complexity and strong, ripe flavours of berry fruits, spices, herbs and nuts.

DRY $45 –V

C.J. Pask Gimblett Road Merlot   ★★★☆

The 2007 vintage (★★★☆) was grown in the Gimblett Gravels, Hawke's Bay, and matured in French and American oak casks. Firm and concentrated, with blackcurrant and spice flavours and hints of thyme and dried herbs, it shows some density and complexity, with firm tannins and good length. Verging on four stars.

DRY $20 AV

Clearview Cape Kidnappers Merlot/Malbec   ★★★☆

The 2007 vintage (★★★☆) is a Hawke's Bay blend of Merlot (76 per cent), Malbec (18 per cent) and Cabernet Franc (6 per cent), made for early drinking. Matured for a year in mostly seasoned French oak casks, it's a fruit-driven style, gutsy and smooth, with dark, purple-flushed colour and plenty of plummy, spicy flavour.

Vintage	07	DRY $20 AV
WR	7	
Drink	09-13	

Coopers Creek Hawke's Bay Merlot   ★★★☆

Coopers Creek's most popular red is typically great value. The 2007 vintage (★★★☆), which includes 12 per cent Malbec, is fresh, fruity and flavoursome, with good colour, generous, ripe plum/berry characters, moderate complexity and firm underlying tannins. Drink now or cellar.

Vintage	07	06	05	DRY $16 V+
WR	7	7	7	
Drink	09-12	09-11	09-10	

Corbans Homestead Hawke's Bay Merlot   ★★☆

The 2007 vintage (★★★) from Pernod Ricard NZ is the best yet, with a touch of complexity and plenty of smooth, plummy, spicy flavour.

DRY $17 –V

Corbans Private Bin Hawke's Bay Merlot/Cabernet Sauvignon   ★★★☆

The 2005 vintage (★★★☆) is from a season which did not produce Corbans' top Hawke's Bay red label (Cottage Block Ruahine). Mouthfilling, with deep, youthful colour, concentrated berry/spice flavours and chewy tannins, it's a slightly austere wine, but likely to be long-lived. Tasted prior to bottling, and so not rated, the 2007 looked excellent, with impressively dense blackcurrant, plum and spice flavours, firm, ripe tannins, and the power and structure to mature well.

DRY $24 AV

Crab Farm Pukera Merlot   (★★★★)

The dark 2006 vintage (★★★★) was grown in Hawke's Bay and matured for 16 months in French oak casks (80 per cent new). Coffee and spice aromas lead into a powerful (14.5 per cent alcohol), still fresh and vibrant wine, gutsy but not heavy, with brambly, spicy flavours, a hint of liquorice, firm tannins and good concentration. Drink now or cellar.

Vintage	06	DRY $25 AV
WR	6	
Drink	09-11	

Craggy Range Gimblett Gravels Merlot   ★★★★★

This is a top buy – superior to many higher-priced Hawke's Bay reds. The 2007 vintage (★★★★★), harvested at 24 brix, includes 13 per cent Cabernet Franc (adding 'spice and complexity'), and was matured for 18 months in French oak barriques (31 per cent new). Classy, with lovely richness and texture, it is deeply coloured, with a fragrant bouquet of plums and spices. Concentrated and supple, with ripe, plummy, distinctly spicy flavours and very fine-grained tannins, it offers great value.

Vintage	07	06	05	04	03
WR	7	6	6	6	5
Drink	10-22	09-18	09-13	09-12	09-10

DRY $30 V+

Crawford Farm New Zealand Merlot   (★★★☆)

From Constellation NZ, the debut 2006 vintage (★★★☆) is a full-coloured Hawke's Bay red. Enjoyable young, it's a 'fruit-driven' style with plenty of berryish, plummy, spicy flavour, fresh, ripe and smooth.

DRY $22 AV

Cypress Hawke's Bay Merlot   (★★★☆)

Estate-grown at Roy's Hill and oak-aged for six months, the debut 2007 vintage (★★★☆) is deeply coloured, with a fragrant, slightly earthy bouquet, and strong plum and spice flavours, ripe and rounded.

Vintage	07
WR	6
Drink	09-10

DRY $20 AV

Delegat's Reserve Hawke's Bay Merlot   ★★★☆

The 2007 vintage (★★★☆) was grown in the Gimblett Gravels and matured for a year in new and one-year-old French oak barriques. Boldly coloured, it has strong plum/spice flavours seasoned with toasty oak, an earthy streak and firm tannins.

Vintage	07	06
WR	6	6
Drink	09-14	09-13

DRY $20 AV

Distant Land Hawke's Bay Merlot/Malbec   ★★★☆

From Lincoln, the 2008 vintage (★★★☆) was matured for a year in French oak casks (30 per cent new). It's a full-coloured wine, mouthfilling, vibrantly fruity, berryish and spicy, with moderately concentrated flavours, showing some savoury complexity, and a well-rounded finish.

DRY $20 AV

Dolbel Estate Hawke's Bay Merlot/Cabernet   (★★★★)

The elegant, savoury 2007 vintage (★★★★) is a blend of Merlot (70 per cent), estate-grown inland at the Springfield Vineyard, and Cabernet Sauvignon from the Gimblett Gravels. Hand-picked and matured in French oak casks (60 per cent new), it is dark, with a highly fragrant, spicy, nutty bouquet, rich blackcurrant, herb and plum flavours, and fine-grained tannins. It shows excellent texture, complexity and length.

Vintage	07
WR	6
Drink	09-15

DRY $30 AV

Doubtless Bay Merlot/Cabernet Sauvignon   (★★★)

Grown in the Far North, the 2006 vintage (★★★) has lightish colour and sweet oak aromas. It's a medium-bodied wine, smooth, with cherry and plum flavours showing some savoury complexity. Drink now or cellar.

DRY $19 AV

Esk Valley Hawke's Bay Merlot   ★★★★

The 2007 vintage (★★★★) of this consistently excellent 'black label' wine was grown in the Gimblett Gravels and matured for 11 months in French oak casks (15 per cent new). Deeply coloured, it's a rich and supple red with strong blackcurrant, plum and spice flavours and a hint of sweet oak. Youthful, mouthfilling and savoury, it's a classy young red for drinking now or cellaring. (This is the last vintage of this label.)

Vintage	08	07	06	05
WR	NM	6	6	6
Drink	NM	09-13	09-12	09-10

DRY $26 AV

Esk Valley Merlot/Cabernet Sauvignon/Malbec   ★★★★

This Hawke's Bay winery specialises in Merlot-based reds. The 2007 vintage (★★★★) is a blend of Merlot (39 per cent), Cabernet Sauvignon (37 per cent) and Malbec (24 per cent), grown in the Gimblett Gravels and barrique-aged for a year. Boldly coloured and gutsy, it has a spicy bouquet and a powerful palate, offering rich coffee and spice flavours with a strong Malbec influence. (The 2008 vintage, grown in the Gimblett Gravels and matured for a year in French oak [20 per cent new], is labelled 'Vineyard Selection'.)

Vintage	08	07	06	05
WR	6	6	7	6
Drink	09-12	09-12	09-12	09-10

DRY $23 V+

Esk Valley Winemakers Gimblett Gravels Merlot/Cabernet Sauvignon/Malbec   ★★★★★

Labelled 'Reserve' up to and including the 2006 vintage (★★★★★), this outstanding red is now sold under the 'Winemakers' label. Dark, vibrantly fruity and bursting with ripe, sweet-tasting blackcurrant, plum and French oak flavours, it is one of Hawke's Bay's classiest reds. Grown in the company-owned Ngakirikiri Vineyard and the Cornerstone Vineyard, both in the Gimblett Gravels, it is matured for up to 20 months in French oak barriques (70 per cent new in 2007). The 2006 (★★★★★) is notably dark, dense and savoury, with impressive complexity and a lovely surge of blackcurrant, plum and spice flavours, deliciously ripe and rich. The 2007 vintage (★★★★★) is a blend of Merlot (54 per cent), Cabernet Sauvignon (33 per cent) and Malbec (13 per cent). Dark and rich, it's a powerful wine with mouthfilling body (14 per cent alcohol) and deep plum and spice flavours, savoury and complex.

Vintage	07	06	05	04	03	02
WR	7	7	7	7	NM	7
Drink	10-20	09-16	09-14	09-16	NM	09-14

DRY $60 AV

Fall Harvest Merlot   (★★☆)

From Constellation NZ, the 2007 vintage (★★☆) is a decent quaffer, not identified by region, with bright, youthful colour. Vibrantly fruity, slightly spicy and smooth, it's a very easy-drinking style.

DRY $13 AV

Farmgate Hawke's Bay Merlot/Cabernet   (★★★★)

From Ngatarawa, the 2006 vintage (★★★★) is a 70/30 blend of Merlot and Cabernet Sauvignon. Rich, complex and supple, with good intensity of blackcurrant, herb and olive flavours, it's a mouthfilling, refined red, for drinking now or cellaring.

Vintage	07	06
WR	NM	7
Drink	NM	09-13

DRY $25 AV

Five Flax Merlot/Cabernet   ★★☆

From Pernod Ricard NZ, the 2007 vintage (★★★) is a very easy-drinking style, plummy and soft, with plenty of flavour.

Vintage	07	06
WR	5	5
Drink	P	P

DRY $15 AV

Floravin Marlborough Reserve Merlot   (★★★★)

From Kathy Lynskey, the 2006 vintage (★★★★) is full-coloured, with slight development showing. Mouthfilling, with strong blackcurrant, plum and herb flavours, seasoned with nutty oak, it is weighty and concentrated, firm and complex. Drink now to 2011.

DRY $35 –V

Forrest Gibsons Creek Marlborough Merlot   ★★☆

The 2005 vintage (★★☆) is full but not deep in colour, with a slightly leafy bouquet and pleasant berry, plum and herb flavours, smooth and fresh.

DRY $20 –V

Frizzell Merlot/Malbec   (★★★★)

The 2007 vintage (★★★★) is a single-vineyard Hawke's Bay red, with some Cabernet Franc in the blend, matured for 18 months in French and American oak barrels. Deeply coloured, with sweet oak aromas, it's a fruity, moderately complex wine with hints of coffee and spices, and very good ripeness and concentration. Fine value.

DRY $20 V+

Glazebrook Regional Reserve Hawke's Bay Merlot   ★★★☆

From Ngatarawa winery, the 2006 vintage (★★★) is tightly structured, with good colour, strong berry, herb and spice flavours and some earthy, coffee-like notes adding complexity.

Vintage	08	07	06	05
WR	6	6	6	7
Drink	09-13	09-12	09-11	09-10

DRY $27 –V

Glazebrook Regional Reserve Hawke's Bay Merlot/Cabernet ★★★★

The 2007 vintage (★★★★☆) from Ngatarawa winery was grown in the Gimblett Gravels (89 per cent) and The Triangle (11 per cent). A blend of Merlot (68 per cent) and Cabernet Sauvignon (32 per cent), it was matured for a year in French oak barriques (50 per cent new). Classy, powerful and firm, it is deep and youthful in colour, with concentrated blackcurrant and plum flavours, a hint of dark chocolate, chewy tannins, and excellent depth and structure. Showing good complexity, it should be long-lived.

Vintage	07	06	05	04
WR	7	6	6	6
Drink	09-16	09-15	09-12	09-11

DRY $27 AV

Goldridge Estate Hawke's Bay Merlot ★★☆

The 2008 vintage (★★☆) was hand-picked and matured for a year in barriques, mostly French. Lightish in colour, it is medium-bodied, with cherry, plum and herb flavours and a hint of sweet oak. A solid quaffer.

DRY $16 –V

Goldridge Estate Premium Reserve Hawke's Bay Merlot ★★★☆

The 2007 vintage (★★★☆) from Matakana Estate offers good value. Hand-picked from a single vineyard and matured for 10 months in mostly French oak barriques (25 per cent new), it is dark, with concentrated plum/spice flavours, a slight herbal thread and chewy tannins. It shows some development, but also good generosity.

DRY $19 V+

Goldwater Esslin Waiheke Island Merlot ★★★★

This stylish but in the past far too expensive wine has recently been halved in price, from $90 to $45. Grown in the Esslin Vineyard and matured for 20 months in French oak barriques (50 per cent new), the 2005 vintage (★★★★☆) is deeply coloured, with strong, concentrated blackcurrant, plum and spice flavours, leathery, savoury and complex. Drink now onwards.

DRY $45 –V

Goldwater Gimblett Gravels Merlot ★★★★

The 2006 vintage (★★★☆) is a Hawke's Bay red, matured in French and American oak barrels. Full-coloured, it's a moderately concentrated wine with berryish, plummy, sweetly oaked flavours, ripe and smooth. Drink now onwards.

DRY $20 V+

Gunn Estate Hawke's Bay Merlot/Cabernet (★★)

From Sacred Hill, the 2006 vintage (★★) is a Merlot-based blend (70 per cent) with light, developed colour and light, green-edged flavours. It's an easy-drinking style, but lacks ripeness and richness.

DRY $17 –V

Hans Herzog Spirit of Marlborough Merlot/Cabernet Sauvignon   ★★★★★

Who says you can't make outstanding claret-style reds in the South Island? Grown on the banks of the Wairau River, matured for two years in new and one-year-old French oak barriques, and then bottle-aged for several years, this is typically a densely coloured wine with a classy fragrance, substantial body and notably concentrated blackcurrant, plum, herb and spice flavours. It is blended from Merlot (principally), with smaller amounts of Cabernet Sauvignon, Cabernet Franc and Malbec, and bottled without fining or filtration. The 2002 vintage (★★★★★) is deep, with some colour development showing. It's a very harmonious, Bordeaux-like wine, savoury and complex, with cassis, herb, spice and leather notes, like a good St Estephe. Drink now onwards.

Vintage	02	01
WR	7	7
Drink	09-21	09-20

DRY $39 V+

Harrier Rise Merlot   ★★★☆

The 2006 vintage (★★★☆) would have been labelled Uppercase, but for a printing error. Grown at Clevedon, in South Auckland, it is full-coloured, mouthfilling and sweet-fruited, with clear varietal character, a slightly earthy streak and very good depth of firm plum/spice flavours.

DRY $22 AV

Hay Maker Hawke's Bay Merlot   (★★★)

From Mud House, the 2007 vintage (★★★) was partly oak-aged. It's a full-coloured wine with lots of plummy, spicy flavour, soft and smooth. A good, drink-young quaffer.

DRY $17 AV

Hihi Merlot/Malbec   ★★★

The 2007 vintage (★★★) is a Gisborne red, grown at Manutuke. A blend of Merlot (82 per cent), Malbec and Cabernet Franc, it was matured for 10 months in oak casks (15 per cent new). Full-coloured, it is mouthfilling, with plenty of plummy, spicy flavour, supported by firm tannins.

DRY $18 AV

Hinchco Paddock Block Matakana Merlot   ★★☆

The 2008 vintage (★★☆) is pale red, in a pleasant, light style with moderate depth of plum and red-berry flavours, offering easy drinking now to 2010.

DRY $20 –V

Huntaway Reserve Gisborne/Hawke's Bay Merlot/Cabernet   ★★★★

The 2007 vintage (★★★★) from Pernod Ricard NZ was grown in Gisborne and Hawke's Bay and matured for a year in French oak casks (48 per cent new). Deeply coloured, with a smoky bouquet, it is ripe and concentrated, with blackcurrant, spice and dark chocolate flavours, toasty and savoury.

Vintage	07	06
WR	7	5
Drink	09-12	P

DRY $23 V+

Hyperion Zeus Matakana Merlot/Cabernet   ★★★

Estate-grown at Matakana, the 2007 vintage (★★☆) was matured for a year in French and American oak casks. Fullish and slightly developed in colour, it's a slightly leafy wine, flavoursome and spicy, with some savoury complexity, but lacking real ripeness and richness. Drink now.

Vintage	07	06	05
WR	5	7	6
Drink	09-13	09-12	09-10

DRY $22 –V

Isola Estate Merlot/Cabernets   (★★★☆)

Grown on Waiheke Island, the 2007 vintage (★★★☆) is a blend of Merlot (55 per cent), Cabernet Sauvignon (40 per cent), Cabernet Franc (4 per cent) and Malbec (1 per cent). Ruby-hued, it is fresh, fruity and firm, with good depth of plum and spice flavours, showing some complexity.

DRY $37 –V

Karikari Estate Merlot/Cabernet Sauvignon/Malbec   ★★★☆

From New Zealand's northernmost vineyard and winery, on the Karikari Peninsula, this is a consistently enjoyable red. The 2005 vintage (★★★☆) is a blend of Merlot (52 per cent), Cabernet Sauvignon (35 per cent) and Malbec (13 per cent), matured for 11 months in American (principally) and French oak casks (35 per cent new). Full-coloured, with sweet oak aromas, it's a warm, medium to full-bodied wine with very good depth of plum, spice and herb flavours, savoury, earthy touches adding complexity and bold, assertive tannins.

Vintage	05	04
WR	6	5
Drink	09-10	P

DRY $28 –V

Kawau Bay Merlot/Franc/Malbec   ★★★☆

From a year in which the top label, Takatu Merlot/Franc/Malbec, did not appear, the elegant, savoury and supple 2006 vintage (★★★★) is a full-coloured, French oak-matured Matakana red, medium-bodied, with very good depth of plum/spice flavours, now showing considerable complexity.

Vintage	06
WR	6
Drink	09-12

DRY $24 AV

Kennedy Point Merlot   ★★★★☆

The classy 2006 vintage (★★★★☆) was grown at four sites on Waiheke Island, fermented with indigenous yeasts and matured for 18 months in French oak casks. Deeply coloured, it is mouthfilling, with strong, ripe blackcurrant, plum and spice flavours, seasoned with nutty oak, in a very elegant, Bordeaux-like style with a firm backbone of tannin. Drink now or cellar.

Vintage	06
WR	7
Drink	12-18

DRY $37 AV

Kew Estate Merlot   ★★★☆

Still on sale, the 2005 vintage (★★★☆) was grown at Patutahi, in Gisborne, and matured for nine months in seasoned American oak casks. It is deeply coloured, generous, plummy and spicy, in a full-bodied, moderately complex style, flavoursome, fruity and firm. Good value.

Vintage	05	04
WR	6	5
Drink	09-10	P

`DRY $22 AV`

Kew Top Flat Reserve Merlot   ★★★☆

The 2005 vintage (★★★☆), still on sale, was grown in the company's elevated Top Flat Vineyard at Patutahi, in Gisborne, and matured for nine months in seasoned American oak casks. It is deeply coloured, with strong, youthful blackcurrant and plum flavours and hints of liquorice and spice. It's a gutsy style, moderately complex, firm and chewy.

Vintage	05	04
WR	6	5
Drink	09-10	P

`DRY $30 –V`

Kim Crawford Hawke's Bay Merlot   ★★★☆

The 2007 vintage (★★★) from Constellation NZ includes 4 per cent Malbec and 3 per cent Cabernet Franc. It's a full-coloured, fruity and flavoursome wine with ripe plum and spice characters and gentle oak and tannins, giving an easy-drinking appeal.

`DRY $22 AV`

Kim Crawford Limited Release Hawke's Bay Merlot   (★★★☆)

A blend of Merlot (93.5 per cent) and Malbec (6.5 per cent), the 2007 vintage (★★★☆) is medium to full-bodied, with full colour, good depth of plummy, spicy flavour and some savoury complexity. It's enjoyable now.

`DRY $30 –V`

Kumeu River Melba's Vineyard Merlot   ★★★★

Named in honour of the family matriarch, Melba Brajkovich, the 2006 vintage (★★★★) is the first for several years (it was previously labelled as Kumeu River Melba). Based on the company's sole surviving plot of Merlot vines at Kumeu, in West Auckland, it is full-coloured, with a spicy bouquet. Youthful, vibrantly fruity and flavoursome, with strong coffee and spice characters, it's a tightly structured wine, best opened 2010+.

`DRY $30 AV`

Lake Chalice Platinum Marlborough Merlot   ★★★☆

Estate-grown in the Falcon Vineyard at Rapaura, the 2006 vintage (★★★☆) was matured for 21 months in oak casks (50 per cent new). Full-coloured, mouthfilling and vibrantly fruity, it has very good depth of blackcurrant, plum and slight herb flavours, with a firm foundation of tannin.

Vintage	06
WR	5
Drink	09-12

`DRY $27 –V`

Lake Chalice Vineyard Selection Merlot   ★★☆

The 2007 vintage (★★☆) is a 3:1 blend of Hawke's Bay and Marlborough fruit. Matured in
tanks and French oak casks, it is a fruit-driven style with vibrant flavours of plums, herbs and
spices, fresh and smooth.

Vintage	07
WR	5
Drink	09-10

DRY $20 –V

Latitude 41 New Zealand Merlot   (★★☆)

From Spencer Hill, the easy-drinking 2005 vintage (★★☆) is a Hawke's Bay wine with fullish
colour, mouthfilling body and decent depth of smooth, plummy, slightly herbal flavour.

DRY $20 –V

Longbush Gisborne Merlot   ★★★

Bargain-priced, the 2007 vintage (★★★) is a full-coloured, fairly gutsy red, still youthful, with
plenty of berryish, slightly spicy and earthy flavour, braced by firm tannins. An excellent quaffer.

DRY $13 V+

Longlands Te Awa Merlot   ★★★☆

From the Te Awa winery in Hawke's Bay, the 2005 vintage (★★★☆) has rich colour and tight,
blackcurrant and plum flavours, showing good concentration and structure.

Vintage	05	04	03	02
WR	6	NM	6	7
Drink	09-10	NM	P	P

DRY $20 AV

Longridge Hawke's Bay Merlot/Cabernet Sauvignon   ★★★

The 2007 vintage (★★★☆) from Pernod Ricard NZ is deeply coloured, with blackcurrant,
plum and spice flavours, showing very good depth, some savoury complexity, and a well-
rounded finish.

Vintage	07
WR	5
Drink	P

DRY $18 AV

Maimai Creek Hawke's Bay Merlot   ★★☆

The full-coloured 2007 vintage (★★★) is a fruit-driven style, fresh, berryish, spicy and smooth,
offering enjoyable, early drinking.

DRY $23 –V

Main Divide Merlot/Cabernet   ★★★☆

The great-value 2006 vintage (★★★★) from Pegasus Bay, matured for two years in French oak
barriques, shows just what can be done in Marlborough with Merlot-based reds. Full and fairly
youthful in colour, it has very satisfying depth of blackcurrant, slight herb and dark chocolate
flavours, savoury and smooth.

Vintage	06	05	04	03	02
WR	6	7	6	7	6
Drink	09-13	09-12	09-10	P	P

DRY $20 AV

Man O' War Waiheke Island Merlot/Cabernet   (★★★)

Grown at the remote, eastern end of the island, the 2006 vintage (★★★) was matured in French (80 per cent) and American oak casks. Fullish in colour, it's a mouthfilling, flavoursome, slightly rustic wine, spicy, leafy and leathery, with some savoury complexity.

DRY $27 –V

Matakana Estate Elingamite Limited Edition Merlot/Cabernet Franc   (★★★★☆)

The powerful, deeply coloured 2007 vintage (★★★★☆) is a Hawke's Bay blend of Merlot (60 per cent) and Cabernet Franc (40 per cent), with vibrant blackcurrant, plum and spice flavours, well seasoned with quality oak (mostly French, all new). It's a highly concentrated, ripe-tasting wine with good complexity, a firm foundation of tannin and obvious cellaring potential.

DRY $59 –V

Matakana Estate Hawke's Bay Merlot/Cabernet Franc   (★★★★)

The dark, generous 2007 vintage (★★★★) is a blend of Merlot (71 per cent) and Cabernet Franc (29 per cent), grown in The Triangle district and matured in French oak barriques (40 per cent new). Brambly and sweet-fruited, it has hints of mint chocolate and coffee and excellent depth.

DRY $29 AV

Matua Valley Ararimu Merlot   ★★★★

Matua's flagship red is grown in The Triangle, in Hawke's Bay. Preceding vintages were Merlot-predominant blends, but the 2004 (★★★☆) is an unblended Merlot, grown in the company-owned Matheson Vineyard. Full-coloured, it's a moderately concentrated wine with berry and spice flavours, showing some savoury complexity, drinking well now. (The 2007 is a Merlot/Cabernet Sauvignon, matured for 18 months in French oak barriques, 70 per cent new.)

Vintage	04
WR	6
Drink	09-10

DRY $40 –V

Matua Valley Bullrush Merlot   ★★★☆

The 2007 vintage (★★★☆) is a single-vineyard red, grown in The Triangle district of Hawke's Bay and matured for 18 months in French oak casks (35 per cent new). Deep and youthful in colour, it is sturdy, with concentrated blackcurrant, plum and slight herb flavours, moderate complexity and some cellaring potential. Open mid-2010+.

DRY $25 AV

Matua Valley Reserve Merlot/Cabernet   (★★★)

The 2007 vintage (★★★) is a Hawke's Bay blend of Merlot (55 per cent) and Cabernet Sauvignon (45 per cent), matured for 15 months in French oak casks. Full-coloured, it is fruity and smooth, with plum/spice flavours, a gentle seasoning of oak and good depth. It's a fruit-driven, moderately complex style.

DRY $20 AV

Maximus Mahurangi River Matakana Merlot   (★★★)

Estate-grown, hand-picked, fermented with indigenous yeasts and matured in French oak barriques, the 2006 vintage (★★★) has fullish, slightly developed colour. It's a medium-bodied wine (11.5 per cent alcohol) with distinctly leafy notes, but also plummy, spicy and earthy, with considerable complexity. Drink now to 2010.

DRY $38 –V

Mill Road Hawke's Bay Merlot/Cabernet Franc   ★★

From Morton Estate, the non-vintage wine (★★) on sale in late 2009 is a green-edged wine with lightish, developed colour and spice, coffee and herb flavours, now fully mature.

DRY $14 –V

Mills Reef Elspeth Merlot   ★★★☆

The 2007 vintage (★★★☆) was estate-grown in Mere Road, in the Gimblett Gravels of Hawke's Bay, and matured for 13 months in French oak barriques (34 per cent new). It's a powerful, firmly structured red with full, youthful colour and generous, spicy, plummy, nutty flavours, showing considerable complexity. However, it lacks the fragrance to rate more highly.

Vintage	07	06	05	04	03	02
WR	7	7	7	7	NM	7
Drink	09-18	09-17	09-15	09-15	NM	09-14

DRY $40 –V

Mills Reef Hawke's Bay Merlot/Cabernet   ★★★

The 2008 vintage (★★★) was barrel-aged for over a year. Full-coloured, with plum, spice, herb and slight coffee flavours, it is fruity and smooth, in an easy-drinking style with good depth.

DRY $18 AV

Mills Reef Reserve Hawke's Bay Merlot   ★★★★

The 2008 vintage (★★★☆) was grown in the Gimblett Gravels and matured in French oak casks (55 per cent new). Full-coloured, it is mouthfilling, with a hint of coffee and very good depth of plum and spice flavours, fresh and savoury.

Vintage	08	07	06	05	04	03	02
WR	6	7	7	7	NM	6	7
Drink	09-12	09-12	09-11	09-10	NM	P	P

DRY $25 AV

Mills Reef Reserve Hawke's Bay Merlot/Malbec   ★★★★

The 2008 vintage (★★★☆) was grown in the Gimblett Gravels and matured for a year in a 70/30 split of French and American oak barriques (58 per cent new). Deeply coloured, it has coffee and spice aromas and flavours, fresh and vibrant, with some complexity and good harmony.

Vintage	08	07	06	05	04	03
WR	6	7	6	7	7	6
Drink	09-12	09-12	09-12	09-11	09-10	P

DRY $25 AV

Mission Hawke's Bay Merlot   ★★★

The 2008 vintage (★★★) is full-coloured and mouthfilling, in an easy-drinking style with good depth of berryish, slightly herbal flavours, fresh, vibrant and smooth.

DRY $15 AV

Mission Reserve Hawke's Bay Merlot   ★★★★

The deliciously easy-drinking 2008 vintage (★★★★) has 'Reserve' only on the back label. A blend of Merlot (85 per cent), grown at Bridge Pa, and Cabernet Franc (15 per cent), from the Gimblett Gravels, it was matured in French oak barriques (35 per cent new). Deeply coloured, it is generous and silky, with strong, ripe blackcurrant, spice and nut flavours, showing good complexity. It's already highly enjoyable.

Vintage	08	07
WR	5	7
Drink	09-15	09-15

DRY $23 V+

Mission Vineyard Selection Ohiti Road Merlot   ★★★

The 2008 vintage (★★★☆) is a single-vineyard wine, grown in Hawke's Bay and matured in French oak barrels. Full-coloured, with a spicy, slightly herbal bouquet, it has very satisfying depth of blackcurrant, plum, spice and slightly nutty oak flavours, showing good balance and complexity.

DRY $18 AV

Moana Park Vineyard Selection Merlot/Malbec   ★★★

The 2007 vintage (★★★☆) is a great buy. A Hawke's Bay blend of Merlot (60 per cent), Malbec (30 per cent) and Cabernet Sauvignon (10 per cent), grown in the Gimblett Gravels and French oak-matured for 16 months, it is deeply coloured, with strong blackcurrant, plum and spice flavours, hints of coffee and dark chocolate, and a smooth finish.

Vintage	07
WR	7
Drink	09-12

DRY $14 V+

Moana Park Vineyard Tribute Merlot   ★★★★☆

The bold, bargain-priced 2007 vintage (★★★★) was grown in the Gimblett Gravels, Hawke's Bay, matured for 16 months in French oak barriques (50 per cent new), and bottled unfined and unfiltered. Deeply coloured, with dense plum, spice and coffee flavours, it's a highly concentrated, firm wine with obvious cellaring potential.

Vintage	07	06
WR	7	6
Drink	09-18	09-16

DRY $20 V+

Monkey Bay Hawke's Bay Merlot   ★★☆

The 2008 vintage (★★★) from Constellation NZ is a deeply coloured, vibrantly fruity red with plenty of berryish, plummy flavour, hints of spices and coffee adding interest, a smooth finish, and lots of drink-young appeal.

DRY $15 AV

Montana Hawke's Bay Merlot/Cabernet Sauvignon   ★★★

Partly oak-aged, the 2007 (★★★) is deeply coloured and vibrant, with a touch of toasty oak and plenty of fresh, smooth flavour. The 2008 vintage (★★★) is full-coloured, with good depth of blackcurrant, plum and spice flavours, showing a touch of complexity.

Vintage	08	07	06
WR	6	7	5
Drink	09-10	P	P

DRY $18 AV

Montana Reserve Hawke's Bay Merlot   ★★★☆

The bargain-priced 2007 vintage (★★★★) was matured in predominantly French oak casks. Still purple-flushed, it is deeply coloured, rich and silky, with deep plum, spice and slight coffee flavours, sweet-fruit delights, good complexity, and strong drink-young appeal.

DRY $24 AV

Morton Estate Black Label Hawke's Bay Merlot   (★★★☆)

Enjoyable now, the 2005 vintage (★★★☆) is full-coloured, with mouthfilling body and moderately rich, plummy, spicy flavour, showing good complexity.

Vintage	05
WR	6
Drink	09-12

DRY $35 –V

Morton Estate Black Label Hawke's Bay Merlot/Cabernet   (★★★)

The 2004 vintage (★★★) was grown at Bridge Pa, in the company's Tantallon Vineyard on State Highway 50, and in the Gimblett Gravels, and matured in French and American oak casks. Fullish and slightly developed in colour, it is spicy, savoury and moderately concentrated, with considerable complexity, but lacks real fruit sweetness and richness.

Vintage	04
WR	6
Drink	09-12

DRY $35 –V

Morton Estate White Label Hawke's Bay Merlot   ★★☆

The 2005 vintage (★★) is mouthfilling, with fullish, developed colour and spicy, herbal, slightly rustic flavours. Ready.

Vintage	05	04
WR	6	5
Drink	09-10	P

DRY $18 –V

Mount Riley Marlborough Merlot/Malbec   ★★★

The fruity, full-flavoured 2007 vintage (★★★) is a blend of Merlot (86 per cent) and Malbec (14 per cent), matured for over a year in French (mostly) and American oak. An easy-drinking style, it has spicy, sweetly oaked aromas and smooth, plummy, spicy flavours, enjoyable young. (I have also tasted a Mount Riley New Zealand Merlot/Malbec 2007 (★★★) with no detailed claims about region of origin, which offered plenty of ripe, plummy, spicy flavour, sweetly oaked and smooth.)

Vintage	07	06
WR	6	7
Drink	09-10	P

DRY $18 AV

Mudbrick Vineyard Reserve Merlot/Cabernet Sauvignon   ★★★★

The 2008 vintage (★★★☆) is a Waiheke Island blend, matured in French and American oak barriques (30 per cent new). Dark, powerful and highly concentrated, with perfumed oak aromas, it has dense blackcurrant, plum, spice, nut and coffee flavours, chewy and firm. Open 2011+.

Vintage	08
WR	7
Drink	10-18

DRY $50 –V

Mud House Hawke's Bay Merlot   ★★★☆

The 2008 vintage (★★★☆) is a youthful, full-coloured red, partly barrel-matured, with some richness of plum and berry flavours, hints of chocolate and herbs and a smooth finish. It's an appealing, moderately complex style.

DRY $21 AV

Nest, The, Hawke's Bay Merlot   (★★★)

From Lake Chalice, the 2008 vintage (★★★) was matured in tanks and French oak barrels. Ruby-hued, it is mouthfilling and smooth, with fresh, vibrant plum and spice flavours, showing good depth.

DRY $20 AV

Newton/Forrest Estate Gimblett Gravels Hawke's Bay Merlot   ★★★★☆

The 2007 vintage (★★★★☆) was grown in the Cornerstone Vineyard and matured in a 4:1 mix of French and American oak casks. Deeply coloured, with a spicy, nutty fragrance, it is sturdy (14.3 per cent alcohol), with strong, vibrant cassis, plum and spice flavours, finely integrated oak, firm underlying tannins, and the power and structure to age well.

Vintage	07	06
WR	5	5
Drink	09-12	09-12

DRY $40 AV

Ngatarawa Alwyn Merlot/Cabernet   ★★★★★

Grown in Hawke's Bay, the 2007 vintage (★★★★★) is a blend of Merlot (80 per cent) and Cabernet Sauvignon (20 per cent), matured for 16 months in French oak barriques. Deeply coloured, it has sweet-fruit delights, with highly concentrated plum, blackcurrant and slight herb flavours, buried tannins, and the power and structure to flourish for a decade.

Vintage	07	06	05
WR	7	6	7
Drink	09-16	09-15	09-14

DRY $55 AV

Ngatarawa Silks Hawke's Bay Merlot   ★★★☆

Priced right, the 2008 vintage (★★★☆) is a deeply coloured red, oak-aged for a year, with strong blackcurrant and plum flavours, an earthy streak and considerable complexity. Drink now or cellar.

Vintage	08	07	06	05
WR	7	6	6	6
Drink	09-12	09-11	09-11	09-10

DRY $20 AV

Ngatarawa Stables Hawke's Bay Merlot   ★★★

An easy-drinking, mid-weight style, the 2008 vintage (★★★) has full, youthful colour and plenty of berry, plum and spice flavour, slightly earthy and smooth.

Vintage	08	07	06
WR	6	7	6
Drink	09-13	09-12	09-12

DRY $17 AV

Nikau Point Hawke's Bay Merlot/Cabernet   ★★☆

From One Tree Hill Vineyards (a division of Morton Estate), the 2005 vintage (★★★) is full-coloured, with plenty of blackcurrant, herb and slight coffee flavour. Ready.

Vintage	05	04	03	02
WR	5	5	6	6
Drink	09-10	09-10	P	P

DRY $17 –V

Nikau Point Reserve Hawke's Bay Merlot/Cabernet   ★★

From Morton Estate, the 2004 vintage (★★) has light, developed colour and slightly rustic, leafy flavours. The 2005 (★★) has fullish, maturing colour and a gutsy palate with firm, developed, herbal flavours. Ready.

Vintage	05	04
WR	5	5
Drink	09-10	09-10

DRY $18 –V

Nobilo Regional Collection Hawke's Bay Merlot   ★★★

Fresh and full-coloured, the 2008 vintage (★★★) is a vibrantly fruity style with plum and spice flavours showing good depth and a smooth, rounded finish.

DRY $17 AV

Okahu Merlot/Cabernet   ★★★☆

The 2006 vintage (★★★☆) is a Northland red, matured for seven months in French and American oak barriques. It's a full-coloured, moderately firm red with finely integrated oak and plenty of ripe, plummy flavour, fresh and vibrant.

DRY $27 –V

Omaka Springs Marlborough Merlot   ★★☆

Handled without oak, this is typically a fruity but light and simple wine, plummy and leafy. The 2008 (★★), American oak-aged for 10 months, is pale red, with berry and herb flavours, very light and smooth. Ready.

Vintage	08
WR	6
Drink	09-12

DRY $19 –V

One Tree Hawke's Bay Merlot   ★★★☆

Made by Capricorn Wine Estates (a division of Craggy Range) for New World and PAK'nSAVE supermarkets, the 2006 vintage (★★★☆) has full, youthful colour and plenty of plummy, spicy flavour, slightly earthy and savoury. Matured for a year in French oak (15 per cent new), it's a finely balanced, smooth wine with a touch of complexity, drinking well now.

Vintage	06
WR	6
Drink	09-12

DRY $19 V+

Onyx Reserve Hawke's Bay Merlot/Cabernet   (★★★☆)

From wine distributor Bennett & Deller, the 2007 vintage (★★★☆) is boldly coloured, with a hint of development. French oak-aged for a year, it's a full-on style, with rich plum and spice flavours, but impresses more with power than finesse.

Vintage	07
WR	7
Drink	09-12

DRY $25 AV

Oyster Bay Hawke's Bay Merlot   ★★★☆

From Delegat's, this red accounts for a big slice of New Zealand's exports of 'Bordeaux-style' wines (Merlot or Cabernet Sauvignon). Winemaker Michael Ivicevich aims for a wine with 'sweet fruit and silky tannins. The trick is – not too much oak.' The 2008 vintage (★★★☆) is dark, with a fragrant bouquet of blackcurrants and spices. Mouthfilling, it's a substantial wine with strong blackcurrant, herb and dark chocolate flavours, supple tannins, and plenty of drink-young appeal.

Vintage	08	07	06
WR	6	7	7
Drink	09-14	09-14	09-14

DRY $20 AV

Passage Rock Reserve Waiheke Island Merlot   ★★★★

The 2008 vintage (★★★★) is a densely coloured, very youthful red with highly concentrated, plummy, spicy flavours, and powerful tannins. It needs another two or three years, but shows obvious potential.

DRY $30 AV

Pegasus Bay Merlot/Cabernet   ★★★★

The 2005 vintage (★★★☆), grown at Waipara, is a blend of Merlot, Cabernet Sauvignon, Malbec and Cabernet Franc, matured for two years in French and American oak casks (30 per cent new). Drinking well now, it has full, fairly developed colour and very good depth of spice, herb and coffee flavours, showing some savoury complexity.

Vintage	06	05	04	03	02
WR	6	7	6	7	5
Drink	09-15	09-15	09-14	09-12	P

DRY $29 AV

Penny Lane Hawke's Bay Merlot/Cabernet   ★★

From Morton Estate, the 2006 vintage (★★) is a blend of Merlot, Cabernet Sauvignon and Cabernet Franc. It has fullish, fairly developed colour and moderate depth of spicy, leafy flavour. Ready.

Vintage	06
WR	5
Drink	09-10

DRY $15 –V

Poderi Crisci Merlot   ★★★

Grown on Waiheke Island, the 2008 vintage (★★★☆) is the best yet. Full-coloured, with a spicy bouquet, it is sweet-fruited, with very satisfying depth of blackcurrant, plum and spice flavours, an earthy streak and good complexity. It's quite forward; drink now onwards.

Vintage	07
WR	6
Drink	10-17

DRY $29 –V

Providence Private Reserve Merlot/Cabernet Franc/Malbec   ★★★★★

Past vintages of this Matakana red were priced around $180, including the full-coloured and fragrant, very elegant and silky-textured 2002 (★★★★★). The 2005 (★★★★★) is a top vintage, beautifully perfumed, with rich, blackcurrant-like flavours, complex and harmonious. If you are a Bordeaux fan with deep pockets, it's well worth trying.

DRY $120 –V

Rannach Merlot   ★★★

Grown at Clevedon, in South Auckland, the 2008 vintage (★★★) has fullish, youthful colour. It's an easy-drinking style, medium to full-bodied, with some savoury complexity. The 2005 (★★★★), still on sale, is the one to buy.

Vintage	08
WR	5
Drink	09-14

DRY $20 AV

Rannach Merlot Reserve   (★★★★)

From an 'almost perfect' season, the 2005 vintage (★★★★) was harvested from seven-year-old vines in the Ness Valley, Clevedon, in South Auckland, and matured for 15 months in French oak barriques. Bold in colour, with a fragrant bouquet, it is rich and smooth, with deep blackcurrant, plum and slight herb flavours, and savoury, leathery notes adding complexity.

Vintage	05
WR	6
Drink	09-14

DRY $30 AV

Redmetal Vineyards Basket Press Merlot/Cabernet Franc   ★★★★

Grown in The Triangle, this Hawke's Bay red is beautifully rich and supple in top years. The 2006 vintage (★★★★☆) is full-coloured, with a fragrant, ripe bouquet of berries and spices. Full-bodied, with blackcurrant, plum and spice flavours, and excellent density and complexity, it's a distinctly Bordeaux-like wine, with good tannin backbone.

Vintage	06	05	04	03	02
WR	6	6	5	NM	6
Drink	09-16	09-13	09-12	NM	09-10

`DRY $39 –V`

Redmetal Vineyards Hawke's Bay Merlot/Cabernet Franc ★★★☆

Made for early drinking, the 2006 vintage (★★★☆) is deeply coloured and mouthfilling, with vibrant plum/spice flavours showing considerable complexity and gentle tannins.

Vintage	07	06
WR	6	6
Drink	09-13	09-12

`DRY $20 AV`

Redmetal Vineyards Mount Erin Merlot/Cabernet Franc ★★★☆

The 2005 vintage (★★★☆), grown in Hawke's Bay, is a 3:1 blend of Merlot and Cabernet Franc, oak-aged for a year. It is moderately concentrated, with ripe, sweet-fruit characters and plum/spice flavours showing good complexity.

Vintage	06	05
WR	6	5
Drink	09-14	09-14

`DRY $29 –V`

Riverstone Merlot/Cabernet Sauvignon/Shiraz (★★☆)

From Villa Maria, the non-vintage bottling (★★☆) on sale in 2009 is an easy-drinking blend of New Zealand, Chilean and Australian wines. Bright and fullish in colour, it's a fruity, smooth red with berry, plum and herb flavours, simple and undemanding.

`DRY $12 V+`

Road Works Waiheke Island Merlot/Cabernet Franc (★★★☆)

From Man O' War, the 2008 vintage (★★★☆) is a gutsy red (14.5 per cent alcohol), full-coloured, with strong, plummy, slightly herbal and earthy flavours, still very youthful. Buy now, drink later.

`DRY $18 V+`

Rongopai East Coast Merlot ★★☆

From Babich, the 2007 vintage (★★★) is a good quaffer with decent depth of blackcurrant, plum and spice flavours, gentle tannins and a smooth finish. It's enjoyable now.

`DRY $15 AV`

Rua Whenua Reserve Merlot/Cabernet Franc ★★★★

The 2007 vintage (★★★★☆) was harvested at Te Awanga, in Hawke's Bay, and matured for nearly two years in French and American oak barriques (60 per cent new). Fragrant and full-coloured, it is a blend of Merlot (60 per cent) and Cabernet Franc (40 per cent), sweet-fruited and savoury, with excellent depth of blackcurrant, plum, spice and nut flavours, still fresh and youthful. A distinctive, complex wine, it's worth cellaring to 2011+.

Vintage	07	06	05
WR	6	NM	7
Drink	10-17	NM	09-15

`DRY $30 AV`

Sacred Hill Basket Press Merlot/Cabernet   ★★★★

Still very youthful, the 2008 vintage (★★★★) of this fine-value red is a blend of Merlot (86 per cent) with minor proportions of Cabernet Sauvignon, Cabernet Franc and Malbec. Estate-grown in the Gimblett Gravels and French oak-aged, it is fleshy and savoury, with strong berry and spice flavours, gentle tannins and good complexity.

Vintage	08
WR	7
Drink	09-11

DRY $21 V+

Sacred Hill Brokenstone Merlot   ★★★★★

This is an often outstanding Hawke's Bay red. Since 2002, the grapes have been sourced entirely from the Gimblett Gravels (mostly the company's joint-venture Deerstalkers Vineyard). The wine spends its first year in mostly new French oak barriques, then another eight months in new and older barrels. The 2007 vintage (★★★★★) is a dark, brooding red, 91 per cent Merlot, with small portions of Cabernet Franc and Cabernet Sauvignon. Concentrated and sweet-fruited, with dense, ripe plum, blackcurrant and spice flavours, and fine-grained tannins, it is still very youthful.

Vintage	07	06
WR	7	7
Drink	10-15	09-18

DRY $65 AV

Saint Clair Marlborough Merlot   ★★★

The 2008 vintage (★★★), grown in the relatively warm Rapaura district and partly barrel-aged, is a mouthfilling, finely balanced wine with cherry, plum, spice and herb flavours, showing a touch of complexity, and a smooth finish.

Vintage	08	07	06	05	04
WR	6	6	6	6	6
Drink	09-11	09-10	09-10	P	P

DRY $21 –V

Saint Clair Pioneer Block 17 Bay Block Merlot   (★★★★)

Grown at Mangatahi, in Hawke's Bay, the debut 2007 vintage (★★★★) was matured for nine months in American oak casks (50 per cent new). Deeply coloured, it is smooth and rich, with concentrated blackcurrant, herb and nut flavours, lots of coffee and spice, and good complexity. Drink now or cellar.

Vintage	07
WR	6
Drink	09-11

DRY $25 AV

Saint Clair Rapaura Reserve Marlborough Merlot   ★★★☆

This is a more wood-influenced style than its 'Marlborough Merlot' stablemate (above). The 2008 vintage (★★★☆) was matured for 10 months in French oak barriques (80 per cent new). Full-coloured, it is fleshy and supple, with blackcurrant, plum and spice flavours, showing very good depth, and gentle tannins. Drink now or cellar.

Vintage	08	07	06	05	04
WR	6	6	6	6	6
Drink	09-12	09-11	09-11	09-11	09-10

DRY $27 –V

Saint Clair Vicar's Choice Marlborough Merlot   ★★☆

The 2008 vintage (★★☆) was partly barrel-aged. Ruby-hued, it is fruity and smooth, with berryish, slightly spicy flavours, in a very easy-drinking style.

Vintage	08	07
WR	6	6
Drink	09-11	P

DRY $19 –V

Salvare Hawke's Bay Merlot   (★★★☆)

Grown in Gimblett Road, the 2007 vintage (★★★☆) is deeply coloured. It's a fleshy red made in a fruit-driven style, with very good depth of fresh, ripe, berryish, gently oaked flavours, and gentle tannins. Drink now to 2011.

DRY $25 AV

Sandspit Cove Saltings Estate Merlot   (★☆)

Grown at Matakana, the 2006 vintage (★☆) has light, developed colour and light, green-edged flavours.

DRY $16 –V

Selaks Founders Reserve Hawke's Bay Merlot   ★★★☆

The 2006 vintage (★★★★) from Constellation NZ is a single-vineyard red, grown at Bridge Pa, in The Triangle, and matured for a year in French oak barriques (60 per cent new). Deeply coloured, with a spicy, slightly earthy bouquet, it shows good power through the palate, with concentrated, brambly, spicy flavours, complex and firm. Drink now or cellar.

DRY $33 –V

Selaks Premium Selection Hawke's Bay Merlot   ★★★☆

A good quaffer, the 2007 vintage (★★★☆) was partly matured in French and American oak barriques. It's a fragrant, medium-bodied style with deep colour, strong, berryish, plummy, slightly herbal flavours and a well-rounded finish. Fine value.

DRY $15 V+

Selaks Winemaker's Favourite Hawke's Bay Merlot/Cabernet   ★★★★

The 2008 vintage (★★★☆) is a blend of Merlot (56 per cent), Cabernet Sauvignon (42 per cent) and Malbec (2 per cent). Grown in Constellation NZ's Corner 50 Vineyard, and matured in French and American oak barriques (partly new), it is full-coloured, with good body and depth of plum and spice flavours, sweet-fruited and supple, and lots of drink-young appeal.

DRY $21 V+

Shipwreck Bay Merlot/Cabernet   (★★)

The 2007 vintage (★★), estate-grown in Northland and oak-matured, is a ruby-hued, medium-bodied red, slightly rustic, with moderate depth of berry, plum and spice flavours. The 2005 (★☆) is light, leafy and past its best.

DRY $18 –V

Sileni Cellar Selection Hawke's Bay Merlot   ★★★☆

The full-coloured 2008 vintage (★★★) is fruity, berryish and slightly spicy, with gentle tannins and satisfying depth, but less concentrated than the briefly barrel-aged, rich, plummy and soft 2007 (★★★★).

Vintage	08	07	06
WR	5	6	6
Drink	09-11	09-11	09-10

DRY $20 AV

Sileni The Triangle Hawke's Bay Merlot   ★★★★

The 2008 vintage (★★★★), in the past labelled 'Estate Selection', is deeply coloured, fleshy and concentrated, with deep, youthful, plum/spice flavours, savoury and complex, and a firm underlay of tannin. Best drinking mid-2010+.

Vintage	08
WR	5
Drink	10-12

DRY $35 AV

Soljans Hawke's Bay Merlot/Cabernet/Malbec   ★★★☆

The 2007 vintage (★★★☆) is a blend of Merlot (62 per cent), Cabernet Sauvignon (23 per cent) and Malbec (15 per cent), matured for 18 months in French and American oak casks. It's maturing well. Full-coloured, it's a firm, claret-style red with mouthfilling body and very good depth of plum, spice and dark chocolate flavours, showing some complexity.

DRY $20 AV

Soljans Tribute Merlot/Malbec   ★★★★

Still on sale, the 2002 vintage (★★★★) is billed as 'without doubt the finest red ever produced by the estate'. A Hawke's Bay blend of Merlot (61 per cent) and Malbec (39 per cent), barrel-aged for 18 months, mostly in new French oak, it is maturing well. Full-coloured, it is ripe and smooth, with strong, plummy, spicy, slightly earthy flavours, showing good complexity.

Vintage	02
WR	5
Drink	09-10

DRY $40 –V

Southern Cross Hawke's Bay Merlot/Cabernet Sauvignon   (★★★)

The bargain-priced 2007 vintage (★★★) is from One Tree Hill Vineyards, a division of Morton Estate. A blend of Merlot (65 per cent), Cabernet Sauvignon (20 per cent) and Cabernet Franc (15 per cent), it is full and bright in colour, with a fresh, spicy bouquet. Mouthfilling, it offers plenty of plummy, spicy flavour, with a moderately firm finish.

Vintage	07
WR	6
Drink	09-11

DRY $13 V+

Spy Valley Marlborough Merlot   ★★★☆

The good-value 2007 vintage (★★★★), which includes 6 per cent Malbec, was fermented with indigenous yeasts and matured for 14 months in French oak barrels (30 per cent new). It's a deeply coloured, fruity red with concentrated plum/spice flavours, slightly nutty and savoury, a hint of coffee, and firm, youthful tannins.

Vintage	07	06	05	04
WR	7	5	6	5
Drink	09-12	09-10	09-10	P

DRY $20 AV

Squawking Magpie SQM Merlot/Cabernet   (★★★★)

Still on sale, the 2005 vintage (★★★★), grown in the Gimblett Gravels of Hawke's Bay, is a refined, generous red with deep, moderately youthful colour and excellent density of brambly, spicy flavours, complex, firm and long.

DRY $40 –V

Squawking Magpie The Chatterer Merlot/Syrah/Malbec   ★★★★

The 2007 vintage (★★★★) is a Gimblett Gravels, Hawke's Bay blend, matured in French oak barriques. Boldly coloured, it is packed with very youthful, plum and spice flavours, fresh and ripe, with a hint of chocolate, and finely balanced oak and tannins. Best drinking 2010+.

DRY $25 AV

Squawking Magpie The Nest Merlot/Cabernet   ★★★★

The 2005 vintage (★★★★) was picked from mature vines in the Gimblett Gravels district of Hawke's Bay. A blend of Merlot and Cabernet Sauvignon, French oak-aged, it is deeply coloured, dense and savoury, with concentrated, spicy, plummy, nutty flavours, showing good complexity.

DRY $40 –V

Stone Bridge North Slope Merlot   (★★★)

Grown in Gisborne and French oak-aged, the 2007 vintage (★★★) is full-coloured, fresh and lively, with vibrant plum and spice flavours, a gentle seasoning of oak, smooth tannins and good depth. Enjoyable now, it's still developing.

DRY $19 AV

Stonecroft Ruhanui Merlot/Cabernet Sauvignon/Syrah   (★★★★)

Grown in the Gimblett Gravels, the 2007 vintage (★★★★) was matured for 18 months in French oak casks (30 per cent new). Fresh and buoyant, it's approachable now but likely to be long-lived, with strong, youthful plum and spice flavours, finely integrated oak, good complexity and firm tannins.

Vintage	07
WR	6
Drink	12-20

DRY $35 –V

Stonecutter Martinborough Merlot   (★★★☆)

The deeply coloured 2006 vintage (★★★☆) was matured for 18 months in French oak casks (30 per cent new). Still youthful, it's a concentrated, distinctly cool-climate style with deep plum, spice and herb flavours, rich and smooth.

Vintage	06
WR	5
Drink	09-12

DRY $27 –V

Stoneleigh Marlborough Merlot   ★★★

The 2007 vintage (★★★) from Pernod Ricard NZ was grown at two sites at Rapaura and matured for a year in French oak casks. Deeply coloured, it is mouthfilling, with strong blackcurrant, plum, herb and spice flavours, a fresh, cool-climate vibrancy and supple tannins. Enjoyable young.

Vintage	07	06
WR	6	5
Drink	09-10	P

DRY $22 –V

Stop Banks Hawke's Bay Merlot   (★★☆)

From a Marlborough-based producer, the 2006 vintage (★★☆) is a pleasant, fruit-driven style with spicy, slightly leafy aromas and flavours.

DRY $18 –V

Takatu Matakana Merlot/Franc/Malbec   (★★★★★)

The silky, generous 2005 vintage (★★★★★) is a splendid debut. A blend of Merlot (72 per cent), Cabernet Franc (22 per cent) and Malbec (6 per cent), it was fermented with indigenous yeasts and matured in French oak barriques (25 per cent new). Richly coloured, it is concentrated and finely structured, fleshy and warm, with sweet-fruit characters and dense plum and spice flavours. Unusually complex, with savoury, earthy notes and a good foundation of tannin, it is highly reminiscent of a fine Bordeaux. (There is no 2006 or 2007, but the 2008 vintage will be released in April 2010.)

Vintage	07	06	05
WR	NM	NM	7
Drink	NM	NM	09-15

DRY $39 V+

Tasman Bay New Zealand Merlot   (★★)

Tasted in mid-2009, the 2005 vintage (★★) is lightish in colour, with a leafy bouquet and fruity, simple, herbal flavours. Ready.

DRY $19 –V

Te Awa Zone 6 Merlot/Cabernet   (★★★★)

Maturing gracefully, the 2003 vintage (★★★★) is a blend of Merlot (61 per cent), Cabernet Sauvignon (37 per cent) and Cabernet Franc (2 per cent), estate-grown in the Gimblett Gravels, Hawke's Bay, and matured for 17 months in French oak barriques. Deep and still fairly youthful in colour, it is fresh and supple, with concentrated, ripe blackcurrant and plum flavours, and coffee and spice notes adding complexity. It's a stylish wine, likely to be long-lived.

DRY $30 AV

Te Kairanga Hawke's Bay Merlot   (★★★☆)

The 2007 vintage (★★★☆) offers excellent value, with full, youthful colour and a fragrant bouquet of coffee and spice. Generous, with very satisfying depth of ripe blackcurrant and slight chocolate flavours, it's a smooth, finely balanced red, drinking well now.

DRY $18 V+

Te Kairanga Regional Selection Hawke's Bay Merlot/Cabernet Sauvignon/Malbec   (★★★)

A good, gutsy quaffer, the 2008 vintage (★★★) is a blend of Merlot (42 per cent), Cabernet Sauvignon and Malbec, barrique-aged for seven months. Boldly coloured, it is vibrantly fruity, plummy and supple, in an upfront style with moderate complexity and a fresh, smooth finish.

DRY $18 AV

Te Mania Three Brothers Merlot/Malbec/Cabernet Franc   ★★☆

The 2007 vintage (★★★) was estate-grown in Nelson. Berryish, plummy and leafy, it's a fruit-driven style, not complex, but fresh, flavoursome and smooth, with drink-young charm. The 2008 (★★☆), matured for 10 months in seasoned French and American oak casks, is full-coloured and fruity, with straightforward red-berry, plum and herbal flavours, fresh and crisp.

Vintage	08	07	06
WR	5	6	5
Drink	09-13	09-12	09-10

DRY $20 –V

Te Mata Estate Woodthorpe Vineyard Merlot/Cabernets   ★★★★

This bargain-priced red is Te Mata's biggest seller. The 2007 vintage (★★★★), estate-grown in Hawke's Bay, is a blend of Merlot, Cabernet Sauvignon and Cabernet Franc, matured for 15 months in French oak casks (new and seasoned). Dark and youthful in colour, it's a distinctly Bordeaux-like wine, savoury and complex, with ripe blackcurrant, herb and spice flavours, showing excellent density. Buy now and drink over the next three years.

Vintage	07	06	05
WR	7	7	7
Drink	09-15	09-14	09-13

DRY $19 V+

Terrain Hawke's Bay Merlot   (★★★)

Good now, the 2007 vintage (★★★) is a full-coloured red with mouthfilling body, blackcurrant and plum flavours showing good depth, and hints of herbs, spices and nuts adding a touch of complexity. (Exclusive to Foodstuffs supermarkets – New World and PAK'nSAVE.)

DRY $13 V+

Te Whau The Point Merlot/Cabernet Sauvignon/Cabernet Franc/Malbec – see Te Whau The Point in the Branded and Other Red Wines section

Thornbury Hawke's Bay Merlot   ★★★★

From Villa Maria, the 2007 vintage (★★★★★) offers irresistible value and is the Best Red Wine Buy of the Year (see page 17). Hand-harvested at three sites in the Gimblett Gravels district of Hawke's Bay and matured for 16 months in French and American oak casks, it is a blend of Merlot (89 per cent), Cabernet Sauvignon (9 per cent) and Malbec (2 per cent). Densely coloured, with a complex, nutty fragrance, it is tight and youthful, very ripe and dense, with layers of blackcurrant, plum, liquorice, spice and nut flavours and lovely texture. A powerful wine with a long future, it's priced very sharply. (Tasted prior to bottling, and so not rated, the 2008 vintage was promisingly dark and concentrated.)

Vintage	08
WR	6
Drink	09-15

DRY $20 V+

Ti Point One – see the Branded and Other Red Wines section

Ti Point Two Merlot/Cabernet Franc   ★★★★

Grown at Ti Point, north of Matakana, this blended red is matured in seasoned French oak casks. Delicious in its youth, it's typically a savoury, Bordeaux-like wine, ripe, earthy and spicy, with rich, smooth flavours, offering excellent value.

DRY $22 V+

True North Merlot   ★★☆

Grown at Doubtless Bay, in Northland, the 2006 vintage (★★☆) is a mature, medium-bodied red with moderate depth of cherry/plum flavours and a hint of spicy oak. It's pleasant now. The 2005 (★★☆) is green-edged, but shows some savoury complexity.

DRY $16 –V

Tuki Vineyard Merlot   (★★★☆)

The 2006 vintage (★★★☆) was grown at the base of Te Mata Peak, in Hawke's Bay, and French and American oak-aged for a year. Full and slightly developed in colour, with a sweetly oaked bouquet, it offers plenty of plummy, spicy, slightly earthy flavour, smooth, savoury and harmonious.

DRY $22 AV

Tuki Vineyard Merlot/Malbec/Cabernet Franc   (★★★☆)

The 2006 vintage (★★★☆) is a fresh, vibrantly fruity Hawke's Bay blend of Merlot (50 per cent), Malbec (33 per cent) and Cabernet Franc (17 per cent). French and American oak-aged, it's a moderately concentrated wine with plummy, spicy flavours, slightly earthy and savoury notes, and a smooth finish.

DRY $22 AV

TW Gisborne Merlot   (★★★☆)

Still developing, the 2007 vintage (★★★☆) is an American oak-matured red with deep, youthful colour and brambly, spicy flavours. Sturdy, with ripe, sweet-fruit characters and slightly chewy tannins, it's full-flavoured and gutsy, with lots of personality.

Vintage	07
WR	7
Drink	09-13

DRY $22 AV

Vidal Hawke's Bay Merlot/Cabernet Sauvignon   ★★★★★

Always a great buy. The 2007 vintage (★★★★★) is a deeply coloured blend of Merlot (46 per cent), Cabernet Sauvignon (39 per cent), Cabernet Franc (12 per cent) and Malbec (3 per cent), grown mostly in the Gimblett Gravels and matured for 15 months in French (80 per cent) and American (20 per cent) oak barrels (15 per cent new). It's a very elegant, Bordeaux-like wine with fresh acidity and rich blackcurrant, plum, spice and nut flavours, fresh and long. The 2008 (★★★★) is a blend of Merlot (53 per cent), Cabernet Sauvignon (36 per cent) and Malbec (11 per cent), 70 per cent barrel-aged. Dark, with ripe plum and spice flavours, it's a finely textured wine with excellent depth.

Vintage	08	07	06	05	04
WR	6	7	7	7	6
Drink	09-15	09-15	09-11	09-10	P

DRY $20 V+

Vidal Reserve Hawke's Bay Merlot/Cabernet Sauvignon   ★★★★★

The price of this distinguished wine recently dropped from $40 to $30. The 2007 vintage (★★★★) is a blend of Merlot (46 per cent) and Cabernet Sauvignon (46 per cent), with a splash of Malbec, matured for 20 months in French oak barriques (64 per cent new). Boldly coloured, with a strong seasoning of toasty oak, it has concentrated, plummy, berryish, slightly chocolatey flavours, showing good complexity and richness.

Vintage	07
WR	7
Drink	09-17

DRY $30 V+

Villa Maria Cellar Selection Hawke's Bay Merlot/Cabernet Sauvignon   ★★★★★

The 2000 (★★★★★) and 2002 (★★★★★) vintages offered exceptional value, winning Best Buy of the Year awards in the *Buyer's Guide*. The 2007 vintage (★★★★★) is a dark, strapping blend of Merlot (47 per cent), Cabernet Sauvignon (40 per cent), Malbec (10 per cent) and Cabernet Franc (3 per cent), grown mostly in the Gimblett Gravels district, hand-picked, and matured for 20 months in French, American and Hungarian oak barriques (25 per cent new). A masculine style with dense, firm flavours of blackcurrants and spices, and firm, youthful tannins, it's once again a great buy.

Vintage	07	06
WR	7	6
Drink	09-15	09-14

DRY $23 V+

Villa Maria Private Bin Hawke's Bay Merlot   ★★★☆

The deeply coloured 2008 vintage (★★★☆) is a blend of Merlot (85 per cent), Cabernet Franc (6 per cent), Malbec (5 per cent) and Cabernet Sauvignon (4 per cent), grown principally in the Gimblett Gravels and matured for a year in seasoned French and American oak casks. A silky-textured wine with generous, ripe, berryish, plummy flavours, a gentle seasoning of oak and smooth tannins, it's already enjoyable.

Vintage	08
WR	6
Drink	09-12

DRY $20 AV

Villa Maria Private Bin Hawke's Bay Merlot/Cabernet Sauvignon   ★★★☆

The 2008 vintage (★★★☆) is a French and American oak-aged blend of Merlot (72 per cent) with Cabernet Sauvignon, Cabernet Franc and Malbec. Dark and youthful in colour, with plenty of ripe blackcurrant, spice and plum flavour, a hint of sweet oak, and gentle tannins giving a smooth, dry finish, it has lots of drink-young appeal.

Vintage	08	07	06
WR	6	6	6
Drink	09-12	09-12	P

DRY $20 AV

Villa Maria Reserve Hawke's Bay Merlot   ★★★★★

This consistently outstanding wine is grown at three company-owned, close-planted sites in the
Gimblett Gravels district – Ngakirikiri, Omahu Gravels and Twyford Gravels – and matured for
18 to 20 months in French (principally) and American oak barriques (40 to 80 per cent new).
The powerful 2007 vintage (★★★★★) is densely coloured, with a fragrant bouquet, saturated
with dark berry fruits and savoury oak. It's highly concentrated, with very fine tannins and an
array of ripe blackcurrant, liquorice, coffee and spice flavours.

Vintage	07	06	05	04
WR	7	7	7	6
Drink	09-19	09-18	09-17	09-16

DRY $51 AV

Villa Maria Single Vineyard Omahu Gravels Merlot   (★★★★★)

The powerful 2006 vintage (★★★★★) was hand-picked in the Gimblett Gravels, Hawke's Bay,
and matured for 18 months in French oak barriques (50 per cent new). It shows great density,
power, complexity and structure. Dark, with notably concentrated blackcurrant, plum, spice
and nut flavours, it is still very fresh and youthful, yet approachable, with supple tannins and a
lasting finish. Open 2010+.

Vintage	06
WR	7
Drink	09-16

DRY $59 AV

Waimarie Muriwai Valley Merlot/Cabernet   (★★★☆)

Drinking well now, the 2006 vintage (★★★☆) was grown at Waimauku, in West Auckland,
and matured for over a year in French oak barrels (one and two-year-old). Merlot (37 per cent)
and Cabernet Franc (30 per cent) dominate the blend, which also includes Cabernet Sauvignon
(16 per cent), Malbec (10 per cent) and Petit Verdot (7 per cent). Full-coloured, although not
dark, it's a medium-bodied style with ripe, berryish flavours, hints of herbs and spices, and some
savoury, earthy complexity.

Vintage	06
WR	6
Drink	09-16

DRY $28 –V

Waimea Bolitho SV Merlot/Malbec   (★★★☆)

Grown in Nelson, the 2006 vintage (★★★☆) is a 3:1 blend of Merlot and Malbec, matured for
10 months in American oak casks (50 per cent new). It has full, slightly developed colour, with
very good depth of spicy, nutty flavour, showing some complexity.

Vintage	06
WR	6
Drink	09-11

DRY $27 –V

Waimea Nelson Merlot/Cabernet   ★★★

The 2006 vintage (★★★☆) is a blend of Merlot (90 per cent), grown on the coast at Kina, and
Cabernet Franc (10 per cent), grown on the Waimea Plains. Fullish, with slightly developed
colour, plummy, spicy, herbal flavours, showing very good depth and some savoury, earthy
complexity, it's an attractive wine, ready now onwards.

DRY $22 –V

Weeping Sands Waiheke Merlot/Cabernets — see Weeping Sands Waiheke Cabernet/Merlot

West Brook Waimauku Merlot/Malbec   ★★★☆

The easy-drinking 2006 vintage (★★★☆) is a 50/50 blend of Merlot and Malbec, estate-grown at Waimauku, in West Auckland, and French oak-matured for nine months. Full-coloured, it's a vibrantly fruity wine with ripe, plummy, slightly spicy flavours, restrained oak, slightly earthy touches adding a touch of complexity, and gentle tannins.

DRY $20 AV

White Cliff Merlot   (★★☆)

The fruity, smooth 2008 vintage (★★☆) is a pleasant, undemanding blend of Australian and New Zealand wines, from Sacred Hill. Ruby-hued, it is berryish and spicy, with a soft finish.

DRY $10 V+

Wild Rock Gravel Pit Red Merlot/Malbec   ★★★★

From Wild Rock Wine Company (a subsidiary of Craggy Range), the 2007 vintage (★★★★) was grown in the Gimblett Gravels, Hawke's Bay, and matured for 14 months in French oak casks (15 per cent new). It's a blend of Merlot (79 per cent), Malbec (11 per cent), Cabernet Sauvignon (7 per cent) and Cabernet Franc (3 per cent). A boldly fruity red with deep colour, substantial body and rich blackcurrant, plum and spice flavours, it's an excellent quaffer, fleshy and sweet-fruited, with slightly chocolatey notes and a seductively smooth finish.

Vintage	08	07
WR	7	7
Drink	09-15	09-14

DRY $20 V+

Wild Rock Hawke's Bay Merlot/Malbec   (★★★☆)

From a subsidiary of Craggy Range, the 2007 vintage (★★★☆) is sold only in supermarkets. Boldly coloured, it is soft and rich, with generous cassis and plum flavours and light tannins. It slips down very easily.

DRY $19 V+

Windmill Merlot/Cabernet   (★★★★)

From Te Awa, the 2007 vintage (★★★★) shows just how enjoyable Hawke's Bay reds can be without oak. A blend of Merlot (90 per cent), Cabernet Franc (6 per cent) and Malbec (4 per cent), it is inky-dark, with loads of plummy, spicy flavour, fresh, concentrated and smooth. It's a boldly fruity style, offering delicious quaffing right now.

DRY $20 V+

Wishart Legend Merlot/Cabernet/Syrah   ★★★☆

The 2005 vintage (★★★★) is a blend of Merlot, Cabernet Franc and Syrah, matured for 20 months in oak barriques. Drinking well now, it's a mouthfilling, full-coloured, spicy, brambly red, showing good concentration and complexity.

Vintage	05
WR	6
Drink	09-12

DRY $35 –V

Wishart Te Puriri Merlot   ★★★

The 2005 vintage (★★★) is a Bay View, Hawke's Bay red, barrel-matured for 18 months. Full-coloured, it is smooth and ready, with good depth of berryish, spicy, slightly leafy and nutty flavour.

Vintage	05
WR	7
Drink	09-11

DRY $20 AV

Zepelin Hawke's Bay Merlot/Cabernet/Franc   (★★★☆)

A single-vineyard red, grown at Havelock North, the 2005 vintage (★★★☆) is a blend of Merlot (50 per cent), Cabernet Sauvignon (25 per cent) and Cabernet Franc (25 per cent). Richly coloured, it is fragrant, with good complexity and depth of blackcurrant, plum and herb flavours and a spicy finish. It should be long-lived.

DRY $39 –V

Montepulciano

Montepulciano is widely planted across central Italy, yielding deeply coloured, ripe wines with good levels of alcohol, extract and flavour. In the Abruzzi, it is the foundation of the often superb-value Montepulciano d'Abruzzo, and in the Marches it is the key ingredient in the noble Rosso Conero.

In New Zealand, Montepulciano is a rarity and there has been confusion between the Montepulciano and Sangiovese varieties. Some wines may have been incorrectly labelled. According to the latest national vineyard survey, between 2005 and 2010 New Zealand's area of bearing Montepulciano vines will expand slightly from 6 to 8 hectares (mostly in Auckland, Hawke's Bay and Marlborough).

Beach House Hawke's Bay Montepulciano (★★★★☆)

Densely coloured, the 2007 vintage (★★★★☆) was grown in The Track Vineyard, in the Gimblett Gravels, and matured for a year in French and American oak casks. Sturdy, it has concentrated, ripe, brambly, spicy, plummy flavours and finely integrated oak, in a very rich and fruity style, with the power and structure to age.

Vintage	07	DRY $45 –V
WR	7	
Drink	09-30	

Framingham Marlborough Montepulciano ★★★

This wine typically has spicy, sweet oak aromas and fresh, vibrant flavours of plums and berries. The 2007 vintage (★★★☆), matured in French and American oak barriques (30 per cent new), is deeply coloured, fruity and supple. It's a medium-bodied red with strong plum and slight liquorice flavours, enjoyable now.

Vintage	07	06	DRY $28 –V
WR	6	6	
Drink	10-15	09-11	

Hans Herzog Marlborough Montepulciano ★★★★★

Typically a giant of a red, overflowing with sweet and ripe fruit flavours. The 2007 vintage (★★★★☆) was fermented with indigenous yeasts, matured for two years in French oak barriques, and bottled without fining or filtration. Deep and youthful in colour, it's a strapping (14.5 per cent alcohol), highly complex wine, nutty, firm and very savoury, although the Montepulciano varietal characters are less clear-cut than in some past vintages.

Vintage	07	06	05	DRY $64 AV
WR	7	7	7	
Drink	09-19	09-20	09-20	

Jurassic Ridge Montepulciano   (★★★★☆)

An excellent debut, the 2008 vintage (★★★★☆) is a strapping red (14.8 per cent alcohol), estate-grown at Church Bay, on Waiheke Island, and hand-picked at 25 brix from first-crop vines. Matured in French oak casks (40 per cent new), it is deeply coloured, rich and sweet-fruited, with concentrated plum, cassis, spice flavours, slightly earthy notes adding complexity, buried tannins, and a rounded finish. Well worth cellaring.

Vintage	08
WR	6
Drink	09-15

DRY $35 AV

Morton Estate Hawke's Bay Montepulciano   (★★☆)

The 2007 vintage (★★☆) is a pleasant, medium-bodied style (11.5 per cent alcohol), with a hint of sweet oak and decent depth of fresh, vibrantly fruity flavour.

Vintage	07
WR	6
Drink	09-11

DRY $19 –V

Omaha Bay Vineyard Matakana Montepulciano   ★★★

The dark 2007 vintage (★★★☆) was matured for 10 months in French oak casks (50 per cent new). It's a gutsy, mouthfilling red (14 per cent alcohol) with strong, berryish, spicy flavours, showing some earthy, savoury complexity, and a firm finish.

Vintage	07	06
WR	6	5
Drink	09-15	09-12

DRY $40 –V

Stafford Lane Estate Nelson Montepulciano   (★★)

Estate-grown and hand-harvested at 22.5 brix at Appleby, the 2008 vintage (★★) was matured for 10 months in French oak barriques (30 per cent new). Light ruby, it's a light, simple red, berryish, slightly spicy and plummy, but lacks real richness and roundness.

DRY $25 –V

Trinity Hill Hawke's Bay Montepulciano   ★★★★

Winemaker John Hancock doesn't believe Montepulciano has a strong future in Hawke's Bay. The 2008 vintage (★★★☆), grown in the Gimblett Gravels, is a fruit-driven style, ruby-hued, with fresh, vibrant, berryish, plummy flavours, and a smooth finish. It's a highly enjoyable, drink-young style.

DRY $20 V+

Weeping Sands Waiheke Island Montepulciano   ★★★★☆

Still a baby, the densely coloured 2008 vintage (★★★★★) was grown by the Obsidian winery at Onetangi. Powerful and rich, with deep, ripe flavours of plums and spices, it is concentrated and complex, with finely integrated oak (French and American, mostly seasoned), and a firm foundation of tannin. It should be at its best 2011+.

Vintage	08	07	06
WR	7	7	6
Drink	10-18	09-15	09-12

DRY $34 AV

Pinotage

Pinotage is overshadowed by more glamorous varieties in New Zealand, with 74 hectares of bearing vines in 2010. After being passed during the past decade by Cabernet Franc, Malbec and Syrah, Pinotage now ranks as the country's seventh most extensively planted red-wine variety.

Pinotage is a cross of the great Burgundian grape, Pinot Noir, and Cinsaut, a heavy-cropping variety popular in the south of France. Cinsaut's typically 'meaty, chunky sort of flavour' (in Jancis Robinson's words) is also characteristic of Pinotage. Valued for its reasonably early-ripening and disease-resistant qualities, and good yields, its plantings are predominantly in the North Island – notably Hawke's Bay and Gisborne – with other significant pockets in Marlborough and Auckland. A well-made Pinotage displays a slightly gamey bouquet and a smooth, berryish, peppery palate that can be reminiscent of a southern Rhône. It matures swiftly and usually peaks within two or three years of the vintage.

Babich East Coast Pinotage/Cabernet ★★★

Over several decades, this honest, bargain-priced red has built up a deservedly strong following. The 2007 vintage (★★★) is full-coloured, fruity, ripe and supple, with the earthy notes typical of Pinotage and good flavour depth. Drink now to 2011.

DRY $12 V+

Babich Winemakers' Reserve Pinotage ★★★★

This is one of the country's best Pinotages. Grown in Gimblett Road, Hawke's Bay, and matured in American oak casks (15 per cent new), the 2006 vintage (★★★★) is dark, with a spicy, earthy bouquet. Gutsy and generous, with concentrated, plummy flavours, the earthy notes typical of Pinotage, and firm tannins, it's full of personality and ready for drinking. The 2005 (★★★★) is still youthful in colour, with strong, ripe plum and spice flavours, earthy and nutty. Ready.

Vintage	06	05
WR	6	6
Drink	09-12	09-12

DRY $25 AV

Hihi Gisborne Pinotage ★★★

The 2007 vintage (★★★) was harvested at 25.6 brix at Patutahi and blended with splashes of Merlot (4 per cent), Malbec (4 per cent) and Cabernet Franc (4 per cent). Barrel-aged for 10 months, it's mouthfilling and spicy, with a slightly sweet American oak influence and firm tannins. A gutsy style, it's a good quaffer.

DRY $18 AV

Hitchen Road Pinotage ★★★

The 2008 vintage (★★★☆) was estate-grown at Pokeno, in North Waikato, and harvested at 25 brix. Oak-matured for 10 months, it's deeply coloured and sturdy (14.5 per cent alcohol), with strong, berryish, spicy flavours, ripe and smooth, and lots of drink-young appeal. Fine value.

DRY $17 AV

Karikari Estate Pinotage ★★★★

Estate-grown in the Far North, the 2007 vintage (★★★★) was matured in American (mostly) and French oak barrels (30 per cent new). It's a substantial red, built to last, with firm, concentrated, spicy flavours, nutty, savoury and complex. Best drinking mid-2010 onwards.

Vintage	07
WR	6
Drink	11-18

DRY $35 –V

Kerr Farm Vineyard Kumeu Pinotage   ★★☆

Kerr Farm's wine is to be enjoyed 'with friends on the verandah for a cruisy afternoon'. Estate-grown in West Auckland and matured in seasoned American and French oak barriques, it is typically an honest country red, berryish, spicy, slightly earthy and leafy.

DRY $20 –V

Marsden Bay of Islands Pinotage   ★★☆

The 2006 vintage (★★☆) was harvested at 25.6 brix and oak-aged for 18 months. It's a deeply coloured, gutsy (14 per cent alcohol) and spicy wine, but now slightly past its best.

Vintage	06
WR	6
Drink	09-12

DRY $24 –V

Muddy Water Waipara Pinotage   ★★★★

'Not for the faint-hearted' (in the winery's words), this is typically a robust red, full of personality. The 2006 vintage (★★★☆) is a strapping wine (15 per cent alcohol), harvested at 25 brix, fermented with indigenous yeasts, and barrel-aged for 16 months. Full-coloured, it is smooth and sweet-fruited, with cherryish, earthy flavours, soft and rich. Ready.

DRY $32 –V

Okahu Pinotage   ★★★☆

The very youthful 2008 vintage (★★★) is a Northland red, estate-grown, hand-picked and matured in a 50/50 split of French and American oak (partly new). It's a dark, vibrantly fruity wine, medium-bodied (12.5 per cent alcohol), fresh, plummy and supple, with plenty of flavour.

DRY $30 –V

Soljans Gisborne Pinotage   ★★★☆

This small West Auckland winery has a strong reputation for Pinotage. The 2007 vintage (★★★☆), barrel-aged for 10 months, is boldly coloured, with vibrant, berryish, plummy flavours, earthy, spicy touches adding complexity, and firm tannins.

Vintage	07
WR	7
Drink	09-14

DRY $18 V+

Te Awa Pinotage   ★★★★

This rates among the country's finest Pinotages. Grown in the Gimblett Gravels district of Hawke's Bay, it is matured for over a year in French oak casks (15 per cent new). The 2005 vintage (★★★★) is full-coloured, mouthfilling and smooth, with ripe, sweet-fruit flavours of plums, spices and liquorice, and finely integrated oak.

DRY $30 AV

Pinot Noir

New Zealand Pinot Noir enjoyed buoyant overseas demand in the year to June 2009, with 687,000 cases shipped – a steep rise from the 139,188 cases exported in 2003. There are now well over 600 Pinot Noir labels on the shelves.

The wines are enjoying eye-catching success in international competitions (which the majority of elite producers, especially in Burgundy, do not enter). Remarkable Central Otago Pinot Noir 2006 won the trophy for champion Pinot Noir at the 2008 International Wine and Spirit Competition in London, and Wild Earth Central Otago Pinot Noir 2006 won the trophy for Top International Pinot Noir, and then the overall trophy for Top International Red Wine, at the UK-based International Wine Challenge 2008.

The 2009 vintage yielded 27,547 tonnes of Pinot Noir grapes, far ahead of Merlot with 11,723 tonnes and Cabernet Sauvignon with 2304 tonnes. The vine is spreading like wildfire. Between 2000 and 2010, New Zealand's area of bearing Pinot Noir vines will expand from 1126 hectares to 4753 hectares.

Pinot Noir is the princely grape variety of red Burgundy. Cheaper wines typically display light, raspberry-evoking flavours which lack the velvety riches of classic Burgundy. Great red Burgundy has substance, suppleness and a gorgeous spread of flavours: cherries, fruit cake, spice and plums.

Pinot Noir over the past decade has become New Zealand's most internationally acclaimed red-wine style. The vine is our second most commonly planted variety overall, now well ahead of Chardonnay and behind only Sauvignon Blanc. Over 40 per cent of the country's total Pinot Noir plantings are in Marlborough (where 8 per cent of the vines are grown for bottle-fermented sparkling wine), and the variety is also well established in Central Otago, Canterbury, Wairarapa, Hawke's Bay, Gisborne and Nelson.

Yet Pinot Noir is a frustrating variety to grow. Because it buds early, it is vulnerable to spring frosts; its compact bunches are also very prone to rot. One crucial advantage is that it ripens early, well ahead of Cabernet Sauvignon. Low cropping and the selection of superior clones are essential aspects of the production of fine wine.

Martinborough (initially) and Central Otago have enjoyed the highest profile for Pinot Noir over the past 15 years. As their output of Pinot Noir has expanded, average prices have fallen, reflecting the arrival of a tidal wave of 'entry-level' (drink-young) wines.

Of the other small regions, Nelson and Waipara, in North Canterbury, are also enjoying great success. Marlborough's potential for the production of outstanding – but all too often underrated – Pinot Noir, in sufficient volumes to supply the burgeoning international demand, is also finally being tapped.

25 Steps Central Otago Pinot Noir ★★★☆

Grown on a terraced site at Lowburn, the 2007 vintage (★★★☆) is ruby-hued and supple, in a middleweight style with ripe cherry/plum flavours, well-integrated oak and plenty of drink-young appeal. The 2008 (★★★) is ruby-hued, with fresh acidity, good but not great depth of cherry and plum flavours, a touch of complexity and gentle tannins.

DRY $35 –V

36 Bottles Central Otago Pinot Noir (★★★)

Grown at Bendigo and oak-aged for nine months, the 2008 vintage (★★★) is a supple mid-weight, ruby-hued, with ripe-fruit characters, decent depth of cherry and spice flavours and some savoury touches adding complexity. It's already enjoyable.

Vintage	08
WR	6
Drink	09-13

DRY $35 –V

99 Rows Martinborough Pinot Noir   (★★★★☆)

From Julicher Estate, the 2008 vintage (★★★★☆) is a great buy. Grown at Te Muna, it was hand-picked and matured for 10 months in French oak casks (15 per cent new). Fragrant strawberry and spice aromas lead into a mouthfilling, intensely varietal wine with a core of sweet fruit, excellent concentration of cherry, strawberry, herb and spice flavours, subtle oak and gentle tannins. A very finely textured red, it's already delicious.

DRY $29 V+

1769 Central Otago Pinot Noir   ★★★★

From Wild Earth, the 2007 vintage (★★★★) was hand-picked and matured for 10 months in French oak. Scented, very generous and silky, with loads of ripe, sweet-fruit flavours of plums and spices, and gentle tannins, it's a good buy. The 2008 (★★★☆) is ruby-hued, floral and supple, in a medium-bodied style with ripe, moderately rich flavour and plenty of drink-young charm.

DRY $25 V+

12,000 Miles Pinot Noir   ★★★

From the Gladstone winery, in the Wairarapa, the 2008 vintage (★★★☆) was matured in seasoned French oak casks. Ruby-hued, it's a very charming, drink-young style with cherry and slight herb flavours, gentle tannins, and good 'pinosity'.

DRY $25 –V

Akarua Cadence Central Otago Pinot Noir   ★★★★☆

Estate-grown at Bannockburn, the 2007 vintage (★★★★★) was picked at 23 to 24.5 brix and matured in French oak barriques (30 per cent new). A very graceful, harmonious red, but also a wine of substance and complexity, it is deeply coloured and richly fragrant, with concentrated plum, cherry and spice flavours and ripe, smooth tannins. Still youthful, but already delicious, it's a drink-now or cellaring proposition.

Vintage	07	06	05
WR	6	5	6
Drink	09-17	09-15	10-11

DRY $45 AV

Akarua Gullies Pinot Noir   ★★★★

An earlier-drinking style, compared to its Cadence stablemate (above). Estate-grown at Bannockburn, in Central Otago, and matured in French oak barriques (33 per cent new), the 2007 vintage (★★★★☆) is an intensely varietal wine, vibrantly fruity, rich and smooth. Beautifully scented and deeply coloured, with a core of sweet fruit, gentle tannins and concentrated cherry, plum and spice flavours, it's already hard to resist.

Vintage	07	06	05
WR	6	5	6
Drink	09-15	09-12	P

DRY $35 AV

Alana Estate Lumiere Pinot Noir   (★★★★)

Made in an 'easy-drinking' style, the 2008 vintage (★★★★) is excellent, if assessed as a sort of Beaujolais look-alike. Ruby-hued, it is sweet-fruited and smooth (in fact, harbouring 5 grams/litre of residual sugar), with generous plum and cherry flavours and gentle tannins in an unabashedly fruit-driven style, delicious from the start.

Vintage	09	08
WR	6	6
Drink	09-11	09-11

MED/DRY $33 AV

Alana Estate Martinborough Pinot Noir ★★★★☆

The 2007 vintage (★★★★★) is dark, silky and sustained, with rich, ripe cherry, plum and spice flavours, savoury and lingering. It's a beautifully fragrant wine, concentrated and supple.

Vintage	07	06
WR	5	7
Drink	09-12	09-16

DRY $60 –V

Alexander Dusty Road Martinborough Pinot Noir ★★★☆

Light ruby, the 2008 vintage (★★★☆) has a floral, scented bouquet. Partly estate-grown, it is smooth, with a subtle oak influence (French, 18 per cent new), some savoury complexity, very satisfying depth of ripe cherry, plum and spice flavours, and lots of drink-young charm.

Vintage	08	07	06
WR	5	NM	6
Drink	10-11	NM	P

DRY $25 AV

Alexander Martinborough Pinot Noir ★★★★

The 2008 vintage (★★★★) is a floral, supple, mid-weight style, showing good complexity and already highly enjoyable. It's an elegant wine with ripe cherry, plum and spice flavours, finely integrated oak (22 per cent new) and silky tannins.

Vintage	08	07	06	05
WR	6	NM	6	7
Drink	10-13	NM	09-10	09-10

DRY $35 AV

Alexandra Wine Company Davishon Pinot Noir ★★★★

The 2007 vintage (★★★★) is a vibrant, supple red, grown at Alexandra. Full and bright in colour, with a core of sweet fruit, it has fresh, concentrated cherry and herb flavours, seasoned with French oak (40 per cent new).

Vintage	08	07	06
WR	5	6	5
Drink	12-13	12-13	10-11

DRY $35 AV

alex.gold Central Otago Pinot Noir ★★★★

From Alexandra Wine Company, the 2008 vintage (★★★★) has deep, cherryish flavours and a strong seasoning of French oak (40 per cent new). It's a richly coloured, savoury and complex wine with a fresh, crisp, almost peppery finish.

Vintage	07	06
WR	6	5
Drink	12-13	09-10

DRY $30 AV

Alexia Wairarapa Pinot Noir   ★★★

On sale at nine months old, the 2008 vintage (★★★☆) is an attractive drink-young style, grown at Opaki, near Masterton, and partly barrel-aged. Ruby-hued, it is fresh and vibrantly fruity, with ripe cherry and plum flavours, gently seasoned with oak.

DRY $25 –V

Allan Scott Marlborough Pinot Noir   ★★★☆

The 2008 vintage (★★★☆) is fresh, vibrantly fruity and supple, with good depth of berry and plum flavours, gently seasoned with spicy oak. Still very youthful, it's a finely textured wine, for drinking mid-2010+.

Vintage	08
WR	6
Drink	09-12

DRY $27 AV

Allan Scott The Hounds Marlborough Pinot Noir   ★★★★

Allan Scott's top red label. A single-vineyard wine, matured in French oak barriques (35 per cent new), the 2007 vintage (★★★★) has a floral bouquet. Fresh and vibrant, it has good density of ripe cherry and plum flavours, overlaid with toasty oak, and a firm backbone of tannin. The 2008 (★★★★) has fresh, strong cherry and plum flavours, oak complexity, and good harmony and richness. Sweet-fruited and supple, it's already delicious.

Vintage	08
WR	6
Drink	09-14

DRY $35 AV

Amisfield Central Otago Pinot Noir   ★★★★☆

Estate-grown in the Cromwell Basin and matured in French oak barriques (25 per cent new), the 2007 vintage (★★★★★) is a distinguished wine, notably dense, rich and supple. Full-coloured, with deliciously ripe, sweet-fruit flavours of cherries, plums and spices and a long, finely textured finish, it's a classy, generous red, still unfolding. The 2008 (★★★★☆) has generous plum and spice flavours, showing good complexity and density, and excellent harmony. It's still youthful; open 2011+.

Vintage	08	07	06	05	04	03
WR	7	7	6	5	6	5
Drink	11-19	10-18	09-15	09-12	09-10	P

DRY $40 AV

Amisfield Rocky Knoll Pinot Noir   (★★★★★)

From Rocky Knoll, a stony terrace within the Amisfield Vineyard at Lowburn, in Central Otago, the debut 2006 vintage (★★★★★) was picked at over 26 brix and matured for 15 months in French oak barriques (44 per cent new). Deep ruby, it's a strikingly rich, complex and harmonious wine, notably concentrated, sweet-fruited and savoury, with supple, silky tannins giving instant appeal.

Vintage	06
WR	7
Drink	11-19

DRY $110 –V

Anchorage Nelson Pinot Noir   ★★☆

The 2008 vintage (★★) is a barrel-aged red, pale ruby, light and smooth, with pleasant, slightly herbal flavours, lacking real ripeness and richness.

DRY $21 –V

Anchorage Pinot Noir Moon Creek Block   (★★☆)

Grown at Motueka, the 2008 vintage (★★☆) is pale, with smooth, light, slightly leafy flavours. Drink young.

DRY $19 –V

Anthem Discover Central Otago Pinot Noir   ★★★

The 2007 vintage (★★★) is a ruby-hued mid-weight with fresh, tight flavours, slightly leafy and smooth. The 2006 (★★★☆) is mouthfilling, with good depth of cherry, herb and spice flavours, slightly nutty and savoury, and gentle tannins. It's drinking well now.

DRY $25 –V

Ara Composite Marlborough Pinot Noir   ★★★★

From the Winegrowers of Ara Vineyard, at the entrance to the Waihopai Valley, the 2008 vintage (★★★★) was matured for 10 months in French oak barriques (20 per cent new). Fragrant and supple, sweet-fruited and lively, it has cherry, plum and spice flavours, showing good texture and complexity. Drink now or cellar.

Vintage 08
WR 6
Drink 09-14

DRY $26 V+

Ara Pathway Pinot Noir   (★★★)

Partly oak-aged, the 2008 vintage (★★★) is a ruby-hued Marlborough red, vibrantly fruity, with fresh cherry/plum flavours, some savoury notes and a rounded finish. It's already enjoyable.

DRY $21 AV

Archangel Central Otago Pinot Noir   (★★★★)

The 2008 vintage (★★★★) is a very elegant, ruby-hued, single-vineyard red, sweet-fruited and supple, with cherry, herb and spice flavours, showing some savoury complexity.

DRY $39 AV

Artisan The Best Paddock Marlborough Pinot Noir   (★★☆)

Verging on three-star quality, the 2006 vintage (★★☆) is light ruby, with pleasant cherry and nut flavours, a touch of complexity and slightly green tannins. It's a light style of Pinot Noir, ready for drinking.

Vintage 06
WR 5
Drink 09-10

DRY $22 –V

Ashwell Martinborough Pinot Noir   ★★★☆

Grown on the Martinborough Terraces, the 2008 vintage (★★★☆) was matured in French oak barriques (50 per cent new). It's a sweet-fruited wine, full-coloured – although not entirely clear – with rich cherry, plum and slight herb flavours, savoury and complex.

Vintage	08
WR	6
Drink	09-14

DRY $40 –V

Ashwell Martinborough Reserve Pinot Noir   (★★★★)

The 2007 vintage (★★★★) has deep, youthful colour and a fragrant bouquet of cherries, olives and herbs. Concentrated and savoury, with plum, spice and herb flavours and good tannin support, it's already enjoyable, but worth cellaring.

Vintage	07
WR	6
Drink	09-13

DRY $40 AV

Ashwell The Quails Martinborough Pinot Noir   (★★)

The fresh, medium-bodied 2008 vintage (★★) was matured in French oak barriques (33 per cent new). Full-coloured, it's a crisp wine, simple and only moderately varietal.

Vintage	08
WR	6
Drink	09-14

DRY $30 –V

Askerne Hawke's Bay Pinot Noir   ★★☆

Estate-grown near Havelock North, the 2007 vintage (★★☆) was matured for 10 months in French oak barriques (35 per cent new). Light ruby, it's a floral wine with cherry, plum and herb aromas and flavours and gentle tannins.

Vintage	07	06	05	04
WR	6	6	6	5
Drink	09-12	09-11	09-10	P

DRY $25 –V

Astrolabe Voyage Marlborough Pinot Noir   ★★★★

The 2007 vintage (★★★★☆) was hand-picked at three sites in the Wairau Valley, one-third fermented with indigenous yeasts, and French oak-aged. A rich, sweet-fruited red, with substantial body and concentrated, well-rounded flavours, it's intensely perfumed and elegant, with fine tannins.

Vintage	07	06
WR	6	5
Drink	09-14	09-10

DRY $29 V+

Ata Rangi Crimson Pinot Noir   ★★★★

This second-tier label is based on young vines in Martinborough and designed for early drinking – within three years of the harvest. Matured in French oak barriques, the 2008 vintage (★★★★) was hand-picked at 23 to 25.5 brix. It's an instantly appealing wine with gentle tannins and rich cherry, plum and spice flavours, showing very good ripeness, complexity and harmony.

Vintage	08	07
WR	7	6
Drink	09-12	09-10

DRY $32 AV

Ata Rangi Pinot Noir ★★★★★

One of the greatest of all New Zealand wines, this Martinborough red is powerfully built and concentrated, yet seductively fragrant and supple. 'Intense, opulent fruit with power beneath' is winemaker Clive Paton's goal. 'Complexity comes with time.' The grapes are drawn from numerous sites, including the estate vineyard, planted in 1980, and the vines, ranging up to 29 years old, have an average yield of only 4.5 tonnes of grapes per hectare. The wine is fermented with indigenous yeasts and maturation is for 11 months in French oak barriques, 25 to 30 per cent new. The 2007 vintage (★★★★★) has dark, dense, youthful colour. The bouquet is fragrant, with plum and liquorice notes; the palate is packed with lush cherry, plum and spice flavours, very fresh, tight and youthful. Powerful, yet graceful, it needs at least another year to develop secondary, savoury, bottle-aged complexity.

Vintage	08	07	06	05	04	03	02
WR	7	7	7	7	6	7	6
Drink	09-20	09-19	09-11	09-13	P	P	P

DRY $65 AV

Ataahua Waipara Pinot Noir (★★★☆)

The single-vineyard 2008 vintage (★★★☆) was hand-picked at 24 brix and matured for a year in seasoned French oak barrels. Floral, fruity and supple, it's a mid-weight style with vibrant cherry, plum and spice flavours, and a touch of savoury complexity.

DRY $36 –V

Auntsfield Hawk Hill Marlborough Pinot Noir ★★★★☆

Hawk Hill is the name of the elevated, north-facing slopes at Auntsfield, on the south side of the Wairau Valley. The 2008 vintage (★★★★), matured in French oak barriques (40 per cent new), is mouthfilling and supple, with deep plum, spice and slight herb flavours, and earthy notes adding complexity. Generous and warm, with the power to age, it should be at its best 2011+.

Vintage	08	07	06	05	04	03
WR	6	7	6	7	5	5
Drink	09-16	09-15	09-14	09-15	09-11	09-10

DRY $44 AV

Auntsfield Heritage Pinot Noir ★★★★☆

The 2007 vintage (★★★★☆) was estate-grown on the south side of the Wairau Valley, in Marlborough, and matured in French oak barriques (65 per cent new). Boldly coloured, with a fragrant, toasty bouquet, it is very powerful and sweet-fruited, with lush plum and spice flavours, strongly seasoned with oak, and earthy notes adding complexity. A big, ripe style, it's built for cellaring.

Vintage	07	06	05
WR	7	NM	7
Drink	09-21	NM	09-20

DRY $75 –V

Aurora Vineyard, The, Bendigo Pinot Noir   ★★★★☆

The savoury, dense 2008 vintage (★★★★★) is a Central Otago red, hand-picked at 24.5 brix
and oak-aged for 10 months. Deeply coloured, with deliciously concentrated plum, cherry and
spice flavours, oak complexity and a fairly firm finish, it's an opulent wine with a core of sweet
fruit and good supporting tannins.

Vintage	08	**DRY $39 V+**
WR	6	
Drink	09-14	

Aurum Central Otago Pinot Noir   ★★★★

Estate-grown at Lowburn, in the Cromwell Basin, and matured for 11 months in French oak
casks, the 2008 vintage (★★★★) is floral and ruby-hued, with lots of charm. Supple and
vibrantly fruity, it offers ripe cherry and plum flavours, finely integrated oak and some savoury
complexity. It's a very skilfully crafted wine, deliciously fragrant and well-rounded, for drinking
now or cellaring.

Vintage	08	07	**DRY $32 AV**
WR	5	6	
Drink	09-15	09-12	

Aurum Madeleine Central Otago Pinot Noir   (★★★★☆)

Named after the winemaker's daughter, the debut 2007 vintage (★★★★☆) is a two-barrel
selection, estate-grown at Lowburn and French oak-aged for 20 months. It's a sturdy, very ripe
and generous red, boldly fruity, with powerful plum and slight liquorice flavours. Still very
youthful, it's well worth cellaring.

Vintage	07	**DRY $85 −V**
WR	7	
Drink	09-20	

Aurum Mathilde Reserve Central Otago Pinot Noir   ★★★★

Estate-grown at Lowburn, in the Cromwell Basin, the 2007 vintage (★★★★) was matured for
14 months in French oak barriques (25 per cent new). Deeply coloured, it's a sturdy red (14.5
per cent alcohol), with rich, sweet-fruit flavours of cherries and plums, finely integrated, spicy
oak and firm tannins. Well worth cellaring.

Vintage	07	06	**DRY $45 −V**
WR	7	6	
Drink	09-15	09-12	

Awa Valley Pinot Noir   ★★☆

Grown at Kumeu in West Auckland, the easy-drinking 2007 vintage (★★☆) was 'hand-picked
from old vines' and matured for 11 months in seasoned oak casks. Light ruby, it has moderate
depth of strawberry and spice flavours, a hint of oak and gentle tannins.

Vintage	07	**DRY $20 −V**
WR	6	
Drink	09+	

Awatere River Marlborough Block 333 Pinot Noir   (★★★☆)

Grown at 333 metres above sea level in the Awatere Valley (hence the name), the 2008 vintage (★★★☆) is a floral, finely textured red, bright ruby, with vibrant cherry/plum flavours and a hint of herbs. Soft and elegant, with a subtle oak influence, it's already enjoyable.

DRY $25 AV

Babich Marlborough Pinot Noir   ★★☆

This wine shows Pinot Noir characters in a fresh, medium-bodied style, enjoyable young. The 2008 vintage (★★☆) is light ruby, with gentle plum and cherry flavours, offering smooth, easy drinking.

DRY $20 –V

Babich Winemakers' Reserve Marlborough Pinot Noir   ★★★☆

The 2007 vintage (★★★☆) is a forward, slightly developed wine with very good depth of cherry/spice flavours, showing some savoury complexity. The 2008 (★★★☆) is ruby-hued, mouthfilling and supple, with cherryish, spicy, moderately complex flavours, showing very good depth. Best drinking mid-2010+.

Vintage	08	07	06	05	04
WR	7	7	7	7	7
Drink	09-14	09-13	09-12	09-12	P

DRY $30 –V

Bald Hills Single Vineyard Central Otago Pinot Noir   ★★★★☆

Estate-grown at Bannockburn, hand-harvested and matured in French oak barriques, the 2007 vintage (★★★★☆) is deep and youthful in colour, with generous flavours of ripe plums and spices, vibrantly fruity, moderately firm and showing good complexity. Still youthful, it's built to last.

Vintage	08	07	06	05	04
WR	6	6	6	7	6
Drink	09-19	11-17	10-16	09-15	09-15

DRY $44 AV

Bannock Brae Barrel Selection Pinot Noir   ★★★★★

Top vintages of this single-vineyard Bannockburn, Central Otago red are outstanding. The ruby-hued 2008 (★★★★☆) was matured for 11 months in French oak casks (35 per cent new), and bottled unfined and unfiltered. Elegant and very finely textured, it has sweet-fruit delights, with strong cherry, plum and nut flavours, supple tannins and excellent complexity.

Vintage	08	07	06	05
WR	5	7	6	7
Drink	10-13	09-14	09-10	09-11

DRY $45 AV

Bannock Brae Goldfields Pinot Noir   ★★★★

Grown at Bannockburn, in Central Otago, and matured in French oak barriques, this is typically a very graceful and supple wine. Already enjoyable but still developing, the 2008 vintage (★★★★) is ruby-hued, with very good depth of ripe cherry, plum and spice flavours, a subtle French oak influence (25 per cent new) adding complexity, gentle tannins, and a lingering finish.

Vintage	08	07	06	05
WR	5	6	6	6
Drink	10-12	09-14	09-10	P

DRY $30 AV

Bel Echo Terroir Portrait Marlborough Pinot Noir   ★★★☆

The 2007 vintage (★★★☆) was grown on the more stony, less clay-bound soils at Clos Henri.
Matured in seasoned French oak casks (60 per cent) and tanks (40 per cent), it is bright ruby,
with fungal, 'forest floor' aromas, ripe, sweet-fruit flavours of cherries and spices, and drink-
young appeal. The 2008 (★★★☆) has a floral, slightly smoky bouquet and good depth of fresh,
vibrant plum and spice flavours, showing some complexity. It's delicious young.

Vintage	08	07		DRY $27 AV
WR	7	6		
Drink	10-13	10-11		

Bell Hill Pinot Noir   ★★★★★

From a 1-hectare plot of vines on a limestone slope at Waikari, inland from Wairapa, in North
Canterbury, this is a rare, highly distinguished red. It is typically a generous wine, powerful yet
silky, with sweet cherry, plum and spice flavours, complex, very harmonious and graceful. (The
2006 vintage was matured for 18 months in all-new French oak barrels.)

Vintage	05	04	03	DRY $95 –V
WR	7	7	7	
Drink	09-14	09-13	09-12	

Belmonte Marlborough Pinot Noir   ★★★

From Forrest, the 2008 vintage (★★★) is light ruby, medium-bodied and supple, with ripe,
cherryish, slightly spicy flavours, showing good varietal character, and a touch of complexity.

DRY $20 AV

Big Sky Martinborough Pinot Noir   ★★★☆

The firmly structured 2006 vintage (★★★☆) was grown in Te Muna Road, just south of the
township, and matured for 10 months in French oak barriques (40 per cent new). Weighty, with
strong flavours of plums and spices, a hint of tamarillo, oak complexity and tight tannins, it's
a savoury style, worth cellaring. The 2007 (★★★★) is a generous, tightly structured red with
full, bright colour. It has strong cherry, plum and dried-herb flavours, with smoky oak adding
complexity and a backbone of firm, ripe tannins.

DRY $39 –V

Bird Marlborough Big Barrel Pinot Noir   ★★★☆

Grown in the Old Schoolhouse Vineyard, in the Omaka Valley, and fermented and matured
in 900-litre barrels, the 2008 vintage (★★★) is a smooth red with vibrant, cherryish, plummy
flavours and a subtle seasoning of oak. It's a fruit-driven style, balanced for easy drinking.

Vintage	08	07	06	DRY $35 –V
WR	5	6	5	
Drink	09-12	09-14	09-12	

Bishop's Head Reserve Waipara Valley Pinot Noir   (★★★)

The 2006 vintage (★★★) is dark and savoury, with cherry/herb flavours showing good
persistence and firm tannins.

DRY $36 –V

Bishop's Head Waipara Valley Pinot Noir   ★★

From Pimlico Vineyards, the 2008 vintage (★★) is a sub-regional blend, matured for a year in French oak barrels (20 per cent new). It has light, slightly developed colour and lacks real ripeness and freshness.

DRY $28 –V

Black Estate Omihi Waipara Pinot Noir   ★★★☆

This is a single-vineyard, North Canterbury label. The 2007 vintage (★★★☆), fermented with indigenous yeasts and barrel-aged for 10 months (30 per cent new), is deeply coloured, with vibrant cherry and herb flavours, generous and supple. It shows good concentration, but the leafy notes detract.

Vintage	07	06
WR	6	5
Drink	10-13	10-12

DRY $40 –V

Black Quail Estate Central Otago Pinot Noir   ★★★☆

Grown at Cromwell, the 2008 vintage (★★★★) is ruby-hued, generous and vibrantly fruity, with ripe, sweet-fruit characters and gently oaked cherry, red-berry and spice flavours, showing good complexity. Drink now or cellar.

DRY $30 AV

Black Ridge Pinot Noir   ★★★☆

A decade ago, this was one of Central Otago's first consistently impressive Pinot Noirs. Grown at Alexandra, the 2007 vintage (★★★★) was hand-picked and French oak-matured. Full-coloured, sturdy and sweet-fruited, it is generous, with rich cherry and plum flavours, some savoury complexity and gentle tannins.

DRY $32 –V

Blackenbrook Vineyard Nelson Reserve Pinot Noir   ★★★☆

The 2007 vintage (★★★☆) was estate-grown, hand-picked at 24 brix and matured for a year in French oak barriques. Mouthfilling, it has good depth of cherry, plum and herb flavours, showing considerable complexity, and firm tannins.

Vintage	07	06
WR	7	6
Drink	09-11	09-11

DRY $33 –V

Bladen Marlborough Pinot Noir   ★★★☆

Firm and youthful, the 2007 vintage (★★★★) is deeply coloured, with rich cherry, plum and spice flavours, a hint of mint, and mouthfilling body.

DRY $33 –V

Blind River Marlborough Pinot Noir   ★★★☆

The 2007 vintage (★★★★) is a floral, silky textured, Awatere Valley red, hand-picked, fermented with indigenous yeasts and French oak-aged. It has deep colour and concentrated, plummy, cherryish flavours, tight and youthful.

DRY $37 –V

Blind Trail Central Otago Pinot Noir   ★★★☆

From Wild Earth, the 2007 vintage (★★★☆) is deeply coloured, with considerable complexity and very good depth. Priced right.

DRY $25 AV

Blue Ridge Marlborough Pinot Noir   ★★★☆

From West Brook, the 2007 vintage (★★★★) is deep ruby, with a scented, ripe bouquet and generous, plummy flavours. Sweet-fruited and flowing, with gentle tannins, it is generous and supple, with loads of drink-young charm.

DRY $29 AV

Boatshed Bay by Goldwater Marlborough Pinot Noir   (★★☆)

The ruby-hued 2008 vintage (★★☆) is medium-bodied, with berryish aromas and fresh, youthful raspberry and spice flavours. Tight, with a hint of toasty oak, it should be at its best mid-2010+.

Vintage	08
WR	7
Drink	09-12

DRY $21 –V

Borthwick Vineyard Wairarapa Pinot Noir   ★★★★

Grown near Masterton, in the Gladstone sub-region, the 2008 vintage (★★★★☆) is a deeply coloured, attractively perfumed red with vibrant cherry and plum flavours, showing excellent depth, ripeness and suppleness. Youthful, with good, savoury complexity and plenty of muscle, it should mature well.

DRY $38 AV

Boundary Vineyards Kings Road Waipara Pinot Noir   ★★★

The 2008 vintage (★★★) from Pernod Ricard NZ was harvested at 24–25 brix and matured in French oak barriques (20 per cent new). Light ruby, with strawberryish, spicy aromas, it is a medium-bodied style with good but not great flavour depth, some toasty, savoury complexity and gentle tannins. It's enjoyable now.

DRY $23 AV

Bracken's Order Central Otago Pinot Noir   ★★★★

Based on grapes grown at Mt Rosa, Gibbston, and matured in all-new French oak casks, the debut 2007 vintage (★★★★☆) is highly scented, spicy, savoury, rich and complex, with excellent ripeness and density. The 2008 (★★★★) is a refined, sweet-fruited wine, floral and supple, with cherry and plum flavours, spicy oak and a rounded, very harmonious finish. Open mid-2010+.

DRY $35 AV

Bracken's Order Small Parcel Central Otago Pinot Noir   (★★★★☆)

The 2008 vintage (★★★★☆) is beautifully floral and supple, with sweet-fruit delights and cherry and plum flavours showing a subtle oak influence, gentle tannins, and excellent delicacy and charm.

DRY $40 AV

Breaksea Sound Central Otago Pinot Noir   ★★★☆

From wine distributor Bennett & Deller, the 2008 vintage (★★★☆) was French oak-aged for a year. Ruby-hued, with fresh strawberry and spice aromas and flavours, it is vibrant and supple, with a touch of complexity, good immediacy, and lots of drink-young charm.

Vintage	08	07
WR	6	6
Drink	10-13	10-13

DRY $25 AV

Brightside Nelson Pinot Noir   ★★★

From Kaimira, the 2008 vintage (★★★) was mostly handled in tanks, but 10 per cent of the blend was matured in French oak barriques. An enjoyable, fruit-driven style, it is ruby-hued, with floral, berryish aromas and fresh cherry and plum flavours, not complex, but showing good depth.

Vintage	08	07
WR	6	5
Drink	09-12	09-12

DRY $18 V+

Brightwater Vineyards Lord Rutherford Nelson Pinot Noir   (★★★★)

The debut 2007 vintage (★★★★) was matured for a year in seasoned French oak casks. Deep and youthful in colour, it has a scented bouquet of plums and herbs. Mouthfilling (14 per cent alcohol) and generous, it shows good concentration of ripe, sweet-fruit flavours, with some toasty oak adding complexity, and a firm finish.

Vintage	07
WR	6
Drink	09-11

DRY $37 AV

Brightwater Vineyards Nelson Pinot Noir   ★★★☆

Ruby-hued, the 2008 vintage (★★★☆) was matured for 10 months in French oak barrels. It's a flavoursome, supple wine, slightly leafy, with very good depth and some nutty, savoury complexity. A drink-young style, it's best opened now to 2010.

DRY $25 AV

Bronte By Rimu Grove Pinot Noir   ★★★★

Estate-grown on the Bronte Peninsula, the 2008 vintage (★★★☆) was matured for 11 months in seasoned French oak barriques. It's a savoury, sweet-fruited wine, mouthfilling, with cherry, plum, herb and spice flavours, gentle tannins, and a well-rounded finish.

Vintage	08	07	06
WR	6	6	6
Drink	09-16	09-15	09-12

DRY $28 V+

Burnt Spur Martinborough Pinot Noir ★★★★

This single-vineyard red is grown south of the township, on heavier soils than those of the Martinborough Terrace. The 2007 vintage (★★★★) was hand-picked and matured for 10 months in French oak barriques. A generous wine, it is fragrant and sturdy (14.5 per cent alcohol), with deep, youthful colour, rich plum/spice flavours and hints of herbs and liquorice. Drink now or cellar.

Vintage	07	06	05
WR	7	7	6
Drink	09-15	09-14	09-13

DRY $44 –V

Cable Bay Marlborough Pinot Noir ★★★☆

Grown in the Brancott Valley and French oak-matured, the 2007 vintage (★★★★) is the best yet. Deep and youthful in colour, it is rich and sweet-fruited, generous and supple, with ripe plum and spice flavours, showing some savoury complexity. It's already highly enjoyable, but has the power to age.

Vintage	07	06	05	04	03
WR	7	7	7	6	6
Drink	09-11	09-10	P	P	P

DRY $34 –V

Cable Bay Reserve Marlborough Pinot Noir (★★★★☆)

French oak-matured for a year, the deeply coloured 2007 vintage (★★★★☆) is a generous Brancott Valley red with cherry/spice aromas seasoned with smoky oak, and hints of prunes and raisins. Powerful, weighty, sweet-fruited and densely packed, it has a creamy texture and long finish.

DRY $55 –V

Cable Station Marlborough Pinot Noir ★★☆

From Cape Campbell, the 2007 vintage (★★☆) was French oak-aged for eight months. Bright ruby, it is fresh and fruity, with plum and spice flavours in a Beaujolais-like style, but lacks real warmth and roundness. The 2008 (★★☆) has cherry and plum flavours, slightly earthy and light.

Vintage	07
WR	6
Drink	09-10

DRY $22 –V

Camshorn Waipara Pinot Noir ★★★☆

From Pernod Ricard NZ, the 2007 vintage (★★★) is deeply coloured, with spice and green-olive notes on the nose and palate, lively acidity and plenty of flavour. It shows good richness and complexity, but leafy notes detract.

Vintage	07	06
WR	5	5
Drink	09-11	09-10

DRY $37 –V

Cape Campbell Marlborough Pinot Noir   ★★★

An enjoyable drink-young style, the 2008 vintage (★★★) is ruby-hued and medium-bodied, with ripe, cherryish, slightly spicy flavours, a gentle seasoning of oak and fresh acidity.

Vintage	08	07
WR	5	5
Drink	09-12	09-11

DRY $25 –V

Carrick Central Otago Pinot Noir   ★★★★★

This Bannockburn label has emerged as a regional classic. The 2007 vintage (★★★★★) was matured for a year in French oak barriques (33 per cent new). Rich and youthful in colour, it is finely scented and flowing, with concentrated cherry, plum and slight coffee flavours, savoury, complex notes and a rich, resounding finish. Dense yet approachable, it's a sophisticated wine, for drinking 2010+.

Vintage	08	07	06	05	04	03	02
WR	6	6	6	7	5	7	6
Drink	09-15	09-15	09-13	09-15	P	09-13	P

DRY $45 AV

Carrick Excelsior Central Otago Pinot Noir   (★★★★★)

The debut 2005 vintage (★★★★★), released in 2009, is from mature, estate-grown vines at Bannockburn. Harvested at over 24 brix, it was fermented mostly with indigenous yeasts, matured in French barriques (30 per cent new), and oak-aged for six months longer than the Carrick Pinot Noir (above). Deep and still youthful in colour, it is beautifully scented, with a spicy, nutty bouquet. Still developing, it is very rich and complex, with deep cherry, plum and spice flavours, balanced tannins and lovely generosity and flow. Drink now or cellar.

DRY $85 AV

Carrick Unravelled Central Otago Pinot Noir   ★★★☆

Designed to be 'easy-drinking, laidback', the 2008 vintage (★★★☆) does not claim to be estate-grown at Bannockburn. Matured for eight months in French oak barriques (15 per cent new), it's a finely textured wine with moderately concentrated, ripe cherry/spice flavours, and greater complexity than you'd expect in this price category. Verging on four stars.

DRY $25 AV

Catalina Sounds Pinot Noir   (★★★☆)

The 2007 vintage (★★★☆) was grown in Nelson and Marlborough and matured for 10 months in French oak hogsheads (10 per cent new). Ruby-hued and fruity, it has good depth of cherry, plum and spice flavours, a hint of herbs, and gentle tannins. It's a moderately complex style, drinking well from now onwards.

DRY $25 AV

Central Schist Central Otago Pinot Noir   (★★☆)

Enjoyable young, the 2008 vintage (★★☆) is a light style of Pinot Noir, floral and soft, with moderate depth of cherry and plum flavours.

DRY $20 –V

Chamberlain Vineyard Pinot Noir (★★☆)

Grown at Motueka, the 2006 vintage (★★☆) was fermented with indigenous yeasts and bottled without fining or filtering. Deeply coloured, with a slight lack of clarity, it has plenty of spicy flavour, but lacks delicacy and finesse.

DRY $39 –V

Charcoal Gully Sally's Pinch Pinot Noir ★★★

Grown at Pisa, in Central Otago, the ruby-hued 2008 vintage (★★★☆) has ripe, sweet-fruit characters, good depth of cherry and spice flavours, light tannins and some savoury complexity.

DRY $29 –V

Chard Farm Finla Mor Pinot Noir ★★★☆

This Central Otago red typically has vibrant cherry/spice flavours, subtle oak and gentle tannins. Grown at Lowburn, in the Cromwell Basin, and matured in French oak barriques, the 2008 vintage (★★★☆) is ruby-hued and sweet-fruited, with moderately concentrated, cherryish flavours, vibrant and supple.

DRY $36 –V

Chard Farm River Run Pinot Noir ★★★

This is a floral, ruby-hued, fruit-driven style, grown at Lowburn, in the Cromwell Basin. The 2008 vintage (★★★) is scented and supple, with soft, berryish flavours and drink-young charm.

DRY $28 –V.

Chard Farm The Tiger Pinot Noir ★★★★

In the past called 'Sugarloaf', this wine is named after the company's 'ebullient cellar door host for 12 years', Keith 'Tiger' Thompson. The Tiger Vineyard at Lowburn, in Central Otago, is a cooler, more elevated site than The Viper Vineyard (below). The 2006 vintage (★★★★) is ruby-hued, very fresh and vibrant, smooth and flowing, with moderately intense cherry/plum flavours. It's not powerful, but elegant and full of youthful charm.

DRY $52 –V

Chard Farm The Viper Pinot Noir ★★★★☆

Grown at a valley floor site at Parkburn, in the Cromwell Basin, the 2006 vintage (★★★★★) is a full-coloured, finely scented Central Otago red. Refined, with substantial body, it offers rich, very ripe cherry/plum flavours, gentle acidity, and a lovely, silky texture.

DRY $52 –V

Charles Wiffen Marlborough Pinot Noir ★★★

The 2007 vintage (★★★), French oak-matured for 10 months, is bright ruby, with fresh, smooth cherry/plum flavours, a hint of herbs and a well-rounded finish. It's an enjoyable, drink-young style.

DRY $27 –V

Charles Wiffen Reserve Marlborough Pinot Noir ★★★☆

French oak-aged for 10 months, the 2007 vintage (★★★☆) is full-coloured, with a spicy, toasty bouquet and good concentration of cherry, spice and slight herb flavours, showing some savoury complexity.

DRY $35 –V

Churton Marlborough Pinot Noir ★★★★☆

Winemaker Sam Weaver wants a 'delicate, refined' rather than 'big, sweet, alcoholic' Pinot Noir. Grown at the company's elevated Waihopai Slopes site and in the Barrow Vineyard, at the western end of the Wairau Valley, and matured for a year in French oak barriques (20 per cent new), the 2007 vintage (★★★★★) is a notably complex style, rich and savoury, with the structure to mature well. Already highly enjoyable, but still developing, it has generous cherry, plum and spice flavours, with hints of herbs and dark chocolate, and a firm backbone of tannin.

Vintage	07	06	05	04	03	02
WR	7	5	6	5	7	6
Drink	10-15	10-12	10-14	P	10-12	P

DRY $37 V+

Churton Waihopai Slopes Marlborough Pinot Noir (★★★★☆)

The 2003 vintage (★★★★☆) was estate-grown 200 metres above sea level in the Waihopai Valley, picked from first-crop vines, matured for 14 months in French oak barriques (50 per cent new), and bottle-aged for four years prior to its release in 2008. Full and mature in colour, with a scented bouquet of herbs and nuts, it is generous and supple, with cherry, herb and nut flavours, showing real complexity.

Vintage	03
WR	7
Drink	09-12

DRY $50 –V

C.J. Pask Gimblett Road Hawke's Bay Pinot Noir ★★☆

The 2006 vintage (★★☆) is full-bodied, with good depth of firm, spicy flavour, but only moderately varietal.

DRY $22 –V

Clayridge Excalibur Marlborough Pinot Noir ★★★★

The generous 2006 vintage (★★★★) was grown on the upper slopes of the Clayridge Home Block, at the top of the Omaka Valley, and matured for 10 months in French oak barriques (33 per cent new). Bright ruby, it has good density of plum and spice flavours, showing impressive ripeness and complexity, and substantial body.

Vintage	06	05	04
WR	5	6	6
Drink	09-15	09-12	P

DRY $38 AV

Clayridge Marlborough Pinot Noir   ★★★☆

The 2007 vintage (★★★☆) is a full-coloured, fresh, vibrantly fruity red with a gentle oak influence, a touch of savoury complexity and gentle tannins.

Vintage	07	06	05	04
WR	5	5	5	5
Drink	09-13	09-12	09-10	P

DRY $29 AV

Clearview Pinot Noir Des Trois   ★★★★☆

From a Hawke's Bay winery, the powerful 2007 vintage (★★★★★) is an intriguing regional blend of Wairarapa, Waipara and Central Otago grapes, matured for 15 months in French oak barriques (one-third new). Deep and fairly youthful in colour, it is finely scented, with mouthfilling body, sweet-fruit delights, and a strong surge of plum, cherry and spice flavours. Very savoury, with a hint of dark chocolate, excellent complexity and richness, it's drinking superbly right now.

Vintage	07	06
WR	7	7
Drink	09-13	09-11

DRY $40 AV

Clearwater Vineyards Waipara Pinot Noir   (★★★)

From Sherwood Estate, the 2006 vintage (★★★) was matured for 10 months in French oak casks. Ruby-hued, it's a moderately complex wine with good depth of cherry, herb and spice flavours.

DRY $28 –V

Clevedon Hills Pinot Noir   (★★★☆)

One of the best Pinot Noirs from so far north, the 2006 vintage (★★★☆) was grown at Clevedon, in South Auckland. Drinking well now, it has strawberry and spice aromas and flavours, and more body than its lightish colour suggests. Sweet-fruited and silky, it shows good texture, harmony and complexity.

DRY $35 –V

Clifford Bay Awatere Valley Pinot Noir   ★★★☆

A middleweight style, maturing well, the 2006 vintage (★★★☆) was matured in French oak casks (35 per cent new). Ruby-hued, it has very good depth of cherry and spice flavours, still fresh and lively.

Vintage	08	07	06
WR	6	NM	6
Drink	09-15	NM	09-11

DRY $32 –V

Clos de Ste Anne Pinot Noir Naboth's Vineyard   ★★★★

This Gisborne red from Millton is one of the country's northernmost quality Pinot Noirs. Grown biodynamically at the hillside Clos de Ste Anne site at Manutuke, the 2007 vintage (★★★★) is richly varietal, with strawberry and spice flavours, showing excellent depth and complexity, ripe, supple tannins and a fragrant, welcoming bouquet.

Vintage	07	06	05	04	03	02
WR	7	5	6	NM	6	6
Drink	09-13	09-12	09-12	NM	P	P

DRY $54 –V

Clos Henri Marlborough Pinot Noir ★★★☆

From Henri Bourgeois, a top Loire Valley producer with a site near Renwick, the 2007 vintage (★★★☆) was matured for a year in French oak barriques (21 per cent new). Ruby-hued, with a slightly earthy bouquet, it is moderately concentrated and supple, with ripe cherry and plum flavours, showing a spicy, savoury, nutty complexity. It's developing well.

Vintage	07
WR	6
Drink	09-15

DRY $39 –V

Clos Marguerite Marlborough Pinot Noir ★★★☆

This single-vineyard Awatere Valley red is hand-picked and matured for a year in French oak barriques (30 per cent new). The 2007 vintage (★★★★) is richly coloured, generous, silky and harmonious, with cherry and slight herb flavours, showing good warmth and density. Drink now or cellar.

DRY $33 –V

Cloudy Bay Pinot Noir ★★★★☆

This is a consistently elegant, intensely varietal red, and the classy 2007 vintage (★★★★★) is the best yet. Grown on the south side of the Wairau Valley, it is a blend of nine Pinot Noir clones, hand-harvested at an average of 24.2 brix from very low-yielding vines (4 tonnes/hectare), and was matured for a year in French oak barriques (40 per cent new). Full-coloured and fragrant, it is mouthfilling (14 per cent alcohol), with ripe cherry, plum and spice flavours, rich, complex and savoury. A harmonious wine, deliciously concentrated and supple, it's still youthful and should flourish with cellaring.

Vintage	07	06	05	04	03
WR	7	6	7	5	6
Drink	10-14	09-12	09-12	09-11	09-11

DRY $51 –V

Coal Pit Tiwha Pinot Noir ★★★☆

This single-vineyard red is grown at Gibbston, in Central Otago. The 2008 vintage (★★★★) was matured in French oak casks (40 per cent new). Deeply coloured, with fragrant plum and herb aromas, it is mouthfilling and supple, with good concentration of cherry, plum, spice and green-olive flavours. Sweet-fruited and generous, it's a drink-now or cellaring proposition.

Vintage	08	07	06
WR	4	5	7
Drink	10-12	09-11	09-10

DRY $42 –V

Coney Pizzicato Pinot Noir ★★★☆

The 2008 vintage (★★★☆) of this Martinborough red is savoury, sweet-fruited and supple, with moderately concentrated, warm, spicy and nutty flavours, showing considerable complexity.

Vintage	08
WR	5
Drink	10-13

DRY $32 –V

Cooks Beach Vineyard Cooks Beach Pinot Noir   (★★☆)

From Cooks Beach Vineyard, on the Coromandel Peninsula, the full-bodied 2006 vintage (★★☆) was matured for six months in seasoned French oak casks. Ruby-hued, with plum, cherry and dried-herb flavours, showing some spicy, savoury complexity, it has a slight lack of softness on the finish, but is verging on three-star quality. Drink now onwards.

DRY $25 –V

Coopers Creek Marlborough Pinot Noir   ★★★

The 2008 vintage (★★★) is ruby-hued, floral and supple, in a buoyantly fruity style with fresh raspberry and spice flavours, showing a touch of complexity. A finely balanced wine with gentle tannins, it's a skilfully crafted, drink-young style, priced right.

Vintage	08	07	06	05	04
WR	6	5	6	6	6
Drink	09-11	09-10	09-10	P	P

DRY $20 AV

Coopers Creek SV Gibsons Run Marlborough Pinot Noir   (★★★★)

A single-vineyard red, grown at the mouth of the Waihopai Valley, the 2006 vintage (★★★★) is full-coloured, with fresh berry, spice and plum aromas, seasoned with quality French oak. Firm, ripe tannins underpin its concentrated flavours, which show good complexity, and the power and structure to age.

Vintage	07	06
WR	NM	6
Drink	NM	P

DRY $26 V+

Crab Farm Hawke's Bay Pinot Noir   ★★★

The sturdy 2007 vintage (★★★) was matured for 16 months in French oak casks (50 per cent new). Full-coloured, with a spicy bouquet, it is mouthfilling (14 per cent alcohol), with strong cherry and spice flavours, firm, ripe and gusty. It's slightly 'dry reddish', reflecting the relatively warm growing environment, but has plenty of depth and personality.

Vintage	07
WR	7
Drink	09-12

DRY $25 –V

Craggy Range Bannockburn Sluicings Vineyard Central Otago Pinot Noir   ★★★★

The floral, full-coloured 2008 vintage (★★★★) was hand-harvested in Felton Road at 24.2 brix, fermented with indigenous yeasts, and matured in French oak barriques (35 per cent new). It's a sweet-fruited wine with strong cherry and plum flavours, seasoned with spicy oak, and good complexity. Drink now or cellar.

Vintage	08	07
WR	6	6
Drink	09-16	09-14

DRY $50 –V

Craggy Range Calvert Vineyard Bannockburn Pinot Noir   ★★★★☆

The 2008 vintage (★★★★☆) was grown in the biodynamically managed Calvert Vineyard in Felton Road, and matured for 10 months in French oak barriques (35 per cent new). Scented and supple, it's a full-coloured wine with good muscle, a core of sweet fruit, and rich plum and spice flavours. A lovely blend of power and approachability.

Vintage	08	07					DRY $50 –V
WR	7	6
Drink	09-16	09-16

Craggy Range Te Muna Road Vineyard Pinot Noir ★★★★☆

The 2008 vintage (★★★★★) of this Martinborough red was hand-harvested at over 24 brix, fermented with indigenous yeasts, and matured for 10 months in French oak barriques (33 per cent new). Deeply coloured, it is finely scented, mouthfilling and supple, with delicious cherry and plum flavours, softly textured and savoury. It's already delicious, but has the muscle and structure to age.

Vintage	08	07	06	05	04	03	DRY $40 AV
WR	7	7	7	7	6	7
Drink	09-16	09-16	09-13	09-12	09-10	09-10

Craggy Range Waitaki Valley Otago Station Vineyard Pinot Noir ★★★☆

Grown in North Otago, hand-picked at 24.6 brix and matured for 10 months in French oak barriques (33 per cent new), the 2008 vintage (★★★★) is richly fragrant and vibrant, with concentrated cherry, herb and plum flavours, fresh, supple and finely poised. Drink now or cellar.

Vintage	08	DRY $45 –V
WR	7
Drink	09-16

Craggy Range Zebra Vineyard Central Otago Pinot Noir ★★★★

The 2008 vintage (★★★★) was grown at Bendigo, hand-picked at 24.6 brix, fermented with indigenous yeasts and matured for 10 months in French oak barriques (40 per cent new). Full-coloured, it is mouthfilling, with concentrated, very ripe cherry and plum flavours, seasoned with spicy oak, and supple tannins.

Vintage	08	07	DRY $40 AV
WR	6	6
Drink	09-16	09-14

Crater Rim, The, Bendigo Terrace Central Otago Pinot Noir (★★★★)

Built to last, the 2008 vintage (★★★★) is a concentrated, single-vineyard red, fermented with indigenous yeasts and matured in seasoned French oak barrels. Warm, spicy and rich, with good, savoury complexity, it is dense and chewy, with presence.

DRY $31 AV

Crater Rim, The, Blacks Lot 7 Pinot Noir (★★★☆)

The deeply coloured 2007 vintage (★★★☆) is a single-vineyard red from Omihi, near Waipara. Fermented with indigenous yeasts and matured in French oak barriques (15 per cent new), it is powerful, savoury and tightly structured, with strong plum, berry and herb flavours.

DRY $52 –V

Crater Rim, The, Canterbury Pinot Noir   (★★★★)

The 2006 vintage (★★★★) was grown at Burnham and Waipara, fermented with indigenous yeasts, and matured in oak puncheons (new and seasoned). Richly coloured, it is full-bodied (14.5 per cent alcohol), with fresh, vibrant cherry/plum flavours, crisp and concentrated. Worth cellaring.

DRY $30 AV

Crater Rim, The, Central Otago Pinot Noir   (★★★★)

From a hillside site at Lowburn, the 2007 vintage (★★★★) was fermented with indigenous yeasts and matured in seasoned oak casks. It's a floral, elegant red with strong plum and spice flavours, finely balanced tannins and earthy, 'forest floor' notes adding complexity.

DRY $32 AV

Crater Rim, The, Omihi Rise Waipara Pinot Noir   ★★★★★

The outstanding, finely structured 2006 vintage (★★★★★) is a single-vineyard red, grown at Omihi and matured for 15 months in French oak barriques (new and seasoned). Bottled unfined and unfiltered, it is rich, with lush plum, cherry and spice flavours, ripe and complex, and a commanding presence in the mouth. The 2007 (★★★★★) is also highly impressive. Deeply coloured, it is very weighty and sweet-fruited, with savoury, complex flavours, ripe, supple tannins and a deliciously soft texture.

DRY $47 AV

Crater Rim, The, Waipara Pinot Noir   ★★★☆

Grown at Omihi and on the Waipara valley floor, the 2007 vintage (★★★★) is a sweet-fruited, richly flavoured wine with gentle tannins and savoury, forest floor notes adding complexity. The 2008 (★★☆) is a multi-site blend, fermented with indigenous yeasts and matured in seasoned French oak barrels. It's a flavoursome wine with some complexity, but also green-edged, with some early development showing.

DRY $37 –V

Crawford Farm New Zealand Pinot Noir   ★★★

From Constellation NZ, the charming 2007 vintage (★★★) is a blend of Nelson and Hawke's Bay grapes. Ruby-hued, it is cherryish and plummy, with a touch of complexity and a soft finish.

DRY $23 AV

Croft Martinborough Pinot Noir   (★★★★)

The 2006 vintage (★★★★) was grown in the Pirinoco Vineyard, hand-picked, and matured for a year in French oak casks (30 per cent new). Full-coloured, it is spicy and savoury, sturdy and ripe, with firm, plummy, nutty flavours, showing good complexity. It's drinking well now.

Vintage	06
WR	5
Drink	09-12

DRY $35 AV

Croney Two Ton Marlborough Pinot Noir   (★★★☆)

The sturdy, good-value 2008 (★★★☆) was hand-harvested from low-cropped vines (5 tonnes/hectare), and matured in French oak barriques (30 per cent new). It shows good concentration, with ripe plum, spice and cherry flavours, firm and still very youthful. Open mid-2010+.

DRY $20 V+

Crossings, The, Marlborough Pinot Noir   ★★★☆

Estate-grown in the Awatere Valley, the 2008 vintage (★★★) was matured for seven months in French oak casks (25 per cent new). An easy-drinking red, it is vibrantly fruity, with ripe cherry and plum flavours, a subtle twist of oak and gentle tannins. Ruby-hued and supple, it's a drink-young charmer.

Vintage	08	07	06
WR	6	7	7
Drink	09-12	09-12	09-12

DRY $20 V+

Crowded House Nelson/Marlborough Pinot Noir   ★★★

The 2008 vintage (★★★) is a light, easy-drinking style, ruby-hued, with smooth cherry and plum flavours, showing a touch of complexity. It's a highly varietal wine, not concentrated, but enjoyable young.

DRY $20 AV

Culley Marlborough Pinot Noir   ★★★

From Cable Bay, the 2007 vintage (★★★☆) is the best yet. A charming drink-young style, ruby-hued and medium-bodied, it has lively cherry, plum and spice flavours, showing good depth, ripeness and harmony.

DRY $20 AV

Curio Bendigo Vineyard Central Otago Pinot Noir   (★★★)

From Mud House, the stylishly packaged, debut 2008 vintage (★★★) was harvested at 24.5 brix and matured in tanks (50 per cent) and French oak barriques. Ruby-hued, it's an off-dry style (5 grams/litre of residual sugar), with fresh acidity and good depth of berryish, slightly spicy flavours. Drink young.

MED/DRY $30 –V

Dancing Water Cabal Waipara Pinot Noir   (★★★☆)

Barrel-aged for a year, the 2007 vintage (★★★☆) is ruby-hued, with cherryish fruit flavours, lively acidity and some spice and 'forest floor' notes adding complexity.

DRY $38 –V

Daniel Schuster Omihi Selection Pinot Noir   ★★★★☆

This producer is now in receivership, but the outstanding 2006 vintage (★★★★★) is the best since 2001 (★★★★★). No longer grown solely in the Omihi Hills Vineyard, the 2006 was from 'selected plots within our Omihi vineyards'. Matured for 15 months in one and two-year-old casks, and bottled without fining or filtration, it is deeply coloured, mouthfilling and fruit-crammed. Full of youthful vigour, it has rich cherry, plum and spice flavours, supple tannins and obvious potential; open 2010+.

Vintage	08	07	06	05	04	03	02
WR	7	NM	7	NM	7	NM	6
Drink	15-20	NM	14-20	NM	09-11	NM	P

DRY $90 –V

Daniel Schuster Waipara Selection Pinot Noir   ★★★★

The intensely varietal 2006 vintage (★★★★) was hand-picked at Waipara and matured for a year in French oak casks (one to four year old). Full-coloured, it is fresh and vibrant, with sweet-fruit delights, mouthfilling body, strong cherry, plum and spice flavours and a subtle seasoning of oak.

Vintage	08	07	06
WR	7	6	7
Drink	12-14	09-10	10-12

DRY $45 –V

Dashwood Marlborough Pinot Noir   ★★☆

Designed for early drinking, the 2007 (★★★) is a buoyantly fruity wine with cherry/plum flavours and supple tannins. The 2008 vintage (★★☆), partly French oak-aged (30 per cent), is a pleasant, easy-drinking style, ruby-hued and floral, with vibrant cherry, plum and slight herb flavours.

Vintage	08	07
WR	6	7
Drink	09-13	09-12

DRY $22 –V

Dawn Ghost Central Otago Pinot Noir   (★★☆)

From an Alexandra-based producer, the 2005 vintage (★★☆), still on sale in 2009, has light, developed colour and green-edged, slightly rustic flavours, showing decent depth. Ready.

DRY $25 –V

Delegat's Awatere Valley Pinot Noir   (★★★★)

Deeply coloured, the 2007 vintage (★★★★) is a cherryish red with rich, sweet-fruit flavours seasoned with toasty oak. It's a powerful, savoury and complex wine, with a firm foundation of tannin.

DRY $39 AV

Delegat's Reserve Marlborough Pinot Noir   (★★★★)

Grown in the Awatere Valley, the 2007 vintage (★★★★) is deeply coloured, with spicy, cherryish, slightly herbal flavours, seasoned with toasty oak, showing good concentration.

Vintage	07
WR	6
Drink	09-12

DRY $28 V+

Delta Hatters Hill Marlborough Pinot Noir   ★★★★

The top label from the vineyard – 6 kilometres inland from Renwick, at the mouth of the Waihopai Valley – the 2008 vintage (★★★★) was 90 per cent oak-aged (barriques, 40 per cent new). Rich and full-coloured, with sweet-fruit characters, it has cherry, plum and spice flavours, woven with fresh acidity, in a vibrant, youthful style, best opened 2011+. The 2007 (★★★★☆) is finely scented, with excellent weight, concentration, complexity and structure, and should mature well.

Vintage	08	07
WR	6	7
Drink	10-14	09-13

DRY $32 AV

Delta Marlborough Pinot Noir   ★★★☆

The 2008 vintage (★★★☆) was 90 per cent matured in barrels (20 per cent new). A good drink-young style, it is ruby-hued, floral and supple, with good depth of ripe cherry, plum and spice flavours, moderately concentrated but intensely varietal. Drink now or cellar.

Vintage	08
WR	6
Drink	09-13

DRY $25 AV

Desert Heart Central Otago Pinot Noir   ★★★☆

The 2007 vintage (★★★★) of this Bannockburn red was matured for 11 months in French oak barriques (30 per cent new). Deeply coloured, it is warm and concentrated, with plum, cherry, spice and toasty oak flavours, good, savoury complexity, and the backbone to age. The 2008 (★★★☆) is bright ruby, with ripe-fruit characters, moderately concentrated berry/plum flavours and gentle tannins. Supple, with a sweet-fruit charm and restrained oak influence, it's already drinking well.

Vintage	07	06
WR	6	6
Drink	09-16	09-15

DRY $37 –V

Desert Heart McKenzie's Run Pinot Noir   (★★★☆)

Grown at Bannockburn, in Central Otago, the ruby-hued 2008 vintage (★★★☆) is forward in its appeal, with cherry and herb flavours, showing some savoury complexity, and supple tannins.

DRY $40 –V

Devil's Staircase Central Otago Pinot Noir   (★★★)

From Rockburn, the debut 2008 vintage (★★★) was released within a few months of the harvest. A drink-young style, it is bright ruby and sturdy (14 per cent alcohol), with plenty of vibrant, cherryish, plummy flavour, very fresh and smooth, showing a Beaujolais-like charm.

Vintage	08
WR	6
Drink	09-11

DRY $22 AV

Distant Land Marlborough Pinot Noir   ★★★

The 2008 vintage (★★★) from Lincoln was hand-picked at Spring Creek, in the Wairau Valley, and French oak-matured. It's a sturdy wine (14 per cent alcohol); with cherry, plum, spice and herb flavours, slightly nutty and firm.

DRY $25 –V

Dog Point Vineyard Marlborough Pinot Noir   ★★★★★

The classy 2007 vintage (★★★★★) was hand-harvested, fermented with indigenous yeasts and matured for 18 months in French oak barriques (50 per cent new). Full-coloured, it is highly fragrant, with ripe plum and spice aromas, seasoned with quality oak. Sweet-fruited and supple, it is very savoury and complex, with lovely texture and harmony. Drink now or cellar.

Vintage	07	06	05	04	03	02
WR	6	5	6	5	6	6
Drink	09-14	09-12	09-13	09-11	09-12	09-10

DRY $39 V+

Domain Road Central Otago Pinot Noir   ★★★★☆

The very good value 2008 vintage (★★★★☆) of this single-vineyard, Bannockburn red was French oak-aged for 10 months. Scented, sweet-fruited and supple, it couples substance and charm, with warm cherry, plum and spice flavours, showing excellent concentration, texture and complexity. It's already delicious. Still youthful, the 2007 (★★★★☆) is sturdy and highly fragrant, with deep, ripe, vibrant cherry and spice flavours, gentle tannins, and power through the palate.

Vintage	08	07	06
WR	6	7	5
Drink	10-16	09-15	09-12

DRY $35 V+

Domaine Georges Michel Golden Mile Pinot Noir   ★★☆

The easy-drinking 2008 vintage (★★☆), grown at Rapaura, in Marlborough, was oak-aged for nine months. Light ruby, it's a supple, mid-weight style with ripe plum and red-berry flavours, not concentrated, but enjoyable young.

Vintage	08	07
WR	5	6
Drink	09-12	09-12

DRY $25 –V

Domaine Georges Michel La Reserve Marlborough Pinot Noir   ★★☆

Hand-picked in the Rapaura district and matured for over a year in French oak barriques, the ruby-hued 2006 vintage (★★) is light in colour, with moderate depth of plum and spice flavours, firm and slightly rustic.

Vintage	06	05	04	03	02
WR	6	6	6	6	5
Drink	09-13	09-12	P	P	P

DRY $30 –V

Domaine Georges Michel Legend Marlborough Pinot Noir   (★★★)

Grown on stony soils at Rapaura, on the north side of the Wairau Valley, and barrel-aged for over a year, the 2007 vintage (★★★) is a full-coloured red with ripe cherry, plum and spice flavours, oak complexity and fairly firm tannins. It shows a slight lack of silkiness and charm, but should reward cellaring.

Vintage	07	DRY $36 –V
WR	6	
Drink	09-14	

Domaine Jaquiery Central Otago Pinot Noir   ★★★

Grown at Wanaka, the 2007 vintage (★★★☆) is a weighty, firmly structured style, spicy and nutty, with good complexity. Worth cellaring. The 2006 (★★☆) is full-coloured, with cherry, plum and tamarillo flavours, showing a slight lack of ripeness, and crisp acidity.

DRY $39 –V

Drumsara Central Otago Ventifacts Block Pinot Noir   ★★★★☆

Grown at Alexandra, in the Ventifacts Block (wind-shaped boulders), the 2007 vintage (★★★★☆) is full and youthful in colour, with fresh plum, spice and green-olive flavours, very vibrant and supple. It shows excellent density and complexity, with the power and structure to age. The 2008 (★★★★☆), matured for a year in French oak casks (30 per cent new), has a lovely, floral bouquet. It's a very graceful, finely poised wine, deliciously sweet-fruited and supple, in a less dense, but riper-tasting, style than the 2007.

Vintage	08	07	DRY $44 AV
WR	6	7	
Drink	09-13	09-12	

Dry Gully Central Otago Pinot Noir   ★★★☆

From Alexandra, the 2007 vintage (★★★☆) is ruby-hued, fragrant and supple, with moderately concentrated cherry, herb and spice flavours in an elegant, middleweight style, enjoyable now.

Vintage	07	06	05	DRY $30 AV
WR	5	6	5	
Drink	09-12	09-13	09-11	

Drylands Marlborough Pinot Noir   ★★★

The 2008 vintage (★★★☆) from Constellation NZ is an attractive mid-weight style with ripe cherry, plum and spice flavours, vibrantly fruity and supple. Enjoyable young, it shows some complexity and good harmony.

DRY $22 AV

Dry River Pinot Noir   ★★★★★

Dark and densely flavoured, this Martinborough red ranks among New Zealand's greatest Pinot
Noirs. Its striking depth, says winemaker Dr Neil McCallum, comes from 'getting the grapes
really ripe' and 'keeping the vines' crops below 2.5 tonnes per acre [6 tonnes/hectare]'. It is
grown in three company-owned vineyards – Dry River Estate, Craighall and Lovat – on the
Martinborough Terrace, and 90 per cent of the vines are over 20 years old. Matured for a year
in French oak hogsheads (20 to 30 per cent new), it is a slower-developing wine than other
New Zealand Pinot Noirs, but matures superbly. The 2007 vintage (★★★★★) is dark and
still purple-flushed. Fruit-packed and very youthful, it has rich cherry, plum and spice flavours,
showing lovely freshness, vibrancy, texture and harmony. It's still a baby; open 2012+.

Vintage	07	06	05	04	03	02	01	00	DRY $82 AV
WR	7	7	7	6	7	6	7	7	
Drink	10-16	09-14	09-17	09-12	09-16	09-10	09-12	P	

Easthope The Centrefold Wairarapa Pinot Noir   (★★★★)

A 'oncer', the 2006 vintage (★★★★) is mouthfilling and concentrated, with deep cherry, plum
and slight dark chocolate flavours, ripe, supple tannins and a mellowing finish. Ready; no rush.

DRY $56 –V

Edge, The, Martinborough Pinot Noir   ★★★☆

From Escarpment, this is the winery's fourth-tier label (behind Kupe, the single-vineyard wines
and the district blend). The fine-value 2008 vintage (★★★★) is a full-coloured, concentrated
wine with cherry, plum and spice flavours, ripe and strong.

DRY $25 AV

Elephant Hill Central Otago Pinot Noir   (★★★☆)

The 2008 vintage (★★★☆) from this Hawke's Bay producer was grown at Alexandra and
barrique-aged for a year. Mouthfilling and supple, it is ruby-hued, with ripe, sweet-fruit
characters and very good depth of vibrant, cherryish flavours, showing some complexity.

DRY $29 AV

Eliot Brothers Marlborough Pinot Noir   (★★★☆)

From an Auckland-based company, the well-made 2007 vintage (★★★☆) is enjoyable now.
Savoury and supple, with full, moderately youthful colour, it has ripe cherry and spice flavours,
showing good varietal character and some complexity.

DRY $20 V+

Escarpment Vineyard Martinborough Pinot Noir   ★★★★

This is the company's third-tier label, behind the single-vineyard wines and Kupe, but the 2007
vintage (★★★★☆) is very impressive. Matured for a year in French oak barriques (30 per cent
new), it is deeply coloured and full-bodied, with concentrated plum/spice flavours, savoury and
complex, and a solid foundation of tannin. It's a rich, youthful wine with a long future.

Vintage	07	06	05	04	03	DRY $50 –V
WR	6	7	6	5	7	
Drink	10-15	10-15	10-12	09-10	P	

Esk Valley Marlborough Pinot Noir   (★★★★)

The debut 2008 vintage (★★★★) was hand-picked in the Wairau and Awatere valleys and barrique-aged for a year. It's a sweet-fruited wine with fresh, ripe cherry and plum flavours, supple and strong.

Vintage	08
WR	6
Drink	09-11

DRY $30 AV

Eve Central Otago Pinot Noir   (★★★)

From Wild Earth, the 2008 vintage (★★★) was estate-grown at Bannockburn and Pisa. Full-flavoured, it has deep ruby colour, with funky, barnyard notes adding complexity and a leafy streak.

DRY $24 AV

Fairhall Downs Single Vineyard Marlborough Pinot Noir   ★★★★

Grown in the Brancott Valley, hand-picked and matured for 11 months in French oak barriques, the 2008 vintage (★★★★) is finely scented, mouthfilling, sweet-fruited and supple. A forward vintage, already delicious, it has gentle tannins and cherry/spice flavours showing good complexity.

DRY $35 AV

Fall Harvest Pinot Noir   (★★)

From Constellation NZ (formerly Nobilo), the 2007 vintage (★★) is a blend of French and New Zealand wines. An easy-drinking style, it's a ruby-hued, cherryish, spicy red with a soft, ultra-smooth finish.

DRY $13 AV

Fallen Angel Central Otago Pinot Noir   ★★★★

The 2008 vintage (★★★★) from Stonyridge Vineyard – far better known for Waiheke Island claret-style reds – was blended from three sub-regions of Central Otago. Floral and supple, it is ruby-hued, with mouthfilling body and strong, ripe cherry, plum, herb and spice flavours, well seasoned with toasty oak. A youthful wine, it shows good complexity and potential; open mid-2010+.

DRY $59 –V

Felton Road Block 3 Pinot Noir   ★★★★★

Grown at Bannockburn, on a north-facing slope 270 metres above sea level, this is a majestic Central Otago wine, among the finest Pinot Noirs in the country. The mature vines are cultivated in a section of the vineyard where the clay content is relatively high, giving 'dried herbs and ripe fruit characters'. The wine is matured for 11 to 14 months in Burgundy oak barrels (50 to 60 per cent new), and bottled without fining or filtration. The 2008 vintage (★★★★★) is very fragrant, complex and savoury, with full, bright colour, sweet-fruit delights, deep, cherryish, spicy flavours and good tannin backbone. Best drinking 2011+.

Vintage	08	07	06	05	04	03	02	01	00
WR	7	7	6	7	7	6	7	7	7
Drink	09-20	09-18	09-17	09-18	09-12	09-11	09-10	P	P

DRY $69 AV

Felton Road Block 5 Pinot Noir   ★★★★★

This is winemaker Blair Walter's favourite Felton Road red. Grown in a single block of the vineyard at Bannockburn, in Central Otago, the 2007 vintage (★★★★★) was matured for 11 months in French oak barriques (30 per cent new), followed by six months in seasoned oak barrels. Deeply coloured, it is mouthfilling and concentrated, with lovely depth of ripe, spicy, plummy, nutty flavours, firm yet supple. It should be long-lived; open 2011+.

Vintage	08	07	06	05	04	03	02	01
WR	7	7	6	7	7	7	7	7
Drink	09-17	09-18	09-17	09-18	09-11	09-10	P	P

DRY $69 AV

Felton Road Calvert Pinot Noir   ★★★★

The deeply coloured 2008 vintage (★★★★☆) was grown in the Calvert Vineyard at Bannockburn – which neighbours and is managed by Felton Road – and matured for 14 months in French oak barriques (30 per cent new). A graceful Central Otago red, it's finely scented, with strong, very youthful plum, cherry and spice flavours, woven with fresh acidity. Elegant and sweet-fruited, it needs time; open 2012+.

Vintage	08	07	06
WR	7	7	6
Drink	09-20	09-18	09-17

DRY $55 –V

Felton Road Central Otago Pinot Noir   ★★★★★

The Bannockburn winery's 'standard' Pinot Noir is a distinguished wine in its own right, and the 2008 vintage (★★★★★) is another top example. Matured for 11 months in French oak casks (30 per cent new), it is very finely balanced, with deep colour and notable richness and harmony. A graceful red, already delicious, it is generous, warm and supple, with deep, ripe cherry, plum and nut flavours, savoury and complex, and good tannin support. Best drinking 2011+.

Vintage	08	07	06	05	04	03	02	01	00
WR	7	7	6	7	7	6	7	6	7
Drink	09-20	09-18	09-17	09-15	09-11	09-10	P	P	P

DRY $46 AV

Felton Road Cornish Point Pinot Noir   (★★★★★)

From the company-owned Cornish Point Vineyard at Bannockburn (originally sold under a separate label), this is always one of my favourite Felton Road reds. The 2008 vintage (★★★★★) was matured for 14 months in French oak barriques (33 per cent new). Deep and youthful in colour, it is perfumed, mouthfilling, sweet-fruited and generous, with lovely depth of cherry, plum and spice flavours, a fine thread of acidity, and a sustained finish. It's a notably elegant wine, with the power to age.

Vintage	08
WR	7
Drink	09-20

DRY $55 AV

Fiddler's Green Waipara Pinot Noir   ★★★☆

Matured for a year in French oak barriques (20 per cent new), the 2008 vintage (★★★☆) is ruby-hued, vibrantly fruity and supple, with very good depth of cherry, plum and nut flavours, showing some savoury complexity. (There is also a Reserve label from 2008, priced at $35.)

Vintage	08
WR	6
Drink	09-14

DRY $25 AV

Forrest Estate Brancott Vineyard Marlborough Pinot Noir   (★★★★)

Made from vines with an average age 'exceeding 20 years', released after lengthy bottle-aging and still on sale in 2009, the 2003 vintage (★★★★) has full, fairly developed colour. It's a mellow, savoury red, full of personality, with rich, mature plum/spice flavours, showing good complexity.

Vintage	03
WR	6
Drink	09-15

DRY $35 AV

Forrest Marlborough Pinot Noir   ★★★☆

This wine rests its case on charm rather than power. The 2007 vintage (★★★☆) has full, bright ruby colour, with fresh plum/spice flavours, ripe, savoury and supple. Drinking well now, it shows good ripeness, body and complexity.

Vintage	07	06	05
WR	6	7	7
Drink	09-15	09-10	09-10

DRY $29 AV

Fossil Ridge Nelson Pinot Noir   ★★☆

French oak-aged for a year, the 2007 vintage (★★☆) has slightly developed colour and moderate depth of cherry, plum and herb flavours, showing a slight lack of ripeness and roundness.

Vintage	07
WR	6
Drink	09-13

DRY $27 –V

Foxes Island Marlborough Pinot Noir   ★★★★

Still on sale, the delicious 2005 vintage (★★★★☆) was estate-grown at Rapaura and in the Awatere Valley. Hand-picked at 23.5 to 25 brix, it was fermented with indigenous yeasts, matured for 14 months in French oak barriques, and bottled without filtering. A fleshy, deeply coloured wine with an abundance of sweet, ripe, cherryish, spicy flavours, 'forest floor' notes adding complexity and velvety tannins, it shows excellent depth and finesse.

Vintage	05	04	03	02	01	00
WR	7	6	NM	7	6	6
Drink	09-10	P	NM	P	P	P

DRY $46 –V

Framingham Marlborough Pinot Noir   ★★★★

This wine is 'feminine', says winemaker Dr Andrew Hedley, meaning it is elegant, rather than powerful. The 2008 vintage (★★★★) was matured in French oak casks (24 per cent new). Already enjoyable, it is full-coloured, ripe and supple, with sweet-fruit flavours, very cherryish and plummy, a subtle seasoning of oak, gentle tannins and good complexity.

Vintage	08	07	06	05	04
WR	6	7	6	7	6
Drink	10-13	09-10	P	P	P

DRY $28 V+

Freefall Central Otago Pinot Noir   ★★★☆

The 2007 vintage (★★★☆) is a fruit-driven style, grown at Bendigo and matured in mostly seasoned oak barrels. Deeply coloured, fresh, ripe and vibrant, it has good depth of cherry and plum flavours, a hint of liquorice and moderately firm tannins.

DRY $30 AV

Frizzell Pinot Noir   (★★★)

From a Hawke's Bay-based company, the 2008 vintage (★★★) was grown in Central Otago. Mouthfilling, sweet-fruited and smooth, it has good depth of plum, cherry and herb flavours, enjoyable young.

DRY $22 AV

Fromm Brancott Valley Pinot Noir   ★★★★☆

Since 2005, this label has replaced the former Fromm La Strada Pinot Noir. Less bold than past vintages, the 2006 (★★★★) is an intensely varietal Marlborough red, ruby-hued, with strong cherry, plum, herb and spice flavours, subtle and savoury, and a good foundation of tannin. It's drinking well now.

Vintage	08	07	06	05
WR	6	6	6	6
Drink	10-16	10-15	10-14	10-13

DRY $45 AV

Fromm Clayvin Vineyard Pinot Noir   ★★★★★

This Marlborough red is grown at the hillside Clayvin Vineyard in the Brancott Valley, matured in French oak barriques (10–20 per cent new), and bottled without fining or filtering. It tends to be more floral and charming than its Fromm Vineyard stablemate. The 2006 (★★★★☆) is full ruby, sweet-fruited and silky-textured, in a highly varietal, 'feminine' style, cherryish and spicy, with supple tannins. It's a forward vintage, for drinking now onwards.

Vintage	08	07	06	05	04	03	02	01	00
WR	6	7	7	7	6	6	6	7	7
Drink	10-16	10-17	09-14	09-15	09-12	09-11	09-10	09-11	09-10

DRY $61 AV

Fromm Fromm Vineyard Pinot Noir   ★★★★★

Winemaker Hätsch Kalberer describes this majestic Marlborough red as 'not a typical New World style, but the truest expression of terroir you could find'. In the Fromm vineyard near Renwick, in the heart of the Wairau Valley, 11 clones of Pinot Noir are close-planted on a flat site with alluvial topsoils overlying layers of clay and free-draining gravels. The wine is fermented with indigenous yeasts and matured in Burgundy oak barrels (up to 10 per cent new). It needs at least four or five years to unleash its full class. The 2006 (★★★★) is a lesser vintage. Moderately concentrated, with ripe cherry, spice and slight herb flavours, firm, savoury and complex, it is more forward than usual; drink now.

Vintage	08	07	06	05	04	03	02	01	00
WR	6	7	6	7	6	6	6	7	7
Drink	12-20	11-19	09-16	09-17	09-16	09-15	09-12	09-11	09-10

DRY $65 AV

Fromm La Strada Pinot Noir — see La Strada Marlborough Pinot Noir

Gibbston Highgate Estate Soultaker Pinot Noir   ★★★☆

The 2007 (★★★★) was grown at Gibbston, in Central Otago, matured in French oak barriques (40 per cent new), and bottled without filtering. Dark, concentrated and firm, it is sturdy and savoury, with strong cherry, plum and spice flavours and the power and structure to age. The 2008 vintage (★★★) is ruby-hued and supple, with berry and herb flavours, showing a touch of complexity.

Vintage	08	07	06	DRY $30 AV
WR	5	6	7	
Drink	09-15	09-16	09-10	

Gibbston Valley Central Otago Pinot Noir   ★★★★☆

The 2008 vintage (★★★★☆) was grown at Bendigo and matured for 11 months in French oak barriques (40 per cent new). Deeply coloured, it is rich, with concentrated cherry, plum, spice and slight herb flavours, finely poised, savoury and long. Best drinking 2011+.

Vintage	08	07	06	05	04	03	02	DRY $42 AV
WR	7	7	7	6	6	6	7	
Drink	10-14	09-14	09-14	09-13	09-12	09-10	09-12	

Gibbston Valley Gold River Pinot Noir   ★★★☆

This is the Central Otago winery's 'lighter' red, made for 'immediate enjoyment'. The 2008 vintage (★★★☆), harvested at Bendigo and Gibbston, was matured for six months in French oak (30 per cent new). It's a floral, vibrantly fruity red with ripe cherry and plum flavours, a touch of complexity, and lots of drink-young charm.

Vintage	08	07	06	DRY $30 AV
WR	7	6	7	
Drink	09-12	09-10	09-10	

Gibbston Valley Le Maitre The Expressionist Series Pinot Noir   (★★★★☆)

A serious wine for the cellar, the debut 2007 vintage (★★★★☆) was harvested from vines over 20 years old at Gibbston, in Central Otago, and matured in French oak barriques (20 per cent new). It's a full-coloured, highly complex young wine, firm yet supple, with concentrated plum and spice flavours, tight, earthy and savoury. It makes no concession to drink-young seduction, but should unfold well for several years.

Vintage	07	DRY $75 –V
WR	7	
Drink	09-15	

Gibbston Valley Le Mineur d'Orient The Expressionist Series Pinot Noir   (★★★★☆)

The 2008 vintage (★★★★☆), estate-grown at Chinaman's Terrace vineyard, at Bendigo, was matured for 11 months in French oak barriques (100 per cent new). Ruby-hued, it is mouthfilling, with ripe cherry and plum flavours, very harmonious, complex and savoury. Drink now or cellar.

Vintage	08	DRY $50 –V
WR	7	
Drink	12-20	

Gibbston Valley Reserve Pinot Noir ★★★★★

At its best, this Central Otago red is mouthfilling and savoury, with superb concentration of sweet-tasting, plummy fruit and lovely harmony. The grapes have been drawn from various sub-regions and vineyards over the years and yields have been very low (under 5 tonnes/hectare). The wine is typically matured in French oak barriques (50 to 70 per cent new). Grown in the School House Vineyard at Bendigo, and matured for 11 months in French oak barriques (60 per cent new), the 2008 vintage (★★★★☆) is full-coloured, scented and supple, with vibrant cherry, plum and spice flavours, ripe, savoury and concentrated. Best drinking 2011+.

Vintage	08	07	06
WR	7	NM	7
Drink	12-20	NM	09-16

DRY $100 –V

Giesen Marlborough Pinot Noir ★★★

The easy-drinking 2007 vintage (★★★) is ruby-hued, with a floral bouquet. Vibrantly fruity, it's a middleweight style, fresh, cherryish, spicy and smooth.

DRY $22 AV

Gladstone Wairarapa Pinot Noir ★★★☆

Still on sale, the 2006 vintage (★★★★) is the best yet. Matured for 10 months in French oak barriques, it is floral and sweet-fruited, with very good depth of cherry, plum and spice flavours. Full-bodied and moderately firm, it shows good intensity and structure, and is drinking well now.

Vintage	06
WR	6
Drink	09-16

DRY $45 –V

Glasnevin Pinot Noir (★★★★☆)

From Fiddler's Green, the 2007 vintage (★★★★☆) was grown at Waipara and matured for 18 months in French oak barriques (30 per cent new). It's a fragrant, ruby-hued red with concentrated plum, spice and slight herb flavours, underlying tannins, good complexity, and the power and structure to mature well.

Vintage	07
WR	7
Drink	09-16

DRY $43 AV

Glazebrook Regional Reserve Martinborough Pinot Noir ★★★☆

From Ngatarawa winery, based in Hawke's Bay, the 2008 vintage (★★★☆) is a supple, ripely flavoured red, based on 11-year-old vines at Te Muna. Bright ruby, it is cherryish, plummy and savoury, with French oak complexity (45 per cent new), very good depth and good cellaring potential.

Vintage	08	07	06	05
WR	6	NM	6	6
Drink	09-14	NM	09-12	09-10

DRY $27 AV

Goldridge Estate Marlborough Pinot Noir ★★

The 2008 vintage (★★☆) was grown at three sites in the Wairau Valley. Ruby-hued, with a hint of development, it's moderately ripe-tasting, with plum, cherry, spice and slight tamarillo flavours, showing solid depth. Ready.

DRY $19 –V

Goldridge Estate Premium Reserve Marlborough Pinot Noir ★★★

The 2007 (★★★★) is a dark, perfumed red, fleshy and sweet-fruited, with rich cherry, plum, spice and olive flavours, supple and finely textured. The 2008 vintage (★★☆) is a drink-young style, light and slightly herbal, with gentle tannins.

DRY $22 AV

Goldwater Marlborough Pinot Noir (★★★)

A mid-weight style, enjoyable now, the 2006 vintage (★★★) was grown in the Awatere Valley. It has lightish, moderately developed colour, with cherry, plum, spice and herb flavours, showing some savoury complexity.

Vintage	07
WR	7
Drink	09-13

DRY $24 AV

Grasshopper Rock Central Otago Pinot Noir ★★★★

Grown at Earnscleugh, in the Alexandra sub-region, the 2008 vintage (★★★★★) offers wonderful value. A single-vineyard red, matured in French oak barrels (30 per cent new), it is deep and rich, with ripe cherry, plum, herb and spice flavours, hints of raisins and coffee, and good, savoury complexity.

Vintage	08	07	06
WR	7	7	6
Drink	09-16	09-15	09-14

DRY $30 AV

Gravitas Marlborough Pinot Noir ★★★★☆

Estate-grown, hand-picked, fermented with indigenous yeasts and matured in French oak barriques, the refined 2007 vintage (★★★★★) is the best yet. Richly coloured, concentrated and fragrant, it has a core of ripe, sweet fruit, with good complexity, finely balanced tannins and a rich finish. It's already delicious, but well worth cellaring.

Vintage	07	06	05
WR	7	6	6
Drink	09-14	09-13	09-12

DRY $34 V+

Greenhough Hope Vineyard Pinot Noir ★★★★★

One of Nelson's greatest reds, at its best powerful, rich and long-lived. It is estate-grown on an elevated terrace of the south-eastern Waimea Plains, where the vines, planted in gravelly loam clays, range up to 28 years old. Yields are very low – 4 to 5 tonnes of grapes per hectare – and the wine is matured for a year in French oak barrels (25 to 50 per cent new). The 2007 vintage (★★★★) is full-coloured, generous and savoury, with plum, spice and slight herb flavours, finely textured and showing good complexity.

Vintage	07	06	05	04	03
WR	7	6	7	5	7
Drink	09-15	09-13	09-14	09-10	09-10

DRY $45 AV

Greenhough Nelson Pinot Noir   ★★★☆

This wine is handled in a similar way to its Hope Vineyard stablemate (above), but without the contribution of as much new oak or fruit from the oldest vines. It is hand-picked from a range of sites and matured for a year in French oak casks (25 per cent new). The 2007 (★★★☆) is ruby-hued and mouthfilling, with cherry, spice and herb flavours, maturing well.

Vintage	07	06	05	04	03
WR	7	6	5	5	6
Drink	09-13	09-12	09-12	09-10	09-10

DRY $26 AV

Greenstone Central Otago Pinot Noir   (★★☆)

From Gibbston Valley, the 2008 vintage (★★☆) is ruby-hued, with mouthfilling body and simple cherry and plum flavours, fresh, ripe and smooth.

DRY $19 –V

Greylands Ridge Central Otago Pinot Noir   (★★★☆)

Grown at Alexandra, the 2008 vintage (★★★☆) is very charming in its youth, with cherry and plum flavours, some savoury complexity, gentle tannins and good harmony.

DRY $36 –V

Greylands Ridge Ridgeback Alex Pinot Noir   (★★★)

Ruby-hued, the 2008 vintage (★★★) is an enjoyable mid-weight style, with ripe, red-berry and spice flavours, fresh and floral.

DRY $25 –V

Greyrock Marlborough Pinot Noir   (★★☆)

From Sileni, based in Hawke's Bay, the 2008 vintage (★★☆) is a floral, supple, light red, with gentle strawberry and plum flavours. It's a drink-young style, priced right.

DRY $14 V+

Greystone Waipara Pinot Noir   ★★★

Ruby-hued, the 2008 vintage (★★★) was fermented with indigenous yeasts and matured in French oak casks (30 per cent new). Floral and supple, it has cherry and herb flavours in a fruity, fairly light style with good varietal character and drink-young appeal.

Vintage	07	06
WR	6	5
Drink	09-12	09-12

DRY $34 –V

Grove Mill Marlborough Pinot Noir   ★★★

The standard of this winery's red wines rarely matches its whites. The youthful 2007 vintage (★★★) is full-coloured but not fragrant, with firm, nutty flavours, fresh but slightly rustic.

Vintage	07	06	05	04	03	02
WR	6	7	7	6	5	6
Drink	09-12	09-11	09-10	P	P	P

DRY $36 –V

Gumfields Marlborough Pinot Noir   (★★★☆)

From West Brook, the ruby-hued 2007 vintage (★★★☆) is very fresh and supple, in a charming style with cherry and plum flavours, gently oaked and finely balanced. It shows good varietal character, with drink-young appeal.

DRY $22 V+

Gunn Estate Pinot Noir   (★★☆)

From Sacred Hill, the 2007 vintage (★★☆) is a blend of 'selected vineyards' in France and New Zealand. Deeply coloured for Pinot Noir, it is smooth and full-flavoured, but not very varietal, with fresh berry and spice flavours. A solid quaffer.

DRY $17 AV

Hans Herzog Marlborough Pinot Noir   ★★★★★

This powerful wine needs at least a couple of years to reveal its class. The 2007 vintage (★★★★★) was harvested at 24.2 to 25.1 brix, fermented with indigenous yeasts, matured for a year in French oak barriques (20 per cent new), and bottled unfined and unfiltered. Highly scented, very ripe and silky, it's a top year, with mouthfilling body (14.8 per cent alcohol) and rich cherry, plum and nut flavours, long and lovely.

Vintage	07
WR	7
Drink	09-19

DRY $50 AV

Harwood Hall Central Otago Pinot Noir   (★★★☆)

Showing greater complexity than most Pinot Noirs in its price category, the 2008 vintage (★★★☆) is a youthful, sweet-fruited wine with good depth of cherry, herb and spice flavours, fresh and supple.

DRY $22 V+

Hawkdun Rise Central Otago Pinot Noir   ★★★☆

The 2007 vintage (★★★☆) is a single-vineyard, Alexandra red with strong plum and herb flavours, threaded with fresh acidity. The riper-tasting 2008 (★★★★) is deeply coloured and mouthfilling (14.2 per cent alcohol), with generous cherry, plum and spice flavours, and the structure to mature well.

Vintage	07
WR	6
Drink	09-15

DRY $38 –V

Hawkshead First Vines Central Otago Pinot Noir   (★★★)

Grown at Gibbston, the 2007 vintage (★★★) was matured in French oak barriques (40 per cent new). Ruby-hued, it has vibrant cherry and herb flavours showing very good depth and considerable complexity, but is green-edged. (Note: 'first vines' means 'our first vines planted'.)

Vintage	07
WR	5
Drink	09-12

DRY $42 –V

Hawkshead Gibbston Valley Pinot Noir ★★★☆

The 2007 vintage (★★★) is a single-vineyard red, hand-harvested at Gibbston, in Central Otago, and matured in French oak barriques (40 per cent new). Full-coloured, it's a sturdy wine with good depth of cherry/spice flavours and some complexity, but also a slight lack of ripeness and roundness.

Vintage	07	06
WR	5	6
Drink	09-12	09-15

DRY $38 –V

Hay Maker Marlborough Pinot Noir (★★☆)

From Mud House, the 2008 vintage (★★☆) is a drink-young style, ruby-hued, with raspberryish, slightly spicy flavours, fruity and smooth.

DRY $17 AV

Heart of Stone Marlborough Pinot Noir ★★☆

The 2008 vintage (★★) from Forrest Estate is light and simple, with soft, cherryish flavours, offering easy, no-fuss drinking.

DRY $18 AV

Highfield Marlborough Pinot Noir ★★★★

The 2007 vintage (★★★★) was hand-harvested at 25 to 27.5 brix, matured for a year in French oak barrels, and 'fined with organic, free-range egg whites'. The bouquet is complex and savoury; the palate is sweet-fruited, with ripe strawberry, spice and olive flavours, showing excellent depth.

Vintage	07	06	05	04	03	02
WR	6	5	7	6	6	7
Drink	10-14	09-10	09-10	P	P	P

DRY $37 AV

Highfield Mill Stream Marlborough Pinot Noir – see Mill Stream Pinot Noir

Hinton Estate Vineyard Central Otago Pinot Noir ★★★☆

Maturing well, the 2006 vintage (★★★★) is one of the finest yet. Grown at Alexandra, it is ruby-hued, elegant and vibrantly fruity, with fresh acidity and cherry, plum and spice flavours seasoned with fine-quality oak. Drink now or cellar.

DRY $35 –V

Hinton Hill Country Central Otago Pinot Noir (★★★)

Grown at Alexandra, in Central Otago, the 2006 vintage (★★★) was 'made to be more approachable, with smoother, lighter tannins'. Ruby hued, it is vibrant and fruity, with plummy flavours woven with fresh acidity.

DRY $23 AV

Homer Marlborough Pinot Noir   ★★★

From Odyssey, the 2008 vintage (★★★) was hand-picked in the Brancott Valley and aged in seasoned oak casks. Deeply coloured, it is generous and fruity, with strong cherry and plum flavours, ripe and gutsy.

Vintage	08
WR	5
Drink	09-12

DRY $20 AV

Hoppers Crossing Central Otago Pinot Noir   (★★☆)

From Auckland-based CPP Wines, the 2008 vintage (★★☆) is a fruity, simple red with a hint of sweet oak and pleasant berry/plum flavours, offering easy, no-fuss drinking.

DRY $20 –V

Hudson John Henry Pinot Noir   ★★★

The 2008 vintage (★★★) is a Martinborough red with cherryish, slightly spicy and herbal flavours. It's a middleweight style with good depth and gentle tannins, already enjoyable.

Vintage	07	06
WR	6	4
Drink	09-11	10-12

DRY $30 –V

Huia Marlborough Pinot Noir   ★★★☆

The 2007 vintage (★★★☆) was matured for 11 months in French oak. Floral, sweet-fruited and supple, it is moderately concentrated, with cherry, plum and slight herb flavours, showing good complexity. It's drinking well now.

Vintage	07	06	05	04	03	02
WR	6	6	6	6	6	6
Drink	09-19	09-11	09-11	09-10	P	P

DRY $36 –V

Hunter's Marlborough Pinot Noir   ★★★☆

Typically a very supple, charming red. The 2007 (★★★★) was picked (partly by hand) in the Wairau Valley at an average of 24 brix, and matured for 10 months in French oak barriques. The best vintage yet of this label, it is fragrant, full-bodied and supple, with strong, sweet-fruit flavours of cherries and plums, and 'forest floor' notes adding complexity. A very harmonious wine, it's already delicious.

Vintage	08
WR	5
Drink	10-13

DRY $26 AV

Hyperion Eos Pinot Noir   ★★

Estate-grown at Matakana, north of Auckland, and French oak-matured for a year, this is one of New Zealand's northernmost Pinot Noirs. The 2007 vintage (★☆) has light, moderately developed colour and hints of bacon, herbs and spices. However, it lacks varietal character and fragrance.

Vintage	07	06	05	04	03
WR	5	7	6	6	4
Drink	09-12	09-11	09-10	P	P

DRY $31 –V

Incognito Pinot Noir   (★★★★)

From Gibbston Highgate, the 2008 vintage (★★★★) was grown at Gibbston, in Central Otago, fermented with indigenous yeasts, matured for 11 months in French oak barrels, and bottled unfined and unfiltered. Floral and ruby-hued, it's a sweet-fruited, supple wine with much more body and depth than its colour suggests. Delicious young, it has rich plum and cherry flavours, subtle oak and gentle tannins. Slightly savoury, with lots of charm and a tight, persistent finish, it should mature well.

DRY $23 V+

Instinct Marlborough Pinot Noir   (★★☆)

From C.J. Pask, the 2008 vintage (★★☆) was hand-picked and French oak-aged for 10 months. It's an easy-drinking wine, light ruby, with fresh strawberry and spice aromas and flavours, and a rounded finish. Drink young.

DRY $20 –V

Invivo Central Otago Pinot Noir   (★★★)

From an Auckland-based company, the 2008 vintage (★★★) was grown at Lowburn, in the Cromwell Basin, hand-picked and partly barrel-aged. It's a ruby-hued, mid-weight style with ripe, sweet-fruit flavours of cherries and plums, gentle tannins, and drink-young charm.

Vintage	08
WR	5
Drink	09-13

DRY $35 –V

Isabel Marlborough Pinot Noir   ★★★☆

This once-outstanding red was originally grown in the close-planted Tiller Vineyard near Renwick, but is now a multi-site blend, including fruit from the company's Elevation Vineyard in the Waihopai Valley, 300 metres above sea level. It is matured for 10 to 12 months in French oak barriques (15 to 20 per cent new), and bottled without fining or filtering. The 2006 vintage (★★★☆) is full-bodied and smooth, with moderately concentrated plum/spice flavours, showing some savoury complexity.

Vintage	06	05
WR	7	6
Drink	09-16	09-17

DRY $35 –V

Jackson Estate Gum Emperor Marlborough Pinot Noir   ★★★★☆

The 2007 vintage (★★★★☆) was grown in the Gum Emperor Vineyard, in the Waihopai Valley. Hand-picked at 24.8 brix, it was fermented with indigenous yeasts, matured in French oak barriques (33 per cent new), and bottled without fining or filtering. Very floral, rich and supple, it is sweet-fruited, with ripe cherry and spice flavours, seasoned with toasty oak, gentle tannins and lovely harmony. It's already highly enjoyable, but best cellared to 2011+.

Vintage	07	06	05
WR	7	NM	6
Drink	09-18	NM	09-15

DRY $55 –V

Jackson Estate Vintage Widow Marlborough Pinot Noir   ★★★★☆

The quality of Jackson Estate's Pinot Noir has shot up since the 2005 vintage (★★★★), the first to be labelled 'Vintage Widow' – a reference to 'our families, often forgotten at vintage'. The 2008 (★★★★☆) was matured in French oak barriques (25 per cent new). Deeply coloured, it shows lovely richness and suppleness, with deep cherry and plum flavours, ripe and rounded, and lots of drink-young charm.

Vintage	08	07	06	05	04	03	02
WR	5	6	5	6	5	5	6
Drink	09-15	09-18	09-12	09-10	P	P	P

DRY $40 AV

John Forrest Collection Pinot Noir   (★★★★☆)

From Bannockburn in Central Otago (the source of 'New Zealand's finest Pinot Noirs'), the 2007 vintage (★★★★☆) is from a season when John Forrest harvested no grapes from the Waitaki Valley. Full ruby, it is mouthfilling and very supple, with vibrant cherry, spice and slight herb flavours, showing good concentration, fresh acidity and impressive complexity. Drink now onwards.

Vintage	07
WR	6
Drink	10-15

DRY $65 –V

Johner Estate Gladstone Pinot Noir   ★★★☆

Grown near Gladstone, in the Wairarapa, the 2007 vintage (★★★☆) is full-coloured, with a floral, slightly herbal, spicy bouquet. It's a supple, forward wine, cherryish, nutty and slightly raisiny. The 2008 (★★★) has full, slightly developed colour, mouthfilling body, plum, cherry and herb flavours and a smooth finish.

Vintage	07
WR	5
Drink	09-10

DRY $37 –V

Johner Estate Gladstone Reserve Pinot Noir   ★★★★

The 2007 vintage (★★★★) is a single-vineyard Wairarapa red, grown at East Taratahi, near Gladstone. Cropped at just 1 tonne per hectare and matured in mostly new oak barrels, it is full-coloured and fragrant, with concentrated cherry, plum and spice flavours and a foundation of firm, ripe tannins. Well worth cellaring.

Vintage	07
WR	5
Drink	09-12

DRY $50 –V

Johner Estate Moonlight Pinot Noir – see Moonlight Pinot Noir

Judge Rock Central Otago Pinot Noir   ★★★★

The 2008 vintage (★★★★) of this single-vineyard Alexandra wine is mouthfilling and well-structured, with rich, ripe cherry, herb and nut flavours and good, savoury complexity. Coupling density with elegance, it's still unfolding; open mid-2010+.

Vintage	08	07	06	05	04	03
WR	6	6	6	6	4	5
Drink	09-15	09-14	09-13	09-12	09-10	09-10

DRY $39 AV

Judge Rock Venus Central Otago Pinot Noir   ★★★☆

The 2008 vintage (★★★☆) from this Alexandra-based producer is a floral, single-vineyard wine with cherry, spice and herb aromas and flavours, showing some complexity, elegance and charm.

Vintage	08	07	06
WR	6	6	5
Drink	09-12	09-11	09-10

DRY $28 AV

Julicher 99 Rows Martinborough Pinot Noir — see 99 Rows Martinborough Pinot Noir

Julicher Martinborough Pinot Noir   ★★★★

Estate-grown on the Te Muna Terraces, the 2007 vintage (★★★☆) was hand-picked at 22 to 25 brix and matured for a year in French oak casks (25 per cent new). Dark, with a distinctly leafy bouquet, it has rich cherry, plum and herb flavours, seasoned with smoky oak, and good complexity and density.

Vintage	07	06	05	04	03	02
WR	6	7	6	5	5	5
Drink	09-14	09-13	09-13	09-10	09-10	P

DRY $39 AV

Junction, The, Front Row Pinot Noir   (★★★)

Grown on the Takapau Plains, in Central Hawke's Bay, the 2007 vintage (★★★) is clearly varietal, with youthful, ruby colour and a cherryish, slightly spicy bouquet, showing some complexity. Ripe and rounded, it's a moderately concentrated red, enjoyable from now onwards.

DRY $30 –V

Kahurangi Estate Nelson Pinot Noir   (★★☆)

The 2008 vintage (★★☆) is a light style, but clearly varietal. Pale and light-bodied, it has fresh, straightforward berry and spice flavours, with gentle tannins. A pleasant, drink-young style.

DRY $22 –V

Kaimira Estate Vintner's Selection Pinot Noir   ★★★

Estate-grown at Brightwater, in Nelson, the 2008 vintage (★★★) was matured for 10 months in French oak barriques (30 per cent new). Ruby-hued, it is mouthfilling (14 per cent alcohol), with ripe, moderately concentrated berry and plum flavours, gentle tannins and a smooth finish.

Vintage	08
WR	6
Drink	09-14

DRY $30 –V

Kaituna Valley Canterbury Pinot Noir   (★★★)

From two vineyards on Banks Peninsula, the 2006 vintage (★★★) is a developed, spicy red with some fruit richness and earthy, herbal touches adding complexity. Ready.

DRY $27 –V

Kaituna Valley Canterbury The Bone Hill Vineyard Pinot Noir   (★★★★)

From a hillside vineyard in the Kaituna Valley, on Banks Peninsula, the 2006 vintage (★★★★) is a scented, supple red, deeply coloured, with cherryish, spicy, slightly nutty flavours and smooth tannins. Mouthfilling and generous, with good complexity, it's maturing well.

DRY $39 AV

Kaituna Valley Canterbury The Kaituna Vineyard Pinot Noir ★★★★★

This striking Canterbury red flows from a warm and sheltered site on Banks Peninsula, south of Christchurch. Of the total area of Pinot Noir vines, a third was planted between 1977 and 1979; the rest was established in 1997. The wine is matured for over a year in Burgundy oak casks (50 to 70 per cent new). Brightly coloured, the 2006 vintage (★★★☆) shows some concentration and complexity, but is less fragrant and well-rounded than a top vintage.

Vintage	05	04	03	02	01	00
WR	7	7	7	7	7	7
Drink	09-12	09-12	09-10	P	P	P

DRY $45 AV

Kaituna Valley Marlborough The Awatere Vineyard Pinot Noir ★★★★

This Marlborough wine is typically powerful, robust and crammed with flavour. Richly coloured, it is scented, with mouthfilling body and a strong surge of cherry, herb and spice flavours, although leafy notes sometimes detract from the otherwise sweet fruit characters. The 2006 (★★☆) is a lesser vintage. Matured in French oak barriques (40 per cent new), it is full-coloured, with plum, herb and rhubarb flavours that lack real ripeness and richness.

Vintage	05	04	03	02	01	00
WR	7	7	7	7	7	7
Drink	09-10	09-10	09-10	P	P	P

DRY $43 –V

Kawarau Estate Central Otago Pinot Noir ★★★

Estate-grown organically at Lowburn, the 2008 vintage (★★) was hand-picked and matured for 10 months in French oak barriques (mostly seasoned). Ruby-hued, it's a light style with plum and herb flavours, lacking real ripeness and richness.

Vintage	08	07	06
WR	6	5	6
Drink	09-12	09-11	09-10

DRY $30 –V

Kawarau Estate Reserve Pinot Noir ★★★☆

Grown organically at Pisa Flats, in the Cromwell Basin of Central Otago, at its best this is a classy, powerful and complex wine. Fermented with indigenous yeasts and matured for 10 months in French oak barriques (30 per cent new), the 2007 (★★★) is earthy and savoury, slightly herbal and nutty, with gentle tannins and some elegance. The 2008 vintage (★★★☆) is ruby-hued, mouthfilling, vibrant and supple, with cherry and spice flavours, showing moderate concentration and good complexity.

Vintage	08	07	06	05	04	03
WR	6	7	7	5	5	7
Drink	10-14	09-13	09-12	09-11	09-10	P

DRY $43 –V

Kennedy Point Marlborough Pinot Noir (★★★☆)

From a Waiheke Island-based producer, the 2008 vintage (★★★☆) was fermented with indigenous yeasts and matured in French oak for 16 months. It's a supple, fruity wine with ripe plum and spice flavours, showing good varietal character, and some savoury complexity.

DRY $35 –V

Kerner Estate Marlborough Pinot Noir   (★★★★)

The stylish 2008 vintage (★★★★) is a single-vineyard, hand-harvested Wairau Valley red, fermented with indigenous yeasts and matured in seasoned French oak barrels. Floral and supple, it is intensely varietal, with ripe cherry and nut flavours, silky textured and showing good complexity and charm. Delicious drinking now onwards.

Vintage 08
WR   5
Drink   09-13

DRY $35 AV

Kim Crawford Marlborough Pinot Noir   ★★☆

The 2007 (★★★) is vibrantly fruity, with cherryish, plummy, smooth flavours. The 2008 vintage (★★☆), aged in tanks and barrels, is a light ruby, pleasant, easy-drinking red, but lacks the richness you'd expect at its price.

DRY $23 –V

Kim Crawford SP Kim's Favourite Marlborough Pinot Noir   (★★★★)

Grown mostly in the Waihopai Valley, the 2007 vintage (★★★★) was only partly oak-aged. Delicious young, it's a softly structured wine with deep cherry, plum and spice flavours, showing good richness and roundness.

DRY $34 AV

Kim Crawford SP Rise & Shine Creek Central Otago Pinot Noir   ★★★☆

Grown at Bendigo and partly oak-matured, the 2007 vintage (★★★☆) has bold, youthful colour. Fruit-packed, but only moderately complex, it has strong, ripe, dark plum and spice flavours, with a hint of liquorice, and supple tannins.

DRY $34 –V

Kina Beach Vineyard Reserve Pinot Noir   ★★★★

Estate-grown at Tasman, on the Nelson coast, the 2007 vintage (★★★★) was matured for 14 months in French oak barriques (one-third new). Ruby-hued, it's an intensely varietal wine with strong cherry, plum, spice and herb flavours, showing good, savoury complexity. Ready; no rush.

Vintage 07
WR   7
Drink   09-15

DRY $40 AV

Kingsmill Tippet's Dam Central Otago Pinot Noir   ★★★★☆

A single-vineyard Bannockburn red, the 2007 vintage (★★★★★) was hand-picked, matured for eight months in French oak barriques (40 per cent new) and bottled unfined. Finely scented, it's a flowing wine with lovely generosity, vibrancy and harmony. Deeply coloured, with impressively concentrated cherry, plum and spice flavours, deliciously savoury and supple, it is already hard to resist.

Vintage 07   06
WR   6   5
Drink   09-14 09-12

DRY $47 –V

Kings Road Waipara Pinot Noir – see Boundary Vineyards Kings Road Waipara Pinot Noir

Kono Marlborough Pinot Noir   (★★★)

From Tohu, the 2006 vintage (★★★) is a ruby-hued, mellow red with supple, cherryish flavours, showing some savoury complexity. Enjoyable now.

DRY $21 AV

Konrad Marlborough Pinot Noir   ★★★

The 2008 vintage (★★☆) is light ruby, with moderate depth of cherry, plum and herb flavours in a smooth, drink-young style. Ready.

Vintage	08	07
WR	4	4
Drink	09-14	09-11

DRY $30 –V

Koru Pinot Noir   ★★★★★

This rare, distinguished wine flows from a tiny, 1.1-hectare vineyard at the foot of the Wither Hills, near Blenheim, in Marlborough. The intensely varietal 2007 vintage (★★★★★) was French oak-matured and bottled unfined and unfiltered. Full, bright ruby, it is finely scented, mouthfilling, rich and supple. Very sweet-fruited, graceful and flowing, it has ripe cherry/plum flavours, deliciously deep, harmonious and silky-textured, in a lush, 'feminine' style of Pinot Noir, for drinking now or cellaring.

Vintage	07	06	05	04
WR	7	7	7	6
Drink	09-22	09-20	09-18	09-15

DRY $78 AV

Koura Bay Blue Duck Awatere Valley Marlborough Pinot Noir   ★★★★

The latest vintages have been silky and sensuous. The 2008 (★★★☆) was estate-grown and matured for 11 months in French oak barriques. Floral, sweet-fruited and supple, it's a moderately complex wine with strong, vibrant, cherry and plum flavours, still youthful; open mid-2010+.

Vintage	08	07
WR	5	6
Drink	09-12	09-14

DRY $25 V+

Kumeu River Estate Pinot Noir   ★★★★

This West Auckland red is different to the floral, buoyant reds grown in the south – less overtly varietal, more earthy and 'red-winey'. The 2006 vintage (★★★★), matured for a year in French oak barriques, was grown in the Hunting Hill Vineyard, across the road from the winery, above Mate's Vineyard. Full-coloured, with a ripe, spicy fragrance and flavours, it is sweet-fruited and savoury, with good density and complexity. The 2007 (★★★★) is vibrant, with plum/spice flavours, slightly earthy and savoury, fairly firm tannins, and good freshness, complexity and structure. Best drinking 2010+.

Vintage	08	07	06	05	04	03	02
WR	6	7	7	5	NM	6	4
Drink	10-15	09-15	09-13	09-11	NM	P	P

DRY $36 AV

Kumeu River Village Pinot Noir   ★★★

Grown at Kumeu, in West Auckland, and French oak-aged for a year, the 2007 vintage (★★★) is medium-bodied and supple, with delicate cherry/plum flavours and earthy notes adding a touch of complexity. Drink now onwards.

DRY $18 V+

Kurow Village Waitaki Valley Pinot Noir   (★★★☆)

An ideal introduction to the North Otago region's reds, the 2008 vintage (★★★☆) is floral and supple, with good depth of ripe cherry and plum flavours, showing some complexity.

DRY $26 AV

Lake Chalice Marlborough Pinot Noir   ★★★

The 2007 vintage (★★★) is ruby-hued, with fresh, smooth berry/plum flavours and a hint of toasty oak in a lively, fruit-driven style.

DRY $23 AV

Lake Chalice The Raptor Marlborough Pinot Noir   (★★★★)

The debut 2006 vintage (★★★★) was harvested by hand at 24.5 brix and matured in French oak barriques (45 per cent new). Full ruby, it is vibrantly fruity and smooth, with gentle tannins and ripe cherry/plum flavours. Elegant, warm and silky, with some savoury complexity, it's delicious young.

DRY $27 V+

Lake Hayes Central Otago Pinot Noir   ★★★★

From Amisfield, the 2008 vintage (★★★★) was matured in French oak casks (20 per cent new). Full ruby, it is floral and vibrantly fruity, with fresh, generous cherry and plum flavours, some savoury complexity, and great drink-young appeal.

Vintage	08	07	06
WR	6	6	6
Drink	09-12	09-10	09-10

DRY $30 AV

Lamont Central Otago Pinot Noir   ★★★☆

The 2006 vintage (★★★★) is a single-vineyard red, grown at Bendigo, and matured for a year in French oak barriques (35 per cent new). It's a classy wine, mouthfilling and savoury, with ripe cherry and spice flavours, showing excellent complexity.

Vintage	06
WR	7
Drink	09-16

DRY $38 –V

La Strada Marlborough Pinot Noir   ★★★★

Made by Fromm, this wine is designed to be ready for drinking upon release, by selecting suitable sites and clones, and 'steering the fermentation towards more fruit expression and moderate tannins and structure'. The 2007 vintage (★★★★) was matured for over a year in French oak barriques (10–20 per cent new). Full-bodied, savoury and supple, it has cherry and spice flavours, showing excellent ripeness, depth, complexity and harmony. It's delicious now.

Vintage	07	06	05	04
WR	7	7	6	6
Drink	09-14	09-13	09-12	09-11

DRY $35 AV

Latitude 41 New Zealand Pinot Noir   ★★☆

From Spencer Hill, the 2008 vintage (★★☆) is a blend of Marlborough and Nelson grapes, fermented with indigenous yeasts and aged 'on' oak (meaning not barrel-aged). Light and slightly developed in colour, it has cherry, spice and slight herb flavours, with a touch of complexity and firm tannins, but leafy notes detract.

DRY $21 –V

Lawson's Dry Hills Marlborough Pinot Noir   ★★★☆

The 2007 vintage (★★★★) was grown at two sites in the Brancott and Waihopai valleys, hand-picked at 24.3 brix, and matured in French oak barriques (25 per cent new). Fragrant and ruby-hued, it has strong plum, cherry and spice flavours, showing some savoury complexity, and supple tannins.

Vintage	07	06
WR	7	5
Drink	09-12	P

DRY $29 AV

Lime Rock Pinot Noir   ★★★

The 2007 vintage (★★★☆) was grown in Central Hawke's Bay and matured in French oak casks. A generous wine with vibrant cherry and plum flavours, a hint of herbs and some savoury complexity, it is ruby-hued, with clear-cut varietal characters and the potential for further aging.

Vintage	07
WR	6
Drink	09-15

DRY $29 –V

Lime Rock White Knuckle Hill Pinot Noir   (★★★★)

The debut 2007 vintage (★★★★) is Lime Rock's reserve wine, hand-harvested in Central Hawke's Bay from 'the tops of the hills and in the Secret Vineyard, where the soils are shallow'. French oak-aged for eight months, it is boldly coloured and notably powerful, with concentrated, lush, sweet-fruit flavours of plums and spices, some savoury oak complexity and obvious cellaring potential.

Vintage	07
WR	7
Drink	09-14

DRY $40 AV

Lindis River Central Otago Pinot Noir   ★★★★

Grown in the Ardgour Valley, 5 kilometres north of Bendigo, the 2007 vintage (★★★★) is full of personality. Matured for 11 months in French oak casks (30 per cent new), it is savoury, supple and finely poised, with concentrated cherry, spice and slight herb flavours, showing good complexity. It's drinking well now.

DRY $35 AV

Lindis River One by One Central Otago Pinot Noir   (★★★☆)

Barrel-aged for 18 months (longer than its stablemate, above), the 2006 vintage (★★★☆) is ruby-hued, with a hint of development. Released in April 2009, it's a savoury, spicy, slightly herbal and nutty red, ready now. (There is no 2007 or 2008.)

DRY $40 –V

Lochaburn Central Otago Pinot Noir   ★★★☆

The 2007 vintage (★★★☆) was matured for 11 months in French oak casks (30 per cent new). Full-coloured and scented, it has very satisfying depth of cherry, spice and herb flavours, showing some savoury complexity, and good length. The 2008 (★★★☆) is floral and supple, with fresh, ripe, sweet-fruit flavours of plums and spices, already enjoyable.

Vintage	07	06
WR	6	5
Drink	09-13	09-12

DRY $35 –V

Lowburn Ferry Central Otago Pinot Noir   ★★★★

Estate-grown at Lowburn, in the Cromwell Basin, the 2008 vintage (★★★★) was matured for 10 months in French oak barriques (20 per cent new). Full-flavoured and firmly structured, it is deeply coloured, with rich, ripe, cherryish fruit flavours and a spicy, savoury complexity.

Vintage	08	07	06	05	04	03
WR	6	6	5	6	NM	7
Drink	10-14	09-14	09-13	09-10	NM	P

DRY $41 –V

Mahi Rive Vineyard Marlborough Pinot Noir   ★★★★☆

The delicious 2007 vintage (★★★★☆) was hand-harvested at a relatively warm site at Rapaura, fermented with indigenous yeasts, barrel-aged for 15 months, and bottled unfiltered. The bouquet is fragrant, with very ripe cherry, spice and liquorice aromas; the palate is mouthfilling (14 per cent alcohol), rich and rounded. Bursting with ripe-fruit flavours, it's a robust wine, savoury and silky smooth, with drink-young appeal, but also the power to age.

Vintage	07
WR	6
Drink	09-16

DRY $45 AV

Main Divide Canterbury Pinot Noir   ★★★★

A consistently rewarding, drink-young style from Pegasus Bay. The 2008 vintage (★★★★) was fermented with indigenous yeasts and matured for a year in French oak barriques. It is full-coloured, very generous and well-rounded, with strong, ripe plum and spice flavours, oak complexity, and a seductively smooth finish. Fine value.

Vintage	08	07	06	05	04
WR	7	6	7	7	7
Drink	09-13	09-12	09-12	09-10	09-10

DRY $25 V+

Main Divide Te Hau Selection Waipara Valley Pinot Noir   ★★★★☆

From Pegasus Bay, the 2007 vintage (★★★★☆) was matured for 18 months in French oak barriques (30 per cent new). Already delicious, but still unfolding, it is a generous, full-coloured

red with concentrated, ripe cherry and plum flavours, finely integrated oak, gentle tannins and a nutty, savoury complexity.

Vintage	07	06	DRY $33 V+
WR	6	5	
Drink	09-15	09-13	

Main Divide Tipinui Selection Marlborough Pinot Noir   ★★★★

From Pegasus Bay, the 2007 vintage (★★★★) was grown on clay slopes in the Brancott Valley, hand-picked, and matured for 18 months in French oak barriques (30 per cent new). Fleshy, rich and supple, it is deeply coloured, sturdy and sweet-fruited, with strong, youthful cherry and plum flavours, gently seasoned with oak.

Vintage	07	06	DRY $33 AV
WR	6	7	
Drink	09-15	09-13	

Ma Maison Martinborough Pinot Noir   ★★★★☆

This rare wine from Leung Estate is based on close-planted, low-cropped vines planted in 1995. The 2007 (★★★★☆) is dark and fruit-crammed, with sweet-fruit delights and very fresh, highly concentrated cherry, plum and slight liquorice flavours. The 2008 vintage (★★★★★) is outstanding. Deep and youthful in colour, it is very rich and sweet-fruited, with a wealth of plum, spice and nut flavours. Sturdy and finely textured, it's already delicious, but well worth cellaring.

DRY $35 V+

Ma Maison Martinborough Pinot Noir Cuvée Sabrina   (★★★★☆)

Made from clone 5 Pinot Noir, matured in seasoned French oak barriques, and bottled unfined and unfiltered, the 2007 vintage (★★★★☆) is deeply coloured and fragrant, with very rich, vibrant cherry, plum, herb and slight liquorice flavours, threaded with fresh acidity. It's a classy, very graceful wine, but needs time to soften; open 2011+.

DRY $70 –V

Ma Maison Martinborough Pinot Noir Cuvée Saffron   (★★★★)

Based on the 10/5 clone, the 2007 vintage (★★★★) was matured for 11 months in French oak barriques of mixed ages, and bottled without fining or filtering. It's a concentrated, supple wine, deep and youthful in colour, with fresh, supple plum and slight herb flavours, showing good complexity.

DRY $70 –V

Ma Maison Martinborough Pinot Noir Reserve   ★★★★

The 2006 vintage (★★★★☆) was based on fruit from the older vines and bottled unfined and unfiltered. It shows strong personality, with ripe, cherryish, spicy, nutty flavours and excellent complexity. Firm and savoury, it's a drink-now or cellaring proposition. Ready now, the 2003 (★★★★) is deeply coloured, with sweet-fruit characters, good concentration of cherry, spice and liquorice flavours, and a rounded finish.

DRY $70 –V

Mansion House Bay Marlborough Pinot Noir   (★★★)

From Whitehaven, the 2007 vintage (★★★) is a charming drink-young style. French oak-aged, it is ruby-hued, with red-berry and plum aromas and flavours, fresh and smooth.

Vintage	07		DRY $19 AV
WR	6		
Drink	09-10		

Manu Marlborough Pinot Noir   (★★☆)

From Steve Bird, the 2008 vintage (★★☆) was hand-picked on the south side of the Wairau Valley, fermented with indigenous yeasts, and oak-aged. It's a slightly earthy and rustic red, ruby-hued, with ripe cherry and plum flavours, offering easy, no-fuss drinking.

Vintage	08		DRY $20 –V
WR	4		
Drink	09-12		

Maori Point Central Otago Pinot Noir   ★★★

Grown at Tarras, north of Lake Dunstan, the 2008 vintage (★★★) was fermented with indigenous yeasts and matured for 10 months in French oak barriques (33 per cent new). Bright ruby, with a floral bouquet, it is vibrantly fruity, ripe and rounded, with moderately concentrated cherry, plum and slight herb flavours, a subtle seasoning of spicy oak, and gentle tannins. It's an attractive drink-young style.

Vintage	08		DRY $29 –V
WR	5		
Drink	09-14		

Margrain Home Block Martinborough Pinot Noir   ★★★★

Typically an impressive red, based on 'vines from our original plantings which surround the winery'. Matured for 10 months in French oak barriques, the 2007 vintage (★★★★) is savoury and complex, with a well-rounded finish. Richly coloured, it has fresh plum, cherry, herb and spice flavours, showing excellent concentration.

Vintage	07	06	05	04	03	02	DRY $52 –V
WR	7	7	7	7	7	6	
Drink	10-17	09-15	09-14	09-12	09-10	P	

Margrain River's Edge Martinborough Pinot Noir   ★★★

Designed for early drinking, the 2008 vintage (★★★), oak-aged for 10 months, was 'barrel selected for its smoothness and charm'. Light ruby, it is fresh and vibrant, with ripe cherry and plum flavours, a touch of oak complexity, and gentle tannins giving a well-rounded finish.

Vintage	08		DRY $28 –V
WR	5		
Drink	09-13		

Martinborough Vineyard Marie Zelie Pinot Noir   (★★★★★)

The gorgeous 2003 vintage (★★★★★) was released in late 2006. A tiny selection of three barrels (700 bottles), it was based on vines now 17 to 28 years old, matured in all-new French oak for 18 months, and bottled without fining or filtration. Full and moderately youthful in colour, it is very finely scented, with silky, highly complex flavours, already highly seductive. It's an arrestingly rich wine (as it should be, given the price), for drinking now onwards. (There is no 2004 or 2005, but the 2006 vintage will be launched in late 2009.)

DRY $175 –V

Martinborough Vineyard Pinot Noir ★★★★★

This was the first consistently distinguished Pinot Noir made in New Zealand. An intensely varietal wine, it is typically fragrant, with sweet-tasting fruit and cherryish, spicy, complex flavours. In the past, it impressed principally with fragrance and finesse, rather than sheer scale, but in recent years the wine has become markedly bolder. Grown on the shingly Martinborough Terrace, it is made from vines ranging from young to 28 years old, and matured for a year in French oak barriques (30 to 35 per cent new). Harvested at 24.8 to 25.1 brix, fermented with indigenous yeasts, and bottled unfined and unfiltered, the superb 2007 vintage (★★★★★) is an instantly likeable red, but it also shows real density and potential. Deeply coloured and finely perfumed, it has very concentrated, beautifully ripe plum, cherry and spice flavours, complex, savoury and finely textured.

Vintage	07	06	05	04	03	02	01	00
WR	7	7	7	6	7	6	7	7
Drink	09-18	09-17	09-15	09-12	09-11	P	P	P

DRY $73 AV

Martinborough Vineyard Te Tera Pinot Noir ★★★★☆

Te Tera ('the other') is designed for earlier drinking than its famous big brother. Based on young and mature vines grown in Martinborough, it is hand-harvested, fermented with indigenous yeasts and matured for 10 months in French oak casks (20 per cent new in 2008). The full-coloured 2008 vintage (★★★★☆), picked at 23.9 to 25.5 brix, is already highly enjoyable, with concentrated, flowing cherry, plum and spice flavours, intensely varietal and silky-smooth. Deliciously fresh, rich and harmonious, it's a top buy.

Vintage	08	07	06	05	04
WR	7	7	7	7	7
Drink	09-12	09-11	09-11	09-10	P

DRY $32 V+

Martinus Estate Martinborough Pinot Noir ★★★★

The 2006 vintage (★★★★) is a savoury, complex style with substantial body (14.5 per cent alcohol). Smooth and ripe, with strong plum, spice and 'forest floor' characters and a hint of liquorice, it's already quite open and expressive.

DRY $40 AV

Matahiwi Estate Wairarapa Pinot Noir ★★★

The 2008 vintage (★★★☆) has strong drink-young appeal. Bright ruby, with a floral bouquet, it is vibrantly fruity, with good depth of fresh cherry and plum flavours, a subtle twist of oak, gentle tannins and a well-rounded finish.

DRY $25 –V

Matakana Estate Marlborough Pinot Noir ★★★☆

The 2007 vintage (★★★★) is the best yet. Matured for 10 months in mostly French oak barriques (one-third new), it is concentrated, with deep, bright colour and strong plum, spice and olive flavours. Sweet-fruited, it has ripe, soft tannins and a smoky, savoury complexity.

DRY $32 –V

Matariki Aspire Pinot Noir   (★★☆)

Enjoyable now, the 2006 vintage (★★☆) was hand-picked in the Gimblett Gravels, Hawke's Bay, and French oak-aged. It's a light style with cherry, herb and spice flavours, a touch of complexity, and gentle tannins. Ready.

Vintage	07	06
WR	6	6
Drink	09-11	P

DRY $20 –V

Matariki Hawke's Bay Pinot Noir   ★★★☆

The 2007 vintage (★★★☆) was hand-picked and matured for nine months in French oak barriques (32 per cent new). Ruby-hued and floral, with concentrated, fresh, ripe, spicy flavours and a moderately firm finish, it shows good warmth and complexity.

Vintage	07	06
WR	6	5
Drink	09-12	09-10

DRY $30 AV

Matua Valley Estate Series Central Otago Pinot Noir   (★★★★)

A single-vineyard wine, grown at Gibbston, the 2006 vintage (★★★★) is deeply coloured, silky and generous, with loads of ripe, plummy, spicy flavour. Savoury and sweet-fruited, it's a 'serious' yet charming red.

DRY $25 V+

Matua Valley Innovator Central Otago Pinot Noir   (★★★)

The ruby-hued, mouthfilling 2007 vintage (★★★) was grown at Gibbston and matured in French oak barriques (35 per cent new). Vibrant, cherryish, plummy and spicy, with fresh acidity, it's a moderately concentrated style, balanced for easy drinking.

DRY $25 –V

Matua Valley Innovator Waimauku Pinot Noir   (★★★)

A rare example of Auckland Pinot Noir, the 2007 vintage (★★★) was estate-grown in West Auckland and matured in French oak barriques (20 per cent new). Deeply coloured, it is plummy and spicy, with fresh acidity and a seasoning of toasty oak. A medium to full-bodied style, it's only moderately varietal, but flavoursome and still developing. Open 2010+.

DRY $25 –V

Matua Valley Reserve Release Central Otago Pinot Noir   (★★★)

Ruby-hued, with good depth of cherry, spice and slight herb flavours, the 2008 vintage (★★★) is a vibrantly fruity, smooth red, with lots of drink-young charm.

DRY $20 AV

Matua Valley Shingle Peak Marlborough Pinot Noir – see Shingle Peak New Zealand Pinot Noir

Maude Central Otago Pinot Noir   ★★★★

The 2007 vintage (★★★★), a regional blend, is scented and vibrantly fruity, with generous, cherryish, spicy flavours, good complexity, supple tannins and deep colour. The 2008 (★★★★) is bright ruby, with ripe, sweet-fruit characters, very good depth of cherry, plum and spice flavours, showing some nutty complexity, and a firm tannin backbone.

`DRY $32 AV`

Mill Road Hawke's Bay Pinot Noir   ★★

From Morton Estate and priced right, the 2007 vintage (★★) is ruby-hued, with light, berryish flavours and a smooth finish. Ready.

Vintage	07	06
WR	6	5
Drink	09-12	09-10

`DRY $14 AV`

Mill Stream Pinot Noir   (★★★★★)

Sold only at the cellar door in Marlborough, the 2007 vintage (★★★★★) is a single-vineyard red, from 'the very best Pinot Noir grapes surrounding Highfield'. Hand-picked at 25 to 26 brix, it was matured for 15 months in new French oak barriques. Richly coloured, with a very ripe bouquet, suggestive of plums, spices and liquorice, it is sturdy (15 per cent alcohol), notably rich and rounded, with beautifully concentrated, sweet-fruit flavours. It's already delicious.

`DRY $60 AV`

Millton Clos de Ste Anne Naboth's Vineyard Pinot Noir –
see Clos de Ste Anne Naboth's Vineyard Pinot Noir

Millton Gisborne Pinot Noir   (★★★)

Grown in the La Cote section of Clos de Ste Anne, the 2008 vintage (★★★) is organically certified. Ruby-hued, it has clearly varietal, strawberry and spice flavours, with a touch of savoury complexity.

`DRY $22 AV`

Misha's Vineyard The Audition Central Otago Pinot Noir   (★★★★☆)

Grown at Bendigo, the 2007 vintage (★★★★☆) is a single-vineyard wine, hand-picked at over 24 brix, fermented with indigenous yeasts, matured in French oak hogsheads (100 per cent new), and bottled without fining or filtration. Deep ruby, it is finely scented and savoury, with sweet-fruit characters and strong cherry, plum and spice flavours, underpinned by fairly firm tannins. A fine debut, it's a complex, harmonious red, for drinking now or cellaring.

`DRY $45 AV`

Mission Reserve Pinot Noir   (★★★★)

The 2006 vintage (★★★★) was grown in the Cromwell Basin, Central Otago, and French oak-aged. Deep and youthful in colour, it is sturdy, with strong, ripe cherry and plum flavours, fresh, fairly firm and still developing. Drink 2010+.

`DRY $23 V+`

Mitre Rocks Central Otago Pinot Noir   ★★★★☆

Grown at Parkburn, in the Cromwell Basin, the 2008 vintage (★★★★★) is very polished and refined. Barrel-aged for a year, it is full-coloured and concentrated, with cherry, plum and nut flavours, beautifully ripe, rich and rounded. It's a skilfully crafted wine, with lovely mouthfeel.

Vintage	08	07	06
WR	7	7	6
Drink	10-17	10-15	10-14

DRY $45 AV

Moana Park Small Batch Pinot Noir   (★★★)

The 2008 vintage was grown in Hawke's Bay, hand-picked, fermented with indigenous yeasts and bottled unfined and unfiltered. A light style with vibrant cherry, strawberry and spice flavours, a hint of herbs and fresh acidity, it is slightly savoury and supple. Ready.

DRY $18 V+

Momo Marlborough Pinot Noir   ★★★☆

A drink-young style from Seresin, the 2008 vintage (★★★☆) was grown at four sites, fermented with indigenous yeasts and matured for 11 months in French oak barriques. Ruby-hued, with cherry, herb and spice flavours with some savoury complexity and gentle tannins, it shows good varietal character and some muscle.

Vintage	08	07	06
WR	5	7	6
Drink	09-11	09-15	09-10

DRY $27 AV

Moncellier Central Otago Pinot Noir   (★★★)

The softly mouthfilling 2008 vintage (★★★) was harvested at over 24 brix, fermented with indigenous yeasts and matured for 10 months in barrels (25 per cent new). Ruby-hued, it's a very easy-drinking style, with moderately concentrated cherry, plum and spice flavours, ripe and supple.

Vintage	08
WR	5
Drink	09-14

DRY $34 –V

Mondillo Central Otago Pinot Noir   ★★★★★

An emerging star. This consistently striking red is grown in a Bendigo vineyard owned by Domenic Mondillo, viticulturist for Gibbston Valley, and made by Rudi Bauer. The 2008 vintage (★★★★★) was matured in French oak barriques (30 per cent new). Fleshy, warm and deeply coloured, with lovely fruit sweetness and a strong surge of cherryish, plummy flavour, rich and rounded, it is a lush, finely crafted wine, very graceful and silky, with excellent weight and persistence.

Vintage	08	07	06	05	04
WR	7	6	5	4	3
Drink	09-12	09-11	09-11	09-10	P

DRY $40 V+

Monowai Crownthorpe Pinot Noir   ★★★☆

The 2007 vintage (★★★☆) was estate-grown in inland Hawke's Bay, hand-picked, and matured for a year in French (90 per cent) and Hungarian oak barrels. Drinking well now, it is full-coloured, fruity and supple, with good depth of strawberry, cherry and plum flavours, and toasty, slightly earthy notes adding complexity. Good value.

DRY $22 V+

Montana Reserve Marlborough Pinot Noir   ★★★☆

The 2006 (★★★☆) was matured in French oak barriques (15 per cent new). It's a warm, savoury wine with earthy, smoky touches adding complexity and moderately concentrated cherry, plum and spice flavours. The 2007 vintage (★★★☆) is immediately appealing, with very good depth of ripe cherry, plum and spice flavours, vibrant and supple.

Vintage	07	06
WR	6	6
Drink	P	P

DRY $28 AV

Montana South Island Pinot Noir   ★★★

Since 2006, this multi-region blend has replaced the former Montana Marlborough Pinot Noir. Grown in Marlborough, Waipara and Central Otago, it is matured in stainless steel tanks, large oak cuves and French and European oak barriques. The 2008 vintage (★★★) is enjoyable young, with gentle tannins and good depth of fresh, smooth plum and slight herb flavours.

Vintage	08	07	06
WR	6	6	6
Drink	09-10	P	P

DRY $21 AV

Montana 'T' Terraces Estate Marlborough Pinot Noir   ★★★★☆

Pernod Ricard NZ's flagship Pinot Noir was in 2007 (★★★★★) grown in the Wairau Valley, mostly at Brancott Estate, hand-harvested at over 24 brix, and matured for 10 months in French oak barriques (39 per cent new). A lovely wine, deeply coloured and strikingly perfumed, rich and silky, it has vibrant plum/cherry flavours, showing excellent concentration, warmth, complexity and suppleness.

DRY $40 AV

Montana Terroir Series Forgotten Valley Marlborough Pinot Noir   ★★★★★

Forgotten Valley is an offshoot of the Brancott Valley. The 2007 vintage (★★★★★) is a youthful, highly attractive red, weighty, with fresh, rich cherry and plum flavours, seasoned with toasty oak. It's an impressively dense wine, finely textured and fragrant.

Vintage	07	06
WR	6	6
Drink	09-10	P

DRY $31 V+

Montana Terroir Series Gabriel's Gully Central Otago Pinot Noir   ★★★★

Grown at Bendigo, in the Cromwell Basin, the 2007 vintage (★★★★) is very vibrant and supple, with full colour and concentrated, ripe flavours of plums and spices, showing good texture and complexity.

Vintage	07	06
WR	7	7
Drink	09-10	P

DRY $39 AV

Moonlight Pinot Noir   (★★☆)

From Johner Estate, in the Wairarapa, the 2007 vintage (★★☆) is designed as an 'easy, accessible wine'. Ruby-hued, with a hint of development, it has slightly leafy aromas and flavours, showing some savoury complexity. Ready.

DRY $22 –V

Morton Estate Black Label Marlborough Pinot Noir   ★★★

The 2007 vintage (★★★), from the Stone Creek Vineyard, is full-coloured, mouthfilling and supple, with cherryish, nutty, moderately concentrated flavours, fresh and savoury.

Vintage	07
WR	7
Drink	09-14

DRY $35 –V

Morton Estate Stone Creek Marlborough Pinot Noir   (★★☆)

The 2006 vintage (★★★) is full-coloured, with cherry, plum and spice flavours showing good depth and a firm finish. Drink now.

Vintage	06
WR	6
Drink	09-12

DRY $22 –V

Morton Estate White Label Hawke's Bay Pinot Noir   ★★☆

The 2007 vintage (★★☆) is ruby-hued and mouthfilling (14.5 per cent alcohol) in a relatively warm climate style, spicy, berryish and firm. Ready.

Vintage	07
WR	6
Drink	09-12

DRY $19 –V

Morton Estate White Label Marlborough Pinot Noir   ★★☆

The 2007 vintage (★★☆) has fullish, slightly developed colour, mouthfilling body and solid depth of plum, spice and herb flavours.

Vintage	07
WR	7
Drink	09-12

DRY $19 –V

Mountain Road Taranaki Pinot Noir   ★★★

The 2008 vintage (★★★), from vines planted in 2004 at Kairau Lodge and Vineyard, near Waitara, was harvested at 22.5 brix and matured for a year in seasoned French oak casks. Just 550 bottles were produced. Enjoyable young, it's a fruit-driven style, ruby-hued and clearly varietal, with ripe cherry and plum flavours, restrained toasty oak, and gentle tannins giving a smooth finish.

DRY $30 –V

Mount Dottrel Central Otago Pinot Noir   ★★★★

Grown at Parkburn, in the Cromwell Basin, this is the second-tier label of Mitre Rocks. The 2007 vintage (★★★★) is deep ruby, with generous, ripe cherry/plum flavours, showing good complexity, and a firm, finely balanced finish. The 2008 (★★★★), oak-aged for nine months, is attractively floral, with ripe cherry and plum flavours, finely integrated oak, considerable complexity and good harmony.

Vintage	08	07	06	05	DRY $35 AV
WR	6	7	6	5	
Drink	09-14	09-15	09-12	P	

Mount Edward Central Otago Pinot Noir   ★★★★☆

Alan Brady and Duncan Forsyth aim for 'elegance, fine texture and an enduring structure' – and are hitting the target. Their 2007 vintage (★★★★★) is deeply coloured, in a mouthfilling, savoury, complex style with fresh, rich, plummy, spicy flavours and a deliciously silky texture.

Vintage	07	06	05	04	03	02	DRY $45 AV
WR	6	6	6	6	6	7	
Drink	09-14	09-13	09-12	09-11	09-10	P	

Mount Edward Morrison Vineyard Pinot Noir   (★★★★★)

The debut 2007 vintage (★★★★★) of this Central Otago red is deeply coloured and powerful, in a voluptuous style, lush and soft, with deep cherry, plum, spice and liquorice flavours, concentrated and silky. It was grown in the company's vineyard at Lowburn.

DRY $65 AV

Mount Edward Muirkirk Pinot Noir   (★★★★★)

From Bannockburn, in Central Otago, the 2008 vintage (★★★★★) is mouthfilling, richly coloured, layered and supple, with very sweet fruit characters and strong cherry, plum and spice flavours, showing lovely texture, complexity and harmony. Savoury and seamless, it's already delicious, but well worth cellaring.

DRY $65 AV

Mount Fishtail Marlborough Pinot Noir   ★★☆

From Konrad, the 2008 vintage (★★☆) is pale ruby, with light cherry and herb flavours and gentle tannins. It's a pleasant, drink-young style.

Vintage	08	DRY $20 –V
WR	3	
Drink	09-14	

Mountford Estate Pinot Noir   ★★★★☆

From a small hillside vineyard at Waipara, Mountford produces bold, rich Pinot Noirs, full of personality. The 2006 vintage (★★★★★) is outstanding. Deeply coloured, it is fragrant, full-bodied (14.5 per cent alcohol) and flowing, with a core of sweet fruit and lovely richness, complexity and harmony. It's a seductive combination of power and finesse.

DRY $64 –V

Mountford Village Pinot Noir   ★★★★

Grown at Waipara, the 2006 vintage (★★★★) is full-coloured (although not entirely clear), with sweet-fruit delights and loads of personality. A powerful wine, it has strong cherry/plum flavours, offering excellent drinking now.

DRY $35 AV

Mount Maude Central Otago Pinot Noir ★★★☆

Grown on steep slopes in the Maungawera Valley, between Lakes Wanaka and Hawea, the 2007 vintage (★★★) was matured for 15 months in French oak barriques (partly new). Full-coloured, it has good depth of cherry and herb flavours, braced by firm, chewy tannins.

DRY $54 –V

Mount Michael Bessie's Block Pinot Noir ★★★★

A single-vineyard red, grown at Cromwell, in Central Otago, the 2007 vintage (★★★★) is a supple wine with ripe cherry, plum and spice flavours, a subtle oak influence, gentle tannins and some savoury complexity.

DRY $39 AV

Mount Michael Central Otago Pinot Noir ★★★

The 2007 vintage (★★★) is an easy-drinking style, full-coloured, with plum, spice and herb flavours, fresh acidity and a smooth finish.

DRY $29 –V

Mount Riley Marlborough/Nelson Pinot Noir ★★★

The 2008 vintage (★★★) was grown in Marlborough (86 per cent) and Nelson (14 per cent), and matured for nine months in French oak casks. It's a pleasant, drink-young style, floral and ruby-hued, with mouthfilling body and gently oaked, vibrantly fruity flavours, fresh and smooth.

DRY $22 AV

Mount Riley Seventeen Valley Marlborough Pinot Noir ★★★☆

Hand-picked in the company's Seventeen Valley Vineyard, south of Blenheim, the 2006 vintage (★★★☆) was matured for 15 months in French (95 per cent) and American oak barriques, new and seasoned. Ruby-hued and attractively perfumed, it's an elegant, savoury style with ripe cherry, plum, herb and nut flavours, underpinned by gentle tannins. Ready.

Vintage	07	06
WR	5	7
Drink	09-10	P

DRY $37 –V

Moutere Hills New Zealand Pinot Noir ★★★

Still developing, the 2007 vintage (★★★☆) is a ruby-hued wine, barrel-aged for 11 months. Floral, vibrantly fruity and supple, it's a mid-weight style with sweet-fruit charm and cherry/plum flavours showing good depth and some savoury complexity.

DRY $40 –V

Mt Beautiful North Canterbury Pinot Noir (★★★☆)

The 2007 vintage (★★★☆) was hand-picked from young vines in the Cheviot Hills, north of Waipara, and matured for 11 months in French oak barriques (30 per cent new). It's a full-coloured red with plum, spice and slight herbal flavours, showing good depth, and some savoury complexity.

DRY $33 –V

Mt Difficulty Central Otago Pinot Noir   ★★★★

This popular red is sourced entirely from Bannockburn vines. The 2008 vintage (★★★★), matured for a year in French oak barriques, is weighty and supple, with full, ruby colour and a floral, spicy bouquet. It's an instantly appealing wine, savoury, sweet-fruited and supple, with vibrant cherry, plum and spice flavours, showing excellent depth and complexity.

Vintage	07	06
WR	7	7
Drink	11-16	09-14

 DRY $45 –V

Mt Difficulty Roaring Meg Pinot Noir   ★★★☆

Grown in the Cromwell Basin (but not entirely at Bannockburn, unlike its stablemate, above) and French oak-aged for nine months, the 2008 vintage (★★★☆) is floral, supple and sweet-fruited, with fresh, ripe cherry/plum flavours, gently seasoned with toasty oak, and some savoury complexity. It's a delicious drink-young style.

Vintage	07	06
WR	7	7
Drink	09-13	09-10

DRY $28 AV

Mt Difficulty Single Vineyard Long Gully Central Otago Pinot Noir   (★★★★☆)

From a vineyard that supplies core fruit for the Mt Difficulty Central Otago Pinot Noir label, this is a more 'feminine' style than its Pipeclay Terrace stablemate (below). The 2007 vintage (★★★★★), matured for 18 months in French oak barriques, is very floral and supple, with lovely, sweet-fruit flavours of cherries and plums, ripe and silky-smooth. It's delicious now.

Vintage	07
WR	7
Drink	09-20

 DRY $90 –V

Mt Difficulty Single Vineyard Pipeclay Terrace Pinot Noir   ★★★★★

A powerful, lush Central Otago red with densely packed, cherryish, plummy flavours, spicy and long. It is grown on a steep, relatively hot slope at Bannockburn, with bony, gravelly soils. Tasted in late 2008, the 2000 was maturing well, building a savoury, nutty complexity, while the star 2002 vintage was still fairly youthful in colour, with beautifully rich plum/cherry flavours, vibrant and harmonious; it's lovely now. There was no 2006 vintage. The full-coloured 2007 (★★★★☆), matured for 14 months in French oak barriques, was bottled unfined and unfiltered. Described by the winery as 'distinctively masculine', it is sturdy, very ripe and sweet-fruited, with a strong surge of plum, spice and liquorice flavours, braced by firm tannins. One for the cellar; open 2011+.

Vintage	07	06	05
WR	7	NM	7
Drink	09-20	NM	11-17

DRY $90 AV

Mt Rosa Central Otago Pinot Noir   ★★★☆

Grown at Gibbston, the 2007 vintage (★★★☆) is a single-vineyard red, French oak-aged. It's a sturdy, full-coloured wine with concentrated, cherryish, plummy, spicy flavours, a distinct herbal thread, and good structure and richness.

DRY $31 –V

Mt Rosa Reserve Central Otago Pinot Noir   ★★★★

Drinking well now, the 2007 vintage (★★★★) is a single-vineyard Gibbston red, matured in French oak barriques (mostly new). Full and youthful in colour, it is weighty and rich, with concentrated cherry, plum and herb flavours, complex, savoury and supple.

DRY $45 –V

Muddy Water Hare's Breath Pinot Noir   ★★★★

From 'a block on limestone slopes at the back of the property', the 2008 (★★★★☆) was hand-picked at Waipara, fermented with indigenous yeasts, and matured for 16 months in French oak barriques (30 per cent new). The best vintage yet, it is fragrant and generous, with full, bright ruby colour, rich, ripe plum and spice flavours, complex and savoury, and the tannin structure to age.

Vintage	08	07	06
WR	7	7	7
Drink	09-15	09-15	09-12

DRY $50 –V

Muddy Water Slowhand Pinot Noir   ★★★★★

Since 2006 (★★★★★), this label has replaced Mojo as the Waipara winery's top red. Based on the oldest vines (clone 10/5), 'tended by slow hands', it always reveals outstanding personality. Hand-picked at 24.7 to 25.4 brix from ultra-low-yielding vines (2.2 tonnes/hectare), and fermented with indigenous yeasts, the 2007 vintage (★★★★★) was matured for 16 months in French oak barriques (30 per cent new). Rich and youthful in colour, it is dense, savoury and silky, with cherry, spice and herb flavours showing lovely depth, flow and complexity. Drink now or cellar.

Vintage	07
WR	7
Drink	09-15

DRY $65 AV

Muddy Water Waipara Pinot Noir   ★★★★☆

The impressive 2007 vintage (★★★★☆) was hand-picked at 22.6 to 25.5 brix, fermented with indigenous yeasts, and matured in French oak barriques (30 per cent new). Richly coloured, it is very fragrant, generous and supple, in a notably savoury, earthy and complex style, delicious now, but with the power and structure to age.

Vintage	07
WR	7
Drink	09-15

DRY $42 AV

Mud House Central Otago Pinot Noir   (★★★☆)

The scented and supple 2008 vintage (★★★☆) was grown at Bendigo and partly oak-aged. It's a vibrant, cherryish and plummy wine, with fresh acidity and very good depth.

DRY $27 AV

Mud House Marlborough Pinot Noir   (★★★)

Enjoyable now, the 2008 vintage (★★★) is a fruit-driven style with vibrant cherry and spice flavours, fresh and supple.

DRY $27 –V

Mud House Swan Central Otago Pinot Noir   ★★★☆

Grown at Bendigo, in the Cromwell Basin, and partly oak-aged, the 2008 vintage (★★★★) is a youthful, deeply coloured red, full-bodied, with a strong surge of cherryish, plummy flavour, gently seasoned with oak. Fruit-packed and supple, it shows good muscle and depth.

DRY $30 AV

Murdoch James Blue Rock Pinot Noir   ★★★☆

Estate-grown just south of Martinborough, the 2007 vintage (★★★☆) was matured for a year in French oak barriques (30 per cent new). Ruby-hued, it is fresh and fruity, with good depth of cherry, plum and herb flavours, gentle tannins and some spicy, savoury complexity. Enjoyable young.

Vintage	07	06	05
WR	6	6	6
Drink	09-13	P	P

DRY $35 –V

Murdoch James Fraser Pinot Noir   ★★★☆

Past vintages were a single-vineyard red, grown on the Martinborough Terrace, but the 2006 (★★★☆) is a blend of the 'very best barrels'. Oak-aged for 18 months, it's a gutsy, firm wine with cherry, coffee and spice flavours, showing considerable development.

Vintage	07	06	05	04	03	02
WR	NM	5	NM	5	4	5
Drink	NM	09-13	NM	P	09-10	P

DRY $65 –V

Murdoch James Pinot Noir   ★★★

The 2008 vintage (★★☆) was blended from grapes grown in Martinborough and other parts of the Wairarapa (although the only front-label references are to Martinborough). Oak-aged for 10 months, it has light, slightly developed colour and fresh, simple berry, spice and herb flavours. Drink young.

Vintage	08	07	06	05	04
WR	6	5	5	4	5
Drink	09-12	09-11	P	P	P

DRY $25 –V

Nanny Goat Vineyard Central Otago Pinot Noir   ★★★☆

The 2008 vintage (★★★☆) is from vines 'up to 350 metres above sea level', described – wrongly – as 'the highest and most southerly in New Zealand'. Floral, ruby-hued and supple, it is moderately concentrated, with ripe cherry and plum flavours, showing some savoury complexity, and lots of drink-young charm.

DRY $35 –V

Nautilus Four Barriques Marlborough Pinot Noir   ★★★★★

The 2007 vintage (★★★★★) was made from four casks chosen from over 120 for 'that special magic'. A blend of three barrels, estate-grown in the Clay Hills Vineyard in the Omaka Valley, and one barrel from the company-owned Kaituna Vineyard, on the north side of the Wairau River, it is rich and youthful in colour, beautifully scented and supple, with lovely fruit sweetness, dense cherry and plum flavours, and great harmony.

Vintage	07	06	05
WR	7	7	7
Drink	09-16	09-16	09-15

DRY $60 AV

Nautilus Marlborough Pinot Noir   ★★★★

The 2007 vintage (★★★★) was hand-picked from six sites, but the majority of the grapes came from clay slopes on the south side of the Wairau Valley. Matured in French oak barriques (new and seasoned), it is ruby-hued, floral, vibrantly fruity and supple, with strong plum and spice flavours and solid underlying tannins. Finely structured, it's an elegant wine, worth cellaring.

Vintage	08	07	06	05	04	03	02	DRY $40 AV
WR	6	7	6	7	6	6	5	
Drink	10-14	09-13	09-12	09-11	P	09-10	P	

Ned, The, Marlborough Pinot Noir   ★★★☆

The 2007 vintage (★★★☆) from Waihopai River Vineyard is full-coloured, mouthfilling, rich and smooth, with plum, spice and slight herb flavours, generous and supple.

DRY $27 AV

Nest, The, Marlborough Pinot Noir   (★★☆)

From Lake Chalice, the debut 2008 vintage (★★☆) was estate-grown in the Wairau and lower Waihopai valleys, and matured for eight months in French oak barrels. Ruby-hued, it's a lightweight style, fruity and supple, with drink-young appeal.

DRY $20 –V

Neudorf Moutere Home Vineyard Pinot Noir   ★★★★★

Neudorf's flagship red is based principally on a block of clone 5 Pinot Noir vines, over 20 years old, in the original estate vineyard at Upper Moutere, in Nelson. The wine is fermented with indigenous yeasts, matured in French oak barriques (usually 35 to 40 per cent new), and is bottled without fining or filtration. The 2006 vintage (★★★★★) is maturing very gracefully. The bouquet is highly perfumed, savoury and nutty; the palate is sensuous and silky, with an array of cherry, spice, herb and slight dark chocolate flavours, showing considerable backbone and muscle. (There is no 2007.)

Vintage	07	06	05	04	03	02	01	DRY $69 AV
WR	NM	6	7	NM	7	6	7	
Drink	NM	09-15	09-14	NM	09-14	09-12	09-10	

Neudorf Moutere Pinot Noir   ★★★★★

Typically a very classy Nelson red. It is grown at Upper Moutere, in the Neudorf home vineyard and the tiny Pomona Vineyard, where the AM 10/5 vines are over 20 years old. The wine is fermented with indigenous yeasts, matured for about 10 months in French oak barriques (20 to 40 per cent new), and is usually bottled without fining or filtering. The 2007 vintage (★★★★) was hand-picked at 23.1 to 25.1 brix. Full and youthful in colour, it is mouthfilling, vibrant and supple, with fresh, rich cherry, plum and spice flavours, a herbal thread, and good complexity and harmony.

Vintage	08	07	06	05	04	03	02	01	DRY $50 AV
WR	6	6	7	7	6	7	6	7	
Drink	09-17	09-16	09-15	09-14	09-12	09-13	09-12	09-11	

Neudorf Tom's Block Nelson Pinot Noir ★★★★☆

This regional blend offers great value. The 2007 vintage (★★★★★), grown at Upper Moutere and Brightwater, on the Waimea Plains, was hand-harvested, fermented with indigenous yeasts, matured for 11 months in French oak barriques (26 per cent new), and bottled unfined and unfiltered. Floral and finely textured, it is mouthfilling, savoury and supple, with rich, ripe cherry and spice flavours, showing excellent complexity, and lovely harmony.

Vintage	08	07	06	05
WR	6	6	7	7
Drink	09-15	09-14	09-13	09-13

DRY $31 V+

Nevis Bluff Central Otago Pinot Noir ★★★☆

Grown at Gibbston and Pisa, in the Cromwell Basin, the 2006 vintage (★★★★) was picked at an average of 24.2 brix and matured for 10 months in French oak casks (25 per cent new). Mouthfilling and supple, with ripe cherry/plum flavours, showing good density and charm, it is a very harmonious wine, enjoyable now.

Vintage	06
WR	6
Drink	08-12

DRY $40 –V

Nevis Bluff Reserve Central Otago Pinot Noir (★★★★☆)

The debut 2006 vintage (★★★★☆) was based on 14-year-old vines at Gibbston and younger vines at Pisa, in the Cromwell Basin, harvested at an average of 25 brix. Matured for 18 months in French oak barrels (half new), it's a ripe, sweet-fruited red with concentrated cherry and plum flavours, seasoned with nutty oak, good complexity and a well-rounded finish. It's already delicious; drink now or cellar. (It was originally released at $58.)

Vintage	06
WR	6
Drink	09-14

DRY $85 –V

Ngatarawa Silks Hawke's Bay Pinot Noir ★★☆

This is the least impressive wine in the Silks range. The 2007 vintage (★★★) is enjoyable now, with smooth cherry, herb and nut flavours, showing some savoury complexity. The 2008 (★★) is light and plain.

Vintage	07	06	05
WR	6	5	5
Drink	09-10	P	P

DRY $20 –V

Nga Waka Martinborough Pinot Noir ★★★★

Typically a refined red, scented and supple. The 2007 vintage (★★★★☆) is dark for Pinot Noir, with a richly fragrant bouquet of plums, liquorice and coffee. The palate is densely packed, very ripe and powerful, with firm tannins. It should be a 10-year wine. There's no doubting the flavour concentration, but has it come at the cost of finesse? Time will tell.

Vintage	07	06	05
WR	6	7	NM
Drink	10+	09+	NM

DRY $45 –V

Nobilo Icon Central Otago Pinot Noir   (★★★)

The 2006 vintage (★★★), grown at Gibbston and in the Cromwell Basin, is a mid-weight style with slightly developed colour, moderate flavour intensity and some savoury complexity.

DRY $24 AV

Nobilo Icon Marlborough Pinot Noir   ★★★☆

The 2007 vintage (★★★) is vibrantly fruity, with plum, cherry and spice flavours, strong and smooth.

DRY $23 V+

Northburn Station Bill's Blend Lot 2 Pinot Noir   (★★★☆)

The 2008 vintage (★★★☆), grown at Bendigo, in Central Otago, is a fruity, drink-young charmer, showing good depth of very ripe cherry/plum flavours, gentle tannins and a well-rounded finish.

DRY $35 –V

Northburn Station Central Otago Pinot Noir   ★★★★

Grown at Bendigo, the 2007 vintage (★★★★) was matured in French oak barriques (35 per cent new). It is full-coloured and fragrant, ripe, spicy and savoury, with a firm backbone of tannin and excellent complexity and density.

Vintage	07
WR	5
Drink	09-11

DRY $42 –V

Northfield Homecreek Waipara Pinot Noir   (★★★)

Matured in French oak barriques (40 per cent new), the 2007 vintage (★★★) is ruby-hued, with plenty of flavour, but green-edged, with a hint of tamarillo and slightly high acidity.

DRY $35 –V

Odyssey Marlborough Pinot Noir   ★★★★

This single-vineyard red is estate-grown and hand-picked in the Brancott Valley and matured in French oak barriques (40 per cent new). The youthful 2007 vintage (★★★★) is weighty, rich and packed with fruit. Mouthfilling and vibrant, it has strong flavours of fresh, ripe cherries and plums, finely integrated oak and good tannin support. Best drinking mid-2010+.

Vintage	07	06
WR	6	6
Drink	09-12	09-11

DRY $30 AV

Old Coach Road Nelson Pinot Noir   ★★☆

From Seifried, the bargain-priced 2008 vintage (★★★) was grown at Rabbit Island and Brightwater, and matured for eight months in French oak barriques (new to three-year-old). Ruby-hued, it is ripely fragrant, mouthfilling and smooth, with satisfying depth of cherry, plum and spice flavours, showing a touch of complexity, smooth tannins and good harmony.

DRY $17 AV

Olssen's Jackson Barry Pinot Noir   ★★★★

This is the Central Otago winery's middle-tier red, but it is usually highly impressive. Estate-grown in The Garden Vineyard, at Bannockburn, the 2008 (★★★☆) was hand-picked at 24 to 26 brix, and matured for nine months in French oak barriques (20 per cent new). Still very youthful, it is full-bodied, ripe and flavoursome, with some savoury complexity and firm tannins, but less concentrated than top vintages.

Vintage	08	07	06
WR	5	6	6
Drink	10-15	10-17	10-17

DRY $42 –V

Olssen's Slapjack Creek Reserve Pinot Noir   ★★★★★

The top label from the longest-established Bannockburn, Central Otago winery is 'made from a careful selection of barrels in those years when the wine is of distinctly superior quality'. The 2007 vintage (★★★★★) was matured for 10 months in French oak barriques (37 per cent new). Densely coloured, it is a complex and generous red with sweet-fruit delights, substantial body (over 14 per cent alcohol) and plum, spice and nut flavours showing great depth.

Vintage	07
WR	6
Drink	10-17

DRY $63 AV

Omaka Springs Falveys Marlborough Pinot Noir   ★★☆

The rich but slightly rustic 2007 vintage (★★★) was matured for 10 months in French oak barriques (one-third new). It's a generous red, full-coloured, ripe and smooth, with earthy, herbal notes and a well-rounded finish. The ruby-hued 2008 (★★) is solid but plain, with simple, berryish flavours and a very smooth finish.

Vintage	08
WR	6
Drink	09-12

DRY $23 –V

Omihi Road SVR Waipara Fields Pinot Noir   (★★★★)

From Torlesse, the 2007 vintage (★★★★) was grown in the Fabris Vineyard and matured for over a year in French oak barriques (50 per cent new). Deep ruby, it's a generous wine with plum, olive and herb flavours, showing good concentration, a savoury, earthy complexity and ripe, supple tannins.

Vintage	07
WR	7
Drink	10-15

DRY $50 –V

Omihi Road Waipara Pinot Noir   ★★★

From Torlesse, the 2007 vintage (★★☆) is mouthfilling, with full, slightly developed colour and plenty of flavour, but green-edged and leafy. Ready.

DRY $30 –V

One Tree Central Otago Pinot Noir   (★★★)

From Capricorn, a division of Craggy Range, the 2008 vintage (★★★) is drinking well now. Ruby-hued, it is fresh and vibrant, with good body and depth of cherry/plum flavours, a gentle seasoning of French oak, and a rounded finish.

Vintage	08
WR	6
Drink	09-12

DRY $19 AV

Opawa Marlborough Pinot Noir   (★★★★)

From Nautilus, the 2007 vintage (★★★★) was hand-picked and fermented with indigenous yeasts. It's a very charming wine, but with substance. Lightly oaked, with a bright ruby hue and floral, red-berry aromas, it is weighty and supple, with sweet-fruit delights, gentle tannins and cherryish, plummy flavours. A delicious, drink-young style.

DRY $28 V+

Opihi Pinot Noir   ★★☆

Grown in South Canterbury, the 2006 vintage (★★★☆) is clearly the best yet. Matured in French oak barriques (10 per cent new), it has ripe, sweet-fruit characters, very good depth of fresh, vibrant, cherryish, plummy flavours, and a well-rounded finish.

Vintage	06	05	04
WR	6	4	4
Drink	09-10	P	P

DRY $25 –V

Orinoco Vineyards Nelson Pinot Noir   ★★★★

Maturing well, the 2006 vintage (★★★★) was fermented with indigenous yeasts and matured for a year in French oak barriques (10 per cent new). Ruby-hued, it is very savoury and spicy, with good complexity and a firm backbone of tannin.

Vintage	06
WR	5
Drink	09-11

DRY $30 AV

Ostler Caroline's Waitaki Valley Pinot Noir   ★★★★

Grown in the Waitaki Valley of North Otago, the 2008 vintage (★★★★) is full of youthful vigour. Mouthfilling and supple, with strong cherry, plum and slight herb flavours, very fresh and vibrant, and good complexity, it's a tightly structured wine, best opened mid-2010+.

Vintage	06
WR	5
Drink	09-16

DRY $49 –V

Ostler Grower Selection Central Otago Pinot Noir   (★★★☆)

From a Waitaki Valley-based producer, the 2007 vintage (★★★☆) was grown in Central Otago, at Gibbston and Lowburn, and matured in French oak casks (20 per cent new). Mouthfilling and full-coloured, with cherry, plum, spice and herb flavours, finely balanced oak and considerable complexity, it's drinking well now.

DRY $35 –V

Overstone Marlborough Pinot Noir   (★★☆)

From Sileni, the 2008 vintage (★★☆) is ruby-hued, with ripe flavours of cherries and plums. Floral, fresh and supple, it's a fruity, uncomplicated style, with drink-young appeal.

DRY $16 AV

Oyster Bay Marlborough Pinot Noir   ★★★☆

From Delegat's, the 2008 vintage (★★★☆) is ruby-hued, with a floral, slightly toasty bouquet. Moderately concentrated, with fresh, ripe plum/spice flavours, it is finely textured, with considerable complexity, and lots of drink-young charm.

Vintage	08	07	06	05
WR	6	6	6	5
Drink	09-13	09-12	09-11	09-11

DRY $25 AV

Palliser Estate Pinot Noir   ★★★★★

A richly perfumed, notably elegant and harmonious Martinborough red, concentrated, supple and attractively priced (reflecting its relatively large volume). Most but not all of the grapes come from the company's own vineyards – Palliser, Om Santi, Clouston, Pinnacles and East Base – where the vines range up to 23 years old. Maturation is for a year in French oak barriques (38 per cent new in 2007). The 2007 vintage (★★★★☆) is richly coloured and finely fragrant, with a strong surge of vibrant cherry, plum, spice and dried-herb flavours, seasoned with toasty oak. Savoury and complex, with ripe, supple tannins, it's an elegant wine, still youthful.

Vintage	07	06	05	04	03	02
WR	6	7	7	4	6	4
Drink	09-15	09-14	09-14	09-10	09-11	P

DRY $42 V+

Palliser Pencarrow Martinborough Pinot Noir – see Pencarrow Martinborough Pinot Noir

Paritua Central Otago Pinot Noir   ★★★☆

The 2007 vintage (★★★☆) from this Hawke's Bay-based winery was grown at Lowburn, Alexandra and Gibbston, and barrel-aged for 10 months. It's a finely balanced, drink-young charmer with strong cherry and spice flavours and ripe, supple tannins. The 2008 (★★★☆) is mouthfilling, with ripe cherry/spice flavours, considerable complexity, fairly firm tannins and very good depth.

Vintage	07
WR	5
Drink	09-13

DRY $37 –V

Parr & Simpson Limestone Bay Pinot Noir   (★★★★)

A single-vineyard Nelson red, grown at Pohara, Golden Bay, the 2006 vintage (★★★★) was matured for nine months in new and older French oak barrels. The bouquet is fragrant and spicy; the palate is medium-bodied, with strong, ripe cherry/plum flavours showing good complexity and a firm backbone of tannin. It's an elegant, savoury wine, for drinking now or cellaring. Priced sharply.

Vintage	06
WR	5
Drink	10-11

DRY $24 V+

Pasquale Hakataramea Valley Pinot Noir   (★★★☆)

Grown in South Canterbury, the 2008 vintage (★★★☆) was fermented with indigenous yeasts, oak-aged for a year, and bottled without fining. It's a medium-bodied red, very fresh and vibrant, with cherry, plum, spice and herb flavours, showing good complexity and depth. It's more leafy than its Waitaki Valley stablemate (below), but more concentrated.

DRY $27 AV

Pasquale Waitaki Valley Pinot Noir   (★★★☆)

The 2008 vintage (★★★☆) was barrel-aged for a year and bottled without fining. Full-coloured, it has a floral, spicy, attractive bouquet, leading into a very youthful wine with moderately concentrated cherry, plum and slight herb flavours, fresh, vibrant and supple.

DRY $27 AV

Pearse & Delaney Central Otago Pinot Noir   (★★★☆)

From a Waipara-based producer, the debut 2007 vintage (★★★☆) is deep ruby, with a scented bouquet. A generous wine, it is vibrantly fruity, with fresh cherry/plum flavours, a subtle seasoning of oak and gentle tannins. It's a moderately complex wine, offering good drinking now onwards.

DRY $35 –V

Pegasus Bay Pinot Noir   ★★★★★

This Waipara red is one of Canterbury's greatest Pinot Noirs, typically very rich in body and flavour. The close-planted vines, planted in stony, sandy soils, range from nine to 23 years old. The juice is fermented with indigenous yeasts and the wine is matured for 16 to 18 months in Burgundy oak barrels (40 per cent new). The 2007 vintage (★★★★☆) is youthful, with deep, bright colour. Deliciously rich, sweet-fruited, complex and supple, it has cherry, spice and herb flavours, fresh acidity and an enticingly scented bouquet.

Vintage	07	06
WR	6	7
Drink	09-14	09-14

DRY $47 AV

🍇🍇🍇

Pegasus Bay Prima Donna Pinot Noir   ★★★★★

For its reserve Waipara Pinot Noir, Pegasus Bay wants 'a heavenly voice, a shapely body and a velvety nose'. Only made in favourable vintages (about one in two), it is based on the oldest vines – up to 23 years old – and matured for up to two years in Burgundy barrels (40 to 50 per cent new). The 2006 vintage (★★★★★) is invitingly scented. Deep and youthful in colour, with concentrated, ripe cherry/plum flavours, showing great delicacy and harmony, gentle tannins and a rich, seductively smooth finish, it offers superb drinking from now onwards.

Vintage	06	05
WR	7	6
Drink	09-16	10-16

DRY $84 AV

🍇

Pencarrow Martinborough Pinot Noir   ★★★☆

This is Palliser Estate's second-tier label, but in top years it is an impressive wine, better than some companies' top reds. The 2007 vintage (★★★☆) is boldly coloured, with mouthfilling body, a restrained oak influence and fresh, strong, vibrantly fruity flavours of plums and herbs.

DRY $22 V+

Peregrine Central Otago Pinot Noir   ★★★★★

This typically outstanding red is also a good buy. The 2007 vintage was grown in the Cromwell Basin (80 per cent) and at Gibbston (20 per cent). The vines' yields are kept low (averaging 5.5 tonnes of grapes/hectare) and the wine is matured for about 10 months in Burgundy oak barrels (35 to 40 per cent new). The 2007 (★★★★★) is delicious now. Richly coloured and concentrated, with cherry, plum and spice flavours, oak complexity and supple tannins, it is fresh, sweet-fruited and long. The 2008 (★★★★) is very finely scented, with moderately concentrated, sweet-fruit flavours, good complexity and ripe, supple tannins. Drink now or cellar.

Vintage	08	07	06	05	04	03	02
WR	5	6	6	6	5	6	6
Drink	09-14	09-14	09-13	09-12	09-10	P	P

DRY $39 V+

Pick & Shovel Central Otago Pinot Noir   (★★★☆)

From Dry Gully, at Alexandra, the floral, supple 2008 vintage (★★★☆) is a highly attractive, drink-young style – and great value. Partly oak-aged, it is ruby-hued, with ripe, sweet-fruit characters and fresh cherry, plum and spice flavours, showing greater complexity and depth than you'd expect at this price.

Vintage	08
WR	5
Drink	10-12

DRY $20 V+

Picnic by Two Paddocks Pinot Noir   ★★★☆

A Central Otago regional blend, the 2007 vintage is an attractive drink-young style, matured for nine months in French oak barrels (30 per cent new). Deeply coloured, with a lifted, aromatic, spicy bouquet, it is fresh and ripe, with very satisfying depth of cherry, plum and spice flavours, a touch of complexity and a smooth finish.

Vintage	08	07
WR	6	6
Drink	10-15	09-10

DRY $28 AV

Pinot NV Pinot Noir   (★★★)

'NV', here, stands for 'envy'. Get it? The 2006 vintage (★★★), grown at Bannockburn in Central Otago, is a robust red (14.5 per cent alcohol), with developed colour and ripe, spicy, nutty flavours, moderately concentrated, but also very firm and a bit grippy. Ready.

DRY $21 AV

Pisa Moorings Central Otago Pinot Noir   ★★★★

Grown in the Cromwell Basin, the 2007 vintage (★★★☆) was fermented with indigenous yeasts and matured for 10 months in French oak barriques (one-third new). It's an elegant, ruby-hued red with moderately concentrated cherry, plum, herb and spice flavours, woven with fresh acidity, and toasty oak adding complexity.

Vintage	07	06	05	04
WR	6	6	5	5
Drink	10-14	10-14	09-11	P

DRY $32 AV

Pisa Range Estate Black Poplar Block Pinot Noir ★★★★★

Grown at Pisa Flats, north of Cromwell, in Central Otago, this is an enticingly scented wine. The 2007 vintage (★★★★★) was hand-picked and matured for a year in French oak barriques (one-third new). A dense, structured style with full colour, substantial body (14.5 per cent alcohol) and impressive concentration of ripe cherry, plum and spice flavours, complex and savoury, it is still fresh and vibrant, with good cellaring potential. The 2008 (★★★★★) is another winner. A powerful, deeply coloured wine, it is mouthfilling and rich, with very ripe, sweet-fruit characters and lovely depth of cherry, plum, spice and slight liquorice flavours. Best drinking 2011+.

Vintage	08	07	06	05	04	03
WR	7	7	7	6	6	6
Drink	10-17	09-15	09-14	09-13	09-12	P

DRY $48 AV

Pohangina Valley Estate Pinot Noir ★★☆

Grown in Manawatu, the 2007 vintage (★★★☆) is the best yet. French oak-aged for nine months, it is deeply coloured, with a spicy bouquet. Mouthfilling, with very good depth of cherry, plum and spice flavours, seasoned with toasty oak, it's a tightly structured wine with fresh acidity and obvious cellaring potential.

Vintage	07	06	05
WR	7	6	5
Drink	09-15	09-13	09-12

DRY $35 –V

Pond Paddock Martinborough Pinot Noir ★★★☆

Grown in Te Muna Road, the 2007 vintage (★★★☆) was hand-picked at 24.5 brix and matured for 11 months in French oak barrels. Deep ruby, with a slightly leafy bouquet and vibrant cherry, plum and herb flavours showing very good depth, it's a moderately complex style, with an attractively silky texture.

DRY $33 –V

Prophet's Rock Central Otago Pinot Noir ★★★★☆

The 2006 vintage (★★★★★), grown mostly at Bendigo, in the Cromwell Basin, was matured for 15 months in French oak barriques (one-third new) and bottled unfiltered. A wine of real stature, it is enticingly fragrant and deeply coloured, with rich, sweet-fruit flavours, concentrated and complex, and ripe, supple tannins. It shows loads of personality. The 2007 (★★★★☆) is delicious now. Deeply coloured, it is rich and complex, with cherry, plum and spice flavours, ripe, nutty and savoury.

DRY $55 –V

Pyramid Valley Vineyards Growers Collection
Eaton Family Vineyard Marlborough Pinot Noir ★★★★☆

Grown on clay slopes on the south side of the Wairau Valley, the 2007 vintage (★★★★☆) is a fleshy, elegant and supple wine with concentrated, ripe plum and spice flavours, savoury and complex, and a silky, sustained finish.

DRY $55 –V

Quartz Reef Bendigo Central Otago Pinot Noir ★★★★★

A bold, fleshy, generous red. The 2008 vintage (★★★★☆) was estate-grown at Bendigo, hand-picked and matured in French oak barriques. Deeply coloured, it is rich and sweet-fruited, with fresh, strong plum and cherry flavours, a hint of liquorice, subtle oak and fine, supple tannins.

Drink now or cellar. The powerful 2007 (★★★★★) is dark, fragrant, sturdy and savoury, with sweet-fruit flavours of cherries, plums and spices, rich and finely textured.

Vintage	08	07	06	05	04
WR	7	7	6	7	6
Drink	10-13	09-12	09-11	09-10	P

DRY $40 V+

Quartz Reef Bendigo Estate Vineyard Pinot Noir ★★★★★

An emerging Central Otago star. Designed for cellaring, it is estate-grown on a steep, north-facing, 'seriously warm' site at the north-east end of Lake Dunstan, at Bendigo Station. The 2007 vintage (★★★★★) is a serious, savoury red. Highly complex, it has deep, youthful in colour and a finely scented bouquet. Powerful, yet also graceful and supple, it has highly concentrated, ripe cherry, spice and nut flavours, with good tannin support, and obvious cellaring potential. The 2008 (★★★★★) is deeply coloured, with dense cherry and spice flavours and ripe, supple tannins giving it early approachability.

Vintage	07	06	05	04	03	02	01
WR	7	6	7	6	7	7	6
Drink	09-13	09-12	09-12	09-10	09-11	09-10	P

DRY $100 –V

Quest Farm Single Vineyard Central Otago Pinot Noir ★★★★

From Mark Mason, co-founder of Sacred Hill, the 2007 vintage (★★★★) was grown in the Cromwell Basin and matured for a year in French oak casks (30 per cent new). Mouthfilling and supple, it's a savoury, sweet-fruited wine with strong, vibrant cherry and plum flavours, offering excellent drinking now onwards. Approaching its peak, the 2006 (★★★★☆) is deeply coloured, concentrated and complex, with rich plum, herb and slight liquorice flavours.

DRY $40 AV

Rabbit Ranch Central Otago Pinot Noir ★★★

The early vintages from Chard Farm set out to introduce a 'new breed of Pinot Noir from Central Otago – affordable, early-drinking, fruit-driven'. The 2008 (★★☆) is a light style, with moderate depth of fresh, smooth plum, herb and spice flavours, enjoyable now.

DRY $22 AV

Ra Nui Marlborough Pinot Noir ★★★

The 2007 vintage (★★☆) is a fruit-driven style, with cherry/plum flavours and a hint of toasty oak. Hand-picked and given an 'aging period in French oak', it was slightly disjointed when tasted in mid to late 2008.

DRY $30 –V

Rapaura Springs Marlborough Pinot Noir (★★★☆)

Fragrant and mouthfilling, the 2007 vintage (★★★☆) from Spring Creek Vintners, oak-aged for nine months, has ripe-fruit flavours showing some complexity, gentle tannins, and very good charm and drinkability. The 2008 (★★★☆) is full-coloured, sturdy and sweet-fruited, with good complexity and depth of cherry/plum flavours.

Vintage	08	07
WR	5	6
Drink	09-12	09-12

DRY $22 V+

Rapaura Springs Reserve Central Otago Pinot Noir   (★★★☆)

The 2008 vintage (★★★☆), matured for 10 months in French oak barriques (partly new), is mouthfilling and supple. Ruby-hued, with buoyant cherry, plum and spice flavours, showing considerable complexity, it's drinking well now.

Vintage	08	DRY $27 AV
WR	6	
Drink	09-12	

Red Tussock Central Otago Pinot Noir   ★★★

From Quest Farm, the 2008 vintage (★★★) is promoted as a 'bistro wine'. Lightish in colour, it is mouthfilling, with satisfying depth of ripe cherry and herb flavours and gentle tannins, offering enjoyable, early drinking.

DRY $25 –V

Redwood Pass by Vavasour Marlborough Pinot Noir   (★★★)

Floral, mouthfilling and supple, the 2008 vintage (★★★) is ruby-hued, with decent depth of ripe cherry, red-berry and spice flavours, and some savoury notes adding a touch of complexity.

Vintage	08	DRY $21 AV
WR	6	
Drink	09-12	

Renato Nelson Pinot Noir   ★★★☆

Drinking well now, the 2007 vintage (★★★★) was grown on the Kina Peninsula and the Waimea Plains, hand-picked at 24.5 brix, fermented with indigenous yeasts and matured for 10 months in French oak barriques (25 per cent new). Full-coloured and weighty, it is concentrated, ripe, cherryish and spicy, with a savoury, nutty complexity.

Vintage	07	06	05	DRY $29 AV
WR	6	5	6	
Drink	09-11	09-10	09-10	

Resolute Marlborough Pinot Noir   ★★★☆

From Winegrowers of Ara, the 2007 vintage (★★★★) was made from vines in the heart of the Ara Vineyard, hand-picked at 23.8 brix and matured for a year in French oak casks (20 per cent new). Ruby-hued, it is graceful and savoury, medium-bodied and supple, with ripe cherry and nut flavours, showing good harmony. Attractively perfumed, it's enjoyable now.

DRY $45 –V

Ribbonwood Marlborough Pinot Noir   (★★★☆)

Already drinking well, the 2008 vintage (★★★☆) is ruby-hued, fragrant and supple, in a light to medium-bodied style with ripe, cherryish, spicy flavours, a touch of complexity and good harmony. (From Framingham.)

DRY $24 V+

Richardson Central Otago Pinot Noir ★★★★★

Still on sale, the outstanding 2006 vintage (★★★★★) was grown at sites in the Cromwell Basin, fermented with indigenous yeasts and matured for 10 months in French oak barriques (40 per cent new). Boldly coloured, it is rich, complex and supple, with dense, well-ripened plum and spice flavours, seasoned with quality oak, and a firm underlay of tannin.

Vintage	07	06
WR	6	6
Drink	09-10	P

DRY $49 AV

Richmond Plains Nelson Pinot Noir ★★☆

Certified organic, the 2007 vintage (★★★) was estate-grown and handled in a mix of new and old oak. Ruby-hued, it has good depth of cherry, spice and plum flavours and a firm, slightly leafy finish. The 2008 (★★☆) is light and smooth, in a drink-young style with cherryish, plummy, herbal flavours.

Vintage	08	07	06
WR	5	6	5
Drink	09-12	09-12	09-10

DRY $23 –V

Rimu Grove Nelson Pinot Noir ★★★★☆

Estate-grown near Mapua, on the Nelson coast, this is typically a rich wine with loads of personality. The 2007 vintage (★★★★☆) was harvested at 23.2 to 26 brix and matured for 11 months in French oak barriques (24 per cent new). Full of personality, it is sturdy, with full, youthful colour and a complex, slightly earthy and savoury bouquet. Weighty, with concentrated, ripe cherry, spice and nut flavours, it is firmly structured and should be long-lived.

Vintage	07	06	05	04
WR	7	7	7	6
Drink	09-21	09-20	09-15	09-10

DRY $45 AV

Rippon Jeunesse Pinot Noir ★★★★

Made from young ('jeunesse') vines (defined as 'under 12 years old') at Lake Wanaka, in Central Otago, the 2007 vintage (★★★★☆) was fermented with indigenous yeasts, matured for 11 months in seasoned French oak barrels, and bottled unfined and unfiltered. Rich and youthful in colour, it is fresh, savoury and concentrated, with sweet-fruit characters and deep, firm cherry, plum and spice flavours. A serious wine with muscle, concentration and complexity, it's built to last. Drink mid-2010+.

DRY $39 AV

Rippon Pinot Noir ★★★★☆

This scented Lake Wanaka, Central Otago red has a long, proud history and is an elegant, 'feminine' style, rather than a blockbuster. The 2007 vintage (★★★★★), picked from mature, ungrafted vines planted between 1985 and 1991, was fermented with indigenous yeasts and matured for a year in French oak barriques (30 per cent new), followed by six months in old barrels. Deeply coloured, it is rich, supple and flowing, with mouthfilling body and strong cherry and plum flavours, savoury and complex. It's a very finely textured wine, with obvious cellaring potential.

Vintage	07	06	05	04	03	02	01	00
WR	7	7	6	6	7	NM	6	6
Drink	10-19	09-15	09-14	09-10	09-14	NM	P	P

DRY $54 –V

Riverby Estate Marlborough Pinot Noir   ★★★

The 2008 vintage (★★★) is a single-vineyard wine, grown in the heart of the Wairau Valley and matured for 11 months in French oak casks (20 per cent new). Mouthfilling, ripe and supple, with decent depth of cherry/plum flavours showing some nutty complexity, it's already enjoyable.

Vintage	08	DRY $29 –V
WR	7	
Drink	09-15	

Riverstone Marlborough/Canterbury Pinot Noir   (★★)

From Villa Maria, the 2008 vintage (★★) is light in body, colour and flavour. Soft and easy, it has fresh, gentle berry and plum flavours. Priced right.

DRY $14 AV

Roaring Meg Pinot Noir – see Mt Difficulty Roaring Meg Pinot Noir

Rockburn Central Otago Pinot Noir   ★★★★☆

The 2008 (★★★★) is a deeply coloured blend of Parkburn, Cromwell Basin (77 per cent) and Gibbston fruit, matured for 10 months in French oak barriques (30 per cent new). Although less concentrated than the 2007 vintage (★★★★★), which shows lovely richness and length, the 2008 offers generous cherry, plum and herb flavours, with the finely textured, silky charm that is the hallmark of this label.

Vintage	08	DRY $39 V+
WR	6	
Drink	09-14	

Rock Face Pinot Noir   (★★★)

From Bishop's Head, the 2008 vintage (★★★) is a fresh, fruity, clearly varietal Canterbury red with moderately concentrated cherry/spice flavours, offering very easy drinking.

DRY $22 AV

Rocky Point Central Otago Pinot Noir   ★★★☆

From Prophet's Rock, the 2007 vintage (★★★☆) is a full-coloured, sweet-fruited red with very good depth of cherry, spice and slight herb flavours. Drink now to 2011.

DRY $32 –V

Rose Tree Cottage Marlborough Pinot Noir   ★★★☆

From Constellation NZ, the 2007 vintage (★★★☆) was matured for nine months in French oak barriques (new and one-year-old). Enjoyable young, it is vibrantly fruity, with cherry, plum and spice flavours, strong and well-rounded.

DRY $24 V+

Rua Central Otago Pinot Noir   (★★★☆)

A drink-young style, the 2008 vintage (★★★☆) is a floral, fruity, smooth-flowing red, made by Akarua. Grown at two sites, including the company's Bannockburn Vineyard, and matured in old barrels, it is ruby-hued, with ripe cherry/plum flavours, gently seasoned with oak, a touch of complexity, gentle tannins and good harmony.

DRY $25 AV

Ruby Bay Vineyard SV Pinot Noir ★★★

The 2007 vintage (★★★) was hand-picked and matured for 10 months in seasoned French oak barrels. Full-coloured, with herbal notes on the nose and palate, it mingles fresh cherry/plum flavours and subtle oak.

DRY $30 –V

St Jacques Nelson Pinot Noir ★★☆

From Blackenbrook, the 2008 vintage (★★★) was matured for a year in seasoned French oak barrels. Drinking well now, it has good depth of fresh berry, spice and herb flavours, with a hint of oak adding complexity.

Vintage	08
WR	6
Drink	09-11

DRY $23 –V

Sacred Hill Marlborough Vineyards Pinot Noir ★★★

The 2007 vintage (★★★) is a ruby-hued, mouthfilling wine with fresh plum/spice flavours. It's not complex, but lively, with good weight, ripeness and length.

DRY $22 AV

Sacred Hill Prospector Central Otago Pinot Noir (★★★★)

The 2006 vintage (★★★★) is a Cromwell Basin red, grown in a Lowburn vineyard owned by Mark Mason, a co-founder of Sacred Hill. Hand-picked, fermented with indigenous yeasts and matured for 18 months in French oak barriques (new and one-year-old), it is ruby-hued and floral, very fresh and vibrant, mouthfilling and smooth, with cherry, plum and spice flavours, showing good complexity.

Vintage	06
WR	7
Drink	09-11

DRY $65 –V

Sacred Hill The Wine Thief Series Dry Run Central Otago Pinot Noir (★★★☆)

Offering lots of drink-young charm, the 2008 vintage (★★★☆) is a single-vineyard red, grown at Lowburn, hand-picked and matured for a year in French oak casks (25 per cent new). Bright ruby, it is floral, fresh, vibrantly fruity and supple, with moderately concentrated cherry and plum flavours, finely integrated oak and gentle tannins.

Vintage	08
WR	6
Drink	09-11

DRY $30 AV

Saddleback Central Otago Pinot Noir ★★★☆

From Peregrine, the 2008 vintage (★★★☆) is a skilfully crafted, drink-young style, hand-picked and matured in French oak casks (20 per cent new). Ruby-hued and floral, with very good body and depth of ripe strawberry and spice flavours, showing some savoury complexity and gentle tannins, it's ready to roll. Verging on four-star quality.

DRY $25 AV

Saint Clair Marlborough Pinot Noir   ★★★☆

The 2008 vintage (★★★) was partly fermented with indigenous yeasts and barrel-aged for eight months. Floral, vibrantly fruity and supple, with a touch of complexity and moderate depth of cherry and spice flavours, it's balanced for easy drinking.

Vintage	08	07	06
WR	6	6	6
Drink	09-12	09-10	09-10

DRY $25 AV

Saint Clair Omaka Reserve Marlborough Pinot Noir   ★★★★

This is Saint Clair's top Pinot Noir. The 2007 vintage (★★★★) was grown mostly in the company's vineyards in the Omaka Valley, and matured for 10 months in French oak barriques (68 per cent new). Deep ruby, it is fresh, vibrant, flowing and supple, with sweet-fruit characters, cherry, plum and olive flavours, gentle tannins and good complexity.

Vintage	08	07	06
WR	NM	6	NM
Drink	NM	09-11	NM

DRY $37 AV

Saint Clair Pioneer Block 4 Sawcut Pinot Noir   ★★★☆

Grown in Marlborough's Ure Valley, 40 kilometres south of the Wairau Valley, the Pinot Noirs from this site are deeply coloured and flavoursome, although sometimes a bit crisp and leafy. The 2008 vintage (★★★☆) was matured for 10 months in French oak casks (50 per cent new). Ruby-hued, it has fresh, vibrant cherry, plum and herb flavours, showing good depth and complexity, supple tannins and a leafy edge.

Vintage	08
WR	6
Drink	09-12

DRY $33 –V

Saint Clair Pioneer Block 5 Bull Block Marlborough Pinot Noir   ★★★★

From clay-rich soils on the south side of the Omaka Valley, the 2007 vintage (★★★★☆) is a dark, full-bodied red, matured for nine months in French oak casks (new and seasoned). Delicious in its youth, it is powerful and sweet-fruited, with deep cherry, plum and spice flavours, supple and harmonious.

Vintage	07
WR	6
Drink	09-11

DRY $33 AV

Saint Clair Pioneer Block 12 Lone Gum Pinot Noir   (★★★★)

Still youthful, the 2007 vintage (★★★★) was grown in the lower Omaka Valley and matured for 10 months in French oak casks (new and older). It has fresh, concentrated, ripe flavours of cherries, plums and spices, seasoned with toasty oak, and a firm backbone of tannin. Best drinking 2010+.

Vintage	07
WR	6
Drink	09-11

DRY $33 AV

Saint Clair Pioneer Block 14 Doctor's Creek Pinot Noir   ★★★★

Formerly sold under a Reserve label, the 2007 vintage (★★★★) was grown mostly in the company's Doctor's Creek Vineyard, south-west of Blenheim. Matured for nine months in French oak barriques (34 per cent new), it's a graceful, supple red with cherryish, slightly spicy flavours, intensely varietal, savoury and finely balanced. The 2008 (★★★★) is full-coloured and sturdy, with ripe plum and spice flavours, generous and sweet-fruited, good complexity and moderately firm tannins. Drink now or cellar.

Vintage	08	07
WR	6	6
Drink	09-12	09-11

DRY $33 AV

Saint Clair Pioneer Block 15 Strip Block Pinot Noir   (★★★★☆)

Full of drink-young charm, the 2007 vintage (★★★★☆) was grown in clay soils in the lower Waihopai Valley, and matured in a mix of tanks and new French oak casks. Full-coloured, it is invitingly fragrant and intensely varietal, with cherry, plum and spice flavours, deliciously fresh, smooth and rich.

Vintage	07
WR	6
Drink	09-11

DRY $33 V+

Saint Clair Pioneer Block 16 Awatere Pinot Noir   ★★★☆

The deeply coloured 2007 vintage (★★★☆), grown in the Awatere Valley, is a medium-bodied style with fresh, vibrant plum and slight herb flavours, showing very good but not great depth. The 2008 (★★★★) is an elegant, youthful red, matured for 10 months in French oak casks (50 per cent new). Bright ruby, it has mouthfilling body, finely integrated oak and strong, ripe cherry, plum and herb flavours, showing good complexity.

Vintage	08	07
WR	6	6
Drink	09-12	09-11

DRY $33 –V

Saint Clair Vicar's Choice Marlborough Pinot Noir   ★★★

Designed as Saint Clair's 'entry level' Pinot Noir, the 2008 vintage (★★☆) was partly barrel-aged for seven months. It's a pleasant, easy-drinking style with light cherry, herb and nut flavours and gentle tannins.

Vintage	08	07	06
WR	6	6	6
Drink	09-11	P	P

DRY $19 AV

Sanctuary Marlborough Pinot Noir   ★★☆

The 2007 vintage (★★☆) from Grove Mill must be 'an attractive, easy-drinking wine', because the back label tells us twice. Light ruby, it has pleasant cherry/plum flavours, showing moderate depth, and a smooth finish. Ready.

Vintage	08
WR	6
Drink	09-12

DRY $17 AV

Sandihurst Canterbury Pinot Noir   (★★★☆)

The 2006 vintage (★★★☆) was grown at Waipara (40 per cent) and on the Canterbury Plains, matured for 10 months in French oak barriques (35 per cent new), and bottled unfined and unfiltered. It's a full-coloured wine, spicy, plummy and cherryish, with a hint of herbs, fresh acidity and very satisfying complexity and depth, although also a slight lack of softness on the finish.

Vintage	06		DRY $38 –V
WR	6		
Drink	09-12		

Sandihurst Central Otago Pinot Noir   (★★★☆)

The vibrantly fruity and supple 2007 vintage (★★★☆) was grown at two sites at Gibbston and matured in French oak barriques (35 per cent new). Ruby-hued, with a floral bouquet, it has cherryish, herbal flavours, showing very good depth.

DRY $30 AV

Sandihurst Waipara Pinot Noir   (★★★)

The 2007 vintage (★★★) was grown at two sites in Waipara and matured for 10 months in French oak barriques (35 per cent new). Ruby-hued, it offers good depth of plum, spice and herb flavours, fresh and firm.

DRY $30 –V

San Hill Pinot Noir   ★★★

The 2007 vintage (★★★★) from Pukeora Estate was grown at altitude at Waipukurau, in Central Hawke's Bay, and French oak-aged for nine months. A big step up from past releases, it's mouthfilling and highly fragrant, with deep colour and strong plum, spice and green-olive flavours, showing good, savoury complexity. The 2006 (★★★) is more herbal and developed, but drinking well now, with some complexity and decent depth of cherryish, spicy flavour.

Vintage	07	06	DRY $24 AV
WR	6	5	
Drink	09-11	09-10	

Savee Sea Marlborough Pinot Noir   (★★☆)

The 2008 vintage (★★☆) is a light to medium-bodied style with pleasant cherry, spice and herb flavours, green-edged, but with a touch of complexity. It's a forward, well-rounded wine, for no-fuss, early drinking.

DRY $18 AV

Schubert Block B Wairarapa Pinot Noir   (★★★★)

Full of personality, the 2006 vintage (★★★★) was grown near Masterton, hand-picked and matured for 16 months in French oak barriques (half new). Deeply coloured, it has a fragrant bouquet of herbs and spices, showing 'forest floor' complexity. Very generous, mouthfilling (14.5 per cent alcohol) and supple, it has good mouthfeel and texture and rich cherry and plum flavours, with a leafy streak.

DRY $60 –V

Schubert Marion's Vineyard Wairarapa Pinot Noir ★★★

Schubert's lower-priced red is based on a selection of clones (mostly Abel and Pommard) designed to produce a 'more fruit-driven style with a softer tannin structure'. The 2006 vintage (★★★☆) was hand-picked and matured for a year in French oak barriques (35 per cent new). Full in colour, with a hint of maturity, it is savoury, spicy and leafy, with herbal notes detracting, but also good flavour depth and considerable complexity.

DRY $40 –V

Scott Base Central Otago Pinot Noir (★★★☆)

From Allan Scott, the 2008 vintage (★★★☆) is a single-vineyard red, grown at Cromwell and matured for a year in French oak casks (25 per cent new). Deeply coloured, it is not highly fragrant but mouthfilling, with fresh acidity and strong, ripe cherry and plum flavours, showing considerable complexity.

Vintage	08
WR	6
Drink	09-13

DRY $35 –V

Secret Stone Marlborough Pinot Noir ★★★

From Foster's Group, owner of Matua Valley, the 2008 vintage (★★★) is mouthfilling and supple, with very satisfying depth of plum and spice flavours, showing good ripeness, complexity and harmony.

DRY $22 AV

Seduction Central Otago Pinot Noir (★★★☆)

From Desert Heart, based at Bannockburn, the 2007 vintage (★★★☆) was hand-picked and matured for 10 months in French oak barriques (30 per cent new). Freshly scented and supple, it's a medium to full-bodied style, ruby-hued, with plenty of berryish, spicy flavour and some savoury notes adding complexity.

Vintage	07
WR	5
Drink	09-15

DRY $28 AV

Seifried Nelson Pinot Noir ★★☆

Matured for 10 months in French oak barriques, the 2008 vintage (★★☆) is light, with cherryish, slightly herbal and spicy flavours, offering smooth, easy drinking.

Vintage	08	07	06
WR	6	6	6
Drink	09-14	09-12	09-10

DRY $21 –V

Seifried Winemakers Collection Pinot Noir ★★★☆

The 2008 vintage (★★★) was grown in Nelson and matured for nine months in new and one-year-old French oak barriques. Ruby-hued, it has fresh, moderately concentrated cherry and spice flavours, seasoned with toasty oak, and supple tannins. Drink now onwards.

Vintage	08	07	06
WR	7	6	6
Drink	09-15	09-14	09-11

DRY $35 –V

Selaks Founders Reserve Central Otago Pinot Noir   (★★★)

The 2006 vintage (★★★) was harvested at Alexandra at 23.8 to 25.2 brix and matured for 10 months in French oak barriques (new and seasoned). Ruby-hued, it has cherry, plum and spice flavours, showing some savoury complexity, but is now fully developed.

Vintage	06
WR	6
Drink	P

DRY $33 –V

Selaks Founders Reserve Marlborough Pinot Noir   ★★★☆

The 2006 vintage (★★★☆) was harvested at 23 brix and matured for a year in new French oak barriques. Full-bodied, with slightly developed colour and very good depth of cherry, plum and spice flavours, strongly seasoned with oak, it shows good complexity, with a moderately firm finish.

DRY $33 –V

Selaks Winemaker's Favourite Central Otago Pinot Noir   (★★★☆)

The 2008 vintage (★★★☆) was harvested at 24.2 brix, fermented partly with indigenous yeasts, and matured in French and American oak barriques. Full-coloured, it is floral, sweet-fruited and supple, with cherry, plum and herb flavours, showing a touch of complexity, and strong drink-young appeal.

DRY $25 AV

Seresin Leah Pinot Noir   ★★★★

Unlike the single-vineyard reds (below), this immediately appealing, lower-priced wine is grown at three sites – the Home Vineyard, Raupo Creek and Tatou – and is less new oak-influenced. The 2008 vintage (★★★★) was hand-picked, fermented with indigenous yeasts, matured for 11 months in French oak barriques (25 per cent new), and bottled without filtering. Deeply coloured, it is generous, ripe and spicy, slightly herbal and savoury, with good density and complexity, and excellent drink-young appeal.

Vintage	08	07	06	05	04
WR	6	7	6	6	7
Drink	09-15	09-15	09-12	09-11	09-10

DRY $37 AV

Seresin Rachel Marlborough Pinot Noir   (★★★★)

The debut 2006 vintage (★★★★) was sourced principally (75 per cent) from the company's Raupo Creek Vineyard, in the clay foothills of the Omaka Valley, supplemented by fruit from Seresin's Tatou Vineyard, at the western end of the Wairau Valley. Matured for 16 months in French oak barriques (30 per cent new) and bottled unfiltered, it's a complex style, very savoury and spicy. Cherryish and plummy, with 'forest floor' notes, it offers satisfying, characterful drinking from now onwards.

Vintage	07	06
WR	7	6
Drink	09-17	09-15

DRY $55 –V

Seresin Raupo Creek Pinot Noir   ★★★★

Grown on clay slopes in the Omaka Valley, the 2006 vintage (★★★★) is a single-vineyard wine, fermented with indigenous yeasts, matured for 15 months in French oak barriques (30 per cent new), and bottled unfined and unfiltered. Very expressive in its youth, it is savoury and sweet-fruited, with an array of berry, spice and herb flavours, showing excellent depth.

Vintage	07	06	05	04
WR	7	6	7	6
Drink	09-17	09-15	09-12	09-11

DRY $45 –V

Seresin Sun & Moon Marlborough Pinot Noir   (★★★★★)

Only 70 cases were made of the 2007 vintage (★★★★★), sold at $120. Designed for the long haul, it was grown in the hillside Raupo Creek Vineyard (80 per cent) and the Home Vineyard (20 per cent), fermented with indigenous yeasts, matured for 17 months in French oak barriques, and bottled unfined and unfiltered. Densely coloured, it has a fragrant, very ripe bouquet of plums and liquorice, leading into a powerful, very youthful palate. Fresh, with rich plum, spice and slight liquorice fruit flavours to the fore, and supple tannins, it is still quite 'primary', needing at least a couple of years to show its best.

DRY $120 –V

Seresin Tatou Pinot Noir   ★★★★☆

Grown in deep gravels at the upper end of the Wairau Valley, the 2005 vintage (★★★★☆) was vinified the same way as its Raupo Creek stablemate (above). Deeply coloured, it is generous and mouthfilling, sweet-fruited and supple, with deep cherry, plum, spice and nut flavours, showing good complexity. It should be long-lived.

Vintage	07	06	05	04
WR	7	6	7	7
Drink	09-19	09-17	09-14	09-11

DRY $45 AV

Seven Terraces Marlborough Pinot Noir   ★★★☆

From Foxes Island, this wine is 'crafted to enjoy its youth in your company'. Hand-picked at an average of 24 brix and mostly matured for eight months in French oak barriques (15 per cent of the final blend was handled entirely in tanks), the 2007 vintage (★★★☆) is a deeply coloured, vibrantly fruity red with strong plum/cherry flavours and gentle tannins. Attractively scented, it has lots of drink-young charm.

DRY $30 AV

Shaky Bridge Central Otago Pinot Noir   ★★★☆

The 2006 vintage (★★★★) is an elegant, intensely varietal Alexandra wine with ripe cherry and plum flavours, fresh, supple and concentrated. The 2007 (★★★☆) is a mid-weight style with cherryish flavours, woven with fresh acidity, and some savoury complexity.

DRY $38 –V

Shaky Bridge Pioneer Series Pinot Noir   (★★★☆)

The 2006 vintage (★★★☆), grown in the Alexandra Basin, is floral and vibrantly fruity, with fresh cherry, plum and slight spice flavours, showing good depth and some savoury complexity.

DRY $25 AV

Shepherds Ridge Vineyard Marlborough Pinot Noir   ★★★☆

From Wither Hills, the 2007 vintage (★★★★) of this French oak-aged red is a floral, finely structured red with vibrant cherry and plum flavours showing excellent ripeness, depth and suppleness. Great value.

Vintage	07
WR	6
Drink	09-10

DRY $20 V+

Shingle Peak New Zealand Pinot Noir   ★★☆

In the past labelled as Matua Valley Shingle Peak Marlborough Pinot Noir, this is now a country-wide blend. Ruby-hued, the 2008 vintage (★★☆) is a pleasant, light red with fresh, strawberryish flavours.

DRY $18 AV

Sileni Cellar Selection Hawke's Bay Pinot Noir   ★★★

Top vintages work well as a drink-young proposition. On the market within six months of the harvest, it's a Beaujolais-style red, made with 'minimal' oak handling. The 2009 (★★★) is ruby-hued, fresh and vibrant, in a simple, charming style with raspberry/spice flavours, slightly savoury and dry.

DRY $22 AV

Sileni The Plateau Hawke's Bay Pinot Noir   ★★★☆

Estate-grown in the inland, elevated Plateau Vineyard at Maraekakaho, the 2007 (★★★☆) has a floral, scented bouquet. Bright ruby, it is youthful, with ripe plum/spice flavours, seasoned with toasty oak, and fairly firm tannins. The 2008 (★★★) has cherry, spice and herb flavours, slightly savoury and toasty.

DRY $35 –V

Sileni Grand Central Central Otago Pinot Noir   (★★★☆)

The 2007 vintage (★★★☆) is a single-vineyard, Bendigo wine with deep, youthful colour and a freshly scented bouquet, cherryish and spicy. Mouthfilling and supple, with very good flavour depth, gentle tannins and some savoury complexity, it offers highly enjoyable drinking 2009–11.

DRY $33 –V

Soho McQueen Central Otago Pinot Noir   (★★★☆)

Still youthful, the 2008 vintage (★★★☆) is exuberantly fruity. Grown at Lowburn and Bannockburn, and matured in French oak casks (40 per cent new), it is ruby-hued, with strong cherry/plum flavours, very fresh and vibrant, and a subtle seasoning of oak.

DRY $40 –V

Soho Marlborough Pinot Noir   ★★★☆

From an Auckland-based company, the 2008 vintage (★★★☆) was matured in French oak casks (33 per cent new). Ruby-hued, it is mouthfilling and vibrantly fruity, with ripe, moderately concentrated cherry/plum flavours, gently seasoned with oak, in a supple, easy-drinking style.

DRY $30 AV

Soljans Barrique Reserve Marlborough Pinot Noir   ★★★

Ruby-hued, the 2007 vintage (★★★) is a light to medium-bodied style, hand-picked and 'aged in secondary wood for 10 months'. Easy, enjoyable drinking, it offers cherry, plum, herb and nut flavours, soft and forward.

Vintage	07
WR	5
Drink	09-12

DRY $29 –V

Soma Nelson Pinot Noir   ★★★☆

The 2008 vintage (★★★) was hand-picked in the Avery Vineyard at Hope and matured for 10 months in French oak barrels (one-year-old). Ruby-hued, it is full-bodied, with cherry and herb flavours showing decent depth, some savoury complexity, and a fairly firm finish.

Vintage	08
WR	7
Drink	09-16

DRY $25 AV

Southbank Estate Marlborough Pinot Noir   ★★★

The 2007 vintage (★★★☆), the best yet, was matured for eight months in small French oak barrels (25 per cent new). Full-coloured, it's a fruit-driven style, with very good depth of vibrant, plummy flavour, a subtle seasoning of oak and gentle tannins.

Vintage	07
WR	7
Drink	09-12

DRY $20 AV

Southern Cross Hawke's Bay Pinot Noir   (★★)

From One Tree Hill Vineyards, a division of Morton Estate, the 2007 vintage (★★☆) is a decent quaffer, with ripe plum and spice flavours, only moderately varietal, but smooth and showing reasonable depth.

Vintage	07
WR	6
Drink	09-11

DRY $13 AV

Southern Eclipse Central Otago Pinot Noir   (★★★★)

From Michelle Richardson, the 2007 vintage (★★★★) is a very elegant, fruit-driven style with mouthfilling body, ripe fruit characters and rich cherry/plum flavours. It's not highly complex, but delicious in its youth.

DRY $35 AV

Spinyback Nelson Pinot Noir ★★☆

From Waimea Estates, the 2007 vintage (★★★) is deep ruby, with plum and herb flavours showing a hint of greenness, some savoury, spicy notes and fairly firm tannins. A decent quaffer.

Vintage	08	07	06	05	
WR	6	7	5	7	
Drink	09-12	09-11	09-10	09-10	P

DRY $18 AV

Spy Valley Envoy Marlborough Pinot Noir ★★★★☆

The 2006 vintage (★★★★) was estate-grown in the Waihopai Valley, hand-picked at 24.5 brix, fermented with indigenous yeasts, matured for 18 months in French oak barriques (25 per cent new), and bottled unfined and unfiltered. Ruby-hued, it is floral, savoury, sweet-fruited and supple, with ripe plum/spice flavours, in a very elegant, intensely varietal style, opening out well with time. Best drinking 2010+.

Vintage	07	06	05
WR	7	6	7
Drink	10-13	09-12	09-11

DRY $55 –V

Spy Valley Marlborough Pinot Noir ★★★★

The 2008 vintage (★★★★) was hand-picked at 23–25 brix, fermented with indigenous yeasts and matured for 10 months in French oak casks (25 per cent new). Weighty and full-coloured, with a spicy, slightly earthy bouquet, it is finely textured, with strong cherry, plum and spice flavours, showing good complexity and harmony, gentle acidity and a backbone of ripe, supple tannins.

Vintage	08	07	06	05	04
WR	6	7	6	6	6
Drink	10-12	09-12	09-11	09-10	P

DRY $29 V+

Staete Landt Marlborough Pinot Noir ★★★☆

This single-vineyard red is typically fragrant and supple. The 2007 vintage (★★★☆) was grown at Rapaura, hand-picked at 24.8 to 26.8 brix, and matured for 18 months in French oak casks (25 per cent new). It's a floral, supple, ruby-hued red with moderately rich cherry, plum and spice flavours, savoury notes adding complexity, and good harmony. Enjoyable now.

Vintage	07
WR	6
Drink	09-14

DRY $39 –V

Stafford Lane Nelson Pinot Noir ★★☆

The 2008 vintage (★★) was hand-harvested at 23 brix and not barrel-aged. It's a simple, drink-young style, with light strawberry and spice flavours and a smooth finish.

DRY $20 –V

Stockmans Station Central Otago Pinot Noir (★★★☆)

From Wild Earth, the 2008 vintage (★★★☆) is a full-coloured red, estate-grown at Bannockburn and Pisa. Cherryish, spicy and savoury, it has good fruit sweetness and complexity, with ripe, supple tannins. Priced right.

DRY $24 V+

Stoneleigh Marlborough Pinot Noir   ★★★☆

The 2008 vintage (★★★) from Pernod Ricard NZ was grown on the relatively warm north side of the Wairau Valley, picked at 23.6 brix, and matured in French oak casks. Bright ruby, it is mouthfilling, with ripe cherry, plum and spice flavours, showing good depth, a touch of complexity, and supple tannins.

Vintage	08	07	06
WR	6	6	6
Drink	09-11	09-10	P

 DRY $24 V+

Stoneleigh Vineyards Rapaura Series Marlborough Pinot Noir   ★★★★

The 2007 vintage (★★★★☆) is deeply coloured and finely scented, showing excellent ripeness, richness and suppleness. It's a complex, finely textured wine with good potential. The 2008 (★★★★) was hand-picked at 23.8 to 25.2 brix and matured for 10 months in French oak casks (42 per cent new). Mouthfilling and smooth, it has cherry, plum and spice flavours, seasoned with toasty oak, showing very good ripeness, complexity and depth. It's a forward vintage; drink now onwards.

Vintage	08	07	06	05
WR	6	6	6	5
Drink	09-11	09-10	P	P

DRY $32 AV

Stonewall Marlborough Pinot Noir   (★★)

From Forrest, the 2008 vintage (★★) is light, simple and smooth, lacking any real depth or appeal.

DRY $19 –V

Stone Paddock Central Otago Pinot Noir   ★★★

From Paritua, the 2007 vintage (★★★) was grown in the Cromwell Basin and matured for nine months in French oak barriques (33 per cent new). Full-coloured, it's an easy-drinking wine with fresh, smooth cherry, plum and herb flavours. The 2008 (★★★) is another drink-young charmer, with mouthfilling body, ripe cherry, plum and spice flavours and gentle tannins.

Vintage	07
WR	6
Drink	09-14

DRY $25 –V

Summerhouse Marlborough Pinot Noir   ★★★☆

The 2008 vintage (★★★☆) is a single-vineyard red, matured for 10 months in French oak barriques. Mouthfilling, it is ruby-hued, with strong, ripe plum and spice flavours, some savoury complexity and finely balanced tannins. Best drinking mid-2010+.

 DRY $30 AV

Surveyor Thomson Central Otago Pinot Noir   ★★★★

The 2007 vintage (★★★★) from this Lowburn-based producer is savoury, with ripe cherry and spice flavours, showing good complexity. The 2008 (★★★★) is a generous red with excellent ripeness, complexity and depth. It's a graceful, savoury wine, showing good 'pinosity' and likely to be long-lived.

 DRY $40 AV

Takutai Nelson Pinot Noir (★★)

The 2007 vintage (★★) from Waimea Estates is an ideal barbecue quaffer. Ruby-hued, showing some development, it has a slightly leafy bouquet, leading into a gutsy, spicy, full-flavoured red, only moderately varietal, with some rustic notes.

DRY $13 AV

Tarras Vineyards Central Otago Pinot Noir (★★★★)

The youthful, deeply coloured 2008 vintage (★★★★) is an elegant red, grown in The Steppes and The Canyon vineyards. Matured in French oak barriques (30 per cent new), it's a mouthfilling wine with excellent depth of warm, spicy flavour and a backbone of firm, ripe tannins.

Vintage	08
WR	7
Drink	10-16

DRY $32 AV

Tarras Vineyards The Canyon Pinot Noir ★★★★☆

Grown at Bendigo, in Central Otago, and matured in French oak barriques (30 per cent new), the 2008 vintage (★★★★☆) is deeply coloured and beautifully scented. Rich and very vibrant, it has strong, ripe, cherryish flavours, finely integrated oak and supple tannins. A graceful, youthful wine, it should reward cellaring; open 2011+.

Vintage	08	07
WR	7	7
Drink	10-18	10-17

DRY $42 AV

Tarras Vineyards The Steppes Pinot Noir ★★★★☆

The 2008 vintage (★★★★☆) is a single-vineyard red, grown at Tarras (a much cooler site than Bendigo, 10 kilometres away), and matured in French oak barriques (30 per cent new). Deeply coloured, it is sweet-fruited, with strong cherry/spice flavours, warm and savoury. It's a dense, rich Central Otago wine with good presence.

Vintage	08
WR	7
Drink	10-17

DRY $42 AV

Tasman Bay New Zealand Pinot Noir ★★

The 2008 vintage (★★☆) was grown in Nelson and Marlborough, and aged 'on' French oak (meaning not barrel-aged). Ruby-hued, it is enjoyable young, with cherry, herb and spice flavours, light and smooth.

DRY $19 –V

Tatty Bogler Otago Pinot Noir ★★★

From Forrest Estate, the 2007 vintage (★★★) was grown in Bannockburn (Central Otago) and the Waitaki Valley (North Otago). It's an attractive mid-weight, with vibrant cherry and spice flavours, some savoury notes and fresh acidity.

Vintage	07	06
WR	6	5
Drink	10-15	09-12

DRY $40 –V

Te Kairanga Estate Martinborough Pinot Noir   ★★★☆

The ruby-hued 2008 vintage (★★★☆) is a highly enjoyable, drink-young red. Based mostly on young vines and oak-aged for six months, it has good varietal character, ripeness and roundness, with fresh, smooth plum, cherry and spice flavours, gentle tannins and some savoury complexity.

Vintage	08	DRY $22 V+
WR	7	
Drink	09-12	

Te Kairanga John Martin Reserve Pinot Noir   ★★★★

The 2006 vintage (★★★☆) is deeply coloured, spicy and nutty, with good complexity, but green-edged and fairly developed. The 2007 (★★★★☆) is a riper style, with good weight, sweet-fruit delights and strong cherry, plum and spice flavours. A powerful wine, it's built for cellaring, but already a pleasure to drink.

Vintage	07	06	05	DRY $50 –V
WR	7	6	5	
Drink	09-16	09-15	09-14	

Te Kairanga Martinborough Pinot Noir   (★★★)

The 2006 vintage (★★★) is ruby-hued, with moderately ripe flavours of cherries and tomatoes and lively acidity. Fresh and supple, with some savoury complexity, it's enjoyable now. (This label has been replaced by the 'Estate' red above.)

DRY $20 AV

Te Kairanga Runholder Martinborough Pinot Noir   ★★★★

This is the middle-tier label. The 2007 (★★★★), matured for 10 months in French oak barriques (25 per cent new), is rich and supple, with sweet-fruit delights and strong cherry, plum and herb flavours. It's an elegant wine, showing good harmony.

Vintage	07	06	05	DRY $29 V+
WR	7	6	5	
Drink	09-13	09-12	09-11	

Te Mania Nelson Pinot Noir   ★★☆

The 2008 vintage (★★☆) was matured in a mix of tanks and barrels. It's a drink-young style, ruby-hued, with light cherry, plum and herb flavours, slightly savoury and very smooth.

Vintage	08	07	06	05	DRY $22 –V
WR	5	7	6	7	
Drink	09-13	09-12	09-12	09-10	

Te Mania Reserve Pinot Noir   ★★★☆

Grown in Nelson, hand-picked and matured for 10 months in French and American oak barrels (30 per cent new), the 2008 vintage (★★★) is sturdy, with satisfying depth of cherry and slight herb flavours, supple and smooth. It's quite forward.

Vintage	08	07	06	DRY $35 –V
WR	5	7	6	
Drink	09-13	09-14	09-12	

Te Mara Estate Pinot Noir   (★★★☆)

The charming 2007 vintage (★★★☆), grown in Central Otago, is floral and ruby-hued, with fresh cherry, plum and dried-herb flavours, some savoury complexity and supple tannins. It's drinking well now.

DRY $36 –V

Terrace Edge Waipara Valley Pinot Noir   ★★★

The attractive 2006 vintage (★★★) is a middleweight style with berryish, slightly herbal and spicy flavours, showing some savoury complexity, and good harmony. The 2008 (★★★) is light ruby, with decent depth of cherryish, plummy, earthy, nutty flavours, showing some complexity.

Vintage	06
WR	5
Drink	09-12

DRY $24 AV

Terrain New Zealand Pinot Noir   ★★

The 2008 vintage (★★), sold in a claret-shape bottle, is a drink-young style with light colour and moderate depth of smooth cherry, plum and herb flavours. Ready.

DRY $13 AV

Terravin Hillside Reserve Marlborough Pinot Noir   ★★★★★

Grown on clay slopes in the Omaka Valley, this exceptional red (until recently labelled Hillside Selection) is harvested from the centre of the slope, fermented with indigenous yeasts, matured for 16 to 18 months in French oak barriques (40 to 55 per cent new), and bottled without fining or filtering. The 2006 vintage (★★★★★) is richly coloured and finely scented. It's a beautifully soft and flowing wine with berry, plum, spice and slight liquorice flavours, very savoury and generous. Showing advanced ripeness and great richness, it's already delicious. (There is no 2007.)

Vintage	07	06	05	04	03
WR	NM	7	7	7	6
Drink	NM	09-13	09-12	09-10	P

DRY $53 AV

Terravin Marlborough Pinot Noir   ★★★★

The 2008 vintage (★★★★) was estate-grown in the Omaka Valley and matured for 11 months in French oak barriques. Deep ruby, it is mouthfilling (14.5 per cent alcohol) and sweet-fruited, fleshy and generous, with very good depth of cherry and plum flavours, and a firm foundation of tannin. It should mature well.

DRY $35 AV

Te Whare Ra Marlborough Pinot Noir   ★★★☆

Estate-grown and hand-picked at Renwick, and matured in French oak casks, this is typically a mouthfilling, supple wine, enjoyable in its youth, with good depth of fresh, ripe cherry, plum and nut flavours.

DRY $36 –V

Thornbury Central Otago Pinot Noir ★★★★

The 2007 vintage (★★★★) from Villa Maria is deeply coloured, in a vibrantly fruity style with cherry and herb notes, fine-grained tannins and excellent flavour depth. The 2008 (★★★★☆) was hand-picked at Bannockburn and matured for a year in French oak barriques (30 per cent new). Beautifully perfumed, it's an instantly appealing wine, full-coloured, with a velvety texture and a strong surge of ripe cherry and plum flavours, rich and rounded.

Vintage	08	07	06	05
WR	7	6	7	6
Drink	09-15	09-14	09-13	09-10

DRY $31 AV

Three Miners Earnscleugh Valley Pinot Noir ★★★☆

This single-vineyard red is grown in the Earnscleugh Valley, between Alexandra and Clyde, in Central Otago, and matured in French oak barriques (30 per cent new). The 2007 vintage (★★★★) is sturdy, spicy and deep-flavoured. Full-coloured, it has fresh acidity, hints of herbs and excellent depth, showing 'forest floor' complexity.

Vintage	08	07	06	05	04
WR	6	6	6	5	6
Drink	09-16	09-11	09-11	P	09-10

DRY $29 AV

Three Paddles Martinborough Pinot Noir ★★★☆

From Nga Waka, this second-tier red is a rewarding drink-young style, and the 2008 vintage (★★★★) offers great value. Matured for 11 months in French oak barriques (25 per cent new), and bottled unfined and unfiltered, it is full-coloured and supple, with warm plum and spice flavours, showing very good depth and complexity, and an underlay of ripe tannins. It's a very satisfying wine, for drinking now or cellaring.

Vintage	08	07	06
WR	7	NM	7
Drink	10+	NM	P

DRY $25 AV

Tiwaiwaka Martinborough Pinot Noir ★★★☆

The 2007 vintage (★★★☆) is a single-vineyard red, grown on the Martinborough Terrace. Ruby-hued, with a hint of development, it's a mouthfilling and savoury wine with firm, spicy, slightly herbal flavours, showing good complexity.

DRY $38 –V

Tohu Marlborough Pinot Noir ★★★

The 2007 vintage (★★☆) was grown in the Waihopai and Awatere valleys, hand-picked and matured in French oak barriques. It has strong cherry/plum flavours and a smooth finish, but lacks real complexity and fragrance. The 2008 (★★★) is a mid-weight style, ruby-hued, with ripe-fruit flavours to the fore, gentle tannins and drink-young appeal.

Vintage	08	07
WR	5	5
Drink	09-10	P

DRY $27 –V

Tohu Rore Marlborough Reserve Pinot Noir ★★★★

The 2008 vintage (★★★★) was grown in the Awatere and Waihopai valleys and selected from the 'very best barrels'. Mouthfilling and generous, it is full-coloured and sweet-fruited, with strong cherry, plum and nut flavours, showing good complexity, supple tannins and a well-rounded finish.

DRY $36 AV

Torea Marlborough Pinot Noir (★★★☆)

Offering good value, the 2008 vintage (★★★☆) is a single-vineyard red, hand-picked in the Brancott Valley and made in a 'fruit-driven style' (meaning lightly oaked). Floral and full-bodied, it has gentle tannins and very good depth of plum, spice and slight herb flavours, showing some savoury complexity. It's delicious young.

DRY $20 Vɪ

Torlesse Waipara Pinot Noir ★★☆

The 2007 vintage (★★★) is ruby-hued, with a hint of development showing. Enjoyable now, it has fresh raspberry, spice and slight herb flavours, showing good varietal character and decent depth. The 2008 (★★) is light and green-edged, lacking ripeness and richness.

DRY $21 –V

Torr Central Otago Pinot Noir (★★☆)

The debut 2005 vintage (★★☆) was matured in French oak barriques (50 per cent new). Fullish in colour, it has slightly leafy, developed flavours, lacking real freshness and vibrancy.

DRY $33 –V

Torrent Bay Nelson Pinot Noir ★★☆

From Anchorage, the 2008 vintage (★★), grown at Motueka, is a pale red with gentle cherryish flavours, light and soft.

DRY $22 –V

Tranquil Valley Marlborough Pinot Noir ★★★

From Huasheng Wines, at Matakana, the 2007 vintage (★★★) is full-flavoured and spicy, with good depth of slightly developed colour, some herbal notes and a firm finish. The 2008 (★★★) is ruby-hued, with a hint of early development. A supple, cherryish red, with good varietal character and a touch of complexity, it's a forward style, already enjoyable.

DRY $25 –V

Tresillian Pinot Noir (★★☆)

Estate-grown in Canterbury, the 2006 vintage (★★☆) was made from young vines. Light in colour, it is fruity and leafy, with a slightly off-dry, smooth finish. Ready.

MED/DRY $28 –V

Trinity Hill Hawke's Bay Pinot Noir ★★★

The 2007 vintage (★★★) was grown at three sites in the cooler hill country to the south and barrel-aged for seven months. Ruby-hued, floral and supple, it's a medium-bodied style with vibrant cherry, plum and spice flavours, a hint of oak and a well-rounded finish.

Vintage	07	06	05	04
WR	5	6	5	4
Drink	09-12	09-10	P	P

DRY $20 AV

Trinity Hill High Country Pinot Noir ★★★★

The impressive 2007 (★★★★) and earlier vintages prove that Hawke's Bay *can* make fine Pinot Noir. Sourced from three vineyards in the relatively cool hill country, south of the Heretaunga Plains, it was harvested by hand at 23.7 to 25.5 brix, and matured for 10 months in French oak barriques (50 per cent new). A classy, medium to full-bodied wine, it is bright ruby, with concentrated, ripe cherry and spice flavours, showing good complexity, and fine, supple tannins. The 2008 (★★★★) is floral and sweet-fruited, with the power to age. The colour is full and bright; the palate offers strong, ripe raspberry/spice flavours, with good density, firm tannins and oak complexity.

Vintage	08	07	06	05	04	03	02
WR	6	6	6	6	5	4	6
Drink	09-15	09-14	09-11	09-10	P	P	P

DRY $39 AV

Triplebank Awatere Valley Marlborough Pinot Noir ★★★☆

From Pernod Ricard NZ, the 2008 vintage (★★★☆) was harvested at 26.5 brix, matured in French oak barriques, and bottled unfined. Full-coloured, it is ruby-hued, scented and supple, in a moderately concentrated style with ripe cherry, plum, spice and slight herb flavours, showing some savoury complexity. Verging on four-star quality, it's a drink-now or cellaring proposition.

Vintage	08	07	06	05	04
WR	6	6	6	5	6
Drink	09-11	09-10	P	P	P

DRY $27 AV

Tukipo River Estate Fat Duck Pinot Noir (★★★)

Grown at Takapau, in Central Hawke's Bay, the 2006 vintage (★★★) is a characterful wine with light, slightly developed colour. Mouthfilling, it is spicy and smooth, with some savoury complexity and good flavour depth. Drink now.

DRY $30 –V

Turning Point New Style Pinot Noir (★★)

From Spencer Hill, the 2008 vintage (★★), grown in Marlborough and Nelson, is based on Pinot Noir (90 per cent), blended with Merlot (5 per cent) and Malbec (5 per cent), to give the 'new style'. Aged 'on' French oak (meaning not barrel-aged), it's a smooth, light dry red with cherry, plum and herb flavours, offering easy, no-fuss drinking.

DRY $16 –V

Tussock Nelson Pinot Noir ★★★

From Woollaston, the 2007 vintage (★★★) was matured for 11 months in French oak barrels (30 per cent new). Full ruby, it is mouthfilling, with plenty of fresh plum, spice and herb flavour. Drink now.

DRY $21 AV

Twin Islands Marlborough Pinot Noir   ★★★

Negociants' red is a drink-young style. The ruby-hued, charming 2007 vintage (★★★) is scented and supple, with fresh raspberry and cherry flavours, gentle tannins, and a deliciously well-rounded finish.

DRY $22 AV

Two Paddocks First Paddock Pinot Noir   ★★★★

Grown in Sam Neill's original Central Otago vineyard, planted at Gibbston in 1993, the 2007 vintage (★★★★★) was matured for 11 months in French oak barriques (30 per cent new). Rich and youthful in colour, it is sweet-fruited, savoury and concentrated, with deliciously deep plum and spice flavours, showing excellent complexity. It's already delicious, but has the structure to mature well.

Vintage	07	06
WR	6	6
Drink	09-14	09-12

DRY $65 –V

Two Paddocks Picnic Pinot Noir – see Picnic by Two Paddocks Pinot Noir

Two Paddocks Pinot Noir   ★★★★

The 2008 vintage (★★★★) is a blend of Alexandra (70 per cent) and Gibbston (30 per cent) fruit, matured in French oak barriques (30 per cent new). Full-coloured, it is already drinking well, with strong cherry, plum, herb and spice flavours, showing excellent complexity. Drink now or cellar.

Vintage	08	07	06	05
WR	6	6	6	5
Drink	10-15	09-14	09-12	09-10

DRY $50 –V

Two Rivers Marlborough Altitude Pinot Noir   (★★★☆)

Grown high in the Awatere Valley (at 333 metres above sea level), the 2008 vintage (★★★☆) was hand-picked in the Aotea Vineyard, fermented with indigenous yeasts, and matured for 11 months in French oak casks (33 per cent new). A buoyantly fruity wine with fresh cherry, plum and spice flavours, showing very good depth, and gentle tannins, it is delicious young.

DRY $30 AV

Two Sisters Central Otago Pinot Noir   ★★★☆

The 2007 vintage (★★★☆) was grown at Lowburn, in the Cromwell Basin, and matured for 14 months in French oak barrels (33 per cent new). Mouthfilling and supple, with cherry, plum and herb flavours showing good complexity and immediacy, it's drinking well now.

DRY $38 –V

Two Tracks Marlborough Pinot Noir   (★★★)

A drink-young style from Wither Hills, the 2008 vintage (★★★) is a ruby-hued red with decent depth of cherry, plum and slight herb flavours, showing good varietal character, and a silky-smooth finish.

Vintage	08
WR	6
Drink	09-12

DRY $24 AV

Urlar Gladstone Pinot Noir   (★★★☆)

Hand-picked from young vines and barrel-aged for a year, the 2007 vintage (★★★☆) of this Wairarapa red is a ruby-hued, mid-weight style with cherry and herb aromas and flavours. It's a strongly varietal wine with some savoury complexity and gentle tannins. Drink now to 2010.

DRY $35 –V

Valli Bannockburn Vineyard Otago Pinot Noir   ★★★★☆

The 2007 vintage (★★★★☆) was harvested at 25.8 brix and matured in French oak barrels (40 per cent new). A rich, flowing red, it is densely coloured, with concentrated cherry, plum and spice flavours, and firm, ripe tannins beneath. The 2008 (★★★★★) is a generous, deeply coloured and mouthfilling wine with rich, ripe cherry, plum and spice flavours, showing excellent structure and complexity.

Vintage	08	07	06	05
WR	7	7	7	6
Drink	10-17	09-16	09-16	09-14

DRY $55 –V

Valli Gibbston Vineyard Otago Pinot Noir   ★★★★☆

The 2007 vintage (★★★★☆) is a fine example of the sub-regional style – generous and supple, with deep colour and concentrated, very fresh cherry, spice and slight herb flavours, showing excellent density and complexity. The 2008 (★★★★) is deeply coloured and concentrated, with the herbal notes typical of the elevated Gibbston sub-region, fresh, vibrant fruit flavours, good texture, and a lingering finish.

Vintage	08	07	06	05
WR	7	7	7	5
Drink	09-18	09-17	09-16	09-12

DRY $55 –V

Valli Waitaki Vineyard Otago Pinot Noir   ★★★☆

The weak point in the range – since the first 2004 vintage, this North Otago red has been clearly overshadowed by its Central Otago stablemates (although the 2004 vintage is still drinking well). The 2008 (★★★☆) is ruby-hued, floral and supple, with vibrant cherry, plum and dried-herb flavours that flow well.

Vintage	08	07	06
WR	6	4	5
Drink	09-15	09-14	09-12

DRY $55 –V

Van Asch Central Otago Pinot Noir   ★★★☆

The 2006 vintage (★★★☆) is gutsy (14.5 per cent alcohol), in a full-on style with strong plum, spice, nut and liquorice flavours. The 2007 (★★★★) is dark and dense, with rich plum and cherry flavours, showing good complexity.

DRY $45 –V

Vavasour Awatere Valley Pinot Noir ★★★★

The 2008 vintage (★★★★) was hand-picked and matured for nine months in French oak casks (35 per cent new). Youthful, with excellent body and depth of cherry, red-berry and spice flavours, seasoned with toasty oak, it is savoury and complex, with finely balanced tannins.

Vintage	08	07	06		DRY $30 AV
WR	7	7	7		
Drink	09-16	09-15	09-11		

Vicar's Mistress, The, Pinot Noir ★★★☆

Full and still youthful in colour, the 2007 vintage (★★★☆) was grown at Waipara and matured in French oak casks (25 per cent new). It's a mouthfilling wine with very good depth of plum, spice and herb flavours, showing some savoury complexity. Drink now or cellar.

Vintage	07	06	05		DRY $35 –V
WR	7	7	6		
Drink	09-13	09-12	09-11		

Vidal Marlborough Pinot Noir ★★★★

The 2007 vintage (★★★★) is an elegant, vibrantly fruity wine with fresh, supple cherry and plum flavours, delicious now. The 2008 (★★★★), matured for nine months in French oak casks (20 per cent new), is mouthfilling, with cherry and spice flavours, rich and rounded.

Vintage	08	07	06	05	DRY $26 V+
WR	6	7	6	6	
Drink	09-11	09-11	09-10	P	

Vidal Reserve Hawke's Bay Pinot Noir ★★★★

One of the region's best Pinot Noirs, in the past labelled 'Stopbank'. The 2007 vintage (★★★★) is a single-vineyard red, grown at Maraekakaho, hand-picked and matured for 10 months in French oak barriques (30 per cent new). Ruby-hued, it is floral and complex, fresh, spicy and full-flavoured, with silky tannins, good length and the structure to age. The 2008 (★★★★) is mouthfilling and concentrated, with rich, ripe plum and spice flavours, showing good complexity.

Vintage	08	07	06	05	04	DRY $30 AV
WR	7	6	6	6	6	
Drink	09-13	09-12	09-11	P	P	

Villa Maria Cellar Selection Marlborough Pinot Noir ★★★★★

Typically a delightful wine, priced sharply, this is often New Zealand's best-value Pinot Noir. Grown in the Awatere and Wairau valleys, it is hand-picked, fermented partly with indigenous yeasts, and matured for nine months in French oak barriques (typically 40 per cent new). The 2008 (★★★☆) is a lesser vintage. Ruby-hued, it is medium-bodied, with cherry, plum and spice flavours and ripe, supple tannins. Sweet-fruited, it's an intensely varietal wine that should reward moderate cellaring, but lacks the richness of a top year.

Vintage	08	07	06	05	04	DRY $31 V+
WR	6	6	7	7	7	
Drink	09-14	09-13	09-12	09-11	P	

Villa Maria Private Bin Marlborough Pinot Noir   ★★★★

Typically an outstanding buy. From a lesser growing season, the 2008 (★★★) was grown in the Awatere and Wairau valleys, and matured for 10 months in French oak barriques (10 per cent new). Ruby-hued, it is vibrantly fruity, with fairly light cherry and plum flavours and a smooth finish.

Vintage	08	07	06	05
WR	6	6	6	7
Drink	09-12	09-11	09-10	09-10

DRY $25 V+

Villa Maria Reserve Marlborough Pinot Noir   ★★★★★

Launched from the 2000 vintage, this label swiftly won recognition as one of the region's boldest, lushest reds. Based on ultra-low-yielding vines (2.5 tonnes/hectare) in the Awatere and Wairau valleys, it is matured for over a year in French oak barriques (35 to 50 per cent new), and bottled with minimal fining and filtration. The 2007 vintage (★★★★★) is deeply coloured, with mouthfilling body and highly concentrated plum, spice and slight liquorice flavours. Rich and finely poised, with ripe, supple tannins, it's still youthful. The 2008 (★★★★☆) is mouthfilling and full-coloured, with warm cherry and spice flavours, showing good complexity, and a smooth, long finish. It's a forward vintage, ripe and rounded.

Vintage	08	07	06	05	04
WR	6	7	7	7	7
Drink	09-18	09-17	09-19	09-18	09-11

DRY $51 AV

Villa Maria Single Vineyard Rutherford Pinot Noir   ★★★★★

The 2007 vintage (★★★★★) is based on vines nestled against the Benmorven foothills, on the south side of the Wairau Valley, and was matured for over a year in French oak barriques (25 per cent new). Powerful and full of potential, it's a youthful, tightly structured wine with rich colour, sweet-fruit delights, and dense cherry, plum and spice flavours.

Vintage	07	06
WR	7	7
Drink	09-17	09-19

DRY $56 AV

Villa Maria Single Vineyard Seddon Pinot Noir   ★★★★★

From an Awatere Valley site even further inland and higher than its stablemate (below), the 2007 vintage (★★★★★) was matured for over a year in French oak barriques (25 per cent new). Richly coloured, it is still very youthful and vibrant, with highly concentrated cherry, plum, herb and spice flavours, refined, long and tightly structured. Best drinking mid-2010 onwards.

Vintage	07	06	05
WR	7	7	7
Drink	09-17	09-19	09-16

DRY $56 AV

Villa Maria Single Vineyard Southern Clays Pinot Noir   (★★★★☆)

Richly coloured, the 2008 vintage (★★★★☆) was matured in French oak barriques (32 per cent new). It's a finely textured wine, warm and concentrated, with rich cherry, plum and spice flavours and a rounded finish.

Vintage	08
WR	7
Drink	09-18

DRY $56 –V

Villa Maria Single Vineyard Taylors Pass Pinot Noir   ★★★★☆

Grown in the upper Awatere Valley, the 2007 vintage (★★★★★) was matured for over a year in French oak barriques (25 per cent new). Richly coloured, it reveals intense, cherryish, plummy flavours, still fresh, tight and youthful, yet deliciously rich and supple.

Vintage	07	06	05	04	03
WR	7	7	7	7	7
Drink	09-17	09-19	09-18	09-11	09-10

DRY $58 –V

Voss Martinborough Pinot Noir   ★★★★☆

Voss is a small winery with a big, instantly likeable Pinot Noir. The 2007 (★★★★☆) is a top vintage. Grown at three sites on the Martinborough Terrace, where the vines are 11 to 19 years old, it was matured in French oak barriques (20 per cent new), and bottled unfined and unfiltered. Deep ruby, it is very fresh and fragrant, with rich, vibrant, well-ripened cherry, plum and spice flavours. Deliciously complex, savoury and smooth-flowing, it has the potential to mature well.

Vintage	07	06	05	04	03	02
WR	7	7	6	5	7	5
Drink	09-13	09-12	09-10	P	P	P

DRY $40 AV

Vynfields Reserve Martinborough Pinot Noir   ★★★★

Certified organic, the 2007 vintage (★★★★★) is a lovely red with an enticingly floral bouquet and deep, bright colour. Concentrated and silky, with a spicy, savoury complexity, it has ripe tannins and a long, seductively smooth finish.

DRY $49 –V

W5 Marlborough Pinot Noir   ★★★

From Mt Olympus, the barrel-aged 2007 vintage (★★☆) is ruby-hued, with slightly leafy flavours in a smooth, easy-drinking style. (W5 stands for 'which was what was wanted'.)

DRY $16 V+

Waimea Barrel Selection Pinot Noir   ★★★☆

The 2008 vintage (★★★☆) was harvested at 24 brix and matured for nine months in French and American oak barrels (partly new). Full ruby, it is mouthfilling and supple, with cherry and plum flavours, showing a hint of sweet oak, and good, savoury complexity. Drink now to 2010.

Vintage	08	07
WR	6	7
Drink	09-13	09-12

DRY $24 V+

Waimea Bolitho SV Nelson Pinot Noir   ★★★★

The powerful 2007 vintage (★★★★) was estate-grown in the Packhouse Vineyard, on the Waimea Plains, fermented with indigenous yeasts and matured for a year in French oak barriques (50 per cent new). Deeply coloured and sturdy (14.5 per cent alcohol), it is sweet-fruited, with concentrated, cherryish, plummy, slightly herbal flavours, seasoned with toasty oak, and a firm finish. It should be long-lived.

Vintage	07				DRY $30 AV
WR	7				
Drink	09-14				

Waimea Nelson Pinot Noir   ★★★

The 2007 vintage (★★★) is deep ruby and mouthfilling (14.3 per cent alcohol), with firm cherry and spice flavours, slightly leafy but showing good depth, and some savoury complexity.

Vintage	07	06	05	04	DRY $20 AV
WR	5	6	7	5	
Drink	09-11	09-11	09-10	P	

Waipara Downs Waipara Pinot Noir   ★★☆

The 2008 vintage (★★) of this estate-grown North Canterbury red is disappointing, with slightly developed colour and green-edged flavours.

DRY $25 –V

Waipara Hills Soul of the South Waipara Pinot Noir   (★★★)

Grown at two sites at Waipara, the 2008 vintage (★★★) is an unoaked, fruit-driven style, ruby-hued, with supple, cherryish flavours, fresh and lively.

DRY $20 AV

Waipara Hills Southern Cross Selection Central Otago Pinot Noir   ★★★★

Grown and hand-picked at Bendigo, in the Cromwell Basin, and French oak-matured, the 2008 vintage (★★★★) is rich and flowing. Sweet-fruited, slightly earthy and savoury, it has impressive depth of cherryish, plummy flavour and good complexity. Best opened mid-2010+.

DRY $37 AV

Waipara Springs Premo Pinot Noir   ★★★★★

Based on some of the oldest vines in Waipara, the 2007 vintage (★★★★★) was hand-picked, fermented with indigenous yeasts and matured for 15 months in French oak barriques (30 per cent new). Dark, finely fragrant, rich and supple, with sweet-fruit delights and highly concentrated cherry, plum and slight herb flavours, seasoned with toasty oak, it should be long-lived.

Vintage	07	06	DRY $36 V+
WR	7	6	
Drink	09-12	09-12	

Waipara West Pinot Noir   ★★★

This small-volume red is mostly shipped to the UK. The 2006 vintage (★★★) has lightish, slightly developed colour. Cherryish and herbal, it is supple, with some complexity. Drink now to 2010.

DRY $26 –V

Waipipi Henry Pinot Noir ★★☆

The 2008 vintage (★★☆), grown at Opaki in the Wairarapa and French oak-aged, has sweet oak aromas, leading into a fresh, cherry and plum-flavoured wine with gentle tannins and drink-young appeal.

Vintage 08	
WR 6	
Drink 09-13	

DRY $25 –V

Wairau River Home Block Marlborough Pinot Noir (★★★☆)

Barrel-aged for a year, the 2007 vintage (★★★☆) is mouthfilling and supple, with ripe cherry, herb and spice flavours, showing good varietal character and some savoury complexity. It's drinking well now.

Vintage 07	
WR 6	
Drink 09-11	

DRY $32 –V

Wairau River Marlborough Pinot Noir (★★★)

Estate-grown in Marlborough, the 2007 vintage (★★★) was matured for 10 months in a mix of tanks (70 per cent) and barrels (30 per cent). Bright ruby, with a slightly toasty and earthy bouquet, it's a smooth, middleweight style with a touch of complexity and cherryish flavours, youthful and well-rounded. The 2008 (★★★) is floral, with fresh, ripe plum and red-berry flavours, not concentrated, but vibrant and supple, a hint of oak and lots of drink-young charm.

Vintage 08	
WR 5	
Drink 09-10	

DRY $23 AV

Waitaki Braids Waitaki Valley Pinot Noir ★★★★

The 2008 vintage (★★★★☆), grown in the Otago Station Vineyard, was hand-harvested, fermented with indigenous yeasts and matured for a year in French oak barriques. Very fragrant, savoury and supple, it is full-coloured, rich and complex, with ripe, sweet-fruit flavours, lovely flow across the palate and a long finish. It's a feminine, graceful style, with lots of class.

DRY $60 –V

Waitaki Valley Wines Grants Road Vineyard Pinot Noir (★★★☆)

The 2008 vintage (★★★☆) has a floral bouquet, fresh, ripe, moderately concentrated plum and spice flavours, gentle tannins and lots of drink-young charm.

DRY $40 –V

Waitiri Creek Central Otago Pinot Noir ★★★★

This label has leapt in quality in recent vintages. The 2007 vintage (★★★★) was grown at Gibbston and Bannockburn and matured in French oak barriques (33 per cent new). It is rich and elegant, with deep colour, strong, plummy, spicy flavours, finely integrated oak and considerable complexity.

DRY $45 –V

Waiwera Estate Pikikiruna Pinot Noir   (★★★☆)

Grown at Golden Bay, in Nelson, the 2006 vintage (★★★☆) has good personality. Ruby-hued, with some development showing, it is mouthfilling, with ripe, sweet-fruit flavours of cherries and herbs, some savoury complexity and gentle tannins. Ready.

DRY $31 –V

Walnut Block Collectables Marlborough Pinot Noir   (★★★)

Barrel-aged for nine months, the 2008 vintage (★★★) is mouthfilling, with fresh, supple flavours of plums, herbs and spices in a fruit-driven style, enjoyable now.

DRY $23 AV

Walnut Block Marlborough Pinot Noir   ★★★★☆

Grown in a single vineyard in the Wairau Valley, the bargain-priced 2007 (★★★★★) was hand-picked and matured in French oak barriques (15 per cent new). Deeply coloured, with concentrated, sweet-fruit delights of plums and spices, and firm tannins, it is fragrant, powerful, harmonious and long. The 2008 vintage (★★★★☆) is full-coloured, mouthfilling and youthful, with ripe cherry, spice and nut flavours showing excellent complexity, texture and length.

DRY $30 V+

Weka River Waipara Valley Pinot Noir   ★★★

Mouthfilling and fairly firm, the 2007 vintage (★★★) is ruby-hued, with a leafy bouquet and plum, cherry and herb flavours, only moderately ripe-tasting, but showing very good depth.

Vintage	07
WR	4
Drink	10+

DRY $33 –V

West Brook Marlborough Pinot Noir   ★★★

The 2007 vintage (★★★) is bright ruby, with fresh, crisp, plummy flavours, showing a touch of complexity.

DRY $22 AV

West Brook Waimauku Pinot Noir   ★★★☆

Here's proof that you *can* make impressive Pinot Noir in Auckland. Estate-grown, hand-picked and matured in French oak barriques (60 per cent new), the 2007 vintage (★★★★) is richly coloured and generous, with concentrated plum, spice and slight coffee flavours, lots of toasty oak – but the fruit depth to match. The 2008 (★★★) is a ruby-hued, medium-bodied wine with ripe plum/spice flavours, good texture and considerable complexity, but currently slightly dominated by toasty oak. It needs time to achieve balance; open 2011+.

DRY $26 AV

Whitehaven Marlborough Pinot Noir ★★★

The 2007 vintage (★★★☆) was matured in French oak casks (33 per cent new). Deeply coloured, it has strong, ripe, plummy, slightly spicy and toasty flavours, fresh and supple. Drink now or cellar.

Vintage	08	07	06
WR	5	7	6
Drink	09-12	09-12	09-11

DRY $30 –V

Wild Earth Central Otago Pinot Noir ★★★★☆

The latest vintages are impressive. Grown in the Bannockburn and Pisa districts, and matured in French oak barriques, the 2007 vintage (★★★★☆) is delicious in its youth – deeply coloured, with beautifully ripe, sweet-fruit flavours, showing impressive concentration. The 2008 (★★★★) is a stylish red, concentrated and supple, with vibrant cherry, plum, spice and nut flavours, showing good ripeness and complexity.

DRY $40 AV

Wild Rock Central Otago Pinot Noir (★★★)

For supermarkets only, the ruby-hued 2008 vintage (★★★) from Wild Rock (a subsidiary of Craggy Range) is a very easy-drinking style, with decent depth of cherry, plum and slight spice flavours, seductively soft and smooth. Drink now.

DRY $19 AV

Wild Rock Cupid's Arrow Central Otago Pinot Noir ★★★☆

From Craggy Range, the 2007 vintage (★★★☆) was harvested at 24 brix and matured for six months in French oak (15 per cent new). Full of drink-young charm, it's ruby-hued, with strong cherry, plum, spice and herb flavours, a gentle seasoning of oak and ripe, smooth tannins.

DRY $25 AV

Wild Rock Struggler's Flat Pinot Noir (★★★☆)

Drinking well already, the 2008 vintage (★★★☆) of this Martinborough red is from a subsidiary of Craggy Range. It is bright ruby, mouthfilling and sweet-fruited, with cherryish, slightly nutty flavours, finely balanced and smooth.

Vintage	08
WR	7
Drink	09-13

DRY $24 V+

Wild South Marlborough Pinot Noir ★★☆

From Sacred Hill, the 2007 vintage (★★☆) is bright ruby, with smooth cherry and plum flavours, but also some green, rustic notes detracting.

Vintage	08
WR	5
Drink	09-10

DRY $19 –V

Wild South Reserve Marlborough Pinot Noir   ★★★

The 2007 vintage (★★★) was mostly estate-grown in the Waihopai Valley, hand-picked and matured in French oak for a year. Bright ruby, it is floral, supple and sweet-fruited, with moderately concentrated cherry/plum flavours, hints of herbs and some savoury complexity.

Vintage	07	DRY $32 –V
WR	7	
Drink	09-13	

Wingspan Nelson Pinot Noir   (★★★)

From Wollaston Estates, the 2007 vintage (★★★) offers good value. French oak-aged for 11 months, it is full-coloured, with a herbal thread running through its strong cherry and plum flavours. A generous, moderately complex red, it's enjoyable now.

DRY $16 V+

Wither Hills Single Vineyard Benmorven Marlborough Pinot Noir   (★★★★☆)

Grown in the Benmorven Vineyard, on the south side of the Wairau Valley, the youthful 2007 vintage (★★★★☆) was matured in French oak casks (40 per cent new). Deeply coloured, with slightly toasty aromas and flavours, it is a powerful, ripe, firm style, fleshy (14.5 per cent alcohol), generous, nutty and complex. Best drinking 2011+.

Vintage	07	DRY $50 –V
WR	7	
Drink	10-20	

Wither Hills Single Vineyard Taylor River Marlborough Pinot Noir   (★★★★☆)

From the Taylor River Vineyard, hard against the Wither Hills, the 2007 vintage (★★★★☆) was matured in French oak casks (40 per cent new). Deep and youthful in colour, with 'forest floor' aromas, it is flowing and concentrated, savoury and supple, with cherry, plum and spice flavours showing excellent ripeness and complexity. It's a very graceful wine, built to last.

Vintage	07	DRY $50 –V
WR	6	
Drink	10-20	

Wither Hills Wairau Valley Marlborough Pinot Noir   ★★★★★

Over the past decade, this has been one of the region's most acclaimed reds. It is grown in two company-owned vineyards – Taylor River and Benmorven – on the south side of the Wairau Valley. The wine is matured in French oak barriques, until recently 50 per cent new, but reduced to 20 per cent in 2008, as winemaker Ben Glover is aiming for wines with 'primary, fragrant fruit in their youth, developing complexity, texture and secondary flavours later, after three years'. The 2008 vintage (★★★★) is full-coloured, with strong cherry, plum and spice flavours, showing considerable complexity. Very fresh, vibrant and fruity, it should be at its best mid-2010+.

Vintage	08	07	06	DRY $34 V+
WR	7	7	7	
Drink	09-20	09-15	09-14	

Wooing Tree Beetle Juice Central Otago Pinot Noir   ★★★★

A top buy. The 2008 vintage (★★★★) is a rich, single-vineyard Cromwell red, hand-picked and matured for 11 months in French oak barriques (35 per cent new). Bold and full-coloured, with strong cherry, plum and herb flavours, showing good, savoury complexity, it's a supple, fruit-packed wine, delicious young.

Vintage	08
WR	6
Drink	09-13

DRY $28 V+

Wooing Tree Central Otago Pinot Noir   ★★★★★

The 2008 vintage (★★★★) of this single-vineyard Cromwell red was hand-picked and matured in French oak barriques (40 per cent new). Full-coloured, it is scented and supple, with ripe cherry, plum and spice flavours, showing excellent depth, and a strong seasoning of smoky French oak.

Vintage	08	07	06	05
WR	6	7	6	7
Drink	09-17	09-16	09-16	09-14

DRY $41 V+

Wooing Tree Sandstorm Reserve Central Otago Pinot Noir   (★★★★★)

Estate-grown at Cromwell, the 2007 vintage (★★★★★) was hand-picked from 'especially low-yielding vines' and given 'extended' aging in French oak barrels. Full and still youthful in colour, it is beautifully scented, elegant and sweet-fruited, with concentrated, vibrant cherry and plum flavours, fresh acidity and supple tannins. Still unfolding, it should be long-lived; open 2011+.

Vintage	07
WR	7
Drink	10-18

DRY $85 AV

Woollaston Estates Nelson Pinot Noir   ★★★

Grown at Upper Moutere and matured for 10 months in French oak barriques (25 per cent new), the 2006 vintage (★★★) has slightly developed colour and, with age, leafy notes are emerging. Savoury and soft, with considerable complexity, it's ready now.

Vintage	06
WR	6
Drink	09-11

DRY $29 –V

Wycroft Forbury Pinot Noir   (★★★)

Grown near Masterton, in the Wairarapa, the 2008 vintage (★★★) was hand-picked and matured for 10 months in French oak casks (30 per cent new). Ruby-hued, it is fresh, fruity and smooth, with good varietal character and moderate depth of cherry/plum flavours, enjoyable young.

Vintage	08
WR	6
Drink	09-13

DRY $30 –V

Yealands Marlborough Pinot Noir   (★★☆)

Light ruby, the 2008 vintage (★★☆) is a drink-young style with gentle raspberry and strawberry flavours, simple and smooth.

DRY $18 AV

Sangiovese

Sangiovese, Italy's most extensively planted red-wine variety, is a rarity in New Zealand. Cultivated as a workhorse grape throughout central Italy, in Tuscany it is the foundation of such famous reds as Chianti and Brunello di Montalcino. Here, Sangiovese has sometimes been confused with Montepulciano and its plantings are not expanding – the 2010 area of 6 hectares of bearing vines (mostly in Auckland) will be slightly less than in 2006.

Heron's Flight Matakana Sangiovese ★★★★

North of Auckland, David Hoskins and Mary Evans are specialists in traditional Italian varieties. Still on sale, their 2005 vintage (★★★★☆) was harvested at 24 brix, after ripening for two weeks longer on the vines than usual, and matured in French oak barriques (50 per cent new). Deeply coloured, it is mouthfilling and sweet-fruited, with blackcurrant, plum and spice flavours, rich and supple. It should be long-lived.

DRY $50 –V

Syrah

Hawke's Bay and the upper North Island (especially Waiheke Island) have a hot new red-wine variety. At the world's second-largest wine show, the International Wine Challenge 2009, staged in the UK, the top trophy for Syrah was awarded to Kennedy Point Waiheke Island Syrah 2007.

The classic 'Syrah' of the Rhône Valley, in France, and Australian 'Shiraz' are in fact the same variety. On the rocky, baking slopes of the upper Rhône Valley, and in several Australian states, this noble grape yields red wines renowned for their outstanding depth of cassis, plum and black-pepper flavours.

Syrah was well known in New Zealand a century ago. Government viticulturist S.F. Anderson wrote in 1917 that Shiraz was being 'grown in nearly all our vineyards [but] the trouble with this variety has been an unevenness in ripening its fruit'. For today's winemakers, the problem has not changed: Syrah has never favoured a too-cool growing environment (wines that are not fully ripe show distinct tomato or tamarillo characters). It needs sites that are relatively hot during the day and retain the heat at night, achieving ripeness in Hawke's Bay late in the season, at about the same time as Cabernet Sauvignon. To curb its natural vigour, stony, dry, low-fertility sites or warm hillside sites are crucial.

The latest national vineyard survey showed that 294 hectares of Syrah will be bearing in 2010 – a steep rise from 62 hectares in 2000. Syrah is now New Zealand's fourth most widely planted red-wine variety, behind Pinot Noir, Merlot and Cabernet Sauvignon, but well ahead of Malbec and Cabernet Franc. Over two-thirds of the vines are in Hawke's Bay, with other significant pockets in Auckland and Northland. Syrah's potential in this country's warmer vineyard sites is finally being tapped.

Ake Ake Vineyard Syrah ★★☆

Grown at the Bay of Islands, in Northland, the easy-drinking 2008 vintage (★★★) was matured in American oak casks (partly new). Full-coloured, with perfumed, sweet oak aromas, it is a medium-bodied red with fresh, ripe plum and spice flavours, seasoned with sweet oak, and a smooth finish.

Vintage	08
WR	5
Drink	09-12

DRY $20 –V

Alpha Domus Hawke's Bay Syrah   ★★★☆

The 2007 vintage (★★★★) is full-bodied, with deep, youthful colour, sweet-fruit characters and rich plum/pepper flavours, clearly varietal, concentrated and smooth.

Vintage	07
WR	5
Drink	09-15

DRY $25 AV

Artisan Fantail Island Oratia Syrah   ★★★

Grown at Oratia, in West Auckland, and French and American oak-matured, the deeply coloured 2006 vintage (★★☆) is medium-bodied, with fresh, vibrant plum/pepper flavours, but also a slight lack of ripeness and roundness on the finish.

Vintage	06	05
WR	4	6
Drink	09 10	09-14

DRY $26 –V

Artisan Fantail Island Oratia Syrah Reserve   (★★★★)

The generous 2005 vintage (★★★★) was estate-grown in West Auckland. Deeply coloured, with a fragrant bouquet of plums and black pepper, it has concentrated, ripe blackcurrant and spice flavours, seasoned with toasty oak, and a finely balanced, smooth finish. It's drinking well now, but also worth cellaring.

DRY $49 –V

Ascension The Bandit Reserve Matakana Syrah/Viognier   (★★★☆)

The debut 2008 vintage (★★★☆) is a blend of Syrah (95 per cent), picked from first-crop vines, and Viognier (5 per cent), from 13-year-old vines. Co-fermented and matured for nine months in barrels (25 per cent new), it's full-coloured, with a perfumed, peppery bouquet. Generous, with fresh, ripe plum, berry and spice flavours and gentle tannins, it's a vibrantly fruity, soft red with lots of drink-young appeal.

DRY $35 –V

Aspire Hawke's Bay Syrah   (★★★☆)

From Matariki, the 2006 vintage (★★★☆) is a Gimblett Gravels red, barrel-aged for over a year. Medium-bodied, with full, bright colour, a floral bouquet, vibrant, gently spicy fruit flavours and some savoury complexity, it's maturing well.

Vintage	07	06
WR	6	6
Drink	09-12	09-11

DRY $20 AV

Aurora Vineyard, The, Bendigo Syrah   (★★★★)

Syrah is unproven in Central Otago, but the 2006 vintage (★★★★) of this rich, vibrant wine is a positive pointer to the future. Boldly coloured, with concentrated flavours of plums, spices and liquorice, woven with fresh, balanced acidity, it shows good complexity and structure. The 2007 (★★★★) was harvested at 26.8 brix from very low-cropped vines (3 tonnes/hectare), and barrel-aged for 10 months. Dense and youthful in colour, it is vibrant, with good fruit sweetness and lush, finely poised, plummy flavours.

Vintage	07
WR	6
Drink	09-12

DRY $32 –V

Awaroa Melba Peach Reserve Syrah   (★★★★★)

Grown on Waiheke, the 2008 vintage (★★★★★) was one of the stars at a major tasting of the island's wines in mid-2009. It's a powerful red, built to last, with a core of sweet fruit and dense, spicy flavours, complex and firmly structured.

DRY $65 AV

Awaroa Syrah   ★★★★☆

The 2007 vintage (★★★★☆) is a dark Waiheke Island red, matured in French oak barriques (50 per cent new). The fragrant, spicy, peppery bouquet leads into a densely packed wine with ripe, concentrated plum/pepper flavours, seasoned with quality oak, and a firm foundation of tannin. It's built for the long haul.

Vintage	07	06	05	04
WR	6	6	7	6
Drink	10-14	10-14	10-12	09-10

DRY $45 –V

Awhitu Greenock Syrah   ★★★☆

Grown on the Awhitu Peninsula, flanking the Manukau Harbour in South Auckland, the 2005 vintage (★★★★) was matured for 14 months in French oak casks (half new), and filtered minimally. Dark, it is powerful, warm and concentrated, with deep blackcurrant, plum and spice flavours, the savoury, earthy notes typical of Auckland reds, and firm tannins. It should be long-lived.

DRY $30 –V

Babich Gimblett Gravels Syrah   ★★★☆

The 2007 vintage (★★★★) is a top buy. Grown in Hawke's Bay, co-fermented with a small portion of Viognier and matured in mostly seasoned oak barrels, it is spicy and silky textured, with strong plum and black-pepper flavours, gamey, savoury notes adding complexity and a floral bouquet.

DRY $20 AV

Babich Winemakers' Reserve Hawke's Bay Syrah   ★★★☆

Grown in Gimblett Road and matured in American oak barriques (20 per cent new), the 2007 vintage (★★★★) is the best yet. The colour is dark and purple-flushed; the palate is packed with fresh, ripe plum/spice flavours, with earthy, savoury notes adding complexity and a rich, smooth finish.

Vintage	07	06	05	04	03	02
WR	7	6	6	6	NM	7
Drink	09-15	09-12	09-10	P	NM	P

DRY $25 AV

Balthazar Gimblett Road Syrah   (★★★☆)

The 2006 vintage (★★★☆) of this Hawke's Bay red has deep, still fairly youthful colour. Mouthfilling, with concentrated, plummy, peppery flavours, it has some rustic notes and slightly grippy tannins, but also plenty of personality.

DRY $39 –V

Beach House Hawke's Bay Syrah   ★★★★★

The classy, youthful 2007 vintage (★★★★★) offers top value. Estate-grown and hand-picked in The Track Vineyard, in the Gimblett Gravels, it was matured for a year in French and American oak casks. Deeply coloured, it is rich and flowing, with sweet-fruit delights and highly concentrated blackcurrant, plum, spice and liquorice flavours, still very fresh and vibrant. Best drinking 2011+.

Vintage	07
WR	7
Drink	09-30

DRY $28 V+

Bilancia La Collina Syrah   ★★★★★

la collina ('the hill') is grown in the company's steep, early-ripening vineyard on the northern slopes of Roy's Hill, overlooking the Gimblett Gravels district of Hawke's Bay, co-fermented with Viognier skins (but not their juice, giving a 2 per cent Viognier component in the final blend), and matured for up to 22 months in all new (but 'low impact') French oak barriques. A majestic red, it ranks among the country's very finest Syrahs. The 2007 vintage (★★★★★) is dark and youthful in colour. Dense, with very fresh and vibrant, ripe blackcurrant, plum, black-pepper and nut flavours, it is savoury and complex, with firm underlying tannins and obvious long-term potential.

Vintage	07	06	05	04	03	02
WR	7	7	7	7	NM	7
Drink	12-16	09-18	09-17	09-16	NM	09-14

DRY $90 AV

Bilancia Syrah/Viognier   ★★★★☆

This Hawke's Bay red is a blend of grapes from vineyards in the Gimblett Gravels district and the company's own block, *la collina*, on Roy's Hill. Co-fermented with Viognier skins and matured in French oak barriques (25 per cent new), the 2006 vintage (★★★★☆) is deeply coloured, with a floral, berryish, spicy bouquet. It is rich and well-ripened, with blackcurrant and spice flavours, a hint of dark chocolate, and excellent density and structure. Drink now or cellar.

Vintage	07	06	05	04	03	02
WR	7	7	NM	6	6	7
Drink	09-15	09-12	NM	09-10	P	09-10

DRY $37 AV

Black Barn Hawke's Bay Syrah   (★★★★)

The graceful, finely textured 2008 vintage (★★★★) is deeply coloured, floral and fruity, with ripe plum, black pepper and slight liquorice flavours, showing some savoury complexity. It's already highly enjoyable, but worth cellaring.

DRY $32 –V

Boundary Vineyards Lake Road Gisborne Syrah   ★★☆

From Pernod Ricard NZ, the 2007 vintage (★★☆) was grown at Patutahi, co-fermented with
Viognier, and matured for five months in French oak barriques (18 per cent new). It's a deeply
coloured, peppery, earthy wine, full-flavoured, firm and slightly rustic. The 2008 (★★☆) is
strongly peppery, but lacks real richness and roundness.

DRY $23 –V

Bridge Pa Vineyard Hawke's Bay Syrah   ★★★★

The 2005 vintage (★★★★) is a floral Hawke's Bay red, matured for nine months in American
and French oak barriques. Estate-grown and hand-picked at Bridge Pa, it is generous and
strongly varietal, with gentle tannins and fresh blackcurrant and plum flavours, slightly earthy
and intensely peppery.

Vintage	05	04
WR	6	7
Drink	09-11	P

DRY $28 AV

Bridge Pa Vineyard Louis Syrah   ★★★★

Estate-grown at Bridge Pa, in Hawke's Bay, this wine is made from lower-cropped vines than the
standard red (above) and American and French oak-aged for a year, instead of nine months. The
2005 vintage (★★★★) is dark, with a smoky bouquet and concentrated plum and black-pepper
flavours, but slightly less seductive and lush than the 2004 (★★★★☆).

Vintage	06	05	04
WR	6	6	7
Drink	09-14	09-14	09-14

DRY $49 –V

Brookfields Back Block Syrah   ★★★

Grown at Ohiti Estate, in Hawke's Bay, the 2007 vintage (★★★☆) was oak-aged for 18 months.
Deep and youthful in colour, it's fresh and vibrantly fruity, with plum and spice flavours showing
very good depth, a light seasoning of oak and gentle tannins. Drink now or cellar.

Vintage	07	06
WR	7	7
Drink	10-17	09-13

DRY $19 AV

Brookfields Hillside Syrah   ★★★★☆

This distinguished red is grown on a sheltered, north-facing slope between Maraekakaho and
Bridge Pa in Hawke's Bay (described by winemaker Peter Robertson as 'surreal – a chosen site').
The 2007 vintage (★★★★★), matured for 18 months in all-new oak casks, is deeply coloured,
with a fragrant bouquet mingling spices and sweet oak. Rich and flowing, it's a generous,
seductive wine with highly concentrated blackcurrant, spice, chocolate and nut flavours, and
ripe, firm tannins. A wine of real power, it should be long-lived.

Vintage	07	06
WR	7	7
Drink	10-18	09-16

DRY $40 AV

Cable Bay Waiheke Island Syrah   (★★★☆)

The 2007 vintage (★★★☆) was matured for a year in French (80 per cent) and American oak casks. It's a medium-bodied style with full colour and a scented bouquet. Smooth-flowing, it has fresh, vibrant, strongly varietal plum and black-pepper flavours and gentle tannins.

Vintage	07
WR	6
Drink	09-11

DRY $35 –V

Church Road Reserve Hawke's Bay Syrah   ★★★★☆

The memorable 2007 vintage (★★★★★) was hand-picked in Pernod Ricard NZ's Redstone Vineyard, in The Triangle (55 per cent), and also in Gimblett Road (45 per cent), and matured for a year in French oak barriques (53 per cent new). Densely coloured, with a voluminous, peppery fragrance, it is highly concentrated yet flowing, with blackcurrant, spice, plum and slight coffee flavours showing lovely richness, ripeness and roundness, and a long, spicy finish. A powerful and complex yet beautifully supple wine, it's already delicious.

Vintage	07	06
WR	6	6
Drink	09-10	09-10

DRY $36 AV

C.J. Pask Declaration Syrah   ★★★★☆

The 2007 vintage (★★★★★), grown in the Gimblett Gravels of Hawke's Bay, has a beautifully floral bouquet, plummy and spicy, with hints of coffee and sweet oak. The palate is bold and rich, with substantial body, deep plum, spice and nut flavours, a silky texture and lovely length.

DRY $45 –V

C.J. Pask Gimblett Road Syrah   ★★★★

This Hawke's Bay red offers consistently fine value. Estate-grown and barrel-matured for a year, the 2007 vintage (★★★★) is dark and highly fragrant, with generous plum, black-pepper and liquorice flavours, well-integrated oak and a firm backbone of tannin. Well worth cellaring.

DRY $20 V+

Clevedon Hills Syrah   (★★★)

Grown at 80–100 metres above sea level in Clevedon, South Auckland, the 2004 vintage (★★★) is fullish in colour, with vibrant, spicy flavours threaded with fresh acidity. It's a tight, moderately ripe-tasting wine with some elegance.

Vintage	04
WR	6
Drink	09-12

DRY $49 –V

Clos de Ste Anne Syrah The Crucible   ★★★★☆

The 2007 vintage (★★★★☆) was grown organically in Millton's elevated Clos de Ste Anne vineyard in Gisborne and matured in large, seasoned oak casks. Still youthful, it is deeply coloured, with substantial body and rich, ripe, intensely varietal flavours of blackcurrants and spices. Slightly earthy and roasted notes add complexity, with a firm backbone of tannin.

Vintage	07	06	05
WR	7	6	6
Drink	09-17	09-15	09-10

DRY $54 –V

Coney Martinborough Que Sera Syrah   ★★★☆

The easy-drinking 2008 vintage (★★★) was matured in oak casks (30 per cent new). Lightish in colour for Syrah, with a fragrant, gently spiced bouquet, it's a medium-bodied wine with satisfying depth of plum/pepper flavours and gentle tannins.

Vintage	08
WR	4
Drink	10-12

DRY $32 –V

Contour Estate Reserve Syrah   ★★★★

Launched from 2007 (★★★★), this consistently rewarding wine is grown on the Takatu Peninsula, at Matakana. The 2008 vintage (★★★★) was matured for 15 months in French and American oak barriques (75 per cent new). Full and bright in colour, it is mouthfilling and youthful, with strong, ripe plum and spice flavours, nutty, savoury and complex. Best drinking 2011+.

Vintage	07
WR	6
Drink	09-12

DRY $38 –V

Coopers Creek Hawke's Bay Syrah   ★★★☆

The 2007 vintage (★★★), which includes a drop of Viognier (1.5 per cent), is full-coloured, fresh and fruity, with satisfying depth of blackcurrant, plum, herb and spice flavours.

Vintage	07	06	05	04
WR	6	NM	5	6
Drink	09-11	NM	P	P

DRY $21 AV

Coopers Creek SV Chalk Ridge Hawke's Bay Syrah   ★★★☆

Grown and hand-picked at a 'very warm' site and co-fermented with a small portion of Viognier (4 per cent), the 2007 vintage (★★★★) was matured in French oak casks (25 per cent new). Fleshy and firm, it's a full-coloured red with rich, ripe plum, black-pepper and slight coffee flavours, showing good complexity.

Vintage	07	06
WR	7	6
Drink	09-12	09-10

DRY $26 –V

Corazon Single Vineyard Syrah   ★★★

Grown at Oratia, near Henderson, in West Auckland, the 2007 vintage (★★★) was matured in French oak casks (20 per cent new). It's a medium-bodied red with good colour depth and peppery aromas and flavours, in a vibrantly fruity and supple style. (There is also a riper, more savoury and complex 2008 vintage, from Hawke's Bay (★★★☆) at $24.95.)

Vintage	07	06
WR	5	6
Drink	09-12	09-10

DRY $20 AV

Corbans Cottage Block Hawke's Bay Syrah   ★★★★☆

Grown and hand-picked in Pernod Ricard NZ's Redstone Vineyard, in The Triangle, the 2007 vintage (★★★★★) was matured for 18 months in French oak barriques (40 per cent new), and bottled unfined and unfiltered. Dark, powerful and concentrated, it is intensely varietal, with complex plum, black-pepper and toasty oak flavours. Tight-knit, strong and youthful, with powerful young tannins, it needs time; open 2011+.

Vintage	07		DRY $39 –V
WR	7		
Drink	10-12		

Corbans Private Bin Hawke's Bay Syrah   ★★★☆

The 2005 vintage (★★★★) was estate-grown in the Redstone Vineyard, in The Triangle, and matured in French oak casks (15 per cent new). Deeply coloured, with a rich, peppery fragrance, it is concentrated and youthful, with firm blackcurrant and spice flavours, seasoned with toasty oak. The 2007 (★★★☆) is dark, with strong, spicy, earthy flavours, showing some complexity, in a slightly more rustic style than its Cottage Block stablemate (above).

DRY $24 AV

Cottle Hill Winery Syrah   (★★☆)

Grown at Kerikeri, in Northland, the 2005 vintage (★★☆) is a relatively light style of Syrah, matured for a year in predominantly French oak barriques (30 per cent new). Ruby-hued, fruity, berryish and distinctly plummy, it lacks real richness, but offers pleasant, easy drinking.

DRY $24 –V

Craggy Range Gimblett Gravels Vineyard Block 14 Syrah   ★★★★★

This label is overshadowed by the reputation of its stablemate, Le Sol, but further proves the power, structure and finesse that can be achieved with Syrah grown in the Gimblett Gravels of Hawke's Bay. The great-value 2007 vintage (★★★★★) was fermented with indigenous yeasts and matured for 17 months in French oak barriques (42 per cent new). Fragrant and highly concentrated, it is deeply coloured, supple and rich, with intensely varietal, very fresh and vibrant blackcurrant/spice flavours, toasty oak adding complexity and ripe, supple tannins. A generous, harmonious wine, it's still youthful, but already drinking well.

Vintage	07	06	05	04	03	02	01
WR	7	6	7	6	6	6	7
Drink	10-22	09-20	09-12	09-11	09-10	09-10	P

DRY $30 V+

Craggy Range Le Sol Syrah – see Craggy Range Le Sol
in the Branded and Other Red Wines section

Crossroads Elms Vineyard Reserve Hawke's Bay Syrah   (★★★★☆)

The debut 2007 vintage (★★★★☆) is a single-vineyard red, hand-picked in the Gimblett Gravels and matured for a year in French oak barriques. Densely coloured, it's still extremely youthful, but bursts with ripe plum, spice and liquorice flavours. Firmly structured, with the power to age, it shows great promise; open mid-2010+.

DRY $40 AV

Crossroads Hawke's Bay Syrah   ★★☆

The 2007 vintage (★★☆) is boldly coloured, with plenty of plummy, peppery flavour, but also slightly rustic.

DRY $20 –V

Cypress Hawke's Bay Syrah   (★★★★)

Estate-grown and hand-picked at Roy's Hill, in the Gimblett Gravels, the 2007 vintage (★★★★) was oak-aged for six months. Finely textured, with good complexity, it's a deeply coloured, aromatic, vibrantly fruity red with plummy, peppery, distinctly spicy flavours, showing some leathery, gamey notes.

Vintage	07
WR	6
Drink	09-10

DRY $25 AV

Dry River Martinborough Lovat Vineyard Syrah   ★★★★☆

Top vintages of this rare red, such as the flavour-saturated 2006 (★★★★★), are among the country's best, with strikingly concentrated, tight-knit flavours. Matured for a year in French oak barriques (30 per cent new), the youthful 2007 vintage (★★★★) is an elegant style, medium-bodied (12.5 per cent alcohol), with deep colour and very fresh, vibrant blackcurrant, plum and spice flavours, strong, supple and harmonious. Drink now or cellar.

Vintage	07	06	05	04	03	02	01	00
WR	6	7	7	6	7	6	7	7
Drink	10-21	09-20	09-15	09-14	09-17	09-10	09-11	09-10

DRY $62 –V

Elephant Hill Hawke's Bay Syrah   (★★★☆)

Grown near the coast, at Te Awanga, the 2008 vintage (★★★☆) is deeply coloured, with an inviting, lifted, spicy fragrance. It has strong plum, black-pepper and herb flavours, vibrant and supple, with a subtle oak influence and good length.

DRY $29 –V

Elephant Hill Reserve Hawke's Bay Syrah   (★★★☆)

Grown at Te Awanga, the 2007 vintage (★★★☆) is a robust, dark red with concentrated flavours of red berries, spices and tar, slightly leafy notes and firm tannins. It shows a slight lack of ripeness and roundness, but is an impressively rich wine, showing considerable complexity.

DRY $45 –V

Esk Valley Hawke's Bay Syrah   ★★★★

The top-value 2007 vintage (★★★★) was hand-picked in the Gimblett Gravels and matured for 18 months in French oak barriques (25 per cent new). Still youthful, it's a dark, powerful wine with concentrated plum and spice flavours, still fresh and vibrant, and supple tannins.

Vintage	08	07	06	05
WR	6	6	7	6
Drink	09-12	09-12	09-12	09-10

DRY $24 V+

Esk Valley Winemakers Gimblett Gravels Syrah   ★★★★★

The 2007 vintage (★★★★★) is the first to be labelled 'Winemakers' (past releases were sold as 'Reserve'). Grown in the Cornerstone Vineyard, Hawke's Bay, it was matured for 21 months in French oak barriques (35 per cent new). Boldly coloured, it's a powerful wine with deliciously deep, ripe flavours of blackcurrants, plums and spices, showing lovely richness, roundness and harmony.

Vintage	07	06	05
WR	7	7	7
Drink	09-17	09-18	09-15

DRY $60 AV

Farmgate Hawke's Bay Syrah   (★★★★)

Generous, with loads of personality, the 2007 vintage (★★★★) was made by Ngatarawa for sale via the Farmgate website. Full-coloured, it is sturdy, savoury and spicy, with excellent ripeness, concentration and complexity and a firm foundation of tannin. Open mid-2010+.

DRY $25 AV

Fromm Syrah Fromm Vineyard   ★★★★☆

The 2006 vintage (★★★★) was estate-grown in the Wairau Valley, Marlborough, and matured for 16–18 months in French oak barriques (10–20 per cent new). Bold and still youthful in colour, with a spicy, nutty fragrance, it is sturdy, with finely integrated oak and ripe berry and spice flavours, concentrated and supple.

Vintage	08	07	06	05	04	03	02	01
WR	6	6	6	7	7	6	6	7
Drink	11-18	10-17	09-16	09-17	09-16	09-13	09-12	09-13

DRY $51 –V

Glazebrook Regional Reserve Hawke's Bay Syrah   ★★★☆

The 2007 vintage (★★★☆) from Ngatarawa is dark, full-bodied and fresh, with a slightly earthy bouquet and strong plum and spice flavours. It's a sturdy, moderately complex wine, generous and firm.

Vintage	07	06	05
WR	6	6	5
Drink	09-13	09-12	09-10

DRY $27 –V

Greystone Waipara Syrah   (★★★☆)

Estate-grown and hand-picked in North Canterbury, the 2008 vintage (★★★☆) is a high-alcohol red (14.5 per cent), matured in French oak casks (65 per cent new). Full-coloured, with a peppery fragrance and gentle tannins, it has very good depth of fresh, spicy, plummy, slightly nutty flavour, but also shows some early development.

Vintage	08
WR	6
Drink	09-16

DRY $46 –V

Gunn Estate Silistria Syrah   ★★★★

The 2007 vintage (★★★★) from Sacred Hill was hand-picked in the Gimblett Gravels of Hawke's Bay and matured for a year in French oak barriques (30 per cent new). Youthful, with aging potential, it is dark and fragrant, with concentrated, ripe blackcurrant, plum and pepper flavours that linger well, and a backbone of fine, silky tannins.

Vintage 07	DRY $33 –V
WR 6	
Drink 12-16	

Harvest Man Syrah   (★★★★★)

From The Hay Paddock, on Waiheke Island, the debut 2007 vintage (★★★★★) was harvested from young vines and matured for a year in seasoned (one and two-year-old) French oak casks. Already delicious, it is full-coloured, ripe, very savoury and harmonious, in a refined, supple style with lovely texture.

DRY $38 V+

Harwood Hall Marlborough Syrah   (★★★☆)

From estate-grown, first-crop vines at Rarangi, the debut 2008 vintage (★★★☆) was co-fermented with Viognier (3 per cent) and matured in French and American oak casks. Full-coloured, with a fresh, peppery fragrance, it is vibrant and supple, with good depth of plum and black-pepper flavours, showing considerable complexity, moderately firm tannins, and a distinctly spicy finish. Best drinking mid-2010+.

DRY $22 AV

Instinct Hawke's Bay Syrah   (★★★)

From C.J. Pask, the debut 2007 vintage (★★★☆) has deep, purple-flushed colour and mouthfilling body (14 per cent alcohol). Vibrantly fruity, with fresh acidity and vibrant plum and black-pepper flavours, it has lots of drink-young appeal.

DRY $20 AV

Iron Hills Syrah   ★★★☆

Grown at Kerikeri, in Northland, the 2007 vintage (★★★☆) was hand-picked at 23 brix and matured in French oak barriques (15 per cent new). Full but not dense in colour, it is supple, with plenty of plummy, spicy flavour, slightly earthy and savoury. An easy-drinking style with lots of personality, it's for drinking now or cellaring.

Vintage 07	DRY $25 AV
WR 4	
Drink 09-12	

John Forrest Collection Syrah   ★★★★☆

John Forrest views Syrah as Hawke's Bay's 'premier varietal'. Grown in the Cornerstone Vineyard, in the Gimblett Gravels, the 2006 vintage (★★★★☆) has deep, youthful colour and a highly fragrant, sweetly oaked bouquet. Mouthfilling (14.5 per cent alcohol) and supple, it has sweet-fruit characters and fresh plum and black-pepper flavours, showing lovely richness and flow.

Vintage	06	05
WR	7	6
Drink	10-15	09-12

DRY $65 –V

Jurassic Ridge Syrah   (★★★★)

Maturing well, the 2005 vintage (★★★★) was grown at Church Bay, Waiheke Island, and matured in French and American oak casks. It's a full-coloured, sweet-fruited wine, with mouthfilling body and plum and spice flavours, peppery and lingering.

Vintage	08
WR	7
Drink	09-14

DRY $30 AV

Kaimira Estate Brightwater Syrah/Viognier   (★★★☆)

The easy-drinking 2007 vintage (★★★☆) is a Nelson blend of Syrah (95 per cent) and Viognier (5 per cent), matured for a year in French oak barriques. Full but not dark in colour, with pungent, peppery aromas, it's a moderately concentrated wine with spice and slight liquorice flavours, fresh acidity and smooth tannins.

DRY $35 −V

Karikari Estate Syrah   ★★★☆

Estate-grown on Northland's Karikari Peninsula, the 2007 vintage (★★★★) was matured in American and French oak casks (30 per cent new). It's a complex, age-worthy wine with a fragrant, spicy bouquet, concentrated plum, pepper and nutty oak flavours, firm and savoury, and a strongly spicy finish.

Vintage	07
WR	5
Drink	10-12

DRY $30 −V

Kennedy Point Syrah   ★★★★☆

A rising star from Waiheke Island. The refined 2007 vintage (★★★★★) was matured for 18 months in French oak casks. Bold and youthful in colour, with a very fragrant, plummy, peppery, slightly earthy bouquet, it is rich and vibrant, with plum, black-pepper and dark chocolate flavours, highly concentrated and complex. Still very youthful, with a long, spicy finish, it should mature gracefully for many years. The dark, finely scented 2008 (tasted shortly after bottling, and so not rated), is powerful, yet elegant and supple, with a complex array of cassis, spice, liquorice and nut flavours.

Vintage	08	07
WR	7	7
Drink	10-15	10-15

DRY $39 AV

La Strada Marlborough Syrah   ★★★★☆

The 2007 vintage from Fromm (★★★★) shows again just how enjoyable the region's Syrah can be. Co-fermented with a small portion of Viognier, it was matured for over a year in oak barriques (10–20 per cent new). Dark and youthful in colour, it has a fresh, lifted, spicy bouquet, with a gentle seasoning of oak. Mouthfilling, vibrantly fruity and supple, it offers ripe, concentrated flavours of plums, spices and black pepper, with earthy, chocolatey hints adding complexity. Drink now onwards.

Vintage	08	07	06	05	04
WR	6	7	7	6	6
Drink	10-14	09-13	09-12	09-11	09-10

DRY $34 AV

Maimai Creek Hawke's Bay Syrah   (★★★)

The gutsy 2007 vintage (★★★) was oak-aged for 15 months. Full-coloured, it is smooth and fruity, with mouthfilling body and plum, spice and slight liquorice and herb flavours, showing good depth.

DRY $23 –V

Man O' War Dreadnought Syrah   ★★★★

Grown on Waiheke Island and matured in French oak barriques (50 per cent new), the 2007 vintage (★★★★) is full-coloured, sweet-fruited and lush, with substantial body and strong, spicy, slightly nutty flavours, showing good complexity.

Vintage	08	07
WR	7	5
Drink	10-18	09-12

DRY $46 –V

Man O' War Waiheke Island Syrah   ★★★☆

The 2007 vintage (★★★★) was grown at the eastern end of the island and matured in French and American oak casks. Already drinking well, it is rich, vibrant and flowing, with deep plum and black-pepper flavours, subtle oak and gentle tannins.

Vintage	08	07
WR	6	5
Drink	10-15	09-11

DRY $28 –V

Marsden Bay of Islands Syrah   ★★★

The 2006 vintage (★★★) was grown at Kerikeri, in Northland, and matured for 15 months in French and American oak casks. Dark and generous, it's gutsy and spicy, with cassis and black-pepper flavours, fairly firm tannins and a spicy finish.

Vintage	06
WR	6
Drink	09-11

DRY $28 –V

Matariki Aspire Syrah – see Aspire Syrah

Matariki Hawke's Bay Syrah   ★★★★

Estate-grown and hand-picked in the Gimblett Gravels and matured for 18 months in French oak casks (56 per cent new), the 2006 vintage (★★★★) is floral, supple and intensely varietal, with fragrant plum/spice aromas and flavours, gentle tannins, earthy, savoury notes adding complexity and a lengthy finish.

Vintage	06
WR	6
Drink	09-12

DRY $27 AV

Matariki Reserve Hawke's Bay Syrah   ★★★★

Still on sale, the 2005 vintage (★★★★) was grown in the Gimblett Gravels and matured for 18 months in French oak casks (55 per cent new). It's a deeply coloured wine, with plum and black-pepper flavours, concentrated, firm and likely to be long-lived.

Vintage	05
WR	7
Drink	09-12

DRY $36 –V

Matua Valley Innovator Syrah/Viognier   (★★★☆)

An attractive mid-weight, the 2007 vintage (★★★☆) was grown in the Bullrush Vineyard, hand-picked, and matured for 18 months in French oak casks (20 per cent new). It's deeply coloured, with vibrant, ripe, brambly, plummy, spicy flavours, showing some complexity.

Vintage	07	DRY $25 AV
WR	7	
Drink	09-12	

Matua Valley Reserve Hawke's Bay Syrah   (★★★☆)

Grown in Hawke's Bay and matured for 15 months in French oak casks (30 per cent new), the 2007 vintage (★★★) is an easy-drinking, mid-weight style with fresh, strong berry, plum and spice flavours, a hint of herbs, moderate tannins and a well-rounded finish.

Vintage	07	DRY $20 AV
WR	7	
Drink	09-16	

Mills Reef Elspeth Syrah   ★★★★★

One of Hawke's Bay's finest Syrahs. The 2007 vintage (★★★★★) was estate-grown and hand-picked at two sites in the Gimblett Gravels – the Mere Road Vineyard (70 per cent) and the Trust Vineyard (30 per cent). Fermented with indigenous yeasts and matured for a year in French oak barriques (65 per cent new), it's a rich, full-bodied style, dark, with ripe, sweet-fruit characters, strong, intensely varietal plum, spice and liquorice flavours, showing good complexity, and silky tannins.

Vintage	07	06	05	04	03	02	DRY $40 AV
WR	7	7	7	7	NM	7	
Drink	09-17	09-15	09-16	09-15	NM	09-14	

Mills Reef Elspeth Trust Vineyard Syrah   (★★★★★)

The distinguished 2007 vintage (★★★★★) is an estate-grown, single-vineyard Hawke's Bay red, hand-picked in the Gimblett Gravels, fermented with indigenous yeasts, and matured for 14 months in French oak barriques (50 per cent new). Dark and sweet-fruited, it has a peppery fragrance and dense blackcurrant, plum and pepper flavours, firm and structured.

DRY $40 AV

Mills Reef Reserve Hawke's Bay Syrah   ★★★★

The 2007 vintage (★★★★), grown in the Gimblett Gravels, Hawke's Bay, was co-fermented with 2 per cent Viognier. Matured for a year in American oak casks (30 per cent new), it's an intensely varietal wine with deep, youthful colour and a fresh, spicy bouquet. Mouthfilling, vibrant and supple, it has blackcurrant, plum and pepper flavours, smooth and strong.

Vintage	07	06	05	04	DRY $25 AV
WR	7	6	7	6	
Drink	09-12	09-10	09	P	

Mills Reef Reserve Hawke's Bay Syrah Unfiltered   (★★★★)

Bottled unfined and unfiltered 'to retain its full complexity and texture', the 2007 vintage (★★★★) was estate-grown in the Gimblett Gravels, Hawke's Bay, co-fermented with Viognier (2 per cent), and matured for a year in a 4:1 mix of French and American oak barrels (50 per cent new). Full-coloured, it has a ripe, peppery bouquet and flavours, showing good, savoury complexity, and supple tannins. It's still very vibrant and youthful.

DRY $25 AV

Mission Hawke's Bay Syrah   ★★★

The 2008 vintage (★★☆), grown at Te Awanga and lightly oaked, is a medium-bodied red (12.5 per cent alcohol), full-coloured and slightly earthy, with berry, plum and spice flavours, showing decent depth.

DRY $16 AV

Mission Jewelstone Syrah   ★★★★☆

The powerful 2007 vintage (★★★★★) is outstanding. Estate-grown in Mere Road, in the Gimblett Gravels of Hawke's Bay, the grapes were harvested at 'great maturity' and the wine was matured for over a year in French oak barriques (50 per cent new). The colour is dense and inky; the bouquet is peppery and toasty; the palate is substantial (14.5 per cent alcohol), very rich and sweet-fruited, with highly concentrated plum and black-pepper flavours and a long, spicy, rounded finish.

Vintage	08	07
WR	5	7
Drink	09-15	09-20

DRY $45 –V

Mission Reserve Hawke's Bay Syrah   ★★★★

(Note: the 2008 vintage (★★★★) has 'Gimblett Gravels Syrah' on the front label, with the word 'Reserve' relegated to the back label.) The bargain-priced 2007 (★★★★★) was grown in the Gimblett Gravels, picked 'very ripe', and matured for 14 months in French (60 per cent) and American (40 per cent) oak barriques. Dark, sturdy, highly concentrated and silky-textured, it was the Best Buy of the Year in the 2009 *Buyer's Guide*, and subsequently won several gold medals, here and overseas. The 2008 vintage (★★★★), less arresting but still offering excellent value, was matured in French oak casks (5 per cent new). Deeply coloured, it is mouthfilling and supple, with good concentration of blackcurrant, plum and spice flavours, savoury and complex. It's already approachable, but has the potential to age.

Vintage	08	07	06
WR	5	7	5
Drink	09-12	09-15	09-11

DRY $23 V+

Mission Vineyard Selection Ohiti Road Syrah   (★★★★)

Grown at Ohiti, in Hawke's Bay, the 2008 vintage (★★★★) was French and American oak-aged for seven months. An excellent drink-young style, with 2 per cent Viognier in the blend, it is deeply coloured, with a very attractive, floral, peppery bouquet and a concentrated, berryish, finely textured palate with supple tannins.

DRY $19 V+

Moana Park Vineyard Selection Hawke's Bay Syrah   (★★★)

Priced sharply, the easy-drinking 2007 vintage (★★★) is full-coloured, with ripe plum and spice flavours, soft and generous.

		DRY $15 V+
Vintage	07	
WR	6	
Drink	09-12	

Moana Park Vineyard Tribute Syrah/Viognier   ★★★☆

The deeply coloured 2007 vintage (★★★☆) was hand-picked in Hawke's Bay, blended with Viognier (1 per cent), fermented with indigenous yeasts and barrel-aged for 18 months. For drinking now or cellaring, it's a smooth wine with blackcurrant, liquorice and spice flavours, showing very good depth.

DRY $20 AV

Morton Estate White Label Hawke's Bay Syrah   ★★△

The 2007 vintage (★★☆) has fullish, moderately youthful colour. It's a gutsy wine with strong, spicy flavours, but slightly leafy and rustic.

		DRY $19 –V
Vintage	07	
WR	6	
Drink	09-15	

Mudbrick Vineyard Reserve Syrah   ★★★★☆

Grown on Waiheke Island, the outstanding 2008 vintage (★★★★★) was matured in American oak casks (50 per cent new). Hand-picked, it is finely scented, with deep, purple-flushed colour, mouthfilling body (14.4 per cent alcohol), a core of sweet fruit, lovely density of blackcurrant, plum and black-pepper flavours, nutty and complex, and fine-grained tannins. It's already delicious, but should be long-lived.

Vintage	08	07	06	05	DRY $50 –V
WR	7	7	7	7	
Drink	09-15	09-14	09-12	09-10	

Mudbrick Vineyard Shepherds Point Syrah   (★★★★☆)

A single-vineyard red, grown at Onetangi, on Waiheke Island, the 2008 vintage (★★★★☆) is dark and powerful (14.5 per cent alcohol), with bold blackcurrant, plum and pepper flavours, seasoned with French oak. It's still very youthful; open mid-2011+.

		DRY $36 AV
Vintage	08	
WR	7	
Drink	09-12	

Murdoch James Saleyards Syrah   ★★★

The 2006 vintage (★★★) is now ready. Blended from Martinborough and Hawke's Bay grapes and barrel-aged for 10 months, it's a medium-bodied wine with moderately ripe plum, pepper and herb flavours.

Vintage	07	06	05	04	DRY $30 –V
WR	NM	6	NM	5	
Drink	NM	09-11	NM	P	

Newton/Forrest Estate Gimblett Gravels Hawke's Bay Syrah   (★★★★★)

The powerful, fruit-packed 2006 vintage (★★★★★) is closer to Australian than Rhône styles of Syrah. Grown in the Cornerstone Vineyard and matured in French (70 per cent) and American (30 per cent) oak casks, it is bold and richly coloured, with dense blackcurrant, plum, spice and black-pepper flavours, seasoned with toasty oak, and an underlay of ripe, firm tannins.

Vintage	06	DRY $40 AV
WR	6	
Drink	09-11	

Ngatarawa Silks Syrah   ★★★☆

The 2008 vintage (★★★) of this Hawke's Bay red is full-coloured and firm, with good depth of plummy, peppery flavour, very fresh and youthful.

Vintage	08	07	06	05	DRY $20 AV
WR	6	6	6	6	
Drink	09-13	09-12	09-10	09-10	

Nikau Point Hawke's Bay Syrah   (★★)

From Morton Estate, the 2005 vintage (★★) has light, developed colour and flavours, plummy, spicy, smooth and ready.

Vintage	05	DRY $17 –V
WR	5	
Drink	09-10	

Ohinemuri Estate Gimblett Gravels Syrah   ★★★☆

The 2007 vintage (★★★☆) of this Hawke's Bay red has full, youthful colour. Fresh and vibrant, it's an intensely varietal, fruit-driven style with strong plum and black-pepper flavours, subtle oak and some nutty complexity. It's enjoyable now.

Vintage	07	06	DRY $25 AV
WR	6	6	
Drink	09-12	09-10	

Okahu Syrah   ★★★★

The 2007 vintage (★★★★) of this Northland red was matured in French and American oak casks (partly new). It's a medium-bodied style (12.5 per cent alcohol), full-coloured and sweet-fruited, fresh and vibrant, with ripe plum and spice flavours, very supple tannins and lots of drink-young appeal.

DRY $30 AV

Omaha Bay Vineyard Huapai Syrah   ★★☆

The 2007 vintage (★★) from this Matakana winery was grown in the Papa Vineyard at Huapai, in West Auckland. Full-coloured, with plum and green-leaf flavours, it is earthy and slightly medicinal, and clearly overshadowed by its Matakana stablemate of the same vintage (below).

Vintage	07	06	05	04	DRY $27 –V
WR	6	5	5	6	
Drink	09-15	09-14	09-11	09-10	

Omaha Bay Vineyard Matakana Syrah   (★★★★)

Still very youthful, the 2007 vintage (★★★★) is dark and fruit-crammed, with rich, vibrant plum and black-pepper flavours, a sweet oak influence and a long, spicy finish. It's a concentrated wine, worth cellaring to 2011+.

Vintage	07
WR	6
Drink	09-19

DRY $30 AV

One Tree Hawke's Bay Syrah   ★★★

From Capricorn (a subsidiary of Craggy Range), the 2005 vintage (★★★) has full, still-youthful colour and a peppery bouquet. Still fresh, it offers good depth of plum and black-pepper flavours, with an earthy streak and considerable complexity, but also a slight lack of warmth and softness on the finish.

Vintage	05
WR	6
Drink	09-10

DRY $19 AV

Paritua Hawke's Bay Syrah   ★★★☆

The dark, full-bodied 2007 vintage (★★★☆) was hand-picked and matured for a year in French oak casks (50 per cent new). It's a powerful, concentrated wine with rich plum/spice flavours and a peppery, firm finish, but with bottle-age some green, leafy notes are emerging. The 2008 (★★★☆) is mouthfilling, with plum and black-pepper flavours showing very good depth, some savoury complexity and balanced tannins. Drink now or cellar.

Vintage	07
WR	7
Drink	09-14

DRY $37 –V

Passage Rock Reserve David's Syrah   (★★★★★)

The rare 2008 vintage (★★★★★) was grown on Waiheke Island and matured in French oak barriques (100 per cent new). Densely coloured, it's a classy, seamless wine, powerful (14.5 per cent alcohol) but not heavy, with beautifully ripe cassis and spice flavours, showing notable density, roundness and harmony.

DRY $100 AV

Passage Rock Reserve Syrah   ★★★★★

Waiheke Island's most awarded wine of late is partly estate-grown and fully matured in American and French oak barriques. A powerful, opulent red, it is seductively rich and well-rounded. The outstanding 2008 vintage (★★★★★) is densely coloured, with a beautifully fragrant, peppery bouquet. It offers highly concentrated plum, cherry and spice flavours, rich, finely textured and flowing.

DRY $50 AV

Passage Rock Syrah ★★★★★

This Waiheke Island red is consistently rewarding. Partly estate-grown and fully matured in American (mostly) and French oak barriques, the 2008 vintage (★★★★★) has bold, bright colour and highly concentrated plum and black-pepper flavours, firm and very youthful. Beautifully ripe and rich, with a solid underlay of tannin and good complexity, it's well worth cellaring.

DRY $35 V+

Peninsula Estate Zeno Syrah ★★★☆

Named after a rock in Auckland's Hauraki Gulf, the characterful 2006 vintage (★★★★) is a Waiheke Island red, matured for 10 months in American oak casks. Full of character, it is richly coloured, weighty and robust (14.5 per cent alcohol), with very ripe liquorice, spice and plum flavours, firm and highly concentrated.

Vintage	06
WR	6
Drink	09-11

DRY $35 –V

Pilgrim Syrah/Mourvedre/Grenache ★★★★★

From Stonyridge, the 2008 vintage (★★★★★) of this Rhône-style blend was estate-grown at Onetangi, on Waiheke Island, and matured for a year in French oak barriques (50 per cent new). Still very youthful, it is floral and dark, with dense blackcurrant, plum and spice flavours, savoury, complex and finely textured, and a well-rounded, very harmonious finish. Drink 2011+.

DRY $85 AV

Providence Matakana Syrah ★★★★

The 2002 vintage (★★★) is savoury and mellow, and the 2004 (★★★☆) is still fresh, with considerable complexity, but the 2005 (★★★★★) is the first distinguished Syrah from this small, highly regarded producer. Richly coloured, it is generous, with ripe cassis and black-pepper flavours, showing lovely texture, complexity and depth.

DRY $130 –V

Ransom K Syrah (★★★★)

The impressive debut 2007 vintage (★★★★), grown at Matakana, is dark and youthful in colour, with a spicy, slightly toasty bouquet. Mouthfilling, with concentrated plum, black-pepper and oak flavours, it's still youthful.

DRY $39 –V

Ra Nui Cob Cottage Reserve Marlborough Limited Release Syrah (★★☆)

A light style, the 2007 vintage (★★☆) is a single-vineyard wine, matured for 20 months in French oak barriques. Full and still fairly youthful in colour, with leafy aromas and flavours, it offers smooth, easy drinking.

DRY $30 –V

Rua Whenua Reserve Syrah   (★★★☆)

The rare 2005 vintage (★★★☆), made from second-crop vines at Te Awanga, in Hawke's Bay, was matured for 21 months in new French and seasoned American oak barriques. Full-coloured, with a fragrant, peppery bouquet, it is vibrant, with fresh acidity and plummy, spicy, slightly oaky flavours.

DRY $33 –V

Sacred Hill Deer Stalkers Syrah   ★★★★★

The 2007 vintage (★★★★★) is a star wine. Hand-picked in the Gimblett Gravels, Hawke's Bay, it was matured for 14 months in French oak barriques (50 per cent new). Dark and dense, with an enticingly fragrant bouquet of ripe berries and violets, it has highly concentrated blackcurrant, plum and spice flavours, with well-integrated, smoky oak and a very finely textured, long finish.

Vintage	07	06
WR	7	7
Drink	10-15	09-16

DRY $50 AV

Sacred Hill Gimblett Gravels Syrah   ★★★☆

The 2007 vintage (★★★☆) of this Hawke's Bay red is mouthfilling, with very good depth of vibrant plum/spice flavours, fresh, youthful and lingering.

DRY $22 AV

Sacred Hill The Wine Thief Series Hawke's Bay Syrah   ★★★★

Still very fresh and youthful, the 2007 vintage (★★★★) was harvested in the Gimblett Gravels and matured for a year in French oak (30 per cent new). It's an intensely varietal, boldly coloured wine with a strong surge of blackcurrant, plum and spice flavours, a delicate seasoning of toasty oak, and finely balanced tannins. Best drinking mid-2010+.

Vintage	07	06
WR	7	7
Drink	09-11	09-12

DRY $30 AV

Saint Clair Pioneer Block 17 Bay Block Syrah   (★★★★)

The dark, very easy-drinking 2007 vintage (★★★★) was grown in The Triangle, Hawke's Bay, and matured for 10 months in French oak casks (half new). Rich, vibrantly fruity and smooth, it has strong, ripe plum, berry, spice and liquorice flavours and gentle tannins. Delicious in its youth.

Vintage	07
WR	6
Drink	09-11

DRY $33 –V

Saltings Estate Matakana Vineyard Syrah   (★★★)

Hand-picked from a sloping site overlooking the Sandspit estuary, the 2006 vintage (★★★) was matured for 16 months in seasoned French oak. It has moderately ripe flavours, plummy and slightly earthy, in a crisp, medium-bodied style.

DRY $26 –V

Salvare Hawke's Bay Syrah   (★★★)

Grown in Gimblett Road and barrel-aged for a year, the fruity 2007 vintage (★★★) is a mid-weight style with bright, youthful colour and vibrant flavours of plums and black pepper, fresh and smooth.

DRY $25 –V

Sandspit Cove Matakana Syrah   (★★☆)

From Saltings Estate, the 2006 vintage (★★☆) was hand-picked and matured for 16 months in new French oak. Fullish in colour, with a slightly leafy bouquet, it's a middleweight style, with moderate depth of plum and herb flavours.

DRY $22 –V

Seifried Nelson Syrah   ★★☆

Grown at Brightwater, on the Waimea Plains, and matured for a year in new and older French oak barriques, the 2008 vintage (★★☆) is a light style, slightly leafy, but fresh and easy-drinking. The 2007 (★★★) is also a bit lean, lacking real richness, but clearly varietal, spicy and floral.

Vintage	08
WR	6
Drink	09-15

DRY $21 –V

Selaks Founders Reserve Hawke's Bay Syrah   ★★★★

The 2006 vintage (★★★★) was matured in French and American oak casks (half new). It's an elegant style, tightly structured and maturing well, with fresh, concentrated blackcurrant, plum and spice flavours.

DRY $33 –V

Selaks The Favourite Hawke's Bay Syrah   ★★★★

Grown partly in the company's Corner 50 Vineyard, the 2007 vintage (★★★★☆) is deeply coloured, with an enticingly fragrant bouquet and ripe blackcurrant, plum and black-pepper flavours, concentrated and gently oaked. Finely textured, spicy and long, it's a great buy. The 2008 (★★★☆) was matured in French and American oak barriques (new and one-year-old). It's an easy-drinking style, fruity and supple, with clearly varietal plum/black-pepper flavours, showing good complexity and depth.

DRY $21 V+

Sérine Syrah   ★★★★

Grown at Kerikeri, in Northland, by Iron Hills, the 2006 vintage (★★★★) was produced in a 'French style', with no use of new oak, fining or filtering. Maturing well, it's a very characterful, savoury red with good weight and depth of ripe, plummy, distinctly peppery flavours, slightly earthy and nutty, and good complexity, texture and harmony.

Vintage	06
WR	6
Drink	09-12

DRY $40 –V

Shipwreck Bay Syrah   ★★★☆

From Okahu Estate, the 2008 vintage (★★★) is a youthful blend of estate-grown, Northland (70 per cent) and Te Hana (north of Auckland) grapes. Full-coloured, with cherryish, plummy, slightly earthy flavours, seasoned with sweet oak, and gentle tannins, it's an enjoyable mid-weight.

DRY $18 V+

Sileni Cellar Selection Hawke's Bay Syrah   ★★★

The floral, easy-drinking 2008 vintage (★★★) was French and American oak-aged. Full-coloured, it has black-pepper and slight herb flavours, a touch of savoury complexity and gentle tannins.

DRY $20 AV

Sileni The Peak Hawke's Bay Syrah   (★★★☆)

A single-vineyard red, grown in The Triangle and French and American oak-matured for over a year, the 2007 vintage (★★★☆) is full-coloured, fresh, ripe, plummy and supple, with gentle black-pepper notes and good fruit sweetness, complexity and depth. It's drinking well now.

DRY $33 –V

Soland Syrah   ★★★

Grown in the tiny (0.8-hectare) Fat Pig Vineyard at Kerikeri, in Northland, the 2006 vintage (★★★★) is dark and mouthfilling, with supple tannins and loads of ripe, plummy, spicy flavour. The 2007 (★★☆) is fresh, vibrant, crisp and peppery, but lacks a bit of ripeness and roundness.

DRY $25 –V

Southbank Estate Hawke's Bay Syrah   ★★★

The 2007 vintage (★★☆) is dark, gutsy and firm, with plum and black-pepper flavours, but slightly rustic.

DRY $20 AV

Squawking Magpie The Chatterer Hawke's Bay Syrah   ★★★☆

Priced right, the 2007 vintage (★★★) is a deeply coloured Gimblett Gravels red with a floral, peppery bouquet. Mouthfilling, it has firm, youthful tannins and strong blackcurrant and spice flavours, showing good complexity.

DRY $25 AV

Squawking Magpie The Stoned Crow Syrah   ★★★★

Densely coloured, the 2007 vintage (★★★★) was grown in the Gimblett Gravels district of Hawke's Bay. Well worth cellaring, it has firm tannins and blackcurrant, pepper and nut flavours, showing excellent concentration.

DRY $40 –V

Staete Landt Marlborough Syrah   (★★★☆)

The debut 2007 vintage (★★★☆) was hand-harvested at Rapaura and matured for 17 months in French oak barriques. The colour is full and moderately youthful; the bouquet is strongly peppery. It's a mouthfilling wine (14.5 per cent alcohol), intensely varietal, with tight acidity woven through its strong plum, black-pepper and nut flavours.

DRY $50 –V

Stonecroft Serine Syrah   ★★★☆

The 2006 vintage (★★★★) is floral and generous. Estate-grown in Hawke's Bay and French oak-aged for 18 months, it is fullish in colour, with strong, spicy, plummy, distinctly peppery flavours, nutty and savoury. A firmly structured and complex red, it's enjoyable now but should also reward cellaring. (The 2007 vintage was matured for 18 months in French oak casks, 10 per cent new.)

Vintage	07	06
WR	5	5
Drink	09-15	09-15

DRY $25 AV

Stonecroft Syrah   ★★★★★

Hawke's Bay winemaker Dr Alan Limmer was the country's first to consistently produce a top-flight Syrah. The early vintages were grown entirely in Stonecroft's stony, arid vineyard in Mere Road, west of Hastings, but the 1998 introduced grapes from the newer Tokarahi Vineyard at the foot of Roy's Hill, which is contributing 'denser, more intense flavours'. Maturation is for 18 months in French oak barriques (50 per cent new). The 2007 vintage (★★★★) is very elegant, with full, bright colour and youthful plum and spice flavours, vibrant and supple. The 2008 (tasted prior to bottling, and so not rated) looked superb – dark, beautifully perfumed, notably ripe and rich.

Vintage	07	06	05	04	03	02	01
WR	6	6	5	NM	7	5	6
Drink	12-20	10-20	09-20	NM	09-15	09-12	09-10

DRY $45 AV

🍇🍇

Stone Paddock Hawke's Bay Syrah   ★★☆

From Paritua, the 2007 vintage (★★★) was grown in Hawke's Bay and matured in French oak casks (20 per cent new). It is deeply coloured, full-bodied and flavoursome, with spicy, nutty notes and a slightly rustic streak. The 2008 (★★☆), matured for nine months in barrels (30 per cent new), is fullish in colour, with spicy, slightly earthy flavours, and offers pleasant, easy drinking.

Vintage	08
WR	6
Drink	09-14

DRY $23 –V

Te Awa Syrah   ★★★★

Boldly coloured, the 2007 vintage (★★★☆) of this Hawke's Bay red is vibrantly fruity, with ripe, sweet-fruit characters and strong plum and spice flavours. It's a moderately complex style, for drinking now or cellaring.

DRY $30 AV

Te Mania Nelson Syrah   ★★☆

The 2008 vintage (★★☆) was hand-harvested and matured for 10 months in seasoned French and American oak casks. Fullish in colour, with peppery aromas, it's a mid-weight style, vibrantly fruity, with fresh acidity and moderate depth.

Vintage	08	07	06
WR	5	6	5
Drink	09-12	09-10	09-10

DRY $22 –V

Te Mata Estate Bullnose Syrah   ★★★★★

Grown in the Bullnose Vineyard, in The Triangle inland from Hastings, in Hawke's Bay, this classy red is based on 11 to 19-year-old vines, hand-picked and matured for 15 to 16 months in French oak barriques (35 per cent new). Unlike its Woodthorpe stablemate (below), it is not blended with Viognier, and the vines for the Bullnose label are cropped lower. The 2007 vintage (★★★★★) is deeply coloured and beautifully perfumed. An elegant wine, it has concentrated, ripe plum, spice and black-pepper flavours, a hint of dark chocolate, and a long, rounded finish. It's still youthful, but already delicious.

Vintage	07	06	05	04	03	02	01	00
WR	7	7	7	7	6	7	7	7
Drink	09-17	09-16	09-15	09-12	09	P	P	P

DRY $44 AV

Te Mata Estate Woodthorpe Syrah   ★★★★

The good-value 2007 vintage (★★★☆) was made by co-fermenting Syrah with a small amount (5 per cent of the blend) of Viognier (a traditional technique of the northern Rhône Valley, designed to add 'a perfumed, floral aroma'). French oak-aged for 15 months, it's the sort of easy-drinking, supple Syrah that would appeal to fans of Pinot Noir. Full-coloured, it has fresh, vibrant plum, spice and pepper flavours, a restrained oak influence, and very good but not great depth. (The price was lowered recently from $25 to $19.)

Vintage	07	06	05	04	03	02
WR	7	7	7	7	6	6
Drink	09-12	09-12	09-11	09-10	P	P

DRY $19 V+

Terrace Edge Waipara Valley Syrah   ★★★

The 2008 vintage (★★☆) was hand-picked, fermented with indigenous yeasts and matured for 10 months in French oak barriques (25 per cent new). It's a spicy and flavoursome red with fresh acidity, but also green-edged, showing a slight lack of ripeness and roundness.

Vintage	07
WR	5
Drink	09-12

DRY $28 –V

Te Whau Vineyard Waiheke Island Syrah   (★★★★★)

The superb 2008 vintage (★★★★★) was hand-harvested from five-year-old hill-grown vines, trained on stakes with no wires, fermented with indigenous yeasts and matured for over a year in two French oak barrels (one new). Dark and highly scented, it is rich and supple, with great fruit sweetness and complexity. Very finely textured, with concentrated plum, spice and roasted nut flavours and buried tannins, it's a Rhône Valley-like red, already delicious, but well worth cellaring.

DRY $69 AV

Ti Point Hawke's Bay Syrah   ★★★☆

The 2008 vintage (★★★☆) is a buoyantly fruity Gimblett Gravels red, hand-picked and French oak-aged for a year, with very good depth of plum and black-pepper flavours, still very fresh and youthful. Deeply coloured and mouthfilling, with gentle tannins, it needs a bit more time.

DRY $22 AV

Tinpot Hut Hawke's Bay Syrah   (★★★☆)

Drinking well now, but still youthful, the 2007 vintage (★★★☆) is a single-vineyard red, grown in the Dartmoor Valley and matured in tanks and barrels. Fragrant plum and pepper aromas lead into a vibrant, fruit-driven style, moderately complex, with plenty of flavour, gentle tannins and good harmony and immediacy.

DRY $29 –V

Trinity Hill Gimblett Gravels Syrah   ★★★★☆

Winemakers John Hancock and Warren Gibson are pursuing a 'savoury, earthy Rhône style'. The 2007 vintage (★★★★☆), grown in the Gimblett Gravels, was hand-picked, co-fermented with 4 per cent Viognier, and matured for a year in French oak barriques (25 per cent new). Deeply coloured, with concentrated, sweet-fruit flavours of blackcurrant and spice, and hints of liquorice and chocolate, it's a plump, slightly earthy and savoury wine, deliciously rich and supple.

Vintage	07	06	05	04	03	02
WR	6	6	5	6	NM	6
Drink	09-17	09-18	09-15	09-12	NM	09-15

DRY $30 AV

Trinity Hill Hawke's Bay Syrah   ★★★☆

The 2008 vintage (★★★★) is an instantly attractive, floral, supple Gimblett Gravels red, blended from Syrah (95 per cent) and Viognier (5 per cent), and oak-matured for 10 months. It has full, youthful colour, with pure, ripe plum/spice flavours, subtle oak and a deliciously silky texture.

DRY $19 V+

Trinity Hill Homage Gimblett Gravels Hawke's Bay Syrah   ★★★★★

Launched from 2002, this ranks among the country's most distinguished reds. Harvested from low-cropped, mature vines, and matured for 18 months in French oak barriques, the 2007 vintage is a densely coloured, majestic red, still very youthful. It has a commanding mouthfeel (14.5 per cent alcohol), with highly concentrated flavours of plums, spices and liquorice, and a foundation of ripe, fine-grained tannins. It's still years away from revealing its full personality; open 2012+.

Vintage	07	06	05	04	03	02
WR	5	6	NM	5	NM	6
Drink	10-18	10-19	NM	10-14	NM	10-12

DRY $120 –V

Unison Hawke's Bay Syrah   ★★★★☆

The 2007 vintage (★★★★), barrel-aged for 16 months, is a dark, powerful red with rich blackcurrant, spice and slight liquorice flavours, drinking well now.

DRY $38 AV

Vidal Hawke's Bay Syrah ★★★★

The 2007 vintage (★★★★☆) was grown in the Gimblett Gravels (93 per cent) and matured for 18 months in French oak barriques (39 per cent new). Dark and youthful in colour, it is mouthfilling, with highly concentrated plum, black-pepper and nutty oak flavours, and lovely texture.

Vintage	07	06	05	04		DRY $25 AV
WR	7	7	6	6		
Drink	09-14	09-11	P	P		

Vidal Reserve Hawke's Bay Syrah ★★★★★

Grown in the Gimblett Gravels, this is typically a dark, opulent wine with dense plum, spice and liquorice flavours, lush and long. A powerful, very ripe style, it needs about four years to show at its best. The 2007 vintage (★★★★☆), matured for 20 months in French oak barriques (25 per cent new), is densely coloured, with fresh, highly concentrated plum and black-pepper flavours, still developing.

Vintage	07	06	05	04		DRY $55 AV
WR	7	7	7	7		
Drink	09-15	09-13	09-15	09-12		🍇

Villa Maria Cellar Selection Hawke's Bay Syrah ★★★★★

A great buy. The 2007 vintage (★★★★★), estate-grown and hand-harvested in the Gimblett Gravels, is a very elegant red, youthful and supple, with vibrant plum and black-pepper flavours, fresh and concentrated. It has a floral bouquet (3 per cent Viognier), with plenty of new French and American oak (44 per cent) and excellent intensity. Drink now or cellar.

Vintage	07	06	05	04		DRY $31 V+
WR	7	6	6	7		
Drink	09-15	09-16	09-12	09-12		

Villa Maria Private Bin Hawke's Bay Syrah/Viognier ★★★☆

The 2007 vintage (★★★☆), grown in the Dartmoor Valley (60 per cent) and the Gimblett Gravels (40 per cent), is a blend of Syrah (95 per cent) and Viognier (5 per cent), barrel-aged for two years. It's a gutsy, richly coloured wine with mouthfilling body, strong plum/spice flavours, woven with fresh acidity, and a hint of sweet oak. Drink now onwards.

Vintage	07		DRY $25 AV
WR	6		
Drink	09-13		

Villa Maria Reserve Hawke's Bay Syrah ★★★★★

The 2007 vintage (★★★★★) is a densely coloured, power-packed, youthful Gimblett Gravels red, matured for 20 months in French oak barriques (56 per cent new). It should be long-lived, with a notably fragrant bouquet of dark berries, tar, anise and violets, bold plum, black-pepper and liquorice flavours, very fine tannins and good complexity.

Vintage	07	06	05		DRY $56 AV
WR	7	7	7		
Drink	09-19	09-18	09-19		

Waimarie Muriwai Valley Syrah   ★★★☆

Hand-picked from young vines at Waimauku, in West Auckland, the 2006 vintage (★★★☆) was matured for over a year in one-year-old French oak barriques. The bouquet is floral and peppery; the palate medium-bodied, with moderately concentrated plum and black-pepper flavours, ripe and supple.

Vintage	06
WR	6
Drink	09-16

DRY $26 –V

Waimea Nelson Syrah   ★★★

The 2007 (★★☆) is full-coloured and sweetly oaked, but lacks real ripeness and richness, with leafy aromas and flavours. The 2008 vintage (★★★) is a single-vineyard red, American oak-aged. It's a mouthfilling wine with perfumed oak aromas and satisfying depth of plum and spice flavours, fresh, vibrant and supple.

Vintage	07
WR	6
Drink	09-11

DRY $24 –V

Weeping Sands Waiheke Island Syrah   ★★★★☆

From Obsidian, the powerful 2008 vintage (★★★★☆) was grown at Onetangi and matured for a year in French (principally) and American oak casks (25 per cent new). Showing excellent density and complexity, it is boldly coloured, sturdy and concentrated, with loads of plummy, peppery flavour, finely integrated oak, ripe, supple tannins and a long, spicy finish. Best drinking 2011+.

Vintage	08	07	06
WR	7	6	5
Drink	10-16	09-15	09-12

DRY $31 AV

Wild Rock Angel's Dust Hawke's Bay Syrah   (★★★☆)

Grown in the Gimblett Gravels, the 2007 vintage (★★★☆) was matured for 14 months in French oak casks (20 per cent new). Deeply coloured, it is mouthfilling and supple, with cherry, plum and black-pepper flavours, showing some savoury complexity and very good depth.

Vintage	08
WR	7
Drink	09-14

DRY $25 AV

Wild Rock Angel's Dust Reserve Hawke's Bay Syrah   (★★★★☆)

The instantly attractive 2007 vintage (★★★★☆) was matured for 18 months in French oak casks (30 per cent new). Classy and rich, it has deep, youthful colour and a scented, intensely varietal, very ripe and peppery fragrance. Its concentrated blackcurrant, plum and black-pepper flavours show a hint of dark chocolate, with gentle tannins and lovely texture.

Vintage	07
WR	7
Drink	09-14

DRY $30 AV

Wild Rock The Underarm Syrah (★★★☆)

Deeply coloured, the 2006 vintage (★★★☆) is a vibrantly fruity Hawke's Bay red with intensely varietal, plummy, well-spiced flavours and gentle tannins. It's a fresh, attractive, drink-young style.

DRY $24 AV

Wishart Alluvion Syrah ★★★

Still on sale, the 2005 vintage (★★★) was grown at Bay View, in Hawke's Bay, and French oak-aged for a year. Full-flavoured and smooth, with plum/spice flavours and hints of tomatoes and herbs, it's a moderately ripe-tasting wine with some complexity.

Vintage	05	04	03
WR	6	6	6
Drink	09-12	P	P

DRY $30 –V

Zepelin Hawke's Bay Syrah (★★★)

Still on sale, the 2005 vintage (★★★) is a single-vineyard wine, grown at Havelock North, in Hawke's Bay. Full-coloured and mouthfilling, with good depth of firm plum and spice flavours, it shows some leafy notes, but also considerable complexity and age-worthiness.

DRY $40 –V

Tempranillo

The star grape of Rioja, Tempranillo is grown extensively across northern and central Spain, where it yields strawberry, spice and tobacco-flavoured reds, full of personality. Barrel-aged versions mature well, developing great complexity. The great Spanish variety is starting to spread into the New World, but is still rare in New Zealand, with 2 hectares of bearing vines in 2004 projected to reach 7 hectares in 2010 (mostly in Hawke's Bay). Trinity Hill has shown what can be done.

Pete's Shed Tempranillo (★★)

From Yealands, the debut 2008 vintage (★★) was grown in the Awatere Valley, Marlborough, and French oak-aged for 10 months. Light in colour, with smooth, gentle strawberry and spice flavours, it's a pleasant, soft red, but lacks any real stuffing.

DRY $23 –V

Trinity Hill Gimblett Gravels Tempranillo ★★★★☆

This is a consistently impressive red, full of personality. The 2008 vintage (★★★★) was grown in the Gimblett Gravels, Hawke's Bay, and matured for a year in French and American oak casks. A fragrant, dark red with deep blackcurrant, dark chocolate, plum and spice flavours, seasoned with quality oak, it's an elegant, vibrant, firmly structured wine, still very youthful; open mid-2010+.

Vintage	08	07	06	05
WR	5	6	7	6
Drink	09-15	09-15	09-14	09-12

DRY $29 V+

Zinfandel

n California, where it is extensively planted, Zinfandel produces muscular, heady reds that can approach a dry port style. It is believed to be identical to the Primitivo variety, which yields highly characterful, warm, spicy reds in southern Italy. There are only 4 hectares of bearing Zinfandel vines in New Zealand, clustered in Hawke's Bay, with no expansion projected between 2004 and 2010. Dr Alan Limmer, of the Stonecroft winery in Hawke's Bay, believes 'Zin' has potential here, 'if you can stand the stress of growing a grape that falls apart at the first sign of a dubious weather map!'

Kemblefield The Reserve Zinfandel   ★★★☆

Still on sale, the 2002 vintage (★★★☆) of this Hawke's Bay wine was estate-grown at Mangatahi and matured for 18 months in French oak casks. Full-coloured, it's a robust red (14.5 per cent alcohol) with brambly, plummy, spicy flavours showing very good depth and some leathery complexity. A concentrated but green-edged wine, it needs a tad more ripeness and warmth.

DRY $50 –V

Stonecroft Zinfandel   ★★★★

The 2007 vintage (★★★★), the best yet, was estate-grown in the Gimblett Gravels of Hawke's Bay. Full and bright in colour, it is floral and supple, with rich plum and pepper flavours. Still youthful, it's full of promise.

Vintage	07
WR	7
Drink	09-20

DRY $55 –V

Zweigelt

Austria's most popular red-wine variety is a crossing of Blaufränkisch and St-Laurent. It's a naturally high-yielding variety, but cropped lower can produce appealing, velvety reds, usually at their best when young. Zweigelt is extremely rare in New Zealand, with 3 hectares planted. (See also Seifried Silvia, in the Branded and Other Red Wines section.)

Hans Herzog Marlborough Zweigelt   (★★★★)

The debut vintage (★★★★) was hand-picked at 23.8 brix and matured for a year in French oak barriques (50 per cent new). Boldly coloured, it has concentrated, berryish flavours, fresh and rich, with a slight medicinal note that is presumably characteristic of the variety.

DRY $35 –V

Index of Wine Brands

This index should be especially useful when you are visiting wineries as a quick way to find the reviews of each company's range of wines. It also provides links between different wine brands made by the same producer (for example, Grove Mill and Sanctuary).